Emotion and Adaptation

EMOTION

AND

ADAPTATION

Richard S. Lazarus

New York   Oxford
OXFORD UNIVERSITY PRESS

Oxford University Press

Oxford   New York   Toronto
Delhi   Bombay   Calcutta   Madras   Karachi
Petaling Jaya   Singapore   Hong Kong   Tokyo
Nairobi   Dar es Salam   Cape Town
Melbourne   Auckland

and associated companies in
Berlin   Ibadan

Published by Oxford University Press, Inc.
198 Madison Avenue, New York, New York 10016-4314

Oxford is a registered trademark of Oxford University Press

Library of Congress Cataloging–in–Publication Data
Lazarus, Richard S.
Emotion and adaptation / Richard S. Lazarus.
p. cm.
Includes bibliographical references and index.
1. Emotions. 2. Adaptability (Psychology) I. Title.
BF531.L37 1991 152.4 – dc20 91–9611
ISBN 978-0-19-509266-0

8 9 7

Printed in the United States of America
on acid-free paper

To Bernice, my impressive wife,
our two wonderful children, David and Nancy,
their fine spouses, Mary and Rick,
and our always lovable grandchildren,
Jessica, Adam, Maiya, and Ava Rose.

Preface

I had the good fortune to publish a book in 1966 entitled *Psychological Stress and the Coping Process,* which to some extent anticipated the movement of psychology over the next 25 years from a behavioristic to a cognitive-mediational outlook. I would like to believe I contributed to the change. Nearly 20 years later, in 1984, with Folkman, I followed this up with another book, *Stress, Appraisal, and Coping.* The central construct of both books, and my research from almost the beginning, was appraisal, which is about how people construe the implications of what is happening in their lives for their well-being.

Since then there has been another remarkable shift (or, rather, an expansion of interest) from psychological stress to emotion. Although stress and coping are still important, social scientists have begun to realize that these concepts are part of a larger rubric—the emotions. A consequence is that appraisal—and coping too—which previously had to deal only with a simple stress dimension from low to high, or a few basic types of stress such as harm/loss, threat, and challenge, had to be refashioned. Appraisal must now be made to account for the differences among distinctive negative emotions such as anger, fright, anxiety, guilt, shame, sadness, envy, jealousy, and disgust and positive emotions such as happiness, pride, love, and relief, as well as some emotional phenomena whose status is problematic such as hope, compassion, and the aesthetic emotions. A modern theory of emotion and adaptation, which is what this book is about, requires propositions about the role of appraisal in each individual emotion.

This book, which I have wanted to write for a long time, was conceived in the light of the above reasoning, and I began to work on it with dedication about four years ago. I wanted to create a rich and complete conceptualization that would make clear the issues underlying the metatheoretical and theoretical decisions that a viable cognitive-motivational-relational theory requires. It turned out to be a remarkably challenging venture, a fascinating experience that once again proves that the best way to learn is to write. As in so many writing ventures, what started out modestly grew and grew as my awareness expanded and I filled in the gaps of my knowledge. I think of this book as a monograph of my late years, a labor of love, one that I want to be the best book on emotion that I could write. Like all such ventures, it can never be truly finished, but conscious of the rapid peaking of professional interest in emotion, I decided not to obsess indefinitely and—with some lapses—closed the book to new thoughts and references as of winter 1990.

Emotion is an interdisciplinary field connecting several life sciences—biology, psychology, sociology, and anthropology. It also has roots in philosophy. I have tried to do justice to the prodigious breadth of subject matter, but the literature, both historical and contemporaneous, research centered and theoretical, is so huge that I have had to be very selective. To my regret, important works have appeared since the winter of 1990, and these would have been relevant. The interesting interchanges between A. W. Kruglanski and commentators in *Psychological Inquiry* (1990, Volume 1, pp. 181–230) addressed the difficult question of how broad and abstract or how detailed a theory should be. And in the same issue (pp. 231–283), interchanges between Michael Lewis and his commentators addressed intentionality and motivation in the context of emotional development. These show how ongoing and fluid the effort at understanding always is. In any case, I hope I will be forgiven for any omissions of work and insights by those whose research I respect. To include the entire literature would have made this book impossibly long, and dull.

This is, fundamentally, an issues and idea book, a theory and a set of propositions about the emotion process and its consequences, not a review. I have often used an instantiation strategy in which a point or theme is illustrated by a specific set of experimental or clinical observations, and have frequently drawn on literary examples that offer dramatic illustrations. It would be an affectation to lay claim to a balanced treatment. In complex, lively, and interdisciplinary fields, even the most scholarly work cannot provide an unbiased account. I am also impressed with the value of debate about issues for both readers and participants, and so I have been unabashedly speculative and sometimes quite opinionated where it seemed appropriate. I hope what I have written will stimulate constructive debate and guide research.

For whom has the book been written? When I began I wanted to reestablish and extend my historical role as an innovator of appraisal theory and research, and to advance a comprehensive cognitive-motivational-relational theory. It was to be an analysis and position statement for colleagues who were afficionados, not a balanced examination of diverse ways of thinking. I wanted it to be clear and to avoid excessive jargon so that people from diverse fields without extensive backgrounds in psychology could read and understand what I was saying. When one writes for knowledgeable colleagues, however, who are ready with inevitable "yes, buts," it is difficult to avoid some jargon, drawn upon in defense of controversial ideas, but I have tried to walk a line between being colloquial and lapsing into academic ostentation.

Despite the passion with which I have presented and defended certain views, what has emerged is also, I believe, a broad contemporaneous treatment of the subject matter of emotion; to present a comprehensive theory is also to address, perforce, a large range of issues, which any ambitious theory must confront. Therefore, I believe the book provides a text that can be read and understood by upper division undergraduate students, graduate students, and professionals. And because the emotions are so central to the work of practitioners in general medicine, psychiatry, clinical psychology, health psychology, social work, and nursing, it should also have utility in these fields as well as in hard-nosed cognitive science and other fields of psychology such as personality, social, developmental, and physiological psychology.

The one subject I have not tried to address, except in passing, is the basic neurophysiology, biochemistry, and genetics of emotion. Though I inveigh against reductionism and avoid taking refuge in neurophysiology, I don't deny that it is relevant to the emotions. Nor have I ignored biology. For example, I hope one of the constructive things I have done, in light of the usual polarity between biological universals and sociocultural, developmental sources of variability, is to try in Chapter 5 to reconcile these positions and find a proper place for both, as any good emotion theory should.

A number of persons whose help in bringing this book into being deserve my gratitude, with the usual reservation that they are not responsible for my failings. Foremost among them is Paul Ekman, who provided me with the resources of his sharp mind and considerable acumen in commenting on early drafts, and who made it possible through a seminar at UCSF in 1988–1989 to have his colleagues and students read and criticize them. I learned much from these dialogues. An NIMH-supported postdoctoral training program during the 1989–1990 academic year, which Ekman and I co-directed at Berkeley, and an outstanding faculty from many universities, including Judy Dunn, Seymour Epstein, Michael Goldstein, John Gottman, Jerome Kagan, Jaak Panksepp, Robert Levenson, Richard Davidson, and Klaus Scherer, as well as Arlie Hochschild, George De Vos, and Mardi Horowitz who gave special lectures, were a tremendous source of inspiration and helped me become aware of and think through much I had not previously thought about.

I spent three months a few summers ago as a Visiting Professor at the University of Heidelberg with my wife, the guest of Professor Reiner Bastine, in what was then West Germany, writing on a rented word processor and lecturing widely on the ideas I was cultivating for this book. I gave lectures at Heidelberg, Mainz, the Free University of Berlin, the University of Amsterdam and the European Congress of Psychology meeting in that city, the University of Geneva, the University of Wurzburg, the University of Munich, and Bamberg University. I express my great appreciation to my hosts on these travels, to those to whom I lectured because of their wonderful, searching questions, which helped me greatly in shaping the formulations that follow, to those at Heidelberg where we resided, and to others such as Professor Lothar Laux and Dr. Hannalore Weber of Bamberg, whose intellectual explorations with me about emotion added greatly to the quality and richness of this book.

A number of colleagues read and commented constructively on portions of the book. Their contribution must not be understated because the kindest thing a colleague can do in academe is to really read and criticize what you write in a sincere effort to help you make it better. Craig A. Smith, who spent two postdoctoral years with me at Berkeley, was most generous of his time in giving me very searching and invaluable criticism on all chapters and making valuable suggestions that I often drew on heavily without identifying them in the text. Eric Gillett meticulously reviewed a number of chapters I was working on while at Heidelberg, and provided me with a much needed psychoanalytic perspective in my struggles to integrate appraisal theory with the unconscious. Eleanor Rosch benefited the manuscript with her unique blend of sophisticated cognitive science and her continuing search for broader and deeper analyses of human meanings in Eastern and Western thought.

The late Irving Janis read and commented wisely and in detail on an early version, and when I learned of his untimely death — a loss to us all — it saddened me very much. I am also very grateful to Joe Campos for the many dialogues we had extending over many months at a late stage of the manuscript. We explored a variety of ideas, theory, and research, and he was a great help to me on many parts of the manuscript, especially with respect to issues of early emotional development, which was not my forte. He also arranged for a modest grant from the Institute of Human Development to aid in the completion of the manuscript, for which I am grateful.

I am also grateful to Joan Bossert, Editor for Oxford University Press, whose dedicated and effective efforts to improve my prose, challenge my reasoning, point up inconsistencies, and clean the manuscript of all sorts of flaws, played an important role in helping to make this book what it is. The thoroughness of her editorial assistant, Louise C. Page, and other staff is also much appreciated.

Most scholars are indebted in ephemeral ways to many students and colleagues whose serious explorations and confrontations with the subject matter leave indelible but difficult-to-specify marks on their intellectual sensibilities. To them I express my everlasting gratitude.

Above all, I salute my wife of 46 years, Bernice, whose vitality, grit, and cheerfulness in the face of physical adversity is inspiring, and who has always cherished and protected my professional commitments, and made it easy to devote so much of myself to writing this book.

Berkeley, California   R. S. L.
May 1991

Contents

PART ONE

Background

Before launching into the cognitive-relational theory, which is the central task of this book, it will help first to explore the complex and wide-ranging subject matter of emotion.

In Chapter 1, I consider the place of emotion in psychology, its recent history, diverse field-centered perspectives on emotion, the adaptational encounter, and the tasks of a cognitive-motivational-relational theory.

In Chapter 2, I consider the variables of emotion and the difficulties of doing research, what the emotions are, whether emotions should be regarded as categories or dimensions, and research and thought about facial expression and physiological activity, which are two features of an emotional response. The chapter ends with a proposed classification system.

✦ 1 ✦

About Emotion

Emotions play a central role in the significant events of our lives. Although they have many characteristics, some behavioral and others physiological, emotions are above all psychological. We feel proud when our loved ones do something worthy. When demeaned, we become angry or ashamed. We experience joy at the birth of our children, anxiety when threatened, and grief at the death of a loved one.

Much of what we do and how we do it is influenced by emotions and the conditions that generate them. Pride and joy about our children revitalize our commitment to advance and protect the well-being of our family. Loss undermines our appreciation of life and may lead to withdrawal and depression. Anger at being wronged mobilizes and directs us toward retribution. When "blinded by rage," our thinking is impaired, which places us at risk. It is even said with good reason that emotions contribute to physical and mental health and illness; positive emotions to health, negative to illness. Surely so powerful a process deserves careful study. From the time of my first contact with psychology, I was sure that we would not understand people unless we understood their emotions.

The primary purpose of this book is to offer a theory of emotion that is cognitive, motivational, and relational, an outlook I have pioneered with respect to psychological stress over the past forty years, and which I will be explaining as I go along. Although I will often take forceful and distinctive positions, my intention is not to be polemical but to point to important issues, raise new ones, and suggest solutions consistent with a coherent and systematic framework for thinking about the emotions.

Given the long and complex history of thought about emotion, it seems almost rash to venture forth with yet another analysis. There has been speculation about the emotions for thousands of years, ranging from brief essays to major works. Recent collections of readings (e.g., Calhoun & Solomon, 1984; Izard, Kagan, & Zajonc, 1984; Plutchik & Kellerman, 1980, 1983, 1986, 1989; Rorty, 1980a; Scherer & Ekman, 1984; and Shaver, 1984) attest to the great current interest.

Since 1960, and especially during the 1980s, the list of monographs would have to include Arnold (1960), Averill (1982), Bearison and Zimiles (1986), Clynes (1977), Frijda (1986), a reissue of Gardner, Metcalf, and Beebe-Center's history (1937/1970), Gordon (1987), Harris (1989), Harré (1986), Hillman (1960), Izard (1971, 1977), Kemper (1981), Lazarus and Folkman (1984), Lewis and Michalson (1983), Lewis and Saarni (1985), Lyons (1980), Mandler (1984), Ortony, Clore, and

Collins (1988), Papanicolaou (1989), Plutchik (1962), Shweder & Levine (1984), Socarides (1977), de Sousa (1987), Thompson (1988), Tomkins (1962, 1963), and Weiner (1986). Before this book appears there will undoubedly be many more, which makes my undertaking daunting, because a modern theory must avoid merely rediscovering what we already know or previously believed. Although there is a real need for a novel integration for many reasons, including epistemological ones, we are a long way from achieving a common framework on which there will be widespread agreement.

In the first two chapters, I intend mainly to rove over the territory of emotion in preparation for the theoretical model. I don't mean to suggest by the term *rove* that the discussion is aimless. Quite the contrary, I will be examining very systematically a number of ideas that are relevant to the emotion process. The topics of this chapter include the place of emotion in psychological thought, diverse discipline-centered perspectives on emotion (such as the individual, the observer, the society, and the biological species), the adaptational encounter as the proper context of emotion, difficult issues that need to be resolved, the tasks of a theory of emotion, and a brief synopsis of the theory.

The Place of Emotion in Psychology

It is inconceivable to me that there could be an approach to the mind, or to human and animal adaptation, in which the emotions are not a key component. Failure to give emotion a central role puts theoretical and research psychology out of step with human preoccupations from the beginning of recorded time. As Plutchik (1962, pp. 3–4) put it so well:

> The emotions have always been of central concern to men. In every endeavor, in every major human enterprise, the emotions are somehow involved. Almost every great philosopher from Aristotle to Spinoza, from Kant to Dewey, from Bergson to Russell has been concerned with the nature of emotion and has speculated and theorized about its origins, expressions, effects, its place in the economy of human life. Theologians have recognized the significance of certain emotions in connection with religious experience and have made the training of emotions a central, if implicit, part of religious training. Writers, artists, and musicians have always attempted to appeal to the emotions, to affect and move the audience through symbolic communication. And the development in the last half century of psychoanalysis, clinical psychology, and psychosomatic medicine has brought the role of emotion in health and disease sharply to our attention.

There was a perplexing resistance to emotion in mainstream academic psychology until the 1960s, especially during the heyday of behaviorism and logical positivism. With few exceptions, the major introductory textbooks seldom managed more than a single chapter on emotion — if that — emphasizing mainly its motivational or drive aspects and its physiology. These texts gave much more attention, however, to perception (and now cognition), learning, motivation, physiology, personality, psychopathology, and social processes. Emotion and adaptation have rarely, if ever, gotten substantial treatment in the standard course curricula of psychology. I hope this situation is now changing.

The de-emphasis of emotion stands in marked contrast to the rich and central place given to the topic by the great dramatists and writers of fiction. Ironically, all but social scientists have recognized that emotions lie at the center of human experience and adaptation. Academic psychologists have seemed little interested in emotion, and because they do not include it in the core curriculum, they could be said to regard it as a highly specialized, perhaps even exotic topic. This is all the more noteworthy when one realizes that emotions are thought to be keys to understanding human problems and psychopathology in clinical work.

Even though clinical theories of psychopathology are centered on emotion, the traditional emphasis has not been on a broad spectrum of emotions, but mainly on *anxiety* (see Chapter 6). Seldom has an emotion other than anxiety been considered a significant causal factor in mental illness. Freudian and reinforcement-learning theory have shared a common view of anxiety as a drive, acquired in the course of development, and connected through association and drive reduction with certain events of living. Anxiety is also said by both theories to motivate pathogenic modes of coping, which succeed in lowering drive tension or distress but are otherwise dysfunctional.

Depression and guilt have sometimes been minor exceptions to this almost exclusive concentration on anxiety as *the* emotion underlying psychopathology. There is much current interest in the etiology and symptomatology of depression, and its treatment, and little current interest in guilt, except perhaps among psychoanalysts. However, depression cannot be regarded, per se, as an emotion; it is a complex state of emotional distress in which sadness, anxiety, anger, and guilt predominate. Helen Lewis (1971) has given *shame* and *guilt* an important place in neurosis, and this, too,is a minor exception to the rule that clinical formulations have centered mostly on anxiety. Even less attention has been given to positive emotions (happiness, pride, love, and relief), which are not usually regarded as relevant to psychopathology.

The mention of positive emotions reminds me that I should, in passing, clear up a common confusion about what makes an emotion either positive or negative. Anger, for example, is commonly classified as a negative emotion, but people often report feeling good about their anger, and clinical practitioners believe that severely depressed persons may be improving when they begin to direct anger outward rather than at themselves. On the other hand, anger—especially when it is acted out—can have harmful social consequences, and when it is not managed well, it may even be physiologically harmful.

An emotion may be considered as either positive or negative, depending on the focus of concern, and there are three possibilities: if we focus on (1) the harmful person–environment relationship eliciting an emotion, negative emotions always point to negative causal conditions, a meaning that should be distinguished from the negative subjective quality and from the negative adaptational consequences. But we may wish instead to focus on (2) an emotion's subjective feel; or (3) its adaptational consequences. These consequences are not always simple, because there may be positive consequences of negative emotions and negative consequences of positive emotions, which makes this criterion a bit muddy. My predilection is to use the terms *positive* and *negative* only to refer to alternative 1 — that is, the beneficial or harmful person–environment relationship, the appraisal of which is what generates an emotion. I deal with this at considerable length in Chapter 3, and with how the judgment is made by the individual in Chapter 4. In any case, the way negative and positive have been defined here is, I think, the most common, implicit use of the terms.

To return to the place of emotion in academic thought, psychology as much as any other life science,* has long had a penchant for separating its subject matter into fundamental and separate analytical categories, which come together in the image of a whole person adapting to the conditions of life. There is nothing particularly strange or irrational in a curriculum that centers on the systematic study of functions such as cognition, motivation, physiological mechanisms, personality, social processes, and their development.

Some of these, however, such as cognition and motivation, more than others, seem to be organismic because they are centered on the way people handle the tasks, opportunities, and problems of living physiologically, psychologically, and socially. Cognitive activity, which refers mainly to diverse forms of thought, whether conscious or unconscious, enters virtually everything we do; we use it to pilot our lives and to be responsive to feedback from the environment that could be relevant for survival. Motivation, which has to do with what we want, wish, or need, and for which I will use the terms *goals* and *goal hierarchies* in Chapter 3, is also an organismic concept in that it deals with what is important to us in our daily lives, which, in turn, guides our choices and influences what we regard as harmful and beneficial.

Although personality, too, is said to be an organismic concept that encompasses adaptation, and indeed is so conceived traditionally, modern personality research has too often strayed from this idea. Personality is seldom explored as a complex, integrated system — as a person struggling to manage transactions with the physical and social environment and being shaped and changed by this struggle. Instead, research in personality tends to be about one or a few traits with little or no attention paid to how they are organized within an individual.

If we are to speak of an organismic concept, one that best expresses the adaptational wholeness or integrity of persons rather than merely separate functions, emotion is surely it. Emotions are complex, patterned, organismic reactions to how we think we are doing in our lifelong efforts to survive and flourish and to achieve what we wish for ourselves. Emotions are like no other psychosociobiological construct in that they express the intimate personal meaning of what is happening in our social lives and combine motivational, cognitive, adaptational, and physiological processes into a single complex state that involves several levels of analysis.

In my judgment, emotion cannot be divorced from cognition, motivation, adaptation, and physiological activity. When we react with an emotion, especially a strong one, every fiber of our being is likely to be engaged — our attention and

---

*I use the term *life science* because psychology has the distinctive feature of being both a biological and social science, and life science is a felicitous way to refer to the study of the adaptational struggles of living creatures.

thoughts, our needs and desires, and even our bodies. The reaction tells us that an important value or goal has been engaged and is being harmed, placed at risk, or advanced. From an emotional reaction we can learn much about what a person has at stake in the encounter with the environment or in life in general, how that person interprets self and world, and how harms, threats, and challenges are coped with. No other concept in psychology is as richly revealing of the way an individual relates to life and to the specifics of the physical and social environment.

The de-emphasis of holistic, system principles in psychology seems to be mainly the result of an analytic and molecular rather than a synthetic way of thinking. The dominant epistemology is based on reductive explanatory laws after the fashion of physics and chemistry in a bygone day. This de-emphasis of organismic and system principles has two major costs.

First, cognition and other fundamental psychological functions are *divorced from human adaptation,* which has indeed been the case in theory and research in cognitive psychology. For example, Norman (1980) complains about the absence in cognitive science of research and theoretical interest in emotion, motivation, individual differences, sociocultural influences, and development and change over the life course. One function, thought, has been divorced from other psychological functions, all of which are usually interdependent in living creatures adapting to their worlds. This divorce is damaging because little that goes on in mind and behavior is not in some way relevant to adaptation, and mind no doubt develops in the process of living and adapting. Indeed, this is why I titled this book *Emotion and Adaptation.* The two concepts are thoroughly intertwined, and one cannot be fruitfully examined without reference to the other.

Second, the search for universal mechanisms does a disservice to *individual variation.* Much of psychology is *normative* in that it concentrates on what people in general are like, and individual differences are only brought in as an afterthought, if not as error. One must remember that, above all, emotions are individual phenomena and display great variations among individuals; although to some extent people share emotional experiences, and general laws can be formulated about the emotion process, an emotion happens to an individual with a distinctive history who wants, thinks, and confronts specific environments, evaluates their significance, and acts as adaptively as possible.

A proper view of (whole) persons as organized systems living in and adapting to their environments also invites—even requires—an *ipsative* or intraindividual perspective (which describes the multiple facets that comprise a person and synthesizes a portrait of how these facets are organized and how the same individual behaves in diverse settings) as well as a normative perspective. In our research designs we should not only compare people with each other, which is normative, we should also study the same persons from one moment to another and across environmental settings, which is intraindividual.

From the standpoint of behaviorism and logical positivism, which until recently dominated psychological thought, it is important not to venture far (or at all) from observables in one's explanatory models (see Fiske & Shweder, 1986). If one truly believed that this was the only proper scientific approach to mind, then emotion, with its admittedly fuzzy, integrating concepts, would have to be regarded as refractory to study. This restrictive outlook left little or no room for concepts of will, intention, planfulness, or the tendency to take account of past, present, and future — all important features of human mental activity. Its sterility led Deese (1985, p. 31) to describe behaviorism, especially radical behaviorism, as "the abolition of mind."

Indeed, not so long ago there was a concerted effort in psychology to dismiss emotion; it supposedly epitomized an unscientific concept characterized by subjectivism and armchair philosophizing. Hillman (1960) describes this effort as the denial of emotion as a legitimate topic of scientific study. The denial took three forms: the recommendation (1) that the concept of emotion be abandoned, (2) that it be subsumed under other concepts, and (3) that polemics be mounted against emotions as "things" that erroneously call for explanation. He quotes Meyer (1933, p. 300), who wrote the following hardly prescient statement:

> Why introduce into science an unneeded term, such as emotion, when there are already scientific terms for everything we have to describe? . . . I predict: the "will" has virtually passed out of our scientific psychology today; the "emotion" is bound to do the same. In 1950 American psychologists will smile at both these terms as curiosities of the past.

As we know, of course, since the 1960s research and thought on emotion have begun to flower rather than wither as Meyer prophesied. Hillman lists many well-known names among those opting for the abandonment of emotion in those earlier days, including Duffy (1941a, 1941b, 1962), Hebb (1954), Koffka (1935), Masserman (1946), and the philosopher Ryle (1949). In a widely read and applauded theoretical review, Brown and Farber (1951) shifted attention away from emotion as an experienced state and complex process by conceiving of it as merely an intervening variable, which is a convenient mental fiction standing between and integrating observable inputs and outputs. Duffy (1962)[1] persisted even into the 1960s in trying to replace the concept of emotion with the unidimensional intervening variable *activation,* which she conceptualized as energy mobilization. Malmo (1959), too, reduced anxiety, with its rich diversity of cognitive-affective contents, to mere activation. And Lindsley (1951) helped to give the concept of activation a major integrative role in psychology by making it possible to think of three key concepts — motivation or drive, physiological mobilization, and alertness — as manifestations of the one basic psychophysiological intervening variable. All these simplifying efforts left emotion as a unidimensional epiphenomenon with no richness or effects at worst, or as a convenient fiction with no substance at best.

The Retreat from Radical Behaviorism and the Rise of Cognitivism

As so often is the case, the elegantly simple, behavioral formulations about emotion as drive or activation, and the corollary idea that adaptive and maladaptive behaviors were merely conditioned responses to drives as a result of drive subsidence, became less and less tenable, because they required all sorts of additional mental variables to make them work as explanatory and predictive accounts. Influential behaviorists, such as Hull (1943) and Spence (Spence & Spence, 1966), kept complicating their models to fit the complexities of the human mind, and only Skinner (1953) consistently stuck to an extreme behaviorist agenda, suggesting that speculations about dispositional properties of persons as mediators of reactions were scientifically unproductive.

By the 1960s and 1970s psychology, unable or unwilling to make do with the oversimplifications it had fostered, had begun to shift from simple stimulus-response (S-R) formulations and away from positivism (cf. Fiske & Shweder, 1986) toward neobehaviorism. In doing so, stimulus-response linkages were transformed into much more complicated stimulus-organism-response (S-O-R) linkages, and the door to speculation was opened wider with renewed interest in the mental structures and processes that might be located in the "black box" of the mind to account for the way people and other animals acted and reacted.

This is not the place to examine in any detail the historical, philosophical, and scientific reasons for this major change in the outlook of the field, and as was evident in back-to-back accounts of this recently by Kendler (1990) and Bolles (1990), there are major disagreements about this shift. I find one of the several reasons suggested by Bolles to be particularly interesting and persuasive — namely, the assumption in S-R reinforcement psychology that all stimuli and all responses are functionally alike in the learning process. About this Bolles (1990, pp. 112–113) writes:

> Reinforcement people say things like "pick an arbitrary operant such as bar pressing" or "choose a representative animal, such as a rat." So we did a lot of paradigmatic experiments, but then when we varied things a little we did not find generalities, we found a lot of specificities. It seems it *does* make a difference what the animal is, what the cue is, what the reinforcer is, and what response is being required. Learning has a vastly richer texture than the old-timers ever dreamed of.

A good example of the intellectual transition away from S-R reinforcement learning to cognitivism was a dramatic change in the original theory of learned helplessness, which had its roots in drive reinforcement, learning concepts, and research with animals (cf. Overmeier & Seligman, 1967; Seligman & Maier, 1967). Seligman (1975) initially applied this outlook to human depression. He proposed that depression was caused by a history of negative life experiences involving lack of control over aversive conditions. These experiences supposedly taught us that we were helpless to control outcomes, and after learning that nothing could be done to alter the negative life conditions, we stopped trying. Seligman called this "learned helplessness" — a term that still survives, though its basic meaning has changed greatly.

Since not everyone reacts with a sense of personal helplessness and depression to a history of negative life experience or a "spate of bad luck," however, the original theory of learned helplessness was ultimately reformulated into a theory about the (cognitive) attributions people make about their control over the conditions of their lives (e.g., Abramson, Garber, & Seligman, 1980). The new version of this theory of depression was no longer recognizable as having much to do with a history of *actual* helplessness but instead was based on *subjective attributions* about helplessness, which have presumably been generalized in the depressed person's mind to become hopelessness about life itself. Besides, as Bolles (1990, p. 113) notes in a wonderfully perceptive comment:

> We usually know nothing about an individual's history of reinforcement, so to cite it as an explanation of some piece of behavior is . . . reductionistic. . . . Most psychologists now know better; they know that to understand the phenomenon they are looking at, they have to look at the phenomenon, not somewhere else.

Psychological stress has undergone a similar transition from formulations emphasizing the objective environment to subjective, cognitive formulations. When it was defined strictly in terms of environmental stimulus conditions (stressors), which bring about behavioral disturbances, subjective distress, and physiological tension, the formulation was basically similar to Duffy's or Lindsley's concept of activation, an outlook that has been increasingly downplayed in recent years.

The older formulation can be traced to Hooke's seventeenth-century engineering input-output analysis of load (a force applied to an object), stress (the way load impinged on the object), and strain (the resulting deformation of the object). Hooke was particularly interested in the elasticity of materials. The inanimate object was said to resist deformation until it breaks. In engineering, strain is disequilibrium or tension in the physical object, just as stress in living creatures is a biological disequilibrium that activates or drives behavioral and physiological efforts to restore the disturbed equilibrium.

The analogy between stress (or strain) and disequilibrium (or activation) was very appealing. Some persons, because they have high stress tolerance, resist psychic distress and dysfunction, just as in Hooke's terms, some substances, because they are elastic, resist breaking. Because it dealt entirely with observables and did not reify the conceptual fictions we put into the mind as explanations, to many this way of thinking seemed more scientific than speculations about mental events. This is what Brown and Farber (1951) were trying to achieve in their formulation of emotion as an intervening variable.

Ultimately, the analogy to load, stress, and strain in engineering, like the activation or drive model in psychophysiology, failed, because psychological stress and emotion cannot be adequately defined without reference to an individual's motivation and the way that individual defines and evaluates relationships with the environment — a process I have been calling *appraisal.* The quality and intensity of an emotional response to the appraised relationship also depends on the *coping process,* because what one thinks and does to alter a troubled relationship with the environment changes either the relationship or the way it is appraised, thereby changing the emotions that flow from it.

The concepts of strain and activation are in no sense equivalent or parallel to the concepts of appraisal and coping. Strain and activation are unidimensional concepts, though the distinctions I have made (e.g., Lazarus & Launier, 1978) among harm, threat, and challenge, and Selye's (1974) distinction between eustress and distress shift the analysis slightly away from a single dimension and toward the idea of different kinds of stress and strain. In any event, the stress process is a complex, multivariate, feedback system, as is the emotion process. Emotion is not unidimensional but refers to a variety of states, each with overlapping but distinctive contents, and so I speak of *the emotions* — that is, as a plural noun rather than a singular.

Cognitive analyses and research on psychological stress (e.g., Janis, 1958; Lazarus, 1966, 1968a; Lazarus, Averill, & Opton, 1970; and Mechanic, 1962/1978) have influenced many psychologists toward subjective, transactional, and process formulations, and away from stimulus-response formulations. These modes of thinking also have brought us closer to a *system theoretical*[2] analysis (cf. von Bertalanffy, 1968; also Lazarus & Folkman, 1984, 1986, 1987), on which I draw in Part Two.

A theory of psychological stress, perforce, takes a large step toward being a theory of emotion, since stress-based emotions are centered on negative conditions of adaptation. To expand psychological stress theory into a theory of emotion requires only that we also consider the conditions under which the person is benefited, and from which positive emotional states are generated. That is, emotions can be described in kind as well as intensity, thereby allowing for a rich variety of kinds of emotion or emotion families (cf. Dewey, 1971). Diverse negative emotional states arise from particular harmful or threatening relationships; positive emotions from particular beneficial ones.

For example, though all negative emotions share the property of being a reaction to thwarting, each of these emotions — that is, anger, fear, guilt, shame, and so on — is also a separate and distinct reaction to diverse forms of thwarting; each involves a different person–environment relationship and pattern of appraisal. Similarly, happiness, pride, love, and relief, though having in common that they arise from beneficial relationships with the environment, are also quite different from each other in the specifics of the relationship and how it is appraised. Once one has sampled the potential richness of the concept of the emotions, psychological stress seems too restrictive as a basis of understanding the processes of adaptation.

Speaking further about the modern penchant for reductive analysis, one could also argue that a common problem has beset all the sciences as a result — namely, that basic theory and research provide the details about microprocesses, which are important, but yield little that has broad utility for understanding and predicting how complex systems function at the molar level, and for influencing in a practical way how these systems act and react. Some aspects of system theory, as we see later, are particularly well suited to the task of bringing the complex set of person-centered variables that affect emotion and adaptation together with the complex set of variables that comprise the environments in which persons must function, and it is especially useful for examining the cognitive processes of decision making on which human adaptive and maladaptive action is predicated.

In connection with cognitivism as explanation, many writers have observed a pendulumlike oscillation between two intellectual traditions, both of which are relevant to emotion: One is based on the outlook of philosophers such as Locke, Hume, and Mills, who promulgated the view that we adapt and develop by copying the "contours of the world" as it exists, to use Gergen's (1985) phrase. The measure of how things are is external reality, which science is seeking to understand. Gergen refers to this as the *exogenic* perspective. The other perspective is the *endogenic*, which locates knowledge within the person, a phenomenological outlook that is consistent with the thinking of philosophers such as Spinoza, Kant, Nietzsche, and Hegel. The measure of how things are is the subjective world of persons. Another way to put this is to say that we can view human life as adapting to the world as it is or as constructing that world out of our minds.

Though he uses terms different from Gergen's, Tomkins (1965) cogently portrayed the same basic ideological polarity in psychology and showed how it also worked in many other areas of knowledge, such as art, politics, and even childrearing. He wrote:

> The issues are simple enough. Is man the measure, an end in himself, an active, creative, thinking, desiring, loving force in nature? Or must man realize himself, attain his full stature only through struggle toward, participation in, conformity to a norm, a measure, an ideal essence basically prior to and independent of man? In Greek philosphy this is the polarity between Protagoras and Plato, between the conception of man as the measure of all things and the conception of Ideas and Essences as the realm of reality and value.

From the 1930s to the 1960s, when the Freudian influence on academic and clinical psychology was great, there was a strong endogenic or intrapsychic focus. The focus later shifted to the environment during the 1970s and is illustrated today in research on major life events, such as death of a loved one or divorce, as the primary sources of change to which the person must adapt. Life events tend to be viewed as adventitious external occurrences (or stressors) rather than as products of continuous transactions that change the functional relationships between a person and the environment and, in so doing, affect that person's emotional life. The reader will see shortly that I take a relational view of the emotions, which is neither exogenic nor endogenic, but consists of a particular combination of both, a compromise or negotiation between the two sets of forces, the outer and the inner.

Gergen (1985) believes that American psychology has for a long time been characterized by an exogenic emphasis, and that scholars in philosophy and psychology, especially in Germany, have wrestled with how to integrate both streams of thought. He suggests that except for a "stalwart band of phenomenologists [p. 269], the endogenic outlook might have died. However, the challenge (for many) has been to transcend the traditional subject-object dualism" (p. 270). If we carry this reasoning into the present domain of concern, we should say that since *both* person and environment are important factors in emotion and adaptation, the oscillation can be ended only when we adopt a truly *relational* (or transactional) approach and find a suitable language for it (see also Lazarus, 1990b).

In the 1960s and 1970s, some psychologists began to recognize that the behavioristic, exogenic outlook drew on an epistemology that was unfriendly to the study of emotion. However, a totally endogenic outlook would be equally unfriendly — and surely in error, too — because it would leave out the social and physical environment in the process of emotion generation. The oscillating extremes of an exogenic or endogenic outlook are efforts to understand human adaptational success and failure exclusively in terms either of universal internal human characteristics, most often manifest in Darwinian, evolutionary terms, *or* in terms of external social and economic conditions that must be manipulated to reduce genetic and acquired inequality. In Chapter 5 I shall attempt to reconcile these biological and sociocultural extremes, which is, I believe, a key requirement of a viable theory of emotion.

Be that as it may, along with others in the 1960s, I was trying to develop a cognitively based, phenomenological approach to psychological stress and coping (Lazarus, 1966). It seemed important then to make an elaborate criticism of the dominant behavioristic outlook, especially radical or extreme behaviorism, and to spend much time and space preparing the epistemological grounds for a cognitive-phenomenological outlook. Today, however, although there are important pockets of resistance, and many psychologists are reluctant to abandon behaviorist values, cognitive views appear to be dominant. The concept of appraisal is now widely used as an approach to stress and emotion. Motivation is coming back as an important construct. And there is no longer much need to assault an S-R psychology that is no longer in control of academic thought.

It is also worth noting that the cognitive movement has gone a bit too far in that thought has almost become equivalent to mind. Although cognition and mind overlap, this equivalence overextends the proper meaning of cognition, which the emphasis on cognition has sometimes implied and invited. In speaking of the role of cognition in emotion and adaptation, we must be clear about the types of cognition, about the other psychological processes that are involved, and about the precise ways in which these processes operate (cf. Lazarus & Smith, 1988).

As I shall try to show in Chapter 3, the so-called cognitive revolution should now be called the *cognitive-motivational-relational revolution* because thought alone is insufficient for an adequate theory of mind, behavior, and emotion. After all, thought has to refer to something — it does not operate in a vacuum — and the cognition of the emotions involves goals, plans, and beliefs and is about the stakes (active goals) and (coping) options a person has for managing the person–environment relationship. Although in 1966 I referred to my psychological stress theory as cognitive and phenomenological, today I refer to my theory of emotion as a cognitive-motivational-relational system of explanation, with *relational* standing for a focus on negotiation with a physical and social world.

Equally important in the recent intellectual movement toward cognitive-motivational-relational formulations was a relaxing of the earlier constraints on the use of constructs in theory, a changing conception of causation and determinism paralleling changes that had already taken place in physics, and a greater pluralism in the scientific paradigms that psychologists were willing to entertain (see Fiske & Shweder, 1986). Modern interest in unconscious processes (see Bowers and his commentators, 1987; Erdelyi, 1985; Guidano & Liotti, 1983), the notion of tacit knowledge (Polanyi, 1966), the concept that what is sensory or perceptual is also, perforce, motor (cf. Neisser, 1985; von Hofsten, 1985), and what is called action theory, which emphasizes goals, intentions, and plans (e.g., Frese & Sabini, 1985) — all reflect a much freer search for understanding how the mind works than was possible in past decades. Although this freedom troubles many, I believe it has been a major stimulant for a renewed interest in emotion.

The changes in outlook referred to here have their modern origins several decades ago in the work of some forward-looking and creative psychologists such as

Asch (1952b), Harlow (1953), Heider (1958), Kelly (1955), Rotter (1954), McClelland (1951), Murphy (1947/1966), and White (1959), to whom we must add their intellectual mentors, Lewin (1935) and Murray (1938), who initiated the modern cognitive-phenomenological movement in North America a generation earlier. Because of their influence, we can now ask with a straight face how persons must be evaluating (appraising) what is happening in their adaptational relationships with the environment to generate a particular emotion. Although the older epistemology refuses to die completely, as is manifested in what might be called "residual behaviorism," psychologists in general are getting more comfortable with this way of thinking.

Ironically, these changes in outlook also brought us back to a kind of "folk psychology" once found in Aristotle's *Rhetoric*. For example, an emotion such as anger is said to be the result of a subjective judgment that one has been insulted or demeaned. Lest the reader come to believe from what I have said that a cognitive emphasis in emotion theory is restricted to either the time of Aristotle or a period following the 1960s with nothing in between, I quote a nineteenth-century philosopher at University College, London, by the name of Robertson, whose work was shown to me by a postdoctoral trainee in the study of emotion. I cannot read this quote without thinking of that wonderful Japanese movie, *Rashomon,* in which the same events are seen through the eyes of several different people sharing them. Robertson (1877, p. 413) wrote:

> Four persons of much the same age and temperament are travelling in the same vehicle. At a particular stopping-place it is intimated to them that a certain person has just died suddenly and unexpectedly. One of the company looks perfectly stolid. A second comprehends what has taken place, but is in no way affected. The third looks and evidently feels sad. The fourth is overwhelmed with grief which finds expression in tears, sobs, and exclamations. Whence the difference of the four individuals before us? In one respect they are all alike: an announcement has been made to them. The first is a foreigner, and has not understood the communication. The second has never met with the deceased, and could have no special regard for him. The third had often met with him in social intercourse and business transactions, and been led to cherish a great esteem for him. The fourth was the brother of the departed, and was bound to him by native affection and a thousand ties earlier and later. From such a case we may notice that in order to [experience an emotion] there is need first of some understanding or apprehension; the foreigner had no feeling because he had no idea or belief. We may observe further that there must secondly be an affection of some kind; for the stranger was not interested in the occurrence. The emotion flows forth from a well, and is strong in proportion to the waters; is stronger in the brother than in the friend. It is evident, thirdly, that the persons affected are in a moved or excited state. A fourth peculiarity has appeared in the sadness of the countenance and the agitations of the bodily frame. Four elements have thus come forth to view.

There is still considerable discomfort with what is called, often snidely, *naive* or *commonsense psychology,* as if scientific concepts should have no connection with ordinary experience. If theory is connected with experience and is, therefore, intuitively believable, it is said to be inadequate, with the parallel implication that a good theory must be abstract and mathematical, as in theoretical physics, and not intuitively obvious. It is also possible to argue that these are two different levels of abstraction and that both levels can be useful in different ways. It is not the level of abstraction that bothers me, but the arrogance that says that the concrete, personally subjective level cannot be good science.

When I began as a student of psychology, there was also much negative comment among some so-called hard scientists to the effect that psychology was not and could not be a science. For all I know, this criticism persists, and unfortunately psychologists still regularly identify with the aggressor — as do psychiatrists — leaning over backwards to prove they are "real" scientists. Social scientists of all stripes keep trying to demonstrate that they live up to the values of proper science, while commonly feeling inferior to the biological and physical scientist. This is unfortunate and has, I believe, held us back.

My view of science is not based on how well we measure psychological variables, though such measurement is plainly essential, or how much we know or can predict, but on an *attitude* toward measurement and inquiry. Any field of inquiry that seeks programmatically to reason about its phenomena, and to build and evaluate understanding through observation, is a science. It uses multiple methods of research, whatever may be available to get at its phenomena, and tries to conceptualize about structure and process within a coherent and self-consistent framework of logical thought. It is the continuous effort to do this that distinguishes science from nonscience, not how successful we are at any given moment. If we try to match our concepts with what we can observe, we are engaged in science. Nor should it surprise us that our present understanding and our ability to predict and influence individual human behavior is modest, especially in light of the complexity of the organisms we study and the processes that are of concern to us. I suppose this is what makes being a psychologist so challenging.

The most important rebuttal to the denigration of folk psychology is that if one believes, as I do, that the way an individual evaluates the personal significance of encounters with the environment is a cause of emotional reactions in that individual, then this is precisely the low-level and concrete explanatory theory psychology must have for the emotions. We need to know what people want and how they evaluate the wide-ranging business of their lives. This is what appraisal is all about. When all is said and done, the concepts of folk psychology can be put to empirical test as readily as any other kind. The main downside of this position is that sometimes people don't know and can't describe what is in their minds, which could produce distortions of what researchers infer is happening. I try to deal with the issue of the unconscious in Chapter 4.

Perspectives on Emotion

I turn now to a number of diverse perspectives on emotion — those of the individual, the observer, the society, and the biological species — which correspond more or less to the various scientific disciplines contributing to knowledge about emotion. Emotion looks different from the vantage point of each of these perspectives. They can be arranged into concentric circles of widening scope, beginning with the most narrow: the *individual* at the center who experiences an emotion; the *observer* (say, a friend, clinical practitioner, or scientist) who pays attention to emotional reactions; the *society,* whose values and institutions shape emotions; and in the broadest circle, the *biological species,* whose genetically given properties shape emotions, too. These perspectives make emotion truly interdisciplinary, with each discipline asking questions that reflect its own field-centered concerns.[3]

The Individual

What happens, especially with a strong emotion, is that we who are experiencing it are often taken over by the emotion; our attention becomes riveted on the harm or benefit and what we must do about it; we are caught up in the charged relationship we are having with the environment, the urge to action, the sensations associated with that relationship, and the reaction it provokes.

Although analysis after the fact, as if we were detached observers of what is happening, is subject to retrospective falsification, it is probably easier to be an observer or to make an analysis of our emotions after the experience has ended than it is during the experience, because an analytic attitude may obliterate or weaken the emotion; intellectualized detachment is itself a powerful method of emotion regulation or coping, as will be seen in Chapter 3. At the moment the emotion is happening, however, our thoughts, motives, action impulses, and physiological changes are focused on and organized around the personal stakes and adaptational requirements of the encounter. When something important is at stake, we pay attention to what seems relevant at the moment and don't want to be distracted by other considerations, giving little opportunity for detached observation as if we were an observer rather than a participant.

We must, of course, be observing ourselves when we experience an emotion, as classical writers have long noted, because we usually remember much, though not all, of what happened. The line between such observation and the experience of an emotion is blurred, because to have and remember an experience also requires perception and judgment. When we remember the experience, however, the perspective taken is more like that of an observer, except that we have access to much more information than an observer—or I should say different sources of information— because we can perceive some of our thoughts, action impulses, and bodily sensations, as well as some of what an observer can also notice. An outside observer, strictly speaking, does not experience the emotion, except perhaps vicariously, but observes evidence of it. I examine the problem of what is observable and unobservable further in Chapter 2.

The all-encompassing nature of some emotional experiences also makes them difficult to ignore. Usually emotions interrupt some ongoing task or activity, which is what leads Mandler (1984) to speak of them as *interrupt* phenomena. Without clarification, however, this designation may be both confusing and misleading and led some years ago to debates about whether emotions organize or disorganize behavior. The issue was resolved by proposing that an emotion organizes behavior around the focal demand that generated it, and also disorganizes the ongoing activity that had been interrupted.

I would prefer not to speak of *organize* or *disorganize* but rather to say that an emotion shifts the focus of attention from what the person was doing before the emotion to some other concern, namely, the focal demand and the emotional experience it creates. What I am saying is that the ongoing activity is not necessarily disorganized (see Hebb, 1949; Leeper, 1948)—though it could be—but only discontinued as an immediate concern; the person's attention is focused on something else that is now intrusive. In short, emotions *focus attention* on some concerns and, by the same token, *distract attention* away from other concerns that are not so pressing, depending on whether one is speaking of the interrupted original activity or the new adaptational demand.

In speaking of shifting attention, or interruption if one prefers, one could say either that the emotion is brought about when an ongoing commitment or behavior sequence is no longer salient or pressing because something new and of greater importance has happened, a statement that refers to the emotion *generating process,* or that the emotional *reaction* itself—for example, the subjective affect, the physiological changes, and the tendency toward some action—turns the attention away from ongoing activity. I think both of these are correct to some extent. Remember, however, that the emotional reaction itself reflects and includes the perception of a changed person–environment relationship, and serves also as a compelling signal that something of significance is occurring. It also motivates subsequent activity, which is organized around this significant occurrence. The person is, in effect, pressed to attend to and deal with a new encounter whose adaptational salience created the new reaction in the first place.

I do not believe that this restatement is mere quibbling, because it points to the functional significance of what is happening in the transaction, including the process generating the reaction rather than merely the reaction itself. When we use the term *emotion,* especially from a cognitive-motivational-relational perspective, we are referring to a great many variables and processes such as the eliciting environmental and internal conditions that produce a person–environment relationship, the mediating process of appraisal of that relationship, the tendency toward action, and the coping process, as well as the response itself, which combines actions, physiological changes, and subjective experiences in a coordinated fashion. When people use the term *emotion* they may have in mind either the whole configuration or one or another of its components.

The potentially disorganizing aspects of emotion—that is, actual fragmentation of thought and action, not just subordination of one activity by another more salient or urgent focus—are, of course, important in themselves. In the 1950s and 1960s, psychologists were very interested in the ways in which strong emotions could *interfere* with rational problem solving and thought. When a person is in a traumatic situation, perception and thought may be impaired, blocked, distracted, even paralyzed. A good example is telling a medical patient about something terribly devastating, such as the presence of an inoperable cancer. Most wise physicians know that what is said after cataclysmic news has been given is often not heard, and so giving any further advice about the management of the illness should wait for a time when the patient is ready and able to listen.

Another example is the tremendous difference between how we function after the appraisal of threat and how we function after the appraisal of challenge. A *threatening* encounter makes one feel uneasy (anxious), which is not only unpleasant but is apt to constrict one's ability to think and perform. The constriction is connected with a strong effort to protect oneself from anticipated danger. In contrast, a *challenge* makes one feel good, and there is apt to be a considerable expansion of one's functioning, with relevant thoughts coming easily and with a subjective impression that one is approaching the zenith of one's powers. The smooth and superior functioning characteristic of challenge and of what Maslow (1971) called "peak experiences" has been called "flow" by Csikszentmihalyi (1976). In sum, threat often involves cognitive impairment, challenge the facilitation of cognitive activity.

An emotion may also be *informative* to the person who experiences it (see, for example, Schwarz & Clore, 1983) — that is, a source of insight into oneself and what is happening. When we react with anxiety, anger, happiness, or whatever, there is usually some awareness and understanding of how the emotion was precipitated as well as of the emotional reaction. We realize immediately, or later after reflection, that we are angry because someone has behaved toward us in a hostile, critical, or unresponsive way, or that we are anxious because the situation threatens us and we are vulnerable. This insight may be useful in helping us deal with recurrent emotional distress and is what clinicians want clients to have in order to better manage their emotional lives.

There are also occasions in which a person is not aware of making an appraisal of harm or threat — which are the bases of negative emotions — either because the social relationship is ambiguous or because the person is engaging in ego-defense. We may not even be aware that we are reacting emotionally because we have misinterpreted our reaction or the conditions bringing it about. As I point out in Chapter 4, it is better to refer to this not as an unconscious emotion, which may be a contradiction in terms, but rather as a misinterpretation or condition of inattention. I recently learned of an academic friend who was monitoring his heart rate because of a problem of ischemia (insufficient oxygen in the muscle tissues of the heart) when his heart rate would reach 150 beats per minute. He was amazed to discover that in departmental faculty meetings, when he had thought he was merely cynically detached from the faculty discussion, he was actually attaining heart rates that approached the point of ischemia, presumably because he was strongly aroused emotionally (not happily, of course) by what was going on. The monitoring of his heart rate was useful because it made him attend to, and properly interpret, what was happening, giving him the opportunity to do something about the problem.

Psychologists have offered theories about adaptationally ambiguous encounters in which the person fails to interpret correctly what is happening. The most notable of these is that of Schachter (1966; Schachter & Singer, 1962), which has generated considerable research and debate (see, for example, Marshall & Zimbardo, 1979; Maslach,1979; Nisbett & Valins, 1972; Reisenzein, 1983; Valins, 1966). This theory states that because emotional arousal is vague and diffuse, what is going on in the social environment provides necessary clues about the emotion being experienced. If we are aroused in a hostile social situation, we label what we have experienced as anger; but if we are aroused in a cheery social situation, we label our emotional and bodily state as happiness.

This line of reasoning about the emotion process is inadequate in my judgment for three reasons: First, it overemphasizes the social environment in the generation of an emotion at the expense of the motivation and thought characteristic of the reacting individual in a relationship with the environment. Second, it makes the cognitive mediation in the emotion process too much a matter of labeling and too little a matter of evaluation and judgment. Although sensing threat can be more or less automatic (see Chapter 4), we often or perhaps typically have to make a complex inference about, or construct an interpretation of, what is happening and its implications for our well-being, which is not mere labeling by association but an evaluation. Third, the reasoning seems backward to me in that it doesn't help to explain why the emotion was aroused in the first place. Although there are undoubtedly exceptions, and although we may not think about or verbalize it clearly, I think we usually react emotionally, and get aroused, because we have sensed something personally harmful or beneficial in our ongoing relationship with the environment. This is not the place to deal in depth with the problems inherent in Schachter's theoretical position. The important point for now is that, if we pay attention, emotions can inform us about psychological processes that might otherwise not have been noticed or their significance grasped.

Emotions also provide *indispensable color* to our lives; we think of emotional experiences as hot, exciting, involving, or mobilizing, and distinguish them from experiences that are routine, cold, and detached. Life without emotion, even painful emotions, would be an exercise in monotony. Negative emotional experiences are aversive, and we seek to remove their causes or regulate the distress when it is above some threshold of comfort or toleration, but when there is too little emotional color, we are bored and seek excitement (Zuckerman, 1979). People seem to differ in the level of emotional excitement that is optimal for their subjective well-being.

The individual perspective also calls attention to inter- and intraindividual variations in emotion. From the interindividual point of view, persons are compared with respect to the emotions experienced in a given context; from the intraindividual point of view, the same individual (or group) is compared across time or occasions. People differ greatly in the emotions they display, and we refer to this as *interindividual* variation. This variation can be explained in either of two ways: First, it may be the result of different personality traits, which lead to different emotions in the same situation. Second, the situations may be different. The fact that the same person may differ in the emotion experienced from situation to situation or moment to moment refers to *intraindividual* variation, and is also explainable in the same two alternative ways. One explanation is that in each instance the person–environment relationship is perceived and evaluated differently because of the action of personality variables; a second is that the situation is actually different in each instance. It is difficult to determine which of these explanations of emotional variability — namely, personality differences or situational differences — is correct in any instance. Both may well apply.

It is also possible that some environmental conditions — those, for example, that are very clear and powerful in their impact and consequences, such as a serious loss or the threat of death — will have a greater effect and produce more uniform reactions, whereas others — those, for example, that are ambiguous and relatively mild in their impact and consequences, such as minor social criticism or an inconvenience — will produce more variable reactions because there is room for diverse interpretations of their personal significance. I would expect that strong emotions would occur only in the most vulnerable persons in these mild loss or threat conditions — for example, in someone whose sense of social esteem is weak and whose need for social approval is great. I have more to say about this in discussing the appraisal process in Chapter 4, which is about how we evaluate the personal significance of adaptational encounters.

One reason why the contrast between intra- and interindividual variations is so important is that they sometimes generate different answers about how emotions are organized. The contrast has been brought home by Epstein (1983, pp. 125–126), who used both strategies and found that, when one strategy was compared with the other, the relationships among the emotions were sometimes different (see also Pervin, 1986). Epstein writes that people who report a higher level of happiness than others also report being more sociable and affectionate, having higher self-esteem, and being more responsive than others to the external world. These between-subject findings are similar to those of Wessman and Ricks (1966), who have also done normative studies of the emotional life over time. In contrast, happiness, viewed from a within-subject perspective, appears to be more often induced by a stimulus and accompanied by increased positive affect along with increased feelings of security, greater reactivity to the environment, and more freedom to be oneself and express what one feels. Presumably, when conditions change, this emotional complex also changes.

If we think carefully about this, we can see that the questions asked in each are different; therefore, the differences in findings ought not to be surprising. Consider, for example, the general question of whether sadness and happiness tend to be correlated. This question as stated is ambiguous. If, for example, it is answered by an *interindividual* research strategy, we are apt to find that the two emotions are correlated positively across persons, which means that those who experience frequent or strong sadness are also likely to experience frequent and strong happiness. If, however, the question is answered by an *intraindividual* strategy, we will find that when a given individual is sad, that individual is not likely to be happy at the same moment or in the same context. In the former perspective, sadness and happiness are positively correlated, but in the latter, they are negatively correlated. There is no contradiction, because the psychological question posed in each case is different. In one, we are comparing different individuals, and in the other, we are comparing individuals with themselves (see Broverman, 1962, and Marceil, 1977, for a more detailed examination of this issue).

It always amazes me that psychologists have been so uncomfortable about individual differences — as if, somehow, science must be entirely normative, and variations among and within people violate science and its search for universal mechanisms (an outlook I shall have more to say about in Chapter 5). I quote from a physicist, de Klerk (1953, p. 4), who wrote about the magnetic properties of metals in a way that suggests that the same problem of individual differences also applies to the physical world:

Some substances, for example, iron and nickel, show a rather complicated magnetic behavior at room temperature. When placed in a magnetic field, they show a magnetic moment which not only is a function of field and temperature, but which also depends on the history of the specimen; that is, it depends on the fields and temperatures in which the substance has been before.

De Klerk's statement, with some slight changes in the variables being referred to, could have been written about individual differences in personal history, resulting in personality variations that play a role in emotions and behavior. The inevitable finding of individual variation, both between and within individuals, challenges the adequacy of our efforts to understand emotion and is one of the issues that must be dealt with by theorists of emotion. The trend today in psychology is to recognize that both sources of variation, the person with a history and the environment that the person confronts, are important, which gives rise to the growing popularity of transactional, process, and system formulations (see Chapter 5).

The Observer

An observer is one who infers the presence of an emotion in another from what is seen and heard. Observers might be friends, enemies, scientists whose business it is to understand the phenomena of emotion, clinical practitioners whose therapeutic task is to help correct or ameliorate clients' emotional dysfunction, or of course, even people who are experiencing the emotion but are also observing themselves. An observer capitalizes on the fact that mammals, people included, communicate on purpose or inadvertently about their emotional lives through their emotional expressions, intentional actions, and what they say about their subjective experience.

Social communication is an important adaptational function of emotion. Herd animals must be able to tell when a predator, who may live among them, is hunting. Mating is often dangerous or impossible without signs of receptivity on the part of the female. The safety of animal handlers in zoos and laboratories depends on their being able to tell when an animal might attack; there have been a number of sad examples of experienced primate researchers who were inattentive or misjudged the situation and lost parts of their anatomy.

Our social behavior is guided constantly by cues that we interpret about the emotions of others, cues that can reveal others' action impulses and intentions. We decode and interpret complex and often conflicting communications and miscommunications that people send and receive in social intercourse. People do not give their trust to someone who seems to feel hateful toward them and could, therefore, intend harm. Verbal compliments or expressions of warmth are discounted if we also sense malevolence. By the same token, we may sense benign intentions in people who on the surface are threateningly direct and tacky, which illustrates the difficulty and complexity of the judgments we make.

An important and sometimes implicit assumption in all this is that we can truly understand other people's states of mind and the implications for our personal well-being by making inferences from signals perceived through our vision, hearing, or other senses. Because these inferences may be erroneous (Ekman, 1985), we must be wary of taking things at face value as appearances may be managed socially for effect or may be the result of a process that is not emotional. From the standpoint of research, the problem is to determine which indicator — or better still, which pattern of indicators — is a reliable source of information about emotion and under what conditions. Multiple indicators can be compared with each other and combined to provide a sounder basis for the judgment (see Chapter 2).

Clinicians have understood well that what is claimed by a client is often suspect because of self-protective or ego-defensive ways of disguising the real meanings of what is happening. The task of distinguishing the truth from attempts to deceive is a daunting one. The principle used for spotting deceptions is the presence of *contradictions,* of which there are several kinds: What a person says at one moment may contradict what is said at another. What a person says may contradict expressive actions, as when anger is denied but nevertheless indicated by facial or bodily gestures or visible physiological changes, such as the reddening of the face. And what a person says may seem unbelievable in light of the situation; often an inference about an emotion in another person is made on the basis of consensual impressions of how people typically react in the same type of situation. Contradictions initiate the hypothesis that things are not what they seem, and the next task, even more difficult than the first, is to make sense of what is going on.

What can we learn ideally from emotional reactions in others (see also Ekman, 1984)? First, given the premise that emotions are rule-based phenomena rather than chaotic, the quality and intensity of an emotion can tell us about ongoing relationships between persons and their environments. I call these *core relational themes* (see Chapter 3). If the emotion is anger, we know that the relationship involves harm, threat, or insult, depending on how we conceptualize anger. If the emotion is anxiety, the relationship involves uncertain threat and the impulse to avoid or escape it. Although the action may be inhibited and even transformed, and there may be other parallel or contradictory actions (cf. Averill, 1983), I assume, along with other cognitive-motivational-relational theorists (e.g., Frijda, 1986), that each prototypic emotion expresses a primary *tendency to act** that is consistent with how a person evaluates the relationship with the environment.

Second, emotions also can tell us about what is important and what is unimportant (i.e., as in a *goal hierarchy*) to a person in an encounter or in life. We do not get emotionally upset about unimportant events. If we do, it is prima facie evidence that something important is going on from our personal standpoint; something of significance is at stake, even if this is denied (see Chapter 3).

Third, by observing how a person characteristically appraises relationships with the environment, and the emotions this results in, we can discover much about that person's *beliefs about self and world* (see Chapter 4). For example, one person may be generally fearful because of a low self-regard. Another person, in contrast, may seem to have a chip on the shoulder, suggesting malevolent beliefs about others.

Fourth, an emotion can tell us about how a person has *appraised* (evaluated) an encounter with respect to its significance for well-being (see Chapter 4). Recurring

---

*Frijda and others use the term *action tendency,* but tendency to act is more euphonious and less jargony.

emotions provide clues about a person's characteristic way of appraising adaptation-ally relevant encounters, and life itself.

Clinical practitioners have long known that no other source of information about their clients' psychodynamics is as informative as the emotions these clients experi-ence, especially the recurrent ones, and the social contexts in which these occur (cf. Lazarus,1990b, in press a). A universal clinical tool is, therefore, to observe the client's emotional reactions in the here and now, and sometimes to have the client reconstruct distressing emotional experiences of the recent or distant past.

These four propositions do not exhaust what can be learned about persons from their emotions, but they are among the most important and have the greatest practi-cal value. I discuss the motives, appraisal process, core relational themes, and action tendencies that might be involved in emotions in Part Two (Chapters 3, 4, and 5), and the specifics for each emotion in Part Three (Chapters 6 and 7).

The Society

What is revealed about persons from their emotional lives is also revealed about social communities in which emotional patterns are widely shared. Emotions, there-fore, are also of interest to sociologists and anthropologists, who are concerned with social systems and culture. This is well illustrated by Smelser's (1963) analysis of panics, riots, fads, and fashions. Although Smelser wrote about collectivities rather than individuals, and he regarded social strains such as unemployment as disequilib-ria in the social system, his analysis parallels in many ways the emotional experi-ences of individuals. In effect, riots can be thought of as social variants of individual anger involving acts of aggression, and panics as social variants of individual fear involving acts of escape or avoidance.

Given this parallel between individual and collective analysis, social scientists can judge the workings of social institutions and their impact on mental and physical health from collective symptoms of emotional distress and dysfunction, just as clini-cal practitioners make similar judgments about individuals. This underlies and is illustrated by some of the classic sociological evaluations of community mental health (e.g., Faris & Dunham, 1939; Hollingshead & Redlich, 1958). Some modern inner-city communities are regarded as severely dysfunctional because of wide-spread poverty, demoralization, and use of illegal drugs (such as heroine and cocaine), which should probably be viewed more as a symptom of the dysfunction than as a cause.

That society shapes the emotional life of the individual is a central theme of *social constuctionist* theories of emotion (e.g., Averill, 1980, 1983), in which it is argued that individual emotional patterns reflect the influences and functions of the social community and involve the acting out of transitory social roles that are sanc-tioned or encouraged by society. In this view, the individual psychological level of analysis and the societal level are intertwined. For example, what are considered appropriate emotions and emotional displays by individuals (Hochschild, 1979) is a product, in part, of social values and beliefs.

It is not difficult to conceive of benign or positive emotional states such as hap-piness, love, pride, and gratitude as helping to preserve the social structure; these emotions obviously can strengthen social bonds. The same point may readily be made for shame and guilt. These negative emotions are generated when overt behavior has deviated from social standards that have been internalized by the individual. Therefore, being deterred from deviancy in the presence of observers by the threat of rejection or abandonment, as in shame, or being deterred from antisocial behavior even when no other person — except perhaps an inner representation of one — is there to see it, as in guilt, helps preserve social institutions by generating prosocial behavior.

It is, however, more surprising to find Averill (1983) also maintaining that, rather than typically being destructive, anger, too, upholds social norms. Based on extensive college student reports about anger episodes, he concluded that anger is usually directed at friends and loved ones, seldom involves overt aggression, is provoked by the appraisal that one has been wronged by another person, is adaptively motivated to prevent a recurrence of the wrong, and usually has an outcome that the angered person regards as beneficial.[4] Averill's data comparing the impulse and the actual response reported, depending on the target of the anger, is presented in Table 1.1

These reports deviate from the expectation that anger engenders aggression against others and, therefore, is destructive to social ties. (See Novaco, 1979, and Tavris, 1984, for an opposing emphasis on the negative social effects of anger.) The issues surrounding anger and its behavioral expressions continue to pose major

TABLE 1.1. Aggressive and Nonaggressive Responses Characteristic of Anger

Response Type	Impulses Felt[a]	Responses Made[a]
Direct aggression		
Verbal or symbolic aggression	82	49
Denial or removal of some benefit	59	41
Physical aggression or punishment	40	10
Indirect aggression		
Telling a third party in order to get back at the instigator (malediction)	42	34
Harming something important to the instigator	25	9
Displaced aggression		
Against a nonhuman object	32	28
Against a person	24	25
Nonaggressive responses		
Engaging in calming activities	60	60
Talking the incident over with a neutral party; no intent to harm the offender	59	59
Talking the incident over with the offender without exhibiting hostility	52	39
Engaging in activities opposite to the instigation of anger	14	19

[a]Expressed as percentage of episodes (N=160) in which response occurred "somewhat" or "very much."

(*Source:* J. R. Averill, "Studies on anger and aggression." *American Psychologist, 38.* Washington, DC: American Psychological Association. Copyright © 1983 by the American Psychological Association. Reprinted by permission.)

questions for research: For example, in what respects and under what conditions do expressed and nonexpressed anger have adaptive as opposed to maladaptive consequences?

In my judgment, there is much merit in the social constructionist position. However, I have the impression that it draws on a partial truth, albeit an important one, and expands this part into the whole, which it is not. For example, social constructionism ignores biological universals in favor of an exclusive reliance on sociocultural forces to explain the emotions, thereby undermining its credibility as a theoretical position.

Nevertheless, though emotional arousal is often useful biologically in helping us mount an effective assault on danger, especially a physical assault, societies have innumerable and complex social constraints on how we react when threatened. Most societies have punitive laws as well as deeply embedded moral impediments against aggression. Restraint, careful planning, cool detachment, and the appreciation of subtle cues and meanings are often the most serviceable strategies of adaptation; becoming overly aroused can get in the way of successful coping, because these cues may be missed in the excitement. People might also be threatened and offended by a group member's tendency to use physical assault, except when it is thoroughly justified.

In an essay titled "Fighting Words," English professor Jane Tomkins (1989, pp. 33–34) describes the morality of violence that characterizes the Western movie, and provides a revealing look at North American social values and the justification of violence:

> The structure of this sequence [described for the movie Shane] reproduces itself in a thousand Western novels and movies. Its pattern never varies. The hero, provoked by insults, first verbal then physical, resists the urge to retaliate, proving his moral superiority to those who are taunting him. It is never the hero who taunts his adversary; if he does, it's only after he's been pushed "too far." And this, of course, is what always happens. The villains, whoever they may be, finally commit an act so atrocious that the hero *must* retaliate in kind. At this juncture, the point where provocation has gone too far, retaliatory violence becomes not simply justifiable but imperative: now we are made to feel that *not* to transgress the interdict against violence would be the transgression. The feeling of supreme righteousness in this instant is delicious and hardly to be distinguished from murderousness. I would almost say they are the same thing.

That the culture of a society and its social structure shape the emotional life of the individual has also become an important theme of cultural anthropology, a field that, like other social sciences in the past, relegated this topic to the sidelines, and of sociology, a field that also has rediscovered the emotions. Reviewing recent work on the anthropology of emotions, Lutz and White (1986) suggest that, to many anthropologists in the past, emotion seemed to belong more in the natural sciences and to be biologically uniform and uninteresting from the standpoint of sociocultural theory. Now, however, anthropologists are beginning to sense a valid tension between the biological concern about what is universal in emotion across cultures and the sociocultural concern about what is shaped by the culture of a people with a distinctive outlook and ways of living. I deal with these questions in depth in Chapters 5 and 9.

The Biological Species

When emotion is viewed from a biological perspective, two themes become salient: The first concerns neurophysiology—that is, the role of different portions of the brain and peripheral nervous systems, and the hormones that serve both as neurotransmitters and as regulators of metabolic and motor activities. The second concerns the operation in a biological species of an inherited emotion process, or *affect programs,* as they are sometimes called. From a phylogenetic point of view, emotions must have promoted species survival to have evolved as they did. Affect programs are the biological analogue of the social constructionist point of view, which seeks an understanding of emotions through their social functions (see Chapter 2).

In this book I do not attempt to address the physiology of the emotions, particularly the role of the brain and its neurohumoral properties. There is a small but growing group of neuropsychologists who are pressing this task, and as the reader will see in Chapter 2, I believe that a sound psychophysiology of the emotions requires, above all, a sound psychological theory about how the emotions work. This is the task I have set for myself, and it would be my hope that others will try to draw the connections between what is known at the psychological level and what is known at the physiological level. On the other hand, I do consider it within my purview here to indicate how biology and sociocultural factors at the macro level combine to influence the emotions, which I do in Chapter 5 and in two chapters on emotional development (Chapters 8 and 9). These give some attention to biological factors, particularly as they are related to temperament. And in Chapter 2, some of the research and thought about the autonomic nervous and hormonal systems, which play an important role in the emotional response pattern, are discussed.

Emotion undoubtedly has many survival-related functions, both social and physiological. Two stand out: Social communication, which I mentioned earlier, is one. Another is to stimulate and sustain psychological and physiological mobilization in the face of essential biological needs that are not being met and challenges from the environment. Emotions can be said to serve as amplifiers, to use Tomkins' (1963) felicitous electronic metaphor, of the cognitive processes that permit an animal or person to evaluate the potential harm or benefit in an encounter with the environment and to cope with it. Thus, a child will often learn more quickly and better in the heat of an emotion than when not mobilized. This principle is illustrated by the ordinarily calm and reassuring mother who intuitively knows that scaring a child vigorously to bring home the dangers of city motor traffic is a good way to avoid depending on the vicissitudes of trial and error in such a life-and-death issue. The danger, of course, is that if the fright is too strong it might also disorganize behavior and thought and so be dangerous in itself.

It is a truism that we pay a price for our animal inheritance, as is implied in this fright example. The human environment for millions of years was one in which survival was threatened primarily by predators and other physical dangers, but the changes in some modern societies over the past few thousand years may have made aspects of the emotion process less useful and even counterproductive under certain conditions. Ethologists refer to this change in utility by the cumbersome phrase "environment of evolutionary adaptedness," which means that humans evolved by adapting to a different environment than the one in which they now live. Emotional arousal is commonly blamed for emotion-produced mental and physical illness, as in the so-called stress disorders (Selye, 1956/1976).

Quite clearly, we must be attentive to the complex strategies of coping with harms and threats, and the emotions they generate, which are capable of suppressing or modifying biologically generated action tendencies such as attack and escape. Thus, what we say about the functional significance of emotion depends on the kind of society and culture we live in or the specific life conditions experienced in sub-groups within that society. The urban life of modern industrial societies — I resist the temptation to refer to what is being called postmodern, which seems to me to be an oxymoron — is probably quite different in respect to how these questions might look from the point of view of less developed societies. In any case, we need to ask when any given emotion will be adaptive or maladaptive, and in what ways — questions I have asked earlier with respect to anger.

Every animal species faces adaptational problems that must be dealt with successfully in order to survive. A central theme of a biological-evolutionary approach to emotion is that there has been a gradual decoupling of adaptive behavior from hardwired reflex actions (see Smith & Lazarus, 1990). For example, when confronted with an image in the sky of a hawklike form, which suggests the presence of a dangerous predator, the fowl studied by ethologist Tinbergen (1951) — in what have become famous experiments — automatically react with alarm. Tinbergen used a cardboard silhouette as an experimental stimulus, and when the movement of the silhouette was reversed so that instead of looking like a hawk it looked like a non-predatory bird, the fowl showed no evidence of fear or alarm. The silhouettes are shown in Figure 1.1.

Similarly, the intraspecies attack behavior of the male stickleback fish studied by Tinbergen depends on there being a bright red spot on the other fish's belly; if the red spot is absent, as it is in the female, attack behavior does not occur. The stimulus materials used in this research are shown in Figure 1.2.

These automatic, reflexive, or neurologically hardwired reaction patterns, which

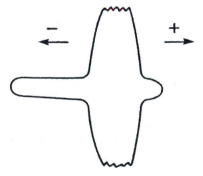

FIGURE 1.1. Silhouette used to study the release of fright reactions in game birds. For explanation, see text. (*Source:* N. Tinbergen, *The Study of Instinct.* London: Oxford University Press, 1951. Reprinted by permission.)

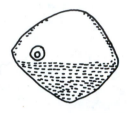

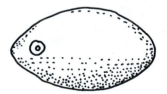

FIGURE 1.2. Models used to test attack responses in male sticklebacks. The four models with red bellies release attack responses. The much more accurate model without coloring does not. (*Source:* N. Tinbergen, *The Study of Instinct.* London: Oxford University Press, 1951. Reprinted by permission.)

in lower species seem to be fully controlled by specific environmental stimulus configurations, provide an important basis for species and individual survival. I have more to say about the evolutionary progression from reflexes to emotion in Chapter 5.

Those who adopt a biological perspective on emotion must resolve the question of what is unique to human emotion and what is shared with other animal species. From an evolutionary point of view, adjacent species on the same limb of the phylogenetic tree share similar neurochemical and, hence, emotional properties. There is also considerable sharing of neural and humoral structures across species. Yet there seem to be important differences, too, in the types of emotion possible in humans compared with infrahuman species. We speak of pride, gratitude, shame, and guilt in humans, and though some writers argue that these are also present in other animals, especially primates, it is difficult to make a case for this that is not anthropomorphic.

Certain emotions probably first emerged in higher species, but when and in what form is not at all clear. Humans, for example, appear to be the only animals that smile and laugh when happy, and almost the only ones that cry when sad. We may also be the most emotional creature in existence, if by this is meant having the richest and most complicated range of emotions and conditions under which to generate them—a result, I believe, of our complex intellectual abilities and social structure. And because the emotions depend on sociocultural factors, our theories about them must encompass *both* biological and social perspectives. Many of the controversies about emotion center on conflicts over differences in these perspectives, and I attempt in Chapter 5 to set suitable biological and social boundaries.

Finally, animal behaviorists, ethologists, and psychologists, unfortunately, are not able to study emotions in infrahuman animals in the same way, or with the same conceptualizations, as they do in humans. For example, at the infrahuman level one speaks of aggression or agonistic behavior rather than anger, and escape or avoidance rather than fear, in deference to the obscurity about what is going on in the animal mind. We can ask people, but not simpler animals, to tell us what they are thinking and feeling. Although many psychologists are distrustful of subjective reports about our mental life, perhaps inordinately so, if we can't depend to some extent on what humans tell us, we lose important information about emotions, because behavior alone is not easy to interpret.

For example, attack behavior does not necessarily permit the inference of anger, nor does avoidance or escape behavior necessarily imply fear. If we turn the issue around, anger, as Averill (1983) suggests, does not necessarily lead to attack (in contradistinction, perhaps, to the impulse or action tendency to do so) any more than fear is tantamount to avoidance or escape. Differences in the methods used with animals and humans, and in resultant conceptualizations, present epistemological problems for any theory of emotion that strives to be biologically universal—that is, to encompass both human and animal species.

The appropriate solution—easier to say than do—is to use more than one response level of analysis as a source of understanding and to check the inferences from one against the other. In human subjects, for example, we can ask about the subjective experience of anger as well as measure facial expression or physiological activity, so that, if anger is denied but the person attacks or shows a facial and physiological response profile associated with anger, we are in a position to second-guess what we are told and infer with some justification that anger has probably occurred.

The Adaptational Encounter as the Proper Context of Emotion

It is not obvious to everyone that the basic *arena* of analysis for the study of the emotion process is the *person–environment relationship*. The basic *unit* of this relationship is an *adaptational encounter* or episode. Sometimes an encounter has to do

with short-term, concrete, and immediate agendas, and sometimes it deals with existential issues extending over a long time, perhaps even over the entire life course.

Encounter boundaries constitute an important problem for emotion theory and
research, and yet this problem has been given little attention. In a valuable review
focused on the concept of *episode* in social psychology, Forgas (1982) examined a
variety of social interactions such as eating in a restaurant, visiting a doctor, and
having coffee with someone; eating in a restaurant, however, may have little or
nothing to do with emotion. If we want to talk about emotions in psychological
terms — that is, to examine what is most meaningful to people — the center of our
interest must not be focused merely on any social interaction, or any setting of interaction, but on the particular aspects of the encounter that have emotional significance.

What is striking about the work of those concerned with episodes is that their
attention has focused mainly on the formal properties of social interaction rather
than on content. More recent work (e.g., Forgas, 1982; see also Forgas & Moylan,
1987) has attempted to remedy this, as will be seen shortly following the discussion
of functional equivalence. We need to narrow our attention to encounters that are
adaptational and thus potentially emotional, to contrast nonemotional social interactions with emotional ones, and to try to understand the functional relationship
between the person and the enviroment that leads to emotion. Our view of encounters also needs to be theory driven.

What I propose is that to engender emotion an adaptational encounter must center on some *personal business,* as it were; it is an ongoing transaction between person and environment having a bearing on personal goals, which are brought to the
encounter and with respect to which the environmental conditions are relevant. The
business has to do with *realizing these goals* as well as *managing the demands, constraints, and opportunities* presented by the environment. I have more to say about
the motivational underpinnings of emotion in Chapter 3.

There has been a growing effort to go beyond the separate, partitioned variance
of person and environment in an encounter, as might be examined in a statistical
interaction, and to find ways of conceptualizing the joint contribution of these two
sets of variables to the reaction. Along with many others (e.g., Tellegen, in press),
Wright and Mischel (1987, 1988) have set the stage for this focus on the person–
environment relationship. They (1988) have noted, for example, that earlier thinkers
writing about traits (such as Allport, Asch, and Murray) warned of the dangers of
examining traits that are removed from the contexts or situations in which they manifest themselves. And in a useful statement about conditional trait approaches that
draws on the notion of functional equivalence, they write (1987, p. 1162):

For more than a decade interactionist approaches have emphasized that personality
assessment requires parallel assessment of situations . . . , and have attempted to
identify the relation between functional equivalence classes of situations . . . , and
categories of behavior. . . . Indeed, one of the greatest challenges both for interactionist research and for our conditional approach is to identify the categories of conditions or "equivalence classes" of situations most relevant to a given behavioral
domain. Historically, empirical studies of "interactionism" have often found it easier
to categorize types of people to whom dispositional statements might apply . . . than

to specify the categories of situations in which important individual differences are most likely to be observed. Without identifying such equivalence classes of situations, applications of conditional models run the same risk as certain previous applications of interactionism, namely, the risk of producing very large numbers of specific context-behavior contingencies whose psychological significance is unknown and that cannot be predicted in advance.

Sorting encounters or relationships into adaptationally relevant equivalence classes is, in fact, what appraisal is all about, as will be seen in Chapter 4. For example, the person must decide whether what is going on is relevant to important values or goals. Does it impugn one's identity? Does it highlight one's inadequacy? Does it pose a danger to one's social status? Does it result in an important loss? Is it a challenge that can be overcome, or a harm that one is helpless to redress? Or is it a source of happiness or pride?

The concept of functional equivalence, or equivalence classes, constitutes an effort to develop a principle to connect properties of persons with environmental conditions in order to define a *person–environment relationship* in adaptational, and therefore emotional, terms. What gives encounters their valence and power to provoke emotion is the person's pattern of *motivation,* which provides the organizing psychological framework for the encounter. For example, when Forgas asked subjects to describe the characteristics of social encounters or episodes, he observed that

Emotional reactions to episodes, such as self-confidence, intimacy, involvement, and pleasantness were more important than objective episode features, suggesting that subjects indeed relied on personally relevant, functional rather than objective, descriptive criteria in their judgments. (Forgas, 1982, p. 74)

There remains the question of whether the boundaries of an adaptational encounter should be defined by the points of change from one emotional state to another, by the business being transacted, or by both. My view of emotion makes these coextensive; the fate of the business at hand, as appraised by the person, and the emotions experienced are conjoined, one being the basis for the other. Thus, when an emotion changes in intensity or quality, the point of transition occurs with a change in the person–environment relationship—in effect, with a change in the *status of the business at hand.* So the boundary problem turns on whether it is more useful to define the encounter boundaries by the emotional state and its changes, or by the status of the business involved in the transaction. These alternatives are really two sides of the same coin.

If we take the business at hand to be the key defining attribute of an adaptational encounter, then even over the course of a single encounter there can be numerous changes in that business. In most adaptational encounters, there are apt to be several or even many kinds of business, which makes the boundary problem even more difficult and complex. The original relational theme—say, dealing with rejection or the threat of rejection—may change in the course of a brief time span to other themes—to being demeaned, feeling that we have transgressed against social standards, that we have acted well, or that we are appreciated by a person we care about. These are

(Wide World Photos)

FIGURE 1.3. Look at this picture and try to infer what the two boys are thinking and feeling on the basis of the situation portrayed and the expressions on their faces. The actual story is printed upside down, below. See whether you have sized up the situation correctly.

"Please, Spade, don't sit down now." The boy at the left burst into tears as his huge collie decides to stage a sitdown strike while being judged in a school pet show. The boy on the right observes sympathetically.

some of the relational themes on the basis of which one reacts emotionally with anger, guilt, sadness, pride, liking, or love. Consider, for example, the challenge presented in Figure 1.3.

There has been little study of the organization and change of the operative goals within complex adaptational encounters. Perhaps there is one overriding theme, but subordinate ones that were latent during the course of the encounter may emerge and gain ascendency. For example, a person may begin the encounter with a concern about selling another person on some course of action, but then become threatened by an unexpected hostile reaction that endangers yet another goal that initially did not seem relevant. Any encounter may also contain two or more contradictory agendas. For example, a person who has experienced anger at having been insulted and who remains resentful may at the same time recognize a social gain in having exposed another's venality, rigidity, or hostility, producing more than one emotional state, based on harm and benefit, depending on which relational theme one attends to.

I recently talked with a student about his orals; he had experienced a number of emotions that illustrate what I have been saying. He was an outstanding and articulate student, but he entered the orals with considerable apprehension and was looking forward to having a chance to demonstrate his competence in the area of psychological stress and coping, which he felt he had mastered. When I chose not to ask him about this but instead asked a difficult integrative question, he became distressed, probably more than he showed, feeling a combination of anxiety and annoyance because his first reaction was that I had let him down. However, he rose to the occasion beautifully and, after a while, realized that my high regard for what he could do led me to challenge him rather than patronize him with an easy question. It took a bit of time for him to see that what I had done was a compliment rather than an offense, but after he did, his emotional reaction seemed to become positive.

What happened in this encounter is that, in addition to surprise because the question was unexpected, the student's original goal, to protect an endangered private and public image, shifted to a challenge of his ability to confront difficult issues with the faculty, and the previous threat-induced anxiety was allayed along with the annoyance. My agenda, in contrast, was not to patronize him, which I believed was unnecessary. This is an example of divergent interindividual and intraindividual appraisals that are possible in the same context and that derive from different personal agendas and perspectives. It is also an example of the changes in operative goals and stakes that may take place in an encounter along with changes in the behavior of the main cast of characters.

To facilitate a comparison between *short-term* adaptational encounters and *long-term* encounters, it would be well to think of a hierarchy of goals in which a short-term goal such as passing an examination in school serves larger order, long-term goals, such as the desire for prestige, high income, and a challenging career (see Ortony & Clore, 1981). For example, failure on an examination could have implications for one's lifelong commitments. In turn, a long-term commitment may require doing well on exams and could make the failure in a brief encounter much more trying and intense — even resulting in a fainting spell — than it would be in the absence of such a commitment. In contrast, a weak long-term commitment may trivialize the immediate failure. Individual differences in the degree and pattern of long-term commitments create variations in the recurrent emotional and mood themes in a person's life, as well as variations in the emotional reactions of the moment.

When we try to understand emotions as the result solely of the immediate adaptational encounter, we fail to consider the figure-ground relationship and are in danger of misunderstanding the quality and intensity of the emotions generated. In a study of adolescent emotions, for example, Klos and Singer (1981) found that the arousal of anger in a parent-child encounter and the repetitive thoughts generated in the encounter were strongly influenced by long-standing, previous interpersonal stress with the parent; emotional reactions were as much affected by background relationships as by the immediate or figural aspects of the encounter.

The imagery of figure and ground still leaves unclear how to define the temporal and spatial boundaries of an adaptational encounter. A spousal argument occurring before a couple leaves for work one morning illustrates the problem. Although actions and words may have set the encounter in motion at the outset, the trouble may have preceded the morning's altercation, in part because the relationship has been chronically strained. Without knowing something more of the history of the relationship, we cannot even attempt to understand the deeper, perhaps unconscious, bases of the strains between the spouses and the individual and joint dynamics at work.

Moreover, the ending or resolution may be far from clear; for example, the argument may have ended merely because both must leave for work, during which it may temporarily drop out of their minds because of new involvements of the business day, only to recur when the couple returns home, perhaps now with brooding silence, hostile gesturing, or brief explosions of anger. Although an episode may at first seem to have had a clear beginning and ending, this is only so superficially. Yet it makes even less sense to muddy the distinction between background and figure, because the emotional states generated in the morning's encounter are not continuous, but have an on-and-off quality tied closely to the actual spousal transactions.

It seems to me that the ultimate solution to the boundary problem must be to break down the business of complex adaptational encounters into their component themes, and to be alert to transitions and the changes they create in the experienced emotion. Each goal or concern that operates in an ongoing emotional encounter constitutes a separate building block, or encounter atom, as it were. If they are not somehow separated in time, we will be mired in confusion about what is going on in the transaction and be unable to study effectively either the emotion process, the emotion-related interface between psychology and physiology, or that between psychology and sociology. Doing this successfully is easier said than done, but it may be essential to good emotion research.

When, for example, we are concerned with the interface of psychological and physiological processes, and we want to link physiological reactions to specific provocations and emotional states, we must measure both variables before there has been a transition to another person–environment relationship with its changed emotional state. The hormones and other chemicals generated by the emotional state linger in the tissues for some time before they have been fully excreted, metabolized, or returned to storage by homeostatic processes. If anger has abruptly changed to guilt or relief or changed in intensity, as when it waxes to rage or wanes to calm indifference, then what we have measured just previously is no longer relevant to the changed state, and we are apt to be misled about the psychophysiological processes. This is more than merely a problem of technology, because in much research the key difficulty is the absence of an adequate theory about the emotion process itself. We need a theory to drive research strategies that might clarify the psychophysiology of emotion (see Chapter 2), among other issues.

The Issues and Tasks of a Theory of Emotion

This might be a good point at which to list the most important, broad, and vexing *issues* that any theory of emotion must address, and for which my cognitive-motivational-relational theory offers some answers at various places in the subsequent chapters. The full list is long, but it is enough here to mention twelve that could help the reader anticipate some of what follows in later chapters.

1. How should the construct of emotion be defined? What should a theory of emotion do? I deal with these issues shortly.

2. Which reactions are emotions, which are not, and by what reasoning should we make the decision? Is startle an emotion? What about surprise? Pain and pleasure? How about empathy and aesthetic emotions? Are frustration, threat, challenge, and hope emotions or are they best regarded as types of appraisal. Many of the issues involved in these decisions are discussed in Chapter 2.

3. Are emotions best thought of as discrete categories—for example, anger, fright-anxiety, guilt, shame, envy, jealousy, sadness, happiness, love, pride, relief, hope, compassion—or as a small set of factor dimensions such as pleasantness and unpleasantness, tension or relaxation, or the like? See Chapter 2 for a discussion of this problem.

4. What, if any, is the role of action tendencies and physiological activity in emotion? Should our answer be like that of Frijda (1986), who suggests that each emotion has its own action tendency, or that of Ortony, Clore, and Collins (1988), who argue that this is an untenable position? What connection, if any, is there between action tendency and physiological activity in emotion? Should physiological activity be a defining attribute of emotion, or are there emotions that have no measurable physiological activity? This also is taken up in Chapter 2.

5. What are the functional interdependencies among emotions such as anger, anxiety, guilt, sadness, relief, and so on? We are told, correctly I believe, that hate (anger) and love (affection) are closely intertwined in human relationships. Depression (which usually involves anxiety, guilt, and sadness) is often said to give way to externally directed anger as a distressed mental patient begins to get well, suggesting that these emotions are also closely related. How can we understand these interdependencies? This is covered in Chapter 3, and again in Part Three.

6. What are the functional relations among what Hilgard (1980) called the trilogy of mind—namely, cognition, motivation, and emotion? I will suggest in Part Two that emotion theories differ mainly in the ways these constructs are deployed, and this has varied throughout the history of thought about emotion. What role, for example, does cognition play in the generation of an emotion? Is it a necessary and sufficient condition? What kinds of cognition are there and do they all influence the emotion process and in the same way? This is dealt with in Chapters 4 and 5, where appraisal is discussed as a key concept of the theory.

7. Biological scientists, and those whose interests center on natural selection and the evolution of species, tend to emphasize species universals in the emotion process, often to the exclusion of variability; in contrast, social scientists and those whose interests center on ontogenesis and learning tend to emphasize the role of society and culture in shaping the emotion process. How can we reconcile biological universals in emotion with sociocultural sources of variabilility? See Chapters 5 and 9 for my proposals.

8. How should we relate the concept of cognitive appraisal to depth psychology and unconscious mental activity? Are the rules of emotion generation different when mental contents are conscious rather than unconscious? This is discussed in Chapter 4.

9. How does each emotion differ in the way it is generated? What are the conditions that distinguish among them? See Part Three, Chapters 6 and 7.

10. How should we understand emotional development? What are the sources of influence? What is the role of biological factors such as temperament? What is the role of learning and personality? The ego-identity or self? This is considered in Chapter 8.

11. What are the effects of emotion on long-term adaptational outcomes such as subjective well-being, social functioning, and health? I deal with this in Chapter 10.

12. How can we influence the emotion process to be less dysfunctional, as in psychotherapy? I deal with this in Chapter 11.

Although many of these issues have been worked and reworked in diverse treatises, my handling of them is necessary for a systematic presentation of the emotions and their conceptualization, which is the intent of this book. In much of my discussion, I believe — at least I hope — that I have added something new to what has been said before. At the very least, I have attempted to present a self-consistent, coherent way of organizing the subject matter of emotion, and to do so it is inevitable that I will go over ground that others too have covered before me.

What of the *tasks* of emotion theory in light of these stated issues? One of these tasks is, of course, to attempt to *define emotion.* It is difficult at this juncture to defend a satisfactory definition of emotion, and each element in the definition might raise as many questions as it answers. A common solution is to give a descriptive definition based solely on the response itself. Most response-based definitions point to three features: physiological turbulence or change; action tendencies that are not necessarily acted out; and subjective experience, which is commonly referred to as *affect.*

No two emotions are identical, of course, because the ideational content depends on the context, which is likely to differ in detail. For example, if I am angry at my boss and angry at my wife, these two emotional states overlap but differ in their ideational content because, perforce, one thinks of wife and boss in quite different ways, though at the moment of the encounter there is some degree of functional equivalence: Both have offended me, and how I react overtly has a great bearing on the future relationship and all that it entails.

In any case, Hillman (1960) suggests that there is considerable agreement on these response aspects in the definition of emotion, and he quotes Drever's (1952) *Dictionary of Psychology* definition as follows:

> *Emotion:* Differently described and explained by different psychologists, but all agree that it is a complex state of the organism, involving bodily changes of a widespread character — in breathing, pulse, gland secretion, etc. — and, on the mental side, a state of excitement or perturbation, marked by strong feeling, and usually an impulse towards a definite form of behaviour. If the emotion is intense there is some disturbance of the intellectual functions, a measure of *dissociation,* and a tendency towards action of an ungraded or *protopathic* character. Beyond this description anything else would mean an entrance into the controversial field.

Although I do not quarrel with most of this, I also believe it is not an adequate strategy to focus solely on the response, because so doing begs a number of fundamental questions. A theory is needed to resolve the issues, a task that a definition such as that of Drever's cannot perform. The basic task of an emotion theory is to find a way to integrate eliciting conditions in the environment and person, mediating processes such as thoughts, motives, action tendencies, and physiological activity, all of which are part of the complex configuration we call an emotion. To accomplish this, several things must be done

First, propositions must be offered about emotion as a general phenomenon — that is, we must describe how the emotion process works and the important variables in this process. These propositions should address two broad matters: (1) The causal variables affecting emotion must be taken into consideration. These include personality characteristics, such as a goal hierarchy; belief systems about self and world; the demands, resources, and constraints of the physical and social environment; the structural and cultural meanings of the society that affect emotion; the person–environment relationships, and knowledge, appraisal, and coping processes. Here emotion is a dependent variable. (2) The effects of the emotion process on short- and long-term adaptational outcomes must be addressed. These include its influence on the development of the self, person–environment relationships of the moment and characteristic of a person, feedback effects on appraisals and coping processes, and the effects of emotion on somatic and mental health. Here emotion is an independent variable.

Second, propositions consistent with the general treatment of emotion must be offered about specific categories or subclasses of emotion such as anger, anxiety, guilt, joy, pride, and so on. These will depend, of course, on what is considered an emotion in the first place. These propositions, incidentally, do not arise out of the thin air but from a combination of logical analysis based on cognitive-motivational-relational theory, a long history of speculations and observations — the wisdom of the ages, as it were — about the conditions of each individual emotion, and recent programmatic research on the appraisals associated with each. One could argue about whether the existing data base, which is often informal and anecdotal, is adequate, but it offers a good start in setting up propositions about the appraisal pattern for each individual emotion. I assume that correlational and experimental research on these patterns, which has already gotten off to a running start, will continue to provide empirical tests of the theoretical reasoning.

After the decision about which emotions to consider, the variables for each emotion must be identified. In addition, the effects of individual (the independent variables) emotions on adaptational outcomes should also be considered when important; for example, the consequences of anxiety are probably quite different from the consequences of anger or disgust, and those of happiness different from those of love.

As independent variables, too, the ways emotions interpenetrate social functioning, subjective well-being, and somatic health must also be explored. Here the focus is on the effects of emotion once generated, and whose total configuration feeds back perceptually and evaluatively to the sentient being and thereby affects the next emotion to be generated.

Without a theory to help us, we are left with the impression that emotion may not be amenable to classical definition at all, and that it might be a good tentative strategy to think of prototype definitions (see also Fehr & Russell, 1984; Leeper, 1965; Rosch, 1978; and Shaver et al., 1987), which acknowledge that some reactions (e.g., anger, fear, guilt) are more prototypical than others (e.g., startle, excitement, surprise, distaste, pain, hunger, and thirst). Excitement, surprise, distaste, and the like are borderline phenomena that resemble sensorimotor reflexes and drives more than they do emotions.

This position about the need for theory to resolve definitional questions creates an epistemological dilemma. Usually definitions identify a phenomenon that can be universally observed and do not include a host of processes that must be explained. Consider the following attempt at definition I made, but never published, four or five years ago in an effort to facilitate finding answers to the difficult questions that cannot be resolved without theory:

> Emotions are organized psychophysiological reactions to news about ongoing relationships with the environment. "News" is colloquial for knowledge or beliefs about the significance for personal well-being of the person–environment relationship. The quality (e.g., anger versus fear) and intensity (degree of mobilization or motor-physiological change) of the emotional reaction depends on subjective evaluations — I call these cognitive appraisals — of this knowledge about how we are doing with respect to our goals in the short- and long-run, and on the action tendency that points to the terms of the relationship. This significance depends on the interplay of a person's goals and beliefs and a provocative environmental context. Emotions are, in effect, organized cognitive-motivational-relational configurations whose status changes with changes in the person–environment relationship as this is perceived and evaluated (appraised).

In this statement, as in response-based definitions, emotional reactions include Drever's (1952) three components: (1) strong impulses to act in certain ways (for example, to attack or flee, to shout with joy, to express warmth to another person, to hide, and so on); (2) a pattern of bodily change coupled with the tendencies to act, which often but not always involves mobilization in the interests of some adaptational end; and (3) an experiential component (often referred to as *affect*) that includes an evaluation or judgment, which includes the contents of *appraisal.* The statement also encompasses the four multidisciplinary perspectives on emotion I discussed earlier, referring to the individual, observer, societal, and biological/adaptational ways of thinking.

The problem posed by calling this a definition is that it presupposes a theory, and therefore, the very issues that must be resolved empirically, such as whether appraisal is both a necessary and sufficient condition of emotion, are part of the assumptions or postulate system of the theory. The answers are given by assertion, as in all theory, so opting for this solution leaves it unclear whether the proposals comprising the theory are subject to confirmation or disconfirmation. And so I offer the statement quoted earlier not as a definition but as a hint of the propositions that comprise the system, which is subject to empirical evaluation.

The Theory in a Nutshell

At this point it may help the reader to have a brief advance statement of the cognitive-motivational-relational theory that is presented in detail in Parts Two, Three, and Four. The theory can be described in terms of five metatheoretical and substantive themes. I review these themes again in Chapter 11, which deals with the practical implications of the whole system.

The five metatheoretical themes are as follows:

1. The theory is a system theory. The *system principle* states tha.. process involves an organized configuration of many variables: antecedent, n.. ing process, and outcome or response. No single variable is sufficient to explain the emotional outcome, and all variables are interdependent. The system variables are outlined at the end of Chapter 5 in Figures 5.2 and 5.3.

2. Emotions express two interdependent principles: one, the *process principle,* referring to flux or change; the other, the *structure principle* (see Chapter 3), referring to the idea that there are stable person–environment relationships that result in recurrent emotional patterns in the same individual.

3. The biological and social variables that influence the emotions develop and change from birth, especially in the early years of life but perhaps also in later life. This is called the *developmental principle;* it also implies that the emotion process is not the same at all stages of life, a topic discussed in depth in Chapters 4, 8, and 9.

4. The emotion process is distinctive for each individual emotion. This, the *specificity principle,* implies what I have already said: that one of the major tasks of emotion theory is to generate subtheories in which the emotion process in each individual emotion — for example, anger, anxiety, pride — is spelled out (see Part Three, Chapters 6 and 7). This is carried out by drawing on Principle 5, which follows.

5. The key substantive theme of the theory is the *relational meaning principle,* which is developed most fully in Part Two, Chapters 3 and 4, and, applied later in Part Three to the individual emotions and to the developmental chapters of Part Four. This principle states that each emotion is defined by a unique and specifiable relational meaning. This meaning is expressed in a *core relational theme* for each individual emotion, which summarizes the personal harms and benefits residing in each person–environment relationship. The emotional meaning of these person–environment relationships is constructed by the process of *appraisal,* which is the central construct of the theory.

The appraisal process involves a set of decision-making components, as it were, which create evaluative patterns that differentiate among each of the emotions; three primary appraisals, which concern the motivational stakes in an adaptational encounter; and three secondary appraisals, which have to do with the options for coping and expectations. The *primary appraisal* components are goal relevance, goal congruency or incongruency, and type of ego-involvement. The *secondary appraisal* components are blame or credit, coping potential, and future expectations. Each individual emotion is distinguished by its pattern of primary and secondary appraisal components. *Coping* also plays an important role in the personal significance of the person–environment relationship and influences the appraisal process, and hence the emotion, through feedback.

Appraisal and coping processes are joint products of personality and environmental variables, which unite in the person–environment relationship; this relationship entails a new level of theoretical analysis, which I speak of as *relational meaning;* this meaning centers on the significance of what is happening for personal well-being. It depends on how the environmental conditions are conjoined with a person's beliefs and goals. The task of appraisal is to integrate the two sets of antecedent variables — personality and environmental — into a relational meaning based on the relevance of what is happening for the person's well-being. We can understand the emotional response in terms of how what is happening is construed by the person from the standpoint of personal interest and adaptation.

If the significance of what is happening involves personal harm or benefit, an emotion is generated that includes an innate *action tendency,* which provides the basis for the unique physiological activity characteristic of each individual emotion. The *coping* process, which may be consistent with or in conflict with the action tendency and may override or inhibit it, is more psychological, planful, and deliberate, and it also influences the actions and physiological pattern.

To summarize the organization of the book, in Part Two, Chapter 3, I go into detail about person–environment relationships, core relational themes, coping, and their motivational underpinnings. In Chapter 4, I am concerned with the ways in which meaning is generated and unconscious appraisals. In Chapter 5, I deal with problems of causality.

In Part Three, Chapter 6, I deal with goal incongruent or negative emotions, and in Chapter 7, I discuss both the goal congruent or positive emotions as well as emotions that are problematic.

In Part Four, Chapter 8 deals with individual differences in emotional development, and in Chapter 9 my concern is with social influence, including the roles of culture and social structure in the shaping of the emotions.

Part Five is concerned partly with emotion as an independent variable. The effects of emotion on health are discussed in Chapter 10, and in Chapter 11, I point to the implications of this theoretical system for three practical arenas — research, assessment, and treatment and prevention.

Summary

The topic of emotion was downplayed in psychology until the 1960s, a decade characterized by the advent of neobehaviorism and social learning theory, a movement toward cognitivism, and greater interest in systems theory. More than any other arena of psychological thought, emotion is an integrative, organismic concept that subsumes psychological stress and coping within itself and unites motivation, cognition, and adaptation in a complex configuration. Emotion theory is also centered on the relationship between a person and the environment rather than either environmental or intrapersonal events alone.

Emotion appears differently as a topic from the point of view of each of four field perspectives — the individual, the observer, the society, and the biological species — and all four viewpoints are essential to a thorough understanding of the emotions. Emotions are experienced by individuals and, through intentional or inadvertent communication, may be inferred by others who are observing; they are a valuable source of information about persons and how they are getting along in their worlds. Society creates patterns of behavior and outlooks that shape the emotions and their expression in the individual. Biological inheritance also shapes the emotion process. Emotion theory has the task of integrating both the social and biological perspectives in understanding how emotions work.

The arena of the emotions is the person–environment relationship, and the basic unit of analysis is the adaptational encounter. One of the important problems in emotion theory is to define the boundaries of encounters, both horizontally and vertically, the latter referring to depth psychology and the unconscious mind. The concept of functional equivalence offers a motivational principle that attempts to locate the business of adaptational encounters in goals that are important to the person and whose salience shifts as the encounter unfolds and changes. Acute emotions arise from specific business in encounters whereas moods have to do with issues having to do with a person's overall life and existential fate. The ongoing business of an encounter and of life itself is appraised by the individual, which is the basis for the emotions experienced.

Chapter 1 ends with an examination of the major tasks of a cognitive-motivational-relational theory and the most important issues that must be addressed by such a theory, including the definition of emotion. These tasks are twofold: (1) to state propositions about emotion as a general phenomenon that describe the workings of the emotion process as well as the important variables of this process, and (2) to suggest propositions, consistent with the general theory, about specific emotions such as anger, anxiety, and pride, which might be regarded as separate subtheories.

In the preceding, emotion is treated as a dependent variable by asking how it is brought about. Emotion must also be treated as an independent variable by examining how it affects social functioning, subjective well-being, and somatic health (see Chapter 10).

Before diving into the cognitive-motivational-relational theory in Part Two, we must still come to terms with issues of emotion research, measurement, and classification in order to decide on the particular emotions to be dealt with later on. I address these issues in Chapter 2.

Notes

1. Actually, Duffy's analysis came to the proposal of abandoning emotion in favor of activation for different reasons than others did, a challenge to a system theory of emotion that I will confront in Chapter 5.

2. When this way of thinking was first proposed, it was called *systems theory* because it was designed to convey the idea of multiple, interdependent systems at different levels of analysis that were part of the agenda of unified science. However, as I am using it, the singular term, *system,* is used rather than *systems,* because I refer only to the emotion process as a system. I alert those readers who are accustomed to seeing the expression *systems theory* that henceforth I will use *system, system theory,* or *system analysis.*

3. There is a fifth perspective, the *developmental,* which I shall not discuss here because I devote two chapters, 8 and 9, in Part Four of this book, to it. The developmental perspective is unique in cutting across these other perspectives and in following a time line from birth to death in the ontogenesis of the emotion process and the variables that comprise it.

4. It is possible that this finding would not have occurred with a lower- or working-class sample, but the comparison was not made. College samples are apt to have a high proportion of students coming from middle-class families that share negative values about, and social constraints against, physical aggression.

❖ 2 ❖

Issues of Research, Classification, and Measurement

This chapter, like the first, is preliminary to the presentation of my theory in Part Two. Its purpose is to examine what makes research on emotion, its measurement, and its classification so difficult and challenging. I believe that the best research draws on theory, which identifies the important research questions and promotes strategies of research and measurement consistent with itself; theory and research strategy are interdependent. Much research, said to be performed without theory, really draws on implicit assumptions about emotion that, even when not stated formally, constitute a kind of primitive theory consisting of causal notions, hunches about how things work, and unstated prejudices about theory and research. A theme that underlies what follows is that without a theory we would be unable to resolve the fundamental issues of classification and measurement on which programmatic research depends.

I consider here five broad issues: the variables of emotion; what the emotions are; emotions as categories or dimensions; current research and thought about universals in the emotion response, which centers on facial expression and autonomic nervous system patterning; and a distinction—favored especially by phylogeneticists—between primary and secondary emotions. I close the chapter with a tentative (working) classification of the emotions, which is necessary for the proper presentation of the theoretical analyses in Part Two and the individual emotions in Part Three.

The Variables of Emotion

A number of specific, molecular variables such as motor actions, physiological changes, and subjective states are functionally united within the molar emotion categories. Molar concepts are created by interpreting peripheral microobservations—such as an action or a physiological change, as a feature of some central, integrative process, such as emotion. To speak of them as features of an emotion is an interpretation—a theoretical inference, if you will. Some of the molecular variables are directly observable and others are not, and we should look more closely at these variables and the interpretive inferences that are required to view them as molar emotional phenomena.

There are four classes of *observable* variables relevant to emotion:

1. *Actions,* such as attack, avoidance, moving toward or away from a place or person, weeping, making facial expressions, and assuming a particular body posture, constitute one class of observables. Some actions, such as facial expressions, might sometimes be said to be volitional and instrumental in that they are performed to create a social effect, whereas at other times the same actions might be said to be expressive, which implies an involuntary process. To suggest either is, in effect, an interpretation, and it is extremely important to recognize when we have made an interpretation and when we are merely making an observation.

When we place the word *instrumental* or *expressive* in front of the word *action,* this juxtaposition implies that a goal or function is involved and the action is instrumental in achieving that goal or function. Even avoidance, which could be said to be an observable action, implies an *intention* because the word *avoidance* suggests that the action's aim is to move the person away from some object or individual. To speak of avoidance is, therefore, to make an inference about an unobservable process that needs to be substantiated. In sum, the phenomena of action are observables, but to say that such actions are either motivated or expressive, or that they derive from or indicate an emotion process, is interpretive and thus involves a kind of theory. There is nothing wrong with this; it is only important to be clear about it.

2. *Physiological reactions,* such as autonomic nervous system activity and its end-organ effects, brain activity, and hormonal secretions, constitute a second class of observables. They are sometimes phenomena of emotion, but at other times they are nonemotional, merely homeostatic adjustments to routine physical activity or effort, as when the heart speeds up in response to changes in the physical climate or as a result of the neurological and metabolic demands of motor activity. Although we can observe some of them without instruments, as when our face reddens or pales, sophisticated instruments now allow researchers to measure many of them well enough to study systematically how they work in emotion. The earlier distinction between molecular variables (which are observable) and interpretive, molar phenomena applies here, too. In other words, when we speak of a physiological reaction as an emotional phenomenon, we are making an interpretive statement.

3. *What people say* about their emotions in reports of being angry, anxious, or proud, when they deny emotion, describe the conditions generating an experienced emotion, or indicate the goals at stake or the beliefs that underlie their reactions — all of these statements constitute a third class of observables. They are an especially valuable source of information about human emotion because they sometimes tell us what may or may not be otherwise in evidence from other sources.

Social scientists are constantly debating the validity of these reports, which can be distorted by the wish to present oneself in a particular light, the failure to grasp what is happening, and self-deception. Nevertheless, the reports themselves can be treated as observables and interpreted in the context of other data. The dependence on interpretive inference applies to all data sources and does not make verbal reports unique as sources of information about the emotion process. As I have already pointed out, to interpret actions and physiological activity as emotional phenomena also requires theoretical inference, and these phenomena are not any easier to manage as data than is what people say about their experience and understanding.

4. *Environmental events and contexts,* including the social, cultural, and physical events under which an emotion occurs, constitute a fourth category of observables. However, when we venture into social structural variables and cultural meanings, relational provocations, and environmental demands, constraints, or resources, and treat these variables as emotional phenomena, we have moved away from simple observables toward interpretative inference and theory.

For example, if we say that an individual responded to a social insult, it is not easy to know why it was or was not regarded by that individual as insulting; if we say that an individual was made anxious by an event, it is not easy to know what it was about that event that was personally threatening or why, because other persons may not have responded to the event in the same way; and if we say that an individual was acting out a particular social role, say, that of father, mother, or child, it is not enough to know merely that this individual is socially defined as father, mother, or child, because the role as subjectively defined by that individual might be quite different.

Let me sum up the main points I have been making. Without an appropriate context and interpretation, none of the molecular phenomena of emotion are emotional per se, because all serve other nonemotional functions. Actions are sometimes emotional, sometimes not. Physiological activity is sometimes emotional, sometimes not. People may deny experiencing an emotion verbally when they are actually feeling angry, frightened, guilty, prideful, or whatever; on the other hand, they may report these emotions without actually experiencing them. Finally, people are often exposed to environmental events and contexts that usually generate emotions, but do not react emotionally or with an expected emotion; on the other hand, they may experience strong emotions upon being exposed to encounters that are normatively nonemotional.

Although the presence of an emotion may be suggested by observable evidence, and we make the appropriate inference readily and routinely in our ordinary lives, to speak of an emotion is to make a theoretical judgment about a highly complicated hypothetical construct, an organized configuration consisting of many variables and processes. This is the main reason why emotions are so difficult to deal with scientifically. The solution is not to write them off or to be hamstrung in doing research, as has been the case in the past, but to apply a careful combination of rational and empirical analysis to sharpen our thinking and deepen our understanding.

There are five classes of *nonobservable* variables relevant to an emotion:

1. *Action tendencies,* which are nonobservables because they refer to private impulses that may or may not be acted out or even recognized (though we might expect, perhaps, to find a clue to their occurrence in measurable increases in muscle tension).

2. *Subjective emotional experiences* (often referred to as *affect*) — say, anger, anxiety, pride, or whatever — which are obviously nonobservable, though we count on having observable clues about them, including verbal reports by the person having the experience.

3. *Person-environment relationships,* which require inferences about the functional connection between a person with particular motives and beliefs and an envi-

ronment with a complex set of demands, constraints, and resources of its own. These two complex subsystems — the *person* and the *environment* — though comprised of observables, are constructs, as when we speak inferentially of structures and processes of personality and the environment. Statements about these subsystems are also usually interpretive.

4. *Coping processes,* though often expressed as actions or thoughts that can be reported, are also complex, molar inferences, which presumably influence emotions via their effects on appraisal. The term *strategy,* which is often used when speaking of coping, implies intentional, perhaps planful, orchestrated action.

5. *Appraisal processes,* which constitute the core construct of a cognitive-motivational-relational theory of emotion, are also knowable only through inference.

The phenomena identified here, both observables and unobservables, form the bases of what I refer to as the emotion system or process. The substance of points 3, 4, and 5 will be developed at length in Part Two.

What Are the Emotions?

Deciding which "emotions" should be considered in a theory and which are nonemotional concepts is a task that is made all the more difficult in the absence of an adequate set of theoretical propositions about the way the emotions work. Although I make numerous proposals about which there is bound to be considerable disagreement, an important objective of the discussions is to explore rational issues having to do with classification and measurement, and to end with a classificatory system to use later in the theory. Five subordinate issues are addressed here: the language of the emotions; three distinctions (between emotion states and traits; among acute emotions, moods, and psychopathology; and among sensorimotor reflexes, physiological drives, and emotions); and whether physiological activity is necessary to speak of an emotion.

The Language of Emotion

Most writers agree that many words should be excluded from the category of emotions. Ortony, Clore, and Foss (1987; see also Clore, Ortony, & Foss, 1987; Johnson-Laird & Oatley, 1989; and Ortony & Clore, 1981, 1989) have made the most systematic recent efforts to "clean up the emotion lexicon," as they put it. To illustrate their outlook, I quote from a recent statement (Ortony, Clore, & Foss, 1987, p. 344):

> Words such as "angry," "fearful," and "grieving," denote emotional states. On the other hand, we think that words like "tearful," "suicidal," "violent," "weeping," and "blushing," all of which were rated very "emotional" . . . do not denote emotions, although certainly they have obvious connections to emotions. But, if words like "tearful," "violent," and "blushing," are not emotions, why did subjects . . . rate them as such? One possibility is that because subjects were not sensitive to the distinction between referring to an emotion and implicating an emotion, they may have responded to terms like "blushing," which strongly implicate emotions, as though they denoted emotions.

I have drawn on this theme at the end of the chapter when I present my classification. There I discuss nonemotions that are often treated as emotions. One reason for the linguistic and conceptual confusion about what an emotion is and is not is that words referring to actions and reactions, without reference to other essential features of the emotion process (such as personal meanings and organismic activities) provide inadequate descriptors. One component, such as violence, cannot be divorced from another component—say, being embittered—without producing ambiguity; violence as an individual coping strategy or a social policy does not reliably connote anger or hatred in those who engage in it.

I doubt, for example, that the person who throws the switch on an electric chair is necessarily angry, though he could be. He might have "psyched himself up," as Hochschild (1979) would say, merely regarding his act as a routine part of the job, or perhaps he was always hostile and enjoys killing, which led him to choose this occupation in the first place. Without more information, we cannot say.

Ortony, Clore, and their associates have presented in their work a hierarchical structure of the emotion lexicon that first distinguishes words referring to internal conditions from those referring to external conditions. External conditions are eliminated, because according to traditional thinking emotions are assumed to be internal. These authors further distinguish internal conditions as either mental or nonmental (e.g., physical and bodily states). Nonmental terms are, of course, eliminated, and the authors finally arrive at a more limited group of *emotion words* that focus on affect, behavior, and cognition.

For these writers, then, emotions are internal, mental, and affective experiences, and emotions are thereby restricted to *affective states,* either as the sole meaning or combined with actions or thoughts. Pure affective states would be illustrated by the word *happy;* affective-behavioral states by the word *cheerful;* affective-cognitive states by the word *encouraged. Nonaffective* states would include behavioral-cognitive states that contain no affective connotations, as illustrated by the word *careful,* and purely cognitive states, as illustrated by the word *certain.*

The term *internal,* as used by these authors, refers to the fact that emotions are, at bottom, psychological experiences. In Chapter 3, the reader will see that I view emotions as relational as well as internal, because we must also pay attention to what provokes them. The distinction is made clearly but in a bit too either-or fashion by de Rivera and Grinkis (1986, pp. 351–352) in the following comment:

> Most theories have treated emotions as if they were internal states. . . . If such a position has merit, it should be possible to demonstrate that the "feel" of different emotions may be related to different relationships between the person and the other. And it should be possible to show that the names of different emotions are not primarily used to refer to particular facial expressions or to particular combinations of pleasant or unpleasant, active or passive feelings, but to different ways in which the person relates to another.

Emotion States and Traits

An emotion *trait* refers to a characteristic of a person, and so is not really an emotion but a *disposition* or tendency to react with one. Saying someone is an angry person (or prideful, or affectionate) does not describe an emotional experience or encounter; an angry person is not always angry but is angry more often than most, especially under particular conditions. An emotion *state,* on the other hand, is a transient reaction to specific encounters with the environment, one that comes and goes depending on particular conditions. For the trait we say someone is an angry person; for the state we say someone is feeling or reacting with anger at a particular time and place.

The concept of an emotion trait (as opposed to state) parallels the traditional concept of *sentiment* or *attitude,* which also is not an emotion but a disposition to react with one. If we dislike someone, we have a greater tendency to experience anger toward that person than toward another. To eventuate in an emotion, a sentiment or attitude must be activated in an encounter with that person, actual or imagined; the anger lies in wait, as it were, for a provocation to make it salient, even one as minor as the mere presence or memory of the person who has previously provoked it. Since the same terms — *anxious, proud, envious,* and so forth — are used to refer to an emotional trait or state, we must be clear about our use of emotion-related language. To feel proud is not the same as to be a proud person, as Ortony, Clore, and associates have repeatedly emphasized.

States and traits are actually closely related, the former (figure) being provoked in a specific context, the latter (background) influencing this provocation. When our concern is with a state, we assume a degree of instability in the reaction (variability); it arises only in certain settings. When our concern is with a trait, we assume a degree of stability in the reaction across contexts (consistency). An emotion trait means that a person possessing it has some personality characteristic that brings the emotional state about or generates it more often or more intensely than in others.

Emotion states and traits are therefore two sides of the same coin; when stability is high, the focus is on trait and state recedes in importance; when instability is high, the focus is on state and trait recedes in importance. Clinical work is centered on unwanted emotion traits (Lazarus, 1989a), and is designed to correct the chronic dysfunction and distress. I will have more to say about this in Chapter 11.

Acute Emotions, Moods, and Psychopathology

It has been traditional in discussions of emotion to make a distinction between acute emotions and moods. Both are types of emotion. The distinction overlaps with what I said in Chapter 1 about adaptational encounters, their focus, and their boundaries. Moods are commonly described with very general terms, such as *happy, joyful, cheerful,* or *carefree, apprehensive, excited, irritable, angry-hostile,* or *melancholy-depressed.*

Although the "feel" of an acute emotion and a that of a mood are quite different, there are a number of difficulties in making a viable distinction between them. Ekman (1984, p. 333) suggests, along with many others, that "moods refer to longer time spans than emotions" do. However, if we distinguish them on the basis of duration by saying that moods are more enduring or stable than acute emotions, although this seems to be often true, some moods seem relatively brief and contextual, thus giving them an on-off character.

If we regard duration or recurrence as implying a personality trait or disposition, which is a common position, I think we are taking a dangerous tack. Some people do indeed have the disposition to be melancholy or cheerful, but most if not all persons can experience moods of both kinds, and so it may be misleading to suggest that moods are always dispositional, in the sense of a personality trait, whereas acute emotions are not. When we say a person is in an irritable or hostile mood, we are not necessarily saying something about personality but rather are saying something about a strong disposition to anger during the period of the irritable or hostile mood — an intraindividual disposition, very different from a personality trait, is putting this individual in a foul mood.

The easily confused issue of *personality* disposition versus *temporal or contextual* disposition is one I touched on earlier in connection with the inter- and intraindividual perspectives in emotion research. It seems to me that a mood should be regarded as a state even though it may dispose the person to react with a relevant, acute emotion. Considering mood as a state, we need to know what it is and how it is brought about. To speak of it as a personality trait or disposition is to look at an altogether different issue.

If we distinguish moods from acute emotions on the basis of the vagueness and lack of a contextual provocation in the mood, we may be more on target. Most moods do not seem to be clearly related to a single object or piece of business in an adaptational encounter, as is the case in acute anger or fear. When we speak of someone's being melancholy or cheerful, it is usually difficult to identify either a specific *object* (as in the target of anger) or *cause* of the state (as in a provocative act), to use Hume's famous distinction.

I suggest that moods have to do with the larger background of one's life, which feels either troubled or trouble free, negative or positive. When life seems good overall, the positive feeling is not necessarily connected with a specific event, though we sometimes point to one when asked. When life seems mostly bad, one feels sad or glum, which also is not necessarily connected with a specific event (see my discussion of sadness as an acute emotion versus a mood in Chapter 6). A good or bad mood, whether or not it has a distinct provocation, depends on how one is doing in the agendas of one's life overall.

In any case, I am inclined to interpret *both* moods and acute emotions as reactions to the way one appraises relationships with the environment; moods refer to the larger, pervasive, existential issues of one's life, whereas acute emotions refer to an immediate piece of business, a specific and relatively narrow goal in an adaptational encounter with the environment. If the fate of this piece of business helps to demonstrate that our lives are misshapen in a larger, existential sense, that we and other humans are basically evil, that life is disorderly and has no meaning, that the fates are against us, we feel bad; alternatively, if we sense that our lives are proceeding favorably — that we are wonderful or masterful, that we are loved or appreciated, that humans are basically good, that life is meaningful, orderly, just, that the fates are with us — we feel good. Though the temporal focus and perhaps the subject matter are different in each, both acute emotions and moods are reactions to appraisals about our well-being. (See also Mayer, Salovey, Gomberg-Kaufman, & Blarney, 1991.)

Heidegger emphasized the existential quality of the person–environment relationship in his discussions of mood in a manner consistent with what I have said here. Moods, for Heidegger, are rooted in the sense of being-in-the-world. About this, Heidegger's interpreter, Guignon (1984, p. 231), writes:

> To be human, as [Heidegger's] term Dasein suggests, is to be "there," caught up [in the world], taking a stand on one's life, active and engaged in ordinary situations, with some overview of what is at stake in living. What characterizes human life in its most natural ways of being is not a relationship between mind and body but a concrete "existing" in a world. Our most natural experience of ourselves is described as "Being-in-the-world," where "world" refers not to the universe studied by physics, but rather to a life-world in the sense in which we speak of "the academic world" or the "world of theater." To be "in" such a world is not like a pencil's being "in" a drawer; it is more like being engaged or involved in something, as is someone who is "into" astrology.

Though it is always dangerous to court a dichotomy, it is difficult to say which type of reaction, a mood or acute emotion, is of greater significance in the psychological economy of the person. However, since moods are concerned with larger, longer lasting, existential issues about the person's life and how it is going, and acute emotions are apt to be brief and evanescent, I venture the thought that moods are transcendentally important in that economy and in how we judge our adaptational status. When one's mood is sour because life seems bad, even positive events can fail to affect our overall mood. Similarly, when one's mood is sweet, presumably because life seems good, negative events are less capable of producing emotional distress.

There is a strong tendency among laypersons and professionals to equate emotion and mood with *psychopathology*. I suppose this has to do with cultural values. Although quiet and sociable people who suppress their negative feelings may suddenly explode to the surprise of everyone, strong negative emotions are highly visible and result in evident trouble for social relationships when they are frequently or consistently expressed. Consider, for example, what Thoits (1984, p. 233) says about emotional distress as a main clinical criterion of psychopathology:

> An examination of the diagnostic criteria for mental disorders indicates that "excessive," "unusual," "bizarre," and "inappropriate" emotions or emotional displays are often major or associated symptoms of disorder. These observations suggest that inappropriate or undesirable feelings and expressive displays play an important part in the recognition and labeling of disturbance. Assessments of distress and disorder appear to be based, at least in part, upon persistent or recurrent deviations from feeling and expression norms. Psychological disturbance might be reconceptualized usefully, then, as persistent or recurrent emotional disturbance or, in extreme forms, as emotional deviance.

Although emotional distress is an important criterion of psychopathology, it is not pathological, per se. Thoits refers rather to emotional deviance, but her analysis remains incomplete without more detail; we must ask about the conditions under which even deviance could be considered pathological. To regard sadness (and other kinds of emotional distress), which constitutes a normal feature of grieving, as pathological, clinicians would say it must be prolonged, inappropriate, or severely dysfunctional. The same state is considered appropriate and useful as a reaction to loss when it is short-lived, realistic, and does not severely impair functioning (cf. Klinger, 1975).

In Chapter 6, I identify sadness, but not depression or grief, as an emotion for two reasons: First, *depression* is usually a composite of several emotions, including sadness, anxiety, anger, and guilt. These emotions — or moods as some might prefer to call them — reflect appraisals of irrevocable loss and hopelessness, existential threat, personal affront, and a moral lapse, in that order, which may all be features of a major depression. In *grief* we also experience a complex mixture of the same emotions. Although logically there is not much difference between depression and grief, depression tends to emphasize the emotional reaction to loss, whereas grief emphasizes the struggle to cope with it. Second, these states, especially depression and even more especially when there is no obvious loss to blame it on, are most commonly treated by laypersons and professionals as hallmarks of psychopathology.

Whether or not an emotion is considered adaptive or healthy, however, is irrelevant to its status as an emotion. We must not confuse the two issues. Statements about pathology and health are professional judgments about the functional and dysfunctional aspects of emotional and coping processes and their consequences. These judgments also entail both interindividual and intraindividual standards of comparison. For example, we may note that a person is severely depressed compared with others (interindividual), but is less so than previously (intraindividual).

Sensorimotor Reflexes, Physiological Drives, and Emotions

The difference between reflexes, physiological drives, and emotions is of great significance (see also Smith & Lazarus, 1990). Reflexes and physiological drives, like emotions, serve as vital adaptational resources in animals (including humans) by arranging for the pairing of adaptive behaviors with survival-relevant conditions, but they are not emotions. If we take seriously that emotions and intelligence are products of evolution and made possible the great flexibility and variability found in the response to diverse adaptational demands, constraints, and opportunities, then the definition of emotion must exclude responses that are hardwired and elicited rigidly and automatically by a specific stimulus.

The hallmarks of a *sensorimotor reflex* are its stimulus specificity and the rigidity of the response. Releasing stimuli elicit or trigger rather fixed action patterns that ensure that the adaptational need signaled by that stimulus is met. The pairing is built into the nervous system, as in the case of the patellar reflex (knee jerk), the pupillary reflex (widening the pupil of the eye in dim light, narrowing it in bright light), and so on. Animals that depend heavily or entirely on reflexes for survival interact with their environments in fairly stereotyped ways.

A good example is the research of Tinbergen (1951), cited in Chapter 1, on the built-in tendency of fowl to react with fear to a cardboard birdlike silhouette, which when moved in one direction made it seem like a dangerous predator, the hawk; when the same shape was moved in the opposite direction, making it look like a nonpredatory bird, the fowl were not threatened and reacted calmly.

Although it promotes survival, this kind of stereotypy has major adaptational costs, especially when compared with the patterns of adaptation of more advanced animals in which more complicated forms of transaction have evolved. For example, I see many deer in the suburban community in which I live because food in cultivated gardens is ample all year long and there are no predators. However, it is not uncommon to come upon a young deer who "freezes" in the middle of the road, an innate reaction to danger, as I approach in my car. Freezing is quite useful when there are predators around, because it is hard to notice a deer that is motionless in the tall yellow-brown grass. However, though it is an innate reflex, freezing in the middle of the road is not useful, especially if the position is held too long or occurs at night when cars move faster and visibility is reduced. Fortunately for the existing deer, though perhaps not for their future evolution, people who live in the community usually drive cautiously and wait until the deer finally moves off. Deer also seem to be sufficiently capable of learning the relevant conditions for the reflex action; the older ones in my community, for example, do not usually stand motionless when an auto approaches while they are crossing. The conditions of life of the deer, living alongside humans in a modern, industrial world without predators, make freezing no longer an adaptive reflex. Instead, the more advanced human species has flexibly adapted, helping the deer survive in spite of their innate patterns.

Simple sensorimotor reflexes were inadequate to the more complex demands that accompanied phylogenetic development toward more complex species, such as the great apes and humans. And as organismic and social complexity increased in more advanced species, it was not possible for each new adaptational demand to be solved by development of a new reflex, so more flexible, context-sensitive response mechanisms evolved.

Physiological drives may be thought of as one of these context-sensitive mechanisms, a more advanced adaptational step than reflexes. They make it possible to meet cyclical homeostatic needs crucial to survival, such as nutrition. The triggers for these drives are provided by feedback from changing internal states — for example, low blood sugar — which indicate the presence of the nutritional need and create psychophysiological tensions that set in motion adaptationally relevant behavior, such as seeking food. These drives allow for more flexibility than do reflexes in respect to how and when the adaptive response is made. Hunger, for example, motivates an animal to eat, but unlike a reflex, it does not dictate the specific behaviors used to obtain, prepare, or consume food. If one strategy fails, another can be tried, which increases the importance of intelligence and learning in survival. A further illustration of the gain in flexibility is that an animal can ignore the signal for a time to deal with even more urgent demands, a property not found in sensorimotor reflexes, which are difficult if not impossible to control at will.

The emotion process, which could be considered a further evolutionary adaptational advance, fulfills many of the adaptational requirements that in simpler species were managed entirely or mainly by reflexes and physiological drives. The progression to more complex species constituted, in effect, an evolution of mind in which emotion, which depends on intelligence, learning, and thought, especially evaluative thought or what I have been referring to as appraisal, became the main functional basis of adaptation. As I indicated in Chapter 1, these functions include social communication, sustained energy mobilization focused on different unmet needs and emergencies that is capable of shifting rapidly from one emergency to another, and above all a high degree of sensitivity to the coping requirements of specific relational demands, which requires intelligence and learning.

Two main changes seem to have occurred in this evolutionary progression: First, as I said, many forms of adaptive behavior were freed from built-in, automatic, reflexive arrangements; and second, adaptation became more dependent on learning and cognitive processes, more variable and complex, and less concrete and stimulus bound. From an evolutionary standpoint, reflexes are the most primitive and rigid of the adaptational resources available to animals, and physiological drives could be said to represent a shift toward increased flexibility and variability.

As the automatic connection between the environmental stimulus and the built-in response loosened, cognitive activity and the formulation of plans began to stand between impulse and action, especially in humans. This has been a frequent ontogenetic theme in modern psychology (see, for example, Werner, 1948; and Freud's distinction between primary and secondary process thinking). Deese (1985) has pointed out that in the early history of neurophysiology an important distinction was drawn between involuntary reflexes and voluntary behavior, the former implying fixed or hardwired, input-output systems, the latter implying volitional behavior and choice. I have more to say about this in Chapters 4 and 5.

In this connection, Plutchik (1980, p. 74) has written that from the "vantage point of evolution, cognition developed in order to predict the future." What he means, of course, is that it is a tremendous adaptational advantage to be able to anticipate what is going to happen and to prepare for it rather than to be locked into the concrete here and now. Some emotional experiences are essentially anticipatory (see Chapter 3), whereas others are reactions to the outcomes of an adaptationally relevant encounter. We learn when it is appropriate to feel anxious, angry, sad, or happy, when to flee or fight, how to deal with the intractable conditions of living, and how to plan ahead in the short and long term. Each emotion expresses a different type of person–environment relationship (see Chapter 3), and in each the individual's well-being is implicated in a different way, depending on how the significance of the encounter is appraised by the individual. But more of this in Part Two.

To add a speculative digression, there is an interesting parallel between this evolutionary transition from animal dependence on rigid response patterns to more flexible ones and the human dependence on stable and secure social patterns. In animal life, order and stability are often the result of biologically driven dominance hierarchies that, once attained, control and moderate intraspecies aggression. Humans can no longer depend on biological arrangements to produce stable social relations. Societal regulation appears to compete with biological regulation in facilitating order and stable relationships among people.

When societies create more misery than satisfaction and no longer produce a viable social order, they begin to fall apart, at which time there is increasing social disorder and new sources of emotional distress. Often people cling to bad government because the order created by them seems a worthwhile price to prevent disorder, which is dangerous and frightening. At this writing we are living through a period in which the social structure of a number of previously stable, authoritarian

Eastern European societies may be shifting from governmental oppression to new political arrangements, but the processes that will occur to produce a new order and the outcomes of the struggle are difficult to predict (see Tuchman's *A Distant Mirror* for a comparison of historical change in the fourteenth and twentieth centuries). In any event, creatures such as humans, with flexible adaptational choices based on intellect and societal arrangements, cannot count on the biological rules that work for less advanced species. Adaptational flexibility is obviously a mixed blessing.

It is not easy to say exactly what has been passed down genetically from forebears and what is learned with respect to the emotion process. Nor is it clear how much loosening of genetically imposed connections between elicitors and emotional reactions has really occurred in humans. Thus, Hebb (1946; 1949; see also Hebb & Thompson, 1954), and others, took quite seriously that chimpanzee and human fears are, in part, the result of inherited tendencies as well as learning. This idea of inherited fears has been somewhat softened today in the concept of "prepared" conditioning, which refers to biological dispositions that make learning some things such as fearing snakes and spiders easier and unlearning more difficult (see Chapter 8). I will also propose in Chapter 5 that there is a strong biological connection between appraisal, once generated, and the emotional reaction, as well as much sociocultural and individual variability in the way we understand and appraise our ongoing and changing relationships with the environment.

Though it can also be relatively primitive and automatic (cf. Le Doux, 1986a), the psychobiological reaction we call an emotion in humans is often very complex. Commonly, for example, it encompasses multiple motives, evaluations of adaptational requirements, foresight and stepwise planning, and a mobilized bodily reaction—all of which make an emotion truly a cognitive-motivational-relational configuration. When meaning became central, even when it was a simple dichotomous judgment of relevance or no relevance, danger or no danger, harm or no harm, benefit or no benefit, emotions achieved much greater flexibility and adaptational power than was possible in relatively rigid, stimulus-elicited adaptational response systems, such as reflexes and drives.

Startle is a good example of the distinction between reflexes and emotions. Some writers have treated startle as a primitive emotion. I believe this is a mistake, because it confuses emotion with reflexes. Startle is relatively fixed and rigid and is best regarded as a sensorimotor reflex. Startle works much like the patellar and pupillary reflexes. This and other reflexes are reactions not to adaptational meaning but to simple afferent stimuli that are universally capable of automatically eliciting them in a neurologically intact person.

A unique study by Ekman, Friesen, and Simons (1985) provides pretty convincing evidence about this. These researchers carefully examined facial and bodily responses to the firing of a blank pistol—a favorite and reliable way to elicit startle—under four conditions designed to test the capacity of cognitive control activities to influence the reaction. In one condition, subjects could anticipate the gunshot; in a second, they could not; in a third, they were told to inhibit the startle reaction; and in a fourth, they were told to simulate the startle reaction in the absence of the gunshot.

Ekman et al. found that anticipating the gunshot did not significantly change the morphology or timing of the reaction, though larger discrepancies were found in its magnitude; that it could not be totally inhibited; and that it could not be very accurately simulated, though here the morphology, timing, and magnitude of the reaction were considerably different as measured; the simulation was correctly distinguished from the real response by observers 60 percent of the time — statistically significant but only a little more than chance.

Although these researchers did not examine the affective state of their subjects by questioning, the most reasonable guess is that people are not frightened when startled, though fear could occur under appropriate circumstances — for example, if a sudden noise is not adequately explained, or if it is explained by a condition portending danger. Moreover, the emotional response to a startle could just as readily be anger, as when the startle stimulus is explained afterward as a practical joke that the victim does not appreciate.

I am tempted to think that the function of the startle reflex is to alert the person to a condition whose personal significance is hinted at but is not yet evident, and which will be subsequently appraised as irrelevant, harmful, threatening, or beneficial. The reader should see Vrana, Spence, and Lang (1988; also Lang, Bradley, & Cuthbert, 1990) for the finding that startle magnitudes in response to unsignaled white noise bursts were larger while subjects were viewing unpleasant photo slides than while viewing pleasant slides.

About this finding I would say that the slides provided a suggestion of the meaning of the startle experience, just as physiological arousal may sometimes be explained by the social context in which it occurs (cf. Schachter & Singer, 1962). In other words, I don't believe the Vrana et al. findings contradict the view that startle is neutral emotionally until the personal significance of the eliciting stimulus has been appraised. Cook, Hawk, Davis, and Stevenson (1991) interpret their recent finding that affective individual differences enhance startle effects as the potentiation of startle by prior emotional states and dispositions. This too is, I believe, consistent with the idea that startle does not involve emotion without added meaning.

In the classification of emotions at the end of this chapter, I refer to startle, and some other nonreflex reactions such as curiosity, surprise, attentiveness, and the "orienting reaction," as *pre-emotions*. They prepare the person or animal to evaluate what is happening (cf. Meyer, 1988; Meyer, Niepel, Rudolph, & Schützwohl, in press). For the reader unfamiliar with the term, the orienting reaction or reflex is what a dog does, for example, when there is a noise or some other event that it doesn't yet understand. It perks up its ears, opens its eyes wide, turns in the direction of the stimulus, and responds bodily with a kind of vigilant attention until the animal can tell whether the stimulus has any significance for action and grasps what is to be done. Acknowledging that this is an initial response to uncertainty, others have also called it the "What is it?" reaction (see Galbrecht, Dykman, Reese, & Suzuki, 1965; Harris, 1943; Sokolov, 1963; Zimney & Keinstra, 1967).

With the preceding discussion as preamble, we can now see the basis for a major generalization about reflexes, physiological drives, and emotions that has been stated earlier by others such as Tomkins (1962, 1963; see also Ekman, 1984). In contrast with reflexes and drives, a true emotion cannot be consistently called forth by any single stimulus. Emotions are generated and controlled by the personal implications for well-being conveyed by relationships with the environment (typically social) and comprehended through an appraisal process that, whether short-circuited or not (see Chapter 4), draws heavily on evolved intelligence and knowledge.

Consistent with this position, Kreitler and Kreitler (1976) have treated the orienting reflex, which is a much-attenuated reaction compared with startle, as a primitive psychophysiological response that alerts the organism to the possibility that something is happening that could have significance for action, but that requires further analysis. Startle does not seem to resemble true emotions in the way it is generated and controlled, any more than does the orienting reflex.

Certain other reactions are comparable to startle in being innate sensorimotor reflexes that have been treated by some writers as emotional states. Classic examples are pleasure, pain, and distaste (distinguished by Rozin & Fallon, 1987, from disgust, which they regard as a true emotion in contrast with the reflex of distaste; see Chapter 6). We are built so that sensorimotor *pleasure,* such as a sweet taste, physical rest, stroking the body, or certain kinds of full stomachs,[1] is almost always elicited by definable physical stimuli in a neurologically intact and receptive person. So, too, with *pain.* One difference between pleasure and pain is that the range of stimuli capable of producing pain is much more circumscribed than that for pleasure. Pleasure is also more modifiable than pain by meaning-related contextual variables.

The qualification that a person be receptive acknowledges that the stimuli eliciting pleasure and pain do not always do so to the same degree. Their power to do so depends on psychobiological conditions that affect receptivity to pleasure, lowered or raised pain tolerance, and perhaps even pain thresholds, though this latter effect is more problematic. As in the case of all sensorimotor reflexes, the degree of modifiability compared with true emotions is always modest. However, even the patellar reflex can be influenced, as anyone knows who has been examined for this reflex by a physician who taps the knee with a rubber hammer to check for evidence of neurological disorder. If we pay too close attention, the reflex may be inhibited, so it is best to attend to something else. Although I consider the distinction between reflex and emotion important, evidence of even a small cognitive effect for reflexes leaves the claim to reflex status in these instances with a modest degree of ambiguity (see also Smith & Lazarus, 1990).

I am not alone in regarding pleasure and pain as nonemotions; Tomkins (1962, 1963), among others, has adopted a similar position. However, when terms like *pleasure* and *pain* are used metaphorically, it seems quite legitimate to regard them as emotional, because there is an extension to personal meaning when we speak of satisfaction, contentment, well-being, relief, and joy, or when we speak of psychic pain, dissatisfaction, distress, and misery. It seems easier to make this metaphoric extension in the cases of pleasure, pain, and distaste than in that of startle.

This discussion is not intended to express any doubt about the well-established idea that the meaning of an injury may increase or decrease the subjective experience of pain (cf. Beecher, as discussed in Melzack, 1961; see also Fordyce, 1988). When we appraise a physical injury and its pain as threatening, we experience an emotion rather than a reflex sensation. More is going on than merely an awareness of the sensation of pain, and the process that is added to change the experience is evaluative — that is, an appraisal. Beecher's observation that badly wounded soldiers seemed to experience less pain than did people with comparable injuries as a result of surgery is a case in point. He speculated that to the soldier the meaning of the injury was that he had survived and was no longer in mortal danger, but to the patient the surgical injury may imply a life-threatening procedure, which is accepted reluctantly as the dangerous, painful, and uncertain price of regaining health.

Similarly, although the bodily sensation of being physically stroked is innately pleasant, the social circumstances — for example, an unwanted sexual demand or even a threatening interpretation of the pleasure itself — can make the same sensation intensely unpleasant, disgusting, or frightening. In these examples, we have moved beyond sensations and perceptions to emotions because they involve personal evaluations, predicated on knowledge (beliefs about how things are).

There is a final point to be made about pleasure and pain, which is of the utmost importance when we examine the development of emotions (see Part Four, especially Chapter 9). From a developmental standpoint it is necessary to acknowledge that, though they are reflexes, pleasure and pain undoubtedly play a central role in the development of the motivational structure on which appraisal and emotion depend. For example, although it is not the only basis of emotional development (see Chapter 9), the infant and young child learn to avoid pain and to seek pleasurable experiences. This learning process has been at the center of emotion theory for centuries. It does not mean, however, that pleasure and pain are emotions, but only that they have a significant bearing on emotional development through the motivational and cognitive activities that ultimately influence the emotions later in life.

Distaste should be treated in much the same way as pleasure and pain. It is a built-in, sensorimotor reflex to offensive substances (e.g., smell, taste) and not an emotion according to the principles thus far discussed (cf. Rozin & Fallon, 1987). On the other hand, *disgust* is ideological — that is, it is a learned meaning that a substance, idea, or action is "offensive" (e.g., ants and grasshoppers as food, or a violation by another person of certain values). As such, disgust is an emotion rather than a sensorimotor reflex.

When we feel disgust socially, we have crossed the line from a distaste reflex to a metaphor for it, even though aspects of the reaction itself — for example, the facial expressions, physiological reaction, motor impulse (vomiting), and subjective reaction (nausea) — overlap with or are indistinguishable from distaste. We may even say to other people of whom we disapprove that they make us "sick." This may not include nausea, but the meaning is fairly clear as a disgust metaphor for distaste. The case for learned distastes, foods "we cannot stomach," seems only slightly less metaphorical than emotions, and it could be said to fall between the two extremes of reflex and emotion.

Although Rozin and Fallon have made a valuable contribution by distinguishing disgust from distaste, and by helping us see the ideological, hence emotional, aspects of disgust, they do not go far enough in providing analyses of the causal personal meanings (appraisals) underlying disgust. Cognitive activity is crucial to the differentiation of an emotion from a nonemotion. The descriptive features of the response alone provide an insufficient basis for the distinction, a point I have made several times before. In short, I am proposing that we can speak of an emotion if cognitive appraisal is a causal factor in the reaction; if it is not, the reaction is something else (see Chapters 4 and 5).

The distinction between reflex and emotion is much like one that has long been made between *feeling* and *emotion*. These terms are often used interchangeably, but I think it would be more precise to speak of feeling as sensory perception, as in feelings of pain, pleasure, and distaste, rather than as emotion. Although we speak constantly about feelings when we mean emotions, and I have sometimes done so a bit carelessly in this book, it is more precise to restrict the word *feeling* to the awareness of bodily sensations and to reserve the word *emotion* for occasions on which there has been an appraisal of harm or benefit. Similarly, although it is fashionable to speak of *affect* rather than *emotion* to refer to the subjective quality of an emotional experience, I think it would be better to use the generic term *emotion* rather than to refer to a single facet to stand for the whole.

Should Physiological Activity Be a Defining Attribute of Emotion?

Now we come to a perennial dilemma, namely, whether physiological activity is necessary to say that a person is experiencing an emotion. The dilemma does not arise in anger and fear because in these emotions physiological activity is evident and readily interpreted as *bodily mobilization* to cope with an emergency. The concept of fight or flight as prototypes for the role of emotion in adaptation originated with Cannon (1939), who spelled out how the autonomic nervous system and the catecholamines secreted by the medulla or inner portion of the adrenal glands work in emergencies. Selye (1956/1976) elaborated on this theme of neurohumoral mobilization to physiologically noxious or demanding stimuli but emphasized the hormones secreted by the cortex or outer rind of the adrenal glands (corticosteroids), which play a major role in anabolic and catabolic activity, especially in prolonged stress.

However, these formulations, which center on mobilization in emergencies, fail to work for the emotion of *sadness* (and certain forms of depression), so anger and fear might be better regarded as special cases rather than as prototypes for all emotions. Sadness and depression, and the hopelessness that is said to generate depression, are the epitome of nonactivation, except in agitated or "crying" depressions, which are also characterized by anger, guilt, and anxiety. In sadness and in many depressions, one has the impression that people so affected have given up and withdrawn from the world into themselves. No effort is made to do anything about whatever has created the distress, presumably because the situation seems hopeless. In this case, incidently, appraisal and coping again seem to make a crucial difference in identifying the reaction as emotional.

A number of theorists have written about the "giving-up" syndrome (see Engel, 1968; Schmale, 1972, who also emphasized its threat to somatic health when prolonged). Klinger (1975), too, has argued persuasively that in the short run sadness and depression can be part of an adaptive process of temporary withdrawal from a failed commitment (which is a good way to define loss; see Chapter 3 on motivation), a psychobiological process of conserving and restoring resources that have been depleted in an unfruitful struggle. This implies that only if the person fails to reengage in the commitments of living and continues to be dysfunctional over an extended period should the process be considered maladaptive. What is a reasonable time to get over a loss is difficult to define precisely, and with better clinical understanding of the grief process in recent years this period has been much extended.

It is also difficult to justify the concept of bodily mobilization in most *positive emotions*. What, for example, should we say about contentment and relief, which represent the opposite of mobilization? In contentment mobilization is presumably unneccessary, and in relief it is lowered rather than raised. Therefore, if mobilization in the form of physiological activity is made a criterion of emotion, we might have to exclude reactions from the emotion rubric that might belong there on other grounds.

If we speak instead of *physiological change* rather than mobilization as an indispensable requisite, we could more easily encompass contentment and relief within the emotion rubric. And because disengagement or withdrawal could be said to produce decreased physiological activity, perhaps sadness, too, can be accommodated with the idea of physiological activity as a necessary criterion of an emotion. This reformulation is consistent with a suggestion made by Kemper (1987) that activation of the parasympathetic nervous system is involved in the demobilization that occurs in relief, and perhaps that in contentment also. For those unfamiliar with the physiology of the autonomic nervous system, the two branches, sympathetic and parasympathetic, operate antagonistically. Becoming excited is usually connected with increased activity in the sympathetic nervous system branch. When we feel relieved, there is reduction in sympathetic activity compared with the parasympathetic, and so Kemper is legitimately able to say about relief that there is increased activity, relatively speaking, in the parasympathetic branch.

We have little actual knowledge about the psychophysiological reactions in most of the response states we call emotions, especially the positive ones. There has been no proliferation of sophisticated studies that draw on multiple physiological response systems, for example, the autonomic, adrenal medullary, and adrenal cortical, as well as other neurohumoral systems (cf. Mason, 1971, 1975; Mason, Maher, Hartley, Mougey, Perlow, & Jones, 1976), though interest has grown in recent years with the development of better technologies and with the neurohumoral research frontier of brain peptides such as the enkaphalins, which are said to inhibit pain.

We might indeed find measurable physiological changes, if we looked for them, in most or all the states we call emotional, even the positive ones and those that seem to be characterized by the subsidence of physiological tension, as in relief or contentment. The problem is made even more difficult because there is no sharp line empirically drawn to distinguish baseline physiological conditions from changes (see Levenson, 1988, for a discussion of baselines). If, indeed, there are physiological changes characteristic of pride, comparable changes might be found in other emotions. To my knowledge, diverse but reliable reports of aches in the "pit of the stomach," "sinking feelings," "clutching in the throat," the "light and airy" feeling of delight, or the "expansiveness" of happiness and pride have never been systematically traced to bodily changes that may well be occurring. We need systematic studies to help us evaluate the hunch that even mild positive emotions like pride involve distinctive physiological patterns. (See Lynch, Bakal, Whitelaw, & Fung, 1991, for a study of chest muscle activity in panic anxiety.)

If the criterion of physiological activity was eliminated from the definition, the concept of emotion would be left without one of the important response boundaries with which to distinguish it from nonemotion. The other response boundary is the motor action tendency presumably generated in an emotion. And although the heat of an emotion seems to be declining in some states such as relief, these states seem far from "cold." Perhaps, too, we should not exclude the cozy feeling of being content and at ease, or the less cozy feeling of being relieved, from the emotion rubric. We need the idea of *embodiment,* which expresses that our entire being, including glands, muscles, visceral organs, and brain are actively engaged in an emotion, and if we dispense with it, a crucial distinction is lost, even if that distinction ultimately comes down to a continuum from little to much, a just-noticeable difference that is almost arbitrary when it is small but important when it is large.

It is, of course, a metaphor to speak of emotions as "warm" or "hot." What does the heat of an emotion consist of? Psychologically, it must depend on having a *stake* in an emotional encounter; having a stake is not being neutral or indifferent. Physiologically, I think it must depend on an *action tendency* that is generated by this stake, and the energy transformations required by it. I believe that Frijda (1986) and others who speak of action tendency, readiness, or impulse as an important feature of an emotion are quite right; these tendencies make an emotion different from a nonemotion.

We should not prejudge whether relief, pride, gratitude, and contentment, for example, are emotions on the basis of uncertainties and lack of research about the physiological activity associated with them. The resolution of these uncertainties depends on analyses of how the body transforms, uses, and conserves energy in adaptational transactions; how these processes are triggered and managed psychologically and physiologically; and how psychological states and processes are affected by physiological states and processes. At present, our conceptualizations of psychosomatic and somatopsychological relationships, which fall within the sphere of what is often called the *mind–body problem,* are woefully inadequate for achieving a full understanding.

Emotions as Categories or Dimensions

I have been treating emotions as discrete categories, an approach that is compatible with the cognitive-motivational-relational theme that each emotion represents a different way in which a person can be harmed or benefited in an encounter. Anger, anxiety, guilt, shame, sadness, disgust, happiness, pride, compassion, relief, hope, and love are examples of categories. The categories of emotion may, of course, be dimensionalized on the basis of their within-category strength, as when annoyance, which is a relatively mild anger, is distinguished from rage, which is an intense anger. Each emotion category is typically represented on a scale from weak to strong without necessarily implying any change in its quality. This begs the difficult question of whether rage is qualitatively different from annoyance. It probably is in certain respects.

However, conceiving of emotions as discrete *categories,* each of which can be placed on a dimension from weak to strong, is very different from thinking of them as *overlapping dimensions,* in which many categories are reduced to a few and their distinctive qualities lost or blurred. In purely dimensional analysis, categories are combined on the basis of shared and divergent properties, usually by factor or cluster analysis. This procedure involves correlating ratings of each emotion to find out which ones rise and fall together across persons, and these correlations provide the basis for a dimensional structure. A dimensional structure can be, and has been, created using any type of response data — for example, facial and vocal emotional expressions, verbally depicted or visual social scenes, and similarities and differences in the meanings of emotion words.

The resulting factor structure is sometimes schematized in dimensional space, for example, as a two-, three-, or four-dimensional arrangement. Dimensions can be organized in a circular pattern (e.g., Plutchik, 1980), a conical pattern (e.g., Daly, Polivy, & Lancee, 1983), or in some other spatial arrangement (see Figure 2.1 for one version), depending on what seems to be the best way to portray how the emotion response is organized psychologically.

There are ongoing debates about whether the factors in this structure should be bipolar or unipolar. For example, in a unipolar structure, pleasantness and unpleasantness are assessed as two discrete variables, each portrayed on a single dimension (unipolar) from high to low; in each such scale, an experience can be more or less pleasant, and independently it can also be more or less unpleasant. In a bipolar structure, in contrast, pleasantness and unpleasantness are treated not as two variables but as a single variable that goes from high to low through a neutral or zero midpoint. In this way, both variables, pleasantness and unpleasantness, are put on a combined, single dimension and treated as opposite poles (bipolar) of the same construct.

The search for the dimensional structure of emotion, as Izard (1977) has observed in his historical review, dates back to Spencer (1890), but is most notably reflected in more recent times in the work of Wundt (1905), Woodworth (1938), and Schlosberg (1941). It was heavily emphasized in Woodworth and Schlosberg's (1954) influential experimental psychology text, but lost favor for many years, until it was revived in the late 1960s with Davitz's (1969) research. Lately it seems to have again achieved a full head of steam (see Russell, 1980, and Watson & Tellegen, 1985, among others; and Dalkvist & Rollenhagen, 1989, for a recent review).

Although there are arguments about how many factor dimensions are necessary or useful to describe the variations in emotional meaning and how they are best arranged spatially, there has also been some consistency over the years despite divergent methodologies. Rarely have more than two to four factors been reported. Wundt (1905) proposed three: pleasantness-unpleasantness, relaxation-tension, and calm-excitement. Two of these dimensions — degree of pleasantness or unpleasantness and degree of excitement or arousal — emerge commonly in factor analyses, though three and sometimes four are commonly proposed. Watson and Tellegen (1985) reported two dimensions: positive and negative affect. Davitz (1969) reported four: activation, relatedness, hedonic tone, and competence.

One must remember that the methodologies employed to study the dimensional structure of emotions differ, and that showing subjects photos of faces to rate the emotions they represent is quite a different task from asking them to rate emotion words as to their similarities and differences. Davitz had subjects check statements such as "There is a heavy feeling in my stomach," or "The world seems no good, hostile, unfair." From these data he produced a "dictionary of emotional meaning," which related emotion words to patterns of psychophysiological reaction and eliciting conditions. In much of the research on the dimensional structure of emotion, the eliciting conditions have been ignored in the rating task. Subjects rate how they think and feel in general. Davitz is an exception, as is the recent research of Shaver, Schwartz, Kirson, and O'Conner (1987).

I am not aware of correlational studies that have considered the stages of an adaptational encounter except one of my own. Folkman and I (1985) obtained emotional ratings at three stages of a college examination: the period of anticipation, the period just after the exam, and the period just after grades were announced. The correlations between positive and negative emotions were nearly zero in the stage of anticipation, −.25 after the exam, and −.50 after the announcement of grades.

How is this possible? That is, how can we be happy and disappointed at the same time? If one does not consider the context of the ratings, in this case the different stages of the exam and the significance of what is happening in these stages, one would expect a strongly negative correlation between, say, feeling happy and feeling disappointed. However, the situation is highly ambiguous before the exam, but it becomes less so after the exam and is quite unambiguous by the time grades are announced. Some have failed and others have done well. At anticipation, therefore, one can be both happy and disappointed, or perhaps I should say that when things are ambiguous one is neither happy nor disappointed; by the end of the exam, however, the psychological situation is much more clarified, and a student who reports disappointment is unlikely also to report feeling happy, the negative correlation having reached .50. Yet even when the meaning of the situation is clear, a perfect correlation would not occur if one is happy about some aspects of the situation and unhappy about others, which may not be reported unless we ask.

In any event, these data suggest that the dimensional structure of emotions is not fixed, as is usually implied by those employing the factor analytic approach, but will change with the context, in this case the stage of an emotional encounter and its relative ambiguity, as well as with the facet of experience to which one is attending. This point undermines a central assumption of those using factor analysis — that the structure is invariant. It also supports what I said earlier about the inadequacy of treating emotions solely from the standpoint of the reaction without reference to the emotion-generating process, its stage, and the conditions influencing it.

Polivy (1981) observes that when students were asked to report emotional reactions, some blending of emotion categories occurred, blurring distinctions among them. She offers several possible explanations. About one of them she writes that it is possible that the majority of college student subjects do not experience discrete emotions long enough to report them as separate experiences. Another possibility is that one emotion triggers another, or different ones may occur simultaneously. An even less plausible possibility, which Polivy seems to take seriously, is that subjects are unable to discriminate one emotion from another; in effect, people don't know what emotion they are experiencing. If this were so, then neither a categorical nor a dimensional analysis of emotion would be justified, which makes this the most nihilistic position that can be taken.

I favor the notion that several or more emotions can occur at the same time, or within a single adaptational encounter, because there are many agendas and thematic facets to a complex encounter; most of the time we do indeed know the emotions we experience, and rarely do we experience only a single emotion. We also use much more than the response "feel" in making the judgment; for example, we also pay attention to the situational meaning in an encounter, which may be even more important and informative than the often ambiguous response feel.

Where does the effort to describe the dimensional structure of emotions through correlational analysis take us? The most extreme and potentially contentious position is that a few basic dimensions of emotion can account for almost all of the reliable variance in the normative emotional response pattern. Thus, Russell and Mehrabian (1977) maintain that 42 different emotion scales can be explained by three factors, with the implication that little meaning is added by using the many emotion terms that fall within the same dimension, such as anxiety, guilt, and shame; they are redundant because what is shared is more important than what is different (see also Russell, Lewicka, & Niit, 1989, for cross-cultural data on this model). This of course requires that we not be concerned about the even more subtle distinctions between meanings — for example, those between righteous anger, vengeful anger, defensive anger, pouting, gloating, irritation, jealousy, contempt, competitiveness, and anger suffused with guilt, shame, or anxiety — because these are even more redundant.

There is merit in simplifying generalizations for the purpose of examining which emotions are closer psychologically or farther apart on a number of factors of meaning, and merit in merely trying to reduce redundancy. Factor analysis can, of course, also be used to develop new content categories. Nevertheless, the search for factors or dimensions sacrifices or blurs important psychological meanings and therefore obscures the emotion process and the conditions influencing it.

Consider, for example, the two-factor solution of Watson and Tellegen (1985, p. 221), shown in Figure 2.1. Notice that four response terms can be found at the six o'clock position at the bottom of the circle — drowsy, dull, sleepy, and sluggish. Presumably these all share the common property of low positive affect, though I agree with Ortony, Clore, and Foss (1987), who question whether drowsy and sleepy are emotions at all, though they are included in Watson and Tellegen's dimensional scheme.

The main critique, however, is that the words in Figure 2.1, though placed in the same position in the circular matrix, do not at all represent the same state, and the differences among them are, perhaps, as important as their similarities. Not only are they products of different generating conditions, they are experienced differently under different conditions.

If, for example, I am drowsy when the day is over, or when awakening in bed, but I have nothing pressing to do but relax, the drowsy state is unconflicted and pleasant. If, however, I am feeling drowsy but I have urgent things to do or I am attending a conference at which I must pay attention, or look like it, then being drowsy is distressing and needs to be fought, sometimes at considerable cost. Nor do I believe that feeling sluggish is ever pleasant, though it is listed in that sphere in the two-factor circle. I suspect that, although these states are more similar to each other in a correlational matrix than they are to other states, the important negative nuance of the word *sluggish* is not conveyed by the terms *drowsy* and *sleepy,* but is an expression of conflict between what I want to do and my body or mind's resistance. Similarly, the words *sorry, blue,* and *grouchy,* sharing the position of five o'clock on the circle, have for me quite divergent relational meanings, which are obscured in this type of analysis.

Much of value is lost by putting these reactions into dimensions, because the simplifying or reductive generalizations wipe out important meanings about person–environment relationships, which the hundreds of emotion words were created to express. If we want to know what makes people or any given person angry, for example, the task is not facilitated—in fact, it is actually undermined—by a preoccupation with the so-called underlying response dimensions, which supposedly transcend emotion categories. Anger, then, becomes only a kind of unpleasant activa-

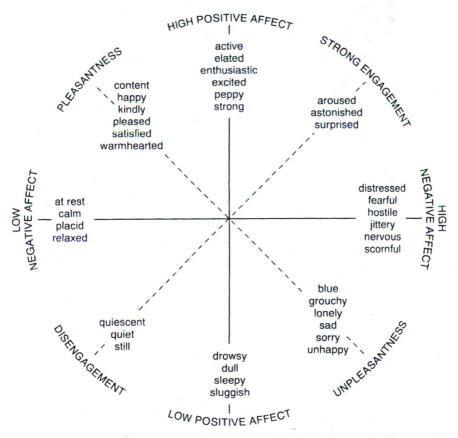

FIGURE 2.1. Watson and Tellegen's two-factor structure of affect. (*Source:* D. Watson and A. Tellegen, "Toward a consensual structure of mood." *Psychological Bulletin, 98.* Washington, DC: American Psychological Association. Copyright © 1985 by the American Psychological Association. Reprinted by permission.)

tion, when in reality it is a complex, varied, and rich relational pattern between persons, one that is distinctive and powerful in its effects on the participating persons and the larger social setting.

Clore, Ortony, and Foss (1987, pp. 751–752) state their criticism of efforts to examine the dimensional structure of emotion words even more sharply than I have when they write:

> Because of the nature of the judgment tasks, such studies often yield rather general dimensions that are not particularly informative with respect to the kinds of questions that ought to concern emotion theorists. For example, the two dimensions (often interpreted as *valence* and *arousal*) most frequently discovered by scaling procedures appear to have no particular relation to emotions. One is simply Osgood's evaluation dimension (*E*), and the other is easily interpreted as a combination of his potency (*P*) and activity (*A*) dimensions (Osgood, Suci, & Tannenbaum, 1957). But these, of course, are universal dimensions in terms of which any concept can be scaled. If this is correct, then nothing unique about the nature of emotions has been discovered unless, perhaps, it can be shown that all and only emotions occupy a unique subregion in the space the dimensions define. . . . Thus, dimensions of this kind are so general that they are quite uninformative with respect to identifying features that distinguish emotions from other things. They reveal no principled definitive differences between emotions (e.g., sympathy) and things having nothing to do with emotions (e.g., food). Nor are they informative with respect to distinguishing one type of emotion, say, *anger* . . . from another type, say *fear*.

Frijda (1986, p. 259) is more charitable in recognizing the two distinctive approaches to emotion: categories and dimensions:

> Emotions are discrete states when considered at the level of actual response readiness — at the level of particular action tendencies. They are states varying along a set of continuous dimensions, however, when considered at the level of response to the event's valence and urgency. They are, in other words, states defined by a restricted set of dimensions when considered at a higher level in the hierarchy of action instigation and action control processes. The dimensional and the categorical view are both valid because they apply to different levels of the emotion process, corresponding to different sets of phenomena.

Linguistic analyses of anger by Heider (1991) and Lakoff and Kovecses (1983) and the work of Shaver et al. (1987) and Storm and Storm (1987), both of whom use treelike taxonomies, combine some of the best features of categorical and dimensional analysis by arranging emotions into a hierarchical structure without sacrificing discrete categories. Shaver et al.'s research has the important advantage of using scripts or story lines in which the eliciting conditions (provocations) of the emotional reaction are included. They quote Fehr and Russell (1984, p. 482) on scripts in a statement with which I obviously agree:

> Although we often speak of fear as a thing, a more apt description may be a sequence of events. . . . [To] know the meaning of the word *fear* is to know some such sequence. It is to know a *script* (Abelson, 1981) [that includes] prototypical causes, beliefs, physiological reactions, feelings, facial expressions, actions, and consequences.

In the first step in Shaver et al.'s research, college students rated 213 emotion terms for prototypicality or "emotionness," drawing on Averill's (1975) Semantic Atlas of Emotional Concepts, which contains 558 words with emotional connotations. On the basis of a cluster analysis of these ratings, they defined five or six clusters representing the "basic" emotion categories. Figure 2.2 presents their arrangement of distinctive emotion categories based on the ratings of emotionness, with overlapping terms falling within the basic categories.

In a second step, students wrote accounts of emotional experiences — some being asked to describe their impressions of typical emotion episodes; others, their impressions of specific, real incidents. After these accounts were coded, the authors determined the prototypical features of the basic emotion categories that had previously been obtained. These were then subjected to further hierarchical cluster analysis* to produce a prototypic diagram for each basic emotion that involved descriptive features of the provoking situation. Because the accounts so clearly resemble what I mean by *core relational themes* (see also Chapter 3 and Part Three), it will be worthwhile to quote in some detail what Shaver et al. (pp. 1077–1078) say about the scripts for each of several basic emotions on the basis of their subjects' accounts:

> If one were to try to convey *fear,* say in a novel or a film, . . . one would want to communicate the threat of harm or death, if possible in an unfamiliar or unpredictable environment and in a situation in which the protagonist is vulnerable or lacking in control; to portray the potential victim's jitteriness and tendency to imagine disaster.
>
> If fear accounts begin with a desciption of events as potentially dangerous or threatening to the self, *sadness* accounts begin with a situation in which the threat has already been realized. The sad person has experienced an undesirable outcome; often he or she has experienced one of the events that the fearful person dreads — death of a loved one, loss of a relationship, or social rejection. Like fear, sadness involves "discovering that one is powerless, helpless, or impotent" to change the unhappy circumstances (cf. Seligman, 1975).
>
> The cognitive antecedents that initiate the *anger* process, as inferred from subjects' accounts, can be summarized as follows: Something (usually another person, in these accounts) interferes with the person's execution of plans or attainment of goals (by reducing the person's power, violating expectations, or frustrating or interrupting goal-directed activities). Alternatively, the person perceives another as harming him or her in some way (inflicting physical or psychological pain). Finally, as de Rivera (1981) pointed out, the angry person makes the judgment that the frustration, interruption, power reversal, or harm is illegitimate — that the situation is contrary to what it ought to be. This last element is the most frequent feature in the anger prototype, occurring in fully 95% of the self anger accounts.

As Shaver et al. (p. 1080) suggest in connection with the category versus dimension issue, people probably judge the similarity or distinctiveness of emotions on the basis of prototypical features rather than where these emotions fall on abstract dimensions such as evaluation, potency, and activity. The same applies to the

---

*This is similar to a factor analysis, both depending on analysis of a matrix of correlations among the measured concepts.

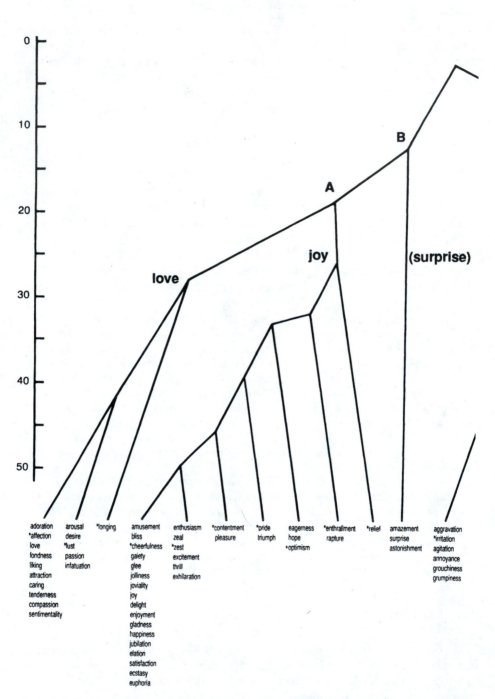

FIGURE 2.2. Cluster analysis of 135 emotion names. (*Source:* P. Shaver, J. Schwartz, D. Kirson, and C. O'Connor, "Emotion knowledge." *Journal of Personality and Social Psychology, 52.* Washington, DC: American Psychological Association. Copyright © 1987 by the American Psychological Association. Reprinted by permission.)

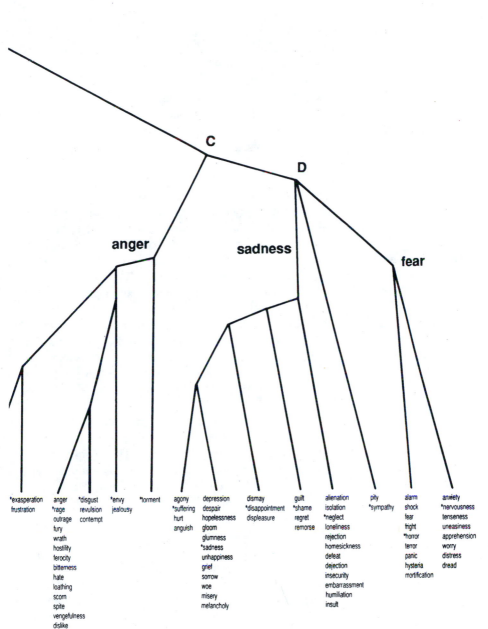

C

D

anger

sadness

fear

*exasperation	anger	*disgust	*envy	*torment	agony	depression	dismay	guilt	alienation	pity	alarm	anxiety
frustration	*rage	revulsion	jealousy		*suffering	despair	*disappointment	*shame	isolation	*sympathy	shock	*nervousness
	outrage	contempt			hurt	hopelessness	displeasure	regret	*neglect		fear	tenseness
	fury				anguish	gloom		remorse	loneliness		fright	uneasiness
	wrath					glumness			rejection		*horror	apprehension
	hostility					*sadness			homesickness		terror	worry
	ferocity					unhappiness			defeat		panic	distress
	bitterness					grief			dejection		hysteria	dread
	hate					sorrow			insecurity		mortification	
	loathing					woe			embarrassment			
	scorn					misery			humiliation			
	spite					melancholy			insult			
	vengefulness											
	dislike											
	resentment											

appraisals underlying each emotion, which are best understood as evaluations of the personal significance of what is happening; in short, the emotional script includes the eliciting conditions that result in either harms or benefits. These authors also note that the prototypes they are describing are parallel with the concepts of a number of cognitively oriented theories, including mine.

A cognitive-motivational-relational theory of emotion must be first and foremost categorical — that is, families of emotions that share a common core relational theme must be identified. Of course, each category itself contains a dimension of emotion strength, which may be fruitfully assessed; the categories, however, come first. I would argue that the primary conceptual and empirical task is to identify the person–environment relationship, appraisal characteristics, and action tendency inherent in each emotion category.

It has often been said that words designating the emotions are ambiguous, and if this is accepted at face value, then the subtle nuances among emotion words, presumably reflecting meaning differences among emotions, do not have to be taken seriously. This is an incomplete and untenable position. To note that a single word is ambiguous as to the emotion referred to is a poor argument when extended to the idea that emotions themselves are ambiguous, or that they cannot be adequately designated. The ambiguity is only true if we limit ourselves to single words that represent the response "feel" or some other part of an emotional whole — for example, the action tendency. The solution is to write a sentence to express an emotional configuration or scenario, which says more than any single word can express. This is exactly what I do in Chapter 3 with what I have been calling core relational themes. They define the essential relational content of each individual emotion. If this is done well, there is little ambiguity in our verbal description of the emotion and its process.

For these reasons, and despite continuing interest and research on it since 1890, I believe that the dimensional analysis of emotion, as it has been traditionally conceived and pursued, can never be at the cutting edge of emotion theory and research. It is fixated too much on factor analytic methodology and too little on systematic theories that can generate variables and conditions to advance our understanding.

Universals in the Emotional Response

Psychologists and other scientists do much research on emotion. My purpose here is not to review that research but to emphasize issues of importance to emotion theory. I have the opportunity later on to refer to research close to my heart because it deals with issues of motivation and cognition in emotion and with emotional development. However, in this chapter, which is concerned with classification and measurement, it would be a serious omission not to illustrate the phylogeneticist's concern with emotional universals. I have therefore chosen to discuss here one of the currently most vigorous and influential approaches to emotion. Though it is focused on two response measures, facial expression and autonomic nervous system patterning, it also addresses issues of classification and measurement from a phylogenetic perspective.

Most lists of individual emotions are based descriptively on response configurations alone. There are, however, occasional exceptions such as Plutchik's (1962, 1980) theory, which is based on propositions about the fundamental (Darwinian) evolutionary, adaptational functions on which the survival of mammals depends. Plutchik lists *protection of self,* associated with escape and fear; *destruction of enemies,* associated with attack and anger; *reproduction,* associated with mating and joy; *reintegration in the group after separation,* associated with crying and sadness; *incorporation,* associated with grooming and acceptance; *rejection,* associated with vomiting and disgust; *exploration,* associated with mapping and expectation; and *orientation,* associated with ceasing action and surprise.

The biopsychologist's interest in the evolutionary functions of emotion is analogous to the social scientist's interest in the role of motivation (or goal hierarchies) in emotion, which defines the business of an adaptational encounter. In effect, evolutionary, adaptational functions in Plutchik's analysis and goal hierarchies in mine provide the theoretical power of motives on which harms and benefits are predicated and on which rest emotional reactions to what happens in an encounter with the environment. Plutchik's analysis has the advantage of a species-based functional rationale for the emotion response, whereas my analysis has the advantage of providing an individualized functional rationale for the emotional response, especially but not exclusively for humans.

Nevertheless, more is needed than a mere linking of emotions with adaptational functions shared by diverse species to help us understand the conditions under which each emotion is generated. We have to say what goals are implicated in *particular* adaptational encounters, how they influence the emotions generated, and what other *contemporary conditions* operate to power, direct, and alter the emotion process. Even if we accept Plutchik's analysis of the functions underlying emotions and are not put off by their lack of clarity and connecting detail (for example, is social rejection really equivalent to disgust and is joy always linked to reproduction—and if so, which phases of reproduction are involved—and is separation the essence of sadness?), an adequate theory of the emotion process and its sources of variation must focus on the phenomena themselves and the contexts in which they occur. (Recall my discussion of reduction in Chapter 1 in which it was suggested that we cannot fully understand a phenomenon by looking elsewhere.)

Research on Facial Expression

Emotional expression, especially as displayed in the face, is the basis of much current research and classification. Other forms of expression are also relevant (e.g., vocal expression as it is studied by Scherer, 1989), but have not been studied as much and may be less informative. A consideration that makes facial and bodily movements theoretically as well as descriptively important is that they are components of the action or action tendency of an emotional state, whether the action is instrumental—that is, purposive or intentional, or purely expressive, though as I said the distinction is not easy to make. If we can identify emotions through expression, then anger or happiness, for example, is said by proponents of facial expression research to be occurring whenever a particular pattern of muscle movement is observed (in the face or in posture and gesture). Certain emotions are said to have their own specific pattern of expression, a criterion that could of course be supplemented and validated by other criteria such as subjective reports of emotional experience and the pattern of physiological change. There is a dangerous temptation in this, which should be resisted, to assume that where a universal facial pattern cannot be demonstrated (as in the cases of guilt and shame), the reaction is not an emotion, and alternatively, that where a pattern seems universal in a species, it is therefore a biologically given engram that should be a criterion of an emotion (see Chapter 5).

Research on facial expression assumes that, although there may be sources of noise such as the operation of social display rules, emotions are often, if not always, revealed in the face. As Buck (1985) put it without equivocation and perhaps too sanguinely, facial actions are readouts of the internal emotional state. Primary or basic emotions are said to express universal biological rules handed down genetically through evolution because they have proved adaptationally useful. They arise from an inherited neural structure, involve a characteristic neuromuscular response pattern, and are correlated with distinctive subjective qualities for each emotion. Since muscle movement patterns in the face are, in effect, expressive of the inner emotional state, we may observe them carefully to "read" the state, which is what animals do in adjusting their behavior to whatever other animals are inadvertently communicating in their bodily expressions.[2]

The idea of a literal readout, however, must be qualified when we realize that we can inhibit and transform both the action tendencies and facial expressions of emotion. Another qualification is that all components of the emotion response serve functional masters other than the emotion process itself. No response component should be regarded as a necessary sign of the presence of an emotion. In addition to inherited expressive patterns, we also have the ability to produce actions and facial expressions of emotions that are not being experienced, as in a stage actor's performance, though it is possible that the actor is experiencing the emotion of the role being played or the facial pattern being produced. In any case, although there is an advantage to decoupling the emotional state from facial and bodily expression, this probably requires some volitional effort, and it also illustrates what I have been saying about the essential flexibility of emotion and coping as an adaptational resource in higher mammals.

Interest in emotional expression was greatly stimulated by Darwin's (1872/1965) important book, *The Expression of the Emotions in Man and Animals,* and by his earlier 1859 masterpiece, *The Origin of Species,* which described the nature and mechanism of evolution. The central theme of evolutionary theory is, of course, that in the descent of man from earlier forms of life, humans and nonhuman animals came to share many characteristics in common—not only their anatomy and physiology, but also their adaptational patterns. Darwin strongly emphasized the similarities—claiming, for example, that nonhuman animals show wonder, curiosity, imitation, attention, memory, reasoning, and a sense of beauty, all of which had once been considered uniquely human attributes. He went so far as to suggest, in what I consider a fanciful idea—though who can gainsay it—that animals had a spiritual sense, which was a precursor of the human belief in God (see Domjan, 1987).

In any case, the way the face expresses emotion was considered innate in the species by Darwin, and is so considered by many modern phylogeneticists. Facial expression is an important basis of the communication and recognition of emotions in other people, just as expression in body movements and vocal sounds also serves these functions in both humans and infrahuman animals. Although the evidence is inconclusive and the conditions that affect the comparison still need to be examined (see Ekman & Oster, 1979), in humans the face seems to be a richer and more dependable source of information about emotion than any other expressive modality, except perhaps verbal reports under nonthreatening conditions (which allow them perhaps to be more trustworthy than otherwise).

There is no need to go into Darwin's theoretical propositions about emotional expression, or into the history of research on facial expression, which has been amply presented elsewhere (see, for example, Ekman, 1971, 1977, 1984; Izard, 1971, 1977; and Tomkins, 1962, 1963). The most widely accepted position is that the face, through a complex and interconnected set of muscles, gives innate expression to the primary emotions that humans inherited in the evolution of the species, and that the pattern of expression for each emotion is universal for that species.[3] In humans there is, in effect, an anger face, a disgust face, a fear face, a happiness face, and so on, although to some extent sociocultural variables can affect the pattern and timing of expression, and an emotional face can be inhibited, disguised, or produced for effect.

It is also worth noting in passing that ecologists and those concerned with animal behavior were also greatly influenced by the Darwinian conceptual framework and have long observed the facial and bodily comportment that signals to other animals their emotional states or intentions. Figure 2.3, for example, is a diagrammatic representation by Lorenz (1963) of fear and anger faces in dogs, which both humans and other animals presumably are able to recognize.

A widely held view today is that the face provides rich information about a person's emotional state, if one knows how to read it. There is, however, disagreement over the extent to which the origins of facial expression are innate, sociocultural, or both. Evidence amassed by recent researchers (see Ekman, 1989; Ekman & Oster, 1979; Fridlund, Ekman, & Oster, 1986) strongly suggests that to a considerable extent facial expressions are part of our hereditary endowment. The arguments tend to center on lists of basic emotions, the specifics of the facial pattern for each emotion, about how fixed or invariant emotions are, what drives them, and about the extent of the correspondence between facial patterns and other response criteria, such as physiological change, instrumental action, and subjective affect; such correspondence is necessary to interpret the facial pattern for its emotional contents.

What gives modern research and thought about facial expression its potential importance for emotion theory is that more than any other response modality the muscle patterns in facial expression have been mapped with great care and objectivity. Although there is more than one system of mapping, this solid base of research is the result of the pioneering work of Tomkins, who greatly influenced two other pioneers I have already cited, Ekman and Izard, who subsequently and painstakingly recorded on videotape and film the face in action during emotions and developed widely used methods for coding the facial action. Ekman's work has been mainly with adults and Izard's with young children. To the extent that the face portrays human emotion, it becomes possible to use its patterns of expression as a strong clue

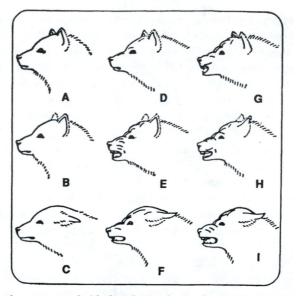

FIGURE 2.3. The dog expresses in his face fear and anger in certain characteristic ways: (a–c) readiness to flee; (a–g) increasing aggression; (e, f, h, i) various combinations revealing ambiguity of intention. People probably do also. (*Source:* Konrad Lorenz, *On Aggression.* Translated by Marjorie Kerr Wilson. Orlando, FL: Harcourt Brace Jovanovich, Inc. Copyright © 1963 by Dr. G. Borothe-Schoeler Verlag, Wien. English translation copyright © 1966 by Konrad Lorenz. Reprinted by permission of the publisher.)

to the presence of emotional states and to examine with high observer reliability its moment-to-moment changes. Ekman's careful observations of facial expression across cultures are illustrated by some examples in Figure 2.4.

If the study of facial expression could indeed provide us with a reliable and valid indicator of what a person is experiencing emotionally from moment to moment, it would offer to the study of human emotion a tremendously important measurement source. The most enthusiastic position, which some writers take, is that, despite the high cost and tediousness of the procedure, we could use the face as the single, unassailable criterion against which to assess all sorts of theoretical questions about the emotion process and the conditions that affect it. A more realistic position would be that because of the complexity of the emotion process and its cognitive-motivational-relational configuration, which includes automatic and deliberate appraisal and coping processes, as well as the many other influences on facial reaction patterns themselves, facial expression should be regarded as one response system among many. Although it is perhaps the most informative of the peripheral response systems, it needs to be supplemented with information from other sources such as the social context, the contents of emotional statements, voice quality, bodily posture, and the like, each serving as data about the complex emotional state being experienced. I believe this is also the way Ekman (personal communication) views it.

Ekman and Oster (1979; updated by Fridlund, Ekman, & Oster, 1986) have provided a very useful analysis and partial review of the evidence about the emotions

Two smiles: left, fulsome; right, uncertain

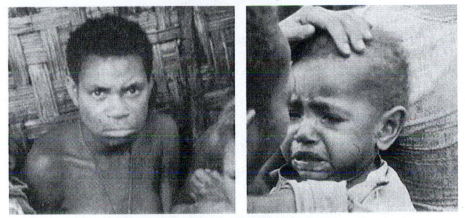

Anger   Distress

Disgust

FIGURE 2.4. Some of Ekman's photos of people in New Guinea. (*Source:* P. Ekman, *The Face of Man.* New York: Garland Publishing, Inc., 1980. Reprinted by permission.)

revealed by facial expressions, particularly on two questions: the *universality* of facial expressions in emotion, and the *validity* of the pattern of expression as an indicator of particular emotions. These authors (1979, p. 531) suggest, for example, that research "in pre-literate cultures has found distinctive facial expressions for anger, disgust, happiness, sadness (or distress), fear, and surprise." Izard also reported evidence for the emotions of interest and shame, which Ekman and Oster, however, regard as artifactual. They also believe that further study could demonstrate universality for other emotional patterns of expression as well.

In a recent review and analysis of the arguments about universals in facial expression, Ekman (1989) states cautiously that the evidence supports the conclusion that there are indeed some universals. He summarizes a large body of evidence across many cultures for universality in the facial expressions of some emotions such as fear, anger, disgust, sadness, surprise, and happiness, but there is uncertainty, he says, about contempt, shame, and interest. He writes in summary:

> Facial expressions of emotion are, in my view (Ekman, 1977), as central to emotion as are the physiological changes or subjective feelings, and thus it would be mistaken to view one as the expression of the other. Also, while people do make facial expressions deliberately to transmit information, most facial expressions of emotion occur, I believe, without such deliberation. That is not to deny their importance as social signals, in either their development or current function.

There are also culturally acquired display rules as well as different social triggers across cultures, but precise methods of facial analysis have not yet been systematically applied to this proposition. As Ekman and Oster put it (p. 532), "There probably are important cultural differences in facial expression, attributable to learning, but precisely what these are and how they come to be are unknown."

The term *display rules* was coined by Ekman and Friesen (1969) to refer to social norms about who can show a particular emotion to which persons and under what conditions. The smile is an interesting and important facial response in the debate about the sociocultural and innate biological sources of control for emotional expression, because if the masking smile of enjoyment under conditions of pain, sadness, disgust, fear, or anger cannot be distinguished from the genuine smile of enjoyment, the interpretation that facial expressions reflect emotions would be seriously challenged. In a recent study, Ekman, Friesen, and O'Sullivan (1988) have observed subtle differences among smiles when people are being truthful and when they are lying. Nurses feigned enjoyment to conceal negative emotions when watching films showing distressing contents, and these smiles were compared with those made to enjoyable films. Differences in the kinds of smiles were detected by visible traces of the muscle actions found in disgust, fear, contempt, or sadness, even when they were trying to mask the negative emotions with a happy face.

Smiles, Ekman writes, should no longer be treated as a single category of emotional expression. There may be a number of different kinds of smile, perhaps as many as 18, which provide different kinds of social signals. After examining the research evidence, he concludes that enjoyment smiles, named the "Duchenne smile" after the pioneering observations and writings of the French neurophysiologist Duchenne (1862), are different from smiles that reflect only efforts at social display (Ekman, Friesen, & Davidson, 1990).

It must be obvious from what I have already said about the mediating role of cognition that I have some reservations about the interpretation of this research; to repeat myself, there is no peripheral response component that should be regarded as an absolute criterion of an emotion, though Ekman's interpretation of Duchenne's smiles seems to suggest, contrary to my position, that true happiness can be distinguished from other states, including feigned happiness, merely by the facial response pattern (see examples of different smiles in Figure 2.4). Research that starts with given patterns of facial expression and defines the state of the person on that basis — as has been common in developmental studies with infants and prelingual children — without providing evidence in addition to the facial expression may well be open to question.*

With respect to the validity of facial patterns as indicators of a particular emotion, Ekman and Oster (1979) have reviewed the problems of validating any particular interpretation of facial expression. In some accord with what I have been saying, they point out that criteria other than the face must be found to suggest the emotion that is being experienced, of which there are four possibilities: One is the report by subjects about the emotion that was experienced. A second is to relate facial expressions to eliciting conditions — for example, positive or negative films, hostile or friendly remarks, and anticipation of a positive or negative experience. A third is to compare changes in voice quality or pitch, body movements, or speech with the kinds of emotion suggested by facial expression patterns. And a fourth consists of autonomic nervous system reaction patterns which I say more about later on. Ekman and Oster (1979, p. 541) observe that "Since there is no single, infallible way to determine a person's 'true' emotional state, it is unfortunate that so few investigators have followed the approach of using multiple convergent measures to gain a more reliable indication of the emotion experienced."

Over the past few decades, no research area in the study of emotions has been more vigorous than the attempt to examine universals in the facial expression of emotion. There is considerable consensus that the face does indeed provide much, perhaps crucial, information about the emotions occurring in a person. If this research can be integrated into cognitive-motivational-relational theories of emotion, which are concerned with variations in emotional experience and reaction as well as universals, and take account of the role of knowledge and appraisal patterns for each individual emotion, and look at emotional development from infancy to adulthood and beyond, there would be an unparalleled opportunity to bring together biological and social science perspectives on the emotion process, and to avoid a common tendency to pit one against the other (see Chapter 5).

Research on Physiological Response Patterns

Seeking physiological response correlates of emotions and facial expressive patterns, or for that matter any correlates, including self-report of emotion content, cre-

---

*I am indebted to Joseph Campos in my department for making this point forcefully in lectures he has given.

ates the dilemma of having to test one set of uncertainties (namely, the emotional significance of facial expressive patterns) against another (namely, the emotional significance of the physiological reaction pattern). In spite of this dilemma, dependable positive findings would have considerable value in showing at least that both levels of analysis reflect overlapping psychophysiological processes. Only a modest number of these studies have been reported to date.

One reason for this dearth of findings is the psychological prejudice of the last few decades that physiological changes in emotion reflect only general arousal (cf. Schachter, 1966; see also Lazarus & Folkman, 1984, for a discussion of this). The concept of general arousal, which is a unidimensional view of emotion compatible with the concept of drive, has also recently lost favor as an organizing principle in psychology. The earlier ascendancy of general arousal over specificity, exemplifying the pendulum swings in intellectual fashions, had been in part the result of disenchantment with the older psychosomatic view, derived from psychoanalytic theory, that ulcers, colitis, hypertension, and the like expressed a particular kind of intrapsychic conflict or attitude (see Chapter 10).

For many reasons, not the least of which was a limited and often otherwise poor data base with inconsistent findings and a change in theoretical fashion, the notion of specificity was replaced by Selye's (1956, 1976) concept of the general adaptation syndrome, which parallels the concept of general arousal by emphasizing a common, orchestrated pattern of physiological changes as the body's main defense against any noxious agent. It was called a *general syndrome* because its core was always the same regardless of the nature of the noxious agent. Ironically, the alternative premise, specificity, now becoming dominant again, is a throwback to the earlier version — namely, that each emotion, such as anger, fear, anxiety, guilt, and joy, involves a specific attitude, conflict, and perhaps a specific pattern of physiological change.

I do not wish to debate in detail the merits and demerits of the general arousal and specificity positions. This has been done by others (e.g., Lacey, 1959; Lazarus, 1966; Lazarus & Folkman, 1984; Levenson, 1988). The issue will also come up again in Chapter 5 in my examination of system theory and in Chapter 10 in my examination of emotions and health. Some recent studies such as those of Schwartz and Weinberger (1980) and Schwartz, Weinberger, and Singer (1981) provide positive results about autonomic patterning in different emotions. A recent study by Ekman, Levenson, and Friesen (1983) also produced evidence of autonomic specificity for disgust, anger, sadness, and fear (see also Davidson, Ekman, Saron, Senulis, & Friesen, 1990, on CNS changes in positive emotions). And among the most thoughtful recent discussions of both the history of this debate and the current evidence for autonomic nervous system specificity is an analysis and review provided by Levenson (1988), who makes a good case for the theory of autonomic specificity while recognizing that the evidence is, as yet, inadequate. He (1988, p. 22) writes:

> It is my belief that the most fruitful model for exploring *autonomic* specificity will prove to be a hybrid [drawing] primarily on the discrete emotions model, but also taking into account the dimension of "intensity. . . ." Given the limited number of studies to date, the inconsistency of findings, and the methodological problems that have characterized much of the work on ANS specificity, there is much to be gained from pursuing separate lines of investigation within both the discrete and dimensional models.

When findings have accumulated from a sufficient number of sound studies representing each model, it should then be possible to evaluate their relative usefulness.

One could argue that autonomic patterns provide the least adequate physiological case for demonstrating specificity, because the neural structure of the autonomic nervous system and its end-organ connections (for example, the digestive tract, endocrine glands, and cardiovascular system) should lead to relatively diffuse reactions in the viscera, especially in the case of sympathetic activation. A more complete approach would include hormonal patterns such as those studied by Mason (1971, 1975; Mason, Maher, Hartley, Mougey, Perlow, & Jones, 1976), as well as autonomic variables. A diagram from Mason (1975, p. 148) of nine neurohumoral systems is presented in Figure 2.5, which illustrates how much more needs to be included within psychophysiological research on emotion than is contained in autonomic data; Mason's 1975 portrait of neurohumoral systems leaves out, of course, the more recently discovered enkephalins, which appear to regulate pain.

I believe that, although the relationship might not be as tight a one as Izard (1990) argues for, facial and other forms of expression and neurophysiological

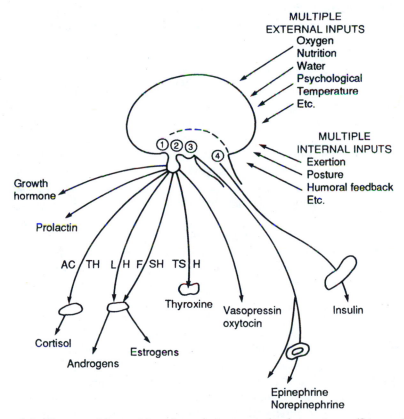

FIGURE 2.5. The assemblage of interdependent neuroendocrine systems. (*Source:* J. W. Mason, J. T. Maher, L. H. Hartley, E. Jougey, M. J. Perlow, and L. G. Jones, *Psychopathology of Human Adaptation*. New York: Plenum Publishing Corp, 1976. Reprinted by permission.)

changes bear a systematic relationship to each other and to the kinds and intensities of emotion that people experience. Why should this be so? A good answer lies in the idea that each emotion involves a particular action tendency — for example, anger with attack, fear-anxiety with avoidance and escape, guilt with making amends, shame with hiding, and so on. Though they can be inhibited and transformed, action tendencies help make the emotion embodied and provide the simplest rationale for a common or shared physiological response pattern for each emotion.

Another rationale might be that there is a common appraisal pattern in every instance of anger, fright-anxiety, guilt, happiness, and so forth, based on a *shared set of adaptational requirements* (see Chapter 5). Anger poses its own special relationship problems, as does fright-anxiety, and so on. Though there will also be some variation in the details — for example, environmental demands, constraints, and resources — their exact personal significance, how they are coped with, and how the environment responds to the coping process are apt to be much more shared within an emotion family than among different families. We might use either the concept of action tendency or the shared adaptational requirements to explain and predict the physiological response pattern associated with each emotion. This requires translating the action tendency and adaptational requirements into physiological activity throughout the body. To date, although Frijda, Kuipers, and ter Schure (1989) have provided some weak data, I am not aware of any systematic effort to do this. I shall say more about this in Chapter 5.

I remain convinced of the potential utility of the idea that each emotion is associated with a specific pattern of bodily response but also suspicious of the empirical case for this for two reasons, both emphasized in Chapter 1. First, methodologically speaking, an emotional encounter only rarely contains a single emotion, and it often rapidly spills over into another encounter with a different business and a different emotional reaction. Therefore, measurement of the autonomic and hormonal response is apt to be confounded by a host of processes whose nature is obscure. Second, without a viable theory about emotional encounters, their motivational business, their cognitive influences, and the action tendencies and coping processes that might shape the adaptational and emotional flow, the problems of studying specificity are magnified, leaving researchers uncertain about what states are actually being measured. Although I regard these problems as daunting, I do not believe they are insuperable, and I am convinced that adequate theory could help prompt the development of suitable research methods to examine emotional response specificity.

Primary (Basic) and Secondary (Derived) Emotions

An important feature of the thinking of phylogenetically centered theorists and researchers, including many who have studied facial expression and autonomic nervous system patterning, is a distinction between basic, or *primary, emotions,* presumably shared within and across mammalian species, and derived, or *secondary, emotions,* which are said to represent some type of combination of the primary ones. The distinction is important because it is made by many researchers and it concerns how emotions should be classified.

Some phylogeneticists (e.g., Ekman, 1977) assume that the primary emotions operate as *affect programs,* which arise from common neurophysiological structures and processes built into the species that, when set in motion, unfold in more or less the same fashion. Ekman (personal communication) now seems to be thinking of affect program as a metaphor rather than as a literal arrangement that rigidly drives and directs the response pattern. I have more to say about affect programs in Chapter 5 when I try to reconcile biological universals with sociocultural and developmental sources of variability in emotion.

Phylogeneticists present lists of the primary emotions that are presumably found in all humans and some animals, as well as those that are secondary either in the sense of being blends (cf. Ekman, 1977; Plutchik, 1980) or combinations, perhaps acquired by association with the primary ones (cf. Izard, 1977; Tomkins, 1981). I note in passing that Scherer (1984a, 1984b) has referred to the concept of *blends* as "palette emotions," referring to the mixing of paint colors on an artist's palette, a concept carefully examined and searchingly criticized recently by Ortony, Clore, and Collins (1988). Some early and classical lists of primaries are very short, as in Watson's (1930) three basic emotions of anger, fear, and love; but other lists are larger, such as Descartes' six basic emotions of wonder, love, hatred, desire, joy, and sadness. Modern lists include Plutchik's (1962, 1980) eight primary emotions — fear, surprise, sadness, disgust, anger, anticipation, joy, and acceptance.

Ekman's (1971) primaries include happiness, fear, surprise, anger, distress, and disgust — to which he has recently added contempt (and as I noted earlier, a few more the evidence for which he regards as equivocal, such as interest, shame-guilt, and embarrassment). Izard (1977) lists ten primary emotions including interest-excitement, enjoyment-joy, surprise-startle, distress-anguish, anger-rage, disgust-revulsion, contempt-scorn, fear-terror, shame-shyness-humiliation, and guilt-remorse. The overlap between Ekman and Izard is, in part, the result of their both being strongly influenced by Tomkins (1962, 1963) and their joint interest in facial expressive patterns. The differences between them probably arise, in part, from the fact that Izard has studied mainly children and Ekman adults. It is a bit perplexing that, despite the common phylogenetic outlook, theorists end up with only modest agreement on what are the basic emotions. To quote a critical comment by de Sousa (1980, p. 142), "The diversity in the lists is warning enough that this is an unpromising strategy."

The terms *primary* and *basic,* along with their synonyms, have at least four different, though overlapping and controversial, meanings — all having a strongly evolutionary flavor. (1) Primary emotions are physiologically elemental and pure; (2) primary emotions are those found consistently across cultures and perhaps in many animal species; (3) primary emotions are those that emerge at birth or at least within the first year of life (see Arieti, 1970; Emde, 1984; Fox & Davidson, 1984; Sroufe, 1979); and (4) primary emotions derive from and express the most important adaptational tasks of animals such as protection from danger, reproduction, orientation, and exploration (see Plutchik, 1980). All these meanings seem to be variants on the common theme of *biological universality.*

I am comfortable with the idea that some emotions are more or less universal within the human species, especially because they are displayed across cultures. However, primary emotions are not necessarily the same across species. Different species (almost by definition) face overlapping but different kinds of adaptational demands, and successful species will have evolved special mechanisms to cope with the particular demands they face in their ecosystems. Those passed down from their forebears but which are no longer relevant to survival will have tended to disappear eventually, especially if they have become costly, whereas new ones will have evolved to meet new needs and demands. One could regard these new mechanisms as just as primary, though perhaps in a different sense, as any that might be shared with other, older species. Therefore, it is reasonable to expect that species have distinct though overlapping sets of primary emotions, but what is primary to one may not be primary to another or as relevant to the other's ecological niche.

How can we resolve these perennial arguments about how many primary emotions there are, and which emotions are primary? If one adopts the biosocial premise that what is important are the fundamental adaptational tasks generated by a mammal's species characteristics, habitat (including culture), and individual motivational agendas, which in turn influence appraisals of the significance for well-being in every transaction with the environment, then the distinction between primary and nonprimary has only limited utility. Although some adaptational tasks may be more vital to survival than others are, the impact of conditions of harm and benefit is not easy to predict without knowing the relative or absolute strength of motives in any species, social group, or individual, in the environments in which they live. For example, humans will often accept the risk of death rather than live under conditions that violate their definition of self or what is minimal for an acceptable life.

Why should one emotion be considered primary and others not? Or, more to the point, in what sense is it useful to argue for the distinction? The phylogeneticists use the concept of primary to promulgate the view that certain emotions emerged through evolution and are shared, say, by all humans and possibly in some form in other animals. From this perspective it makes sense to retain the distinction just for the purpose of marking the pattern of evolutionary development across species. On the other hand, it puts considerable emphasis, perhaps too much, on continuity in evolution and heredity. Recently Ortony and Turner (1990) have made extensive criticisms of the concept of primary emotions, and though I am not always sanguine about the concept, I am also not in agreement with all of what these authors say.

There are other arguments in favor of the distinction. For example, it is also possible that newer portions of the human brain might not easily and completely override older portions that still govern the energy transformations and homeostatic regulations so important in emotions as well as in nonemotional adaptations (see also Henry, 1986; Le Doux, 1987; MacLean, 1949, 1975; Panksepp, 1982, 1986). For example, although we might be able to influence heart action, especially indirectly, it is unlikely that we can stop our hearts from beating or put them into fibrillation. Heart activity is controlled largely by involuntary mechanisms of the midbrain.

Therefore, species-programmed emotions may be harder to transform or control than those shaped more by what is learned from the society and its culture. Freud regarded the aggressive instincts pessimistically as extremely difficult to override by social or intrapsychic controls, which in his judgment is why humans are constantly killing each other and displaying the most terrible cruelty and brutality, as well as enjoyment of it.[4] Brain damage and the primitivations resulting from drugs such as alcohol also potentiate inherited emotional patterns normally regulated by higher brain centers. When we are not intact or "ourselves," so to speak, we are more vulnerable to primitive, biological tendencies, an idea expressed in the Freudian concepts of primary and secondary processes, and of regression.

It might be more useful for certain purposes to consider that many human emotions—for example, guilt, shame, pride, gratitude, nostalgia, and regret—may have emerged on the basis of greater human cognitive and social complexity, and that these may be unique to humans and just as peremptory but no less primary in the process of survival. Whether and how these newer, emergent emotions are built into the human nervous system are not at all clear.

It seems to me that the utility of the distinction between primary and nonprimary rests on the purposes for which one makes it—for example, the extent to which one is more interested in phylogenetic continuity, species variation, or the social and psychological context of the human emotion process and its variations. My main complaint with the distinction is that when too much is made of it, when it becomes the main concern of theory and research because a phylogenetic perspective calls the tune, the functional importance of the so-called nonprimary emotions in humans is understated. They are treated as merely derivatives rather than as psychologically, socially, and even biologically fundamental in their own right.

A Working Emotion Classification System

I come now to the last step before turning to the chapters dealing with my cognitive-motivational-relational theory—namely, to present a working classification of the emotions on which to draw in Part Three, which deals with the individual emotions. Its basis is largely rational and hence has a certain arbitrariness. A key test I have used for inclusion as a bonafide emotion family is sharing with other variants of that family a common *core relational theme*, which in turn is comprised of a particular *primary and secondary appraisal pattern*. Each emotion family is also characterized by an *action tendency* or impulse, though as we have seen, this is particularly problematic in sadness, happiness, pride, and hope. Other key tests are linguistic, depend on the distinction between states and traits, and exclude reflexes and physiological drives.

Before proceeding to the classification system, we should say something about who is making the appraisals that combine into a core relational theme. Most emotions stem from an interpersonal transaction—for example, by a married couple, lovers, parent and child, two friends, a worker and boss, two people engaged in some economic exchange, and so on. In these transactions the emotion process is not likely to be the same in each person. When *A* offends *B,* it is *B* who feels angry. When *B* retaliates, it is now *A* who feels angry, sad, guilty, or whatever.

When I speak of a relationship, as in a core relational theme, that theme and the appraisals producing it are often different for each individual person in the encounter, sometimes extremely so, even though it occurs in the same transaction. *A* sees things from *A*'s point of view; *B* sees them from *B*'s point of view. Often these perceptions and appraisals are in tune with each other, but often not with realism. We must always specify who is doing the appraising, what is being appraised, and what it is about that individual and the external conditions that contribute to the appraisal process. A third perspective, as we saw in Chapter 1, is that of an observer, C, who is interested in both A's and B's appraisals as the transaction unfolds. This third perspective provides still another set of cognitions about what is happening between A and B.

I want the reader to understand that I do not regard my list of emotions as a final one but only as an approximation that is subject to change with further analysis and observation. There is bound to be a degree of arbitrariness about this, given what we know. Remember, however, that this is a working classification. I am quite willing to say that the list can be expanded or contracted on the basis of more that we might learn. The emotion concepts discussed are divided into four categories:

   1. Emotion families resulting from a primary appraisal of *goal relevance* and *incongruence,* the classically negative emotions, which refer to diverse forms of threat, delay, or thwarting of a goal or a conflict between goals.
   These include anger, fright-anxiety, guilt-shame, sadness, envy-jealousy, and disgust. I regard contempt as a variant of anger, combined with an attempt to denigrate.
   2. Emotion families resulting from a primary appraisal of *goal relevance* and *congruence,* the classically positive emotions, which refer to diverse forms of goal attainment or the movement toward it.
   These include happiness/joy, pride, love/affection, and relief.
   3. *Borderline emotions,* whose status in each case is somewhat equivocal.
   These include hope, compassion (for empathy/sympathy), and aesthetic emotions. Evidence by de Rivera et al. (1989) suggests I should add elation and gladness, which if replicated would certainly be appropriate. Contentment, too, might be considered here.
   4. *Nonemotions,* which are often treated as emotions but I believe shouldn't be, as I elaborate below.

A number of terms clearly connote emotional reactions — that is, though they may convey emotional content, they are ambiguous as to meaning or fail one or another of the basic tests of an emotion and the lexical considerations discussed earlier; therefore, they should not be treated as belonging to an emotion family. I have grouped them here into six categories: complex states, ambiguous positive states, ambiguous negative states, mental confusion, contentless excitement or arousal, and pre-emotions.

Complex states. Grief and depression are overlapping and important emotion-related concepts, though they cannot be viewed as distinctive emotions. What makes them difficult to classify is that they are each complex, including more than one emotion. Grief also has the implication of a coping process, as I have indicated.

Ambiguous positive states. Included here are expansiveness, awe, confidence, challenge, determination, satisfaction, and being pleased. Expansiveness implies a positive emotional involvement, as in happiness or joy, love, triumph, pride, and so forth. It is not, per se, an emotion but an attitude that generates emotion, or a response to an emotion such as happiness or pride and its provoking conditions. Confidence is also a positive attitudinal state that is probably linked to several positive emotions, which are not specific in content. Determination, too, implies an emotional commitment, but without any clear content. It is even ambiguous as to whether the state of mind is positive or negative; we can be determined to deal with adversity or to seek and sustain benefit.

Challenge is a special case. Although it has emotional implications, as expressed in terms like enthusiasm, excitement, exhilaration, and even happiness or joy, I doubt that it is useful to refer to challenge as an emotion any more than its opposite, threat, which belongs in the ambiguous negative category. Threat, for example, is better regarded as an appraisal that leads to anxiety, anger, jealousy, and so on, but should not be thought of as an emotion. Parallel with this, challenge is an appraisal that one can gain and grow from a demanding encounter or set of encounters. I do not think it generates a specific emotion, but rather several somewhat different emotions that have already been considered. I also recognize the potentially controversial nature of this decision.

Ambiguous negative states. The list of negative states that are ambiguous includes threat, frustration, disappointment, helplessness, meaninglessness, and awe. Awe is classified as positive and negative because it can be either, depending on contextual and cognitive considerations. Some writers list frustration as an emotion, but this strikes me as incorrect. Frustration, like threat and challenge, is involved in emotion as an appraisal, even descriptive of an emotion-provoking person–environment relationship, but is not itself an emotion. Helplessness, like frustration, describes a person–environment relationship; though it sometimes is referred to as a feeling, I see little reason to identify it as an emotion. I would argue similarly in the case of meaninglessness.

Functional mental confusion. Two common terms, *bewilderment* and *confusion,* have emotional overtones, but refer to what I have called here mental confusion; they are bound to have emotional correlates and consequences without being emotions in themselves.

Contentless excitement or arousal. Although Tomkins treats it as an emotion, excitement as well as upset, distress, nervousness, tension, and agitation fall within this category. All clearly have emotional overtones. However, the main shared meaning is diffuse, unidimensional arousal without unambiguous emotional content. These words are apt to be used in the context of stress rather than for identifying a particular emotion with a particular content, and so I have chosen to exclude them.

Pre-emotions. I use this term to refer to cognitive states—namely, interest, curiousity, amazement, anticipation, alertness, and surprise—that appear to have some heat or arousal, but seem to me to fall within the rubric of an orienting response that indicates a watching or waiting for the evidence on which appraisal of personal significance depends. Startle might be considered here too.

Summary

Research on emotion is difficult to accomplish because many of the emotional variables on which we depend consist of nonobservables. The chapter began with a listing of these variables, both observable and nonobservable.

There are some important rational tests of what are bonafide emotions and nonemotions, and I have drawn upon the work of Ortony, Clore, and colleagues

ing emotional states and emotion terms that also have cognitive and behav-
ferents. In addition, there are a number of classic distinctions to be made
emotions and nonemotions. These include emotion states and traits that, like
sentiments and attitudes, are dispositions, not emotions. Traits imply stability in
reactions across circumstances, and states imply contextual variation; they are opposite sides of the same coin.

The commonly made distinctions among acute emotions, moods, and psychopathology were also drawn. Acute emotions arise from specific business in
encounters, whereas moods have to do with existential issues of a person's overall
life and fate. Both acute emotions and moods are reactions to the way the fate of the
encounter business and the business of life, respectively, are appraised by the individual. Psychopathology — as in the case of depression — although usually involving
emotional distress, is a professional judgment that is independent of emotion as a
reaction and requires its own special criteria.

In the course of evolution, organisms have shifted for survival from dependence
on rigid sensorimotor reflexes, in which a releasing stimulus elicits an adaptational
response, to physiological drives, which were somewhat more flexible than reflexes
in the timing and nature of the response, and ultimately in advanced mammals to
emotions, which provide the highest degree of adaptational flexibility and variability. Emotions evolved in conjunction with the evolution of intelligence, and the
capacity to learn from experience.

A number of reactions that have sometimes been considered emotions are best
regarded as innate reflexes, including startle, which is akin to the orienting reflex
and curiousity in that it could be treated as a pre-emotion, along with curiosity, pleasure, pain, and distaste. These are not themselves emotions, but they may set the
stage for an emotion when they are followed by an appraisal or analysis of the significance of what is taking place in the person–environment relationship for personal well-being. Feelings, too, are best regarded as built-in sensorimotor reflexes,
though the word is often treated as an equivalent of emotion.

Physiological activity should be a defining attribute of emotion, even in difficult
cases like sadness, and in positive emotions such as contentment and relief. The
main reason is that without the criterion of "heat," which is a metaphor for involvement or stakes in an encounter, emotion would not be distinguishable from other
forms of behavior. Action tendencies, and the physiological activity they generate,
are important bases for differentiating emotion from nonemotion.

Emotions are best regarded as categories that can be put on a dimension of
intensity. The reduction through factor analysis of the vocabulary of emotion to a
few basic dimensions, however, loses important relational meanings inherent in our
rich vocabulary of emotions. The advantages and disadvantages of categorical and
dimensional analysis of emotion were examined closely.

I also discussed some of the research and thought of the phylogeneticists who
have focused on universals in the emotional response and have produced a very
influential program of research that investigates facial expression and autonomic
response patterns in emotion. I argued in favor of a specificity position — that each
emotion had its own pattern of expression and physiological activity.

Arguments about primary or basic emotions and secondary or derived emotions, characteristic of the phylogenetic outlook, were also examined. Although I can see value in this distinction, if one wishes to identify emotions that have a phylogenetic history in contrast with those that seem to have arisen de novo in humans, the danger of this phylogenetic stance lies in underplaying what is considered secondary when, in reality, emotions such as guilt and shame, as well as others such as pride, are as important to understanding humans in their society as are those emotions that are considered primary.

We are now prepared to explore theoretical propositions about the emotion process from the perspective of a cognitive-motivational-relational point of view, which I provide in Part Two.

Notes

1. I qualify here because some full stomachs, as in the case of indigestion, make one feel overfull, distressed, and even ill.

2. This view is not unchallenged. Fridlund (in press) emphasizes the use of facial and bodily expression as social tools for dealing with adaptational transactions with other animals. They are, in a sense, manipulative signals, displays that communicate intention, and therefore are important sources of *information and disinformation* about which other animals must be vigilant. He assumes that social displays, and vigilance by other animals about their significance, evolved together because an animal that can sense another animal's next move (as when competing for access to a female or deciding whether to attack) would be more fit to survive than one who cannot. Fridlund's analysis is interesting and provocative. It suggests that there are some conditions under which the face may not be a good readout of emotions, a point that most researchers of facial expression concede in the concept of *display rules* (see Ekman, 1977).

3. I am aware that a few proponents of facial expression in emotion even regard them as the central causal mechanism in the emotional experience rather than as merely an innate peripheral response when an emotion is generated (cf. Tomkins, 1962, 1963, 1981; Izard, 1977). I have ignored this view because it has never attained widespread acceptance (see also Matsumoto, 1987, for a methodological analysis of research on this), and it seems to deemphasize what I consider to be the central process in emotion, namely, cognitive appraisals of the adaptational significance of the encounter. In this peripheral quality it is analogous to Zajonc, Murphy, and Inglehart's (1989) recent claim, which I also ignore, that blood temperature and pattern have causal significance in the generation of emotion. Nevertheless, for a different view, see Izard (1990).

4. Herein lies an irony. Why is it useful to argue that human anger and aggression arise genetically from other mammalian species in phylogenesis when it is so different in form and content from the observed phenomenon in those species? What is it here that is innate? Animal lovers regard it as an insult to animals to speak of persons as animallike because humans kill indiscriminately, while animals kill mainly to eat and to protect themselves and their young. In dominance struggles, animals mainly threaten and display, usually ending their battle when the opponent has withdrawn.

Humans, at least many of them, on the other hand, seem to gain much pleasure from the suffering of others, from vengeance, from cruelty. The classical Greeks, among the most cultivated of peoples in history, manifested great cruelty while creating the most sensitive and impressive art, literature, philosophy, and science. Something seems wrong with the evolutionary interpretation of human anger and aggression because it emphasizes mainly the similarities rather than the differences, which are striking, between the human and animal versions.

If we are to charge the similarities to genetics and evolution, to what do we charge the differences? One possibility is that our memories and time-binding capacities teach us to kill vanquished enemies out of rational self-interest, because otherwise they might return some day to overthrow us or exact vengeance, a cognitive capacity lacking in other animals. Another possibility is the appearance of new innate patterns in humans. Still another possibility has to do with the kinds of societies some peoples have created. For example, the United States exceeds all other countries in which records are kept in annual homicide deaths by a very large margin, perhaps as much as four to one compared with its nearest competitor. In any case, it is not enough to rely simply on evolutionary models and universalities without also trying to explain and identify the conditions between — and within — species variations.

PART TWO

The Cognitive-Motivational-Relational Theory

We are now ready to examine the central ideas of a theory of emotion that draws on concepts I hinted at but did not detail in Chapters 1 and 2. These concepts fall into three categories.

First, the *antecedent variables* consist of environmental conditions of an adaptational encounter and a person's characteristics, which interact to produce appraisals of the person–environment relationship. The relevant *environmental* variables include demands, resources, and constraints with which a person must deal, and imminence, uncertainty, and duration as some of the formal conditions that provide information about what is being faced. The most important *personality* variables affecting emotion are motives and beliefs about self and world that have been acquired through the course of living.

Second, *mediating process* variables fall into three main classes—namely, appraisal, action tendencies (or action readiness, to use Frijda's 1989 term), and coping. *Appraisal,* which is an evaluation of the significance of what is happening in the person–environment relationship for personal well-being, and which is influenced by both environmental and personality variables, is the central construct of the theoretical system. Primary appraisals refer to whether what is happening is personally relevant; secondary appraisals refer to coping options and prospects. Patterns of appraisal of the person–environment relationship coalesce in the concept of *core relational themes,* which have to do with the diverse forms of harm or loss, threat, and benefit; there is a distinctive core relational theme for each emotion. *Action tendencies* provide the link between an emotion and its physiological response pattern. And *coping processes* alter the person–environment relationship either in reality or in its appraised meaning, both of which, in turn, change the prior emotional state.

Third, *outcomes* are divided into the short and long term. *Short-term* outcomes consist of the immediate response components of emotion—that is, the actions and action tendencies, physiological changes, and subjective states, which are usually referred to as affects. *Long-term* outcomes consist of the ultimate effects of recurrent or chronic emotional patterns on social functioning, subjective well-being, and somatic health. I shall save discussions of long-term outcomes for Chapter 10, which is concerned with emotions and health.

These variables, whose interplay comprises the emotion process, constitute a complex system of interdependent variables. If we view what is happening in emotion and adaptation as a flow of events taking place over time (process), each variable can play more than one role in an emotion, sometimes as antecedent, sometimes as outcome, and sometimes as mediating process, though not at the same instant, a metatheoretical principle called "reciprocal determinism" by Bandura (1978, 1982). At the end of Chapter 5, I provide a brief discussion of system theory and a schematic diagram of how it works in emotion. In the meantime, my task is to spell out how the emotion process works in general by drawing on the variables of the system and describing their role in this process.

Chapter 3 deals with the person–environment relationship, the role of motivation in defining the harms and benefits involved, and how this relationship is changed by coping. Chapter 4 deals with the functional relationships between cognition and emotion. Chapter 5 is concerned with issues of causality.

◈ 3 ◈

The Person–Environment Relationship, Motivation, and Coping

This chapter is about the changing person–environment relationships that result in emotion. It is the place to begin a theory of emotion, because appraisal, which is the central construct of the theory, is always about these relationships, whether they are realistically or unrealistically evaluated by a person or merely imagined, and whether they are novel or recurrent.

The plan for the chapter is as follows: I must first make clear what it means to speak of relationships having emotional significance, the motivational principle (which underlies what is a harm or loss, threat, or benefit), to think of emotion as a process; in addition, I examine the way coping influences the relationship; and finally I pursue the powerful idea that each emotion has a distinctive core relational theme.

The Rationale for a Relational Theory

The fundamental idea of a relational theory of emotion is that we cannot understand the emotional life solely from the standpoint of the person *or* the environment as separate units. Although most or all emotion theories could be said to be relational, this idea is often implicit and underplayed, especially in simple input-output analyses, with the result that not enough attention is actually paid to what relationship means in the context of emotion.

Two kinds of relationships may be distinguished. In the first, we think of a relatively *stable arrangement* between a person and the environment. Marriage is such a relationship at a societal or sociological level, but at the psychological level, we think of stable mutual affection or resentment as relational. The second kind of relationship consists of relatively unstable or *transient arrangements* that are in flux from one moment to another; with the flux come changes in the emotional state. Here, too, there are societal or sociological versions—as in the playing of social roles that may change from context to context—and psychological versions—as when attitudes change, making for altered appraisals that transform the consequent emotions.

If we take the idea of relationship seriously, a language of relationships is required in which the two complex subsystems, person and environment, are conjoined and considered at a new level of analysis. The separate identities of the two subsystems are then lost in favor of an emergent condition, described as one or another relationship with its own relational meaning. Relational meaning is at a different level of abstraction than the individual sets of variables that have come together to produce it. There is already an implicit concept that corresponds to this idea, which I refer to later in this chapter as the *core relational theme.*

I can illustrate the relational meanings that underlie emotions with the concepts of threat, insult, and enhancement of ego-identity, each of which lead to a different emotion — namely, anxiety, anger, and pride, respectively. If we feel threatened, insulted, or benefited — these are, of course, appraisals — the relational meaning of each does not stem from either the person *or* the environment; there must be a conjunction of an environment with certain attributes and a person with certain attributes, which *together* produce the relational meaning.

More concretely, we are threatened and anxious only if we also want something that is endangered in a particular environmental setting and we believe we lack the power to attain it; we are insulted and angry only if someone slights us and we want this person's respect and regard; another person might be unable to effectuate an insult. We feel ego-enhancement and proud only if we are identified with or can take credit for something that we regard as socially valued.

In other words, relational concepts such as threat, insult, or ego-enhancement, with their respective emotions — anxiety, anger, and pride — lose their meaning when applied to an environment without regard to the persons who transact with it. Similarly, the relational meaning is lost when these concepts are applied to persons who have no regard for the environmental conditions that bring these relational meanings about in persons for whom they are relevant.

This seems to be a difficult idea for modern social scientists to grasp, perhaps because they have been reared professionally to venerate analysis and the partitioning of variance (as in analysis of variance) as the ideal model for scientific understanding. To speak of relationship and relational meaning is to move toward a synthesis in which the parts lose their identity at a higher level of abstraction.

When I was a young man in college, it seemed strange to me that two gases, hydrogen and oxygen, when combined in a particular way (H_2O), produced something altogether unlike either gaseous component. Only one particular combination of the two elements (two molecules of hydrogen and one of oxygen) will result in water, which adds to the value of the chemical analogy for relational meaning and emotion. The new emotional meaning at the molar, relational level has no resemblance to the elements that combine to produce it, just as water as a liquid or as ice is an entirely different substance from the separate gaseous substances that produce it.

Too much psychological analysis in the recent past has centered on what the environment or stimulus does to us — as if we were passive creatures, acted on rather than actively seeking things we want and contributing to the outcome. A simple input-output analysis focuses only on negative or positive events in the environment *or* on intrapsychic (within the person) drives, wishes, or impulses. In the case of negative emotions, a person is presumed to be in an environment in which the input is threatening without regard to what might make it so to that particular person. In the case of positive emotions, the environment is said to offer something beneficial without regard to what might make it so to a given person.

A better model for emotion would envision more than a person simply reacting to an environment—which, of course, is often the case; it would also account for the person selecting an environment, moving toward one that has positive value and away from one that has negative value. As the reader will shortly see in my discussion of the motivational principle, harms and benefits depend on goal commitments, which reside in the person and are either thwarted or facilitated by the behavior of the environment.

Some environments are almost always harmful or beneficial for the people living in them. As I suggest later, all persons, and certainly many or even most of those sharing a given cultural outlook, have motives and cognitive characteristics in common that create similar vulnerabilities. Therefore, some occurrences will be reacted to as more or less harmful or beneficial to virtually everyone, or to large classes of persons, and thereby serve as common provokers of emotion.[1] This repeats what I said in Chapter 1 about the very powerful events that arise from either internal or external sources, which to some extent may level individual differences, in contrast with the effects of weak and ambiguous events.

The data of Tompkins (1959) provide a good example of powerful events, in this case the actual danger inherent in military activities, and the incidence of emotional dysfunctions. Tompkins shows a clear and strong association between these two variables, which is not the same as saying that the dysfunction is likely or inevitable, but only that there is increased statistical risk—the greater the objective danger, the more the casualties. This is shown in Table 3.1.

Also, some wants (or goals) are more urgent than others, so their presence increases the likelihood that the people possessing them will feel harmed, threatened, or benefited. For example, some individuals possess insatiable needs for love, approval, or success, and such needs make these individuals vulnerable to negative emotional experiences. Therefore, just as some environments are generally destructive, people can generate their own harms, threats, and joys. Compared with others, these people more readily judge that they have been or might be harmed or benefited.

Nevertheless, despite the existence of powerful environmental and personality influences that are, in themselves, capable of shaping emotional states, the relational

TABLE 3.1. Relation Between Actual Danger and Incidence of Neurosis Among Combat Flyers

Duty	Relative incidence of neurosis	Relative flying hours per casualty in these duties
Night bombing	12.0	160
Day fighting	6.0	188
Night fighting	3.4	231
Coastal reconnaissance	3.3	360
Training	1.1	1,960

(*Source:* V. H. Tompkins, "Stress in aviation." In J. Hambling (Ed.), *The Nature of Stress Disorder*. Springfield, IL: Charles C Thomas, 1959. Reprinted by permission.)

principle — that we will not feel threatened unless the environment is refractory to our wants, and that we will not feel benefited unless our wants can be satisfied under the existing environmental conditions — still applies. For example, in Tomkins's data (Table 3.1) the correlation between objective danger and relative incidence of neurosis still leaves ample room for individual differences in reaction; no doubt, more men escaped being casualties than did not, though the probability of being a casualty rose with added increments of danger.

In effect, universal statements about environmental or personality-centered provokers of emotion are, theoretically incomplete. They do not specify the *conditions* that are harmful or beneficial for any given *type of person* or, conversely, the *types of persons* for whom *particular environments* are especially harmful or beneficial, and they do not help us understand the varieties of emotional patterns that result. The bottom line is that the quality and intensity of an emotion are products of actual, anticipated, or imagined adaptational encounters with an environment, which are appraised by the individual as having either positive or negative significance for well-being.

The Motivational Principle

Because an emotion depends on the person–environment relationship, we must turn now to the concept of motivation, for a credible account of the role of this relationship in the emotion process cannot be given without reference to the goals that help define it. The concept of motivation is essential for a proper understanding of what makes an encounter with the environment result in good or bad outcomes from an individual point of view.

Emotions are first and foremost reactions to the fate of active goals in everyday encounters of living and in our lives overall. Even before considering appraisal, which lies at the center of my theory, we have to think about what it is that is appraised when an emotion is generated, which, I suggest, must consist of harms and benefits, actual or potential, real or imagined. I refer to this with the somewhat portentous term, the *motivational principle,* to emphasize the fundamental role played by motivation in defining the harms and benefits on which emotions depend (see Pervin, 1983).

The Motivational Principle Viewed Historically

The idea that positive emotions derive from goal attainment, conditions that facilitate attainment, or smooth progress toward it, and negative emotions from goal thwarting, threat of this, or delay, has been around a long time. Aristotle (384–322 B.C.; modern source,1881) suggested that it was not goal attainment that generated pleasure but the normal exercise of any function, an idea that remained prominent in medieval Europe. It is noteworthy that goal attainment is often disappointing in comparison with the satisfaction derived from striving toward some goal, as Goethe's famous line intimates: "Man never is but always *to be* blessed" [italics added].*

---

*I know too little of Asian traditions to try to locate ideological parallels there.

In ancient and medieval tracts on emotion, less attention was paid to harm and benefit than to pleasure and pain, and a hedonic emphasis is also to be found in some modern treatments, one of the most prominent being the Freudian concept of the pleasure principle. Pervin (1982) suggests that theories of motivation have mainly been based on a hedonic or pleasure principle. As I said in Chapter 2, however, pleasure and pain are sensory states. They are probably very important in the development of emotions, however, because they teach the child what is safe and what is noxious. Being burned by a match once, or seeing someone else react to a burn, helps us grasp that a hot flame to the body is something to be avoided.

Yet to refer to satisfaction and dissatisfaction is to build a metaphor out of the sensation of pleasure and pain. To have pain- or pleasure-centered emotions requires that the sensory state be evaluated or appraised as to its significance for well-being (cf. Lazarus & Smith, 1988; Smith & Lazarus, 1990). Without the ability to experience sensory pleasure and pain it is unlikely that psychic pleasure and pain—that is, satisfaction and distress—would play such major roles in the human psychic economy. Because of the natural contingencies that result in conditioning, and because of the development of (cognitive) expectations that generate satisfaction and distress, sensory pleasure and pain ultimately get transformed into motives or goals, which are, in part, the developmental consequences of these innate physiological reflexes (see Chapter 2).

The historical role of motivation as a basis of emotion has been reviewed by Gardner, Metcalf, and Beebe-Center (1937/1970, p. 197), who wrote:

> The doctrine that the passions are essentially conative [motivational] is common to all writers of [the seventeenth century] and goes back to Aristotle and the Stoics. It is especially prominent in Malebranch, who finds them rooted in the natural inclination of man to the good, and in Hobbes, who connects them empirically with the two antithetic forms of endeavor, appetite and aversion. It remained for Spinoza to reduce the conative tendencies which find expression in emotion to the one fundamental striving of self-conservation, to conceive this striving as the individual's very being, and to derive from it all human actions and passions.

Augustine (c. 430, quoted in Gardner et al., pp. 97–98) offers a version of this theme about the importance of motivation in emotion that emphasizes will or volition, a cornerstone of the church doctrine in the Middle Ages regarding moral choice:

> For what are desire and joy but a volition of consent to the things we wish? When consent takes the form of seeking to possess the things we wish, it is called desire; when it takes the form of enjoying the things we wish, it is called joy. In like manner when we turn with aversion from that which we do not wish to happen, this volition is termed fear; and when we turn away from that which has happened against our will, this sort of will is called sorrow. And generally, in respect of all that we seek or shun, as a man's will is attracted or repelled, so it is changed into these several affections.

I might add that the ancient Greek Stoics offered another philosophical theme that relates to what I have said about emotion and motivation, namely, that inner peace, harmony, integrity, and the absence of suffering are possible only with the renunciation of worldly commitments. Renunciation is another way of speaking of the abandonment of standard human goals. This renunciation is similar to the Buddhist quest for nirvana, is found in Ellis's (1962) clinical rationalism, and is illustrated by Shafii's (1985) attempt to link Moslem Sufism, meditation, and psychotherapy.

Despite language differences and conceptual detail, motivation in one form or another, sometimes only implicitly, has long been presumed to be crucial to emotion. For example, Plutchik (1980) emphasized the evolutionary, biological functions found in all animal species that are basic to survival. These functions are tantamount to drives such as hunger, thirst, self-protection, and reproduction. Others speak of intentions instead of motives, as in the attitude change theory of Ajzen and Fishbein (1980; see also Fishbein & Ajzen, 1975). My own preference is to use the language of goal commitments and goal hierarchies, which, like intentions, seems particularly appropriate when speaking of humans (cf. Wrubel, Benner, & Lazarus, 1981).

The Modern Meaning of Motivation

I use the term *motivation* in two interrelated senses, namely: (1) as a personality trait and (2) as a reaction to a set of environmental conditions.

Motivation as a Personality Trait. The first sense has to do with what a person typically wants or finds aversive. Adults arrive on the scene of adaptational encounters with well-established and relatively stable value and goal hierarchies, and motivation in this sense refers to a personality *trait*. A goal hierarchy is established in an individual developmentally. Changes in it usually involve a struggle and occur typically only after the failure of goal commitments, which may result from, say, social change or when commitments prove to be unserviceable. This may happen very early in life as the person is developing an ego-identity, or late in life when capacities and roles change. When motives are viewed as traits, they are latent, being merely dispositions to strive for goal attainment if and when a disposition is engaged by suitable environmental circumstances.

To refer to the strength of a goal commitment in the trait sense is a way of speaking of its importance and the price we are willing to pay to attain it compared with other goals. A *goal hierarchy* provides the individual with a basis for evaluating personal harms and benefits. For any given individual, such a hierarchy provides the basis for what is considered most or least harmful or benefical. There would be no emotion if people did not arrive on the scene of an encounter with a desire, want, wish, need, or goal commitment that could be advanced or thwarted. The stronger or more important the goal, the more intense is the emotion, other things being equal.

Values refer to what we consider desirable or undesirable, good or bad, but they do not necessarily get acted on, so if we treat them as motives, they are weak motives at best. For example, we may consider it good to be honest, have children, or be rich, but circumstances may not encourage us to try to actualize these values. The term *value,* and even *goal,* does not say much about the effort we are willing to invest in striving to attain what we believe is valuable; one can have goals that are relatively weak or unimportant. I like the term *goal commitment* because it implies that energy will be expended in the pursuit of the goal with some degree of persistence and in spite of thwarting, delay, stress, and distress. *Commitment* is also a term used by Brickman (1987), who proposed that it gives meaning to negative and positive experiences of life and organizes how one lives and what one lives for. In his usage, however, the term refers to an overarching set of ideas about oneself and the world to which one is committed, rather than being one goal among many.

I should also add that goal hierarchies have both horizontal and vertical structure. Not only do individuals invest in different goals, such as achievement, affiliation, a certain kind of ego-identity (horizontal structure), but within each goal the person's desires are probably organized around narrow goals on the one hand, and very broad, global goals on the other (vertical structure). Values are probably related to more global goals, which is probably why they don't translate into action very well.

Therefore, to understand a person's emotional response fully it would seem important to know which narrow goals people think are at stake in an encounter (horizontal) and how they think these are related to more global goals within the goal hierarchy (vertical). Thus, two people will react with different appraisals and different resulting emotions to an event — say, doing poorly on a school assignment — even when they agree that it is an achievement-related task. Even though achievement is a strong (trait-centered) commitment in both persons, one may view the assignment as a crucial test of the probability of future success, whereas the other doesn't see this incident as having much diagnostic importance. So not only is it useful to know to which goals in the goal hierarchy a person is committed, but there is also much to be gained by knowing the functional connections and meanings characteristic of each subgoal within that hierarchy and the steps necessary to attain it.

Dealing with the difference between values and goals, Biernat (1989) has written that

> Motives energize, orient, and select behavior. That is, they make one active in pursuing a goal, sensitive to cues relating to a goal, and quick to learn what is necessary to reach a goal (McClelland, 1985a & 1985b). . . . Values do not serve these functions . . . , but they can influence self-conscious behavioral choices and evaluations of other people. For example, persons high in the value for achievement, as opposed to those low in the value, are more easily influenced by expert authority . . . and form more negative impressions of persons described as unsuccessful.

McClelland, Koestner, and Weinberger (1989) have also struggled with the distinction between values and goals or motives. Their analysis centers on achievement motivation, a topic with which McClelland has long been identified. Whereas other researchers have used questionnaires to measure the achievment motive, his measure of "need achievement" is based on stories or fantasies given in the Thematic Apperception Test. McClelland et al. suggest that the TAT measures *implicit* achievement motivation in contrast with *self-attributed* achievement motivation, or what Biernat means by *values,* which are measured by questionnaires or direct interviews. Self-attributed motives, they argue persuasively, represent surface beliefs about desirable goals, and are not the same as implicit motives, about which a person may be unaware or only dimly aware.

The two methods of measuring achievement motivation seldom correlate significantly with each other, according to McClelland and his associates. Implicit motives, assessed by fantasies or stories, appear to be better at predicting behavioral trends over time — for example, the frequency of achievement-related activities, or what Skinner referred to as *operant behavior*. Self-attributed motivation, on the other hand, correlates better with immediate choice behavior and a conscious concern to do things well.

McClelland et al. propose that self-attributed motives reflect what others in the society consider valuable. By implication, these are conscious aspects of an individual's self-concept, so when one is asked about them, the answer assumes a consciousness of one's important personal values. In contrast, implicit motives are more or less unconscious or preconscious and are more primitive, being centered in the midbrain rather than in the cerebral cortex. In Chapter 4, I consider the distinction between deliberate, conscious ways of generating meaning and automatic (unconscious or preconscious) ways. And in Chapter 11, where I am concerned with assessment, I illustrate a questionnaire method that Novacek and I (Novacek & Lazarus, 1990) have been using to assess individual differences in motivation, as well as McClelland's TAT story approach. McClelland et al. (1989, p. 700) sum up their views of implicit and self-attributed motives as follows:

> The data can be reasonably interpreted to support the generalization that implicit motives are acquired earlier in life on the basis of important nonverbal affective experiences, whereas the self-attributed motives are acquired later, after the development of language, on the basis of more explicit instructions as to what is important from the parents. The key theoretical point is that the implicit motives appear to have been acquired on the basis of affective experiences and so remain aroused by them later in life, rather than by salient social incentives. Similarly, the self-attributed motives were acquired from social, linguistically conceptualized instructions and remain responsive to them in adulthood.

This distinction invites us to imagine that in any adaptational encounter there might be one kind of appraisal based on deliberate, conscious evaluations about the stakes in that encounter, and a different kind of appraisal based on automatic, preconscious, or unconscious evaluations. This implies the possibility of two emotional processes at different psychological levels — in effect, a conflict between them within the same mind. I know of no research that explores this intriguing possibility, nor do I know whether and how it might be addressed in research. I will deal with unconscious appraisals in Chapter 4. The distinction also suggests a familiar contrast between two modes of child socialization — namely, what adults say about how to think and act (sometimes called *formal education*) and what adults model as appropriate modes of thought and action (sometimes called *informal education*). I shall say more about this in Chapter 8.

Motivation as a Reaction to Environmental Conditions. The term motivation is used in a second sense to mean the actual mobilization of mental and behavioral effort in a particular encounter to achieve a goal or to prevent its thwarting. In this sense, motivation is reactive to the demands, constraints, and resources presented by the environment. There is a cognitive component here, too, because to be reactive to the environment is to perceive it, have knowledge about it, and evaluate its implications for personal well-being.

This reactive kind of motivation becomes a feature of the emotion process, because an emotion, once generated, involves a compelling urge toward action (as in Frijda's 1986 concept of action tendency), whether this urge is conceived of as an innate feature of the emotion or as a coping strategy that is sensitive to and shaped by the adaptational requirements of the person-environment relationship. Mobilized into action, the person must now attend to the environmental signs revealing the possible or probable fate of the goal in the encounter and also must attend to what to do about it, which is the point at which emotions are generated.

This second meaning of motive is therefore *transactional* or relational rather than dispositional or trait centered—that is, it depends on a suitable environment to draw out the dispositions involved in a motive trait, which was the first sense I spoke of earlier. *Transaction* means simply that a person with a motive trait is engaged in business with an environment that is relevant to that person's habitual goals. Persons who have the motive trait or disposition to achieve are turned on in this respect only by finding themselves in an environmental context relevant to achievement. If the environment is irrelevant to achievement, the motive trait remains only an inactive disposition.

Another way to put this is that they have an achievement-related *stake* in the encounter but not in other encounters that are irrelevant to the motive trait. It takes both the trait and the right environment to mobilize the mental or physical effort that makes for a motivational stake. What I have just said is a standard treatment of motivation as a dispositional (trait) variable, activated transactionally as a stake by a range of appropriate environmental conditions that might be said to be functionally equivalent (see Lazarus, 1990b). This conception was greatly influenced by McClelland (see McClelland, Atkinson, Clark, & Lowell, 1953), who had proposed that the appropriate environmental context to activate the achievement motive is one that encouraged competition against a standard of excellence.

The juxtaposition of a motive trait and a relevant environmental context can also be viewed from an interindividual or an intraindividual perspective. From an interindividual perspective, achievement as a goal is stronger in some persons than others, which makes it easier for the former to engage in achievement strivings. If, on the other hand, we use an intraindividual perspective, we would have to say that the achievement goal is stronger than other goals within a given person's goal hierarchy.

The two meanings of *motivation*—a latent motivational disposition and a transactional state—are both important for understanding the emotion process. In the first meaning, the goals with which a person arrives on the scene of an encounter set the stage for the possibility of thwarting (harm) or gratification (benefit). Emotion does not occur until the person appraises that either of these two outcomes has occurred or is to be anticipated.

Dispositional or *trait motivation* serves as an antecedent condition of emotion. As Emmons and Diener (1986) have shown, goal importance and goal attainment are the best predictors of the time people spend in situations and of whether the emotions in those situations are positive or negative. Emmons (1986) further demonstrated that positive emotions are strongly related to personal goal striving and past fulfillment, whereas negative emotions are associated with a low probability of future success in these strivings or with conflicts about the goals being strived for.

In *transactional motivation,* when a harm or threat has actually generated a negative emotion — say, anger, anxiety, shame or guilt — the person is now motivated in a new sense to do something about the negative condition. This is the meaning of *emotion as a drive* (Lazarus, 1968a). The point is reminiscent of the discussion in Chapter 1 of the organizing and disorganizing aspects of emotion: When ongoing patterns of behavior are interrupted by new adaptational requirements, either because a goal is suddenly put in jeopardy or because new opportunities for gratification have emerged, the person's preoccupation shifts toward the new adaptational requirements. With a change in the original business of the encounter, the person must now mobilize to deal with the new business.

That there are two alternative but interrelated ways in which motivation is involved in the emotion process makes it absolutely necessary to be clear about what we are referring to when the concepts of motivation and emotion are being considered. The existence of these alternative ways also complicates the task of describing and keeping separate conceptually and empirically the interdependent variables and processes of an emotional encounter. I will say more about the distinctions and interdependencies of motivation, emotion, and cognition in Chapter 5.

To sum up the motivational principle, we can say that, other things being equal, the stronger or more important the goal commitment activated in an encounter, the more the effort invested, the greater the amount of emotional satisfaction associated with progress toward its attainment, and the greater the emotional distress associated with its thwarting. Subjectively appropriate movement toward attainment of a goal is tantamount to benefit and positive emotional states; thwarting of a goal, the threat of this, and unexpected delay are tantamount to negative emotional states. Emotions, therefore, seem to depend, as the motivational principle implies, on having a strong goal commitment that is thwarted or favored by life conditions, and either positive or negative emotions result from whether the outcome of the encounter is positive or negative (see Chapter 1 for a discussion of positive and negative emotions).

Individual and Group Differences

Because of our common biological makeup, some goals are widely or universally shared. Other goals, however, are the products more of learning and social development than of biology, and these vary in importance among different groups whose individual members share a common culture and social structure. Societies treat some values and goals as desirable while subordinating others, which is one way in which these societies help to shape the emotional lives of their members.

Nevertheless, in spite of shared influences, and because of the interaction of divergent life experiences with biological inheritance, there is considerable individual variation in goal hierarchies within the same society, even when it is monolithic — but especially when it is multilithic.* For some people, a particular goal, such as achieving success, is of paramount significance, whereas for others that goal is relatively insignificant or its significance suppressed. A proper understanding of emotion depends on having a grasp of inter- as well as intraindividual differences in the organization of goals.

Psychologists concerned with emotion often treat these statements about individual differences as truisms. Nevertheless, the role of differences among individuals in motivation has occasionally been tackled in empirical research. For example, Vogel, Raymond, and Lazarus (1959) demonstrated that students with a strong commitment to achievement and a weak commitment to affiliation showed a larger psychophysiological stress reaction under conditions in which academic performance was being evaluated than these same students did when they were being evaluated socially by peers. The reverse pattern of commitments also led to the obverse stress reaction pattern: high stress for social evaluation, and low stress for performance evaluation. In other words, stress is high when a goal commitment is strong and low when a goal commitment is weak.

Bergman and Magnusson (1979) later demonstrated that Swedish male high school overachievers, rated by their teachers as extremely ambitious, secreted more adrenalin in an achievement-demanding situation than did other boys in the same class. And Kasl, Evans, and Niederman (1979) studied the importance of commitment as a risk factor for infectious mononucleosis among West Point cadets. A combination of high academic motivation and poor academic performance predicted vulnerability to infection.

This principle of individual differences in motivation, and its psychobiological consequences, is important because variations in goal hierarchies from person to person, from group to group, and within the same person from time to time or from occasion to occasion contribute to great emotional diversity. The principle implies that one person will be threatened in the same environmental context in which another is edified and still another is indifferent. This is taken so much for granted that formal statements about it are commonly omitted in discussions of emotion, or are dealt with in only a cursory fashion.

Thus, if a theorist says that loss generates sadness, or that an unexpected event results in surprise, to make practical use of this generalization a researcher or clinician must identify for any individual or group what is a loss and how important it is to the individual or group being studied. Goal hierarchies of individuals and groups have to be assessed to define what is a loss in order to test predictions empirically: Degree of loss-induced sadness depends on the strength of attachment; degree of offense-induced anger depends among other things on the need to protect one's ego-identity.

It is a testable proposition that the more vulnerable a person's ego-identity the greater the disposition to anger, other things being equal. One may, of course, have a strong ego-identity and yet be made angry by an unjustifiable and strong attack by

---

*I realize that there is no such word as *multilithic* in the dictionary, but the neologism is the best antonym for *monolithic*, which refers to a society that has only one outlook, to which all or most members subscribe. This latter word is in the dictionary, and in this context the meaning, I hope, will be clear.

someone worth being bothered by; on the other hand, someone with a vulnerable identity might respond with anger to even a mild provocation, one that others might hardly notice or react to. But more about this in Chapter 6, where negative emotions such as anger are discussed.

Goals/motivation always unneeded to a "self" [handwritten note in margin]

Motivation and Self or Ego-Identity

The topic of human motivation brings to mind Hilgard's (1949) treatment of the self as a unifying principle, which organizes multiple motives and specifies their relative importance and thresholds of engagement. He noted, for example, that there could be no concept of defense mechanism without a self to defend. The reader will see in Chapter 4, when I discuss the process of appraisal, and in Chapters 6 and 7, which deal with the individual emotions, that I place great stock in two ideas: first, that a personal stake in an encounter is a crucial feature of the emotion process; second, that ego-identity (a term I prefer to *self*) is involved in every emotion, though typically in different ways. These two motivational qualities are what makes an emotion and the thoughts that generate it hot rather than cold. I also argue in Chapter 8 that emotions require some elemental or emerging sense of ego-identity to advance and protect. This is being written at a time when psychology is celebrating, so to speak, the centennial of William James's *The Principles of Psychology* (1890). Discussing James's emphasis on the self as a part of what he refers to as the "ignored James," Markus (1990, p. 182) writes:

> Very early in the volume [James's *Principles*], in the chapter on the stream of thought he writes (I, 226), ". . . the personal self rather than thought might be treated as the immediate datum in psychology. The universal conscious fact is not feelings and thoughts exist but I *think* and *feel*. No psychology, at any rate, can question the existence of personal selves." James claims that consciousness is always personal consciousness. (I, 226) "The only states of consciousness that we naturally deal with are found in personal consciousness, minds, selves, concrete particular I's and you's."

Markus (1990, p. 182) goes on to point out the vital role James gave to the self in his writing on emotion:

> Whenever a stimulus implicates the self-system, the ensuing processes are likely to be influenced by the nature of the self. For example, apart from the fear induced by loud noises or bright lights, or the felt pleasure produced by a sweet taste, there are likely to be few emotions that do not directly implicate one's self. From James' chapter on emotions, it is evident that feelings are not pure bodily states. What is experienced depends on the nature of the "I" doing the experiencing. If I feel sad, the nature of my sadness will depend on the nature of my "I" and the nature of the empirical self or "me" that is its referent. And so it is with motivation. The motives for achievement, affiliation, power, are not pure, impersonal, or instinctual entities that vary among people only in amount. If "I" want to win, the precise nature of my motivation—its power, its specificity, its behavioral consequences, in short, everything interesting about it—depends on the shape of my "I" at that moment, which, in turn, is some selection from the domain of "me" and "mine." The "me" and the "I" together

then provide the context and the ground for mental life. And to a greater or lesser degree, all aspects of mental life will bear this personal touch.

The development of self or ego-identity, which I discuss in Chapter 8, is undoubtedly an important feature of emotional development in the young child. A self or ego organizes motives and attitudes into hierarchies of importance, which may persist for a lifetime or a large portion of it (Allport, 1937). Goals are not disconnected from each other, and decisions must be made about which goal to center on and which to subordinate or suppress. Threats to any personal goal are, at bottom, threats to oneself. It makes little sense to speak of goals that are part of the self and goals that are not, because all are in some way a property of the person. Thus, the self or ego-identity is in large part a motivational concept, and goal hierarchies are organized by an executive agency of the personality, which coordinates and regulates in action what a person desires or builds into a self-schema that is differentiated from the rest of the world.

The reader will have noticed here, and later will again, that I have alternated among the terms *self, ego, identity,* and *ego-identity.* I recognize that there is a long and complex history of ideas about self, ego, and identity, and much overlap as well as divergence in the meanings of these terms (see, for example, Lapsley & Power, 1988; and a review by Klein, 1990). Although the emphasis may shift among ideas we hold about ourselves as beings, which consist of a set of beliefs, schemata, meanings, or commitments, and an executive agency of the personality to direct thought and action, I use a variable terminology because of the great overlap in what the words *self, ego,* and *identity* connote for the emotions.

In my later treatment of the individual emotions in Chapters 6 and 7, the reader will see that I have used the language of ego-involvement and ego-identity rather than the language of self, especially in discussions of anger, anxiety, and shame, anger being a reaction to a personal slight or insult, anxiety a reaction to existential threats that involve essential meaning, and shame a reaction to failure to live up to one's ego-ideal.

Why do I prefer the term *ego-identity* to *self?* The problem with the term *self,* as I see it, is that it is usually used to describe what is within the boundaries of the skin, whereas Erikson's (1950, 1963) concept of ego-identity encompasses the *person-in-the-world,* which includes roles, relationships, and functions in society. So when I can I will use ego-identity in the future, except when the context makes it awkward or when I am referring to someone else's ideas that are centered on the term *self.* Now and then I will show my ambivalence by using both.

A brief word, too, about the types of ego-involvement I shall refer to in Chapter 4, and in Chapters 6 and 7, which deal with the individual emotions. I conceive of six types of ego-identity to which a person may be committed. The six, shown in Table 3.2, comprise what is meant by ego-identity and are: (1) self- and social esteem, which involves commitment to certain social roles; (2) moral values; (3) ego-ideals; (4) essential meanings and ideas; (5) other persons and their well-being; and (6) life goals. All of these types of ego-involvement are collections of narrower goals, brought together as broad abstractions that encompass the many goals of our everyday lives. Any given type of ego-identity may be involved in some individual

TABLE 3.2. Types of Ego-Involvement[a]

---

1. Self- and social esteem
2. Moral values
3. Ego-ideals
4. Meanings and ideas
5. Other persons and their well-being
6. Life goals

---

[a]Ego-involvements refer to commitments, which might be thought of as goals that fall within the rubric of what we usually mean by ego-identity.

emotions and not in others. As is indicated in Chapters 6 and 7, certain emotions depend on one or another type of ego-identity. For example, guilt depends on moral values and shame on ego-ideals.

While on the subject of self and ego, allow me to digress momentarily to address the concept of an "empty self," a sociopsychological view of our times recently proffered by Cushman (1990). Drawing on many writers such as Geertz (1973), Gergen (1985), and Sampson (1983, 1985, 1988), Cushman advances the idea that after World War II, Western industrialized peoples, especially those in the United States with its strong commitment to consumerism, began to lose their connection with family, society, and its values, so that the self was emptied of these traditional contents on which it normally is predicated and had to stand on its own.

What has been lost, according to Cushman, is a set of emotional tools traditional cultures use for integrating people within the society. These tools help the sick by providing a "web of meaning" that includes stories, songs, beliefs, rituals, ceremonial objects, costumes, and potions that reconnect the person to the cultural frame of references within the society. The modern person is said to be alienated from the social world—that is, to have an empty self. In Chapter 11 the implications of my emotion theory and metatheory for psychotherapy will be discussed. In addition to the standard functional difficulties for which people seek professional help, one of the frequent problems confronted by psychotherapists is existential emptiness and lack of commitment (see also Kohut, 1971, 1977, 1984). About this sort of thing, Cushman (1990, p. 604) writes:

Inner emptiness may be expressed in many ways, such as low self-esteem (the absence of a sense of personal worth), values confusion (the absence of a sense of personal convictions), eating disorders (the compulsion to fill the emptiness with food, or to embody the emptiness by refusing food), drug abuse (the compulsion to fill the emptiness with chemically induced emotional experiences), and chronic consumerism (the compulsion to fill the emptiness with consumer items and the experience of "receiving" something from the world). It may also take the form of an absence of personal meaning. This can manifest as a hunger for spiritual guidance, which sometimes takes the form of a wish to be filled up by the spirit of God, by religious "truth," or the power and personality of a leader or guru (Cushman, 1984). For instance, one of the most *au courant* of New Age therapies is *channeling*, an experience in which an individual is said to be entered by the soul or spirit of another "entity," usually thought to be a god, who then speaks "important truths." The wish to be spiritually filled up and guided can make the individual vulnerable to the deceptive practices of restrictive religious cults (Cushman, 1986), charismatic political leaders (Kohut, 1976) . . . , unethical psychotherapists, or even highly authoritarian and controlling romantic partners.

Differentiation of self* and other may be a very fundamental property of living things. This property is displayed even by plants, which use complex protein discrimination mechanisms. A basic principle of immunology is that organisms attack alien tissues, which presupposes the ability to make the distinction. Although it can go wrong, as in autoimmune diseases and allergies, animals could not survive without a process, whether cognitive or neurochemical, that is in some sense analogous to what psychologists speak of as the process of distinguishing self and other. I would be skating on thin ice in this analogy if I were seeking to equate mental activity with what happens at the neurochemical level — which would be a form of reduction against which I inveigh in Chapter 5 — but an analogy is not an equation, and I find it compelling.

It is not a great leap from the preceding to the corollary idea that emotions, which represent reactions to evaluations of relationships with the environment, depend to some extent on an organizing principle in which self is distinguished from non-self, or ego-identity from non-ego-identity, and without which there could be only the vaguest sense of harm, threat, the benign, or the beneficial. To what extent in the growing child do emotions depend on the development of a sense of self or non-self, identity or non-identity? This is a theoretical and research issue of great moment, which I turn to in Chapter 8, and touch on in Chapter 4.

The very concept of relationship implies self and other, and before a relationship can be considered relevant to well-being, one must be in a position to respond at some level to the question, "Beneficial or harmful to what or to whom?" The answer to this question is the basis for specifying the specific harms and benefits that distinguish and define each individual emotion. In complex species, such as humans, a further distinction — "Beneficial or harmful in what sense?" — must also be made. In effect, my view of self or identity does not obviate the motivational principle, which requires that we also specify the biological and social conditions that influence the ways in which any person or animal can be benefited or harmed. This view of the importance of the self or identity is reinforced later, in Chapter 4, in my treatment of appraisal as an evaluation of the implications of what is happening for personal well-being.

Some readers may regard the emphasis on the motivational basis of personal harm or benefit as a premise for an entirely self-centered emotional life. However, we also become committed to the well-being of others whom we care about and feel responsible for, as well as to ideas, values, and conditions of life. Because of these commitments, if the well-being of other persons — for example, a child, parent, or other loved one — is at stake, or if ideas and values that we cherish are endangered, lost, or demeaned, we react just as emotionally — that is, with just as much anxiety,

---

*The reader can see that when it is juxtaposed with the term "other," self is more euphonious than ego-identity, so I use it here.

anger, guilt, shame, sadness, or pride—as when our own personal well-being is at stake. Indeed, in a very important sense, it is. We need not resolve the question of whether or not altruism is involved in this to accept the point.

Emotion as a Process

Theory and research must take into account the fact that person–environment relationships and the emotions they result in are processes in transition from moment to moment as the conditions of our lives change. Although a person may recurrently experience certain emotions—as we see, for example, in angry, anxious, or guilt-ridden personalities—the study of emotions is primarily the study of change and flow over time and across occasions (see Lazarus, 1989a). This is what it means to speak of emotion as a process.

Recently I saw a production of Puccini's opera *Madame Butterfly*, which seems to me to provide a good fictional illustration of emotion as a process: The emotional state of the heroine changed markedly during the drama as the fortunes of her life, as she appraised them, also changed. The opera also illustrates how emotions about the same events may differ among the participants in the drama.

At the start of Act I, the audience is led to expect tragedy from the marriage of a beautiful Japanese teenage girl, Cio Cio San—Madame Butterfly—to an American naval officer who values seduction, conquest, and short-term pleasure more highly than fidelity, and who has already announced to the American Consul in Japan that he regards this cross-cultural relationship lightly and really wants someday to marry an American.

We see Cio Cio San initially as apprehensive and dismayed as her uncle, a Buddhist priest, denounces and curses her for abandoning her own religion and people. After the wedding, and before she and Lieutenant Pinkerton retire to bed, her affection and contentment seem to grow with Pinkerton's seductive reassurances and her own misguided hopes. I have seen another version of this opera in which the performer puts more apprehension into this scene, as if to indicate that Cio Cio San has some recognition of her dismal future prospects.[2] Some women, perhaps hyperconscious of male sexual exploitation, might at this point in the story experience cynical anger at Pinkerton's male chauvinism, in addition to vicarious apprehension for Butterfly or contempt at her self-victimization; a stage director or diva could enhance or understate these themes by manipulating visible signs of hope, love, and apprehension in the performance of the role. As to mixed emotions for the audience, I felt sad, angry, and apprehensive, depending on whether I was paying attention to Cio Cio San or Pinkerton, and even exhilarated at the performance. At times it was difficult to hold back tears, for reasons which will always remain complex and probably obscure.

In the second act, we discover that Pinkerton has left three years earlier to return to the United States, but Cio Cio San expresses a persistent belief and hope that he will return, a coping pattern that looks like denial given the circumstances. In what is probably the most famous aria in the opera, "Un bel di" (one fine day), she creates an elaborate and rosy fantasy of what will happen when he returns, as surely (she believes or rather hopes) he must. In a deeply moving scene, when the American

Consul, Sharpless, brings a letter from Pinkerton that should have shattered her faith, at first she seems not to want to hear, but when she is forced to confront the truth (Sharpless asks her what she would do if Pinkerton never came back), she becomes momentarily despairing and talks of suicide.

Suddenly, Pinkerton's ship appears in the harbor, and Butterfly reacts with unmitigated joy. She and her maidservant, Suzuki, decorate the house with flowers in the expectation of Pinkerton's arrival, but Suzuki remains appropriately apprehensive (because, presumably, she senses the truth, as the audience does also). We know that Pinkerton is now married to an American and wants the child that Butterfly is raising. At the end of the act, there is a scene of quiet but strained musical and visual beauty in which Butterfly, her son, and Suzuki station themselves almost motionlessly at the doorway overlooking the waterfront and wait for Pinkerton.

At dawn, as Act III begins, Pinkerton still has not arrived. As Butterfly retires, Pinkerton and his new American wife enter, along with the Consul to plan how to deal with her. In due time, Cio Cio San discovers that Pinkerton has come back only to ask her to give up the male child that resulted from their lovemaking. In great despair she tells Pinkerton to return for the child in half an hour, and after sending the boy out to play, she kills herself in the Japanese ritual of seppukku. Pinkerton's voice is heard calling in the distance as Butterfly dies.

As in most stories, this one reflects numerous emotional transitions. Butterfly's emotions shift from apprehension to contentment, hope mixed with denial, despair, joy, contempt, and ultimately to final despair and the act of suicide. As the audience, we suffer with Cio Cio San, weep for her — and dread her moments of joy, because we know that they are based on a false appraisal — but we can also enjoy the whole experience, probably because we are able to keep enough psychological distance to be personally protected. Nevertheless, we are drawn into the emotions portrayed by the characters in their situations, a process that is also facilitated by the music.

We suspend the reality that we are merely watching a fictional story, even the reality that the singer (as one I once saw) playing Butterfly may look at least 50, not 15, and be portly rather than slender and delicate, as Puccini intended her to be. Our emotional involvement despite these distractions attests to the brilliance of the drama and music, the skill of the actors, director, and set designers, and our capacity to identify with the characters in the drama. The reader might wish to consult a recent interchange between Walters (1989) and Frijda (1989) exploring reasons we react emotionally to a movie or play while we sit personally removed from the story's strife in a theater or in our home. In Chapter 7, I again give consideration to this remarkable human capacity in connection with the aesthetic emotions.

Puccini readily manipulates the audience's emotions. He shows his great command of the psychology of audiences in the scene in which he has Butterfly engage in vehement denial before displaying distress about the information presented by the American Consul that Pinkerton will not return. Her desperation is revealed more by the denial, followed by momentary, frantic despair, than if she had simply wept or expressed anger at the Consul for his terrible message. Somehow Puccini correctly sensed that Suzuki's disbelief further adds to the poignancy of the scene. We also understand why what is being experienced leads to different emotions in Butterfly, her servant Suzuki, her lover Pinkerton, and ourselves, the audience. A cognitive-motivational-relational theory tries to explain all this, not just in a theater but in real life, by its central propositions.

We can better understand how an emotion is generated and unfolds if we examine in some detail the *stages* of the process. There are four: anticipation, provocation, unfolding, and outcome.

The Anticipation

Disaster researchers distinguish among three stages of a natural disaster: warning, confrontation or impact, and postimpact. These stages parallel the ones I have identified—except for provocation, which applies only to individual emotional encounters that depend on some event that generates the emotion process. Although there is often no stage of anticipation—as in a sudden earthquake or explosion—the stages include anticipation, because we often experience cues or warnings that an emotional encounter is upcoming or imminent that lead to expectations about things to come. These expectations are important in the emotion process.

With modern meteorological techniques, for example, hurricanes can to some extent be forecast, and people get warnings that they are in danger before the storm has struck. Of course, disasters mainly involve negative emotions, and I don't mean to suggest by this comparison that emotions are always negative or that their flow can be readily predicted or forecast. The concept of stages in disaster, however, provides a useful model not only for negative emotions but for positive emotions as well.

Warnings—whether they are the result of technical knowledge that can be disseminated by television, radio, newspapers, and word of mouth or are based on inferences from personal experience—greatly change the psychological situation compared with that of a person who has no advance signs with which to read the future. The psychological implications of warnings have been well described by Breznitz (1984) in a book titled *Cry Wolf* (a reference to the Aesop fable by the same name), in which the author examines the sometimes disastrous loss of credibility generated by repeated false alarms.

Having a warning of an upcoming harm or benefit is a powerful adaptational tool, especially in humans, who are able to think in terms of past, present, and future, and to engage in *anticipatory coping*. To anticipate the future permits us to prepare for it and sometimes to change things to prevent or ameliorate harm. I have more to say later in this chapter about how coping can influence the subsequent emotional state.

Because anticipating the future creates expectations about it, we are not neccessarily neutral before an emotional encounter. A cognitive-motivational-relational theory of emotion regards such expectations, or beliefs, as antecedent causal factors in the emotional response. For example, positive expectations increase the likelihood of disappointment (and therefore of sadness and anger), whereas negative expectations can make a negative outcome seem even positive ("It could have been worse"), or a positive outcome seem negative ("It could have been better"). People sometimes set low levels of expectation defensively—that is, to increase satisfaction or reduce disappointment with the outcome even when it is poor (see, as examples, Lewin, Dembo, Festinger, & Sears, 1944; and Janoff-Bulman & Brickman, 1982).

It is tempting to suggest that there may be distinct emotions for anticipation and outcome, though they may occur simultaneously. Anxiety is, par excellence, an anticipatory emotion, because by definition it is a response to possible future harm. By contrast, relief is an outcome emotion, because it depends on encounters having worked out better than expected (see Gordon, 1987). The trouble with this line of reasoning, however, is that anticipation and outcome are commonly intertwined. For example, if we are disappointed, and perhaps saddened, the bad outcome has implications for the future as well (cf. Lazarus, 1966). This is why psychological stress so often consists more of threat, or the anticipation of harm, than harm per se (see also Nomikos, Opton, Averill, & Lazarus, 1968, who showed that anticipation is commonly much worse than the actual reality). So we may be saddened, which refers to an outcome, but perhaps we are also hopeful or anxious at the same time, which refers to an anticipation.

Furthermore, any outcome can be anticipated and reacted to emotionally before it has actually occurred. Thus, we can be sad in advance merely because we anticipate that things will work out badly, and we can work ourselves into a rage about what we imagine will happen. When things actually turn out well, we experience joy, relief, or chagrin instead of anger; the joy, relief, or chagrin, incidentally, is as much the result of our negative expectation as it is the result of the actual outcome. Anticipatory coping may also be subtle and ongoing rather than being restricted to extreme conditions of threat. Our courses of action and the situations we choose to place ourselves in, too, may be strongly influenced by how we anticipate reacting to the eventual confrontations, rather than by a strong present emotional reaction. In any event, because of our tendency to think both forward and backward in time, the interesting and sometimes useful distinction between anticipatory and outcome emotions often breaks down in practice (see Folkman & Lazarus, 1985, for additional discussion of this).

The Provocation

A provocation is any occurrence, in the environment or within the person, that is judged by that person as having changed the person–environment relationship in the direction of harm or benefit, failed to change an existing harmful relationship, endangered an existing favorable relationship, or forecast a favorable or unfavorable one in the future.

An external or internal event does not by itself constitute a provocation, unless it also signifies a change in the person–environment relationship for better or worse. Thus, a clear insult by another person is not a provocation to anger unless the person attacked takes seriously what is said or done and treats it as a damaging insult. Although many or most others might regard the "offending" action as a provocation for anger, this evaluation (or appraisal) depends on the personality of the victim and the social conditions that surround the action. In fact, an act by another person, or even the absence of a desired or expected act, which few would regard as an insult, may be interpreted as such by someone in great need or with certain personality traits — say, persons who are said to "carry a chip on their shoulder."

Since an emotional provocation cannot be either external *or* internal, but depends on how an initiating occurrence bears on the person–environment relationship, we are forced to abandon, or at least greatly modify, the traditional input-output, or stimulus-response, formulation of emotion. This formulation must be replaced by a view of the person (or animal) as an active agent rather than a passive recipient in transactions that have relevance for personal well-being. People arrive on the scene of an emotional encounter seeking certain conditions or outcomes and having certain expectations, ways of attending to and interpreting what happens, and ways of coping. To some extent, they even choose the environmental contexts and time frames in which their transactions will take place.

It is often said that an emotion can be generated by the mere *memory* of a prior emotional state or occasion, which presumably illustrates an internal rather than environmental provocation. However, a relational interpretation differs importantly from the tradition in which the memorial provocation is viewed as entirely internal. A memory of an emotional experience is reconstructed in a different way each time it is activated. Two considerations will help explain this. First, as we grow older new schemata are always being formed, so the reconstruction of the past tends to change. Second, we need to consider the adaptational context in which a memory is activated. From a relational viewpoint, the memory does not arise by happenstance but is in some way functionally connected with what is going on at the moment. The current transaction, or some feature of it, has somehow triggered the appropriate memory. The feature responsible for the memory could be the emotional response pattern, the psychological situation and personal meanings that have generated the emotion, which are similar in some sense to what happened in the earlier encounter, some fragment or element of the situation such as the other person's appearance or demeanor, or the organized configuration or interpretive scenario of all these components of the emotion process.

Each fragment or component seems to connote the entire scenario. That is, all the elements combine psychologically into a complex emotional story or script, and though a researcher might center attention on only one element, it is always a part of a larger configuration that provides the personal meaning that connects the two encounters, the one in memory and the current one (cf. Vitz, 1990). My own disposition is to focus on what I regard as the crux of an emotion, namely, its *appraised significance* for the individual's well-being, which in molar terms is expressed as the *core relational theme* of the encounter (see the sections on relationships later in this chapter). In accordance with my emphasis on motivation in emotion, J. A. Singer (1990) also argues persuasively and provides data suggesting that what is crucial in eliciting a memory is its relevance to "the attainment or nonattainment of an individual's long-term goals."

Because it is a kind of meaningful plot or scenario, I believe that the core relational theme helps us remember past emotional experiences better than when there is just a jumble of images and disconnected thoughts from the past—without a plot. When I watch old television movies, for example, it often takes me quite some time into the movie to decide whether or not I have seen it before, sometimes until well into the story. I say to my wife, "Have we seen this movie?" and often she will say she doesn't know. Then suddenly both of us will recognize that we did indeed see it before. For a long while I didn't grasp why this was so. However, I think what happens is that often at the outset the events and characters being portrayed are without interconnection, meaningless until the plot has been revealed, and so we fail to remember them — they are like nonsense syllables without a meaningful connecting link — and they do not help us to recall the movie. The plot carries the emotional thread — the relational theme of the story — and the instant it is revealed we remember that we have seen it before.

Rholes, Riskind, and Lane (1987, p. 92) make a similar point about cognition and emotion when they write about their research findings on the effects of cognitive priming and mood on memory:

> The effect of mood on memory retrieval may be at least partially accounted for in the following way. An emotion-producing event, such as a failure, occurs and produces both an affective state and a set of relevant cognitions (e.g., self-devaluation). The cognitions produced by the event then directly prime, or semantically cue, other items in long-term memory (e.g., life experiences) that are associated with them, thus increasing their recall accessibility. In other words, it may be mood-related cognitions, rather than affect per se, that at least in part influence memory retrieval. This cognitive process, of course, is not necessarily incompatible with state dependent learning. It is conceivable that both can operate at the same time.

Laird (1989) has also pointed out that the effects of mood on memory are described no differently from the effects of cognitive variables, which should be perplexing only to those who regard mood (and emotion) as singularly different from cognitive activity. Implicit here is that moods and emotions are complex events, with the response word *mood* being used to stand for certain components of the whole, such as arousal, and not others, such as thoughts or meanings. Though he leaves out coping, Laird provides the useful service of listing six easily distinguished components of emotion: the eliciting event, the appraisal of that event, patterns of autonomic response, expressive behavior, instrumental action, and the subjective feeling. These are always connected and interdependent in an emotion, which is one reason we think of it as a system (see Chapter 5), and any or all of these components could produce the mood effects on memory or be the basis of the retrieval of a memory in an adaptational encounter. But the most potent source of memory, I think, is the core relational theme — a gestalt[3] that carries the emotional meaning (see also Lewis & Williams, 1989).

This formulation accords with what I have already said about emotion and memory (cf. Forgas & Bower, 1987, 1988; and Isen, Shalker, Clark, & Karp, 1978), with what I will have to say about the role of cognition in emotion in much more detail later (see Chapters 4 and 5), and about the effects of emotion or mood on subsequent thoughts, actions, and emotions (see Chapter 10). The theoretical debates about the role of mood in the retrieval of memories and the role of memory in mood stem from treating mood as a disembodied response component or element divorced from the more global personal meanings that are causal and indigenous to it.

In her short story, "The Aliens," Carson McCullers suggests the dormant nature of some kinds of emotional work, such as grieving, which are evoked unexpectedly from time to time by some familiar fragment suggesting the lost loved one rather than being a constant state of mind. Using the metaphor of an orchestral piece, she wrote:

> Grief is like a subordinate but urgent theme in an orchestral work — an endless motive asserting itself with all possible variations of rhythm and tonal coloring and melodic structure, now suggested nervously in flying-spiccato passage from the strings, again emerging in the pastoral melancholy of the English horn, or sounding at times in a strident but truncated version down deep among the brasses. And this theme, although for the most part subtly concealed, affects by its sheer insistence the music as a whole far more than the apparent major melodies. And also there are times in this orchestral work when this motive which has been restrained so long will at a signal volcanically usurp all other musical ideas, commanding the full orchestra to recapitulate with fury all that hitherto had been insinuated. But with grief there is a difference here. For it is no fixed summons, such as the signal from the conductor's hand, that activates a dormant sorrow. It is the uncalculated and the indirect.

A myriad of unsolved problems concerning what connects the two emotional occurrences, the current transaction and the one in memory, are raised by this analysis. One could argue, for example, that many or even most emotional encounters are repetitions of relational troubles and triumphs of the past, which are central to the person rather than peripheral and which involve basic adaptational themes, such as being loved or rejected, being powerful or powerless, or overcoming or being traumatized by adversity, loyalty or treachery, loss or gain, failure or success, and the like, even if the connection is not at all obvious.

This line of reasoning is akin to the Freudian concept of repetition compulsion (cf. Breger, Hunter, & Lane, 1971; Horowitz, 1976), in which unresolved emotional difficulties of the past keep recurring in the present in order to undo them. I don't consider the mechanical features of the concept of repetition compulsion useful as a model, but the principle that there is a functional connection between a memory or a dream about the past and what is happening in the present, illustrated in the presumed role of day residues in night dreams, seems important and useful. People define most encounters in which they engage as new, yet there must be general schemata in a person's mind for deciding whether similar or different appraisals and coping processes are called for. Neurosis can be regarded as a manifestation of rigidity with respect to the past, and healthy coping implies being flexible and changing when appropriate.

The reason for my cryptic qualification earlier about the nonobviousness of the connection between a past and present encounter is simply that what makes two experiences similar is not at all clear. The problem of stimulus similarity was a long-standing source of perplexity in learning theory. The issue was begged in Freud's clinical observations about Little Hans, Hans's father, and the horse that symbolized his father and was the object of his phobia. Why did a horse represent the father? We cannot say, although clinical intuition makes it seem somehow understandable, at least after the fact, that a stallion is a powerful male, presumably like the father as fantasized by Little Hans, though there are probably other subjective features in common that would also make the connection comprehensible. To my mind, stimulus similarity cannot be understood without reference to the relational meaning that underlies it, which is often idiosyncratic to the individual.

The Unfolding

With the start of an emotional reaction in person *A,* the second stage of an emotional encounter — namely, its unfolding or flow — now begins. What happens is that *A*'s emotional reaction (let's say it is anger) has an effect on *B.* *B* might react to *A*'s anger by being pleased, guilty, shamed, angry, or maybe even indifferent. Since *B*'s reaction is expressed in words and other actions, *A* will, in turn, probably react to *B*'s visible response, and so on back and forth until the encounter is ended by one or the other person's leaving the scene or by resolution of the issue at stake. One way of coping with the threat of *B*'s response is, of course, not to notice it as such or to pretend not to notice it.

How each party to the transaction reacts and is left emotionally at the end depends on what has happened and their respective goals and beliefs. Even if *B*'s reaction is ambiguous, irrelevant, unnoticed, or not visible, *A* will also probably react to his or her own actions and emotional state. An emotional encounter is an unfolding event that is typically characterized by many complex and fleeting cognitive, motivational, emotional, and coping processes in consequence of which changes take place in the person–environment relationship for *each* participant.

The Outcome

The outcome of an encounter — that is, the fate of the business at hand — results in an emotional state that reflects how we have appraised what has happened from the point of view of our well-being. Emotional outcomes are based on whether or not our goals and expectations have been realized, and in what ways. The emotional state conveys what has happened to anyone who understands the process. A successful theory of emotion should allow us to connect, on the basis of the rules proposed, the emotion process with the emotional reaction, and to reason both ways about it. That is, the observer can reason back from an emotional reaction to the process that brought that reaction about; conversely, if we begin with the variables that generate the emotion process, we should be able to explain or even predict the emotional reaction.

An emotional encounter ultimately comes to an end, or perhaps we should say that it moves on to other business. Maybe nothing has been resolved, but the relational theme provoking the emotion has ended for the moment, if not for all time. There are recurrent themes — life has a way of involving us in similar business again and again — and by the time we are mature, most of the kinds of business we are going to handle over the course of our lives have already been experienced, defined by stable personal values, goals, and beliefs, that shape our encounters with the world.

Since we experience countless emotional encounters, there is apt to be considerable discontinuity between specific encounters and our overall state of mind. Therefore, depending on whether it is or is not representative for the person, a single emotional encounter may say relatively little, but occasionally very much, about that person's overall subjective well-being, social functioning, and somatic health, though the cumulative effects of many encounters should have great significance with respect to what they say about persons and the world in which they live.

Coping

I said earlier that emotions are always in flux, because encounters with the environment constantly change, generating new relational information whose significance must be appraised. Many of the changes affecting appraisal are the result of coping processes whose function is to alter a troubled person–environment relationship or to sustain a desirable one.

Coping, as I define it, consists of cognitive and behavioral efforts to manage specific external or internal demands (and conflicts between them) that are appraised as taxing or exceeding the resources of the person (Lazarus & Folkman, 1984, 1987). Though it may flow from emotion and be aimed at changing the conditions of the emotion or the emotion itself, coping also directly and indirectly affects subsequent appraisals (reappraisal), and it is therefore also a causal antecedent of the emotion that follows (Folkman & Lazarus, 1988a). Coping affects the emotion process in two ways:

1. Some coping processes change the actual relationship, as when an attack or aggressive display wards off or demolishes an enemy. My colleagues and I have called this *problem-focused coping*. These are in a sense action-centered forms of coping. If a neighbor's tree is producing emotional distress because it drops leaves in our yard, we might try to induce the neighbor to cut the tree down or trim it. If this succeeds, there is no longer a problem and subsidence of the emotional distress should follow, assuming that the distress does not have some other basis — expressed, for example, in the familiar vulgar statement, "I hate his guts." (Obviously there is more to the relationship than just leaves.) Coping efforts, of course, often fail to ameliorate the source of stress and distress, and sometimes even provoke more stress and distress; moreover, these efforts may be excessive in relation to the problem they are addressing, with costs that exceed the potential benefits (see Schönpflug, 1985; Schönpflug & Battmann, 1988).

2. Other coping processes change only the way in which the relationship is *attended to* (e.g., a threat that one avoids perceiving or thinking about) or *interpreted* (e.g., a threat that is dealt with by denial or psychological distancing). I call these *emotion-focused* or *cognitive coping* strategies, because they involve mainly thinking rather than acting to change the person–environment relationship. They are by no means passive, but have to do with internal restructuring, sometimes even to the point of changing a commitment pattern that can't be actualized. Even though they do not change the actual relationship, they change its meaning, and therefore the emotional reaction. For example, if we successfully avoid thinking about a threat, the anxiety associated with it is postponed. And if we successfully deny that anything is wrong, there is no reason to experience the emotion appropriate to the particular threat or harm — say, anxiety, anger, guilt, shame, envy, or whatever. In

Chapter 11, sample items from eight factors in the Ways of Coping Questionnaire (Folkman & Lazarus, 1988b), which is one approach to measuring the coping process, will be presented.

The reader should note that there is some overlap between appraisal (see Chapter 4) and cognitive coping. The overlap is that *coping* refers to what a person thinks and does to try to manage an emotional encounter; and *appraisal* is an evaluation of what might be thought or done in that encounter. Both change emotional meanings, so that the concepts are difficult to disentangle in practice, especially in the absence of a context to help us differentiate them. Appraisal influences the coping strategy, and coping changes appraisal by virtue of what it does to the person–environment relationship, the deployment of attention, or the appraised meaning of that relationship. Cognitive coping is, in effect, an appraisal in its own right, though it is self-generated and sometimes ego-defensive.

The importance of coping in emotion has been largely underestimated, I believe, for two reasons: First, the concept has been mainly associated with psychological stress, a field of theory and research whose extensive overlap with emotion has not always been appreciated. Second, over many decades coping has been viewed as a response to emotion—that is, as motivated by emotion. For example, in the drive-reinforcement theories of learning that once dominated psychology, anxiety was said to activate conditioned "coping" responses, both instrumental and ego-defensive, because they had previously succeeded in reducing the anxiety (drive or tension). In psychopathology, a more adaptive alternative to a neurotic defense cannot be learned until its conditioned link to anxiety reduction has been loosened so that the person can confront the source of anxiety and learn a better way of handling it (cf. Dollard & Miller, 1950; see Chapter 11).

The view I am proposing is that, although coping does indeed flow from emotion and is often directed at the regulation of emotional distress (as in emotion-focused coping), it also directly follows an initial appraisal of harm, threat, or challenge and can modify the subsequent appraisal, thereby changing or even short-circuiting the emotional reaction (cf. Lazarus & Alfert, 1964; and Opton, Rankin, Nomikos, & Lazarus, 1965). The term *short-circuiting* implies an analogy to an electric current that has been shunted somewhere else.

If, for example, we respond to a provocation to anger (e.g., an insult) with a reappraisal, whether defensive or based on evidence that we had misunderstood the other person's intent, our anger subsides or at least is prevented from becoming full-blown rage. Defensive reappraisals (or *ego-defenses* in psychoanalytic language) can be learned and made automatic as a way of dealing with a similar provocation in an individual, say, who is unable to mount anger without great anxiety because anger is itself threatening. It is as if that individual wants to view other persons' provocations as benign or nonexistent. A subsequent cue that is suggestive of an attack from someone now triggers the defense, which short-circuits the anger so that it is obviated, suppressed, or repressed. It is therefore unwise to conceptualize coping solely as a response to emotion, though it often is, and if we include in the emotion the appraisal processes that generated it, coping may also be said to influence the quality and intensity of subsequent emotions. I have more to say about short-circuiting in Chapter 4.

Empirical support for the position that coping mediates the emotional response can be found in a study by Folkman and Lazarus (1988b), in which negative and positive emotions were assessed at the outset of stressful encounters and then again at their conclusion, both reported on retrospectively. The pattern of coping used by subjects to deal with the encounter was also assessed. We found that certain coping strategies, both problem-focused and emotion-focused, were associated with improvement in the emotional state from the beginning to the conclusion of the encounter, which means that negative emotions such as anger and anxiety were decreased and positive emotions such as happiness and confidence were increased.

If we assume what cannot be proven in this study because of its retrospective design — namely, that the pattern of coping caused these changes — the findings are consistent with what I have been saying here about coping and emotion. A recent prospective study by Bolger (1990) provides even stronger evidence. Croyle and Ditto (1990) have also provided some experimental support for two oft-stated ideas about denial as a form of coping (e.g., Lazarus, 1983), first that denial is a common initial reaction to very threatening information, and second that it is most likely to be used by those who both believe the threat and have no problem-focused way of coping with it.

There is another sense in which coping is important in the emotion process, namely, in respect to *action tendencies*. These tendencies are usually thought of as biological urges to act that distinguish one emotion from another. Consider, for example, the emotions of anger and fear. Attack seems to be biologically linked to anger in both humans and nonhuman animals, just as avoidance and escape appear to have a biological link to fear. However, as I noted in Chapter 1, Averill (1983) disputes this for anger in humans, arguing that people infrequently report attacking the objects of their anger. On the other hand, Averill's subjects could have had strong impulses to attack that were inhibited because of social or intrapsychic pressures.

If we accept this reasoning, then there is potential overlap, as well as conflict, between coping and the action tendency characteristic of certain emotions. One might think of the biological impulse to attack as an analogue of coping — that is, it is one of nature's built-in forms of coping when an animal is endangered. The coping process can, in effect, augment or inhibit the impulse to attack — the former occurring when the process is compatible with the action tendency and the latter occurring when it is in conflict with the action tendency (say, when there are social or personally acquired taboos against it).

Little previous attention has been given to the overlaps and differences between biological action tendencies and coping. Biologically engendered action tendencies are automatic, nondeliberate, and primitive. I think, therefore, that it is better *not* to refer to them as coping, because coping is a much more complex, deliberate, and often planful psychological process; unlike innate action tendencies, coping draws heavily on appraisals about what is possible, likely to be effective in the specific context, and compatible with social and personal standards of conduct (e.g., display rules, action rules). We need to know more about how a person evaluates and controls action tendencies and how the biological impulse is transformed into a sophisticated coping strategy.

As I said in Chapter 2, the concept of action tendency helps us understand some of the response characteristics of emotion. Other writers, too, conceptualize the expressive and physiological characteristics of emotion, and perhaps even the ideational aspects, as products of these action tendencies. For example, Frijda (1986, p. 71) writes that "Emotions, then, can be defined as modes of relational action readiness, either in the form of tendencies to establish, maintain, or disrupt a relationship with the environment or in the form of modes of relational readiness as such" (see also Arnold, 1960, and de Rivera, 1977, for similar ideas).

On the other hand, as I also observed in Chapter 2 (see also Ortony et al., 1988), it is difficult though not impossible to suggest an action tendency for problematic emotions such as sadness, and mild positive ones such as contentment, relief, and pride. We must give more attention to the concept of action tendency, especially when considering physiological mobilization and change in emotion, as well as to the coping process, which plays such an important role in subsequent emotion by affecting appraisal and reappraisal.

Laux and Weber (1991) have recently suggested that each emotion, or better still, each cognitive-motivational-relational configuration, might differently influence the coping process — for example, when managing an anger encounter compared with one involving anxiety, shame, or guilt. These researchers, with some success, have been seeking to show that emotion-specific coping patterns exist in married couples, patterns that occur, they suggest, because the *intentions* of the marital partners are apt to differ in these encounters.

Laux and Weber's idea that the intentions underlying coping differ for each emotion suggests the fascinating possibility, inherent in a cognitive-motivational-relational theory, that to properly understand coping we must also understand the specific goals being threatened, both those that the person brings to the encounter and those that emerge during the encounter. Thus, anger encounters compared with those centered on anxiety are more likely to be dealt with by escalation of anger-aggression, self-promotion, or defensiveness (protecting one's self-image), thereby vigorously demonstrating rather than concealing anger; anxiety encounters, on the other hand, are apt to be dealt with by strategies aimed at preserving the relationship in the interest of obtaining reassurance and emotional support. In anxiety encounters the partners seek emotional closeness and are more apt to apologize, show concern, or engage in efforts to present a self-picture of one who needs help.

With the exception of this ongoing research, the connection between coping and intentions or goals has not been of interest to those working on the coping process. Yet how the person copes depends not only on the coping possibilities and how they are appraised but also on what a person wants to accomplish in the encounter. Moreover, new agendas arise from the ongoing flow of events in the adaptational encounter. More than one goal is apt to be involved in each encounter, and these are apt to change in primacy and salience (see Chapter 1). The study of coping should never be divorced from motivation, though it has been in recent research and theory, including my own. This injunction is a consequence of the insight that emotions are complex configurations of cognition, motivation, and relational patterns of adaptation that empower the coping process.

Person–Environment Relationships Bearing on Emotions

Before turning to the theory of core relational themes, I should explore briefly some of the ways in which others have thought about relationships relevant to emotion in humans and infrahuman animals. The issue we have to deal with now is how to decide about what are the appropriate relationships to consider.

How Emotional Relationships Have Been Conceived

The full range of relationships relevant to emotion must be very large, but we lack systematic enumeration and classification. Species characteristics undoubtedly constitute a powerful factor. For example, an animal that is prey to many other animals sharing the same habitat is exposed to dangers that a predator with few or no natural enemies is not. Habitat will also have an important bearing on person–environment relationships affecting well-being. For example, persons who live in a community with a significant crime problem will have somewhat different emotion-relevant relationships with their environment than will those who live in a peaceful community. Cities in the United States constitute a dangerous environment compared with, say, many European cities and with rural and suburban communities. Women who fear rape in North American cities will arrange different patterns of activity than will those who do not. In humans, habitat also includes culture and social structure, which influences the emotions by shaping relationships and the meanings that affect well-being. I shall have more to say about this in Chapter 9.

Writing from an ecological perspective, Baron and Boudreau (1987) offer a pleasing metaphor that could help emotion and adaptation theorists grasp the idea of person–environment relationships more clearly. Using Gibson's (1966, 1979) concept of affordances to refer to the instantaneous perceptual recognition by an animal species that a female is receptive, a tree is for cooling off, a field is for grazing, a nipple is for nursing, these authors use a lock and key metaphor—the same that microbiologists use today in speaking of how proteins, drugs, and viruses bind to neural receptors—to refer to how a particular person and a particular environment mesh or fit. They write:

> From an affordance perspective, personality and the environment are related in complementary fashion, similar to the relationship between keys and locks. Personality, in this metaphor, is a key in the search of the "right" lock, whereas the environment, including other people, is the lock waiting to be opened so that its affordances can be realized. . . . Personality, from this perspective, is defined jointly by the range of social affordances people can activate as keys and the range of opportunities for unlocking what people offer to other people.

At the first mention of Gibson, whose views others and I have drawn on (and I do again in Chapter 4), I should qualify that Gibson's concept of affordances does not assume that perception is something mediational going on in the person or infrahuman animal, or in the retina or nervous system, but that adaptational meaning is inherent in the "optic array"—that is, in the environmental pattern of light that conveys definite information about the nature of that environment, and which makes effective behavior possible, not something that needs to be interpreted (see, for example, Neisser, 1990). As an aside, it is interesting that cognitive psychologists and those concerned with individual differences draw so heavily on Gibson's theory, often without realizing that he did not regard perception as interpretive.

A relational view of emotion runs into the possibility that there are as many emotions as there are specific ways in which one can be harmed or benefited. At first blush these possibilities seem unlimited and an invitation to chaos. That there is an unlimited number of emotions is a logical possibility that does not appear to have had many adherents, though William James (1890) was one. Instead, classical and modern thinking organizes emotions into families such as anger, fear, and so forth, within which each instance can be slightly different while sharing a common prototypical feature (see Chapter 2).

For example, although there are many forms of anger — such as righteous anger or indignation, gloating, pouting or hurt anger, defensive anger, and vengeful anger — which imply different person–environment relationships — we assume that they all fall under a common category based on shared features, which include provocation and pattern of response. Similarly, one could distinguish, as did H. Lewis (1971), numerous forms of shame such as embarrassment, mortification, shyness, and humiliation, all of which involve a failure to live up to a demanding ego-ideal, but which also differ in important relational details.

Though animal behaviorists usually refer not to anger but to aggression or agonistic behavior, it is noteworthy that variations in anger are probably also applicable to infrahuman animals. One can, for example, differentiate defensive aggression (mother defending young), predatory aggression (killing prey for food), and intraspecies aggression (dominance struggles within the same species). Expressively, and perhaps physiologically, each looks quite different, and each form of aggression also has its own provocations. For example, a stalking lion is the picture of controlled tautness and stealth; a mother defending her young may, depending on conditions, present a display of menacing rage (see Eibel-Eibesfeldt, 1970; Moyer, 1968, 1976, 1986; Washburn & Hamburg, 1968).

It is difficult to say how much similarity there is across species in emotions and the relationships they imply, and it would be easy to be misled about this by superficial similarities at the behavioral level that might not conform to inferred psychological processes. Some human emotions may well have emerged for the first time in the evolution of the human species; perhaps this applies to pride, shame, and gratitude, assuming that these states don't exist in infrahuman animals. Because we can talk to humans but not to animals, it is difficult to make unequivocal statements about emotions that are shared or not shared across species, and one does so with great risk.

For example, a dog may display what we think is guilt or shame — ears down, slinking away from the evidence of its incontinence — but what we are observing may well be fear or anxiety over possible disapproval. Of course, we could also say that guilt (and shame) are forms of anxiety (see Chapter 6). And we could look at social context, behavior (e.g., social action and expression), and physiological patterns in making inferences about this (see, for example, Hebb & Thompson, 1954, for a rich discussion of the uses of observing animal behavior in social psychological research).

Animal behaviorists and psychologists concerned with human emotion some-times argue, with good reason, that infrahuman animals experience some emotions in common with humans. For example, there are signs of anger (in contrast with aggression or attack) and jealousy in chimpanzees, including even temper tantrums and sulking. Griffin (1984) makes a case for complex and flexible patterns of adaptive behavior in relatively simple creatures, such as birds, that suggest goal-directed actions and plans. Thus, even so-called instincts, or behavior that is said to be "released" by certain stimuli called elicitors, can be interpreted as purposive and goal directed—implying the capacity for emotions, though the jump to emotion, as to intention, is obviously inferential. For example, a mother bird's "broken wing" displays are directed toward distracting a predator away from her offspring. During this feigned injury, in which it appears badly impaired, the mother is

> clearly controlling its behavior and modifying it in detail according to what the intruder does. It looks frequently at the intruder, continues in one direction if the intruder follows, but flies in a well-coordinated fashion back to the intruder's vicinity if he does not. Furthermore, if the intruder comes too close, the bird always recovers its coordinated locomotion. There are many well-orchestrated complexities to the behavior, and its adjustment to the circumstances strongly suggests intentional reactions to the situation rather than crippling confusion. (Griffin, 1984, p. 90)

When Plutchik (1980) expresses wariness about the meaning of emotion terms across different cultures and persons, which is a legitimate concern, he also fails to point out that the common inferences phylogeneticists make across species, and from animal to human, could be equally, if not potentially more, misleading. It troubles me that psychologists who urge a science-centered outlook and are so ready to denigrate self-report in humans as a source of information about mental life can also be so reluctant to express the same reservations about other sources of information that are just as or even more subject to inferential error.

A major task of relational formulations is to develop a basis for classifying person–environment relationships and the emotions they generate. Most existing efforts, however, focus on environmental and personality factors separately, though some rudimentary relational languages can be found (see, for example, de Rivera, 1977; de Rivera & Grinkis, 1986). Murray (1938), too, was reaching for such a relational language in his phenomenological analysis of personality in terms of the needs that characterized the person and the environmental presses that that person faced. Although needs and presses separate the person and the environment as systems, Murray's concept of *themas*, which combine needs and presses, is a good example of the attempt to bring the separate sets of variables together in a relational, meaning-centered fashion.

A relational, transactional emphasis, which asserts that "the actor and the situation are indivisible as a unit" (Forgas, 1982, p. 61), brings what I have been saying into the orbit of earlier writers, such as Koffka (1935), who distinguished between the external, or geographical, environment and the internal, behavioral or subjective, environment. The subjective environment was also the centerpiece of Lewin's field theory (1935, 1951), and a number of other distinguished personality, clinical, and social psychologists, including Murray (1938, pp. 39-40), have proposed that "the organism and its milieu must be considered together, a single creature-environment interaction being a convenient short unit for psychology." For the reader wedded to sociology, a compatible position would be *symbolic interactionism,* which also gives an important place to the relational meanings carried by social interaction and, to anticipate the subject matter of Chapter 4, the cognitive representations that these interactions imply.

Two of the broadest modes we can use to classify person–environment relationships center on the *input.* One of these makes a distinction between positive and negative emotions, but does not clarify which of several bases for the distinction should be used (see Chapter 1). The other is concerned with whether the person is harmed or benefited in the relationship. These modes offer too broad a classification to be serviceable by themselves in distinguishing the different ways a person can be harmed or benefited and the specific emotions that might result.

Another broad classification, approach versus avoidant emotions, is centered on the *output* or response and refers to the action impulse generated by the transaction (see also Frijda, 1986). Fox and Davidson (1984, p. 354) suggest that "approach-withdrawal is an underlying behavioral dimension upon which affective subsystems have evolved," a sort of fundamental psychobiological dichotomy. They draw on the phylogenetically centered writings of Bowlby (1969), Schneirla (1959), and others to support their argument (see also Arnold, 1960; Lewin, 1935; Miller, 1944).

The response tendencies under this schema are overbroad in that they imply grouping a number of emotions in a way that is inconsistent with the way we understand these emotions. One can see, for example, that anger and love are very different states with very different impulses to action, and they are united under the concept of approach in Fox and Davidson's analysis. Yet we approach to attack as well as to express and receive affection. And sometimes we withdraw to enjoy something quietly as well as out of fright, sadness, or shame — these withdrawals being quite different in character and meaning, as well as in their associated emotions.

In effect, the dimension proposed is insufficient to allow us to differentiate among the many different kinds of emotion that we must take into account. I have already noted that Frijda (1986; Frijda, Kuipers, & ter Schure, 1989) makes a case for the importance of specific action tendencies or forms of action readiness as a key feature of each emotion (see also de Rivera, 1977, for another categorization). In the case of Frijda, and that of de Rivera, the concept of action tendency does not suffer as others do from overbroad categorization. If anything, Frijda et al.'s (1989, p. 214) list of action readiness variables (shown in Table 3.3) contains too many variables whose status as action tendencies is uncertain.

When all is said and done, the *relational meaning* of the adaptational situation — that is, the implications for well-being of the person–environment relationship — is my candidate for the basis of a classificatory system. This meaning also includes both the input and the response side of the equation. The relational meaning and action tendency for each emotion will be examined in some detail in Part Three. All writers, such as myself, who see emotion as involving relational meaning, and who insist that emotions are always about something, are taking a cognitive-motivational-relational position by implication. Some state this very clearly, as when Bedford (1956–1957, pp. 303–304) writes:

TABLE 3.3. Action Readiness Variables: Study 2

Variable[a]	Item
Approach (Moving toward)	I wanted to approach, to make contact.
Be with (Moving toward)	I wanted to be or stay close, to be receptive to someone.
Protection (Moving away)	I wanted to protect myself from someone or something.
Avoidance (Moving away)	I wanted to have nothing to do with something or someone, to be bothered by it as little as possible, to stay away.
Attending	I wanted to observe well, to understand, or I paid attention.
Distance (Rejection)	I wanted to keep something out of my way, to keep it at a distance.
Rejection (Rejection)	I did not want to have anything to do with someone or something.
Disinterest	Things going on did not involve me; I did not pay attention.
Don't want	I wanted something not to be so, not to exist.
Boiling inwardly (Moving against)	I boiled inside.
Antagonistic (Moving against)	I wanted to oppose, to assault, hurt, or insult.
Reactant (Moving against)	I wanted to go against an obstacle or difficulty, or to conquer it.
Interrupted (Interruption)	I interrupted what I was doing, or I was interrupted.
Preoccupied (Interruption)	I could not concentrate or order my thoughts.
In command	I stood above the situation; I felt I was in command; I held the ropes.
Helping	I wanted to help someone, to take care of someone.
Disappear from view	I wanted to sink into the ground, to disappear from the Earth, not to be noticed by anyone.
Inhibition (Inhibition)	I felt inhibited, paralyzed, or frozen.
Blushing (Inhibition)	I blushed or was afraid to blush.
Submitting	I did not want to oppose, or I wanted to yield to someone else's wishes.
Apathy (Hypoactivation)	I did not feel like doing anything; nothing interested me; I was apathetic.
Giving up (Hypoactivation)	I quit; I gave up.
Shutting off (Hypoactivation)	I shut myself off from the surroundings.
Helplessness (Helplessness)	I wanted to do something, but I did not know what; I was helpless.
Crying (Helplessness)	I cried, had to cry, or wanted to cry.
Excited	I was excited, restless, could not sit still.
Exuberant (Exuberance)	I wanted to move, be exuberant, sing, jump, undertake things.
Laughter (Exubereance)	I laughed, had to laugh, or wanted to laugh.
Rest	I felt at rest, thought everything was O.K., felt no need to do anything.

[a]Dimension names are given in parentheses to distinguish alternative items intended for the same dimension.

(*Source:* N. H. Frijda, P. Kuipers, and E. ter Schure, "Relations among emotion, appraisal, and emotional action readiness." *Journal of Personality and Social Psychology, 57.* Washington, DC: American Psychological Association. Copyright © 1989 by the American Psychological Association. Reprinted by permission.)

Emotion concepts are . . . not purely psychological: they presuppose concepts of social relationships and institutions, and concepts belonging to systems of judgement, moral, aesthetic and legal. In using emotion words we are able, therefore, to relate behaviour to the complex background in which it is enacted, and so to make human action intelligible.

Not all person–environment relationships are central to the emotion process, though they may well be relevant. For example, we contrast passive-dependent with aggressive relationships between persons; competitive, self-centered relationships with those characterized by mutuality or community; symbiotic with independent relationships; and rigid relational patterns with flexible ones. (See also Hinde & Stevenson-Hinde (1988) for analyses of relationships within families.) How one classifies person–environment relationships depends on one's analytic purposes, and most of these do not direct us toward the elementary psychological relationships that underlie each of the emotions — say, anger, anxiety, pride, and so on. For this we need a specific kind of theory. I propose to talk about the concept of core relational themes in this connection (see also Smith & Lazarus, 1990; and Lazarus, 1990b).

Core Relational Themes

Person–environment relationships come together with personal meaning and the appraisal process (to be discussed in Chapter 4) in the concept of *core relational themes.* Appraisal involves an appreciation of a particular harm or benefit in the relationship with the environment, with its manifold implications for well-being, action, and coping. Within the cognitive-motivational-relational framework, each negative emotion should suggest research questions about the necessary and sufficient core relational themes at the *molar level,* as well as the necessary and sufficient appraisal components specifying the harms or benefits, and what could be done about them, at the *molecular level.* The latter combine into patterns to produce the core relational themes as a kind of convenient summary, much like the themas of Murray (1935). Considering knowledge and appraisal in terms of *both* molecular components and molar themes provides a clearer understanding of the relationship between appraisal and emotion than a study of either would yield in isolation.

Although person–environment relationships must be sensed and evaluated personally (appraised) by an individual to generate emotions, we can nevertheless speak of them without reference to cognitive activity for the time being if we simply assume for future reference that it is the relationship as appraised subjectively that counts rather than the objective or actual relationship as it is presumably viewed through the eyes of observers.

A core relational theme is simply the central (hence core) relational harm or benefit in adaptational encounters that underlies each specific kind of emotion. There are diverse kinds of harmful relationships, each of which constitutes a core relational theme leading to a distinctive negative emotion. There are also diverse kinds of beneficial relationships, each of which constitutes a core relational theme leading to a distinctive positive emotion. Each individual emotion or emotion family is defined by a specific core relational theme. When its implications for well-being are appraised by the person, each thematic relationship produces an action impulse consistent with the core relational theme and the emotion that flows from it.

The premise that each emotion has its own particular core relational theme, appraisal pattern, and action tendency has led to a number of clinical research studies on what is called the content-specificity hypothesis, which means that specific emotion traits are associated with specific sets of ideas, or *cognitive distortions* as Beck and Weishaar (1989) call them, about oneself and the world (see Derry & Kuiper, 1981; Kuiper & Derry, 1982). Although this hypothesis centers on psychopathology, research on it suggests that ideas like core relational themes have an emerging empirical data base. Beck and Weishaar identify a number of cognitive profiles for each of a number of psychological disorders, some of which have divergent emotional patterns (see also Clark, Beck, & Stewart, 1990).

Although content specificity as a correlate of an emotional trait does not prove cognitive causality—in fact, Beck and Weishaar (1989, p. 23) even caution, surprisingly, that "Cognitions do not 'cause' depression or any other psychopathological disorder but are an intrinsic part of the disorder"—different ways of viewing harm or threat are likely to underlie each negative emotion. Beck (1987), using an acquired stress-diasthesis model—which means that in early development certain traits were acquired (in another version they could be inherited) that under stress make the individual vulnerable to later distress and dysfunction—has argued that depression is the result of certain negative cognitions people have about themselves before the stress-induced onset of the depression. Although depression is usually a complex of several emotions, research contrasting the divergent concerns of depressed and anxious patients parallels the notion that each emotion has its own core relational theme, appraisal pattern, and action tendency. Studies by Clark, Beck, and Brown (1989), Greenberg and Beck (1989), Hammen, Marks, Mayol, and deMayo (1985b), Hammen, Marks, deMayo, and Mayol (1985a), and Strauman and Higgins (1988) illustrate the search for stress-diathesis variables in emotion.

Although I will discuss in detail the core relational themes for each emotion in Chapters 6 and 7, it will help at this point to illustrate more concretely what the most important of these are as postulated in the theory. Table 3.4 contains a list of the core relational themes for each emotion in the classification scheme presented in Chapter 2.

The idea that there is a distinctive core relational theme for each emotion has been expressed in different but informal ways by numerous writers on emotion, sometimes with an emphasis on a single specific emotion. I believe that there is considerable agreement about these themes, though there are also arguments about some of them, such as anger, particularly in the details. As we saw in Chapter 2,

TABLE 3.4. Core Relational Themes for Each Emotion

Anger	A demeaning offense against me and mine.
Anxiety	Facing uncertain, existential threat.
Fright	Facing an immediate, concrete, and overwhelming physical danger.
Guilt	Having transgressed a moral imperative.
Shame	Having failed to live up to an ego-ideal.
Sadness	Having experienced an irrevocable loss.
Envy	Wanting what someone else has.
Jealousy	Resenting a third party for loss or threat to another's affection.
Disgust	Taking in or being too close to an indigestible object or idea (metaphorically speaking).
Happiness	Making reasonable progress toward the realization of a goal.
Pride	Enhancement of one's ego-identity by taking credit for a valued object or achievement, either our own or that of someone or group with whom we identify.
Relief	A distressing goal-incongruent condition that has changed for the better or gone away.
Hope	Fearing the worst but yearning for better.
Love	Desiring or participating in affection, usually but not necessarily reciprocated.
Compassion	Being moved by another's suffering and wanting to help.

research also suggests that people have a pretty good idea about many of these themes, especially prototypical ones, when they are asked about them in research (cf. Shaver et al., 1987).

After arriving at the term *core relational theme,* I became aware of the writings of Luborsky (especially 1984), in which the concept of "core conflictual relationship theme" (CCRT) is discussed. I am not sure whether my term was influenced by earlier contact with Luborsky's work, but there are some overlaps as well as differences. Luborsky is referring to the central and recurrent interpersonal scenario of a troubled person, which displays emotional dysfunction and which needs to be grasped by a therapist on the basis of evidence revealed in psychotherapy. An example of a conflictual interpersonal scenario might be a constant need to assert oneself with other persons, including loved ones, that usually leads to disapproval or rejection by the other person whose approval is important and, as a result, to withdrawal by the needy person who has been thwarted—an example of what has often been called a "vicious circle."

Luborsky's CCRT is also similar to Horowitz's analysis (1988, 1989) and his role-relationship model (RRM). Horowitz's version portrays a schema or scenario of the self in interaction with another person. For any given individual, there can be many such schemata, which are based on the patient's history, concepts of self, wishes, sources of threat, and context. Horowitz's RRM and Luborsky's CCRT are attempts to construct a portrait of the individual in troubled relationships with other important persons in the patient's life, which could help the therapist and patient understand dysfunctional and distressing emotions.

The differences between Luborsky's CCRT or Horowitz's RRM and my Core Relational Theme have to do with the distinction between emotion traits and states. Luborsky and Horowitz are concerned with emotion traits, because in their work clinically dysfunctional and emotionally distressing consequences, which are stable, are addressed in psychotherapy. I have had occasion to discuss this distinction elsewhere (Lazarus, 1989a); remember, a state perspective focuses on unstable, contextual conditions of emotion generation; a trait perspective, on the other hand, emphasizes what is stable (that is, recurrent reactions). Each is valid in its own right, depending on the question at hand.

There remain many unresolved questions about the role of the molar concept of core relational themes, and about the molecular appraisal components that contribute to them, in the generation of emotion. However, these are better addressed in my discussion of the appraisal process in Chapter 4.

Interdependencies Among the Core Relational Themes

Why is it that love and anger (hate is the more commonly given opposite) are so closely intertwined in our emotional lives? For that matter, what makes it possible for sadness and anger, guilt and anger, pride and anxiety, and so on, to flow from the same emotional encounter and social relationship, one often rapidly superseding the other? We are told convincingly, for example, that love and hate are close cousins, that anger, fear-anxiety, guilt, shame, envy-jealousy, and sadness-depression on the one hand, and happiness, pride, love, hope, relief, and compassion on the other hand, all flow from each other and mix together. Why are there important interdependencies among emotions, or rather, among the processes generating and changing them?

If one has been demeaned by a loved one, there is apt to be anger. However, the anger, when displayed, tells the loved one that he or she has acted hurtfully, and an apology or manifestation of affection may turn the emotion into relief, guilt, anxiety, or love in the wink of an eye. At one moment, there is anger, sometimes bitter anger, and in another moment, there is love. In other words, where there is love there is apt to be "hate," and where there is hate, there is apt to be love or the desire for it. In this vein, it has been suggested by psychoanalysts that what we hate in another is what we are apt to reject unconsciously in ourselves. Anger may also turn to sadness, anxiety, or guilt, depending on what is communicated and how it is appraised and coped with.

The explanation of these interdependencies is really quite simple, and there is no magic involved. It is that we are likely to feel anger most at those for whom we also feel love because the relationship is so important to our well-being. When a loved one disappoints us we feel angry, even though we would prefer to feel love. In this kind of relationship, positive and negative emotions are, in a sense, opposite sides of the same coin; both indicate strong personal involvement. Positive appraisals potentiate love and affection, whereas negative appraisals potentiate anger, sadness, anxiety, guilt, shame, or jealousy, depending on what is happening and how it is appraised. In other words, both reactions, though obviously opposite, are directed toward a person whose attitudes and behavior are of great moment to us. We have such a high stake in the other person that negative and positive emotions are, in a sense, cut from the same cloth and are likely to arise more easily than with someone about whom we are relatively neutral.

These seemingly paradoxical interdependencies among core relational themes, and the emotions they serve, highlight the motivational principle. We could also use the word *power* to express this theme; because we have ceded power over us to another, what that person does with respect to us becomes all the more important (cf. Kemper, 1978).

Finally, when a relationship is no longer serviceable, we must engage in an active coping struggle, akin to grief, to disengage from it so that the psychological pain or distress of disappointment no longer has the power to generate anger, anxiety, sadness, guilt, shame, or jealousy, just as it also no longer generates positive emotions such as happiness and pride. Live relationships are potentially emotional ones, both positive and negative, whereas dead relationships can no longer engage our emotions one way or the other.

Summary

In this chapter I have been examining the person–environment relationship and what makes it a source of positive and negative emotions. A fundamental premise is that to understand emotions we must spell out the particular person–environment relationships that underlie each of the emotion categories. I referred to the concept that defines these relationships as core relational themes, which express the key relational harm or benefit underlying each class of emotion, positive and negative, and each specific emotion within these classes.

Much of this chapter was devoted to the role of motivation in emotion, because a fundamental premise of a cognitive-relational-motivational theory of emotion is that we react emotionally only when we have a stake in the outcome of an encounter. In other words, emotion depends on what is important to us — in effect, our individual goal hierarchies.

I examined two facets of motivation, the stable goal commitments that people bring with them to an adaptational encounter as traits, and the more fluid, transactional concept of stakes in the outcome of an encounter. I also discussed the distinction made by McClelland and his colleagues between self-attributed motivation, which seems more like a conscious value that depends on language and abstract thought and on what is learned from the society, and implicit motivation, which seems more akin to unconscious or preconscious urges that depend more on the primitive, emotional, and unspoken experiences of early childhood.

The chapter reviewed the role of motivation as an antecedent condition of emotion and the way it has been viewed historically. I argued that theory must take into account individual differences in goal hierarchies, and that this had to be seen as an aspect of an individual ego-identity or self. The underlying premise is that emotions make no sense without a consideration of person–environment relationships and the motivational business that underlies them.

The person–environment relationship is always changing, along with the emotions it generates, which makes emotion a process. The emotion process may be readily divided into four stages: a provocation, unfolding, outcome, and when there is a warning, anticipation. Although emotion may be viewed structurally (that is, from the standpoint of stable traits, as when we speak of angry, anxious, or guilty persons), it must be studied primarily as a process.

The person–environment relationship keeps changing, in part because of coping activities. In deference to this, I also discussed two coping functions: problem focused and emotion focused. The former changes the relationship, and hence the emotion, by actively doing something to either the environment or the person. The latter changes the relationship by attention deployment, as in avoidance, or by altering the personal meaning on which the emotion is predicated. While action tendencies may have some of these effects, they are innate dispositions, whereas coping is more deliberate, complex, and psychological, and can override the action tendency by inhibiting or redirecting it, sometimes in an elaborate, time-sequenced set of plans. Coping must also be considered within the framework of motivation, because one's active goals in an adaptational encounter strongly influence the choice of coping strategies.

Throughout my discussion of the person–environment relationship, the role of coping in this relationship, and the role of the motivational principle in defining what is harmful, threatening, and beneficial for any given individual, I constantly alluded to the key construct of a cognitive-motivational-relational theory of emotions — namely, appraisal. I have deferred dealing with appraisal in detail because this process is always about person–environment relationships that depend on coping and motivation. Having covered the person–environment relationship, the coping process that changes it, and the motivational principle, which, in part, defines the adaptational business of every encounter, I turn to cognition and emotion, especially the concept of appraisal, in Chapters 4 and 5.

Notes

1. This the rationale for Selye's term *stressor*. It is also the rationale for life event lists, which identify life changes, such as bereavement and divorce, as powerful sources of stress and distress. If some events are likely to generate stress in those exposed to them, we can call them *stressors*. On the other hand, how stressful they are and in what ways depend on appraisal and coping processes, and many events that are rarely stressful for some persons are capable of generating stress reactions in others who are vulnerable to these events.

2. Writing about denial as a way of coping with the imminent threat of death, Weisman (1972; see also Hackett & Weisman, 1964) has used the graphic expression, "middle knowledge" to refer to the fact that somehow such persons sense that they are terminally ill, even if everyone around them engages in denial.

3. This term was once used — around the 1920s — by a group called *gestalt psychologists*, one of whose tenets was that an experience or action was best understood as a configuration, a whole, a *gestalt*, rather than as a sum of smaller elements or components. My occasional use of the term *holistic* partakes of this idea.

✦ 4 ✦

Cognition and Emotion

Cognitive activity is taking place all the time, even in sleep, as manifest in dreams; perhaps it occurs as long as we are not comatose but we cannot really be sure. Because there are at least three different ways to speak of cognitive activity in the emotion process, it is important to be as precise as possible about how the concept is used. As I see it, these ways have to do with (1) the functional and temporal role of cognition in emotion; (2) the contents and formal qualities of the cognition; and (3) how meaning is achieved.

1. With respect to its *functional and temporal role,* I will argue that cognitive activity causally precedes an emotion in the flow of psychological events, and subsequent cognitive activity is also later affected by that emotion. The causal cognitive activity continues into the emotional response itself as an integral feature. That this is not a tautology is discussed in Chapter 5 when I deal with issues of causality. Feedback from the emotion process, which includes the causal cognitive activity and the emotional state itself—having been perceived and further evaluated by the experiencing person—also influences subsequent psychological states and processes, including emotion, in a continuous psychological flow.

In effect, the temporal and functional role of cognitive activity in an emotion depends on where in this flow we make our observations. In our analyses and research, cognition is sometimes the independent and sometimes the dependent variable; similarly, emotion is sometimes the independent and sometimes the dependent variable. In this chapter, I am concerned with how knowledge and appraisal influence the emotions rather than how emotion affects cognition, which I deal with in Chapter 10.

2. The most important cognitive *content* in the emotion process consists of *knowledge* (that is, beliefs about how things work in general and in the specific adaptational encounter) and *appraisals* of the significance of the person–environment relationship for personal well-being, whether about a specific encounter or life as a whole. Perceptions of our thoughts, action tendencies, bodily changes, and the subjective feel of the emotions we experience are additional contents of cognition that are part of the emotion process and contribute to knowledge and appraisal. Although most of us are accustomed to think of it as objective truth, knowledge does not necessarily refer to this but rather to what people *take to be* objective truth, which is a phenomenological position. The relationship between a public or private truth is an important issue that requires further philosophical examination, but it would take me too far afield to elaborate on it here.

Certain *formal qualities* of cognitive activity are also relevant to the emotions, because they have to do with how we comprehend and regulate emotional transactions. There are two main kinds: One consists of *cognitive styles,* as they are often referred to, which are consistent ways in which people perceive and relate to their environments. The classical ideas of Klein (1958, 1964; see also Holzman & Gardner,1959) on "levelers and sharpeners" (those who gloss over details and distinctions and see large wholes versus those who center their attention on details and distinctions), and Witkin's (1965; see also Witkin, Dyk, Faterson, Goodenough, & Karp, 1962) analyses of "psychological differentiation," have had substantial influence in personality and clinical research. Both of these programs of research had a close affinity with psychoanalytic and developmental thought and treated cognitive styles as functionally related to ego-defense and neuroses, exemplified clinically, for example, in the writings of Schafer (1954) and Shapiro (1965).

Another kind of formal cognitive activity has to do with its *functional manifestations at different stages of development.* Such stages in the development of ego-functioning and intelligence were of concern to Freud (1957b), Piaget (1952), and Werner (1948, 1957). This was expressed in ideas about the progression from concrete and relatively simple forms of thought in early childhood to more advanced, abstract forms characteristic of the adult, a progression that has important implications for adaptation and maladaptation. Loevinger's (1976) efforts to assess ego-level in adults, which I will touch on in Chapter 10, are an outgrowth of theories of cognitive development.

3. A central problem in understanding the role of cognitive activity in emotion is how meaning is achieved and changed in an adaptational encounter. Later in this chapter, and again in Chapter 5, which deals with causality, I distinguish between *two modes of appraisal:* one automatic, unreflective, and unconscious or preconscious; the other deliberate and conscious. There may well be other modes (cf. Leventhal, 1980, 1984), but the contrast between these two is especially important. The cognitive activity of observing and evaluating at both these levels may also be contrasted with what Heidegger (see Benner & Wrubel, 1989; also Guignon, 1984; and Taylor, 1985) identified as "being in a situation," and what Merleau-Ponti (1962, 1968) referred to as "embodied intelligence," both of which seem to be less distanced than when we act as an observer of ourselves.

At this juncture I hasten to make a point about meaning and cognitive activity that I do not want the reader to miss or forget — namely, that innate discriminations and the biologically fixed responses tied to them, if that is a proper way to put it, should probably not be considered cognition even though they constitute an adaptive distinction between danger and no danger. When the fowl studied by Tinbergen (1951) got frightened by the hawklike cardboard model and not by the gooselike model, an experiment I mentioned in Chapters 1 and 2, this was probably an innate reaction pattern or reflex, not a real evaluation. The discriminative meaning is, in effect, a property of the nervous system of fowl and presumably requires little or no actual experience and learning.

To treat this built-in and rigid response to an environmental signal as cognition weakens the concept by overextending it, something I myself have been guilty of doing (e.g., Lazarus, 1982). What looks superficially like judgment is not, and even if the adaptational consequences are similar, I think it is wise to exclude reflexlike processes from what we are calling cognition. Not to do so is to overlook the phylogenetic principle, offered in Chapter 2 and again in Chapter 5, that human emotions depend on intelligence and evaluation, which constitute an evolutionary step beyond sensorimotor reflexes and physiological drives. The essence of a cognitive approach is that emotion is largely a learned response, especially as regards *meaning* — that is, it is a response to changing or recurrent judgments about oneself in the world.

After some general remarks in the next section about cognition, the history of thought surrounding it, and its relevance to emotion, Chapter 4 proceeds along the following route: I discuss appraisal in considerable depth, including its adaptational function, situational versus generalized appraisals, the transition of appraisal theory from stress to the emotions, the distinction between knowledge and appraisal, and the six primary and secondary components of appraisal that shape the emotional reaction. The final and focal section of this chapter looks at two modes through which meaning is achieved; first, the modes are contrasted, and then their implications for life-span development are examined. The chapter ends with an examination of unconscious appraising.

Rationale and a Bit of History

As I indicated in Chapter 1, cognitive-mediational approaches now appear to dominate the field of emotion, although the functional relations between cognition and emotion are subject to vigorous debate. Depending on how broadly one defines it, a cognitive emphasis can be found in the writings of Aristotle, Spinoza, Hume, Dewey, Brentano, Scheler, Heidegger, Sartre, Bedford, Kenny, Thalberg, and Solomon, to go down the list of classical and modern philosophical writers excerpted in Calhoun and Solomon's (1984) useful reader (see also Rorty, 1980a, for a different reader). Freud and McDougall focused mainly on drives, but they touched on cognitive issues, too, and if one's interpretation of cognition is broad enough, they, too, could be included. Alfred Adler was clearly a cognitivist, as were other neo-Freudian and psychoanalytic ego-psychology writers.

Many theorists and researchers now accept the premise that adult human emotion can best be understood in cognitive terms. Explicitly cognitive formulations of emotion theory have been presented since 1960 by a number of psychologically oriented social scientists, including Arnold (1960), Averill (1982), Bandura (1977b, 1982), Bearison and Zimiles (1986), de Rivera (1977), de Sousa (1987), Epstein (1983), Frijda (1986), Gordon (1987), Harris (1989), Lazarus (1966, 1990), Lazarus and Folkman (1984), Leventhal (1984), Mandler (1984), Ortony, Clore, and Collins (1988), Roseman (1984), Scheele and Groeben (1986), Scherer (1984a, 1984b), Smith and Ellsworth (1985, 1987), Smith and Lazarus (1990), Solomon (1980), and Weiner (1985, 1986). Undoubtedly there will be more. Although they vary in emphasis and detail, all accept the central idea that emotions are mediated by cognitive activity (see also a review by Dalkvist & Rollenhagen, 1989a).

As I have already indicated, the cognitive emphasis was not greatly in evidence in academic psychology in the years preceding the 1970s and 1980s, though as Solomon (1980, p. 271) points out: "The idea that emotions are akin to judgments and within the bounds of human responsibility is a very old theory." The classical and medieval philosophers of emotion not only emphasized conation (motivation or will), but they were often interested in perceptual and cognitive transformations of human experience. Modern-day clinicians who do cognitive therapy — such as Beck (1976, 1987), Ellis (Bernard & DiGuiseppe, 1989; Ellis, 1962), Meichenbaum (1977; Meichenbaum & Cameron, 1983), and others — emphasize the rational control of the emotions. Ellis draws, for example, on the writings of Greek philosophers such as Epictetus, who wrote in the *Enchiridion* (1956, p. 19) that "Men are disturbed not by things, but by the views which they take of things." Shakespeare often echoed the same theme, the best example of which, from *Hamlet,* Act II, Scene 2, is "For there is nothing either good or bad/but thinking makes it so" (see also Greenberg & Safran, 1987; Safran & Greenberg, 1991; and Guidano & Liotti, 1983, for treatments of this by other cognitive therapists).

What is strange about all this is not the cognitive emphasis but the stubborn effort by radical behaviorists, beginning with the turn of the century and covering over seventy-five years, to sell psychology on the belief that it is without scientific merit to treat thought as a causal mediator of our emotional and behavioral reactions (cf. Bolles, 1974; Mahoney, 1989). The advance of cognitive explanations, however, has now gone so far that there is a dangerous tendency to equate cognitive activity with mind, a trend I have already commented on.

About cognition, motivation, and emotion in the Middle Ages, Gardner et al. (1937/1970, pp. 103–104) wrote:

> As regards their [i.e., emotions] relation to cognition, there is a diversity of views, or at least diversity of emphasis. All agree that apprehension accompanies the modification [of conative tendencies], but while some writers show a disposition to regard the apprehensions of some good or evil as an antecedent condition of the emotion, others lay stress on the 'intention' of the object, that is, its favorable or unfavorable relation to tendencies in the individual, and dwell on the function of apprehension in promoting or checking these tendencies.

Notice that in this quotation, cognitive activity is regarded as a source of constraint or control over self-centered and presumably primitive biological impulses, which was a major "ethical" preoccupation in the Middle Ages. The outlook of this period in Western culture was dominated by Church concerns about morality and human rationality — as a reflection of God's nature — an outlook borrowed from the ancient Greeks whose ideals of reason and moderation were largely Apollonian (from the god Apollo).

Medieval writer John Gerson, as cited in Gardner et al. (1937/1970, p. 104), argued that there is no cognition that is not also affection, and no affection that does not include cognition; both are interdependent and operate together. Current debates about the relationship between cognition and emotion, with the position sometimes taken that cognition and emotion are separate neural functions, make this statement by Gerson all the more striking. Some would argue that no knowledge is totally cold or unemotional, because there must always be some emotional involvement in its construction.

I take the view that although emotion always involves cognition — that is, personal meaning of some sort — cognition can be relatively cold when there is *minimal self-involvement or low stakes* in what is thought; cognition may also be hot or emotional. As I suggest later in Chapter 11 (see also Lazarus, 1989c), an ideal of mental health is the harmonious integration of the three main constructs of mind — cognition, motivation, and emotion — disconnection among these constructs, which most commonly results from self-protective ego defenses but also from brain damage, is tantamount to psychopathology.

In addition to pursuing the position that having an emotion requires a goal commitment (see Chapter 3), and that emotional judgments are necessarily personal and involving, Solomon (1980, pp. 274–275) presses the cognitive theme vigorously. I greatly enjoy the following statement he made about peripheral, viscerally centered approaches for its pithy analogies and biting sarcasm:

> Emotions are defined primarily by their constitutive judgments, given structure by judgments, distinguished as particular emotions (anger, love, envy, etc.) as judgments, and related to other beliefs, judgments, and our knowledge of the world, in a "formal" way, through judgments. No alternative theory, it seems to me, has ever made the slightest progress in explaining the central features of emotion, as opposed to their red-in-the-face and visceral cramp symptomatology. Anger, for example, is to be analyzed in terms of a quasi-courtroom scenario, in which one takes the role of judge, jury, prosecuting attorney and, on occasion, executioner. The object of anger is the accused, the crime is an offense, and the overall scenario is one of judgmental self-righteousness. (One might add that the court is almost always of the kangaroo variety, with self-esteem taking clear priority over justice.)

To document the widespread emphasis on cognitive factors in emotion would lead to an endless succession of quotations, and obviously, the case cannot be made simply by reference to authority. Although I am not attracted to some of what he wrote about emotion, no one is clearer and more convincing about the fusion of cognitive and relational features in emotion than Sartre (1948, p. 51–52):

> It is evident, in effect, that the man who is afraid is afraid *of* something. Even if it is a matter of one of those indefinite anxieties which one experiences in the dark, in a sinister and deserted passageway, etc., one is afraid *of* certain aspects of the night, of the world. And doubtless, all psychologists have noted that emotion is set in motion by a perception, a representation-signal, etc. But it seems that for them the emotion then withdraws from the object in order to be absorbed into itself. Not much reflection is needed to understand that, on the contrary, the emotion returns to the object at every moment and it's fed there. For example, flight in a state of fear is described as if the object were not, before anything else, a flight *from* a certain object, as if the object fled did not remain present in the flight itself, as its theme, its reason for being, *that from which one flees*. And how can one talk about anger, in which one strikes, injures, and threatens, without mentioning the person who represents the objective unity of these insults, threats, and blows? In short, the affected subject and the affec-

tive object are bound in an indissoluble synthesis. Emotion is a certain way of apprehending the world.

The reasoning in Sartre's statement, which I think is impeccable, leads me to regard appraisal not only as the cause of an emotion but also as an integral feature of the emotional response itself. As Sartre argues, if the agent that one fears or that one regards as the source of a personal offense ceases to be seen as harmful or threatening, the emotion simply dissipates; if this appraisal is rejected, the emotion on which it depends no longer exists.

Although this position presents some difficulties having to do with separating cause from effect in the traditional Aristotelian sense, I believe it is the only reasonable position that can be taken if, indeed, one says as I do that emotion is always a response to meaning. Moreover, if we adopt the reasoning of reciprocal determinism (Bandura, 1978) and recognize that in nature causes overlap with effects and are separable only in a temporal sense or for convenience of analysis, we should not be troubled by including the causal cognitive activity within the emotional reaction itself. This doesn't mean, however, that emotion is equivalent to cognition, because other processes such as motivation, impulses to act, and physiological changes are also involved (see Chapter 5 for a more detailed analysis of this).

While I am on the subject of the emphasis on cognition and meaning, an age-old bit of wisdom is that humans are meaning-generating creatures who require a sense of relatedness to other humans and to the world. This is related to but not the same as the more limited meaning analysis implied by the concept of appraisal. I bring it up now to point out how continuous and important in human existence is the search for meaning, both broadly as a definition of our lives and narrowly as an evaluation of what is happening in a particular life encounter for personal well-being.

In any case, some people ask questions or brood whereas others do not, and conscious questioning or brooding may occur in some periods of a person's life and not others; however, personal meaning is important for everyone. The need to achieve meaning in life, despite the vagueness of the concept, is probably one of the factors motivating interest in history, archeology, and anthropology. Given the propensity of all human cultures to generate beliefs about the meaning of existence and about God or gods, meaninglessness is probably a fundamental source of threat and existential anxiety.

This theme is promulgated by many writers including Frankl (1959), whose approach to psychopathology draws heavily on it. It may well be useful to think of specific harms and threats as organized around broad existential themes even if these themes are not consciously acknowledged. To push the point a bit further, fear of psychological disorganization and death has long been regarded as the major ideological and emotional force in human existence. Becker (1973) interpreted all of the creative works and institutions of human life as a way of coping with the inevitability of death—that is, as an implicit denial of death. Our value systems and mythologies, our notions of an afterlife, and our search for order as opposed to chaos can be understood as reassurances against the existential threat of chaos, nothingness, or meaninglessness (see also Florian & Snowden, 1989, for an analysis and data on the values of different ethnic groups and their members' interpretation of death).

In his autobiography, *Timebends,* Arthur Miller writes of a sear~
that is suffused with denial, or as it might better be termed, illusior
sion of denial and illusion (Lazarus, 1983), I pointed out that a prim
erature and drama throughout the ages is that life is intolerable withou~
the differences between denial and illusion are often subtle and difficult to vi~w.
simply in terms of psychopathology. People are constantly struggling to perpetuate
their diverse myths about life, other people, and their society. Miller writes as follows
(p. 542) about the theme of his play *The Price,* which is about two brothers who
come together after a long estrangement to divide the estate of their deceased father:

> Despite my wishes I could not tamper with something the play and life seemed to be
> telling me: that we were doomed to perpetuate our illusions because truth was too
> costly to face. At the end of the play Gregory Solomon, the eighty-nine-year-old used
> furniture dealer, is left with the family's possessions, which he has purchased from
> the brothers; he finds an old laughing record and, listening to it, starts laughing
> uncontrollably, nostalgically, brutally, having come closest to acceptance rather than
> denial of the deforming betrayals of time.

Appraisal

My early writings about appraisal were centered on psychological stress rather than
emotion. In having to tailor the concept of appraisal to emotion, considerable refine-
ment of the concept was necessary, especially to accommodate the many different
individual emotions and the cognitive evaluations needed to distinguish among
them. I will examine the transition to emotion theory shortly to highlight what
makes the appraisal process in the emotions so different from that in psychological
stress, in which it must distinguish among only three states: harm or loss, threat, and
challenge, or in some approaches, merely high or low activation.

Appraisal and Psychological Stress

My colleagues and I have written about two basic kinds of appraisal — primary and
secondary — to differentiate between discrete and complementary sources of knowledge on which evaluation of the personal significance of an encounter rests (see, for
example, Lazarus, 1966, 1981a; Lazarus & Folkman, 1984, 1987; Lazarus &
Launier, 1978).

Primary appraisal concerns whether something of relevance to the person's
well-being has occurred. Only if a person has a personal stake in an encounter — say,
a short- or long-term goal such as social or self-esteem or the well-being of a loved
one — will there be a stressful response to what is happening. To anticipate recent
changes in this concept, primary appraisal has now been expanded to include three
components: *goal relevance, goal congruence or incongruence,* and *type of ego-
involvement.* I have more to say about these components later.

Secondary appraisal concerns coping options — that is, whether any given action
might prevent harm, ameliorate it, or produce additional harm or benefit. The funda-

.nental issue being evaluated is: "What, if anything, can I do in this encounter, and how will what I do and what is going to happen affect my well-being?" (see Janis & Mann, 1977, for a parallel analysis). To distinguish among the individual emotions, three secondary appraisal components are needed — namely, *blame or credit, coping potential,* and *future expectations.* I return to these later.

Because all encounters with the environment are continually changing and generating feedback about the psychological situation, primary and secondary appraisal are also continually changing, which is why emotions are always in flux. Feedback about the environment, or from one's own actions and reactions, constitutes new information to be evaluated. I refer to the process of further evaluation as *reappraisal* (Lazarus, 1966). It is distinguished from appraisal only by coming later, and so it is basically no different from other kinds of appraisal except for its history and the self-generated feature of cognitive- or emotion-focused coping, which, like defenses, are appraisals that are constructed by the mind to regulate emotional distress or protect one's ego-identity (see Chapter 3). The term *reappraisal* also implies the continuous nature of a person's evaluations of transactions with the environment and emphasizes their responsiveness to feedback.

The Adaptational Function of Appraisal. Classical thought about perception and modern approaches to cognition define cognitive science as having to do primarily with how an environmental display gets attended to, registered, encoded, transformed, stored, and retrieved, leading to decision making. The framework is largely *veridical* in that interest centers on the match between knowledge, action, and the objective world; *normative* in that the focus is on how people in general rather than individually deal with the environment; and *cold* rather than hot in that there is little interest in emotions, personal beliefs, motives, and the sociocultural factors influencing cognitive activity (see, for example, Norman, 1980, for a cognitivist's complaint about this). Cognitive psychology (with certain exceptions such as Frese & Sabini, 1985; Kahneman, Slovic, & Tversky, 1982; and Neisser, 1967) has never managed to assimilate an alternative perspective, once referred to as the "New Look" movement of the 1940s and 1950s, which emphasized *nonveridicality* and implied that cognitive activity could signify or result in psychopathology, *selectivity,* i.e., individual differences in what a person attends to and the transformation of environmental information by factors such as motivation, selective attention, and ego-defense, which make cognitions *hot.*

A problem that must be resolved is to what extent and in what respects any given appraisal depends on *environmental realities* or *personality factors.* If one emphasizes selectivity and adopts a purely phenomenological stance that meaning is in the eye of the beholder, then the role of the objective environment is of little interest. If one makes the alternative assumption of veridicality, then meaning lies entirely in the environmental configuration and the person must extract it to grapple successfully with life and world. Gergen's (1985) exogenic and endogenic perspectives, which I discussed in Chapter 1, fit here nicely, as does a related analysis by Tomkins (1965) of ideological polarities in science, literature, and art.

These positions are extreme, and the truth lies somewhere in between. We could not have been successful as a species, or as individuals, if our knowledge and appraisals were often not in good fit with the environmental realities; yet to a considerable extent, we must also realize our individual, societal, and species agendas. One might add that the capacity to put a favorable light on our prospects despite gloomy realities, to sustain illusions, to hope against hope, to maintain positive morale, and to keep trying are survival-related processes that help us mobilize and sustain adaptive efforts (see Andrews's 1989a discussion of the romantic, ironic, tragic, and comic visions of reality; also Breznitz, 1983; Goleman, 1985; Lazarus, Kanner, & Folkman, 1980; and Taylor, 1989; Taylor & Brown, 1988, on positive illusions and self-deceptions).

To integrate the two seemingly contradictory perspectives requires ultimately that we spell out the lawful connections among subjective appraisals, the objective environment, and personal agendas. I think the best generalization to be made about this is that healthy people normally, and more or less successfully, perceive and understand their worlds with remarkable objectivity—they are good at reality test- ing—yet also manage at the same time to minimize distress and maximize a positive outlook on life. Paterson and Neufeld (1987) have drawn upon the reality-testing aspect of this thesis in emphasizing three objective situational determinants of threat appraisal: the severity or clear danger of an event, its imminence, and the probability of occurrence. Their view that the objective world is often stressful would not make sense unless there were, on the average, considerable correspondence between the environmental conditions and appraisals of personal significance. (For a searching examination of this issue in the context of the match between social perception and social reality, see Jussim, 1991).

Nevertheless, because the environment is enormously complex and not every- thing can be attended to, and because it is often ambiguous, we attend to and process it selectively in ways that are, in a sense, programmed by goal hierarchies and what we believe about ourselves and the world. There are also many realities, not a single one, and we must not fall into the habit of thinking of personality factors as neces- sarily distorting reality. Instead, out of several possibilities, personality factors influ- ence which realities are relevant; thus, an apple is a food, but it can also be a weapon if you throw it hard enough, or it can be a toy if you are a juggler.

Arthur Miller illustrates this selectivity in *Timebends* (p. 252):

> The Arab calls the Crusaders "accursed"—as did the Jews of medieval Europe, who were so frequently massacred by them on their way to redeem Jerusalem, the City of God—while the Christian image of the Crusader is all nobility, the epitome of the ideal man. Which view is properly history?

The task of evaluating what is happening with respect to the implications for personal well-being is a continuing struggle to balance both sets of forces—the environmental realities, and personal interests. The primary function of appraisal is to *integrate* the two as effectively as possible without giving short shrift to either. Just as in script-based semantic theories of humor (e.g., Raskin, 1985), personal goals and beliefs constitute one script and the environmental stimulus configuration another; appraisal, like the punch line of a joke, reconciles them. In psychopatholo- gy, one set of characteristics, either the environmental realities or personal agendas, dominates at the expense of the other. In health, they are maintained in reasonable balance.

In this connection, Alloy, Albright, Abramson, and Dykman (1990) offer the stunning proposition, and review some of the evidence for it, that people who are depressed are more realistic than those who function well and with optimism (see also Lewinsohn, Mischel, Chaplin, & Barton, 1980). On this, Alloy et al. (1990, p. 82) write:

> Depressed individuals may be suffering from the absence or breakdown of normal, optimistic biases and distortions. Maladaptive features of depression such as low self-esteem, negative affect, decreased persistence, poor coping with stress, and hopelessness may be consequences, in part, of the absence of healthy personal illusions. There is, in fact, one clinician who long ago appreciated this possibility. To quote from Sigmund Freud's (1917/1957) *Mourning and Melancholia:* "When in his [the depressive's] heightened self-criticism he describes himself as petty, egoistic, dishonest, lacking in independence, one whose sole aim has been to hide the weakness of his own nature, it may be, so far as we know, that he has come pretty near to understanding himself; we only wonder why a man has to be ill before he can be accessible to a truth of this kind."

A related explanation of individual differences in the evaluation of common experiences comes from the concept of *personal control*—that is, the control one has over what is happening in an encounter. There is some rather solid evidence that people prefer to have control over events and decisions in their lives (see Averill, 1973; Miller, 1980; Rodin, 1980; Weinberg & Levine, 1980; also Parkes, 1989, for an analysis of research on control in an occupational context; Bryant, 1989, for a four-factor model of perceived control; and Mirowsky & Ross, 1990, for a comparison of control and defense). It has been widely assumed that control is tantamount to health and lack of control is pathogenic or an inevitable source of distress.

However, the assumption that feeling responsible for the conditions of our lives is beneficial to health and morale has also been challenged in interesting ways. Some research suggests that personal responsibility for undesirable conditions may be harmful and that there can be excessive belief in personal control based either on delusion or guilt—in other words, self-defensive forms of coping. The confusion, Mirowsky and Ross (1990) argue, stems from the failure to recognize that much of the research on this issue focuses on a sense of personal responsibility for or control over only bad outcomes, leaving out responsibility for good ones. With a strong data set, their research suggests that lack of control over both good and bad outcomes is associated with depression. They write (1990, p. 81):

> According to control theory, fatalists are more depressed than instrumentalists. This view is supported. Defense theory holds that self-blamers are more depressed than self-defenders. This view is not supported. We expected that the basic hypotheses of both control and defense theories would be supported, but they were not. Self-defenders, self-blamers, and fatalists do not differ significantly in their average depression. In our results, absence of a sense of control over good outcomes, over bad outcomes, or over both is associated with depression.

Folkman (1984) has made a subtle analysis of the appraisal-related concept of controllability, pointing out that although being in control is often evaluated as favorable, there are many exceptions. If, for example, in the absence of solid evidence about the value of different forms of surgery for breast cancer, we can choose to have a radical mastectomy, a modified radical, or a lumpectomy, we are also in the unenviable position of having to take the blame, which is more than mere causal responsibility, for the negative consequences of that decision (see Chapter 6). Many persons would rather have someone else decide, because for them control is a double-edged sword. A literary variant of this theme may be found in a story by Leschak about a violent summer storm. Leschak (1989, p.76) writes:

> It required a conscious, sweaty effort to focus my thoughts. I forced myself to be fatalistic. Either a tree would hit us or it wouldn't. That simple axiom was comforting. It acknowledged that the situation was out of our hands. If there was an aspen with our names on it, well, *c'est la vie.*
>
> I temporarily relinquished any command over my life and fate. I had no control; therefore, I had no responsibility. With no responsibility I had no problem. I couldn't calm the wind or deflect a falling tree; there was nothing I could do. Since the matter was out of my hands, perhaps it was in someone else's. This mind-set is the essence of supplicatory prayer. All that remained was to exercise my faith—to believe that we wouldn't get nailed, to be utterly convinced that it couldn't happen to us.

Concerning deviations of appraisals from the environmental realities, it is at present unclear how well we can measure the objective environment to which individuals respond (see, for example, Lazarus, 1990b). The only method that has been devised for describing the objective environment is based on a consensus of people who live in this environment, and Repetti (1987) has provided the useful service of producing a scale measuring the social environment at work, which is evaluated consensually and which can be used to compare an individual's picture of that environment with that of the consensus.

Her scale consists of four factors: a *global* one with items expressing such ideas as "people seem to take pride in the organization," "few people ever volunteer," "supervisors tend to talk down to employees"; an *intimacy* factor illustrated by the item "people take an interest in each other"; a *support* factor illustrated by the item "How much does your immediate supervisor/or other people at work go out of his/her/their way to do things to make your work life easier?"; and a *job satisfaction* factor illustrated by the items "work is really challenging" and "the work is usually very interesting."

Although this is a sound and interesting approach, it is not certain that the issues defining the social environment for people in general are germane to the central concerns of any given individual in whom we might be interested. Nevertheless, it is possible to use such a scale to compare an individual's perceptions and appraisals with those of a normative consensus. Repetti's findings suggest, actually, that the objective quality of the social environment is related to the mental health of employees but an individual's evaluations—that is, the subjective appraisal measure—are an even stronger correlate of depression and anxiety than the consensual (objective) perception. I will present Repetti's scale in Chapter 11 in my discussion of assessment.

Sometimes appraisal is realistic, and sometimes it is not. A factor in this might be the damaging effects of emotion. There is abundant evidence that emotions can disrupt thought and lead to erroneous conclusions (see Chapter 10). Another factor, however, is that we think or act in a seemingly irrational way simply because of erroneous belief premises that underlie otherwise perfectly sound reasoning. For example, Henle (1962, 1971) found that, when errors of syllogistic reasoning were made by her students, they were based on unstated value and belief premises that made these "errors" understandable and logical. An erroneous appraisal of "objective" conditions may therefore be the result of commitments and beliefs, sometimes unstated or unrecognized, without the presence of any emotional disruption of the reasoning process.

In any case, appraisal is the process most proximal to a person's emotional state, because it reflects what the person understands and cares about. It will, therefore, give a more intimate and dependable picture of the emotional life than distal antecedents such as personality traits and characterizations of the objective environment. Appraisal becomes even more important as a construct when, through self-deceptions or on the basis of different beliefs and patterns of commitment, there is an incongruity between how the person construes things and the actual conditions. Though normatively people are more often accurate than inaccurate in their judgments, no theory of emotion can be complete without reference to the cognitive activity that mediates between encounters and emotional reactions and integrates the two sets of variables, the environment and the person.

Appraisal as Process and as Style. An evaluation of the significance of what is happening for well-being is not static; once achieved an appraisal does not necessarily remain fixed. Rather, it should be regarded as a tentative and changeable cognitive construction, which emerges and reemerges out of ongoing transactions on the basis of conditions in the environment and within the person, and it is more or less subject to modification as conditions and persons change. This is what it means to speak of appraisal *as a process,* and to some extent it even applies to relatively stable beliefs and motives. In our daily lives we are constantly engaged in a struggle to make sense of what is happening to us, to seek an understanding that preserves the psychological structures we have forged over the course of our lives, and to revise our goal commitments and beliefs when they are no longer serviceable. When such change involves expansion of one's possibilities and areas of engagement, it is sometimes referred to as personal growth.

Although appraisal should be studied as a process, people also develop what might be called relatively stable *appraisal styles* — that is, dispositions to appraise ongoing relationships with the environment consistently in one way or another, especially under conditions of ambiguity, for example, by typically putting events in either a positive or negative light (see Smith, Novacek, Lazarus, & Pope, unpublished). Ancient wisdom has it and there is abundant modern evidence to favor the idea that some people are optimists and others pessimists (cf. Antonovsky, 1979, 1987; Scheier & Carver, 1987; Scheier, Matthews, Owens, Magovern, Lefebvre, Abbot, & Carver, 1989; and Scheier, Weintraub, & Carver, 1986). Consistent styles of appraisal have been little investigated. They reflect relatively stable patterns of commitment and belief in an individual, as well as individualized patterns of cognitive coping with threat. I will discuss assessment strategies for a cognitive-motivational-relational theory in Chapter 11 and will provide some examples of how appraisal style may be measured.

Stable styles of relating to the world reflect one side of a person's "vision of reality," to refer again to Andrews (1989) and his predecessors, and another style can emerge as a result of deliberate effort, conversion experiences, trauma, or psychotherapy, just as Jung (1933) postulated that the subordinated side of the personality would emerge and become dominant later in life. Quoting from a newspaper story, Andrews (1989, p. 814) illustrates the multiple levels of the psychological makeup of persons with a case history of Walter Mondale, who chose a deliberate style reversal in his 1984 presidential campaign:

> This reversal of form was the product of hours of intense rehearsal, self-criticism, and coaching. . . . (Mondale's advisers understandably made a point of giving full credit to the candidate.) "It was Walter Mondale. He did it. . . . " And some aides tried to play down the importance of the planning. All the advice given to him was, "Be yourself. . . . " But the key question Mondale had to answer before he walked on stage was which "self" he should be. On the one hand, there was Fighting Fritz . . . , so strident on the stump that his voice whined while his arms waved and his neck muscles bulged. Then there was Friendly Fritz . . . , a man of wry wit, crisp speech, and relaxed charm.
>
> The quotation begins with a description of conscious, even laborious role-rehearsal. Then, perhaps fearing that this will seem manipulative, Mondale's aides offer us simultaneous and contradictory notions of "the self": The candidate is portrayed as playing a part, and yet also as "being himself." As if this were not enough, we are then told that "he (Mondale) did it!" Who is this "he"? Not the role player, nor the self he is advised to be, but still another meta-self — not unlike the "storyteller" — who has somehow orchestrated the entire process of role choice. Finally, the reporter underlines the existential irony of attempting to simply "be" one's real self while simultaneously experiencing a choice of potential selves.
>
> When Mondale elected to be a hostile-dominant warrior or a friendly dominant charmer, he was creating a vision of reality as well. Regardless of which identity he adopted, it was the *chooser of identities* (the storyteller) that was constant. Thus, at the level of self as content, we can identify with any or all of the . . . personality styles or world views, but at the level of self as process, we can come to see ourselves as more the storyteller than we are the characteristics in the scripts we write. When we make this shift of perspective, we enhance our personal freedom as well.

The concept of appraisal styles is a variant of the distinction made in Chapter 2 between emotion states and traits. When there is instability in the way a person appraises transactions with the environment over time or across occasions, we speak of appraisal as a state (or process) in that it changes with the circumstances; however, when there is stability, we speak of appraisal as a trait or style. Because there is usually some instability and some stability, too, both concepts reflect different perspectives on the same phenomenon, one focused on variation or change, the other on stability.

Situational versus Generalized Appraisal. Appraisal is influenced by and directed at *specific* encounters or settings; Bandura's (1977a, 1982) concept of self-efficacy
fits in well here. On the other hand, appraisal may consist of *generalized* patterns
(cognitive and motivational traits) that transcend a specific encounter but that may
be regarded by a person as relevant to it. To explain and predict the emotion process, we require an examination of both generalized cognitive dispositions and situational cognitive activity. And to be clear about how this works, we must recognize
that generalized outlooks, such as trust or distrust, confidence in one's competence
or the lack of it, and the like, affect acute emotions by their influence on situational
knowledge and appraisals.

The distinction between cognitive activity that is limited to a particular context
and that which is generalized and applies over many encounters is a very important
one. The latter consists of stable knowledge and beliefs that a person has acquired
over a lifetime. These cognitive traits or styles of thinking transcend the specifics of
what is happening in a transaction (cf. Peterson, Seligman, & Vaillant, 1988), influence situational knowledge and appraisal, and affect the kind and degree of emotion
experienced.

A pioneering effort to study generalized beliefs about the control one can exert
over situations was made by Rotter (1966, 1975). His well-known scale, derived
from social learning theory, measured whether a person places the locus of control
internally or externally (in the environment), and it stimulated much research on
control as a psychological variable. It also influenced the creation of a host of other
personality measures—of self-esteem (Rosenberg, 1965), mastery (Pearlin &
Schooler, 1978), hardiness (Kobasa, 1979), optimism (Schier & Carver, 1987),
sense of coherence (Antonovsky, 1979, 1987), constructive thinking (Epstein &
Meier, 1989), depressive attributional style (Peterson, Semmel, von Baeyer,
Abramson, Metalsky, & Seligman, 1982), and appraisal style (Smith et al., unpublished).

A schema, belief system, or script consists of generalized knowledge about a
concept or an experience. It is, in Epstein's (1980) terms, a personal theory guiding
what we notice and remember and how we interpret new experiences. Janoff-
Bulman and Timko (1987) have also used this type of formulation to analyze the
coping process of denial, and Andrews (1989a) has reviewed individual differences
according to four broad visions of reality or world outlooks—the romantic, ironic,
tragic, and comic—an evaluation of which, he suggests, could facilitate our understanding of personality, subjective experience, and the best therapeutic approach for
each kind of psychopathology (cf. Brickman, Rabinowitz, Karuza, Coates, Cohen,
& Kidder, 1982; Messer & Winokur, 1980, 1984; and Schafer, 1976).

My general point is that, if a person believes that other people cannot be trusted,
or that one must always perform perfectly in every situation to be worthy of respect,
the emotion process will differ from that of another person who does not share these
beliefs. A similar premise that counterproductive beliefs underlie depression and
anxiety is found in Ellis's and Beck's therapeutic writings and procedures, which I
have already mentioned. Therapy is designed to change these beliefs to overcome
dysfunctional and distressing emotional states (see Chapter 11).

Early Research on Appraisal. Extensive research performed in the 1960s in my Berkeley laboratory (see Lazarus, 1968a; Lazarus, Averill, & Opton, 1970) provided evidence that the way persons construe what is portrayed in a stressful motion picture film influences their psychophysiological reactions while watching. One of the methods used in this research was to construct sound tracks, or orientation passages played before the film was shown, which were designed to encourage either denial of the threatening features of what was being depicted or intellectualized detachment from it. In contrast with neutral control and threat-enhancing passages, denial and intellectualization sharply lowered subjective ratings of distress as well as heart rate and skin conductance, which were continuously recorded during the film.[1]

The ideas for these passages had originally come from ego-defense theory, but they were also concretely based on interviews with the participating subjects who had viewed the stressful films without sound tracks or orientation passages. Many of them seemed to make extensive use of denying and intellectualizing modes of cognitive coping with the threatening film content. They would say, for example, that it didn't bother them (denial) or that the film was interesting and informative (intellectualized detachment), even when they were showing marked physiological evidence of stress. In one study, participants were also invited to lower the level of involvement in the stressful film or to increase it; interviews were used to identify how this was accomplished (Koriat, Melkman, Averill, & Lazarus, 1972). A common way to produce greater involvement was to identify subjectively with the victims of the distressing procedure portrayed in the film, whereas distancing from the victims, for example, by dehumanizing them had the opposite effect. Table 4.1 shows the extent to which these strategies were employed in both conditions.

As this research progressed, our theoretical emphasis gradually moved from ego defense to the broader concept of cognitive appraisal and reappraisal by means of which people constantly evaluated the realities of their experience and also protected themselves from threat. The reason for our change in emphasis was that we realized that not all such evaluation is ego-defensive, and appraisal therefore seemed to be a more basic process and defense one form of it.

The capacity of soundtracks and orienting statements to lower stress levels, both in self-report and in autonomic nervous system reactions, is illustrated in a study I undertook with Alfert (1964) in which subjects viewed a film showing a distressing surgical procedure called *subincision.* Without anesthesia and with a stone knife, older males cut deeply into the penis and scrotum of adolescents as part of a tribal "rite of passage." The film shows a series of these procedures, the insertion of maggots into the wound, and other ceremonial activities.

The denial passage advised the viewer before the film was shown that this procedure was not significantly threatening, painful, or dangerous, and that the adolescents looked forward to it all as an important step to adulthood. Figure 4.1 compares the skin conductance curves, averaged for the group of subjects who viewed the 17-minute film, in a control condition in which there was no orientation passage, a denial orientation passage played before the film was viewed, and a denial commentary passage that was played during the film viewing. It is clear that these denial statements, which presumably changed appraisals of what was happening by provid-

TABLE 4.1. Percentage of Subjects Who Used a Particular Strategy for Involvement and Detachment, and the Percentage Who Listed That Strategy as Their First or Principal Choice

	Involvement Group		Detachment Group	
	% Used	% 1st Choice	% Used	% 1st Choice
Involvement strategy				
1. I tried to relate the scenes to a similar experience I had or was witness to.	42.5	20.5	28.9	2.6
2. I tried to imagine that it is happening to me.	72.7	49.0	60.5	42.1
3. I tried to imagine that it is happening to somebody I know.	27.5	5.5	36.8	13.2
4. I tried to think about and exaggerate the consequences of the accident.	50.0	11.5	34.2	11.8
5. Something else. Specify_____	37.5	13.5	31.6	13.6
Detachment strategy				
1. I constantly tried to remind myself that it was a film rather than a real occurrence.	57.5	39.0	55.3	28.9
2. I watched the film concentrating on the technical aspects involved in its production.	50.0	18.5	55.3	26.3
3. I concentrated on the details involved in the cause of the accidents and possible ways of their prevention.	10.0	0.0	18.4	5.3
4. I told myself that the workers were actually responsible for what happened.	20.0	10.0	7.9	0.0
5. I tried to adopt a humorous attitude towards what happened.	17.5	2.5	34.2	7.9
6. I told myself that such accidents are inevitable.	0.0	0.0	5.3	0.0
7. Something else. Specify_____	57.5	30.0	28.9	13.2

(*Source*: A. Koriat, R. Melkman, J. R. Averill, and R. S. Lazarus, "The self-control of emotional reactions to a stressful film." *Journal of Personality, 40.* Durham, NC: Duke University Press. Copyright © 1972 by Duke University Press. Reprinted by permission.)

ing interpretations of this strange, esoteric, and disturbing ritual, markedly reduced the stress of watching the film.

Our evidence had clearly pointed to the power of cognitive processes to shape an emotional reaction, just as in an earlier decade in which different interests prevailed, the evidence pointed to the power of emotion to disrupt cognitive processes (see Erdelyi, 1974; and Lazarus, 1966). In short, the direction of effect goes both ways, with emotion influencing cognition and cognition influencing emotion (Lazarus, 1982, 1984a, 1991a; Lazarus, Coyne, & Folkman, 1982).

This research was followed by extensive experimental studies in other laboratories in which appraisal was manipulated in situations involving diverse stresses, for example, aggression anxiety (Geen, Stonner, & Kelley, 1974), electric shock

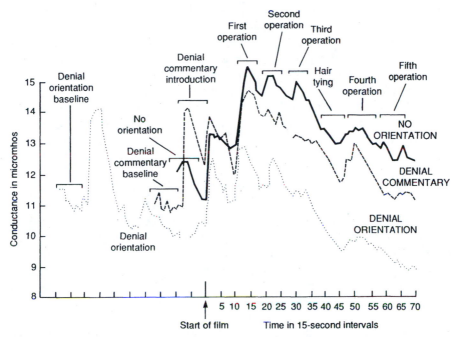

FIGURE 4.1. Skin conductance curves for the denial orientation, denial commentary, and no prior treatment conditions. (*Source:* R. S. Lazarus and E. Alfert, "The short-circuiting of threat." *Journal of Abnormal and Social Psychology, 69.* Washington, DC: American Psychological Association. Copyright © 1969 by the American Psychological Association. Reprinted by permission.)

(Bloom, Houston, Holmes, & Burish, 1977; Holmes & Houston, 1974), and failure threat (Bennett & Holmes, 1975). Neufeld (1975, 1976; Dobson & Neufeld, 1979) performed a series of studies in which signal detection methods were employed to distinguish between stress that was experienced and stress that was only claimed. Still later research by Krantz (1983) focused on secondary appraisal (of coping possibilities) in a college examination. A series of studies by Breznitz (1984), both naturalistic and experimental, also demonstrated the power of appraisals generated by false alarms about disaster to influence emotional distress and coping, and revealed some of the conditions influencing these appraisals.

The Transition of the Appraisal Concept from Stress to the Emotions

Though early research provided numerous examples of the influence of appraisal on the presence and intensity of the stress reaction, it did not address the *quality* or *content* of the resulting emotion — for example, anger, fear, guilt, or pride. Nevertheless, the further inference that appraisal would shape the quality of the emotion just as it did the intensity of the stress reaction was appropriate, though it required empirical confirmation.

In recent years, the concept of appraisal has undergone considerable transformation in the direction of much greater detail. The appraisal decisions that must be made by a person for a particular emotion to occur are now being identified. I call these *appraisal components*, and will discuss them shortly. Research on cognitive factors in emotion has been burgeoning and will be cited in the subsection that follows. In Chapter 10, I shall cite some recent approaches to the measurment of appraisal. About research on appraisal and the emotions, Frijda, Kuipers, and ter Schure (1989, p. 212) have concluded that it "has produced sizable support for this approach by demonstrating strong relations between emotions and cognitive appraisal structures. . . . The cognitive approach to emotions therefore appears to be well established."

Knowledge versus Appraisal. Two different kinds of cognitive activity were mentioned earlier — namely, knowledge and appraisal. Although both are important in the emotion process, their respective roles are quite different (Lazarus & Smith, 1988).

Knowledge is required to act appropriately when we are harmed or threatened, or when conditions are beneficial. If because of the failure of knowledge, harm and benefit are not recognized as such, and if the possibilities and consequences of action are overlooked, the person is potentially in trouble. As I am using the term, knowledge refers to our understanding of the way things are and work in general as well as in a specific context. General knowledge consists of established ideas and beliefs about ourselves and the world (see Epstein, 1983; Gilbert, 1991; Ross, 1977), whereas contextual or situational knowledge consists of the way we understand what is going on in any particular encounter. The two are interdependent, because what we know about a particular encounter, and how we act and react to it, is derived partly from what is presented to us and partly from general knowledge, which is drawn upon through various attributional and inferential strategies (Heider, 1958; Nisbett & Ross, 1980). In turn, what we know in general comes from what we learn from particular encounters.

Knowledge can sometimes be verbalized, but it can also be tacit (cf. Polanyi, 1966) and even unconscious, either in the sense of being unnoticed or unnoticeable, or in the more controversial Freudian sense of being kept out of awareness through ego-defenses. Knowledge can be elemental, concrete, and limited in scope, or complex, abstract, and broad; it can also be accurate or inaccurate. I say more about this later in my discussions of how meaning is achieved and unconscious appraisals may come about.

The second type of cognitive activity, *appraisal*, consists of a continuing evaluation of the significance of what is happening for one's personal well-being. Without personal significance, knowledge is cold, or nonemotional. When knowledge touches on one's personal well-being, however, it is hot, or emotional (Abelson, 1963; Folkman, Schaefer, & Lazarus, 1979). The character of personal and self-involving meaning is nicely expressed by Kreitler and Kreitler (1976, pp. 77–78):

> Meaning generation is regulated by two focal questions: "What does it mean?" and "What does it mean to me and for me?," "In what way does it affect me?," "Am I concerned in any way?," "Should I be concerned?," "Am I involved personally?," "Should I be involved?," "Is any action required on my part?," "Am I to act or not?"

"In which sense(s) does it or may it affect (or concern) my goals, my norms, my beliefs about myself, and my beliefs about the environment or any of its aspects?" Evidently, the formulation "What does it mean to me or for me?" is merely a label summarizing these different variants of the question.

This conceptualization of personal meaning is closely related to what I mean by appraisal. The most important theoretical and research issues deriving from an analysis of meaning in any encounter concern the questions that a person must ask and answer — that is, the primary and secondary appraisals for each individual emotion. (See Chapters 6 and 7 for the application of these concepts to individual emotions.)

Primary appraisal — which, as the reader will remember, addresses whether and how an encounter is relevant to a person's well-being — is similar to Kreitler and Kreitler's question about whether the situation affects the person. It is primary because it provides the emotional heat in an encounter; it is based on the personal relevance of what is happening, which in turn depends on goal commitments and transactional stakes in a particular environmental context. Some of the key issues are: Is there harm or threat or am I to be benefited? What kinds of harm or benefit are involved?

Secondary appraisal, which is an evaluation of the person's options and resources for coping with the situation and future prospects, is similar to Kreitler and Kreitler's question about whether action is required, and if so, what kind. Because secondary appraisal is necessary to define the full adaptational significance of the encounter, it often has a crucial influence on which individual emotion is experienced. Some of the key issues are: Are my coping resources adequate to manage things? How will it work out? Am I helpless? Who or what, if anything, is to blame or to be credited for the things that have happened or will happen to me? What can I do, or do I need to do, and what are the consequences of doing it? And so on.

Of the many issues about the role of cognition in emotion, the one most widely overlooked and misunderstood is the difference between knowledge on the one hand and appraisal on the other, as expressed in Kreitler and Kreitler's analysis and in what I have just said. Writers who draw on the appraisal concept commonly fail to recognize that appraisal is not about what people know or believe about emotion in the abstract, or about how things work in the living world — that is, the causal attributions they make — but is about how one evaluates the *personal significance* of what they know or believe.

Although knowledge is the cold cognitive stuff of which personal meaning is made (Lazarus & Smith, 1988), it is not an appraisal with its personal heat until the implications for personal well-being have been drawn. As such, mere knowledge does not result directly in emotion. Another process (appraisal) is required, which involves an evaluation of whether and how what is happening is harmful or beneficial, and if so, in what way. Kreitler and Kreitler (1976, pp. 16–17; see also Bar-Hillel, 1955; and G. Miller, 1953) illustrate that personal meaning cannot be reduced to knowledge,

as is well known to every dinner guest who is uncertain about the dessert, expecting either his beloved strawberry shortcake or his adored peach Melba. Normally, fear and anxiety do not stem from the mere existence of open alternatives but from what some of these alternatives imply. This is evident when one considers, for instance, the following pairs of alternatives: "either dessert will be served or burglars will interrupt the dinner party." Conversely, even very precise information does not nec-essarily — through its precision and adequacy — stabilize the system and reduce fear and anxiety, as is psychologically evident from the information, "Tomorrow you will be executed." This demonstrates that the core concepts of information theory, name-ly, the number of alternatives, their respective probabilities, and their eventual reduc-tion to bits of information, have far less psychological relevance than their actual meanings.

The failure to appreciate this point about personal meaning and appraisal has helped make Kahneman, Slovic, and Tversky's (1982) work on heuristics and biases in judgment and decision making so influential. It needs to be said again and again — in contradistinction to the normative and veridical emphasis in cognitive psychology — that thinking is not necessarily objective, as I noted earlier, especially when strong social and personal values are at stake.

The confusion about knowledge and appraisal comes home to roost in recent conceptualizations of cognitive activity in emotion and in empirical research on this. The confusion can be illustrated by examining some of the best-known cognitive dimensions, some of which are instances of knowledge rather than appraisal, some of which are components of the emotional reaction rather than antecedents of it, and some of which are appraisals, or at least come closer to being hot evaluations of the significance of what is happening for personal well-being.

The cognitive dimension of intrinsic pleasantness, proposed by Scherer (1984a, 1984b) and others (Frijda, 1986; Frijda, Kuipers, & ter Schure, 1989; Manstead & Tetlock, 1989; Smith & Ellsworth, 1985; Tesser, 1990), illustrates the three sources of confusion. This dimension is defined by Scherer (p. 307) as "the inherent pleas-antness or unpleasantness of a stimulus, and is not dependent on the relevance to goals of an organism at that particular moment." Precisely because this cognitive dimension is, in Scherer's own words, independent of the organism's goals, it should be regarded merely as *knowledge*, which has to be evaluated further with respect to its personal significance before it will result in an emotion.

A good example of knowledge needing an appraisal for emotion generation is painful muscle fatigue. As I have said, pleasure and pain are sensory states, not emotions; they lead to emotions only when their significance is evaluated, the quali-ty of the resulting emotion depending on the nature of the evaluation. Muscle pain will be appraised positively by an athlete who believes it is a desirable goal of con-ditioning or practice; however, it will be evaluated negatively when it occurs in a competitive race, because in this context the pain and fatigue indicates endangered prospects of victory. It is also negatively evaluated when the pain signifies physical impairment or illness to the person, how negatively depending on its judged serious-ness as a threat to life and functioning. In other words, the perception of pain can have positive or negative emotional significance depending on how it is appraised.

Strictly speaking, the qualitative properties of an emotional reaction such as pleasantness or unpleasantness are not dimensions of appraisal but should be consid-ered as descriptive components of the *response*. They are the result of appraisal, not the cause of the emotion. They do, of course, provide information for subsequent appraisal, as in the previous example of the ways an athlete might appraise muscle pain. But they are not, per se, appraisals. There is a long history of confusion about this point (e.g., Frijda & Philipszoon, 1963; Osgood, 1966; J. Russell, 1980; Schlosberg, 1952; as reviewed in Smith & Ellsworth, 1985).

In making a distinction between knowledge and appraisal, I do not wish to suggest that the two cognitive processes follow predefined sequences (as Scherer, 1984a, 1984b, does in his concept of "stimulus evaluation checks"). Knowledge and appraisal are best regarded as different aspects of one instantaneous process, temporally though not qualitatively difficult to separate. I have made the same point about primary and secondary appraisal, which are also functionally interdependent in the emotion process and may simultaneously occur, or take place in reverse order, rather than necessarily following a preordained temporal sequence (Lazarus, 1966).

The vast majority of the actual cognitive dimensions studied by emotion researchers deal with *causal attributions,* a form of knowledge rather than appraisal. The attribution dimensions explored by Weiner (1985) and others—for example, locus of causality, stability, controllability, intentionality, and globality, as well as analogous cognitive dimensions such as causal agency (Roseman, 1984; Scherer, 1984a, 1984b), locus of responsibility (Smith & Ellsworth, 1985), the probable motives of the causal agent (Scherer, 1984a), perceived fairness or legitimacy (Roseman, 1984; Scherer, 1984a, 1984b; Smith & Ellsworth, 1985), and locus of control (Manstead & Tetlock, 1989; Smith & Ellsworth, 1985)—are examples of knowledge not appraisal. The key point is that these attributions or forms of knowledge do not have the same personal implications for well-being for everyone under all circumstances, and it is these implications that have emotional relevance. To predict consequent emotions requires that implications for well-being in the case of any particular individual or group, in some given setting, be specified.

The earlier quote from Kreitler and Kreitler about *certainty* and *uncertainty* further illustrates the apposition to which I have been pointing. I invite the reader to reread their statement again on pages 145–146. Uncertainty is not an appraisal dimension, though it is often treated as such (cf. Smith & Ellsworth, 1985; Roseman, 1984), because it provides only a factual basis for personal meaning, not the meaning. This becomes clearer when we recognize that sometimes uncertainty adds to a threat, but at other times it is reassuring since it leaves room for hope. How uncertainty is appraised personally makes all the difference.

Another interesting example is *locus of causality,* which has obvious relevance for the kind of emotion generated but stops short of appraisal or personal meaning. Several studies (e.g., Ellsworth & Smith, 1988a; Weiner, Graham, & Chandler, 1982) show that when harm is attributed to someone other than oneself there is a greater probability of anger compared with guilt, the latter being linked to the attribution of causality to oneself. However, more than mere locus of causality is needed for anger or guilt—an evaluation of blame is necessary. Though they overlap with locus of causality, these concepts are by no means identical, as recently noted by McGraw (1987) and Shaver (1985). I deal with them shortly.

In adults, knowledge of or inferences about intentionality, legitimacy, and controllability combine with locus of causality in complex ways that affect whether *other-blame* or *self-blame,* therefore anger or guilt, will occur. For example, under conditions of harm, people will be held less accountable for their actions when these actions are interpreted as unintentional, just, or unavoidable (Pastore, 1952; Shaver, 1985; Weiner, Amirkhan, Folkes, & Verette, 1987). Although words can be used in many ways, blame most often implies resentment, which is much more an appraisal than a cold cognition about who is responsible for an outcome. A similar argument can be made about credit, which is crucial to the positive emotion of pride. Not to recognize this is to perpetuate the confusion between knowledge and appraisal.

For this reason, as will be seen below and in Chapters 6 and 7, I have drawn on the attribution of *accountability* — that is, responsibility for a harm or benefit as well as the attribution of whether a person could actually have controlled his or her actions. If *control* is attributed to oneself or another person for a harmful act, then accountability becomes blame; if control is attributed to oneself or another person for a beneficial act, then accountability becomes credit.[2] In other words, here is an example of how a hot appraisal of credit or blame draws on the cold knowledge of accountability and control (see also Tennen & Affleck, 1990, for an examination of the adaptational consequences of self versus other blame).

The conclusion that must be drawn from this analysis is that some cognitive dimensions are true appraisal processes because they directly refer to evaluations of personal well-being, while others refer to knowledge and require the additional step of an appraisal of their personal significance. Accountability and imputed control are examples of knowledge or attributions, while blaming and crediting exemplify true appraisals because their implications have to do directly with personal well-being; they are, therefore, hot cognitions, as it were. Another important implication is that knowledge is a *distal* variable in the emotion process compared with appraisal, which is *proximal* (cf. House, 1981; Jessor, 1981).

The links between knowledge and emotion are looser and more variable than those between appraisal and emotion. It should therefore be possible to demonstrate that the latter are more dependable and necessary compared with the former in predicting individual differences in emotional reactions. I note, for example, that Weiner (1985) acknowledges that attribution-emotion relationships (i.e., knowledge-emotion relationships) are not at all invariant, which implies that something else, such as appraisal, is needed (see also Weiner & Graham, 1989, for the use of attributional analyses for the emotions of pride, gratitude, guilt, anger, and compassion). Weiner (1985, p. 564) writes:

> A word of caution . . . is needed. Given a causal ascription, the linked emotion does not necessarily follow. . . . Hence, the position being espoused is that the [attribution] dimension-affect relations are not invariant, but are quite prevalent in our culture, and perhaps in many others as well.

Attribution theorists can to some extent explain and predict emotions probabilistically on the basis of shared or prevalent values about variables such as locus of causality, but what is still missing is a concern with cross-cultural variations and individual differences in the ways causal attributions are appraised. For example, the personal implication drawn from attributing failure on a school exam to lack of effort or ability appears to be quite different for Western and Asian students, with consequent differences in the emotional reaction. Western students appear to be more threatened by the personal implication of lack of ability, Asians by lack of effort.[3] Westerners even use lack of effort as an excuse for failure. Similarly, although many persons in the same society may share a common interpretation of lack of ability or effort, there are undoubtedly great individual differences within a society. In a pluralistic society such as ours, this is apt to be even more so. The meaning could also change in a given individual over the life course. To truly understand and predict the emotional reaction requires, in my view, that the theorist and researcher favor (proximal) appraisals over (distal) knowledge.

This may be illustrated by research of Baumgardner and Levy (1988), which examined individual differences in self-esteem in the ways ability and effort are interpreted with respect to personal significance. They found that when someone performed poorly on an examination, persons high in self-esteem viewed that person as greater in ability if effort had been expended than they did if effort had been withdrawn intentionally; persons low in self-esteem did not make this discrimination about effort and ability. This suggests, as I have been arguing, that individual differences in personality can lead to different interpretations of the personal significance of effort and ability, with resulting differences in appraisal and the emotions generated.

The same point has been expressed by Wollert (1987, p. 226) who writes, in connection with the understanding of clinical depression:

> I would argue that identifying the content of an attribution—for example, that failure is attributed to internal factors—is not sufficient to achieve a full understanding of depression. We must also know what this attribution means to the person who makes it. Does it signify the triggering of a critical or a protective self-evaluation? Does it mean that goal-directed efforts should be abandoned or, perhaps, even redoubled? If these associations were more clearly mapped out, the role of attributions in the development of depressive disorders would also probably be clarified.

Primary and Secondary Appraisal Components. I am now ready to examine the six appraisal components, which I will use in Chapters 6 and 7 to explore the appraisal pattern for each individual emotion. These have been chosen with two purposes in mind. First, I aim to integrate my earlier work on psychological stress theory with the present cognitive-motivational-relational theory of emotions (for example, one of the secondary appraisal components refers to conditions relevant to coping). Second, I have also drawn on concepts that either borrow or parallel the burgeoning work of others on appraisal and emotion.

There are three forms of primary appraisal and three of secondary appraisal, which overlap with some of the cognitive dimensions proposed by Frijda (1986), Roseman (1984), Scherer (1984a, 1984b), and Smith and Ellsworth (1985, 1987). These can be considered components of appraisal (Lazarus & Smith, 1988) rather than of knowledge. The three *primary appraisal* components are goal relevance, goal congruence or incongruence, and type of ego-involvement.

Goal relevance refers to the extent to which an encounter touches on personal goals—that is, whether or not there are issues in the encounter about which the person cares or in which there is a personal stake. If there is no goal relevance, there cannot be an emotion; if there is, one or another emotion will occur, depending on the outcome of the transaction.

Goal congruence or incongruence refers to the extent to which a transaction is consistent or inconsistent with what the person wants—that is, it either thwarts or facilitates personal goals. If it thwarts, I speak of goal incongruence; if it facilitates, I speak of goal congruence. Goal congruence leads to positive emotions; goal incongruence to negative ones. The specific emotion depends, however, on additional secondary appraisal components.

Type of ego-involvement refers to diverse aspects of ego-identity or personal commitments. I listed six in Chapter 3 including self- and social-esteem, moral values, ego-ideals, meanings and ideas, other persons and their well-being, and life goals, all collected within the rubric of ego-identity. As we will see in Chapters 6 and 7, ego-identity is probably involved in all or most emotions, but in different ways depending on the type of ego-involvement that is engaged by a transaction. To illustrate with several examples: In anger, one's self- or social-esteem is being assaulted; in anxiety, the threat is existential (to meaning structures in which one is invested); in guilt, it is violation of a moral value one is sworn to uphold; in shame, it is a failure to live up to one's ego-ideals; in sadness, it is loss of any or all of the six types of ego-identity; in happiness, it is an overall sense of security and well-being; and in pride—a kind of opposite of anger—it is an enhancement of the self- and social-esteem aspect of ego-identity; and so on.

The three components of *secondary appraisal* are *blame or credit* (which can be external—that is, directed at someone else—or internal—that is, directed at oneself), *coping potential,* and *future expectancy.*

Blame and *credit* derive from knowing who is accountable or responsible for frustration; if this knowledge is accompanied by the knowledge that the frustrating act was under the accountable person's control, credit or blame is assigned.

Coping potential refers to whether and how the person can manage the demands of the encounter or actualize personal commitments (cf. Folkman & Lazarus, 1980, 1985; Folkman, Lazarus, Dunkel-Schetter, DeLongis, & Gruen, 1986; Folkman, Lazarus, Gruen, & DeLongis, 1986; Folkman & Lazarus, 1990; Lazarus & Folkman, 1987). I emphasize that coping potential is not actual coping but only an evaluation by a person of the prospects for doing or thinking something that will, in turn, change or protect the person-enviroment relationship.

Future expectancy has to do with whether for any reason things are likely to change psychologically for the better or worse (i.e., becoming more or less goal congruent).

This is a good place to emphasize one more time that the concepts of blame and credit, and those of accountability and imputed control, illustrate the interplay of knowledge and appraisal in the generation of an emotion. Accountability and imputed control are components of knowledge; blame and credit are components of appraisal. Knowledge is often indeterminate with respect to personal implications and does not generate emotion without a further process of evaluation of its personal implications for one's well-being. (See also a complex and subtle attributional analysis of the effects of praise and blame by Meyer [in press], which shows that how it is taken by the recipient and observer depends on the context and cognitive maturity.) Knowing that we are accountable for something socially valued does not create pride unless we have also accepted credit for it. For example, we cannot readily take credit if what has happened was accidental. Similarly, others frustrating us does not result in blame unless we also believe that they were in control of their actions; if they couldn't have done otherwise under the circumstances, we resist blaming them and feeling anger toward them, though we may cast around for others to blame. We will see how this works specifically in anger, pride, and other emotions in Chapters 6 and 7.

Notice that the appraisal components are ordered in such a way that they proceed from very broad decisions—for example, whether or not there will be an emotion (goal relevance), whether the emotion will be positive or negative (goal congruence or incongruence)—gradually narrowing down to a precise discrimination between one emotion and another. As the options are narrowed, it becomes possible to say that only one emotion is possible in this context. This decision-tree pattern will be used in Chapters 6 and 7 in identifying the appraisal patterns for each individual emotion.

Since I argue that appraisals are not sequential (unlike Scherer's 1984a, 1984b, analysis), why do I use a decision-tree format, which invites the image of a person going stepwise down the list of appraisal components until the specific desiderata of a single emotion have been reached? The answer is that a decision-tree format helps the reader to understand the theoretical or explanatory logic of appraisal but does not describe how a person goes about appraising in the real world. It is a didactic device rather than a portrayal of how things work. There is, of course, no established answer about how appraisal decisions are actually made. However, I would like to make two points about this:

First, we do not have to go through the entire appraisal process every time a new adaptational encounter is faced. When we have previously learned the contingencies between certain conditions and their consequences for well-being, instantaneous appraisals will then be made in response to minimal cues, based on our knowledge of these contingencies. Much in life is a restatement of past struggles, which as a feature of our personal history is an integral part of the emotion process (see Chapter 8). In effect, many appraisal decisions have already been all but made, and need only the appropriate environmental cue to trigger them. Deliberation is not needed to appraise these instances, because the appraisal patterns have, as it were, already been set in advance.

Second, goal hierarchies and belief patterns prime the person to be sensitive to some circumstances and not others. This priming is a prior process that speeds up the appraisal and makes it selective. This is better addressed in the next section, however, under the rubric of meaning.

In any event, even though I have presented it and used it in Chapters 6 and 7 as a decision tree, we must not see the appraisal process as a sequential or stepwise process of scanning the components in any fixed order. Very rapidly, perhaps even simultaneously, we draw on a variety of stored information about the environment, person variables, and their relational meaning. How this is done remains something of a mystery, but we must indeed automatically do something similar to what I have described, or else the emotion process would not be adaptive and our emotional lives would be much more chaotic than they are.

How Meaning Is Achieved[4]

I confess that my discussion of appraisal, especially without considering specific examples of particular emotional reactions — a task saved for Part Three — leaves me with a feeling of incompleteness. Perhaps my unease stems from the way I have been speaking of appraisal, which seems too predicated on notions about adult, deliberate, and reflective thought. I have previously stated (cf. Lazarus, 1982, 1984a) that the concept of appraisal does not imply rationality, deliberateness, or consciousness of the cognitive processes involved in emotion. Therefore, we should look more carefully now at how meaning is achieved.

Here a basic theme is that there is *more than one way of knowing*. I quote Benner and Wrubel (1989, p. 41) on Heidegger's views about knowing:

> According to Heidegger, a person is a self-interpreting being, that is, the person does not come into the world predefined but becomes defined in the course of living a life. A person also has, Heidegger proposes, an effortless and nonreflective understanding of the self in the world. People can have this understanding because they are always situated in a meaningful context and because they grasp meaning directly. This is not to say that people are not capable of thinking reflectively or conceptually. But deliberative, abstract thought is not the only way in which people encounter the world. In fact, one would not know what to do with such abstract, conceptual thinking if one were not situated in a meaningful context. But it is easy to see how one could believe that all knowledge was reflective knowledge, because whenever one stands outside of a situation, one is in a reflective position. Heidegger's concern was to illuminate what kind of knowing occurs when one does not stand outside of the situation, but is involved in it. This concern was preeminent because it seemed to him that most of a person's being was engaged in particular situations.

In Heidegger's analysis, we grasp the situation directly in terms of its meaning for the self, which is what I believe most commonly happens in appraisal. This notion overlaps with what Baron and Boudreau (1987) mean when they borrow the concept of affordances; it is also related, though not identical with, what is meant by embodied intelligence (Merleau-Ponty, 1962, 1968) and tacit knowledge (Polanyi, 1966).

In speaking of embodied intelligence, I keep thinking of my peculiar but common experience with the keyboard of my word processor. I learned to touch type many years ago, and I am skilled and fast. My fingers hit the right keys automatically most of the time as any good typist would. Recently, at someone's urging, I tried to identify where the letters were on the keyboard from memory and failed miserably. I could not even say whether many of the letters were on the right or left side. Yet, in some odd way, my fingers "know" so well that I make few mistakes even when typing rapidly. People can also make grammatically correct statements without being able to state the rules, and they can also state rules, for example, about grammar or how to type or ride a bicycle, when they are unable to put the rules into practice. In other words, there is, as Brewin (1989, p. 380) put it, a "dissociation between verbal knowledge and task performance."

One way the Heideggerian theme of "being in" a situation expresses itself today in theories of cognition is in a widely held proposition that there are two different modes (perhaps systems) of appraisal: one *conscious, deliberate, and under volitional control,* the other *automatic, unconscious, and uncontrollable.* I suppose that *automatic* and *unconscious* might not necessarily be conjoined, though they often are when discussed. Thus, Kihlstrom (1987) has suggested as criteria for the automatic mode of meaning generation that the process is unintentional, involuntary, effortless, autonomous, and outside awareness.[5]

If we take the distinction between the two modes of meaning generation seriously, we can believe contradictory things simultaneously—for example, that flying in an airplane is safe and that it is also very dangerous. The thoughts of persons like me on takeoffs and landings are preempted by the automatic processing that treats these events as dangerous; at the same time, I know at a conscious level that in a probabilistic sense they are safe. If some unusual sound or motion occurs, I become instantly vigilant. Yet there is an important part of me that knows—and the statistics on fatalities reveal—that in the main I am safer in a commercial airplane than in a host of daily contexts in which I live, such as driving my car, about which I have the illusion that I am in control. About this sort of thing Brewin (1989, pp. 381–382) writes:

> Such a system would be able to account both for conditioning in animals and for the irrational nature of some human fears and phobias. One would only have to assume that with irrational fears the person's conscious recollection of events did not correspond to the representation of them that was automatically created by the system mediating nonconscious causal perception. This might occur for a number of reasons. For example, the critical event or events might have occurred very early in childhood during the period of infant amnesia. Other events might be so distressing that they were defensively excluded from consciousness. Discrepancies might also arise because the nonconscious representation is theoretically based on the full array of sensory input, plus related material in memory, whereas because of processing limitations, the conscious representation would be based on a much smaller amount of information. . . . [Here Brewin points out that under emotional conditions, or in shock, perception and memory might be impaired.] Furthermore, social pressures may operate to influence the conscious interpretations that people form of their experience.

What does it mean to speak of automatic and unconscious modes of appraising in contrast with deliberate and conscious modes? The terms *primary process* and *secondary process* were used by Freud to refer to primitive, wishful logic in very young children on the one hand, and reality-oriented, ego processes, which develop later in life through maturation and experience with the world, on the other. Rational rules govern secondary process thinking, whereas irrational rules govern the primary process; thus, primary process thinking is fragmented, condensed, and magical—as it is in dreams and psychosis.

Freud was not the only theorist to think in this way. Werner (1948, 1956) distinguished between developmentally *primitive* and *advanced* cognitive processes for achieving the same adaptational outcome. For example, one child may be able to "tell time"; when the mother says to get up at 6:30 A.M., the child reads the clock with a sophisticated grasp of the additivity of numbers. When that child says it is 6:30 A.M., it understands what a half hour means, or what five minutes means, and that if you add five minutes to the time, it becomes 6:35. Another child also can "read" the clock and rises on cue, perhaps even being able to say it is 6:30 in the morning. However, the child has little understanding of what this means, or about the additivity of time; this child has simply learned the names of significant times and recognizes them on the clock. Both children achieve a performance outcome that looks the same if one doesn't examine it too closely; however, in one case the process is developmentally primitive, and in the other it is developmentally advanced.

Piaget (1952) was also a developmental pioneer who charted the epigenetic stages of cognitive development. In consequence of two broad adaptational processes — *accommodation,* in which children adjust to the requirements of the physical world, and *assimilation,* in which they transform that world in accordance with their own needs — *abstract* forms of thought emerge and ultimately gain ascendence over earlier *concrete* forms in the course of development. These abstract forms permit us to gain cognitive distance from the concrete here and now. Realistic and symbolic thought replace stimulus-bound, impulsive action, help the adult achieve a sense of past, present, and future, and provide a measure of control over person–environment relationships and the capacity to engage in future planning, all of which make possible the remarkable adaptations of which the human adult is uniquely capable.

If we are to fully comprehend how emotions are generated, I think we need to give more attention than we have to relatively inarticulate processes like "resonances" between wishes or fantasies and what is actually encountered, even in adults, as well as to complex, abstract matchings and functional equivalences. For want of a better term, *resonance* refers to an amorphous or ineffable sense of connection between what is in us and something in the outer world. Shepard (1984) has used the term *resonance* as a metaphor in connection with Gibson's affordances (see also Trevarthen, 1979, and Trevarthen & Hubley, 1978, on intersubjectivity). Shepard (1984, p. 433) wrote:

> Instead of saying that an organism picks up the invariant affordances that are wholly present in the sensory arrays, I propose that as a result of biological evolution and individual learning, the organism is, at any given moment, tuned to resonate to the incoming patterns that correspond to the invariants that are of significance for it. . . . Up to this point I have not departed significantly from what Gibson himself might have said. Moreover, with the notion of selective tuning I can encompass the notion of affordance and thus explain how different organisms, with their different needs, pick up different invariances in the world.

This sounds much like automatic processing. I believe the process of emotion generation is often automatic rather than deliberate and volitionally controlled. It is not possible to say with any confidence what proportion of appraisals and emotions are based on either mode of cognitive activity, and perhaps most adult appraisals involve a mixture of both. In all likelihood, too, we have probably underestimated the importance of resonances or automatic processing even in the adult emotions. Though they can be so equated, we should resist equating the automatic with the primitive, because automatic processing can involve complex, abstract, and symbolic significances that through experience can be condensed into an instant meaning. I return to the distinction between automatic and deliberate modes of meaning generation in Chapter 5 when I discuss arguments about the causal role of cognition in emotion, and note several other emotion theorists, namely, Buck (1985), Leventhal (1984), and Scherer (1984a, 1984b) who make a similar distinction.

Sometimes our initial appraisals are hasty and unreflective, but if given time and opportunity, we engage in *reappraisals* that result in a different evaluation than the one we began with (see also Le Doux, 1986,1989). This is well illustrated by an experiment conducted in my Berkeley lab by Folkins (1970), which at the time got less attention than I thought it deserved. Different subjects awaited an electric shock for various periods of time, 30 seconds, a minute, several minutes, and more, and their subjective distress and psychophysiological reactions recorded. At the outset each subject was flashed a sign saying "shock in 30 seconds"; "shock in 1 minute"; and so on for each of the time conditions.[6]

Stress reactions were found to be greatest in the briefest waiting-time period, but less in 3- or 5-minute waits. Interviews showed that alarm was generated in those subjects with the short waiting periods and that this alarm was mitigated by all sorts of reappraisals when enough time was given. For example, subjects in the groups with 3- and 5-minute waiting periods used the longer time to reappraise what was going on in the experiment, saying to themselves that the professor conducting the study would not dare to truly injure them and that shock from an inductorium couldn't be a valid cause for alarm. In effect, when time was short, subjects felt an elemental dread, but with sufficient time for deliberation and reappraisal, they considered all sorts of realistic and reassuring thoughts, which reduced the experienced stress and distress. There is a great temptation now to call this *cognitive coping.*

In the early 1950s there was also much interest in experimental demonstrations of what was often called *autonomic discrimination* without awareness, or *subception* as McCleary and I referred to it in one of these demonstrations (Lazarus & McCleary, 1951). The word *subception* was used to indicate that what was being studied was not conscious perception but a selective, learned discrimination of danger without the person being aware that it had occurred.

Our study followed several others, most notably one by McGinnies (1949), who had demonstrated that galvanic skin responses (GSRs) were greater for emotional or threat words, such as *whore, bitch,* and *raped,* than for neutral words presented tachistoscopically (a device that varies exposure speed or brightness) and too rapidly for conscious recognition. This finding seemed to have demonstrated that the message of the threat words had somehow been recognized without subjects being aware of it. However, one could argue that McGinnies' subjects might well have been motivated to withhold their report of the socially taboo words, or even to doubt their presence in the laboratory of an upright professor, thereby accounting for the difference in GSR to threat and nonthreat words.

So McCleary and I conditioned a set of nonsense syllables to a painful electric shock, and in a later session compared GSRs to these syllables and to nonsense syllables that were never associated with shock. We used nonsense syllables to get around the problem of subjects' withholding reports of taboo words, and to generate threat we conditioned some of the syllables to a painful electric shock. We found that even when subjects were incorrect in their report about which syllable had been flashed on the screen — because the speed was below their recognition thresholds — they gave a larger GSR to the shocked syllables than to the nonshocked ones.

This seemed to demonstrate that there could be a discrimination between threat and no threat even when there was no awareness of the stimulus actually presented, as indicated by an incorrect identification of that stimulus by the subject. Moreover, inasmuch as there was no reason to withhold reports of what had been seen, because the stimuli were nonsense syllables rather than socially taboo or threatening words, the subception experiment seemed to leave little doubt that discrimination between threat and no threat had occurred at a preconscious or unconscious level, as evidenced by the selective GSR. Put differently, subjects were making an automatic appraisal without awareness, even when a correct deliberate evaluation was not possible, because the syllables were presented below the threshold of conscious recognition and the one that was reported was in error. These findings are presented in Figure 4.2.

What followed from this research is still interesting for me to recall. There were virtually no challenges to the methodology and findings of the subception research.[7] However, there were numerous challenges to the interpretation that an unconscious process was somehow involved. The most important and influential of these were by Bricker and Chapanis (1953), Eriksen (1956), and Howes (1954), to which I responded as effectively as I could (Lazarus, 1956).

What I find most interesting is that, as I intimated in Chapter 1 and as will again be evident in Chapter 5, research findings rarely if ever settle theoretical issues in psychology, especially those that depend on epistemological and ideological differences. Although I think the subception research was the most effective experimental demonstration of the existence of the two modes of cognitive processing, and of the unconscious nature of some appraisals, psychologists in those days were simply not ready to assimilate the idea of the unconscious, especially if it contained the dynamic Freudian implication that ideas are kept defensively out of awareness, or even preconsciously processed. Actually, when McGinnies summarized some of the research in this area, called then the "New Look in Perception," he actually phrased the concept of the unconscious dynamically as follows: "It seems well established, then, that the perceptual 'filtering' of visual stimuli serves, in many instances, to protect the observer as long as possible from an awareness of objects which have unpleasant emotional significance for him" (cited by Lazarus & McCleary, 1951, p. 114).

Reservations about this kind of analysis still remain among psychologists today, though the more benign version of unconscious, which presumably has to do with what is not or cannot be attended to, seems now to be more widely accepted. Although usage here has been inconsistent, there is a tendency for many psychologists now to use the term *preconscious* for the more benign meaning of an idea that

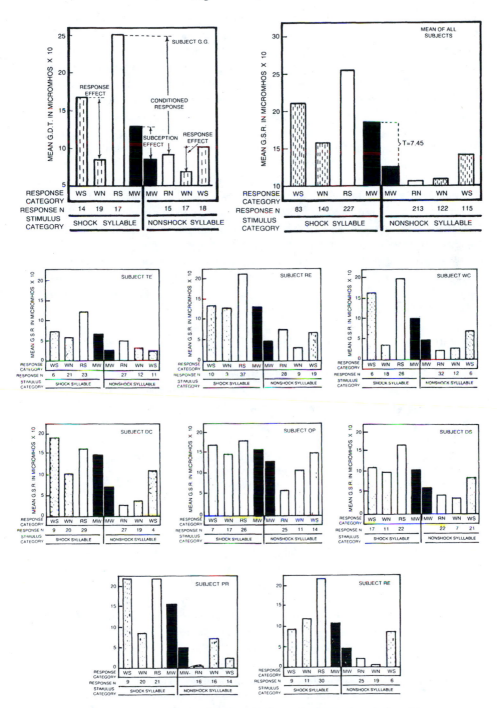

FIGURE 4.2. GSR data from final test period. (*Source:* R. S. Lazarus and R. A. McCleary, "Autonomic discrimination without awareness." *Psychological Review, 58.* Washington, DC: American Psychological Association, 1951.)

is is not attended to and so remains close to consciousness and probably accessible with effort, and to reserve the term *unconscious* for an idea or process that is inaccessible, perhaps as a result of an ego-defense. The reader will see later and in Chapter 11, in which I talk about psychotherapy, that even clinical psychologists and psychiatrists are divided about the accessibility of unconscious mental contents.

Now, roughly forty years later there is a new groundswell of interest in preconscious modes of evaluation in contrast with conscious modes, particularly in the field of social cognition, which is producing a considerable body of research and theory. This research and theory seem to have begun with a concern about how people form evaluative impressions of others and how these impressions affect social interaction. There is growing evidence that these evaluations are often made without awareness — that is, automatically or preconsciously. The evidence and the theory involved has been reviewed by Uleman and Bargh (1989; see also Bargh, 1990). I comment here only on some of the features that might be salient (see also Fazio, Sanbormatsu, Powell, & Kardes, 1986; and Fiske, 1982).

Preconscious evaluation of social events seems to be made for simple categorical distinctions such as *good* or *bad* rather than for finely graded analogical distinctions. This is consistent with the idea that conscious, deliberate, and volitional evaluations, which have the advantage of language, may be more finely graded than unconscious, automatic, and involuntary ones, which are apt to be hasty and vague. The latter are often regarded as primitive, developmentally earlier, and subcortical (cf. Le Doux, 1989).

That there are two modes of meaning generation helps us understand how it is possible for values and goals to influence what is attended to and to result in appraisals of social harm, threat, and benefit automatically and without reflection. Social psychologists Jones and Thibaut (1958, p. 152) express this as follows:

> If we can successfully identify the goals for which an actor is striving in the interaction situation, we can begin to say something about the cues to which he will attend, and the meaning he is most likely to assign them.

The underlying theme that emerges from all this, which in social cognition is not usually explicitly directed at the emotion process but could be, is the question of how plans and goals (cf. Miller, Galanter, & Pribram, 1960; Schank & Abelson, 1977) influence evaluations in ordinary adaptive social interchanges. I want the reader to see here that what psychologists concerned with social cognition are struggling with — namely, how personal meaning is extracted from person–environment relationships — is fundamentally the same as what cognitive-motivational-relational theorists of emotion are dealing with. Allow me to document this parallel by quoting Bargh (1990, p. 100) who brings the relevant variables together as follows:

> Therefore, the mechanism proposed here by which the social environment may possibly control judgments, decisions, and behavior is the formation of direct and automatic mental links between representations of motives and goals in memory (and consequently the goals and plans associated with them) and the representations of the social situations in which those motives have been frequently pursued in the past.

The result of this automatic associative link is for the motive-goal-plan structure to become activated whenever the relevant triggering situational features are present in the environment. The activated goals and plans then presumably guide the social cognition and interaction of the individual, without the person's intention or awareness of the motive's guiding role.

This type of analysis seems vital to emotion theory, and the connection with such theory should be made explicit: To feel an emotion such as anger, anxiety, guilt, shame, sadness, joy, or pride, and so forth, the process of knowing — whatever form it might take, whether automatic or deliberate — must get the person to the specific core relational theme or meaning associated with a given emotion. We may arrive at the appraisal and core relational theme via an automatic, unconscious process of knowing in the Heideggerian sense or via deliberate, self-controlled, abstract cognitive analysis. Regardless of the manner through which one gets there, however, to experience the particular emotion the processes of knowing must lead to the relational meaning psychobiologically connected with that emotion (see also Chapters 3 and 5).

The adaptational consequences of conscious and unconscious appraisal processes are also probably different. An important difference is that because unconscious appraisals are often less accessible, and therefore more or less refractory to rational analysis, especially when they are the product of ego-defense, the person who depends on them is probably more vulnerable to poor decision making and coping, and thus to psychopathology. I will have more to say about this in Part Five.

Implications for Life-Span Development

Before leaving this very important set of issues about the organization of cognitive activity in the emotional process, I should also set the stage for a consideration in Chapter 9 of the developmental aspects of the idea that there is more than one way in which meaning is generated. In recent years, there has been renewed interest in both early cognitive-motivational-emotional development and, more broadly, life-span development which extends to old age. The contrast in the two modes of meaning generation has profound implications for emotions in infants and young children compared with adults, and this should be touched on briefly here. My discussion earlier of the six components of appraisal sounds as though I believe that the appraisal process draws only on advanced and complex types of cognitive activity, which are appropriate only for adults and probably not for infants and young children.

For this to be so would leave me in an untenable position about how emotion is provoked in children, especially if the very young child could not grasp the social and intrapsychic meanings on which certain emotions depend — for example, who is to be held accountable for a frustration and whether the responsible person could have controlled the damaging actions? Do infants grasp these meanings somehow by some kind of automatic, involuntary, and nonreflective cognitive activity? Can a young child sense that its ego-identity is threatened or that someone should be blamed? How early in life can a child impute control or its absence to someone who seems accountable? The answers to these and other questions profoundly affect which emotions can be experienced by young children of different ages.

Some tentative answers are beginning to emerge from studies of infants. For example, research with infants (Stenberg & Campos, 1990; Campos, 1988–1989) suggests that at 3 months a baby shows only distress in response to restraint; at 4 months, however, there seems to be unmistakable anger in the baby's demeanor and facial expression, and the baby looks at the wrist that is restraining it, suggesting an elemetary grasp of external accountability. At 7 months, the baby looks at the face of the person whose hand is the source of restraint. Now it would appear that the baby has accurately personified the external source of the frustration. I doubt, however, that such a baby can yet judge whether the other person restraining it should be blamed in an adult sense for the frustrating act. And is there some elemental sense of self in this process? If we take seriously the work of Bahrick and Watson (1985; see also Papousek & Papousek, 1974), we would have to say that at 5 months the baby seems aware of the contingency between its movements and what is shown of this movement on a TV monitor, so it presumably has an emerging sense of self.

In the light of these observations, perhaps we should say that anger in a very young child is different, or differently elicited, than it is in an adult for whom the inference about control is important. Nevertheless, it appears that many of the six primary and secondary appraisal components are within the meaning-generating capacities of infants even though the infants cannot evaluate these components in the complex and abstract ways characteristic of the older child or adult. Remember, it is meaning that counts in emotion, not how that meaning is achieved. I return to this point in Chapters 6 and 7, when I discuss the appraisal patterns for each emotion, and again in Part Four when I discuss the developmental perspective.

With respect to later life-course development, I have been much influenced by Labouvie-Vief, Hakim-Larson, DeVoe, and Schoeberlein (1989), who also examine the idea that there are at least two general ways of deriving adaptational meaning: one relatively primitive and concrete and similar to automatic, unconscious, and involuntary processing; the other more abstract and symbolic and similar to deliberate, conscious, and voluntary processing.

These authors make the point that the ways in which meaning is achieved are usually considered to be organized hierarchically, the automatic mode coming first in child development but later being overridden by rational, distancing, emotion-regulating, and symbolic cognitive manipulations. Hierarchical analyses are found in Freud (1957) in his discussion of primary and secondary process, in Piaget (1976, 1980) in his discussion of accommodation and assimilation, and in Werner (1957; see also Werner & Kaplan, 1963) in the distinction between physiognomic and formal-technical modes of thought.

Labouvie-Vief et al. (1989, p. 283) summarize the traditional, hierarchical developmental view as follows:

Most theories of development portray the progression from childhood to adulthood as the gradual dissociation of two forms of meaning, as the individual adapts to a collective language of symbols. Through this process of dissociation and hierarchization, meaning systems that originate in the organismic, the sensorimotor, the figurative, the dynamic, and the personal, are gradually displaced by those that are abstract, conceptual, stable, conventional, and impersonal. Indeed, it is often assumed that the former are a characteristic of immature thought.

They also cite Langer (1942, p. 292), who writes:

Everything that falls outside the domain of analytical, propositional, and formal thought is merely classed as emotive, irrational, and animalian. . . . All other things our minds do are dismissed as irrelevant to intellectual progress; they are residues, emotional disturbances, or throwbacks to animal estate [and indicate] regression to a pre-logical state.

Piaget considered that inner speech is inferior or childish, and that rather than establishing truth, it is individual and not communicable. With developmental advances, the person gives up private, individual symbols and adopts those that are collective (cf. Watkins, 1986). Freud (1957), too, treated primary process as primitive and pathogenic. It must ultimately be given up in the healthy adult in favor of secondary process or realistic, abstract thought. Labouvie-Vief et al. believe that Piaget overemphasized accommodative forms of coping in development by suggesting that ultimately the child comes to subordinate inner fantasy and personal agendas to the requirements of external reality. This implies that with maturity one becomes more focused on the environment and its demands, constraints, and resources.

A few Freudians (e.g., Kris, 1952) also wrote about regression in the service of the ego and creativity. In such regression, we reach down into our primitive, childish selves, as it were, which is fine so long as we ultimately come back to secondary process thinking and use primitive processes realistically. A fascinating experiment by Wild (1965) illustrates this concept of creative intellectual functioning by psychologically healthy persons, which though it may seem superficially pathological, represents regression in the service of the ego.

Matching teachers, schizophrenic patients, and art students on intelligence, education, sex, and age, she compared the ways they handled word association and object sorting tasks. Task performance was observed under three conditions: (1) the standard test instructions that encouraged spontaneous thought, (2) a condition of regulated thought using instructions to take the test as a conventional, orderly person would, and (3) as modeled after a whimsical or fanciful person who is capable of novelty and originality, in other words, a condition of unregulated thought.

Wild found that art students could function with pleasure and enthusiasm in a freer, more spontaneous and unregulated fashion when appropriate than either teachers or schizophrenics could. The students could express relatively primitive forms of cognitive activity, for example, combining a balloon with a tobacco pipe and calling it, imaginatively, a bubble pipe. Wild suggests that it takes a strong, healthy ego to think of and express seemingly crazy ideas comfortably—implying, too, that the primitive and the adult ways of achieving meaning exist side by side, as it were, and most important, that they can combine functionally in adaptation.

Although the two modes of meaning generation are typically referred to as primitive and advanced, with the latter ultimately overriding the former smoothly and without conflict in the course of psychological development, Labouvie-Vief et al. suggest that the integration of the modes is a dialectical result of a continuing struggle for integration. One may also think of them as, instead of being hierarchical, organized rather in a parallel or horizontal arrangement in which both continue to operate, perhaps in conflict or as smoothly integrated in the mentally sound adult.

Although the two modes of thought emerge sequentially and may be in conflict when fully developed, one of the tasks of development is to somehow integrate them to the extent possible, permitting persons to draw adaptively on each in the ordinary course of living. The authors speak of this as "reconnection," or as Turner (1973) calls it in Piagetian terms, "re-centering" — that is, reconnecting logical thought with an organismic core of meaning. In sum, we have the option of viewing the two (or more) modes of meaning generation as hierarchical, with one overriding the other as development proceeds, or as parallel, with the potential for conflict or integration, as complementary forms of knowing that emerge and operate together on the basis of a dialectical struggle of living (see also Lerner & Gignac, in press, and Lerner & Lerner, 1983, for an analysis of the emotional life in aging, and Alexander & Langer, 1990, for diverse views of the higher cognitive stages of human development).

The Unconscious Mind

Although there would be some naysayers, largely on the basis of its methodological refractoriness to proof (cf. Eriksen, 1960, 1962), there is probably more widespread interest and acceptance of the idea of unconscious mental activity among academic psychologists today than ever before. I believe that psychology, especially the subtopics of emotion and adaptation, would be seriously impaired without reference to unconscious or preconscious processes.

The great current interest in this has no doubt been encouraged by the vigorous theoretical and research activity of cognitive, social, and clinical psychologists, and the greater freedom to speculate about the mind. Searching examinations of the meanings of unconsciousness can be found in a number of recent volumes, including those of Erdelyi (1985), Frese and Sabini (1985), Greenberg and Safran (1987), and Guidano and Liotti (1983). An article by Bowers (1987), with commentaries, and a special journal issue (Brody, 1987), which presents diverse analyses of the place of unconscious processes in psychology, illustrate this current interest.

As Erdelyi (1985) and many others have pointed out, there are at least two meanings to *unconscious*. One meaning is the more or less bland idea that we are simply not aware of many of the thoughts and thought processes that influence how we act and feel. The second is the more controversial Freudian concept of ego-defense, in which it is assumed that some cognitive processes are actively kept out of awareness to cope with threat and to avoid emotional distress.

However, herein lies a theoretical dilemma. In Freud's (1936) concept of signal anxiety, ego-defense is treated as a response to emotion rather than as a cause (see Chapter 3). But what tells the mind to activate a defense? To ask this without an implicit homunculus (that is, an imaginary mind within the mind that controls things and that can be carried to an infinite regress), what is the mechanism that triggers the defense? Psychoanalytic theorists have assumed that defense requires the existence of unconscious anxiety, which acts as the signal of danger. The notion of an unconscious emotion, in contrast with an unconscious appraisal or coping process, is logically and empirically very awkward. The awkwardness comes from obscurity about how an emotion, which is an experience as well as a process, can be unconscious. There would be no problem if we assumed that the defensive process and its ideational contents were unconscious but the emotional experience conscious. As Oatley (1988, p. 15) puts it, "It is ideas that are stored, not affect. Goals may be unconscious. Emotions are not usually repressed in this way (although there are phenomena like being angry but not knowing it)."

Gillett (1990; see also 1987a, 1987b) has attempted to refute Freud's signal theory (as I did earlier in Lazarus, 1966). Gillett proposes a distinction between the "triggering of defense" and the process of "motivating the defensive effort." He makes use of my distinction between primary and secondary appraisal, which makes it possible to dispense with the concept of unconscious anxiety in the theory of intrapsychic conflict. All it takes to initiate a defense is an appraisal of threat.

Consider what it means to speak of *threat*. When we anticipate a harmful transaction, we engage in secondary appraisal, which has to do with options for coping, which in turn are conducive to anticipatory coping with the upcoming harm. However, based on what we have learned, we also anticipate the probable success or failure of our coping effort, which is a part of secondary appraisal. Although threat is sufficient to activate the coping process, both the anticipation of danger (primary appraisal) and the anticipation of our probable success or failure in coping (secondary appraisal) are necessary for determining the emotional state of anxiety.

In those cases in which we anticipate with great confidence that we will be successful in avoiding the danger, there need be no anxiety; there are no first inklings of anxiety to trigger the (defensive) reappraisal. However, in those cases in which we anticipate the actuality of the harm, this anticipation (of harm) is quite sufficient to generate coping or defense. We don't need to experience a little bit of anxiety to trigger coping or defense; we merely make a primary appraisal of threat and a secondary appraisal (or expectation) of whether we can manage it. We don't need to postulate unconscious anxiety to serve as a signal that triggers the coping or defensive process.

In research with colleagues in the 1960s (e.g., Lazarus & Alfert, 1964; Opton, Rankin, Nomikos, & Lazarus, 1965), some of which I described earlier, I referred to the effects of changing experimentally the way subjects interpreted the threatening contents of movies as the *short-circuiting* of threat. In these studies, denial or intellectualizing statements, made before the movie, significantly lowered the stress levels observed during the stressful film compared with a control condition, as measured both by self-report and by autonomic nervous system indicators.

The idea of short-circuiting is a metaphor for an electrical charge that is shunted away from the main circuit, and hence is said to be short-circuited. In short-circuiting, an emotion such as anxiety is not experienced when it is expected, because the threatening meaning has been made benign, usually by some kind of ego-defensive process. Short-circuiting may be thought of as a metaphor, as already discussed, for the triggering of defense without anxiety having to play a role. The decision about the danger, and the defense against it, was, in effect, made earlier in the person's life as a result of prior learning and contemporaneously only requires the right cue to elicit it.

Bargh (1990) has drawn on this idea, too, though seemingly unaware of this prior usage and research. He quotes a passage from Wilensky (1983, pp. 24–25) that adds fuel to the idea that the entire meaning system inherent in an appraisal might be triggered automatically, without deliberate or voluntary processing (p. 104):

> If a standard plan is associated with a goal that occurs in a particular situation, it would be more efficient to associate this plan directly with that situation and select the plan at the same time the goal is detected. This would permit the planner to "short-circuit" part of the planning algorithm and suggest a plan immediately upon noticing a significant situation.

In any case, most cognitive psychologists today seem to accept that there is unconscious processing of information and ideas and that some degree of effort may be required for retrieval. This is Erdelyi's first meaning of unconsciousness. However, many of these same psychologists have doubts about or even reject the concept of ego-defense as a basis of unconsciousness, which is the second meaning.

Writers differ about how accessible to consciousness ideological contents are, but it is common to differentiate the unconscious contents and processes into deeper, inaccessible layers and more surface, preconscious layers (see also Epstein, 1984, 1990). Brewin (p. 380) notes, for example, that these mental contents may be preconscious merely because we choose not to attend to certain things or because they are a part of the "enormous number of sensations, images, and so forth, which are automatically filtered out of the material potentially available to our limited consciousness." These contents will become accessible readily if we are alerted to their presence (see also Broadbent, Fitzgerald, & Broadbent, 1986).

Even clinical psychologists who accept the idea of ego-defense differ among themselves about how accessible the unconscious or preconscious contents of the mind are. Whereas Freudians assume that most of these contents will remain forever unconscious, or can only be made conscious with immense and prolonged effort, others (e.g., Ellis, 1962; also see Bernard & DiGiuseppe, 1989; and Beck, 1976) assume that they can be accessed more readily with modest effort.

Gillett (1987a, 1987b) also opts for a structural position about this, seeing non-experiential mental entities and processes as incapable of becoming conscious under any conditions because of the relationship of the mind-brain functioning. Preconscious mental contents can usually become conscious, and repressed mental contents can become conscious if the repression is lifted by powerful experiences or psychotherapy and insight. Even in the case of potentially voluntary or conscious appraisals, the appraisal content could be either conscious or preconscious — that is, as I pointed out earlier, close to consciousness and probably accessible with effort.

This implies a third meaning of unconscious mind (e.g., Gillett, 1987a, 1987b), namely, that one can only be aware of the *contents* of mental activity but not the mental *processes* by which these contents are achieved. Neisser (1967) seems to have made the same point; we cannot access most of the cognitive processes involved in registration, storage, and transformation of our experience, but we can be aware of some of their products. Gillett notes, historically, that Lashley, too, a neurophysiologist, made the claim that all mental processes are unconscious and only the contents — which are the product of these processes — are capable of becoming conscious. Sandler and Joffe (1969) first introduced this distinction between experiential mental contents and nonexperiential mechanisms, structures, and energies into psychoanalysis; later they and Wallerstein (1983) argued that the nonexperiential realm is not part of the unconscious. This seems to me to be a reasonable way of thinking of what is available to conscious and what is not.

Implications for Unconscious Appraising

I assume that an encounter with the environment may be appraised as harmful or beneficial, hence emotion-generating, without the person being aware of the operative motivational and cognitive agendas or of the environmental influences that have contributed to the appraisal. From the point of view of depth psychology, which centers on ego-defensive processes, the analysis of core relational themes offered in Chapter 3 and used later in Part Three, which deals with the individual emotions, is much too pat. What is missing is a consideration of individualized cognitive-motivational-relational configurations that operate idiosyncratically as hidden, irrational, or distorted meanings shaping our appraisals of interpersonal and intrapersonal relationships, and therefore generating emotions that seem not to fit the observations of bystanders, for whom there might be a consensus about what is taking place. When hidden premises and processes are at work, individuals react with intense anger, say, when there does not seem to be adequate provocation, and likewise with sadness or depression, anxiety, guilt, or shame. Conversely, because of these hidden premises and processes, individuals may fail to display or experience emotions that would ordinarily be called for under conditions of harm or threat.

In his review of two psychoanalytic books on emotions and memory in psychoanalysis — one by Erdelyi (1985), which I have already cited, and another by Wegman (1985) — Oatley (1988) has made a nice analysis of the importance of goals or wishes in Freudian language, making the central point that Freud was laying the ground for a psychology of intention, and that it is intentions that serve as important sources of threat in connection with a disapproving environment or personal value system (superego). The way he puts this (Oatley, 1988, p. 11) is worth quoting in the context of my discussion of threat and defense, and what I have said in Chapter 3 about motivation:

> Memory does indeed have a central place in psychoanalysis, but the key to Freud's theorizing about it is his treatment of it as related to human goals, wishes as he called them: how we sometimes act as if we had an intention but deny it. Freud's methods were methods for investigating goals and plans, by listening to patients' stories. A story makes sense only when the goals and plans of the actors are understood. Yes, Freud was interested in restoring memories, but the interpretations that psychoanalysts offer to fill gaps in a story do not fill any old gaps. They fill specifically those gaps left

by missing intentions. They suggest goals that might have been forgotten or denied, but which might make sense of otherwise incomprehensible sequences of action.

Expressed in terms of core relational themes, persons reacting this way have appraised the relationship unconsciously and automatically, if one prefers, and differently from how they view it consciously and under volitional control or how others view it. Therefore, the emotions experienced or displayed seem to make little or no sense, because the intentional premises are hidden. Even when conditions are reassuring and should make for a sense of security, we react with anxiety; even when the social conditions seem to others to be benign or supportive, instead of a friendly response anger is observed; even when there is no evident reason for self-blame, guilt is nevertheless experienced; even when there seems to be reason for rejoicing, instead we react with sadness or depression; and so on for any and all kinds of emotion, both positive and negative. It is as if we are reacting to a different world than that indicated by actual conditions as judged by others or ourselves consciously. For reasons that are obscure to the person involved, a different feeling is experienced than that which seems appropriate. Although there are many relatively simple reasons why this could be so—for example, cultural and individual differences or confusions about signals—a frequent and self-consistent explanation centers on the operation of ego-defenses.

Throughout my discussion of subtle meanings and vertical or depth analysis of the emotion process, there has been an assumption, not always made explicit, that conscious meanings may differ dramatically from those operating below the surface as a result of processes of defense. The danger of an exclusively surface analysis of an emotion, especially if it is based solely on what a person reports, is that we will mistake what is observed because it is on the surface for what is happening at a deeper, presumably unconscious or preconscious level.

Defenses, I assume, change appraised meanings, but the meaning postulated for each emotion may still apply if it is to be drawn on in our analysis of emotional transactions, whether or not a person is aware of the presumably unconscious meaning. This possibility leads me to the striking proposition that two appraisals might occur at the same time, one unconscious and another conscious, and, in a sense, both could be valid. One way in which this might take place is expressed in the idea of ambivalence. Another is to speak of different mental stages for the same event, stages in which there are conscious intrusions of the contrary emotional process (cf. Horowitz, 1976). For example, in one stage after a loss or trauma, a person engages in denial and experiences emotional numbing, whereas in another stage the traumatic experience surfaces and enters intrusively into a person's thoughts and actions.

Depth psychologists point to unconscious conflicts, especially in childhood, which set a person on a lifetime course of distorted interpretations and which, as Wachtel (1977) has suggested, have been reinforced and sustained by others during development in childhood. In the language of the Freudians, these phenomena are viewed as the result of unresolved conflicts, which though inaccessible to awareness, remain active somehow in shaping contemporary appraisals. Jung used the term *complexes* to refer to them; Freud's term for this in psychotherapy was *transference,* a process by which troubled patients react to the therapist as if he or she were a parent; Sullivan spoke of *parataxic distortions,* in which a person reacts to others as if they were parents.

Whatever conceptual language one uses for the distortion of the emotional process by images and ideas that reflect intentions lying below the surface, people carry around with them private and recurrent personal meanings that lead them to react inappropriately to an encounter with a sense of betrayal, victimization, rejection, abandonment, inadequacy, or whatever. They appraise their relationships in accordance with private and commonly unrecognized meanings that engender the core relational themes for anger, anxiety, guilt, and so on, which they alone conceive as applying to their transactions.

But what happens to the emotion generation process when it is kept unconscious as a result of a process of defense? Does it remain silent? Does it go away? Does it influence what is going on consciously? Of course, we don't know, but we can suppose one or another answer. Freud tried to explain neurotic symptoms as the return of the repressed, thereby adopting the position that some or all defenses are unsuccessful in containing the impulse or wish that is offensive. If there were no symptoms to note in the form of distressing emotions and dysfunctions, we could not know about the defense. A number of personality psychologists are currently seeking ways to distinguish among those who present themselves positively and are psychologically healthy and those who present themselves positively but who are personally unsound as a result of defenses or self-presentational strategies (see D. A. Weinberger, 1989).

Depth psychologists have not gotten very far in conceptualizing and demonstrating how unconscious processes work in influencing appraisal in our daily lives. The writings of Horowitz (1988, 1989), Luborsky (1977, 1984), and the Psychotherapy Research Group, Department of Psychiatry, Mount Zion Hospital and Medical Center (e.g., Sampson, Weiss, Mlodnosky, & Hause, 1972; Silberschatz & Sampson, 1991; Weiss, 1971, 1990) exemplify efforts to concretize this complex process in clinical terms.

The empirical problem posed by reliance on the idea of unconscious processes is that when it is the result of hidden agendas, an appraisal is difficult to assess accurately, and even more difficult to trace to its unconscious meanings and developmental origins. On the other hand, if appraisals are assessed by self-report methods, there is the danger that what is obtained is superficial, and therefore will not lead to successful predictions of manifest emotions. It is easier to observe evidence of idiosyncratic emotional reactions than to understand what they are all about.

As I noted in Chapter 1, clinicians use a number of clues about this—for example, the presence of symptoms of intrapsychic struggle, seemingly irrational reactions, contradictions in what is reported by a client from time to time, or between what is reported and behavioral and physiological reactions. These clues generate only the suspicion that something obscure is going on in the appraisal process, and further exploration is needed to reveal what this is.

Most of the programmatic research done in the study of the cognition-emotion relationship has been directed at readily observed processes operating on the surface of awareness. Depth psychologists, however, who emphasize unconscious determinants, will doubt that the real meanings underlying emotions can be deciphered without in-depth, intensive clinical examination. I suspect that they are partly right, which is why I have attempted to integrate appraisal theory with the notion of an unconscious. The problem with doing this is the difficulty of knowing when the emotional manifestation is a result of one or another of the levels at which the process can be examined. I have no special answer for this conundrum.

Summary

The use of cognitive concepts—such as learning, perception, and judgment (as well as concepts relating to motivation and hedonism)—in studying emotion has a long history and goes back to ancient and medieval times. There are numerous ways of speaking of cognitive activity, but for a cognitive-motivational-relational theory of emotion what is most relevant is the process of obtaining meanings out of an adaptational encounter, especially meanings having to do with the personal significance for well-being of what is going on. This is what defines the concept of appraisal. A complication for this kind of theory is that because of overlaps and interdependencies among the three constructs of mind—motivation, cognition, and emotion—it is difficult precisely to distinguish among them; yet each of these constructs has irreducible meaning, and all three play special roles in adaptation.

Drawing on my cognitive theory of psychological stress, there are two kinds of appraisal: primary, which concerns whether or not something of relevance to a person's well-being has occurred, and secondary, which concerns the coping options in an encounter. Extensive research from my laboratory and those of others in the 1960s and 1970s has documented the roles of appraisal and coping in the stress reaction, and more recent evidence has supported the inference that appraisal also has causal significance in the quality and intensity of emotions.

Appraisal has the adaptational task of integrating the realities of environmental demands, constraints, and resources with personal interests without giving short shrift to either. Well-functioning people generally are good at reality testing yet manage at the same time to minimize emotional distress and maximize a positive outlook. Individual differences result from the fact that there are many realities to respond to, as well as from self-protective or ego-defensive mechanisms that distort reality. Appraisal is both variable and stable (as in appraisal styles) in any given person, both being opposite sides of the same coin.

Much confusion has resulted from the failure to distinguish two kinds of cognitive activity in studying emotion—namely, knowledge and appraisal. Knowledge has to do with beliefs about how things work in general and in specific contexts. Appraisal is a personal evaluation of the significance of this knowledge in a particular encounter or existentially. Knowledge is apt to be cold, appraisal hot and more proximal to emotion because it has to do with what a person has at stake in an encounter or in life.

I postulate six appraisal components in the emotion process, three primary and three secondary. Primary appraisal components include goal relevance, goal congruence or incongruence, and type of ego-involvement. Without goal relevance or something at stake there is no prospect of an emotion. Particular ego-involvements distinguish among certain emotions such as anger, guilt, and shame, but not in case of sadness. The secondary appraisal components of emotion are blame or credit, coping potential, and future expectations. These appraisal components will be used in Chapters 6 and 7 to specify the cognitive appraisal patterns for each individual emotion, both those that are goal incongruent or negative and those that are goal congruent or positive.

Appraisal implies nothing about rationality, deliberateness, or consciousness. A central postulate for dealing with this issue is to say that there is more than one way of knowing, and in the generation of an emotion these ways may be in conflict or may be contributed to simultaneously by two kinds of appraisal processes — one that operates automatically without awareness or volitional control, and another that is conscious, deliberate, and volitional. We shall see in Chapter 5 that this way of thinking helps us deal with numerous confusions about the causal role of cognition in emotion.

Developmental psychologists have typically viewed the two modes as hierarchically organized; that is, the child begins life by drawing on automatic, unconscious, and involuntary modes, but these are said to be overridden in maturity by deliberate, conscious, and volitional modes that create distance from the concrete here and now. It is possible, however, that maturity and health are characterized instead by laterally coexisting automatic and deliberate processes, which must be integrated so that the person can draw on both modes of knowing harmoniously and without sacrificing either accurate reality testing or personal commitments. Perhaps these two modes can exist side by side, as it were, in conflict or in harmony, thus leading to different construals of person–environment relationships at different levels of the mind — the conscious, the preconscious, and the unconscious. Emotion theory must struggle with these alternatives and must perhaps give more attention than it has in the past to relatively inarticulate processes such as resonances between wishes, or fantasies about what is encountered, as well as to deliberate and volitional processes in the generation of emotional states.

To deal with unconscious mind and many of the dilemmas of the emotional life, emotion theory must be constructed vertically as well as horizontally; that is, it must deal with what is going on at conscious, preconscious, and unconscious levels of mental activity. In the final section of the chapter I explored what it means to speak of unconscious mind and attempted to relate this to appraisal.

Notes

1. Recently, however, despite much other supporting evidence, Steptoe and Vogele (1986) failed, for reasons that are obscure, to confirm some of the details of what we, and many others, too, found with orienting statements.

2. I am indebted to Professor M. Perez of the University of Freiburg, Switzerland, for suggesting this way of handling blame while I was a visiting professor at the University of Heidelberg, FRG, during the summer of 1989. Invaluable discussions of issues like this one took place during a seminar in Geneva in June 1989 that also involved other scholars and advanced students of emotion such as Klaus Scherer, Nico Frijda, and Shlomo Breznitz.

3. It would be better to refer to particular cultures and nations from Asia—for example, Chinese, Koreans, Japanese, Vietnamese, and so on—for these are by no means alike as implied in the collective term, Asians. However, cross-cultural data on the significance of ability and effort in these cultures are not to my knowledge yet available.

4. This material on how meaning is achieved overlaps extensively with that in my recent article entitled "Cognition and Motivation in Emotion" (Lazarus, 1991a) in the *American Psychologist*. Both discussions were written at the same time.

5. Some readers will think that I am being too sanguine about this approach to the achievement of meaning, and I am aware that there is currently an ongoing debate about whether awareness is necessary for what is called *evaluative conditioning* (see, for example, Baeyens, Eelen, & van den Bergh, 1990; Levey & Martin, 1990; and Shanks & Dickenson, 1990, all in the same issue of *Cognition and Emotion*). I mention the issue here only because it seems to be regarded as important by a number of cognitive psychologists.

6. The experiment used a between-subject (group) design rather than repeated measures within subjects, so that different groups were made to wait different amounts of time.

7. There is one exception to this statement, a study by Chun and Sarbin in 1968, which led to a brief interchange (see Lazarus, 1968b).

❖ 5 ❖

Issues of Causality

I begin this chapter with a deferred topic, namely, the overlaps and distinctions among the three constructs of mind — cognition, motivation, and emotion — which could not have been effectively dealt with earlier, before each had been examined as a portion of the emotion process.

There follows a difficult set of issues concerning causality in the emotion process. Three main issues stand out: The first has to do with causality itself and I deal with it very briefly; the second, on which there is vigorous debate, has to do with whether and how cognition plays a causal role in emotion, and I deal with it at greater length in conjunction with appraisal. My position is that appraisal is a necessary and sufficient condition but that the knowledge on which appraisal rests is necessary but not sufficient; this needs further clarification and defending. The third concerns how to reconcile biological universals with learned sociocultural, developmental sources of variability in the emotion process.[1]

The final topic of the chapter concerns the system principle as it is applied to the cognitive-motivational-relational theory; because the basic system variables for emotion in general have now been discussed (though not yet applied to the individual emotions), I am able to close the chapter with an overview of the emotion process in system analytic terms.

Overlaps and Distinctions Among the Constructs of Mind

The existence of overlap among the three constructs of mind discussed in Chapters 3 and 4 — cognition, motivation, and emotion — results in some uncertainty about whether they are discriminable in psychological analysis. For example, the dual meaning of motivation — as dispositional and transactional — makes it easier to reduce emotion, unwisely I believe, to motivation, because arousal, which is part of the transactional meaning of motivation, seems to overlap with emotion, which also has an arousal feature. This problem needs to be addressed a bit more before proceeding.

Differences between emotion and motivation can easily be obscured, because, when motivation is transactional — that is, when it is defined as situational arousal or mobilization to overcome obstacles — the two constructs have overlapping psychophysiological correlates; in other words, when a person is aroused physiologically, we cannot automatically say whether it is because of motivation or emotion

171

unless we have additional information about what is going on. The overlap has also led some to regard both arousal (and drive), and its labeling on the basis of existing social conditions, as necessary to arouse an emotion, in what is often referred to as the *two-factor theory* (Schachter & Singer, 1962). Nevertheless, we can separate the two constucts if we recognize that goal-based activation bears only a modest resemblance to the complex, cognitive-motivational-relational configuration of an emotion. Emotion occurs only when a motivational stake has been appraised.

The developmental interdependence of emotion and motivation adds further confusion to the distinctiveness of the two constructs. Emotions play a role in the development of motivation; from pleasure and pain we learn to want conditions that have previously resulted in positive emotions to occur and to want to avoid conditions that have resulted in negative emotions. This overlap also tempted earlier writers to subsume motivation under emotion, or vice versa. In my view, this is not a good solution; though in nature they are always conjoined and interdependent, emotion and motivation are both needed as separate and distinct concepts.

Motivation also overlaps with cognitive processes. For example, values and goals contain cognitive components in that they depend on feedback, interpretations, and regulating decisions, in addition to having developmental connections with deficit or drive states (see Lazarus, 1968a; Lazarus, in press a; and Tetlock & Levi, 1982). For example, achievement goals include knowledge about the possibility (or probability) of their attainment, the steps needed to attain them, the obstacles that must be overcome, and so forth. We generally do not strive for what is clearly unattainable. Choices must be made among the goals we can and will commit ourselves to in any given situation, and often a set of plans is required that is based on an understanding of the means that serve desired ends (goals). Thus, goals do not consist merely of diffuse drive tensions, but typically call for perceptions, judgments, planning, and decisions.

In sum, motivation in nature is a fusion of activation and goal direction, just as emotion is a fusion of motivation, knowledge, and appraisal of the person–environment relationship (see also Lazarus, Coyne, & Folkman, 1982, for a discussion of this). Motivation without cognition is merely activation without knowledge and direction. Emotion without cognition is merely activation or drive. Nevertheless, the evident overlaps between motivation, emotion, and cognition should not lead us to reduce motivation to cognition, any more than emotion should be reduced to cognition or motivation. There remains a substantial core of distinctive and essential meanings in each construct that is not reducible.

Causality in the Emotion Process

To say that emotion is a result of appraisal clearly implies a causal linkage (see also White, 1990, for a detailed discussion of causation). In philosophical jargon, this treats the cognition-emotion relationship as *synthetic* rather than purely *logical or analytic* in causality. Synthetic here means that certain patterns of appraisal *cause* particular emotions; the logical form requires a different phraseology — namely, that certain patterns of appraisal logically *imply* particular emotions without any necessary causal ascription.

If the description of each emotion is to include the cognitive appraisal that generates it as well as its behavioral and physiological correlates, as when anger was said in Chapter 4 to include an image of the offense and of the blameworthy person (or object), and this offense and blame were also said to cause the anger, then *both* kinds of causal relationship between cognition and emotion, the synthetic and the logical, apply, which avoids an either/or position. This reasoning is consistent with the metatheoretical concept of *reciprocal causality* and with my reluctance to overemphasize material causes.

Because emotion is a complex configuration that draws on and fuses motivation and cognition in any adaptational encounter, another issue concerns the *direction of causality* in the cognition-emotion relationship. Appraisal influences emotion, but the resulting emotion also influences later appraisals reciprocally. Remember that emotion, as I see it, always includes cognition — it is a response to a particular kind of meaning — but impersonal meaning is not emotional. Since an emotion always includes cognition, which is its cause according to Sartre (see Chapter 4), to say that emotion also influences cognition seems at first to be almost a meaningless tautology, particularly if we do not specify what the emotion includes or does not include when we refer to it as causing something.

Social scientists sometimes get uncomfortable about the inclusion of appraisal, the cause of an emotion, in the emotion itself; that is, they are hesitant to see appraisal as a portion of the effect. One reason for the discomfort is the traditional reliance on the Aristotelian logic that one concept, A, cannot also be another concept, B, and we are in the habit of thinking of cause and effect as inviolately separate. This outlook, by the way, also encourages the proposition that emotion and cognition occur in separate portions or systems of the brain, which is another way to distinguish them materially. I shall say more about this later.

To resolve this dilemma about cause and effect, we need to recognize that emotion is a superordinate concept that includes cognition in a part–whole relationship, but the reverse is not true. The cognitive activity, A — namely, blaming someone for an offense — combines in an emotion with physiological reactions and action tendencies, B, to form an organized configuration, AB. The blame causes the emotion, anger, and is also a continuing part of it. To say that anger (AB) — which includes thoughts of blaming someone for an offense (A) — is the cause of the angry reaction (AB) makes no sense unless we realize that a component of the configuration, A, can produce another subsequent AB, of which A is an essential part. When we say that we experience an emotion such as anger, which includes the causal cognitive appraisal as well as the behavioral and physiological reaction, and this anger, in turn, influences subsequent emotional states, we are simply saying that, as a result of feedback, part of the emotional state influences subsequent appraisals and the emotional state they provoke in a causal time series.

This analysis is essentially no different in form than the germ theory of disease. If a disease-causing microbe is present in a vulnerable organism, there is a high probability that the disease will occur. The disease, which I am treating as analogous to emotion, also includes the microbe that, when overcome by the body's defenses, disappears or becomes dormant like a spore. In effect, one of the causes, the microbe (organismic vulnerability is another cause), must remain present during the disease just as the cognitive cause must remain present in the emotion as long as the emotion lasts; however, when the cognitive cause disappears, or is no longer salient, the emotion disappears, too. There is no tautology in this.

I should not try to go much further in the discussion of causality, because there is so much that would need to be covered to justify a full treatment. There is, for example, the analysis by Aristotle of material, efficient, formal, and final causation; the last of these means that behavior must be explained on the basis of the sake for which it occurs, or in my language, on the basis of goals or purposes. I have always had an affinity for this position, as I have with Rychlak's (1981a, 1981b) treatment of free will and his emphasis on the guidance of behavior by its purpose or goal, which he expresses in the concept of "telosponse."

In the last stages of writing this book an instructive article on free will and determinism appeared by Sappington (1990), which reviews a number of recent analyses of the problem of free will and determinism, including those of Bandura (1989), Sperry (1988), and Tageson (1982), as well as others. Bandura, for example, speaks of environmental constraints on the behavior of persons, which implies determinism, but also suggests that such persons are also capable of self-influence or choice; Bandura sees no incompatibility ultimately between the idea of human agency and determinism. The cognitive-motivational-relational theory I am espousing in this book is also essentially deterministic in its framework, though such determinism includes the capacity of the person to choose appraisals on the basis of individual goals and belief systems about self and world.

Contextualism and Mechanism in Emotion Theory

Social science has long struggled with an important contrast between two ways of achieving scientific understanding, contextualism and mechanism. The tension between them is instructive for our understanding of emotion.

From a *contextualist* point of view, an emotion, as well as other psychological phenomena, can only be understood by reference to the particular setting or context in which it occurs. The contextual variables in the emotion process include the demands of the immediate environment (which are primarily social), constraints on thought, feeling, and action, the resources available to the person, as well as personality variables such as motives and beliefs. Contextualists (e.g., Sarbin, 1982), dialecticians (e.g., Riegel, 1975), and those devoted to phenomenology and hermeneutics (e.g., Heidegger & Husserl; see Dreyfus, 1982, 1991; Jennings, 1986; and Taylor, 1985) have all expounded on this theme. Unfortunately, just as mechanists are hidebound in their own way, contextualists insist that mechanism be totally rejected in favor of their world view; yet contextualism does not lead to general explanations about how things work, and it is difficult to translate this view into empirical research strategies that go beyond descriptions of the phenomena of interest.

The *mechanistic* view has long dominated the physical and biological sciences, and it has helped us understand and control the physical world. It is best described as a search for universal mechanisms or fundamental laws for understanding the natural world. Following Pepper (1942), its root metaphor is the machine. Whether biological, psychological, social, or physical, a mechanism is a universal cause-and-effect arrangement that works the same way in any context.

Mechanism is illustrated by the servo or feedback principle, which operates in the common household thermostat and in the body's homeostatic processes for preserving its chemical equilibria; for example, when the presence of suger in the blood indicates depletion beyond some specified level, we experience hunger, and when the blood's water content goes below a given level, we experience thirst. In speaking of appraisal as a necessary and sufficient condition of emotion, I have also adopted a mechanistic approach to understanding, which says that a given pattern of thoughts will always yield a particular emotion.

When we consider where each epistemological outlook leads, certain issues about the emotion process are clarified. In *mechanism,* the emphasis is on universality, structure, and process. A complete scientific understanding of how things are and work requires a grasp of both structure and process. Generally *structures* refer to the more or less stable arrangement or patterning of parts in a system; a *process* refers to the functions carried out by the parts — that is, what they do and how they interact and change.

The mechanically minded reader might think of an internal combustion engine as an example.[2] The automobile engine has many parts (structure), all connected into a system that determines how energy is transformed from its latent form in gasoline to the synchronous turning of the wheels (process). The geological structures of our physical environment (e.g., hills, riverbeds, foliage) and the geological processes (e.g., the flow of water and wind, upheavals of the earth's surface) are also good examples of the interplay of both structures and processes. The structure of the land directs wind and water flow; this in turn erodes the structure in the long run, which is what happens when river channels and valleys are formed. A psychological system, too, may be described in terms of structures and processes; we speak of the stable attributes of the person that affect emotional reactions as personality structures, and changeable states such as wanting, thinking, and feeling as personality processes.

The contrast between structure and process suggests the more familiar contrast between emotion as a *state* or a *trait,* which I spoke of in Chapter 2. As a *state,* emotion is always in flux, changing from one context or moment to another. No two emotional events are ever the same; if I am angry, this cannot be understood solely by reference to other occasions in which I was angry, but requires an examination of the special context in which the present anger occurred. The anger is always unique in certain respects, which emphasizes contextualism, but it is also like all other anger episodes, too, in some ways, which emphasizes universal mechanisms.

As a *trait,* on the other hand, emotion is a structural property of the person–environment relationship. Strictly speaking, a trait cannot be an emotion, because it is a disposition to react with one rather than being one. Said differently, it is a prediction about the frequency, intensity, or environmental contexts in which a particular individual is likely to experience a given emotion state. When the same emotion recurs, as is frequently the case, we speak of angry, guilty, shameful, or happy persons. To the extent that it recurs across circumstances, or follows a common pattern of generation, an emotion can be viewed as expressing more or less stable features of a person's psychological makeup, of an environment (e.g., an assaultive spouse or employer), or, I think more accurately and completely, of a person's stable relationship with the environment. One person may feel anger again and again in basically the same environmental context as that in which another person recurrently feels anxiety or guilt (see Lazarus, 1989a).

If one is mainly interested in what it is about the person (trait) that disposes that person to anger, one seeks the universal rule within the person. If one is mainly interested in social situations (contexts) that make people angry (state), one seeks the universal rule in sociocultural processes. If, as I would argue, the explanation is said to lie in the conjunction of person and environmental forces, we must seek the universal rule or mechanism in the person–environment relationship in an adaptational encounter, which is the proper arena in which to study emotional reactions. By now the reader knows that the psychological unit of this arena on which I center my analysis of emotion is the core relational theme, which is arrived at through the process of appraisal.

Crucial features of the emotions are sacrificed if either the mechanistic or the contextualist perspective is carried to an extreme. In the search for universal mechanisms we pay attention to the ways people are alike, making generalizations that apply to everyone in any time or place. We also try to classify contexts on the basis of their capacity to produce a particular emotional state in a particular type of person. We might observe, for example, that anger always occurs in a particular kind of person–environment relationship, one in which we make the evaluative judgment that we have been insulted or demeaned. We can generalize only if we ask how situations are *functionally equivalent* in their capacity to generate emotional states, and how a particular experience of anger, though different in certain ways from other anger experiences, is comparable to others in what brings it about and how it looks and operates.

However, when we make this kind of useful generalization, we also must overlook or de-emphasize variations in the emotions experienced on different occasions. This is what contextualism is all about. Hermeneutics, which is a form of contextualism, is overly concerned with uniqueness and context, and mechanistic science is overly concerned with universal principles that transcend variable contexts. When generalizations about emotion are qualified by contextual variables, our analyses are made more complicated, but this also increases our ability to explain and predict the inter- and intraindividual variations.

It is my opinion that extreme contextualism — the "ism" makes it a doctrine rather than merely being a sensible awareness of the importance of contexts — cannot be accepted as a complete science, because it undermines the search for generalizations about the phenomena of emotion; and extreme mechanism as a doctrine undermines an appreciation of the variations in the phenomenon and its complexity. As will be seen at the end of the chapter, this is an argument for a system theory approach to the emotion process.

Three Issues about the Causal Role of Cognition

To say that cognitive activity is a sufficient condition of emotion means that it is capable of causing an emotion, but that other factors do so, too. To say it is a necessary condition means that there can be no emotion without cognitive activity. The latter is a stronger statement about causality. These statements are, however, both incomplete as given because we must consider more than one kind of cognitive activity — namely, knowledge and appraisal (see Chapter 4, and Lazarus & Smith, 1988).

My proposal in Chapter 4 was that *knowledge,* which includes both accurate and inaccurate beliefs about how things are and work, is *necessary* for an emotion to occur, because the significance of transactions for one's well-being rests on such knowledge. However, knowledge is *not sufficient* to produce an emotion, since a personal evaluation (appraisal) is required for an emotion to occur, and this appraisal depends not only on the facts as apprehended (i.e., knowledge) but also on an evaluation of how these facts affect one's well-being. Some sense of ego-identity and, for want of a better term, self-interest in what is happening must be added to knowledge to produce an emotion. *Appraisal* of the significance of the person–environment relationship, therefore, is both *necessary and sufficient;* without a personal appraisal (i.e., of harm or benefit) there will be no emotion; when such an appraisal is made, an emotion of some kind is inevitable.

Although there is considerable agreement that appraisal is a sufficient condition of emotion — that is, it will often result in and shape an emotion — many theorists argue against the proposition that it is necessary. The argument is often fuzzy, because protagonists typically write too broadly about cognitive activity without making the functional distinction between knowledge and appraisal. For example, in an important edited book about cognition-emotion relationships, Izard, Kagan, and Zajonc (1984, p. 5) write: "There is no argument as to whether cognition is a sufficient cause of emotion; the question is whether cognition is a necessary cause." Hoffman (1985) makes the same point in suggesting that little is to be gained by postulating in advance that cognitive evaluation is always necessary. The kind of cognition is not made clear.

Why is there opposition to the proposition that appraisal is a necessary condition of emotion? Three difficulties are posed by the naysayers, erroneously in my view: (1) In giving thought processes a central role in shaping emotion, emotion is said to be left cold and bloodless. (2) Infants and nonhuman animals react emotionally without having the capacity, it is said, for the complex thought necessary to make an appraisal. Drugs, too, and other physiological conditions like fatigue and illness, result in changes in mood and other emotional consequences, which is often interpreted to mean that emotion can be generated without cognitive mediation. (3) Emotional reactions are often, or perhaps even usually, rapid or almost instantaneous. This speed makes it is difficult to account for them on the basis of a complex process of obtaining and processing information from the environment, which cognitive psychologists have typically described as proceeding in relatively slow, sequential steps, having modeled them on the digital search, storage, and retrieval of computers. The issue can best be stated, I think, by asking whether there is only one mechanism for achieving meaning. I shall now address each of these issues in turn.

1. Does Cognitive Causation Make Emotion Cold and Bloodless?

Tomkins (1981, p. 306) treats the idea of cognitive causation as an overintellectualized way to make hot emotions cool and pallid, and others have made this same logical error, which is to assume that cognitive approaches subsume emotion under cognition or make it equivalent to cognition. This is a straw man. The more precise and restricted proposition in cognitive causation is that emotion has cognitive causes and components, not that emotion is merely a form of cognition. When one says, as Solomon (1980, p. 271) and Sartre (1948, p. 52) do, that emotions are akin to judgments, or a certain way of apprehending the world, these statements, especially when taken out of context, do indeed make it seem as though the heat of emotion has been circumscribed.

I think the best rejoinder to those who criticize the proposition that appraisal is necessary on this basis is that emotion depends on and contains knowledge, but it also includes other (hot) components such as a heightened sense (appraisal) that one has a personal stake in an encounter, action tendencies, and physiological changes that stem from this sense. In short, *to emphasize cognitive activity in the emotion process does not equate emotion with cognition.*

Another straw man is the result of misunderstandings about the ambiguous phrases, the "primacy of emotion" (Zajonc, 1980, 1984) and the "primacy of cognition" (Lazarus, 1982, 1984a), used in earlier debates about the role of cognition in emotion. Some readers interpreted these phrases as suggesting, erroneously, either that emotion was more important than cognition, or vice versa, that cognition was more important than emotion. I certainly did not intend to imply by primacy that one is more important psychologically than the other.

Some of those who accept these straw man arguments have offered as a solution the idea that emotion and cognition are *separate systems,* governed by separate anatomical structures of the brain (cf. Zajonc, 1980, 1984). This position has been especially appealing to those who think of emotion as an innate process and those who are comfortable reducing mental activity to neurophysiology (see Panksepp, 1982, 1986). Le Doux (1989), too, favors the anatomical and functional independence of emotion and cognition. When he writes (1989, p. 278) that "the systems can also function independently" I have somewhat less discomfort than when he writes (1989, p. 279) that "affective computations can be performed without the assistance of cognitive computations."

In the absence of a qualification that affective computations are evaluations of danger or benign conditions, and therefore are cognitive processes, such a statement seems unsound to me even if the evaluations are primitive, as long as they depend to some extent on experience rather than innate reflexes. Le Doux seems to imply learning in the same article when he writes (1989, p. 271) that "the core of the emotional system is thus a mechanism for computing the affective significance of stimuli." Expressions such as "computing" and "affective significance" surely imply meaning, evaluation, or cognitive processing of some sort even when conducted at the level of the amygdala in the brain, and I think it is a careless usage to speak of an affective system as though it involved no cognitive activity. Thus, part of the problem is to be much clearer about what we mean by cognition and to overcome the notion, evaluated a little later on, that there is only one way in which evaluation or meaning can occur (see also Chapter 4).

To argue against viewing cognition and emotion as separate systems, however, does not gainsay the concept of system but only quarrels with one way of organizing it. Later in the chapter, in dealing with system theory, I suggest that it is indeed useful to speak of an emotion system, an organized complex of variables and processes that makes the emotions different from other psychological activities — for example, those involved in ordinary, nonemotional living and adapting (cf. Duffy, 1941a, 1941b).

One difficulty with a solution that makes cognition separate from emotion is that emotion and cognition are each so complex, and their mechanisms spread so widely over the central and peripheral neural pathways that, in my opinion, it is difficult to argue convincingly for separate systems as though there were a special brain organ for each. Today neuropsychologists also seem to think of the brain in terms of telephonelike circuits instead of electrochemical fields that might diffuse somewhat and involve diverse portions of the brain. I'm not sure whether either of these analogies is completely sound or whether either will be the ultimate way in which we will understand brain function. Despite much recent progress, we are a long way from understanding how this most complicated organ (or organs) works.

The argument is reminiscent of much earlier debates about *mass action versus localization of brain function,* and pendulum swings about this have been endemic. Right now, localization is in the ascendency. Although emotions and cognitive activity can be disconnected functionally, as when we are engaged in ego-defensive maneuvers such as distancing or intellectualization, or under certain conditions of brain damage (cf. Sachs, 1987), separatism could be carrying neural localization and specificity too far, a sort of neuropsychological *deus ex machina.*

A second difficulty is that the functioning of living creatures is generally integrated rather than fractionated. Mind is usually rapidly coordinated and directed, with each adaptational function operating interdependently rather than going off in diverse directions at once. There is a long and reasonable tradition of thinking of health as integration and pathology as conflict and fragmentation. In my view, the separatist solution keeps us from asking the right questions, which have to do with the kind of cognitive activity that is causally involved in the emotion process, how it works, and how the processes involved in the emotions are coordinated in the mind.

The separation of cognition and emotion has been a long tradition in the Western world, going back to the ancient Greeks and continuing through the Middle Ages in the Catholic Church and into the present. The Apollonian Greek ideal, which the medieval Church also adopted, enthroned rationality as godlike. Passion was regarded as animallike, and the Church enjoined its parishioners to control their animal natures by reason.

In the counterculture of the 1960s, and in the romanticism of Rousseau and others, the relationship was briefly reversed by the outlook that in the industrial world humans had become overly constrained by rational values and societal rules at the expense of their humanity. Therefore, we must struggle to get in touch with our emotions, which had been suppressed. (A number of modern experiential psychotherapies also adopt this view; see Chapter 11.) Here too, as in classical and medieval times, emotions and cognition are separated and contrasted rather than being seen as interdependent and fused.

Perhaps we have become entrapped by this ideology when we think of mind and brain today. Psychophysiological research on emotions up to recent times centered on lower and mid-brain structures such as the reticular activating system and the hypothalamus (cf. Averill, 1974). Emotion was treated as a primitive gut reaction, so to speak, and only recently has there been much interest in the limbic system and cerebral cortex in the emotion process. We are beginning to catch on that higher forms of cognitive activity are important in emotion. Leeper (1970, pp. 156–157) put it this way:

> Older psychological thought assumed also that emotions are lower-order processes, partly because emotions were pictured as dependent on subcortical mechanisms and the autonomic nervous system, whereas perceptions and cognitive activity generally in the higher vertebrates were pictured as dependent on the neocortex and on the somatic nervous system.
>
> However, any such neurological dichotomy can be dismissed fairly surely. The new discoveries about the influences of the brainstem reticular formation were merely part of the evidence showing the interdependence of cortical and subcortical functioning both in cognitive activities and in emotional processes.
>
> Indeed, since emotional functioning is most developed in creatures like man and chimpanzees, less in dogs, and still less in chickens, it may even be that the neocortical part of the brain has been as crucial for emotional characteristics as for traditionally recognized sorts of perception, learning, and thinking.

In sum, our cultural traditions and philosophical biases have reinforced the concept of emotion and cognition as separate systems, with emotion as primitive and cognition as advanced in both a phylogenetic and an ontogenetic sense, despite the very real possibility that this is not the best model for thinking of the emotion process.

2. Can Emotion Be Generated Without Cognitive Mediation?

The answer to this question depends on evidence that emotions are experienced in the absence of the capacity for relevant knowledge and appraisal. Obviously, if *infants and young children* — as well as *infrahuman animals* — experience emotions without being able to evaluate what is happening in their adaptational encounters, or if *physiological states* could produce emotions directly without cognitive mediation, it would be difficult to argue that cognition is a necessary condition of emotion. Izard, Kagan, and Zajonc (1984, p. 2) write that neurally mediated "afferent [sensory] information can be transformed directly into emotion without cognitive activity." However, because of methodological difficulties that make the question very difficult to resolve, not the least of which is identifying the emotional experience itself from what we observe, evidence is not easy to generate. On the basis of peripheral responses whose significance is not very clear, we are forced to surmise about the cognitive capacities and processes used by infants and young children, about cognitive activity in nonhuman animals, and about mediating appraisals accompanying physiological states such as those produced by drugs.

The Case for Infants and Young Children. In Chapter 8, I will cover the ground of emotional development more thoroughly, so here I touch on only a few key points somewhat lightly and in a way that overlaps with what I have already said in Chapter 4 about cognitive mediation. A number of developmental psychologists (e.g., Emde, 1984; Izard, 1978, 1984; Fischer & Pipp, 1984; Sroufe, 1984) believe that infants are not capable of a wide range of emotions at birth, but that emotions emerge at from about two to four months of age, with some appearing earlier than others. The earliest emotional state said to be displayed by infants is diffuse upset, followed by wariness or interest, then happiness, anger, and later fear. Shame and guilt probably arise much later because of their dependence on an advanced under-standing of complex social relationships (see also Dunn, 1988; Harris, 1989), but there is not much developmental observation on which to rely, and many phyloge-neticists do not even regard them as primary emotions.

As Lewis and Saarni (1985), and many others, have pointed out, too, there is an important distinction between emotional *experience* and *expression,* which later gets integrated into an emotional configuration. There is no problem in conceding that children give early evidence of expressions that look emotional, but this is not to say that infants necessarily experience emotion before they can grasp the significance of what is happening for their well-being. Above all, the issue of whether and when infants and very young children experience emotions, and which ones, is an unset-tled one that should not be casually foreclosed.

Much has been made of smiling in the newborn, but Emde's (1984, p. 82) obser-vations that very early smiling does not seem to be related to external events should make us wary of claims, based on facial reactions, that infants experience emotion before they are capable of the most primitive kind of appraisal. Although this seems to be a reasonable position that has empirical support, an analysis by Ekman, Friesen and Davidson (1990), which I cited in Chapter 2, also cautions us that there may be different kinds of smiles, which could signify quite different psychological states and processes. And so, regardless of how one views the adequacy of the evi-dence, interpreting smiles may be more complex and difficult than is ordinarily assumed, and observers could be fooled about their emotional meaning.

Moreover, it does not make good sense, in my view, to say that the ability to communicate with words is crucial to experiencing an emotion. Actually, very young, preverbal children have emotions that cannot be assessed through verbal reports. That children appear to express emotions and show associated physiological changes that imply that they are having emotional experiences quite early in life, even if not represented in consciousness or describable by them in words, can be reasonably well documented, as in Dunn's (1988) ethologically oriented research.

Dunn and Munn (1985), for example, observe that emotional conflicts with the mother are very common and escalate from 14 months to 24 months, as shown in Table 5.1. The frequencies of some of the child's emotionally loaded responses are shown in Table 5.2. Later on, in Chapter 8, I provide some concrete illustrations of verbal interchanges from Dunn's research that suggest how sophisticated the young child's grasp of the rules of emotion can be.

In other words, a substantial case can be made even without use of verbal report that children are capable of making cognitive appraisals quite early and, in fact,

TABLE 5.1. Totals and Mean Frequencies of Conflict Incidents per Family

Conflict Incidents	Mean Frequency at Various Ages (Months)				
	14	16	18	21	24
Sibling conflict					
Study 1 (N = 328)	10.3	8.2	11.7	11.5	11.2
Study 2 (N = 656)	–	–	8.0	–	7.6
Child–mother conflict					
Study 1 (N = 298)	5.8	8.2	9.2	12.0	12.5
Mother–sibling conflict					
Study 2	–	–	3.0	–	4.7

(*Source:* J. Dunn and P. Munn, "Becoming a family member." *Child Development, 56.* Chicago: University of Chicago Press. Copyright © 1985 by The Society for Research in Child Development, Inc. Reprinted by permission.)

rapidly learn important lessons in the early months about the significance of encounters for their well-being. But what about early infancy? Campos and his associates (e.g., Bertenthal, Campos, & Barrett, 1984) have shown that an infant's appraisal of the danger of height depends on experience with locomotion (crawling), which occurs developmentally very early. Only when the child has begun to crawl does it react with fear of height in the experimental situation of the visual cliff, in which the child is directed to cross a transparent table top that creates an illusion of height-induced danger.

These data strongly suggest that, as a result of the experience of crawling, babies must first appraise in an embodied sense, as it were, that there is a danger of falling

TABLE 5.2 Study 1: Changes in Behavior during Sibling and
Mother–Child Conflict during the Second Year

Child's Response	No. of Incidents at Various Ages (Months)				
	14	16	18	21	24
Sibling conflict in which child appeals to mother					
Looks at mother, fusses, holds up arms	16 (6)	3 (3)	6 (3)	1 (1)	–
Looks at mother or observer, points at sibling, vocalizes protest	–	8 (5)	13 (6)	7 (2)	2 (1)
Makes verbal protest on sibling transgression	–	4 (1)	9 (3)	26 (6)	20 (6)
Mother–child conflict in which child expresses anger or laughter					
Expresses anger	2 (2)	7 (4)	8 (4)	17 (5)	17 (6)
Laughs at mother or observer	9 (3)	20 (5)	29 (6)	35 (5)	37 (6)

Note: Numbers in parentheses = N.

(*Source:* J. Dunn and P. Munn, "Becoming a family member." *Child Development, 56.* Chicago: University of Chicago Press. Copyright © 1985 by The Society for Research in Child Development, Inc. Reprinted by permission.)

and being hurt in order to experience the emotion of fear in the visual cliff experiment. Babies who have had a previous falling experience, or a near fall in which the mother has spoken or acted with alarm when the child is poised at the edge of a precipice or at the top of a staircase, are more likely than others to show fear. If the mother smiles from the seemingly "dangerous" side of the visual cliff, the baby is less fearful and may even move to the deep side of the cliff or sometimes even crawl around the outside edge to avoid it (see Figure 8.2). Later on, with additional experience and maturity, the same baby will gingerly cross over the visual cliff, which means it has passed on further to a stage of coping, which requires much more understanding of the world.

The fact that I have not yet dealt much with issues of emotional *development* makes this discussion perforce incomplete. In Chapter 4, I made what I consider the extremely important distinction between complex, deliberate, volitional, and unconscious modes of meaning generation on the one hand, and simpler, automatic, involuntary, and unconscious (or preconscious) modes on the other, as illustrated, for example, in the notion of resonances. Yet my discussion of appraisal components could seem like backsliding to a view of appraisal as deliberate and reflective, which applies only to adults under certain conditions rather than to infants.

Although in Chapter 4, citing Stenberg and Campos (1990) and Bahrick and Watson (1985), I digressed briefly to point out that infant anger, for example, might operate differently than later, adult anger, I repeat here the statement that the appraisal components I have been discussing, and will continue to use in Chapters 6 and 7, not be viewed as necessarily high-level forms of information processing when meaning can be achieved in other, developmentally more elemental ways. It is wise to defer discussion of many of the issues of development until Chapter 8 in Part Four. Nevertheless, I think it is tenable and worth reemphasizing here that the 4-month-old infant may have elemental sense of goal relevance, self or ego-identity, goal incongruence, and external accountability when anger is generated; the capacity for imputed control, hence blame, could easily be lacking; it may be important only in adult anger but not in very young children.

How appraisal develops and how emotions come about will remain a difficult and controversial set of issues, and we should expect divergent conceptual solutions to be debated for a long time, because we cannot make the observations necessary to resolve the issues cleanly, and because social scientists have divergent theoretical and metatheoretical predilections. My concern here has been to show that it is reasonable to propose that appraisal is a necessary and sufficient cause of the emotions, and that the emergence of different emotions in infants and young children at different ages reflects the growth of understanding about self and world, on which adult appraisals are predicated.

The Case for Infrahuman Animals. A comparable argument can be made that even relatively simple *animals* may have a far greater cognitive capacity to evaluate the significance of what is happening than is often assumed. The pattern of behavior in the broken-wing displays of birds described by Griffin (1984), which suggest well-orchestrated, appraisallike, conditional complexities and maneuvers that are flexibly responsive to the situation as it changes, is clearly relevant here (see

Chapter 3). Simple animals, such as the fowl and fish studied by Tinbergen (1951), are capable of discriminating danger from benign conditions on the basis of environmental "releasers" that seem little dependent on experience. Although one must be wary of either/or treatments of genetics and learning, as Beach (1955) has admonished, innate neurological reflexes become less important in higher species such as humans in favor of more variable and flexible patterns of discrimination based on intelligence, a theme developed more fully later in this chapter.

The Case for Physiological States. A corollary of separatism and reduction is the assumption, which I am inclined to challenge, that brain activity can influence emotion without cognitive mediation, or perhaps more to the point, that to understand emotion psychologically requires that we study neurochemical processes. The penchant for reducing psychological processes such as emotion to neurochemical ones is well illustrated in the interpretation of how *physical conditions* such as fatigue and illness, or drugs such as cocaine, lithium, and caffeine, affect moods and acute emotions.

Microbiologists say, for example, that *cocaine* produces euphoria by flooding the synapses (spaces between nerve cells) with chemicals such as dopamine and norepinephrine, which facilitate neural transmission. This is one prominent theory of the drug effects. However, the question of whether the effect on mood is direct or mediated by how these chemicals influence the appraisal process remains unresolved.

Presumably as a result of increased ease of neural transmission, which facilitates adaptive functioning, cocaine is also said to result in enhanced self-confidence and a sense of security and personal power. From a cognitive-mediational point of view, no wonder the person feels euphoric, given the temporarily enhanced and subjectively perceived functional power. Like the emotion-focused coping processes I discussed earlier, this is a phony high, because nothing has really changed in the person—environment relationship, and after a short time — when the neurotransmitters are back to normal or are at subnormal levels — the person crashes and becomes emotionally depressed.

The point I am making about cocaine — and it could also be made about any other drug — is that drugs do, of course, affect moods and acute emotions, but it is perfectly reasonable to propose that their influence on the brain of a sentient being never occurs independent of cognitive activities such as appraisal, unless that being is comatose.

Many years ago (Lazarus, 1966, p. 398) I cited a study by Symington et al. (1955) suggesting that certain forms of unconsciousness, as a result of surgical anesthesia or when dying, eliminates the adrenal effects of psychological stress. For example, patients who were dying from injury or disease showed a normal adrenal cortical condition, as assessed during autopsy, as long as they had remained unconscious during the death process. In contrast, patients who were conscious during the fatal disease process and died showed adrenal cortical changes. Moreover, Gray, Ramsey, Villarreal, and Krakaner (1955–1956) showed that general anesthesia, by itself, did not result in a significant adrenal cortical reaction.

This research, along with the observations of Mason and his colleagues (1976), which I cited in Chapter 2, suggest that it may be an *awareness* of the psychological significance of illness, which implies appraisal, that results in the adrenal cortical response described by Selye (1956/1976). It has always surprised me that because of their potential importance for theory these findings have not been discussed more by those concerned with stress and appraisal.

It is not easy, and it may never be possible methodologically, to separate the role of cognitive appraisal from what is happening at the neurochemical level. Without a demonstration that drug effects on the emotions (mood included) occur in the absence of mediating cognitions, evidence of these effects does not tell us how they work or in any way undermine the proposition that cognitive mediation is a necessary condition of emotion. Although many of my colleagues would prefer me to adopt a less extreme position, there is clarity and utility in taking the strong position that appraisal is causally necessary in emotion. A reasonable but less attractive alternative is that there are two principles of emotion generation: one operating through cognitive mediation, the other producing effects independent of appraisal. This issue is unlikely to be resolved easily, and we will continue to find theoreticians arrayed on both sides of the fence.

How then could physiological states such as fatigue, illness, and drugs play a causal role in the emotions? I suggest that the primary role of physiological states is to *potentiate* emotional states, not to cause them directly, which requires a sensing of a harmful or beneficial person–environment relationship. Fatigue and illness, and other debilitating bodily conditions, increase the potential for either generalized distress or negative emotional states such as anger, sadness, and the like, depending on the particular core relational theme that is generated. Positive physical states — for example, feeling rested or the return of energy after illness — increase the potential for positive emotional states such as happiness, pride, and love; which of these states occurs will depend on the core relational theme — influenced, of course, by what is happening in the person–environment relationship.

I think of the many times I have awakened at 4 A.M. only to begin a process of ruminating about the tasks and responsibilities I must take on the next day. The tasks seem endless and overwhelming, a source of anxiety. Ultimately I fall asleep and wake with a very different subjective sense, especially after getting started and having some coffee. I have always believed that this commonly experienced phenomenon stems from the vulnerability that comes from being sleepy, tired, and unalert. The anxious mood associated with this is potentiated by the temporary physical limitations for coping with what will seem to most of us quite manageable when one is alert or mobilized. The same reasoning applies to the premenstrual syndrome (PMS) in connection with a young woman's monthly ovulation cycle, which is much in media attention. The varying physical states in the cycle, based no doubt on hormonal changes, influence appraisals, and hence moods.

In other words, physical states serve, as do moods (see Chapter 1), as dispositions, whose capacity to generate particular emotions depends on the mediating appraisals the dispositions result in for managing transactions with the environment, whether actual or anticipated. They are not direct causes but depend, as emotions always do, on how what is happening is appraised. They tell us we are on top of things, without defining the specific adaptational agendas, or that our resources for coping are undermined because we are momentarily lacking in energy and reserve, and so, routine demands seem to tax or exceed our adaptational capacities more than in the normal course of events.

In the foregoing discussion, alert readers will have recognized the ubiquitous philosophical issues of mind and body and reductionism. For some, mind can be reduced to the basic principles of physiology; thoughts and actions are explained as neural activities, which in turn might be further reduced to cellular and microbiological processes, and I suppose ultimately to particle or subatomic physics if we take seriously the dream of a unified science. Deese (1985) observed that reductionism dominates science today but was shared by only a small minority of seventeenth-century scientists and philosophers. As usually stated, however, it offers no explanation without reference to the psychological conditions (e.g., environmental, intrapsychic, or relational) that influence thought and action. It is, as I see it, merely a form of pointing to the next lower level of analysis.

Reductionism, when it is relevant to emotion, is mainly limited to physiology, because it is still relatively molar compared with chemistry or physics; physiology centers on brain structure and function and on the macro hormonal substances that influence and are influenced by nerve cells—for example, the cortical and medullary hormones of the adrenal glands and the recently discovered neuropeptides (e.g., enkaphalins), which are used by the body in the relief of pain and are sometimes called natural opiates. Discovery of neural receptors where morphine and other drugs act was an important step in understanding how the nervous system works. Further reductive steps are not usually attempted, because the molar concepts of mind and behavior do not lend themselves easily to the molecular concepts of microbiology.

There are many arguments against reduction of social science to biological and physical science, and it would not be worthwhile to develop them all here in a long digression. Some discussion of this fundamental epistemological problem will help us be clear about this, however. It is relevant here because so much of what is written about the emotions presumes that understanding them requires the study of the brain. In the most extreme version of this, psychological theory must be in accord with beliefs about the brain, though these beliefs—characteristically referred to as knowledge—keep changing; if it is not in accord with physiology, psychological theory must, perforce, be wrong.

The main problem with reductionism, in my view, is that concepts at the different levels of analysis are not parallel; one doesn't map the other so that meaningful functional links can be drawn between them. For example, the concept of the reticular activating system made a meaningful connection with earlier thinking about drive, attention, and mobilization at the behavioral level, but in current thinking activation seems inadequate to explain complex processes of adaptation, especially when cognitive mediation is said to be involved (cf. Neiss, 1988; Anderson, 1990).

With respect to the mapping of one level of analysis by another, too little is known about the physiology of the brain at this time to match up well with the psychological processes of appraisal and coping. A trend toward greater interest in cortical and limbic system research on the cognitive processes involved in emotion (cf. Henry, 1986; Le Doux, 1986a, 1986b, 1989; Panksepp, 1982, 1986, 1990) and in split-brain cortical research on emotion (e.g., Fox & Davidson, 1984) is taking place, but it is too early to tell how far this will go in narrowing the gap between the physiological and behavioral levels of analysis. The further one goes in the molecular direction away from molar concepts of mind, the more remote seem to be the functional connections between them.

I don't want to be misunderstood here. In spite of the problems presented by thoughtless reductionism, I believe it is quite appropriate and valuable to build bridges across scientific levels of analysis. Though an opponent of reduction, Parisi (1987) has suggested that finding a functional link is often very useful, as when a chemical or surgical treatment is the best way to deal with a psychological dysfunction. Problems arise, however, when we seek to explain what is happening at a molar level by literal reference to the molecular. We must not try to explain the psychological on the basis of the physiological, and vice versa, nor adopt the erroneous view that the higher level reflects "nothing but" what is going on at the lower level. To do so not only inhibits and demeans the study of the molar level, but also makes an implicit if not explicit claim, which could be damaging to our search for understanding, that the theory of mind and behavior must conform to what is believed at any given time about the brain. Besides, if we believe as I do that higher levels of analysis involve emergent properties that are not present at lower levels, then we can never hope to fully explain the phenomena of one level by invoking the basic principles formulated when studying the phenomena of a lower level.

In contrast, with one-way reductive analyses that descend from molar to molecular levels, one can locate bidirectional causal links. For example, although we usually assume that the psychological response depends on physiological processes, the reverse can also be true. This striking idea was suggested recently by Erdelyi (1985) in passing, and very searchingly examined by Parisi (1987) in a discussion of Freud's effort to place psychology within a natural science framework, an effort that Parisi says failed. The failure occurred because the clinical observations, which formed the basis for Freud's analysis of hysterical conversions, demonstrated, ironically, that neurology could not account for the observed paralyses and anesthesias. The symptoms did not, in effect, conform to known nerve pathways. Parisi (1987, pp. 237–238) put it as follows:

> Freud reached a conclusion that there can be no hope of tracing these phenomena back or down to biological roots. Without espousing some sort of mysticism or dualism, he effectively concluded that psychological phenomena are not reducible to biological phenomena. . . . Ideas are causal in the formation of symptoms and behavior. As Rychlak (1981a) pointed out, this constitutes a reversal of the normally conceived causal stream in which ideas, behaviors and symptoms reduce to physiology. What Freud witnessed in Charcot's clinic and in his later work with Breuer (Breuer & Freud, 1985) was that symptoms reduce to ideas.

A final argument might be made, which I could jokingly refer to as "reverse reductionism," from a different point of view than that of Parisi's. The argument goes as follows: Brain physiology, without knowledge of psychological functioning, is merely anatomy. Physiology is all about the functions of the nervous system, and to apply to behavioral functions it must have psychological referents. So instead of the usual proposition that we need to know about the brain to understand the emotions, a proper case could be made for the opposite proposition that there can be no knowledge of brain physiology without a sophisticated grasp of how and why we act and react as we do, the emotions included. Even if we try to explain behavior on the basis of neurophysiology, which I reject as bad science, to understand the brain requires that we have something psychological to explain, meaning the rules about how we act and react. In effect, a physiologist, much less a neuropsychologist, needs to know about the mind in order to know about the brain.

3. Is There Only One Mechanism for Achieving Meaning?

An apparent dilemma, contained in the proposition about the cognitive causation of emotion, results from the fact that emotion is often or, perhaps even usually, an almost instantaneous response to a provocation. A very rapid response seems to obviate sequential "information processing"—once the dominant view of cognitive psychologists—which, in an analogy to the computer, involves a time-consuming sequence of digital scanning of meaningless inputs from multiple sources in the environment and within the person in order to generate relevant meanings on which adaptive choices of action depend. If this were the only process of meaning generation, there would, indeed, be a dilemma: Animals (people included) must often react at virtually the instant of input relevant to their well-being, especially danger. If we were built any other way, we would not long survive.

There are two possible solutions: One is to assume that the process of appraisal must be capable of operating through mechanisms far more simple and rapid than those implied by traditional cognitive psychology; a second is to assume that emotion does not depend on cognitive activity at all—in effect, that there is a separate emotion process operating independent of cognition.

I have already argued against the second solution. The position I believe is the most reasonable and self-consistent is that there must be more than one kind of appraisal. Some emotions are the result of time-consuming, deliberate, volitional, and conscious forms of reasoning, which draw on our abstract, symbolic capacities, whereas others are the result of automatic, involuntary, and unconscious cognitive activity that is very rapid. I discussed this at considerable length in Chapter 4. And although most cognitive scientists began with a seriatim, conscious conception of information processing, for quite some time they have been interested in parallel processing, which is a variant of one of the solutions to the problem of meaning generation discussed later.

Other emotion theorists seem to have come to a similar conclusion following public debates about cognition-emotion relationships (cf. Baars, 1981; Ellis, 1985; Kleinginna & Kleinginna, 1985; Lazarus, 1981b, 1982, 1984a; Leventhal & Scherer, 1987; Scheff, 1985; Slife, 1981; Zajonc, 1980, 1984). The issue of how cognition and emotion are related has a long history (see also Bolles, 1974; Hilgard, 1980, for further analyses).

One example of advocacy for the idea of different levels of cognitive processing in emotion can be found in Buck's (1985) distinction between analytic and synthetic cognition. In *analytic cognition,* there is a buildup of meaning from originally meaningless bits in a stimulus display through linear scanning and digital analysis. In *syncretic cognition,* there is analogue detection of ecologically significant information, which is similar to Gibson's (1966, 1979) view of how perception works. Here adaptational meaning is instantaneously achieved without reflection or multiple operations.

A comparable view is found in Leventhal's (1984) distinction between schematic and conceptual processing. In *schematic processing,* which is the simpler of the two, when knowledge has been consistently appraised in the past in a particular way by a person, probably as a result of positive or negative adaptational outcomes, connections between knowledge and appraisal are formed that are functionally inseparable and seemingly fused and instantaneous. The evaluation occurs automatically and without complex cognitive activity.

In *conceptual processing,* complex knowledge structures and appraisals shape emotions through abstract, conscious, and deliberate forms of reasoning. This could well follow predefined stages, though I said earlier that the idea of such stages, as in Scherer's (1984a, 1984b) concept of stimulus evaluation checks, is problematic (see also Baron & Boudreau, 1987; and Shepard, 1984, on resonances). Leventhal has also suggested a third, more primitive level of cognitive processing, *sensorimotor,* which might be similar to what I said in Chapter 4 about resonances, or embodied intelligence (cf. Leventhal & Scherer, 1987).

In any case, cognitive activity can occur in simple, primitive, and very rapid fashion, or in more complex and multiple-process fashion, which would also be slower. In his discussion of empathic emotions, Hoffman (1984), too, assumes that several kinds of cognitive activity, some relatively primitive, some highly advanced, can take place in emotion, perhaps even at the same time.

That there is more than one mode of meaning generation has gained added credibility as a result of attempts to trace neurophysiological pathways of evaluative cognitive activity in the brain. Although my views on reduction make me wary of citing it as support, the point may be illustrated by the work of Le Doux (1986a, 1986b, 1989; see also Lazarus and others on Le Doux, 1986a), merely to suggest that what is believed by physiologists about the way the brain works is at least consistent with the thesis about more than one way to achieve meaning. Le Doux (1989, p. 271) writes:

> Regardless of whether one favours a cognitive, feedback, or central theory of emotion, the core of the emotional system is thus a mechanism for computing the affective significance of stimuli. As this mechanism is the precursor to conscious emotional experience, it operates, by definition, outside of conscious awareness.

And consistent with what I said in Chapter 4 about two modes of appraisal, Le Doux (1989, p. 274) adds:

> Thus, the amygdala receives sensory inputs from the thalamus both directly and by way of the cortex. The thalamo-amygdala projections appear to be involved in the processsing of the affective significance of relatively simple sensory cues, whereas the cortico-amygdala projections are necessary when complex stimuli are processed.

In effect, the study of neurophysiological pathways suggests that there is a primitive or subcortical neural pathway for emotional processing from the thalamus to the amygdala of the limbic system, which can function independently of neocortical involvement. This permits rapid, crude, and even hasty judgments about danger in the environment, a defensive reaction that can later be aborted if it proves false in more detailed cognitive analysis, which is a kind of neurophysiological analogue of appraisal and reappraisal. Le Doux (1986a, p. 241) writes:

> What possible role in emotional processing might be served by pathways that provide the amygdala with "quick and dirty" representations of peripheral stimuli? First, the rapid arrival of crude stimulus information may be sufficient to initiate defensive (and other emotional) reponses organized through efferent connections of the amygdala. Since the stimulus information is crude, however, defense responses may be initiated inappropriately in some situations. But false-positive responses to threat probably have more survival value than false-negative responses. The defensive reaction can be aborted once it is determined, on the basis of more detailed perceptual analysis (provided by way of cortico-amygdala connections), that the threat is not real. Postponement of defense until the cortical sensory systems have analyzed the stimulus, however, could be costly.

If, indeed, we take seriously that there is more than one kind of cognitive activity in emotion, the point that instantaneous emotion makes specious my proposal that cognitive activity is necessary for an emotion to occur is vitiated. It is, in effect, important not to equate cognitive activity with relatively slow, progressive, stepwise generation of meaning from meaningless stimulus bits, or with deliberate, volitional, and conscious appraisals, and instead to recognize that emotional meanings can be generated in more than one way.

I conclude that it is not so outrageous to argue that meaning is *always* (a high-risk word) involved in emotion, because most if not all mammalian creatures are capable of simple, learned evaluations of elemental categorical distinctions of harm, threat, and benefit. There is no logical or empirical reason why cognitive activity should not be regarded as a necessary condition of emotion.

Biological Universals and Sociocultural Variability in the Emotion Process

A major problem that must be faced by any theory of emotion, and certainly a cognitive-motivational-relational one, is how to provide enough room to accommodate the obvious biological, social, and individual contributions to the emotion process. Let me put this another way: For emotions to play their vital function in human adaptation, the emotion process must be variable and flexible enough to permit intelligence, learning, and judgment to shape the response to adaptational business and, at the same time, to operate in accord with biological species principles. So the theory must detail how psychobiological *and* sociocultural factors operate in the emotion process.

A Reconciling Solution

The proposed solution, which extends what I said in Chapters 1 and 2, by means of which I want to reconcile biological universals with sociocultural sources of variability, is to make one fundamental premise and two subpremises. The *fundamental premise* is that in order to survive and flourish, animals (especially humans) are constructed biologically so that they are constantly engaged in evaluations (appraisals) of their changing relationships with the environment. Appraisals involve detection and evaluation of the relevant adaptational conditions of living that require action. These appraisals determine the emotional state, which involves efforts to respond adequately to the adaptational implications of what is happening.

Phylogenetically more advanced species, such as humans, are in a position to make deliberate, complex, abstract, and symbolic evaluations; simpler species make perhaps as many evaluations, but these are less complicated. Similarly, ontogenetically more advanced or developmentally older individuals will depend on more complex modes of meaning generation compared with young children. A finite set of relational and appraisal components and patterns must be proposed, such as the list I offered in Chapters 3 and 4, which I will apply in Chapters 6 and 7 to each emotion family.

What then is the genetic-biological contribution to universals in the emotion process? It lies, I think, in a principle stated as the *first subpremise* in the form of an "if-then" formula:

1. *If* a person appraises his or her relationship to the environment in a particular way, *then* a specific emotion, which is tied to the appraisal pattern, always follows. A corollary is that *if* two individuals make the same appraisal, *then* they will experience the same emotion, regardless of the actual circumstances. I think of this as a *psychobiological principle,* which provides for universals in the emotion process of the human species and probably applies to other animals, too. In other words, we are constructed in such a way that certain appraisal patterns and their core relational themes will lead to certain emotional reactions. This biological principle is similar in function to the concept of *affect programs,* which I will comment on shortly, though my version of it is highly flexible, especially with respect to the input; therefore, there is considerable variation in the exact details of the emotional response.

The psychobiological principle is essential for a cognitive-motivational-relational theory of emotion, because it implies a degree of universality — or commonality — in the emotion process, which seems evident observationally. One of the striking features of human life is that throughout history, and across very diverse cultures and conditions of life, the same basic themes and emotions seem to recur. This invites us to think about universals in the emotion process, does not obviate individual variations, and requires us to sort out what is universal and what is variable.

What, then, are the sociocultural, personality, and individual developmental contributions to variability in the emotion process? They lie, I think, in the *second subpremise,* which is laid out in two logical steps:

2a. Personality, which includes what is important to the individual person (i.e., a value and goal hierarchy) and a set of beliefs acquired over the life course, especially in childhood, is forged — one might say here that it is constructed by the individual in an effort to create meaning out of social influences — by living in a particular society and culture and by selectively internalizing some of its values, meanings, and social rules.

2b. Individual variability in the emotion process is predicated on differences in how people appraise their person–environment relationships, which is the "if" of the "if-then" formula. Appraisal is always influenced by the confluence of what is in the environmental display and the personality, which jointly affect the knowledge an individual has in general and about the specific situation. This knowledge is always being evaluated with respect to its personal significance. In other words, inter- and intraindividual differences in emotion occur because of variations in the ways persons construe what is happening in an encounter, and in life in general.

The intersection of the sociocultural and biological themes, which is expressed in personality, may be further clarified as follows. The "if" in the statement provides for flexibility and complexity in the emotion process and the adaptation it facilitates, which is made possible by intelligence and culture. The "then" in the statement provides the biological universals which link appraisal to the quality and intensity of the emotional response. When the "if," which is tied to environmental variables and personality, varies, so does the emotion experienced, as mediated by different appraisals.

Imagine, for example, two persons who have been treated inconsiderately in a social transaction. If one of them interprets the other person's behavior as an unwarranted personal offense, that individual will get angry; if the other person interprets the same behavior as a consequence of a personal tragedy (for example, being terminally ill or dealing with a spouse with Alzheimer's disease), the emotion might be compassion based on empathy. Once the appraisals have been made, the emotional response is a foregone conclusion, a consequence of biology. However, there are many determining factors in the "if," which result in considerable sociocultural and individual variation. In ongoing encounters between a person and the environment, the "if" can also be rapidly changed by virtue of a change in the person–environment relationship and by coping, which is aimed at producing such change. This formulation provides for both flexibility and variability as well as a degree of psychobiological invariance, without making one captive to the other.

Now that I have identified the response to appraisal as a species-linked psychobiological principle, what should be said about culture as a factor in the shaping of emotions? This is a highly important and fascinating issue, and I have more to say about it in Chapters 8 and 9 which deal with development. If we find that a culture lacks words for emotions that are common in other cultures, does this mean that people in that culture will not experience the emotion for which there is no word? At present, we don't have a solid basis for answering this question, but it is possible to speculate in a way that is consistent with observation and the formulations offered here.

Our own culture has many more words for negative emotions than for positive ones, and of the former anger provides a richer vocabulary than disgust, shame, and envy (see Chapters 6 and 7). It is possible that an examination of these vocabularies, aside from what they might tell us about human nature, could also be instructive about our cultural values about each emotion (see also Heider, 1991; Lakoff & Kovecses, 1983).

Calhoun and Solomon (1984, p. 34) refer to a statement by anthropologist Jean L. Briggs that certain Eskimo tribes do not feel, much less express, anger. And Levy (1973, 1978, 1984) suggests that Tahitians have few words for sadness, longing, or loneliness. These concepts are said to be "hypocognized" in that culture — that is, not much attended to in language and thought. Guilt, too, is scarcely recognized in Tahiti, according to Levy. Although Tahitians seem to have a concept of severe grief and lamentation, they describe the experience of loss as fatigue, sickness, or other kinds of bodily distress. On the other hand, anger and shame are "hypercognized," meaning that there are many words for these states and much attention is paid to them.

The problem is to decide whether Tahitians are: (a) reacting with sadness (or if we want to consider another example, guilt) but labeling the reaction with a distinctive, culturally based word; (b) experiencing sadness but denying it; (c) reacting with no emotion (which seems belied by their bodily complaints); (d) reacting with an emotion other then sadness, which for argument's sake could be called bodily distress; or (e) responding emotionally to different circumstances than people of other cultures where the experience of sadness is common.

My own predilection is to say that regardless of what a culture emphasizes or de-emphasizes about the emotional life, all the core relational themes, and the emotions connected with them, that are common to humans are apt to have been experienced by adulthood, because people are inevitably caught in certain fundamental negative or positive person–environment relationships regardless of whether they can verbalize what these are, and regardless of whether an emotion is recognized or labeled as such. Thus, most people experience anger, shame, guilt, happiness, pride, relief, love, and so on, even if they label these emotions in some other way or don't pay much attention to them. We are biologically constructed in this way, and so we get into similar social relationships across cultures and over human history. In every culture, the key relationships underlying all the important emotions are experienced along with their associated emotions whether or not the culture has a word for them.

In saying this, I am not denying the power of language; rather I am emphasizing that emotions are primarily psychobiological and not so much linguistic phenomena. If we appraise a person–environment relationship in a way that defines the core relational theme of an emotion, we will experience the biologically appropriate emotion whether or not the language used provides a verbal label for it, and whether or not there is a verbal label that corresponds with the one given to it in some other culture.

The preceding proposal flows from principle (1), which focuses on the "then" part of the "if-then" formula. Appraisal is not merely a trick of language or reflection, but is an evaluation, often elemental and without awareness, of the significance of what is happening for our personal well-being, corresponding to a core relational theme. We often sense this significance without being able to put words to the process. Language plays a role, and certainly sharpens the appraisal and its analysis, but not an exclusive one. The biological principle only says that the fundamental meanings are given to a species as sources of each emotion, but the social conditions that generate these meanings are still to some extent culturally variable and learned. If we recognize that someone has slighted us, we will feel demeaned and react emotionally, probably with anger; this is the way we are built. This may be the case even if the interpersonal scenario is smoothed over or qualified, though not if we change its meaning.

How, then, does culture shape an emotion? I think the best general answer is that it helps us identify the signs of being loved, when there has been enhancement of one's identity (pride), the conditions of existential threat (anxiety), when we have been demeaned (anger), when we have failed to live up to an ego-ideal (shame), when we have violated a moral proscription (guilt), what an altruistic gift is (gratitude), and so on. In short, just as culture teaches us when each core relational theme has occurred, it teaches us the results of these themes in the form of species-prescribed emotional responses. I have much more to say about how social and cultural variables influence appraisals and emotions in Chapter 9.

Parallels and Contrasts with the Concept of Affect Programs

In psychoevolutionary thought about emotion, there already exists a concept that is parallel with the psychobiological principle embodied in the "then" of the "if-then" formula — namely, the concept of affect programs. Few theorists (mainly Ekman, 1977; Tomkins, 1962, 1963) have actually used the term formally, and with only modest elaboration. However, some idea of this sort is, I believe, commonly assumed by psychobiologists who are interested in emotion. In what follows, I try to explore some of the dilemmas inherent in this idea and to offer a way of thinking that is speculative but seems plausible to me.

At its most inflexible, an *affect program* is a complex neurochemical and behavioral response system, programmed in the brain, that when properly triggered by the right neurological button, so to speak, runs off more or less as preordained. Ekman (1977, p. 57) has written that the "term 'affect programme' refers to a mechanism which stores the patterns for these complex organized responses, and which when set off directs their occurrence." Presumably the program coordinates, perhaps sequentially as well as structurally, the thought, action impulses, and physiological processes that constitute an emotion. In effect, an anger response will look similar in all humans, and perhaps to some extent in all animals capable of them, as will a fear response, and so on.

Although the triggering, directing, or organizing mechanisms could conceivably have been acquired (cf. Ekman, 1977), the usual implication is that the pattern of emotional response is genetically preprogrammed and stored, as it were, in the brain. As I said in Chapter 3, coping is a separate concept from action tendency in that it is much more the result of learning and deliberate choices among strategies. More recently, Ekman (personal communication) has softened his original position on this, which had implied innate psychobiological programming. He seems now to regard the concept of affect program as a metaphor rather than a material, neurohumoral and peremptory program. However, if we put this together with his concept of the Duchenne smile as a built-in indicator of true happiness, some inconsistencies remain to be resolved, and I am not convinced that metaphor here is as useful as assuming that there is, indeed, something that is biologically given but capable of great flexibility and adaptive functioning.

Ultimately, the assumptions underlying affect programs encourage phylogeneticists to speak of emotion blends or combinations that seem unique to humans, such as guilt, shame, and pride, and that are so important intrapsychically and in social functioning. If the emphasis is on what is presumably universal, innate, and displayed in the face or body, then reaction patterns that don't conform to this set of criteria are either not emotions or are, perforce, combinations or blends of basic emotions.

Ekman (1971) gives the example of an effort to conceal anger with a smile that makes us look smug, a blend of happiness and anger. When this sort of thing happens often, society will give it its own name—that is, smugness. However, what might be a blend to one theorist is a primary emotion to another. Plutchik (1980) treats contempt as a blend of anger and disgust, while Ekman (see Ekman & Friesen, 1986, 1988; Izard & Haynes, 1988) believes he now has some evidence of its universality, which would promote it to the status of a primary emotion.

How rigidly organized an affect program is has really not been examined carefully, and this issue lies at the heart of the explanatory competition between biological and social science approaches to emotion. And how much of the total emotion process it preprograms is another aspect of the issue. If the entire emotion process is highly rigid and preprogrammed, then ontogenetic—that is, sociocultural, experiential, and contextual—variables could play an important role in emotion only or mainly with respect to the eliciting stimuli or triggers, which would influence the appraisal process, and perhaps also with respect to turning off the emotion or moving on to another. That is the heart of my earlier "if-then" analysis.

How peremptory an affect program is, and how subject it is to modification and control *during its course,* remains obscure. Affect programs may be presumed to be inherited in the species and influence appraisal, though Ekman (1977) considers them also to be influenced by learning and social influence. When we engage in coping, even emotion-focused coping in which the meaning of an encounter is changed, the affect program is turned off or changed, because the feedback from the coping process changes the appraisal. This can happen almost instantly.

If we accept the most rigid and extended version of the idea of affect programs—namely, that once elicited, an emotion runs its whole course—and that ontogeny plays its role largely in the rules of emotion generation rather than in the emotion process itself, we can accommodate both variability and universality in the emotion process. Start the machine in the right direction, and the program plays itself out as prearranged by the inherited structure of the nervous system, until something happens to turn it off or change it. Push the anger button and we get anger; push the fear button and we get fear. Just what can be modified in the running and turning off needs to be made clear. One could propose that a *changed appraisal,* which is sometimes occasioned by the coping process, results in a different button push and a new affect program as an all or none process.

There are fewer difficulties in interpreting what is happening in a rigid version of affect programs within a species than in interpreting across species. It is difficult to say, for example, to what extent anger in a chimpanzee, in a monkey, or in an African lion is the same, or whether such anger resembles human anger, or whether it should be called anger at all. Writing about the social significance of animal studies, Hebb and Thompson (1954, p. 554) wrote some time ago that:

In the rat, for example, there is little need of such a term as "anger" for describing the animal's behavior. A rat is aggressive or he is not, and the aggression has about the same pattern in different circumstances. The same seems true of the dog, although occasionally he shows something that may be homologous with the primate's sulking. But with the chimpanzee, it is essential to distinguish anger from chronic malice if the animal is to be handled safely. The peculiarly human patterns of temper tantrum and sulking occur frequently. The causes of aggression are more varied in the dog than in the rat, and far more varied in the chimpanzee than in the dog. Finally, the period of emotional disturbance following a brief stimulation also increases from rat to dog to chimpanzee (the chimpanzee Fifi, for example, sulked for three weeks over not getting a cup of milk, first showing outright anger, then refusing to accept milk from anyone for a day or so, and continuing for three weeks to refuse it from the one who had denied it to her).

The social psychologist Heider (see Benesh & Weiner, 1982, p. 889) has made the same point with a very different emphasis in the following perceptive query:

How should one reconcile the "ought" component of anger with the fact that animals can get angry? Is not "ought" something that belongs to a more abstract level? Does a dog defending his territory think, "This is my property. I have a right to it. Other dogs ought not to come here."?

The difficulty of answering this question is expressed in the reluctance of ethologists to speak of anger in animals at all, using instead the more neutral and behavioral term, *aggressive* or *agonistic behavior*. Heider's query also underscores that we must still identify the conditions generating anger in people, which are apt to be different from those of a dog and might even be somewhat different among individual humans, though still reducible to some common theme.

If we seek, as I do, a more flexible way of viewing affect programs—a term that seems to me too inflexible in its usual implications because of the connotations of the word *program*—to spell out the psychobiological link between appraisal and the emotional response, it is possible to imagine an arrangement of the components of the emotion process as relatively independent and responsive to the particular adaptational requirements connected with an ongoing transaction, and yet one that would produce the *appearance* of an innate, organized, and universal emotion process. In this view, which I favor, each component would function in a more flexible way, though still following biological constraints having to do with the demands for energy and homeostatic load in any action sequence.

In this option I think of the emotion system as highly structured but complex and flexible. Under a particular set of circumstances, the affect program or system always contributes to the same effects in whatever response measure one is interested in, but each of these effects is brought about by only one of several factors in the total configuration. Thus, in fright it may always or usually be the case that there is an acceleration of heart rate, but other factors such as practiced breathing, physical exertion, and so on, also contribute to the observed heart rate so that what we observe in fright could range from substantial acceleration to perhaps even a deceleration when contrary processes overwhelm the "programmed" effect. And if we held these other factors constant, we would always or usually see fright-induced acceleration, just as when we are angry we would always or usually expect the action tendency of attack.

In effect, the several response components of an emotion, once provoked, must be coordinated — which is one way to think of a system — yet operate with some degree of independence, depending on the immediate person–environment demands, constraints, and resources that are brought into play in any adaptational transaction. Perhaps a basic response pattern exists for each emotion, which is easily obscured by "noise" from other adaptational processes. For example, in anger the basic pattern might include desire for retaliation, revenge, or the removal of the offending agent. However, in one instance of this pattern the impulse is denied or inhibited, whereas in another it is unconflicted and in clear consciousness. These versions would look different to an observer. If there is a universal psychobiological pattern, it could easily be obscured by all this other coping activity.

Frijda (1986, p. 83) points out clearly in his discussion of action tendencies that there is danger in conceiving of affect programs as too fixed and peremptory. He writes:

> To the extent that action programs are fixed and rigid, action tendency loses much of its meaning. The situation merely elicits action; action readiness only exists to the extent that inhibition can block action execution. To the extent that the program is flexible, however, action tendency, and action readiness generally, become meaningful concepts. Flexible programs are those that are composed of alternative courses of action, that allow for variations in circumstances and for feedback from actions executed. In such programs, wishes, intentions, and aims have become independent of particular actions. Action tendency acquires the properties of a plan (see Schank & Abelson, 1977; and Wilensky, 1983) or, more precisely, of a plan placed into readiness by the initiating signals. With such a structure, it is meaningful to speak of emotions.

The problem with this view is that the more an action tendency takes on the characteristics of a flexible plan, subject to feedback, the more it approximates what I mean by *coping*, which is a much more deliberate and psychological concept than innate action tendencies, and the less the response pattern will seem universal. Frijda's greater recent use of the term "action readiness" (Frijda et al., 1989) may reflect some concerns on his part with the rigid implications of action tendency or impulse, given the wide variety of actions that accompany each emotion. In any case, the distinction between innate fixed action and flexible action based on feedback and plans reveals the difficulties inherent in the concept of affect program and its workings.

There appear to be five essential psychobiological components and processes in emotion: perception, appraisal, coping actions (as in locomotion), physiological activity that may involve mobilization, and homeostatic process involving anabolic and catabolic activities. Each also serves adaptational requirements other than emotional ones. We do not experience an emotion merely in response to heat, cold, fasting, or exercising even though homeostatic processes essential to survival are set in motion and coordinated in these situations (cf. Mason, 1975). However, if we appraise the heat or cold as a harm, threat, or benefit, then we will react emotionally. And this emotional reaction involves the same response components and processes that are integral features of other forms of adaptation, coordinated by changing adaptational requirements. When components of the emotion process serve nonemotional functions, they may easily be interpreted emotionally, even when no emotion is actually involved.

Ekman (1977) points out that each kind of facial pattern, such as the raising of eyebrows, can be employed for other purposes—for example, for greeting and for expressing surprise as well as an unequivocal emotion. He refers to these as emblems. Izard (1978) acknowledges that emotional expressions can take place in the face of an infant many months before they are organized into affect programs that can be elicited. Thus, the facial configuration of a smile does not necessarily mean the infant is happy or experiencing joy, because facial motor actions, including smiling, can serve other functions that are nonemotional, and do so developmentally before they can indicate a social reaction (cf. Emde, 1984, p. 82). In spite of this argument, however, Izard assumes a tight linkage among the diverse response components of an emotion and between each of them and the adult emotional experience (see Chapter 8).

There is a real dilemma here, and of course we don't truly know how all this works, which is why we must try to make a good guess, one that takes into account what we observe and can eventually be evaluated in specifically designed research. Even computer programs today are highly flexible, "smart" as some would say. They are always highly algorithmic but the algorithms are flexible, and allow for alternative courses of action whose direction depends on the conditions met along the way. They have statements along the lines of: If A happens, then do this; if B happens, then do that; otherwise, do something else. Such conditional statements embedded within one another can produce some very complex, context-sensitive results.

However things work, the way the response components are organized in emotion must allow for flexible patterns of reaction, because each also functions in the service of many other adaptational tasks. They are brought together in the service of whatever ongoing transaction is important to well-being—say, when a goal is endangered or its attainment is facilitated. This adaptational flexibility needs to be more emphasized in emotion theory. Fixed programming without the option of flexibility is for relatively simple organisms that are not capable of abstract thought and decision making. In more advanced species, especially humans, through evolution, hardwired·affect programs have given way to a complex and flexible process. This is precisely the way functionalists usually conceive of the role of emotion in more advanced mammals—that is, as having progressed away from innately given, rigid adaptational processes and as increasingly dependent on higher cognitive capabilities.

In trying to appreciate this idea, it helps to think of the impressive research of Lehrman (1964), an ornithologist whose careful observations and experiments on the reproductive cycle of the ring dove did much to change the way social scientists thought about the concept of instinct. The rigid recruitment of complex patterns of behavior, which was once called *instinct,* was assumed to be innate and built into the nervous system, but this view, in its original form, has all but been discredited.

The reproductive cycle of ring doves was traditionally considered instinctual because it displays a predictable, *stereotyped pattern*—which, on closer inspection, turns out to be quite modifiable and dependent on the nature and timing of environmental and hormonal stimulation.

The seemingly stereotyped pattern looks like this: When a male and female ring dove with no previous breeding experience are placed together in a cage with a glass bowl and some nesting material, courtship occurs; the male struts about, bows, and coos at the female. After some hours, they select the glass bowl (or any other concave place), crouch in it, and give distinctive coos. The male gathers materials for the nest, and the female constructs the nest while standing in the bowl. After a week or so of this nest building, during which copulation has also occurred, the female seems to become strongly attached to the nest as evidenced by the fact that she resists being dislodged. She is about to lay her eggs. Seven to eleven days after the onset of courtship, she produces the first egg, usually around five o'clock in the afternoon. She sits on the egg, then lays another one, usually about nine the next morning. During that day, the male typically takes a turn sitting, and thereafter the two birds sit alternatively, with the male sitting about 6 hours during the middle of the day and the female the rest of the time. In about 14 days the eggs hatch, and the parents feed the young a liquid secreted from the lining of their crops (a pouch in their gullet). When the young are about 10 or 12 days old, they leave the nest but continue to beg for and receive food from the parents until they are about 2 weeks of age, at which time the parents become increasingly unwilling to feed them, and the young are forced to learn to peck for grain on the floor. This terminates the reproductive cycle. When the young are about 25 days old, the male again starts the courting behavior, and the entire cycle lasting 6 or 7 weeks begins again as before.

This behavior seems much like the homing of pigeons or the migration of fish and birds in its apparent universality and biologically stereotyped details, and it illustrates the kind of seemingly built-in patterns that led early investigators to postulate instincts. Lehrman's research, however, might serve as a useful lesson to those who are convinced that emotions can be understood in terms of built-in affect programs, which are similarly said to be stereotyped.

Lehrman helped identify the actual internal (hormonal) and external influences, which bring about each aspect of the pattern sequentially. The hormonal influences are illustrated by the fact that when the female ring dove is first placed in the cage, her oviduct weighs about 800 milligrams, but when she lays her eggs after having proceeded through courtship and nest building, it weighs about 4,000 milligrams. Similarly, gradual changes occur in the birds' crops that are necessary to prepare them for feeding the young, and in the males' testes, preparing them to copulate.

Lehrman's research has also shown that the pattern of behavior in the reproductive cycle, though having a large hormonal component, is also highly dependent on environmental events or stimuli that trigger the secretion of these hormones if they occur at the right moment, which in turn help initiate the appropriate actions. For example, if the birds are placed in a cage in which there are nesting materials and two eggs already laid, the birds do not sit on them but act as if the eggs were not there. Instead of sitting, they proceed in sequence to court, build their own nest, lay their own eggs, and only then sit on them. The lone female lays no eggs; she needs

FIGURE 5.1. Pattern of reproductive behavior in ring doves. There is an interplay of internal and external factors, in step-by-step progression, from the initial courting and nest-building behavior through the final care and feeding of the young. (*Source:* John L. Howard. In Daniel Lehrman, "The Reproductive Behavior of Ring Doves." *Scientific American, 211.* New York: Scientific American. Copyright © November 1964 by Scientific American, Inc. Reprinted by permission.)

the sight of the male. A lone male has no interest in nesting materials, eggs, or young; he must be stimulated by the female. The complex interplay of environmental and hormonal influences in the reproductive cycle is illustrated in Figure 5.1.

Thus, the total behavior pattern is by no means entirely preprogrammed from within; though each component has considerable programming, it depends also on the timing of many environmental events that set in motion the internal (hormonal) ones, which control the behavior necessary for nest building, copulation, egg laying, and feeding of young. In short, instinct is merely the disposition to respond in some given fashion to some suitable external stimulus, and if the term is meant to refer to a complex, fully preprogrammed pattern, it is misleading. For the reproductive behavior cycle of the species to take place, exactly the right combination of stimuli, hormonal changes, and mutual actions is required, each occurring at the proper moment.

I believe that this revised conception of biological factors in adaptive behavior (which are no longer seen as strictly innately controlled sequences of action) represented a major step forward from earlier ideas of rigid, built-in patterns that unfold. It encourages scientists to elaborate the interplay of both biological and social forces in the control of adaptation. It is also a good model for thinking about affect programs. If we take it seriously, we must now think in terms of much more complexity and flexibility and less completely preprogrammed processes. It no longer makes sense to think of a "button-push" metaphor for whatever it is that leads to the complex sequence of reactions in an emotion.

If we accept this functionalist position, how then can we understand that each emotion, like the ring dove's reproductive cycle, seems to be organized into a universal configuration, or at least widely shared, complex response sequences within a single species? Emotions, like the ring dove's reproduction cycle, do seem to have a universal, stereotyped, and partly peremptory character (cf. Averill, 1974), and this common appearance deceives us into believing that once set in motion, the working of the entire emotion process is innately preprogrammed. Without having to go back to the most rigid and simple concept of affect program, a reasonable solution might be that this *appearance* of biological universality arises in part because each emotion family contains two features in common, regardless of particular details:

1. There is a common core relational theme and appraisal pattern for the adaptational encounter. All instances of the emotion family of anger, for example, share a common apprehension of what is happening, with of course variations around this central theme. Likewise, when we are happy, there is a common core relational theme and appraisal pattern, and so on, for each positive and negative emotion family. The variations within each kind of emotion are not as important in defining the family as are the shared cognitive properties. Nevertheless, if and when people find themselves in the psychobiological situation conveyed by one or another core relational theme, they will experience the emotion that is biologically preordained. This restates the psychobiological principle.

2. There are also the common intent and action impulses defined by the core relational theme and appraisal pattern — for example, restoring one's wounded ego, perhaps by revenge; expiating guilt; hiding one's failure to live up to an ego-ideal; preserving the meaning whose loss is threatened; and so forth (see also Frijda, 1986). The impulse to attack in anger, for example, provokes a particular motor pattern and

psychophysiological responses that reflect how the mind and body must be organized to deal with one's plight, which results from having been insulted or
demeaned. In effect, each kind of emotion comprises a distinctive cognitive, motor,
and physiological response configuration that is defined by the common adaptational (psychological and physiological) requirements of the person–environment relationship, as these are appraised.

The configuration, which combines (1) and (2), looks similar whenever it is produced. It is not necessary to conceive of it as a hardwired program of sequences;
rather, it is a functional arrangement that has neurophysiological determinants and is
also greatly dependent on what, as a result of learning, humans and other species
think they must do to manage the adaptational requirements of the relationship, as
given by their biological natures. These requirements are more or less similar across
individuals within a species, and perhaps to some extent even across species. The
innate aspects of this, and its rigidity, will be greater for phylogenetically simpler
species than for advanced and complicated species, the latter relying more on learning and intelligence for their adaptational decisions, which increases the variability
and tends to obscure the commonalities.

And so the emotion reaction pattern appears, and to some degree is, built into
the species. Each emotion does, indeed, engender a more or less similar pattern of
physiological change, homeostatic process, perception, appraisal, and coping action.
What is inherited may not be the response configuration or affect program but the
basic psychobiological capacities and mechanisms of the system's operation, the
rules of elicitation and control of each separate component, and the functional interdependence of the system's components for any basic kind of adaptational
encounter. These rules and functional interdependencies are played out in the role of
appraisal and coping, the psychophysiology of locomotion (say, in attack or flight),
how locomotion affects energetic and homeostatic processes, and how the elements
of locomotion and homeostasis are coordinated over time. Where action is inhibited,
which also requires effort, the physiological process will look different.

The emotion process I am describing would still produce continuity within and
perhaps between species and a pattern of reaction that would be more or less specific to each emotion family. It would also allow for the emergence of new forms of
organization among the components as new types of relationships, relevant to well-
being, come into play with the evolutionary development of the brain and the elaboration of new social structures. With this kind of system, we could also more easily
understand how emotions shared among similar mammals could appear universal,
or *primary* in the language of the phylogeneticists. The universality stems in some
measure from the common adaptational tasks as these are appraised and configured
into core relational themes.

Conceiving of emotion in this way has the added advantage of encouraging
investigators to explore the relational and cognitive conditions under which a given
kind of emotion is generated and transformed by coping during the ordinary flow of
events in adaptational encounters. It would relieve us of the need to force this flow
into a procrustean and too-simple computer metaphor in which pushing this or that
button releases the whole, seriatim, universal, built-in response configuration. It

would allow us to ask whether different forms of each emotion category — say, righteous versus defensive anger — should be given different names to reflect their special cognitive and adaptational features, or whether these variations are best retained within the same generic emotion family on the premise that what is shared is more important than what is not. Above all, this conception would allow us to encompass both the biological universals and sociocultural sources of variability as aspects of the emotion process without doing a disservice to either.

From a broad philosophical perspective, a flexible arrangement, which eschews rigidly fixed patterns in higher organisms, is also more in keeping with recent movements in biology. Although biology has gotten increasingly molecular, biologists interested in development have also become increasingly restive about bottom-up analyses of the principles of organization in adaptive systems, and more interested in top-down principles. They have become more and more aware of the importance of intercellular organizing principles that bear some analogy to what I said earlier about goals (and intentions) and threats to a system's well-being, which require intelligence to manage. Quoting Sydney Brenner in *Science,* for example, R. Lewin (1984, p. 1327) has written that:

> At the beginning it was said that the answer to the understanding of development was going to come from a knowledge of the molecular mechanisms of gene control. I doubt whether anyone believes that anymore. The molecular mechanisms look boringly simple, and they don't tell us what we want to know. We have to try to discover the principle of organization, how lots of things are put together in the same place. I don't think these principles will be embodied in a simple chemical device, as it is for the genetic code.

What I have said about the key organizing principle in emotion — namely, that it is based on adaptational agendas of species and individuals — is quite analogous to what Brenner said. These agendas are engaged and modified by the changing relationships with the environment, and they depend on central, cognitive appraisal processes, by which people evaluate the significance of what is happening for their well-being. This principle cannot be derived from the DNA chain of a species or from a bottom-up examination of a species' physiology at a still more molar level; it requires a top-down examination of how a person or other animal must deal with the environment that is being faced.

Emotion as a System of Interdependent Variables and Processes

In Chapter 1, I said that there has been a movement away from linear stimulus-response formulations toward those in which the mind mediates the person's reactions. An even more advanced approach called *system(s) theory*[3] has also begun to take the place of earlier ways of thinking. McGuire (1983, pp. 20–21) has described a system approach in contrast with more traditional styles of thinking with respect to its relevance for social psychology. He writes:

Both the convergent and divergent styles are "unilinear" in depicting some variables as independent and others as dependent with the main causal flow from the independent to the dependent. The contextualist theory of knowledge on the other hand calls for a contrasting systems style that allows knowledge representations more adequately to reflect the complexities of the real-world situations being represented which have reciprocal links and remote feedback loops that allow multiple and bidirectional causal paths. Hence a systems stylist includes a complex set of variables within the research design. While initially some may be conceptualized as independent, others as mediating, and still others as dependent variables, all are allowed to covary naturally. This is necessary to detect complex relationships, including multiple causal pathways whose relative contribution to the covariance can be shown to fluctuate from one to another of the differing contexts established by other variables in the design.

Besides starting with a multiplicity of interrelated independent, mediating, and dependent variables, the systems stylist typically presents a low profile to the participants, for example, observing persons in a natural situation or presenting open-ended probes that allow a wide range of participant-chosen responses instead of limiting the participant to multiple-choice response options on a researcher-chosen dimension. . . . The systems style also encourages employment of time-series designs in which participants are measured on the variables at several different times in order to trace complex, bidirectional causal pathways among the variables.

The reader should understand that a system implies that any variable can serve as an antecedent, mediator, or consequent in a process, depending on the point at which one enters the flow of psychological events. For example, although personality variables are usually treated as causal antecedents of an emotion, along with environmental variables, they can change with emotional experience and so be effects, too—as can the environmental configuration, which can be changed by the person.

What we think of as stable in the components of the system may not be nearly as stable as we are inclined to believe. Indeed, personality is formed in the course of human development, but it, too, can be changed, thereby becoming a set of outcome variables as well as antecedents. Similarly, emotional states may result in illness, but illness, once it has occurred, can also affect the person's emotional state. This reciprocality is also a feature of what I mean by *transaction* and *relationship*. I hasten to add, however, that although personality is sometimes an antecedent variable and sometimes a consequent, as indicated earlier and in the principle of reciprocal determinism, it can never be both at the same time (see Bandura, 1978; Phillips & Orton, 1983). This would constitute a form of illogic.

Moreover, a person is not merely a passive being responding to inputs from the environment, as implied in stimulus-response or linear thinking. To some extent we actively select the environments to which we respond, and we attend selectively to this or that aspect of the environment depending on our personal agendas. An overemphasis on input is also a weakness of the computer analogy of the mind, which must be programmed to do what it does, but it doesn't initiate action unless that action is already part of the program, or told to do so. Mediating processes, in contrast with moderator variables, emerge, *de novo* and creatively, out of transactions with the environment.

System principles have two important implications for emotion theory, as I have been trying to press home: (1) Emotion cannot be adequately defined externally in terms of environmental variables or as a simple response to such variables, nor internally as an impulse or conflict between impulses; and (2) the quality and intensity of an emotion depends on a variety of mediating processes. The theoretical or research task is then to specify the variables and processes of interest and their patterns of mutual influence.

This leads us to the issue of costs and benefits with respect to antecedent variables and mediating processes. If, for example, the personality and environmental antecedents account for as much variance in emotion response as do mediating process variables such as appraisal and coping, the latter being very costly and difficult to study, reasonable doubt could be raised about the value of using the costlier process measures. An assumption of my theoretical analysis is that mediators such as appraisal and coping are more proximal and, therefore, have a larger payoff in prediction than distal antecedents.

This assumption could be tested by comparing the success of predictions from both types of variables. When I (e.g., Lazarus & Folkman, 1987, for a summary) or others (e.g., Larrson, 1989; Larrson, Kempe, & Starrin, 1988) have been able to make this kind of comparison, the antecedent variables appear to be much weaker than the process variables in predicting emotional outcomes. One reason for this, I believe, has to do with limitations in the typical measurement of traits, which tends to ignore the situational contexts in which traits operate (see Lazarus, 1990b). Cost, however, is not the only value to be considered; it is possible to seek predictive efficiency at the expense of thorough understanding. In any event, a system analysis requires complex rather than simple research designs.

Much of what I have been saying here expresses what protagonists of systems theory have been saying for roughly two decades. Evered (1980, p. 7) has put it as follows:

> Traditional causal thinking which underlies much of modern science has not proven adequate for the task of understanding change, and increasingly one senses that it never can. The assumption of an *independent external* and *antecedent* factor, a set of factors that "causes" changes seems far too simplistic. . . . As Bertalanffy puts it: "We may state as characteristic of modern science that this scheme of isolable units acting in one-way causality has proved to be insufficient." Hence the appearance, in all fields of science, of notions like wholeness, holistic, organism, gestalt, etc., which all signify that, in the last resort, we must think in terms of systems of elements in mutual interaction. . . .
>
> Until quite recently the prevailing view of science . . . incorporated a bias to generic, past-oriented, antecedent explanation. In the past two or three decades, however, the culturally infectious influences of existentialism, phenomenology, gestalt psychology and systems thinking have influenced science toward a more present-oriented, interactive and perceptual view of science — at least in some areas of the social sciences.

Those committed to contextualism and/or hermeneutics, which are centered on description and process, may find it strange that I should also draw on a more or less traditional cause-and-effect frame of reference in which there are antecedent, mediating, and consequent variables, despite my advocacy of fluid system analyses and process formulations. A system analysis does not accept traditional causality, though it is multicausal, process-centered, and flexible in what is an antecedent or a consequence. The surprise should stem from the impression that one is not supposed to be both contextual, transactional, and phenomenological on the one hand, and also mechanistic on the other. Yet if we were to depend entirely on description and post-hoc explanation, we would be forever mired in tautology. Because the only way to get out of the circle is to demonstrate that a given mediating process such as cognitive appraisal can in some degree be predicted by antecedent variables that are measured in advance, an appropriate metatheory for emotion is a blend of two epistemologies that are normally presented as at odds with each other (see Lazarus & Folkman, 1987).

I hope it is clear that I do not want to espouse any single epistemology in blind opposition to the useful tenets of other ways of thinking which have traditionally been viewed as incompatible. My stance does not arise out of bland eclecticism, but rather from the belief that each epistemology arose for good reasons and contains a portion of the truth. Even the operational emphasis of behaviorism has the positive value of alerting social science researchers to the importance and difficulties of measuring psychological variables and evaluating the validity of concepts. Determinism, with its oversimple cause-and-effect analysis, protects us from slavish contextualism. And contextualism, with its potential chaos, protects us from having to operate within a strictly mechanistic and reductive science. Although linear models are inadequate to grapple with reciprocal influences, they do point us toward the idea of temporal flow, without which it would be impossible to study process and change. The protagonists of each epistemology have argued as though no integration among them is possible, and have tried to reduce to absurdity the alternative formulations. Nevertheless, I believe that the mechanistic and contextual views can comfortably coexist, and even supplement each other.

When all is said and done, there remains one major puzzle in thinking of the emotions from a systems point of view. In Chapter 1, I had noted an earlier tendency of psychology to write off emotion as a legitimate topic for theory and research, and I mentioned efforts such as those of Duffy (1941a, 1941b, 1960) to replace it with the unidimensional variable of *activation,* defined by Duffy as "energy mobilization." Before I summarize my system theory analysis of the emotions, allow me to digress a bit about Duffy's views, which in many respects overlap with mine, despite her advocacy of a single dimension of activation to replace the concept of emotion.

Most important in Duffy's challenge to the concept of emotion is her view that there is nothing special about emotion, and that what we are describing when we deal with emotional responses is simply "all of life." And because in Chapter 4 I criticized the treatment of cognition and emotion as separate systems, I must here consider whether or not we should think of emotion as an important system of variables and processes in its own right rather than as a vacuous concept, as suggested by Duffy.

Duffy (1941b) saw that psychology was concerned with adaptational activities by means of which an organism maintains its internal equilibrium in the face of threatened disruption from internal and external pressures. The essential properties of adaptational responses are direction, reactions to relationships, and the idea with which she wants to replace emotion — namely, energy level or mobilization. When we think of Duffy today, it is this latter point we remember, the way she tried to dismiss emotion as energy level, and we tend to assume that it was a behavioristic predilection that influenced this proposal. However, if we read Duffy's (1941b) statements about adaptation, they could have been written by any cognitive-motivational-relational theorist, an aspect of her viewpoint we have forgotten. Duffy writes (pp. 188–189):

> If the individual is to reach his goal, he must respond to certain relationships in the situation. His response can be appropriate only if it represents adequate discrimination of those relationships which are relevant to his purposes. This discrimination need not be conscious, or to speak more accurately, the individual may respond appropriately to relationships of which he could not give a verbal report, and which he may not be aware of responding to as such.
>
> By "response relationships" I refer to the fact that stimuli have *meaning* for the individual. This meaning is, of course, a function of their relationship to the goal of a particular response cycle; the same stimuli would have different meanings in different cycles of behavior. They might also have different meanings if they occurred in conjunction with a different set of surrounding stimuli. And their meaning would be different if the past experience of the responding individual had been different, for it is on the basis of his past experience that the individual arrives at a tentative interpretation of, or meaning for, the present stimulus situation. We may say, then, that the behavior of the individual is directed toward present stimuli, not as discrete and independent entitites, but as *related to each other,* as *related to the individual's past experiences,* and above all, as *related to the individual's present goal* [emphasis in the original].

Let us consider one of Duffy's examples in which she questions whether there is any difference between a person running from a street corner to his or her house as fast as possible on a whim and a person standing on the corner of the street seeing smoke coming out of the roof of that person's house, and then sprinting to the house in a panic. About this Duffy writes (1941a, pp. 287–288) that

> *all* behavior is motivated. Without motivation there is *no activity*. . . . The responses called "emotional" do not appear to follow different principles of action from other adjustive responses of the individual. Changes in internal or external conditions, or in the interpretation of those conditions, always result in internal accommodations. The responses made are specifically adjustive to the situation and are not subject to classification into such categories as "emotional" and "non-emotional. . . . " All responses — not merely "emotional" responses — are adjustive reactions attempting to adapt the organism to the demands of the situation. The energy level of response varies with the requirements of the situation as interpreted by the individual. Diffuse internal changes (especially in the viscera) are involved in the production of these changes in energy level. But continuous visceral activity, with accompanying changes in energy level, is a function of life itself, not merely a function of a particular condition called "emotion."

I think this is an interesting and reasoned position. However, in my view, even though the two events would look pretty similar, say, in respect to autonomic activity, I think there is a world of difference between them, which makes me call the first example nonemotional and the second one emotional. The reason the two examples given by Duffy are different is that, in the second, a distinct system has taken over and is providing motivation for the reaction. The emotion system is following some of its own rules, which is what I am trying to delineate in this book. Many of the behavioral components of the two examples overlap, but the ways in which they are organized are not the same, and they draw differently on motives and beliefs, appraisals, and coping processes; appraisals are also associated with special subjective states such as anger, anxiety, pride, and so on, that are distinctive to the emotions. The emotion system is in place in our species to ensure that the truly important things in life, adaptation and survival, get taken care of.

More must be said about this, however, because I argued earlier in this chapter that we must not think of cognition and emotion as separate systems of the mind and brain, and that the concept of an innate emotion program as usually imagined is too rigid. I may now be seen as taking a position that is inconsistent with what I said earlier. However, to say that the emotions constitute a system or set of subsystems is not to separate cognition, motivation, and emotion but to postulate a special kind of system that when it is engaged draws on all three of these constructs of mind as part of the total process. And when I say that each component of the system or systems serves other masters, as I did in discussing Lehrman's work on the reproductive cycle of the ring dove, and when I say that the system is organized flexibly by adaptational requirements as these are appraised, I am simply saying that the system is a relatively loose arrangement made up of many psychobiological processes that operate in ways consistent with the laws of biology and physics.

Then, too, there are many other models of adaptation, some of them in what is currently called social cognition—for example, health-belief models, social information-processing models, value-expectancy models, all systems in which a person engages in appraisallike evaluations to determine whether the situation is relevant to goals, to identify barriers or facilitators of action, and to sort out, select, and enact what has to be thought and done from the available courses of action. All of these models are quite rational in focus and tend not to be concerned with emotion in any way.

So to justify my argument in Chapter 1 that emotions are a central organizing construct in human adaptational affairs requires that emotion be seen as a system or set of systems in its own right. This is the position I have taken throughout this book. Emotions are not merely "all of life" but a distinctive and organized pattern of reaction. Though we can approach an understanding of human adaptation without discussion of the emotions, a wholy rational and biological analysis falls far short of capturing the essence of the human animal, of which emotion is a complex part.

I would like to close this chapter by spelling out more clearly but briefly what it means to adopt a system analytic view of the emotion process (Lazarus & Folkman, 1984, 1986, 1987). The cognitive-motivational-relational analysis thus far offered refers, in reality, to a multivariate system, which consists of a number of causal antecedents, mediating processes, immediate emotional effects, and long-term effects, all acting interdependently. I offer here two illustrations, Figures 5.2 and

CASUAL ANTECEDENTS	→	MEDIATING PROCESSES Time 1...T_2...T_3...T_n Encounter 1...2...3...n	→	IMMEDIATE EFFECTS	→	LONG-TERM EFFECTS
Personality variables		Primary appraisal		Physiological changes		Somatic health/illness
Values or commitments Beliefs (existential sense of control)		Secondary appraisal		Positive or negative feelings		Morale (well-being)
		Reappraisal		Quality of encounter outcome		Social functioning
Environmental variables		Coping				
(Situational) demands, constraints, resources (e.g., social network) Ambiguity of harm Imminence of harm		Problem-focused Emotion-focused Seeking, obtaining and using social support				
		Resolutions of each stressful encounter				

FIGURE 5.2. A theoretical schematization of the emotion system. (*Source:* R. S. Lazarus and S. Folkman, *Stress, Appraisal and Coping.* New York: Springer Publishing Company, Inc., 1984. Reprinted by permission.)

5.3, which are organized somewhat differently and which emphasize different aspects of the system of variables that make up emotion and the emotion process. Figure 5.2 (Lazarus & Folkman, 1984) has been presented several times in different publications and has the virtue of showing the main variables of the system, presented as antecedents, mediating processes, and short- and long-term outcomes. In this figure the flow of events is barely suggested in the references to Time 1 . . . Time *n,* and Encounter 1 . . . Encounter *n.*

Figure 5.3 (from Smith & Lazarus, 1990) provides a slightly different sense of the flow of events in the emotion process from top to bottom. The reader will notice at the top of Figure 5.3 what amounts to *antecedent* variables of the emotion process of two kinds: intraindividual factors and situational ones. Personality factors such as commitments and beliefs, in interaction with situational factors, lead to a situational construal which, as we proceed downward, eventuates in an appraisal outcome, the mediating process that is the proximal cause of all that follows, including coping and the emotional response state. The antecedent personality variables interact with each other in initiating the emotion process; for example, a strong goal commitment plays a different role when accompanied by beliefs that we are adequate and likely to be effective than beliefs that we are inadequate and likely to be ineffective. Similarly, a goal will be operative only in an environmental context in which the person has a goal-relevant stake in the transaction — that is, when there are environmental demands, constraints, or resources that bear upon it.

The emotional response configuration, as it is characterized in Figure 5.3, includes overall an appraisal outcome action tendencies, a physiological response

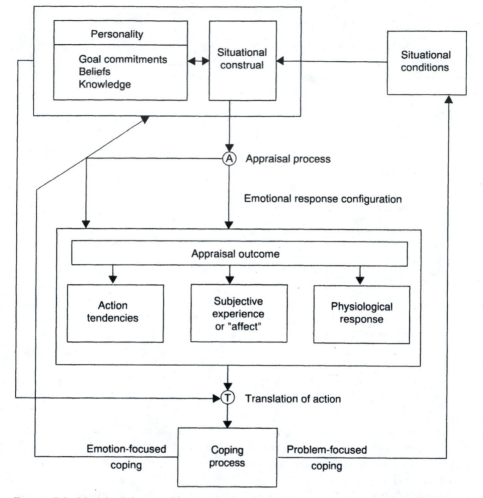

FIGURE 5.3. Model of the cognitive-motivational-emotive system. (*Source:* Modified from C. A. Smith and R. S. Lazarus, "Emotion and Adaptation." In L. Pervin (Ed.), *Handbook of Personality: Theory and Research.* New York: Guilford Press, 1990.)

pattern, and a subjective experience that is typically referred to as affect. All this is translated further into coping processes that enter the chain after appraisal, and their results feed back to the appraisal process to produce a reappraisal (not shown in figure), which further influences the emotional response state. What the person does to cope makes an important contribution to whether an emotion will occur, which emotion, and how strong it will be. If a cognitive coping process of denial is brought to bear successfully, for example, even under conditions of great threat a benign rather than distressed emotional state could result.

In speaking of appraisal and coping as processes, I am implying change over time and across environmental contexts. Appraisal and coping are mediators because they are not present as variables at the outset, but arise *de novo,* as I said, out of the transactional context. Since they are responsive to the conditions that prevail at that moment, they are difficult to predict. The idea of process or time is not shown in Figure 5.3. However, by repeatedly observing the same person's emotional reactions in slices of time or across encounters that are connected according to theme (e.g., bereavement), we can provide a picture of the emotion process — that is, the flow of events and the conditions influencing this flow. If, for example, we diagrammed the factors involved in the emotion process in an individual as a series of diagrams, we would have a three-dimensional portrait of that emotion process as it unfolds over time rather than as a single static moment. Because I am alergic to flow charts — believing that they often obscure as much as they reveal — I have not tried to create a series of charts to express what is happening at each moment in an ongoing emotional transaction, though this could be done if one wished.

Anyway, one of the implications of a system process analysis is that each variable affects each other variable in that system. In Figure 5.3 we see that personality factors, for example, influence both appraisal and coping. If we examine only antecedents, without reference to appraisal and coping, or if we fail to recognize that emotional reactions provide feedback to the other variables in the system, the picture we will have for any given individual's emotional flow will be at best incomplete or at worst distorted.

Finally, what is presented above is mainly centered at the psychological level of analysis, but as I noted early in this chapter, emotion is a multidisciplinary concept that also draws on the societal and physiological levels. To have a complete picture, we can simultaneously view the variables and processes of emotion at three levels of analysis: the societal, the psychological, and the physiological (as in Lazarus & Folkman, 1984, p. 308). Behavioral or psychosomatic medicine operates at the juncture of psychological and physiological processes. Sociopsychological studies — that is, those that examine how the social structure affects individuals and their emotions — and psychosocial studies — that is, those that examine how psychological processes affect the social structure — operate at the juncture of the social and psychological levels of analysis.

Other theorists may make different individual choices with regard to variables and processes that seem most pertinent and promising to them, or may conceptualize their interplay in the emotions differently than I have. I suggest, however, that until we learn to work within a system framework, our grasp of the emotion processes will be inadequate. Furthermore, there seems to be a current *zeitgeist* in which similar variables and processes are cited by a large number of writers and researchers. I would like to believe that the convergence we are seeing reflects the analytic power of the variables and the theoretical systems into which they are placed, rather than being merely a product of current fashion.

Summary

In this chapter I have addressed the most controversial issues underlying whether and how cognitive activity plays a causal role in emotion. I took up three main issues — namely, how we should think of cause, whether appraisal is a necessary as well as sufficient cause, and how we might reconcile biological universals with learned, sociocultural, and developmental sources of variability in emotion. Finally, I considered the metatheoretical contributions of a system analysis to emotion theory.

With respect to causality itself, I argued briefly for both synthetic and logical or analytic forms of causality. I addressed the uncomfortable issue of an analysis in which cognitive activity as cause continues as an essential component of the emotional effect. I drew on the concepts of reciprocal causality and temporal flow to show that there was no illogic or inherent circularity in this position. In addition, I examined contexualism and mechanism as ways of thinking about emotion theory and tried to show that this metatheoretical distinction is relevant to the distinction between emotion state (contextualism) and trait (mechanism). In my opinion, both metatheoretical outlooks make an important contribution to the understanding of emotion.

With respect to the substantive role of cognition in emotion, I proposed that knowledge is a necessary but not sufficient condition of emotion, and appraisal is both necessary and sufficient. Three misunderstandings have led to doubt or rejection of this position by many writers, and each of these was examined in turn:

First, it is a straw man to assume that cognitive causation makes emotion cold, calculating, and bloodless, based on a false premise that to speak of cognition as causal is to equate emotion with cognition.

Second, it is mistaken to believe that the proposition that cognition is a necessary cause of emotion is mooted by the claim that emotion occurs without cognitive mediation. Indeed, this cannot be shown and is implausible. Nor can it be shown that the effects of physical factors (such as drugs on mood) occur in the absence of cognitive mediation. It is not possible, nor the best theory, to say that emotional experience occurs in the absence of appraisal.

A school of thought has arisen that treats emotion and cognition as separate brain structures and functions. Although I agree that the two can be separated, as in ego-defense and certain forms of pathology, these functions are normally, or at least in the ideal case, highly interdependent, which is the position I have argued in this chapter.

In this connection, I believe it is also unwise to reduce psychological processes to neurophysiological ones, and as Erdelyi and Parisi have pointed out, not only is one poorly mapped by the other, but Freud has made an important case that the direction of the causal relationship is often reversed. Recent research and understanding of brain physiology are more promising than in the past in the examination of cortical and limbic system pathways for appraisal processes, but the dangers of reductionism remain in evidence. In any case, modern neurophysiology provides no basis, in my view, for the argument either that the emotion system and the cognitive system are separate, or that an emotion can occur in the absence of cognitive mediation.

Third, the fact that emotion is brought about rapidly is not grounds for invalidating the proposition that appraisal is a necessary condition of emotion. There is now widespread agreement that there is more than one way in which appraisal generates meaning, as was reviewed at some length in Chapter 4.

With respect to the need to reconcile biological universals with sociocultural variability in the emotion process, I offered a basic premise and two subpremises.

The basic premise is that in order to survive and flourish, mammals, especially humans, are constructed biologically so that they are constantly engaged in evaluations (appraisals) of their changing relationships with the environment with respect to the significance of these relationships for well-being.

The subpremises were presented in the form of "If-then" statements. First, if a person appraises his or her relationship with the environment in a particular way, then a specific emotion, which is tied to that appraisal pattern, always follows. I think of this as a basic psychobiological principle, which accounts for the universals in emotion. Second, individual variability in the emotion process is predicated on differences in how people appraise their person–environment relationships; this variability is influenced strongly by what is learned in the course of development from sociocultural influences. This affects the "if" in the "If-then" formula. Flowing from this, I also argued that most people, regardless of the cultures from which they come, experience all the core relational themes underlying each emotion, but that they learn from the culture what constitutes, say, a demeaning act, a loving act, an unselfish gift, a failure to live up to one's ego-ideal, a moral infraction, and so on.

This account has some parallels with the concept of affect program, and I examined how peremptory affect programs are in the emotion process, opting for a relatively loose and flexible system that is predicated on the appraised adaptational requirements of each core relational theme and correlated emotion, and the psychobiological rules linking the various physiological processes that come together in an emotion.

Drawing on a flowchart I have used elsewhere, I close the chapter with an account of a system analysis and its use in emotion theory as a set of interdependent variables and processes.

Notes

1. Discussions of causality with respect to appraisal overlap considerably with those in my recent article entitled "Cognition and Motivation in Emotion" (Lazarus, 1991a) in the *American Psychologist*. Both discussions were written at the same time.

2. These illustrations of structures and processes come from a book, now out of print, by R. S. Lazarus and A. Monat (1979).

3. See note in Chapter 1 for an explanation of why I use the singular, system theory or system approach, in contrast with the traditional usage, systems theory.

PART THREE

Individual Emotions

In the first chapter, I pointed out that a theory of emotion must do two things: (1) offer a general treatment of the emotion process, identifying the system variables that must be considered, and (2) apply this treatment to individual emotions. In Chapter 2, I discussed numerous issues concerned with defining emotions and classifying them. In Chapters 3, 4, and 5, I offered the major principles and propositions about emotion as a general concept. Now, in Chapters 6 and 7, I must spell out how the theoretical system works for each individual emotion.

Before proceeding, I should point out that rarely if ever are there adaptational encounters in which there is only one emotion. Usually, there is more than one piece of business, which is apt to change with the flow of events. Imagine, for example, going into your boss's office in hopes of getting a promotion and a raise. When you sit down, the boss says unexpectedly that the company is now under great financial pressure, and some people will be let go, including you. Although you began with one piece of business, getting a promotion and raise, it has now shifted dramatically to holding onto your job, with all that this might imply. Implications might include an angry picture of the world as unjust, the denigration of oneself and one's abilities and the shame this generates, anxiety about future employment and economic security, having to confront a loved one or others about having lost one's job, and defensiveness designed to maintain ego-identity and social esteem.

Our emotional lives are very complex, both in the multiple goals that are operating at any given time and in the changes taking place from one moment to the next. Nevertheless, to preserve clarity, each analysis in Chapters 6 and 7 centers on a single, individual emotion rather than on the juxtaposition of emotions and the flow that takes place in nature as the encounter unfolds and changes.

Although it is useful to seek consensual data from verbal reports and other types of response, as in the studies by Shaver et al. (1987) and Storm and Storm (1987), which were cited in Chapter 2, I believe there is no substitute for a theoretically driven, rational analysis of the meanings inherent in each emotion. I have tried in this part to use the concept of a core relational theme, the six appraisal components discussed in Chapter 4, and the concepts of action tendency and coping as the cognitive-motivational-relational basis for each emotion.

The reader will remember that three of the primary appraisal components are goal relevance, goal congruence or incongruence, and type of ego-involvement. The three secondary appraisal components include blame or credit, coping potential, and future expectations. Thus, for each emotion, there are at most six appraisal-related decisions to make, sometimes less, creating a rich and diverse cognitive pattern with which to describe the relational meanings which distinguish any emotion from each of the others.

When one considers the clinical data on the psychopathology of the emotions (e.g., Socarides, 1977), and the questions addressed in Chapter 4 about unconscious appraisals and defense, the resulting analysis may appear too simple — I hope not simplistic. I will supplement the simplifying generalizations somewhat at the end of the discussion of each emotion to point up the intrapsychic complexities arising from deeper, unconscious, and defensive processes, as well as the subtle shades of meaning inherent in our rich vocabulary of emotions.

The discussion of each emotion in the next two chapters follows a common outline: First, a set of propositions about the core relational theme, appraisal pattern, and action tendency is given. This is followed by a list of other terms falling within the emotion, a brief discussion of dynamics (the flow of events after experiencing the emotion), and brief comments about common kinds of psychopathology.

Chapter 6 deals with goal incongruent (negative) emotions and Chapter 7 with goal congruent (positive) emotions, as well as those that are problematic for various reasons.

❖ 6 ❖

Goal Incongruent (Negative) Emotions

The main emotions that result from goal incongruence include anger, fright-anxiety, guilt-shame, sadness, envy-jealousy, and disgust. The hyphens denote two different emotions that are closely related or at least have been traditionally regarded as such. My discussion of anger will be considerably more detailed than the discussion of other emotions, because anger is in many ways so complex, socially important, and conflictful, and because many of the issues surrounding anger apply to all emotions. For example, the subtle differences in the meaning of emotion terms are particularly well illustrated in anger. Though many of the same points apply equally to the other emotion families, it would become repetitive and boring if they were made compulsively for each, so where possible, I have used anger as a general model — recognizing, of course, that no individual emotion can play a prototypical role for all issues.

Anger

Anger is one of the most powerful emotions, if we consider its profound impact on social relations as well as effects on the person experiencing this emotion. In humans, the social meanings and folkways that generate, sustain, and regulate anger can be elemental and forceful as well as remarkably complex and subtle. Aristotle's approach to anger pointed the way to a modern, folk-centered, cognitive-motivational-relational theory of emotion. Indeed, Aristotle could be called the first cognitive theorist of the emotions, and his analysis makes implicit use of the ideas of relationship, appraisal, and action tendency. He writes in the *Rhetoric* (1941, p. 1380):

> Anger may be defined as a belief that we, or our friends, have been unfairly slighted, which causes in us both painful feelings and a desire or impulse for revenge.

Lyons (1980) points out, to the surprise of classical readers, that Aristotle discusses the emotions in the *Rhetoric* rather than in *De Anima*, revealing his view of the importance of emotion in public speaking and his interest in how emotions could be manipulated by orators and politicians. This is illustrated in the following quotation from the *Rhetoric* (1941, p. 1380):

Take, for instance, the emotion of anger: here we must discover (1) what the state of mind of angry people is, (2) who the people are with whom they usually get angry, and (3) on what grounds they get angry with them. It is not enough to know one or even two of these points; unless we know all three, we shall be unable to arouse anger in anyone. The same is true of the other emotions.

During the 1950s and 1960s, aggression was considered the response to the frustration or thwarting of a goal commitment, with anger being viewed as the motivator (drive) of aggression. It was mainly aggression rather than anger that was studied in those days. One of the problems with this outlook is that the frustration of a goal may be followed by *any* negative emotion, such as anxiety, guilt, shame, sadness, envy, or jealousy. To the extent that there is a possibility of *future harm,* which translates to threat, a likely result is anxiety; when negative conditions are *irrevocable* (entailing helplessness) and without the assignment of blame, a likely result is sadness; when they are *blamed on oneself,* a likely result is guilt or shame, or anger at oneself; and when there has been harm or loss to ourselves and *others are not victimized,* a likely result is envy or resentment toward the ones who remain unscathed or have benefited.

Therefore, it is of the utmost importance to specify what makes the provocation of adult anger different from other negative emotional states, all of which derive from harm, loss, or threat. One attribution distinguishing anger from other negative emotional provocations is whether blame is directed at someone or something other than ourselves; when harm or loss is *blamed on another person,* a likely result is outwardly directed anger; when it is blamed on oneself, the result is anger at oneself, as if we were an external object.

To blame persons, rather than simply hold them accountable or responsible for the harm, requires also that we believe that they could have acted differently, that they had control over the offending action. And so imputed control becomes another crucial attribution feeding anger, as will be seen. The inference is that the other person acted with volition, which is another way of saying without proper regard for our sensibilities, or even maliciously.

Both accountability and imputed control are forms of knowledge or attribution rather than appraisals, and blame is the appraisal that grows out of them in the context of threat and frustration. The rules that govern the provocation of anger may well be different for infants and young children, which is why I previously spoke of adult anger. Another special theme of anger is that a particular goal must be frustrated rather than any goal — namely, the preservation or enhancement of ego-identity.

Please bear in mind that in most of the research and thought on aggression, which has been primarily behavioristic, the differentiation of anger from other negative emotions has not been of widespread interest, which helps explain the acceptance of the overly simple frustration-aggression hypothesis with its extension to anger. To remedy this, some writers proposed that for anger to occur, the frustrating act had to be interpreted subjectively as arbitrary or malevolent, which implied an inference on the part of the angry person about the offender's intentions (cf. Pastore, 1952). This proposal is a precursor of present-day cognitive-motivational-relational ideas, which restate Aristotle's concept of anger as a reaction to a personal slight or insult — in effect, an assault on one's ego-identity.

The form this idea took in the 1950s emphasized the variables of arbitrariness and the intent to harm, and a certain amount of research confirmed its importance in the provocation of behavioral aggression, if not anger. If frustration was created inadvertently by a sympathetic person who did not intend to do harm — for example, someone who was handicapped and confined to a wheelchair — attack following a frustration was less likely (in contrast to when the same frustration was perpetrated inconsiderately or malevolently). Store clerks, for example, who make us wait unacceptably long for service because they are hard pressed by other customers or tasks, and who have not acted in a hostile or inconsiderate fashion, frustrate us but are less likely to provoke anger than is being ignored, say, because of a frivolous and extended personal telephone conversation.

Never settled in this research was whether anger had actually occurred in the nonblameworthy condition but had merely been inhibited from overt expression, or had never even been aroused in the first place. What little research had been done on malicious intent and on the tendency to react as if one had been insulted or demeaned went out of fashion before any consensus had been achieved about the core relational theme for anger (however, see Ohbuchi & Kambara, 1985, on apologies; and Torestad, 1989). The argument had been between those who looked to cognitive mediation as explanation and those who preferred a more behavioristic way of thinking, which emphasized observables and parsimony. Broad epistemological issues, such as the scientific status of the subjective concepts of appraisal and intention, make a consensus about this still difficult to achieve.

Despite changes in the dominant outlook, Berkowitz (1989) has persisted in the theoretical position that anger is not restricted to those situations in which one's personal or social identity is demeaned. He proposes that any frustration of an expected gratification will suffice, though he acknowledges that arbitrariness, inconsideration, and malevolence increase the intensity of the anger and its probability. Berkowitz (1989, p. 71) goes even further by saying that "any kind of negative affect, sadness as well as depression and agitated irritability, will produce aggressive inclinations and the primitive experience of anger before the higher order processing goes into operation."

That this is hardly the last word on how anger is provoked is reflected in a recent research analysis by Carlson and associates (e.g., Carlson, Marcus-Newhall, & Miller, 1989, 1990; and Carlson & Miller, 1988). Citing mostly laboratory research, they examined the effects of situational aggression cues on aggression with metaanalytic procedures, which summarize the findings of numerous studies. Unfortunately, their analysis did not reach back before 1966 to the days when intent to harm was of interest; the research they review tends to center on the frustration-aggression hypothesis, much of it stimulated or performed by Berkowitz, and few studies in which the dependent variable was anger rather than aggression were included.

In any case, their analysis supports a cognitive rather than a drive interpretation of anger-aggression (see also Tedeschi, 1983; Tedeschi, Smith, & Brown, 1974).

Recognizing that (p. 156) the "nature of the relationship between frustration and aggression has historically been the source of much controversy, with many researchers contending that thwarting per se is unrelated, or at best weakly related to aggressiveness," Carlson and Miller (1988) favor the theory that an intentional attack, such as an unwarranted insult, is a prime factor in aggression, and presumably anger. They write (p. 157):

> Given that a person has been insulted or criticised, the "dominant response" is generally to counteraggress. The nonsocial stessors [meaning the presence of weapons, unpleasant physical characteristics, and aggressive statements] may, therefore, augment drive and thus multiplicatively increase aggression above the level that would normally result following the receipt of an insult or criticism.

It seems to me that Carlson and Miller's argument turns the Berkowitz position completely around. Instead of saying that frustration is primary in anger and aggression, with social factors merely adding to it, they suggest that insult is primary, with nonsocial factors merely adding to it.

An advantage of the Berkowitz position is that it unites human aggression (anger being more debatable) with infrahuman aggression and anger in human infants, and makes it unnecessary to assume a phylogenetically advanced type of process in humans. For behaviorists, this position also has the advantage of not requiring inferences by the victim of frustration about the intentions of the other persons who are the sources of the frustration. A disadvantage is that it reduces human adult anger to the immature forms found in human babies and lower animals, and therefore may obscure important differences in the phenomena of anger in different species and at different stages of development. I remind the reader of what I said in Chapter 4 and have intimated here about the developmental aspects of an emotion such as anger. An appraisal-centered analysis of anger (and other emotions, too) is based on meanings that emerge with development and in evolution, and my account is mainly about adult human anger.

On the surface, the cognitive-motivational-relational approach to anger I am advocating, with the emphasis placed on the goal content of preserving one's ego-identity, creates a special problem even in the adult version. It seems to overlook the anger we experience if we see someone assaulting a helpless person, for example, a child. Why, if ego-identity is what is at stake in adult anger, do we react with anger? Of course, we also react with horror, with anxiety about what it means that such a thing could happen, and perhaps even with guilt or disgust, too. My answer is that sometimes anger is a vicarious reaction to a real societal danger. The abuse of a helpless child also assaults cherished values or meanings to which we are committed — for example, a basic fairness, integrity, and a just world (Lerner, 1970, 1980) — and which have become aspects of our ego-identity.

And if we have to wait in line for something we want, even if no one tries to sneak in ahead of us, the frustration of waiting is often sensed as an offense against us. We believe we should be treated better and perhaps that celebrities and the wealthy are not subjected to the same indignity. In the case of missing a golf putt, it is usually our own incompetence that should be blamed, and so we do the uniquely human thing of berating ourselves as if we were an external object of blame, or do the opposite, which is to find someone or something else to blame. I think all of these instances involve more than mere frustration and reflect who we want to be and how we are being treated.

The importance I attribute to assaults on ego-identity in the provocation of anger also points to certain personality variables that undoubtedly contribute to the readiness to become angry. An action that is an offense to one person because of a vulnerable ego-identity need not be an offense to another who can readily ignore or reinterpret the behavior that could be offensive. This doesn't mean that only those with vulnerable integrities get angry — the tendency is probably universal — but rather that the personality trait is a contributing factor, especially when the provocation is mild. Remember the epigrammatic advice that *a soft answer turneth away wrath.*

This emphasis also allows us to account for changes in personal vulnerability to anger as a result of fatigue or a recent history of being demeaned, a point that is reminiscent of James Joyce's short story, "Counterparts," in *Dubliners.* After the protagonist's ego is much buffeted over the course of the day, on returning home to find his wife out and only a cold supper waiting for him, he assaults his defenseless child in retaliation. This pathetic compensatory action cannot, of course, change anything but his wounded identity, but it symbolizes much that is characteristic of human anger, including its intrapsychic functions.

Dominance hierarchies in a large number of animal species are also relevant. When animals test their place in the hierarchy but are defeated — in the human context we might say they were deprecated, embarassed, or shamed — they will often take their defeat out on one lower in the hierarchy that is readily defeated. Displaced aggression is often observed serially from the top to the bottom of the hierarchy. I am convinced I see such behavior in my Welsh Corgie who, incidently, is female and, though loving to people, doesn't get along well with other dogs.

The sociobiologist might argue that Joyce's story is a manifestation of a displacement process, which connects the human motive of preserving and enhancing ego-identity to dominance struggles in simpler species. I am comfortable with this as long as we don't say that the human version should be understood as *nothing but* the process taking place in the infrahuman one. We don't refer to egos in the latter, nor do we need to. It is still necessary to study the conditions under which this process operates and how these conditions vary across species to achieve an adequate understanding. Simply drawing the parallel is not enough.

A human emotion such as anger, with its complex personal meanings, as well as other emotions such as anxiety, shame, and guilt, can be transformed readily by cognitive (or emotion-focused) coping processes, leading to remarkably flexible reappraisals of blame and the other key meanings underlying each emotion. Humans are perversely gifted at using these self-serving meaning manipulations, which are both a blessing and a curse. To make sense of what people feel requires, I believe, that we examine how they think and act to cope with the demands, constraints, and resources presented by their environments and to actualize personality characteristics such as goals and belief systems — all of which affect appraisal and coping processes and therefore the specific emotion that is experienced.

Core Relational Theme

I propose that a *demeaning offense against me and mine* is the best shorthand description of the provocation to adult human anger. An offense that is deemed arbitrary, inconsiderate, or malevolent contributes to the impression that we have been demeaned; the angry person has suffered what is taken to be damage or threat to ego-identity, whether this is recognized consciously and admitted or not. In effect, the word *offense* refers not merely to the frustration of a goal, though frustration certainly has emotional significance, but it carries a special significance — namely, a slight or injury to one's identity. This is how I believe adult anger arises. Even a mere frustration may carry with it the implication that we are less significant or worthy of esteem than we would claim or wish. Otherwise, we would react with an emotion different from anger.

Appraisal Pattern

A good way to portray the combination or pattern of appraisal components distinguishing anger from other negative emotions is to use the strategy of a *decision tree,* an analysis in an "if-then" form, which moves progressively from the most general and elementary distinctions — for example, between emotional and nonemotional encounters — to the distinction between negative and positive emotions, and finally to what makes the provocation to anger different from all other negative emotions.

So that there is no misunderstanding, let me repeat myself about using this decision-tree format before proceeding further. By ordering the appraisals for each negative emotion in a sequence from the general to the particular, I am not suggesting that the evaluative decisions made by a person in real life necessarily follow a sequence. As I noted in Chapter 4, a great many of the evaluative decisions have already been made in a person's past, save for the cues that activate them currently (as in short-circuiting). I am using the decision tree for explanatory reasons, not to describe how the appraisals are made in nature. It allows me to follow the theoretical logic of a progressive narrowing of appraisals to a specific emotion as a *didactic device* rather than a portrayal of how people actually go about appraising.

I begin the analysis of the pattern of appraisal in anger with *primary appraisal* components — namely, goal relevance, goal incongruence, and type of ego-involvement.

1. *Goal relevance* is crucial for all emotions, anger included. If a goal is at stake in an encounter, then an emotion will be generated, but if there is no active goal, and none emerges as salient during the encounter, there will be no emotion.

2. *Goal congruence* or *goal incongruence* is crucial to whether the emotion that is generated will be positive or negative. If there is (a) *goal congruence,* the consequent emotion will be positive; if there is (b) *goal incongruence,* then any negative emotion is possible, including anger, which also depends on at least three additional components, which are discussed as components of secondary appraisal.

3. The basic motive to preserve or enhance self-esteem against assault, which is one *type of ego-involvement,* must also be activated for anger to occur. Thus, if this facet of ego-identity has been assaulted or threatened, conditions are set for anger to occur; if it is not involved, anger will not occur. Remember, my position is that

anger depends not merely on frustration, but on a personal slight or a demeaning offense. Frustration leads to anger only when the frustration communicates that we have been taken to be less than what we are, sometimes directly in word or deed, and sometimes because of the manner in which the frustration occurs. Without this special meaning, frustration could equally well produce anxiety, guilt, shame, sadness, envy, jealousy, or disgust.

Certain *secondary appraisal* components are also crucial to an anger provocation as distinguished from any other negative emotion.

4. A key secondary appraisal component is *blame,* which depends on who, if anyone, is taken to be accountable for the damage or threat to our identity. If the accountability is internal—that is, if we hold ourselves responsible—we experience either anger at ourselves, guilt, or shame. If none is held accountable, sadness rather than anger is a candidate. Anger at another person or object occurs *only* if the direction of accountability is external. Even this, however, is not sufficient to predict anger, because external accountability also occurs in fright-anxiety, envy-jealousy, and disgust. Ultimately, imputed control is also crucial for anger in contradistinction to all other negative emotions by providing for blame.

Blame rather than mere accountability is crucial for anger, just as credit is for pride.[1] Therefore, control must be attributed to whomever we blame for a frustration. If the people who frustrated us are not thought to be in control of their actions, no blame can logically be assigned to them, though we create blame out of whole cloth, so to speak. If, however, the people who frustrated us are capable of having acted otherwise, then they are likely to be blamed. If they could not help themselves for the harm they have done, either there is no legitimate blame, or the blame is inhibited for other reasons; for example, there are some persons we don't want to be angry at because of the power they hold over us, whether this power is willingly granted or not. But more of this later under dynamics.

To continue a previous example, store clerks who make us wait while they talk to a friend on the telephone, assuming it is not an emergency, make us angry because they have chosen not to treat us as we require. They have control over their actions, and their inconsideration demeans us. Imagine, however, the scenario in which we begin to rage over such a slight, then discover that the clerk was actually talking at length to a doctor in an emergency room where her child had been taken after an accident. Now the anger suddenly turns to guilt, shame, or shared anxiety, because control cannot legitimately be imputed to the distraught mother. Store clerks who can't help themselves for other reasons—for example, because there are too many customers—are also blameless and do not warrant our anger.

However, since we are still frustrated, we might then reserve our anger for management or some other institution, or even ourselves for having been foolish enough to get caught in this anomalous position. Self-blame may be warranted, for example, when we have left our holiday shopping for the last minute. Making the judgment about who, if anyone, should be properly blamed can be complex and difficult, because there are so many environmental levels at which it is possible to assign accountability and control, and hence blame. The more complex the society, the more difficult is the judgment, but the more potential targets there are. When the specifics of accountabililty and control are ambiguous or too complex to interpret, we may direct our anger to the "system." Here is an obvious place where sociocultural variables may play an important role in the dynamics of anger (see also Chapters 4 and 9).

When things go badly, it is also common to search for an external source of blame even when it is not readily in evidence, in order not to have to accept it ourselves. Since the world has mistreated us, we feel less significant as persons than we would like to feel, and so we find someone or something else to blame. To feel angry as a result of this kind of projection may also provide a sense of self-righteousness and even power, which is better than feeling that we are helpless or that there are no rules. In thinking about externalizing blame in this way, we have suddenly turned our attention to the process of *coping* with the harm or threat to which we have been exposed. It is worth repeating that the words we use for the complex cognitive, motivational, and relational configurations we refer to as emotions often refer to action tendencies or coping processes, which as I said are integral components of the emotion process.

When we kick a stone on which we have tripped, or smash our golf club on the ground after missing a putt, we are, in reality, attacking someone whose identity may be unclear. Emotions are normally interpersonal, whether in reference to a real person or to an imagined one. That person may represent someone we resent for other reasons (or perhaps unconsciously), the anger toward whom has been displaced onto an inanimate object. Engaging in such a process may also affirm a meaning in which we are invested—for example, people we dislike or fear. The action may also serve as a mild self-confirming punishment; when we kick the stone we are apt to injure our foot or produce pain, and when we bang the golf club it may break. Even without it being interpreted as a defensive reversal of blame, the high frequency of these behavior patterns suggests that the psychodynamics of anger depend heavily on coping and appraisal processes (see Folkman & Lazarus, 1988a, 1988c, 1990), which alone provide good reason for moving away from a simple input-output explanation to a system theory analysis.

If accountability and imputed control are directed at oneself rather than another, guilt or shame is experienced instead of anger, or alternatively, *anger at oneself* (as if one were another person). Though guilt and shame have often been interpreted as anger at the self, in my judgment these are not the same processes. If no agency, either internal or external, can be blamed, the reaction is apt to be an emotion other than anger, guilt, or shame—for example, sadness (especially if the loss is irrevocable), anxiety (which always involves ambiguous threat), or an emotional state that does not fall within a clear emotion family, and for which we use vague terms like frustration, disappointment, or merely distress because we can specify no clear core relational theme.

Ambiguous experiences are like "acts of God" in insurance contracts; the damage has been done, but none can be blamed. If control is not imputed to God, we need not blame God for evil; if it is, we might be angry at God or angrily reject the whole idea of God. The mind, however, works differently from the rules of business law, and people often try to find someone or something to blame, which makes anger a very frequent emotion, even under ambiguous conditions, as long as the victim of a slight can find a scapegoat.

Although only four appraisal components seem necessary to describe the cognitive-motivational-relational rudiments of anger, and to differentiate anger from other emotions such as sadness, guilt, or shame (Lazarus, 1991b), added secondary appraisal components help in distinguishing anger from other emotions, and one kind of anger from another. It will be fruitful, therefore, to examine the last two secondary appraisal components in our consideration of anger — coping potential and future expectations. Note that coping potential refers to an appraisal rather than to actual coping.

5. I suggest that anger, in contrast with fright and anxiety, is potentiated by an appraisal that the demeaning offense is best ameliorated by attack; in effect, the individual evaluates her *coping potential* of mounting an attack favorably, which is also the innately given action tendency. If this were not so, and to the extent that the person is in control of her actions, then attack would be inhibited or another emotion would take place. Coping potential overlaps with Bandura's (1977a, 1982) concept of self-efficacy.

In this connection, when endangered, animals threaten if they sense they can overpower or bluff an adversary, but withdraw or flee when they sense that the opponent is too dangerous. The decision appears to be made quickly, and the animal may shift back and forth between attack or flight, depending on the changing competitive conditions. The form of adaptation that predominates also seems to have species determinants, because some animals are timid and others are ferocious. Most animals display a degree of tentativeness about responding to challenges with flight or attack — a sensible reluctance, as it were, to commit themselves irrevocably (see White, 1974).

This suggests that fear and anger are opposite but interdependent sides of the same adaptational coin, and that an appraisal about coping prospects is usually involved in decisions about which adaptational strategy to pursue. This interdependence and oscillation also provide a phylogenetic basis for the anxiety that often accompanies human aggression — that is, the apprehension that an attack places us in danger, either from the object of the attack or on the basis of moral or idealized self-concepts (see also Chapter 3).

We must take seriously that various contextual factors that influence coping possibilities influence whether a person will react with fright, anxiety, or anger. This is exemplified in Henry James's fascinating story *The Turn of the Screw*. In this story, malevolence, which I have earlier identified with anger, produces anxiety instead. The governess who is caring for two children begins to experience apprehension about ghosts from the past that seem to shape what seems increasingly to be malevolent behavior on the children's part, and she becomes increasingly anxious, as does the reader — or the viewer of the excellent film version of this story, *The Innocents*. At this point, the story takes on a chilling quality, and we are made vicariously fearful or uneasy rather than angry. That the malevolence results in anxiety rather than anger in this context is, I think, the result of the uncertainty of the threat, and therefore the lack of a basis for confidence in a coping decision. The governess and we the audience do not know who is responsible for the threat, or what can be done about it, so anxiety, not anger, is the appropriate emotional reaction.

6. If the negative conditions generating anger can be overcome or ameliorated

TABLE 6.1. Appraisals for Anger[a]

Primary Appraisal Components

    1. If there is goal relevance, then any emotion is possible, including anger. If not, no emotion.

    2. If there is goal incongruence, then only negative emotions are possible, including anger.

    3. If the type of ego-involvement engaged is to preserve or enhance the self- or social-esteem aspect of one's ego-identity, then the emotion possibilities include anger, anxiety, and pride.

Secondary Appraisal Components

    4. If there is blame, which derives from the knowledge that someone is accountable for the harmful actions, and they could have been controlled, then anger occurs. If the blame is to another, the anger is directed externally; if to oneself, the anger is directed internally.

---

    5. If coping potential favors attack as viable, then anger is facilitated.

    6. If future expectancy is positive about the environmental response to attack, then anger is facilitated.

---

[a]Appraisal components sufficient and necessary for anger are 1 through 4.

by attack with safety, there remains a question about the later consequences of this coping strategy, which is another way of speaking about *future expectations.* This appraisal component, like coping potential, also overlaps with the environmental aspect of Bandura's (1977a, 1982) concept of self-efficacy, which has to do with whether the environment will respond favorably to the coping action. Anger and attack may have to be paid for later by retaliation or by social disapproval and even punishment. Future expectancy and coping potential overlap in some respects, but differ in the type of constraint. In coping potential, the issue is whether one can mount a viable attack; in future expectations, the issue is whether there will be any benefit or whether the costs of attack produced by the environmental response exceed the benefits.

    A summary of the appraisal decision tree for anger is given in Table 6.1.

Action Tendency

Although it is often inhibited for personal and social reasons, few would argue with the proposition that the innate action tendency in anger is *attack* on the agent held to be blameworthy for the offense (cf. Averill, 1980, 1982, 1983). I don't want to get into the perennial issue of how peremptory the impulse to attack is; many writers have taken sides on this, pitting biology against psychosocial forces. Freud was quite pessimistic about human destructive tendencies and the difficulty of sublimating or otherwise controlling them. Obviously, the impulse to attack must be a strong and perhaps universal one, though it is often kept under tight control or transformed. It also appears possible to be very angry, to have a powerful impulse to exact vengeance, and nevertheless to act benignly and constructively on the basis of threat, enlightened self-interest, or strongly internalized ethical values.

    As I pointed out in Chapters 2 and 3, an action tendency expresses a biological urge that is generated as part of the cognitive-motivational-relational configuration, but in anger the forms of attack and its control or redirection also fall into the sphere of the coping process. Once we get away from innate action tendencies, the coping process may lead to strategies of attack that seem, from the standpoint of secondary appraisal, to maximize the possibilities of success. These may be carried out planfully over a considerable period of time, as is illustrated in the Dumas novel, *The Count of Monte Cristo,* in which the count plots a complicated skein of cold yet hateful vengeance against those responsible for his long imprisonment. Coping is far more psychological than are innate action tendencies—it is more planful, deliberate, and rational, is more dependent on skills, and is shaped by a knowledge of the tactical as well as strategic possibilities inherent in the long-term relationship as well as in the specific encounter.

Other Terms

A large number of words fall within the emotion family of anger, perhaps more than for any other emotion, which may say something about our culture or about human nature. Some of these, such as *rage, outrage, fury, wrath, ferocity, indignation, irritation, annoyance,* being *appalled,* and *hatred,* differ from one another at the very least in the intensity of the indicated reaction, though subtle shades of meaning also distinguish many of them as well. For example, *indignation* and *outrage* clearly imply having been wronged, whereas *irritation, rage,* and *fury* do not. *Spite* implies a particular kind of hostile motivation. Other words (for example, *pouting, gloating, vengeance, stubbornness, disdain, sarcasm,* and *petulance*) are characterized by an emphasis on particular actions, actions that may also communicate deeper psychodynamic meanings and possibilities.

For many action words, the relational meanings are subtly diverse; for example, *gloating* connotes the verbal or expressive enjoyment of another person's comeuppance. *Sarcasm* has some overlap with gloating, but lacks the sense of pleasure at the other's bad fate. I implied earlier that, along with the four basic appraisal components of anger, gloating also involves an attempt to enhance an injured or vulnerable personal identity, which could be the result, perhaps, of an earlier history of having been demeaned, "adding insult to injury," an inordinantly heightened goal relevance (e.g., a greater identity stake), or greater goal incongruence (the harm is considered more severe). The savoring of another's discomfort, injury, or defeat (i.e., schadenfreude; see also envy) is experienced by the person who gloats as a well-deserved vindication, which also serves to enhance a damaged ego-identity. The mocking might be seemingly polite and subtle or might be ventured with malignant scorn and smiling satisfaction.

From a psychoanalytic point of view, Whitman and Alexander (1968) have written about gloaters as "sore winners." They view gloating as based on the childhood envy of more successful siblings, perhaps also modeled on a parent who gloated. Presumably as a result of an imagined or realized victory over an adversary, gloating creates the illusion that we are superior, thereby increasing our sense of personal justice or vindication. In this psychoanalytic formulation, superiority is a defensive illusion against the opposite construal—namely, that we are inadequate and in a one-down position. This kind of reasoning also implies that emotions such as anger, anxiety, envy, jealousy, joy, and pride are really quite interdependent (see also Arlow, 1957, on the relationship between smugness and gloating).

On this point, notice that subtle appraisal changes can tranform an emotion from envy to anger if the person who has what we want rubs our noses in it, as it were, or from anger to anxiety if the angry expression of the envy seems to have offended the other person in such a way that we now become anxious lest we have gone too far (as in "aggression anxiety"). In Chapter 3, I briefly discussed the interdependencies among the core relational themes and the emotions they produce, which result from the stakes that they sometimes share and the changed appraisals that the flow of events may create.

In contrast with gloating, *pouting* arises from a tendency to feel inadequate and dependent, which results in inhibition of overt attack and its transformation into a mild reproach designed to obtain or preserve succor from another. It expresses the idea that we have been disappointed by another person from whom more was expected or hoped. In pouting, we are in a one-down position with respect to the person who has dissappointed us, but we cannot afford to attack in order to enhance our wounded integrity as we do when we gloat.

Thus, pouting expresses not only reproach, but neediness, which is why it is so commonly seen as childish, and certainly quite different from sarcasm which can be an uninhibited, spicy, or witty verbal expression of anger, almost but not quite akin to contempt. Whatever makes the person not dare to attack for fear of further alienating the person whose approbation and concern are still needed creates the coping strategy of pouting. From the standpoint of its developmental origins, and formulated within a psychoanalytic perspective (Adatto, 1957), the aim of pouting is an attempt, recapitulating childhood, to force one's mother (lover, offspring, etc.) to pay attention.

To distinguish pouting from gloating in the appraisal process, we need only draw on the secondary appraisal components of an unfavorable *coping potential* and *future expectations,* which contribute to anxiety and weaken anger and the tendency to attack. What makes the dynamics of pouting different from other forms of anger is the threat (and its anxiety) of what an uninhibited expression of anger is thought to produce — namely, retaliation and loss of succor.

Personality traits involving helplessness and inefficacy or their opposite, a sense of mastery or control, should contribute to the appraisals underlying gloating or pouting. In the same vein, some people are not given much to aggression anxiety or can easily overcome it, whereas others are made extremely anxious by their own anger. In addition, some encounters are more conducive to gloating, as when the angry victim feels, for the moment at least, powerful and safe, and other encounters are more conducive to pouting, as when the person toward whom we might feel angry is too powerful to attack — for example, someone whose approbation and affection are greatly valued and desired (cf. Kemper, 1978). Although a boss with control over our job or salary may also be threatening, we are not likely to pout when we are not given patronage, because this would make us look childish in a work context in which we prefer to look masterful.

As already implied, pouting and gloating could be viewed as *coping strategies* rather than as emotions, though I think both also involve anger. This suggests overlap or interdependency between coping processes and emotions, especially when the emotion words we use emphasize the language of action, as in gloating, pouting, sarcasm, disdain, spite, stubborness, and petulance. I conclude that emotion and coping refer to distinguishable but functionally interdependent features of a common adaptational process. Here, as well as earlier, I express reservations about isolating one function or quality of a complex emotional state and ignoring the other functions or qualities.

Other words such as *scorn, dislike, feeling smug, arrogance, hatred,* and *bitterness* also illustrate subtle variations among relational meanings. *Indignation* and *outrage* suggest righteous, justifiable anger against injustice; these anger states draw on the components of *type of ego-involvement, blame,* and *coping potential.* And although one can feel hatred, the word contains the additional connotation of a stable sentiment about another person or group, bordering on a trait or disposition rather than necessarily being an acute emotional reaction.

In jealousy, a good case could be made for a combination of the core relational themes for both anger and envy. Though anger is one of its hallmarks, I treat jealousy later as a separate emotion, related to but not the same as anger or envy. Loathing seems to contain both horror and disgust, but I have treated the latter as a separate emotion on the basis of Rozin and Fallon's (1987) recent work. Arrogance and smugness, especially the latter, seem to combine contempt (hence anger) with pride, and bitterness combines anger with sadness, but could also imply a trait or disposition, as in a bitter person. Contempt seems to involve denigration as well as anger. It is treated by Ekman and Friesen (1986, 1988; Ekman & Heider, 1988; also Izard & Haynes, 1988) as a primary emotion in its own right, as I noted in Chapter 2.

When I say "combined," I mean by this a combination of *separate* emotions, each with its own core relational theme, rather than what is often meant by the term *emotion blend. Blend* is often used in a very special sense by some writers, who distinguish primary or basic emotions and secondary or derived emotions. When I say that smugness is a combination of contempt and pride, I mean that to feel smug is to feel both contemptuous of those who are below us *and* proud to be superior. The content is not changed from the original emotions that were blended, and so I think *combination* is a better word for this than *blend.*

All of these emotion words seem to contain anger — either at their core, subordinated to other emotions, or focused on aggressive actions of a particular sort. Each, however, contains additional meanings that could be taken into account depending on our purposes, and without which we would lose clinically valuable information about what is happening in the person–environment relationship and how it is appraised. A special emotion category could validly be created for each word, though I am not sure that this would often be a practical solution, as I indicated in Chapter 2. Yet if my impression that the various relational meanings carry important information about emotions — for example, the person–environment relationship they imply and the psychological makeup of persons experiencing them — then there will be occasions on which we cannot afford to abandon them completely in favor of reduction to the broader category of anger. The choice between expansion or reduction of emotion categories depends on one's theoretical and research purposes.

Dynamics

I have already noted that anger is often inhibited rather than expressed, especially when the person toward whom one feels anger is powerful and might retaliate. In these cases, we will be misled if we take the surface appearance as the totality of the emotional state. Freud wrote extensively about the anger felt by the young boy toward his father, who is a competitor in the family triangle (the Oedipus complex), and the threat of castration (symbolic or real) as punishment for his hostile wish. He proposed that, to feel safe, the boy ultimately represses the hostility and by a process of unconscious identification internalizes the father's outlook, and more generally that of the male gender.

Does the appraisal involving anger still exist following the anger's repression? Although this is difficult to answer, except by making certain assumptions, I think the answer is that sometimes it does and sometimes it does not. I struggled with this issue briefly also in Chapter 4, citing the Freudian concept of the return of what is repressed as symptoms. It disappears when the defense is totally successful; it continues to exist when provoked if the defense is unsuccessful, as when we say, "I tried to tell myself I was not angry," or when the defense is not well consolidated and so works some of the time but not others (see also Lazarus, 1966). I believe that we must avoid the outdated Freudian concept of energy, which treats repressed anger as undischarged energy that continues to exist even when there is no provocation, and recognize that what does not disappear is the disposition to feel anger under particular conditions that reflect the beliefs, urges, and conflicts of an individual for whom anger is an important personal characteristic.

Sometimes, as I said earlier, we inhibit the expression of anger against superiors lest they punish us for it on the job, or against someone we love lest they retaliate, or against someone we love to whom we have ceded power. Often this is done deliberately and consciously, but it may also occur without awareness. Though we may avoid the appearance of anger for safety and security by appearing cooperative, anger can be expressed subtly and indirectly in passive-aggressive tactics by means of which we undermine a boss's objectives by goofing off, playing sick, and manifesting stupidity in the conduct of our job or in response to the advice of a professional that we find threatening.

Many nursery rhymes originating in eighteenth-century England express cleverly disguised hostility to the English crown because to express it openly was dangerous. For example, the baby on the tree top in "Rock-a-bye Baby" is said to be the illegitimate child of the hated and feared King James. The king wanted to have this child inherit the throne, but if that took place — so the rhyme goes — baby, cradle (meaning the throne), and all (the whole dynasty) would come crashing down. Today our children enjoy this very seditious message without having a glimmer of its historical significance, but it would have been exceedingly risky to express such sentiments in King James's day had they not been disguised and tranformed into a seemingly harmless ditty. As we all know, anger when expressed can be useful; it can also be very dangerous (see Tavris, 1984), and if not controlled may not only be counterproductive but over the long run may even endanger our physical health and well-being (for example, Keinan, Ben-Zur, Zilka, & Carel, unpublished, on patterns of anger and long-term health; Williams, Haney, Lee, Yi-Hong Kong, Blumenthal, & Whalen, 1980, on anger's relation to heart disease; and Spielberger, Johnson, Russell, Crane, Jacobs, & Worden, 1985, on its consequences for long-term health).

The power of coping to influence anger reactions in anger-provoking encounters has also been studied by Hart (1991), whose findings on adolescents suggest that there is less anger when the emotion-focused coping process of "focusing on the positive" is emphasized, but that those who engage in wishful thinking in interpersonal anger-provoking encounters show exaggerated anger. Here, as in other research, the emotional consequences of being exposed to anger provocations is mediated by coping activity whose adaptiveness depends on contextual factors such as the nature of the stressful encounter.

And what are we to make of competitive striving and zealotry in the context of what I have said about the emotion of anger? Are these defensive manifestations of anger, or does this stretch the meaning of the term too far? People who are deeply involved in competition are sometimes said to be acting out feelings of anger in socially acceptable ways, and zealots are said to be acting out personal hatreds while imputing to themselves socially constructive motives. Consider, for example, the late Ayatollah Khomeini's urging that Salman Rushdie, writer of *The Satanic Verses,* a novel that many Moslems considered offensive, be murdered. Though Khomeini always seemed to me to be a bitterly angry man, as judged by facial expressions, words, and actions, the idea that zealots are acting out personal anger in any given instance is a difficult thesis to prove. We should be concerned about some of the scientific difficulties inherent in a depth interpretation of the emotion process in which meaning transformations of the motivation for action are presumed to take place without awareness.

It might also be useful here to pursue the suggestion I made in Chapter 3 that coping strategies and intentions are closely linked, and that they may depend on the individual emotion being experienced. In that discussion, I cited Laux and Weber's (1991) list of intentions (or goals) underlying coping with anger episodes in married couples, which included, among others, self-promotion, defensive self-presentation, and seeking emotional closeness (or protecting the relationship).

That numerous intentions are possible means that the coping strategies for achieving them could take many forms, depending on what is at stake in the encounter and on the emotion that has been generated. To illustrate how this might work in the case of anger, I will contrast two of many possible intentions—namely, to protect the relationship or to preserve and enhance one's wounded ego-identity—and consider some coping alternatives for each.

Let us say that a person, A, has slighted his friend, B, and that B is privately smarting with anger from a wounded ego-identity. At this point in the transaction, B has at least the two coping alternatives just mentioned, either to repair his wounded sense of identity or preserve the relationship with his friend A. If the major goal is to *preserve the relationship,* perhaps because it is already threatened and might not survive further assault, or because B is particularly threatened, perhaps more so than the partner, by the loss of the friendship because of his own vulnerable identity, his dependence on the partner who has protected him, or a history of poor relationships that have failed, how can this goal be accomplished? One coping strategy might be for *B* to *conceal* the negative appraisal and the anger that it provoked. In that way, there will be no counterattack to escalate what harm has already been done.

Arrayed against the intention to preserve the friendship is the fact that *A*'s offense has undermined an already vulnerable ego-identity in *B*. A person is even more vulnerable to insult if there is already a weak identity. To ameliorate this, an effort to *protect, save, or enhance one's identity* is needed. The coping strategy used depends on whether one is playing to an outside audience of persons who may have witnessed the offense or to the inner audience of one's own ego. One strategy might be to *escalate the conflict* by showing anger and seeking revenge — in effect, to risk all to preserve or enhance one's wounded identity.

A compromise is also possible in which mild anger or reproach (pouting) is shown to the partner, along with evidence of being hurt, which in a more needy extreme might include supplications ("look how you have hurt me without provocation; please show me more kindness, respect, etc."). With this compromise there might be a chance to preserve the relationship and one's integrity, too. An alternative might be for *B* to show anger lest he lose even more by displaying cowardice and neediness. Personal and cultural values operate silently here in the choice of the strategy to manage troubled social transactions. These transactions contain many coping possibilities, depending on personal goals and beliefs about resources and judgments concerning human relationships.

I don't mean to suggest that *B* stands there mentally reviewing each strategy, but merely that some or all of the alternatives, and the considerations underlying their use, are probably available in his mind. Some of the alternatives will have higher or lower thresholds of activation in light of personal and social goals, values, constraints, and life experience. The specifics of the anger encounter, including how clear and forceful the provoking slight was, the expectations that were generated based on the history of the relationship, and the background of other recent events in the person's life, are also relevant to the choice. The temporal flow of emotion, which includes appraisal and coping processes, changes in the relationship, and the emotion experienced, may, and often does, continue until resolution or disengagement. This flow is apt to be experienced differently by each participant because of differences in their goals and beliefs, which, in turn, depend on personal histories and circumstances. In complex transactions, the emotions may undergo transitions ranging from anger, anxiety, and guilt to shame, sadness, affection, relief, and disengagement, or any combination of these at the same time, with changes sometimes occurring very rapidly.

These changes can be analyzed microanalytically as separable but an interconnected series of transactions, each with its own scenario, identifiable personality and situational antecedents, appraisals, and coping processes whose consequences feed back and shape reappraisals with their own new personal meanings and the emotional changes these engender (see the discussion of the emotion process in Chapter 3). The picture I have drawn for anger can also be drawn for every other individual emotion, each with its own dynamics.

The complexity of the problem in the case of anger and how to cope with it is also illustrated by the fact that there are many ways of conveying anger socially, and these ways have to do with the intentions a person has in the emotional encounter, the sociocultural outlook about anger and its expression, and the history of the inter-personal relationship. Thus, although we often express anger with verbal attacks, or with physical assaults, we may also convey that we are angry by coldness, by slow, calculated speech, and by inattention. It takes considerable social skill to read accu-rately what is being conveyed by another, and sometimes the correct inference can only be made by intraindividual comparison — that is, by knowing the person so well that exceptional patterns stand out by virtue of their being unusual for that person.

Pathology

Obvious examples of what is regarded as pathological anger include unrestrained and recurrent violence toward others, verbal and physical abusiveness toward chil-dren and spouses, perpetual bitterness and unrelenting disillusionment, the tendency to carry a proverbial "chip on the shoulder" in which the person overinterprets oth-ers' actions as demeaning, and the inability to inhibit the expression of anger. Persons who engage in disguised and destructive patterns of anger such as passive-aggressive behavior display another kind of pathology. There is also an opposite pattern in which a person feels but is unable to express anger even when it is appro-priate and useful. What makes these patterns pathological, at least potentially, is that they are recurrent and contribute to dysfunction and distress. They produce mal-adaptive consequences by defeating the pursuit of important goals, alienating others whose support is valued and needed, and sometimes result in violence that could lead to punishment or worse.

As with all judgments of this sort, it is not always easy to say when anger is or is not pathological. One test would be the fit between the emotional reaction and the provoking circumstances. Another would be the adaptational consequences. Anger that destroys the one who is angry would be an obvious example. In some instances, anger is justified by the offense, but expressing it may expose the person to retalia-tion, or it may be expressed in such a poorly formulated way, as when we speak of *blind rage,* that it is self-destructive.

One of the most interesting self-destructive versions of anger is when it is used to defend a personal identity but externalizes the blame even when some of the responsibility is better accepted by the self in the interests of doing something con-structive. If a victimized group externalizes the blame, its members are apt to feel better about themselves but may miss ways to adapt more successfully in spite of their social handicaps. Victims often don't do anything to change things for them-selves, because taking responsibility for oneself is not usually compatible with the psychology of being a victim. Anger and certainly rage have to be controlled, pur-poseful, and realistic to have constructive value, and a defensive analysis of the real-ities will often only perpetuate the status quo, or make it worse, even if in the short run it makes the victims feel better.

In contrast, self-blame — that is, when it is limited to a specific encounter and is what Janoff-Bulman (1979) called *behavioral self-blame* — could be a valuable kind of coping, for if we can see how we have failed, we have a good chance of doing better next time (see Bulman & Wortman, 1977). On the other hand, *characterolog-*

ical self-blame, in which failure is attributed to personal inadequacies, with the implication that messing up is inevitable, is clearly counterproductive and hence pathogenic. Neither attributing accountability and blame to the self when this is not realistic, nor inappropriately blaming others, is likely to be adaptive.

Fright-Anxiety

One cannot help but be struck by the tendency in psychology to regard anxiety as the key emotion in both healthy adaptation and psychopathology, especially the latter. Anxiety is a unique emotion, because its hallmark, *ambiguity* (of the available information) or *uncertainty* (the resulting psychological state), which I believe stems mainly from its existential underpinnings, all but immobilizes us with respect to coping. This emotion came to be theoretically synonymous with the idea of uncertain threat, which Averill (1988, p. 264) describes as follows:

> Ask a person who is afraid what he fears, and generally he can tell you; ask him what he would like to do, and he can tell you that, too. By contrast, the person who is suffering an anxiety attack cannot say what he is anxious about, or what he wants to do.

To survive, humans need to impose meaning on events in a confusing world, to provide a map, as Averill puts it, of one's relationship to that world. Anxiety arises when existential meaning is disrupted or endangered as a result of physiological deficit, drugs, intrapsychic conflict, and difficult-to-interpret events. The threat involved is symbolic rather than concrete. If the threat is mild, and the structures that are endangered not very central to the person's identity, the result is apt to be mild uneasiness. If the threat is severe and the meaning structures central, the result is apt to be a full-blown anxiety attack and a personal crisis of major proportions. This has been said many times in diverse ways (e.g., Lazarus & Averill, 1972).

Anxiety is also widely treated as a primary, often *the* main, motivating force in human affairs. Early in Freud's theorizing, anxiety was said to arise when there is danger of being overwhelmed by stimuli; threat of castration, which could also be a metaphor for loss of potency against the demands of living, exemplifies this potential. Being overwhelmed or traumatized is also the central message of Goldstein's (1939) "catastrophic reaction," which he described as a consequence of brain damage that produces psychophysiological incompetence. And though it is cast quite differently from Freud's treatment, the modern preoccupation with control, mastery, or efficacy overlaps this Freudian idea in important ways, but leaves out the psychosexual features central to Freudian psychoanalysis.

The religious philosopher, Tillich (1959), and other existential psychologists and philosophers (e.g., May, 1950; May, Angel, & Ellenberger, 1958) helped popularize a conception of anxiety as unique among the emotions in that it is the result of the threat of nothingness or nonbeing, a kind of psychological death. Becker (1973), too, conceived of anxiety as the dread of death, the denial of which was said to motivate all human enterprise. Humans build, said Becker, in order to deny their ultimate death. While Freud emphasized conflicts over oral, anal, or phallic impulses as the main sources of anxiety, Becker emphasized being permanently trapped in a decaying body, which, by dying, destroys one's ego-identity. Religion is one way to gain a sense of immortality, which may reassure us against the existential anxiety. Regardless of how it has been portrayed, there has been a great penchant for viewing anxiety as a main engine of mind.

Not all psychologists make a distinction between fear and anxiety, as I do, and quite commonly a single term, say, *fear,* is used for both. I use the term *fright* for reasons that will soon be clear. Fright and anxiety are focused on the threat of a future harm. In my judgment this obscures striking differences between them, and so in my discussion I have separated them and their appraisals. There is room for taking two alternative tacks on this: One is to assume that anxiety and fright are forms of one emotional state with the same basic machinery, as it were, though they differ in important respects and therefore are variants within the same emotion family; the other tack is to propose that they are different emotions altogether. I can see advantages to both ways of handling the matter.

Core Relational Themes

Fright, as I shall henceforth term fear, involves threats that are concrete and sudden; therefore, it is a more primitive reaction than anxiety. The core relational theme is the concrete and sudden danger of *imminent physical harm.* Because of this concreteness and suddenness, I prefer the term *fright* to *fear,* which in common usage has come to be ambiguous, referring sometimes to specific, harmful social and self-related consequences, and at other times to concrete physical dangers. As with anxiety, uncertainty or ambiguity is always a feature of fright because the harm is always in the future. However, since the danger is concrete and sudden and there is little time to reflect, uncertainty is not as prominent in fright as it is in anxiety, where the threat is symbolic, existential, and ephemeral.

In fright we are scared about the immediate prospect of sudden death or injury. I say immediate because, although we may be anxious about death, we are not frightened about it, because it seems vague and a long way off; we can put it out of mind except under circumstances of acute danger, as when the aircraft in which we are traveling suddenly hurtles temporarily, thank heaven, toward the ground with all its engines having lost power, which has happened now and then. The near miss cannot help but remind us of our mortality.

The core relational theme of *anxiety* is *uncertain, existential threat.* The uncertainty about what will happen and when obviates any clear idea on the part of the person of what to do to prevent or ameliorate it. We are nagged by abstract, ambiguous, and symbolic threats to our ego-identity. Anxiety, in contrast with fear or fright, always entails existential danger and uncertainty (Lazarus & Averill, 1972).

This distinction between fright and anxiety is also supported by the research observations of Hibbert (1984) and McNally (1990) that panic patients (when they are anxious) seem threatened by bodily harm, whereas anxiety patients are threatened by personal inadequacy when they are anxious. The emphasis on existential threat in anxiety is also consistent with Spielberger's empirical findings (Spielberger, Gorsuch, & Lushene, 1970) that anxious persons, more than others, are faced with threats to their ego-identity (he uses the term *self-esteem*) but do not perceive physical dangers as any more threatening than do persons low in trait anxiety. Spielberger thus seems to be agreeing that anxiety, at least in the trait sense, is predominantly an existential emotion.

Freud suggested that the causes of "neurotic" anxiety lie within the person in the form of unacceptable impulses but that the causes of "objective" anxiety lie outside the person as actual dangers. This distinction makes less sense when we take a relational approach to emotion. Threat is always a product of the interplay of personal *and* environmental conditions, even when it has to do with unacceptable impulses that arise from within; these impulses are appraised as dangerous because they are in conflict with environmental constraints and taboos, or with an internalized version of the environment. The mechanisms underlying objective and neurotic anxiety must, therefore, be basically the same. Nevertheless, it is always appropriate to ask a more fundamental question — namely, to what extent has an appraised threat been evaluated realistically? If one wishes to use these terms, it would make more sense merely to say that neurotic anxiety, in contrast with objective anxiety, is an unrealistic appraisal of danger regardless of its source.

Appraisal Patterns

Following the same basic decision-tree format used for anger, the *appraisal* components for *fright-anxiety* are presented in Tables 6.2 and 6.3. I have not duplicated its details here to reduce repetition.

Fright may be the sole emotion in which primary appraisal component 3, *ego-involvement,* is absent or irrelevant in the generation of the emotion, at least directly, and so with this absence the potential emotions involved narrow to *fright.* I should add that fright itself can potentiate threats to one's ego-identity, as when we are demeaned, made guilty, or shamed by experiencing fright. Thus, we may experience existential threat after or during a fright encounter, but ego-identity is not directly relevant to the generation of fright itself.

On the other hand, if the *type of ego-involvement* engaged in an encounter is

TABLE 6.2. Appraisals for Fright[a]

Primary Appraisal Components

1. If there is goal relevance, then any emotion is possible, including fright. If not, then no emotion.

2. If there is goal incongruence, which is a threat to bodily integrity by a sudden, concrete harm, then only negative emotions are possible, including fright.

---

3. Ego-involvement is typically not relevant to the generation of fright, though it may be important in the appraisal of the significance of how one reacts to the fright encounter.

No secondary appraisal components are essential; blame is irrelevant, coping potential is uncertain, as is future expectancy.

---

[a]Appraisal components sufficient and necessary for fright are 1 and 2.

TABLE 6.3. Appraisals for Anxiety[a]

Primary Appraisal Components

1. If there is goal relevance, then any emotion is possible, including anxiety.

2. If there is goal incongruence, then only negative emotions are possible, including anxiety.

3. If the type of ego-involvement is protection of personal meaning or ego-identity against existential threats, then emotion possibilities narrow to anxiety.

No secondary appraisal components are essential. Blame is irrelevant, as implied in 3, coping potential is uncertain, and future expectancy uncertain.

[a]Appraisal components sufficient and necessary for anxiety are 1 through 3.

protection of the ego-identity or personal meaning structures one has created against existential threat, the emotion possibilities narrow to *anxiety*.

No *secondary appraisal* components are essential for anxiety, but it may be worthwhile to enumerate their possible role. *Blame* (appraisal component 4) is certainly irrelevant, and if we blame someone, the expectable emotions are anger, guilt, shame, or jealousy. If we don't know what is going to happen or when, which is consistent with an existential threat, *anxiety* is the likely emotion.

These appraisal components are capable of distinguishing fright from anxiety and both of these emotional states from other emotions, both positive and negative. I do not believe that additional secondary appraisal components add much to the distinction between fright and anxiety, but they might contribute modestly to increases or decreases in anxiety.

Although the hallmark of anxiety is uncertainty, the source of danger is often perceived as external; knowing what is going to happen and when it will happen provides a way of overcoming anxiety temporarily by taking concrete action or engaging in anticipatory coping. The existential source of threat in anxiety provides a strong motivation to objectify it, either appropriately or inappropriately, by reference to sources of external and concrete danger, such as loss of a job, failure to pass an exam or to be hired after a job interview, being rejected or ostracized, and so on.

Indeed, there is evidence (Gal & Lazarus, 1975) that acting against danger, even when there is little or nothing effective to be done, is more reassuring than uncertainty and inactivity, just as externalizing blame is psychologically more comfortable than internalizing it. Freud spoke of neurotic anxiety as being in a free-floating state that could be attached to this or that concrete threat even when it had intrapsychic origins. However, even when a person attributes anxiety to external conditions, the basic source is always existential and consists of threat to meaning structures to which we have become committed.

Coping potential (5) is uncertain in both fright and anxiety. If we could avoid or escape the sudden danger, fright would be aborted or rapidly mitigated. If we could prevent or overcome the existential threat, anxiety, too, would also become moot. The problem, of course, is that, since the real danger in anxiety is existential, no sooner have we overcome an objectified threat such as an exam or a social performance than another threat has taken its place. Vulnerability to anxiety consists of our existential relationship to life and the world, the nature of which we may only dimly appreciate.

The presence of *anxiety* suggests that an existential threat has not been success-fully controlled by emotion-focused (cognitive) coping activity; if it were con-trolled, the anxiety would be short-circuited. Aside from the changes in meaning associated with cognitive coping, we seem to be relatively helpless to deal with anx-iety, which may be the most ubiquitous human emotion, except to learn how to tol-erate it. Under conditions of sustained or recurrent physical danger, such as in military combat, in contrast with sudden dangers that pass, we frequently draw on magical solutions, superstitions, and denial, as suggested by Grinker and Spiegel's (1945) observations of combat air crews during World War II. These ways of changing meaning are forms of cognitive coping, which the psychoanalysts speak of as ego-defense.

Future expectations (6) are also uncertain in fright *and* anxiety. Because the appearance of danger is sudden, it is difficult to develop expectations about what will happen in a frightening encounter. The emotion doesn't usually last long, and it may give way to uneasiness when the danger is prolonged or recurrent. In anxiety, the nature of the threat is uncertain, again obviating a role for future expectations, except those generated by cognitive coping efforts to think positively; besides, if expectations are positive rather than negative, there would be no rational reason for anxiety.

Action Tendencies

In both fright and anxiety, the action tendency is avoidance or escape, in contrast, say, with approach and attack. Since the harm is imminent and concrete or external in fright, the impulse to get away from the obvious danger is unconflicted. On the other hand, because of uncertainty about what is happening in anxiety, including its existential source, the appropriate action is by no means obvious. There is, in effect, no concrete harm to avoid or flee, which makes anxiety more of an ache than an acute pain, metaphorically speaking, and difficult to control. It is an action tendency without a concrete goal, and so it is experienced as vague and diffuse, an effort to get away without anything specific to get away from.

Other Terms

A substantial number of other terms, though fewer than in the case of anger, fall within the fright-anxiety emotion family. Those associated with *fright* include hor-ror, terror, and fear; those associated with *anxiety* include unease, concern, appre-hension, and worry; some, such as dread, alarm, and panic, are ambiguous in usage and can refer to either fright or anxiety. Horror may combine fright with loathing or disgust, as when we react to a decayed body or a threatening supernatural image. Awe, when a negative experience, seems to be a blend of fright and amazement, but when it has a positive quality, it is almost the same as wonder.

It has frequently been suggested that worry is different from anxiety in that worry is usually consciously directed at concrete concerns in daily adaptation rather than at existential sources of threat. I am not sanguine about this suggestion, because it separates one objectified feature of an anxiety state, conscious concerns about specific demands, from the total cognitive-motivational-relational configuration. Worry can be treated as an attempt to make existential anxiety concrete and external in order better to deal with it. The separation of worry from anxiety would be justified only if worry were not usually correlated with the rest of the anxiety configuration, a proposition I tend to doubt.

As with anger, anxiety-fright words carry multiple connotations having to do with the intensity of the reaction, its source, ambiguity, action tendency, and mixtures of other meanings, as in panic, horror, and awe. These terms may be used somewhat differently across individuals and in different contexts, though it is reasonable to suggest that there is a common core of shared meaning.

Dynamics

More than any other emotion, psychological research has centered on how anxiety influences adaptational outcomes such as subjective well-being, social functioning or performance, and somatic health or illness. As such, it is almost a synonym of psychological stress (cf. Cofer & Appley, 1964), which is largely centered on threat (Lazarus, 1966). From the 1950s to the present, the focus of interest was on anxiety as a source of interference in skilled performance, and a large number of psychologists are still doing research on *test anxiety*, which is viewed both as an educational and personal problem. A central research issue has been the conditions under which threat and the anxiety it provokes have positive or negative effects on functioning, and the mechanisms of these effects. Because test anxiety is experienced by people who are prone to be threatened (trait anxiety) by taking tests or being evaluated, it would be more precise, I think, to speak of *test threat*. I have more to say about this in Chapter 10, which deals with emotion and health.

Pathology

What is the pathology of *fright?* Unduly fearful people, including phobics, could be said to display pathological distress and dysfunction. These symptoms are said by behaviorists to be the result of conditioning, and the strategies of treatment are aimed at deconditioning. Panic is also regarded by some as an inherited neurochemical disorder. Psychodynamic theories treat phobias as products of ego-defense, a symptom of unconscious conflict. I discuss treatment strategies in Chapter 11.

All sorts of intrapsychic strategies are used to control anxiety, which makes it difficult to assess what is really happening on the basis of what is observed on the surface. For example, counterphobic strategies of coping with threat may lead to a superficial picture of courage, boldness, or fearlessness instead of fright or anxiety. Denial and intellectualization as coping strategies may create a positive psychological portrait, when, in reality, the person using them might be deeply troubled. It is as if the person claims to have no problems, only symptoms (cf. Shapiro, 1965; see also Weinberger, 1990). One must get below the surface to make an accurate assessment of these coping styles and the sources of threat for which they are designed. I discuss attempts such as these to assess variables and process in Chapter 11.

It is an open question how successful denial or repression of anxiety on the one hand and vigilance or distancing on the other are in sustaining adequate functioning. Clinicians often assume that both are dangerous, especially suppression or denial of anxiety. They are said, for example, to result in so-called posttraumatic stress disorders in which dysfunction may not be evident during the period of acute stress but may appear at a later time. The conventional wisdom is that immediately following trauma, a person should be given an opportunity to vent and explore what happened lest the trauma be buried in the mind and later reemerge to result in psychopathology. When anxiety-inducing threats overwhelm the person's coping resources, we speak of *trauma* or *crisis* rather than stress.

Guilt-Shame

Guilt and shame are usually treated as overlapping emotions. Guilt has received more attention (Zahn-Waxler & Kochanska, 1990) but there seems to be increasing interest in shame (Lindsay-Hartz, 1984; Lynd, 1958; Wicker, Payne, & Morgan, 1983; Scheff, 1990a, 1990b). The new interest is also reflected in efforts to assess proneness to shame and guilt as a personality trait (e.g., Harder & Lewis, 1986; Tangney, 1990). Both are said to involve thoughts or actions that violate a social proscription that has been internalized (see also Klass, 1981; and McGraw, 1987).

Traditional psychoanalytic thought has been criticized for not making enough of the distinction between these two emotions, which on closer inspection reveal different person–environment relationships.[2] H. Lewis (1971), who gave close clinical attention to guilt and shame, has suggested that *guilt* arises from internalized values about right and wrong (that is, what parents and society would like the person to be) and *shame* arises from one's ego-identity (that is, discrepancies between what persons are and what they would like to be). The treatment of shame-based clinical syndromes has been the concern of a new book by Kaufman (1989). The same question about their distinctness as emotions, in which one could argue for two variants of one basic emotion, occurs here as it did in the case of anxiety and fright.

Core Relational Themes

Guilt is generated by having done, or wanting to do, something we regard as morally reprehensible, a formulation which can be shortened merely to *having transgressed a moral imperative.* Guilt is felt when we believe we have acted in a morally deficient way, all the more so if in so doing we have wronged or harmed an innocent other. There need be no actual transgression, for even a fantasized sin can produce guilt. Nor does another person have to be physically present to result in the feeling of guilt; it is enough that we have observed ourselves in a transgression.

Although this is the way I characterize guilt, several alternative emphases have appeared in theoretical treatments of this state of mind. In an extensive treatment of guilt, which focuses on its social and developmental origins, Zahn-Waxler and

Kochanska (1990) point out that theories have varied as to whether guilt is considered innate or learned, functional or problematic, a state or trait, or whether affective, behavioral, or cognitive components are emphasized.

These authors characterize three different main emphases as follows: (1) In the psychoanalytic view guilt feelings are conceived of as a reaction to unacceptable impulses in oneself and traced to hostile and sexual impulses in childhood that are repressed as a result of fear of punishment and loss of parental love; (2) guilt feelings are said to be based on prosocial feelings and empathic concern over the distress of others, which evolve developmentally into wanting to do well by others (see Hoffman, 1982a); and (3) guilt feelings are primarily cognitive and not present in very early childhood but are aroused when the children learn to perceive and understand the social significance of violations of standards of conduct (see Wicklund, 1975). I see these views of guilt as an emotion as overlapping, because — in the terms of the core relational theme I set forth earlier — transgressing a moral imperative is always involved in guilt feelings, even when its dynamics and origins are conceived somewhat differently.

Shame is generated by a *failure to live up to an ego-ideal.* We feel disgraced or humiliated, especially in the eyes of someone whose opinion is of great importance to us such as a parent or parent-substitute, who was the original source of the demanding ego-ideal. Because it is so difficult to distinguish between social and self-disgrace — both are regarded as functions of the superego in Freudian language, and both represent a form of threat and anxiety — shame and guilt are easily confused, though subjectively and behaviorally they seem quite distinct.

In shame, another person whose approbation is important to us views and presumably is critical of our failure. We have, in effect, disappointed that person, typically a parent (of course), the internalized version of that person's ego-ideal, and therefore ourselves as well. As with guilt, if we merely believe we have failed to conform to our idealized identity, this is enough to generate the feeling of shame. A parent figure need not actually be physically present to see our "shame" or even still be alive; it is only necessary that we imagine how that figure would react to what we have done or not done.

Let me back up a bit here and restate the relational principle of Chapter 3. Both shame and guilt, and other emotions, too, in my view, are based on social relationships; all of us, especially children, frequently personify what happens to us, even the physical world. It is usually other persons who are given credit or blame for what happens to us, and we act with the sense that others are watching and judging what we do.

When I say that shame is based on an internalized ideal, and guilt is based on a moral transgression, this doesn't mean that another disapproving person is not involved, either in actuality, in anticipation, or wholly in fantasy or imagination. The shamed person may see the disapproving image of a mother, father, or someone else, and this could be an inaccurate image or a distortion of how these persons might actually have reacted. Although emotions can seem to arise privately and without others being around, I think they always involve other persons, and the emotion process draws on past and present relationships with such persons. Emotions are social phenomena. This is especially the case with guilt and shame;

the conflict is always about a disapproval for a moral transgression or for failure to live up to an ego-ideal.

Appraisal Pattern

The appraisal components for guilt and shame, respectively, are presented in Tables 6.4 and 6.5, and these should be consulted.

If *blame* (component 4) is internal—that is, the responsibility for the moral transgression resides in oneself, and we accept that we had control over the action—the remaining emotional possibilities narrow to guilt. All negative emotions that involve an external agent such as anger, envy, jealousy, and disgust are eliminated. Sadness is eliminated because no agent can be blamed. Shame is obviated because its goal content has been ruled out.

And so we have reached a single emotion after four appraisal steps. Minor contributions are also made by additional appraisal components. For example, if we recognize that we can expiate guilt through an apology, then this *coping potential* (5), which could lead to apology—the more abject the better to make amends—helps mitigate guilt. And if the *future expectation* (6) is that atonement will restore our moral stature, or that we will live up to our ego-ideal more successfuly in the future, both guilt and shame could be mitigated somewhat if, indeed, we expect to translate this positive expectation into coping acts. We often do this in our coping fantasies.

A paradox about guilt suggested by Freud is that most guilty-feeling people are less blameworthy in actuality than the average person. Guilt-ridden personalities berate themselves for little or nothing, and feel more blameworthy than others, which may make them less likely to engage in thoughtless or reprehensible acts that violate moral standards. Presumably we often act with the intention of preventing distressing guilt or shame. It is not clear how frequently we do this or how important this kind of anticipatory coping is in preventing guilt and shame.

For Freud, therefore, guilt was mainly a neurotic obsession rather than a reality-

---

TABLE 6.4. Appraisals for Guilt[a]

Primary Appraisal Components

    1. If there is goal relevance, then any emotion is possible, including guilt.

    2. If there is goal incongruence, then only negative emotions are possible, including guilt.

    3. If the type of ego-involvement is to manage a moral transgression, then emotion possibilities narrow to anger, anxiety, guilt, and disgust.

Secondary Appraisal Components

    4. If blame is to oneself, then emotion possibilities narrow to guilt.

---

    5. If coping potential is favorable, then guilt may be expiated by apology or making amends.

    6. If future expectations are favorable, then guilt may also be mitigated or reduced.

---

[a]Appraisal components sufficient and necessary for guilt are 1 through 4.

TABLE 6.5. Appraisals for Shame[a]

Primary Appraisal Components

1. If there is goal relevance, then any emotion is possible, including shame.

2. If there is goal incongruence, only negative emotions are possible, including shame.

3. If the type of ego-involvement is to manage a failure to live up to an ego-ideal, then the possible emotions narrow to anger, anxiety, shame, and disgust.

Secondary Appraisal Components

4. If blame is to oneself, then the possible emotions narrow to shame.

5. If coping potential is favorable, then shame can be mitigated by promising to redouble efforts to live up to an ideal.

6. If future expectations are favorable, then shame may be mitigated or reduced along with the threat of abandonment.

[a]Appraisal components sufficient and necessary for shame are 1 through 4.

based self-perception, and needed to be overcome in psychotherapy. Mowrer (1976), however, took the opposite position — that people who feel guilty have actually been moral transgressors, and that psychotherapy should be oriented to the exploration of actual sins that the person should avoid in the future to be successfully helped.

According to H. Lewis (1971), rejection or abandonment is the basic threat underlying shame developmentally and is the assumed punishment for the failure to live up to parental standards, which have been internalized. This implies that people who are vulnerable to recurrent shame are especially concerned with rejection and abandonment, a causal process, however, that is apt to be unconscious. We recognize the experience of shame without necessarily being aware of its familial, developmental roots or its underlying motivation.

Action Tendencies

The core relational themes for guilt and shame point to differences in the action tendency in each. In *guilt,* the impulse seems to be to expiate, atone, or make reparation for the harm that has been done to another and perhaps to seek punishment, all the more so when the harm to the other person is severe and unjustified. Though this may be a universal action tendency, emotion-focused coping strategies are available that could undercut it. For example, thoughts about the injured party can be avoided. Another way to cope with a guilt-centered encounter is to deny control or to project the blame onto the other person so that we do not have to accept it ourselves. This is facilitated by dehumanizing the victims so that we do not have to feel distress at their suffering (Bernard, Ottenberg, & Redl, 1965; Lazarus, 1985). The reader may recall that the same cognitive coping process, called *projection* by psychoanalysts, also applies to anger and anxiety, and the blame for both may be turned from oneself to a concrete, externalized source, which is easier to handle psychologically in that form. If these coping strategies are successful, there is no reason for guilt.

I propose that the action tendency in *shame,* in contrast with guilt, is to hide, to avoid having one's personal failure observed by anyone, especially someone who is personally important. To publicly expose one's failure to live up to an ego-ideal is to risk disapproval and quite possibly even rejection. In our research on coping (Folkman, Lazarus, Dunkel-Schetter, et al., 1986), we found that if a person's stake in a stressful encounter is the well-being of another person, a common strategy of coping is to seek social support; on the other hand, if the stake is the preservation or enhancement of one's self-esteem or social standing, seeking social support is eschewed, because we feel shame about having such a self-serving goal.

This finding is particularly interesting in light of past research on anxiety and shame. A well-known study by Schachter (1959) showed that when laboratory subjects awaited what they expected to be a painful electric shock, they preferred to wait with another subject facing the same stressor rather than alone. Schachter drew on this finding in proposing that social affiliation is motivated by anxiety. However, in a later study by Sarnoff and Zimbardo (1961) in which the awaited stressor was to engage in socially embarrassing acts, subjects preferred to wait alone.

The principle that guilt makes us want to atone publicly, whereas shame encourages us to hide, seems to be consistent with the findings on choosing to wait alone or in company, and seeking social support in anxiety- but not in shame-generating situational contexts. In short, if we extrapolate from this research, the two closely related emotions, guilt and shame, are distinguished not only by the person–environment relationship and the appraisal pattern contributing to it, but also by the action tendency associated with each. Though circumstances might well modify this, shame makes us want to hide, whereas guilt makes us denounce ourselves to the world.

Other Terms

Remorse emerges consistently as a synonym for guilt, and feeling repentent, sorry, bad, and apologetic also seem to fall within the same emotion family. Notice that the terms of *remorse, feeling sorry,* and *feeling bad* center on the feeling state and its cognitive supports, but the words *repentant* and *apologetic* center on the action tendency. Therefore, these terms are not synonyms, strictly speaking, for they refer to different aspects of a guilt-centered relational configuration. Feeling sorry and bad are also too ambiguous to identify formally as guilt; one can feel sorry about something without accepting responsibility or blame. We say we feel bad about another's misfortunes, which might be true, but we do not always feel bad about our role in it.

Alternative terms for *shame* are humiliation, embarrassment, mortification, chagrin, and feeling ridiculous, each of which has somewhat different connotations. H. Lewis (1971) also includes shyness. Although Shaver et al. (1987) list regret within a subcluster of sadness, which includes guilt and shame, and Storm and Storm (1987) include it with guilt and feeling sorry, regret (like feeling sorry) is too ambiguous in relational meaning to be included within either the guilt or shame families with confidence, unless there is other evidence of its exact meaning. Like many so-called emotion synonyms, shame-related words are also not all alike in their relational meanings. Perhaps the most obvious difference lies in the intensity of the reaction: Chagrin and embarrassment seem rather mild and are often used in a casual way, while humiliation and mortification are strong reactions.

Dynamics

Some apologies for *guilt* are based on institutionalized practices that do not engage the emotions but serve as pro forma ways of behaving properly. We can say we are sorry without having blamed ourselves in the least for what has happened, and we often use statements about being sorry as a strategy of coping with guilt. Consider, for example, people who always seem to be apologizing or saying they are sorry. Such statements are not true attempts to expiate guilt but efforts to ingratiate, probably made by persons who have strong doubts about their social acceptability. When there has been a moral transgression that has harmed someone, a statement that one is sorry does not always satisfy the injured party, because the process of protecting the self against blame may be transparent to the victim; however, the failure to mollify with a pro forma apology may be remedied if the guilty party appears sufficiently abject before the victim (see Ohbuchi, Kameda, & Agarie, 1989, for discussion and research on apologies).

The transactions here, or interpersonal games as Eric Berne (1964) would have called them, are sometimes complex, involve posturing, and are capable of satire. For example, the guilty person gives an abject apology, but the victim still appears unmollified, at which point the guilty person grows angry and accuses the victim of exaggerating the problem out of hostility, leading both parties to make efforts to "forgive and forget" in order to bring about the restoration of the status quo.

Both emotions, guilt and shame, are said to encourage prosocial behavior that matches high social standards. *Guilt* is commonly viewed as a motivator of proper conduct, since it is a distressing emotion. Perhaps more accurately, it should be said that we avoid guilt by acting morally, though, as I have already said, the empirical case for this seems weak. Some parents are guilt inducers; that is, they use guilt to socialize their children (a comment often made, sometimes half-jokingly, about American Jews of European origin, as well as about certain other groups). *Shame,* too, is distressing, and it presumably motivates the person to live up to ego-ideals imposed by parents and internalized by the child. It is also said that Japanese parents socialize their children with the (shame) threat that they will be disapproved of, or that they make the mother unhappy, if they do not measure up to certain standards. (See Chapter 9 for further discussion of cultural differences relevant to emotion.)

Pathology

Clinical descriptions of shame- and guilt-centered neuroses have been provided by H. Lewis (1971, p. 18), who writes from a psychoanalytic perspective that it "is a commonplace that the outbreak of neurotic symptoms is fostered by the difficult experiences of life: disappointment, failure, defeat, helplessness and moral transgression." Feelings of shame or guilt may also lead to poor social judgments about relationships with others. Persons suffering from characterological guilt or shame (these states are recurrent) may display overweening perfectionism, chronic anxiety, recurrent self-reproach, and a negative ego-identity. In addition, those suffering from characterological shame may also display an oversensitivity to rejection by others, which is sometimes coped with by hostility and scorn, and which in turn leads to disturbed interpersonal relations.

Writing about shame from a psychoanalytic point of view, Levin (1971) comments on the painful nature of shame as an emotion and discusses the way the person's ego is pressed into defensive maneuvers to limit exposure to shameful encounters, to repress the reaction, to withdraw emotionally from close relationships, and to cope defensively by anger and aggression. He uses the term *shame anxiety,* which implies that much effort goes into protecting oneself against the threat of being criticized and rejected.

Levin also notes that, unlike guilt-ridden clients who are apt to cry out and want to look into the sources of their distress, shame-ridden clients hide the truth behind defensive coping strategies that get in the way of treatment. They also assume that the therapist, like their parents, rejects them, and they may run away from therapy overtly or by the use of complex resistances.

Perhaps I should also mention again the issue of unconscious emotion, because in psychoanalytic writing, guilt, especially in the so-called phenomenon of "moral masochism," is a frequently mentioned "unconscious affect." In Chapter 4, I intimated that unconscious emotion poses logical problems, and, with respect to the theory of signal anxiety, I suggested that the concept of threat appraisal as a precursor to coping and defense does away with the need for a self-contradictory concept of unconscious emotion.

Although masochism is often regarded as a sexual perversion (see disgust), it is moral masochism, meaning the need to suffer as a defense against unconscious guilt, that is the center of considerable attention in psychoanalysis. In moral masochism, patients are said to be unconscious of both the guilt and the fact that they seek suffering (see also Gillett, 1987a, 1987b). So-called masochistic defenses operate either by reducing conscious guilt or by preventing its generation. In Chapter 4, I also said that defense is capable of being triggered by appraisals that lead to the emotion of guilt, and that this defensive process has to be unconscious. The person learns to anticipate when a given type of appraisal will generate guilt, and then the defensive process automatically prevents the guilt-inducing mental content from becoming conscious. It is, therefore, unnecessary to postulate unconscious guilt, just as it is unnecessary to postulate unconscious anxiety, because the defense can respond automatically to an unconscious guilt-inducing wish, a cognition which is appraised as threatening, before any emotional guilt is created. I called this short-circuiting in Chapter 4.

Finally, I should not leave guilt and shame without referring to one of their occasional consequences, namely, suicide. It is a bit risky to speak of this as pathological without qualification, because there seem to be cultural differences in the conditions of life that provoke suicide. For example, in Japan it is not uncommon for suicide to follow great shame after a person has failed to live up to a social obligation. Other suicides result from loss, as well as shame, as when Madame Butterfly performed seppukku after she had lost all hope of a socially and personally approved life, and when businessmen in the United States destroyed themselves after having lost everything in the stock market crash of 1929. It appears that extreme loss and hopelessness result in suicide for some, whereas great and irrevocable shame does so for others, though this too can be interpreted as loss of "face."

Sadness

Sadness is an especially interesting and obscure emotion. It is usually said to be linked to a loss such as the death of someone we love, the failure of a central life value or role, or the loss of the positive regard of another. The concept probably embraces several overlapping states that have to do with the conditions of loss and whether or not it can be dealt with, states which can be thought of as falling along a dimension of coping with loss or threat of loss that might be called *degree of engagement.*

At the high end of the engagement dimension, the actuality or threat of loss results in other emotions characterized by the potential for active coping, and to the extent that one is not helpless to change things, efforts are mounted to avoid loss, restore what has been lost, or manage the distress; these efforts are apt to be accompanied not so much by sadness but by anger, anxiety, guilt, shame, envy, or hope, which are the *emotions of adaptational struggle.* A similar view, cast in terms of coping stages, may also be found in treatments of coping with loss by Horowitz (1976), Klinger (1975), Marris (1975), Shontz (1975), and Wortman and Brehm (1975).

For example, to seek help and emotional support and to make efforts to recover the lost object by one means or another, including fantasy and denial, are common patterns of coping in the first hours, days, weeks, and even months after the death of a loved one. Gradually, as these efforts fail to restore the loss, the person must come to terms with it through what is typically a long and complex process of *grieving.* Depending on the stage and dynamics of the struggle, a complex of other emotions that includes anger, guilt, and anxiety plays a prominent role, with or without sadness. This complex is typically referred to as *depression,* with its psychopathological implication, or *grief,* with its active and prolonged coping struggle.

Sadness belongs at the low end of the dimension of engagement and involves *resignation* rather than struggle, at which time the person has been moving toward acceptance of and disengagement from the lost commitment. The emotion at this stage may be more akin to wistfulness than deep sadness. I propose that sadness only occurs at fleeting moments, or in general when it is acknowledged that nothing can be done to restore a loss. Therefore, sadness is a step toward resignation, which emerges from a difficult coping struggle in which the emotional outlook is often contradictory, fragile, and changing. As long as the person is not subjectively helpless, negative emotions other than sadness are more likely to occur. Marris (1975) argues that loss threatens stable lifelong meanings, even when change is being sought, and that grieving is the process of coming to terms with the loss, especially the loss of meaning. When grieving is successful, old and cherished meanings are retained and integrated with more serviceable new ones, which are more appropriate for the new life conditions.

Core Relational Theme

As I have already pointed out, the core relational theme in sadness is not just loss, but *irrevocable loss;* in other words, there is a sense of helplessness about restoration of the loss, which is why I used the term *irrevocable.* I avoid the term *hopelessness* in this context, because when a person feels hopeless about the implications of the loss there is apt to be depression rather than sadness.

If and when resignation or acceptance has occurred, the associated emotional distress is ultimately attenuated or, for the most part, has disappeared. When a person becomes resigned to the loss, the sadness is obviated, because the person has given up the lost commitment. It is part of the past, and if and when the loss is remembered, what remains is mostly calm memory and wistfulness. Whether or not this happens probably depends on the quality of the adjustment that has been made to the changed life conditions.

If the loss is not considered irrevocable, then anger, anxiety, guilt, shame, envy, or hope, which are associated with possibilities of restorative actions, are more likely to be the emotional reactions. This reasoning suggests that sadness is typically a temporary state of mind until it is worked through. When sadness becomes more or less permanent in those persons for whom resignation or acceptance is not possible, we might better speak of depression or impacted grief.

Grief and depression, which are also reactions to loss, must be distinguished from sadness, and from each other. In grieving, the emphasis is on attempting to cope with loss, and several emotions are apt to be involved, typically sadness, anger, anxiety, and guilt. In depression, which centers not just on loss but rather on the implications of loss for our whole life, we also feel perhaps worthless (guilty and shameful), anxious, and angry, depending on the nature and stage of the coping process. In other words, like grief, depression involves several different emotions. Grief should be defined, I believe, as a process of coping with loss, and depression as a complex emotional response to grief, with overtones of sadness in it.

In depression, the loss has been generalized to the whole of life, which is what *hopelessness* means clinically in contrast to *helplessness.* When this state of mind occurs, the person sees no positive reason for continuing to be engaged in living. To use the metaphor of figure-ground, as I did in Chapter 3 in the discussion of acute emotions and mood, helplessness refers to the figure — that is, the specific loss — and hopelessness is the generalization of implications of irrevocable loss to the whole of life, which makes it existential.

When the loss is the death of a loved one or the failure of a major commitment such as a life role, which may occur in old age (see Shneidman, 1989), it is no surprise that the impact of this loss is largely existential. Given a lifelong commitment — say, to a marriage in which the partners have become so interdependent that little life space for either person existed outside the relationship — it is no surprise that its end through death or divorce would bring a sense of great loss and the grieving that accompanies it. This is illustrated by the fact that consensually the most stressful life event on the Holmes and Rahe (1967) list is death of a spouse. It is a good hypothesis, however, that, where one or both partners in the relationship have extensive outside commitments that are not shared, there should be less tendency to react to loss in so generalized and existential a way. And given a lifelong commitment to work and career, which has become almost a definition of self, it is no surprise that retirement or disability that defeats work would also bring a sense of great loss, and grieving, too.

On the basis of this analysis, sadness should be treated as a distinctive emotion, one that overlaps with but is different from depression. The difference, I believe, lies in giving up on the idea of restoring the loss in the case of sadness, and making new commitments. The existential misery of grief and depression is that resignation, a state close to acceptance, has not been reached, and other commitments do not yet seem serviceable. In sadness, though there is unhappiness, there is no sense of struggle — in contrast with anxiety, anger, and other negative emotions. Sadness is, par excellence, a passive emotional state. We know little about the role of resignation and acceptance as forms of cognitive coping with loss, or about how they help to shape the emotion of sadness.

Appraisal Pattern

The appraisal components for sadness are presented in Table 6.6.

The *type of ego-involvement* (appraisal component 3) that is distinctive of sadness is a loss that diminishes the scope of one's ego-identity. Not all losses are of this sort (for example, minor ones), but most important losses result also in a loss of ego-identity. Sadness may also be unique in that any of the six types of ego-identity may be involved. This is why the loss could be of such diverse kinds: self-esteem and social status, persons and their well-being, a moral value, ego-ideal, meaning

TABLE 6.6. Appraisals for Sadness[a]

Primary Appraisal Components

1. If there is goal relevance, then any emotion is possible, including sadness.

2. If there is goal incongruity, then only negative emotions are possible, including sadness.

3. If there is a loss to any type of ego-involvement — e.g., esteem, moral value, ego-ideal, meanings and ideas, persons and their well-being, or life goals — sadness is possible.

Secondary Appraisal Components

4. If there is no blame, then sadness is likely; if blame is external or internal, then other emotions such as anxiety, guilt, or shame are likely.

5. If coping potential is favorable, that is, the loss can be restored or compensated for, then sadness may not occur, or will be associated with hope.

6. If future expectations are favorable, then sadness is associated with hope and not hopelessness and depression.

[a]Appraisal components sufficient and necessary for sadness are 1 through 5.

and ideas, or life goals. These types of ego-involvement are concretely represented in what happens to loved ones, one's job, reputation, social or occupational roles, occupational success, and so on. Ego-identity is usually involved in any or all of these. Any major loss, especially one that is important in defining who we think we are in the world, will produce the potential for sadness. Thus, one can say that if loss to one's ego-identity occurs, conditions are set up for sadness to occur, though certain secondary appraisals are also crucial.

Sadness and anxiety are therefore similar in that they both have a strong existential aspect; the difference is that in anxiety, a sense of loss (of meaning) has not yet occurred but is imminent. In sadness, the loss (of meaning) has already occurred and is irrevocable.

Sadness will also occur *only if no blame* (component 4) can be specified, meaning there is no accountability and control is irrelevant. If blame is external or to oneself, other emotions such as anger, anxiety, guilt, and shame are more likely to occur instead. Remember that sadness only occurs when the person's focus is on the loss that has occurred; other negative emotions such as anger, guilt, and shame are centered on dealing with the agency responsible for the harm that has occurred.

Sadness is unique as an emotion in that we rely on *coping potential* (5) to isolate it from other negative emotions: If there is something that can be done to undo the harm or restore the loss, the emotion will not be sadness but one that involves a struggle to change a goal incongruent condition—for example, anger, anxiety, guilt, shame, envy, jealousy, disgust. If, on the other hand, nothing can be done and the person is helpless against the loss, sadness is the only indicated emotion, which is implied in the core relational theme for sadness, irrevocable loss.

Finally, sadness occurs only if the grieving person senses or believes that the future offers hope for the cessation of distress and a restoration of positive conditions of life. In contrast, when depression occurs, the future expectation is bleak and empty, and there is no hope. In effect, if the *future expectation* (6) is hopeful, we sense that we can work through the loss, come to accept it as irrevocable, and recommit ourselves.

I have some uncertainty about the status of sadness, which I want to express at this juncture, because, as I said, we are not likely to feel sad for very long unless we are also depressed, which then opens the possibility of pathogenic implications. In addition to this, I want to make three points.

First, we often use the word *sadness* rather loosely and freely, not to express emotion but as a pro forma social acknowledgment that something bad has happened to someone. We think or say something like "I feel sad about what happened to you."

Second, when we experience loss, we rarely feel a single emotion such as sadness. We grieve, are angry, anxious, guilty, envious, even hopeful, and defensive—all as part of the struggle to cope with loss. Although there may be elements of sadness in this complex state, the sense of irrevocability of loss does not come easily and takes time. Perhaps this is a function of our cultural predilection to want to control and manipulate the world; if so, people in more fatalistic cultures might experience sadness more readily or sooner. Anyway, by the time we become ultimately resigned to the loss and have come to accept it, the sadness may be all but gone, or it may occur as a fleeting and mild component of one's mental state, reserved perhaps for special occasions such as anniversaries, nighttime fantasies, lonely vigils, or wistful or nostalgic moments.

Third, it might be more accurate to treat sadness, like its opposite, happiness, as a *mood* rather than as an acute emotional state (see Chapter 3). Sad states are not, I think, usually focused on a single encounter but merge with the existential quality of life in reflecting a general relationship with the world, in the sense of the ground in a figure-ground relationship (see Chapter 3). Notice that if we treat sadness as a mood, then we are relieved of having to resolve certain difficult issues such as specifying an action tendency; it may be inappropriate to attribute an action tendency to a mood, because moods are diffuse and are seldom consistently or solely related to a specific adaptational encounter or to any single facet of one.

Action Tendency

I have already considered the issue of trying to force all emotions into the mold of built-in action tendencies. We have come to the first major case in which there is difficulty in postulating an action tendency. In sadness there seems to be no clear action tendency — except *inaction,* or withdrawal into oneself — that seems consistent with the concept of a mood. Withdrawal from the environment would also be consistent with the postural stereotype of sadness as downcast, as if one is pulling away from everyone and expressing motorically the shrinkage of one's identity in the world. I think it is appropriate to call this withdrawal an action tendency, but it also seems to be a very different version of withdrawal than that in avoidance or escape, or in shame, which is more active.

If the loss is irrevocable, there is indeed nothing against which to mobilize. It is as if we normally strive to remove any trace of sadness if it occurs or is imminent by trying to overcome it with coping actions tantamount to other emotional states. This gives sadness a deceptive and ambiguous quality; on the one hand, it has an easily grasped and consensual core relational theme and pattern of appraisal; on the other hand, the action tendency and physiological response pattern in sadness are obscure. When sadness is sustained and is about one's life in general, we are likely to call it *depression* or *despair.*

Other Terms

There are many words to express the various features of sadness as an emotional experience, including *anguish, hopelessness, gloom, unhappiness, grief, woe, misery, melancholy, blue, down, low, moping, desolate, devastated, heartbroken, mournful, forelorn, gloomy, despair, sorrow, melancholy, apathy,* and *nostalgia.* Some of these, such as *melancholy, apathy, heartbroken, hopelesssness,* and *despair,* are used to connote depression and grief. Some, such as *unhappiness,* carry no connotation about provocation. Some, such as *heartbroken* or *mournful,* imply loss. Still others, such as *despair* and *apathy,* imply an existential crisis without implicating anything in particular as causal. As is the case with other emotion families, the many terms for sadness suggest that we need special appraisal components and diverse nuances to distinguish among the relevant relational meanings. It is also noteworthy that a scan of all these terms reveals the absence of any action-related concepts, which are found in all other emotion families that result from goal incongruence.

Dynamics

If sadness is a mood that has no action tendency except inaction, then it will also not result in problem-focused coping, though it will generate much emotion-focused coping, which our research has shown is encouraged when the person believes there is nothing that can be done to alter the troubled relationship (e.g., Folkman & Lazarus, 1980, 1985; Folkman, Lazarus, Dunkel-Schetter, et al., 1986). To the extent that weeping implies a struggle to cope, it should be more likely in grief and agitated depressions than in sadness. We know rather little about weeping, which seems particularly connected with losses and being reunited with someone whom we thought we had lost or felt threatened that we would lose.[3]

The seeming paradox of *crying at a happy ending* and at nostalgic moments (see Winterstein and Bergler, 1935; and Feldman, 1956) is consistent with this idea. Weiss (1952, 1986) suggests that crying at a happy ending illustrates a change in the social situation that makes it safe for a person to experience previously *warded off emotions.*

Silberschatz and Sampson (1991) provide an example of a person watching a movie about a love story in which little emotion is experienced when the lovers quarrel but is moved to tears at the happy ending in which they are reunited. What is said to happen is that the moviegoer has identified, unconsciously perhaps, with one of the lovers. When they are separated in the movie, the viewer is threatened by the impulse to feel sad and, therefore, intensifies his defenses against sad feelings. When the lovers are reunited in the story, however, there is no longer a reason to feel sad and he can afford safely to experience sadness, and so abandons the defense against the previously warded-off feeling. The authors suggest that in psychotherapy, patients make many similar unconscious decisions to permit themselves to experience feelings that previously were warded-off (see also Gassner, Sampson, Brumer, & Weiss, 1986, and Weiss, 1986, for empirical research; Sampson, Weiss, Mlodnosky, & House, 1972; Weiss, 1971, 1986, 1990).

Therefore, we might say that, like smiling (see Chapter 2), there is more than one function of crying. One must consider also the stage of grieving over loss at which sadness occurs. According to what I have been saying, sadness, in contrast with emotions involving active coping, occurs at a late stage of grieving, perhaps near its conclusion, and after many emotional variations and ups and downs in the grieving process.

One could argue that sadness has the evolutionary function of provoking efforts at succorance from others. This is usually said about grief (see Averill, 1968) rather than sadness, which seems more withdrawn and quiet than grieving. All in all, sadness appears to pose some fascinating and unique questions, which leave its dynamics more unsettled than in the case of other emotion families that result from goal incongruence.

Pathology

Given what I have been saying about sadness, it may be contradictory to identify pathological forms. The concept of pathology fits depression (which although emotional is not a true emotion) better than it does sadness. In depression, there are rich clinical observations laced with diverse examples of dysfunction and unconscious motivational, cognitive, and coping processes.

If we consider only depression-related states, we might consider pathos as pathological (discussed from a psychoanalytic point of view by Winterstein & Bergler, 1935), and perhaps nostalgia, discussed by Kleiner (1970) which is described as a bittersweet mood linked to loss and the yearning for lost objects and is seen as the result of incomplete grieving. So-called smiling depressions in which the person seems unable to tolerate sadness or depression and, therefore, defends against it by constant cheerfulness and even hypomania, represent another possibly pathological form of sadness.

I mentioned suicide in my discussion of guilt and shame, and it should also be mentioned in connection with depression. From my point of view, suicide should be considered a strategy of coping with intractable life conditions. For some it carries complex, culturally or religiously based overtones — for example, moral lapse or weakness, hopelessness, or irrationality and mental illness. Aside from religious considerations, the main argument against this coping solution is that life often changes for the better, especially for young persons, and the depression associated with loss and hopelessness may lift. Suicide ends all chance of this.

Most of us are shocked by the suicide of someone we know or love, and it is difficult to approach it without great distress, conflict, ambivalence, and guilt, especially when suicide is taken to be (or is) a wordless accusation that we have not cared enough or have not been suitably attentive to the suicidal person's needs. This is one of the reasons why failed suicide is often called a cry for help. In any case, the point needs to be made that suicide is associated with depression as well as with intractable guilt and shame, and although the conditions bringing it about differ, hopelessness and despair constitute a bottom line for the act, whether or not the judgment leading to suicide is based on a realistic evaluation that one's life should be ended.

Envy-Jealousy

Envy and jealousy are usually considered together, yet I think they should be treated as separate emotions, as I do here, on the basis of the person–environment relationships and the appraisals for each. The ten commandments inveigh against coveting, and envy has long been regarded with moral suspicion (obviously for good reason, when one considers not only the misery involved in the feeling but also its potential destructiveness in human social relationships). Especially when it involves jealousy, envy can also include anger and potential attack. Jealousy is always an interpersonal triangle. When the person whose yearned-for affection — or some other valued commodity — is, in the eyes of the jealous one, misdirected to the rival (which may be viewed as treachery, rejection, a loss, or the threat of loss), jealousy is experienced with one of its hallmarks, anger.

Smith, Kim, and Parrott (1988) have made the interesting suggestion that the reason for the confusion about the two emotions, and the tendency to treat them as overlapping, lies in the fact that in the English language the term *jealousy* may denote *either* jealousy *or* envy, whereas envy tends to be used in only the sense of negative social comparison. In any case, when the rival is both envied and resented, envy and jealousy occur together. The important point is that the appraisal pattern in the two states can be clearly differentiated, as Smith, Kim, and Parrott (1988) show in their research, which warrants treatment of them as separate emotions. For some recent research and thought about envy and jealousy, the reader should consult Clanton and Smith (1977), Hupka (1981), Lynd (1961), Mathes, Adams, and Davies (1985), Salovey (1990), Salovey and Rodin (1986), Stearns (1989), White (1981), and White and Mullen (1989).

Core Relational Themes

The core relational theme for *envy* is *wanting what someone else has*. The core relational theme for *jealousy* is *resenting a third party for loss* or *threat to another's affection*. The triangle involving a rival is a crucial component of jealousy. I should qualify here that although romantic love is probably the most common context for jealousy, threat to any cherished value by a rival could provoke that emotion; thus, a professor can be jealous of a colleague who gets a scarce grant by pulling strings.

Appraisal Patterns

The appraisal components for *envy* are presented in Table 6.7.

Although we can *envy* a person anything that is considered desirable, if we believe that we need and deserve what another person possesses and are little or nothing without it, it becomes a *type of ego-involvement* (component 3) that makes it distinctive among the other negative emotions—except for jealousy, which may combine envy with blame. In effect, if we are ego-involved in what someone else has, envy is potentiated; if we are not, then there is less reason for envy, perhaps

TABLE 6.7. Appraisals for Envy[a]

Primary Appraisal Components

  1. If there is goal relevance, then any emotion is possible, including envy.

  2. If there is goal incongruency, then only negative emotions are possible, including envy.

  3. If what is possessed by another involves a major lack in any of the six types of ego-involvement, the possible emotions narrow to envy.

No secondary appraisal components are essential; however, if future expectancy is not hopeful, then there are apt to be feelings of sadness or even anger, depending on the coping process and the appraisals that this generates.

---

[a]Appraisal components sufficient and necessary for envy are 1 through 3.

none. Type of ego-involvement probably doesn't matter; we can envy anything that we value, but, of course, we value most the kinds of issues that comprise our ego-identity. An interesting question from this perspective is whether we can have envy without ego-involvement; if so, surely it would be mild and without great importance.

Blame (4) has no bearing in distinguishing envy from most other negative emotions, because whether or not the envied person is responsible for the good fortune is largely irrelevant for envy. We envy whether or not we give credit to that person for the good fortune we envy, or blame for our lack. However, this very irrelevancy makes envy different from jealousy, in which *another is held blameworthy* for what one lacks or has lost, which is why anger is so important a feature of jealousy.

If we believe that we can change the goal incongruence, then we are mobilized (with strong yearning) to seek what we envy; therefore, a favorable *coping potential* (5) contributes to the envy, because if the situation is hopeless we are more likely to feel sad and depressed rather than envious. Envy is not a passive condition as is sadness.

If our *future expectations* (6) about what we yearn for are hopeful—for example, that we can have what another possesses—then envy is sustained; if the situation is hopeless, we are apt to give up envy and feel discouraged and sad, or engage in emotion-focused coping such as disparaging what we can't have, as in the Aesop fable of the sour grapes.

The appraisal components for *jealousy* are presented in Table 6.8.

Although it is an open question, I suspect there is always ego-involvement in an encounter involving jealousy, and it probably overlaps greatly with the type of ego-involvement in anger. If the *type of ego-involvement* (3) is a desire for another's contested favor or affection without which we see ourselves as little or nothing, jealousy is particularly relevant, though anger, anxiety, guilt, shame, and sadness are not ruled out.

As in the case of envy, jealousy implies a lack or loss in ego-identity, which is possessed by another, making it even more galling. The lack or loss could involve

TABLE 6.8. Appraisals for Jealousy[a]

Primary Appraisal Components

    1. If there is goal relevance, then any emotion is possible, including jealousy.

    2. If there is goal incongruity, then only negative emotions are possible, including jealousy.

    3. If the desire for another's affection or favor, which is threatened to be or has been taken by another, constitutes a major threat to any of the six types of ego-involvement, jealousy is favored.

Secondary Appraisal Components

    4. If there is external blame, then the possible emotions narrow to jealousy.

    5. A favorable coping potential helps modestly to keep jealousy alive but is not crucial.

    6. A negative but not hopeless future expectation likewise helps modestly to keep jealousy alive but is not crucial.

[a]Appraisal components sufficient and necessary for jealousy are 1 through 4.

any of the six types of ego-involvement, esteem, moral values, ego-ideal, meanings and ideas, other persons and their well-being, and life goals, but I guess that most important in jealousy is our sense of personal value (in effect, our self-esteem or social status), which is damaged when another fails to grant us affection and favor that we believe is necessary to our well-being.

If there is *blame* (4) and the direction is external, the likelihood of jealousy is increased, but one still cannot rule out anger, anxiety, and even shame, along with the jealousy which always involves two other persons, with at least one of them being blameworthy for the threat or loss.

If the *coping potential* (5) is unfavorable but hopeful, jealousy with its anger and impulse for revenge is kept alive. If the coping potential is hopeless, then either the love object must be relinquished along with its attendant negative emotions, or destructive acts could follow.

If the *future expectation* (6) of achieving the loved one's favor is negative but hopeful, jealousy is sustained. If we believe we can live without a favorable outcome in the jealous triangle, this expectancy may mitigate jealousy and encourage more adaptive solutions.

Implied in both envy and jealousy is the potential for action to ameliorate the situation in contrast with the helplessness and inaction of sadness. An additional and crucial attribution in jealousy, which is not present in envy, is imputed control, hence blame, directed to either the rival or the one who is favored by the loved one. One could argue from this that jealousy is nothing more than anger, centered on the goal of wanting another's favor, which is why envy and jealousy are so often conjoined. The feeling of anger in jealousy, which is one of its most outstanding features, is usually absent, or suppressed as irrational, in envy. The angry feeling and its causation are similar to standard anger.

Nevertheless, in spite of the special yearning feature of jealousy, with its sense of loss or threat of loss of another's favor, it is probably best for theoretical reasons to keep its connection with envy intact and treat it as a special case of treachery-based anger, as well as a form of coping with loss or the threat of loss of favor. Therefore, I see the emotion family of envy-jealousy as involving two correlated but separate relationships with the environment, which depend on different appraisal patterns. This justifies the tradition of putting them together in hyphenated form, as I have also done in the case of guilt-shame, but treating them separately with respect to core relational theme and appraisal pattern, as I have here.

Some writers have contrasted the goal incongruence in each of these emotions, suggesting, for example, that *envy* involves something that one does not have, or never had, whereas *jealousy* involves the threat of loss of what one once possessed or thought was possessed. In Tov-Ruach's (1980) coping-centered account of jealousy, for example, the jealous person's message is twofold: namely, "Look at me!" (a plea for attention) and, as in the notion that attempted suicide is a cry for help, "Catch me if I fall!"—a demand for succorance and protection, perhaps similar to pouting. This demand may also be associated with blame and resentment, or may lead to resentment when it remains unfulfilled. In a very thoughtful analysis of jealousy and its connection with envy, Neu (1980) quotes Spinoza (1949, Part III, Proposition XXXV) on the union of envy and anger in *jealousy*, as follows:

If I imagine that an object beloved by me is united to another person by the same or by a closer bond of friendship than that by which I myself alone held the object, I shall be affected with hatred toward the beloved object itself, and shall envy that other person. . . . This hatred toward a beloved object when joined with envy is called "jealousy," which is therefore nothing but a vacillation of the mind springing from the love and hatred both felt together, and attended with the idea of another person whom we envy.

Neu also suggests that sometimes envy is malicious, in which case it is fused with anger, and at other times admiring, in which case the person wants to become more like the other, or more worthy of the good things the other possesses. The former has been called *schadenfreude,* which is a German word for joy at another's suffering, and pain at another's success.

With respect to the threat of loss in *jealousy,* which also provides, I believe, an important rationale for treating it as a separate emotion, Neu quotes Freud (1922, p. 223) as follows:

Normal jealousy . . . is compounded of grief, the pain caused by the thought of losing the loved object, and of the narcissistic wound, in so far as this is distinguishable from the other wound; further, of feelings of enmity against the successful rival, and of a greater or lesser amount of self-criticism which tries to hold the subject's own ego accountable for his loss.

This quotation also points up the idea I have expressed before that rarely are emotions single-theme experiences. Emotional encounters are normally complex and have multiple themes or facets, which generate more than one emotion.

Envy-jealousy appear to be universal human emotions.[4] I believe they may occur also in infrahuman mammals. Though it is always risky to impute emotions to animals, many a dog owner has observed reaction patterns that suggest jealousy, as when dogs actively get in the way when spouses, to whom they are attached, fondle their bedmates; sometimes dogs even growl at, threaten, or attack the rival. Not surprisingly, similar patterns are observed in nonhuman primates, which are highly social and intelligent beings. Perhaps one reason psychologists give more attention to jealousy than to envy—and drama and literature are filled with classic examples (e.g., Othello)—is that triangular human relationships so often lead to violence. Envy can be destructive intrapsychically, but society is endangered when jealousy leads to intense anger and violence.

Action Tendencies

The action tendency for *envy* is to seek and possess the positively valued person, though that impulse would be difficult to translate into a clearly demarcated motor pattern. The subjective state of this seeking might be described as one of yearning, wishing, or wanting, making it akin to the yearning of hope, which I treat in Chapter 7 as a separate emotion.

Anger, with its impulse to attack, is the most prominent action tendency in *jealousy,* though anger's more hopeful side should also involve yearning and whatever is also the action tendency in love, which I also discuss in Chapter 7. If we take seriously Freud's view of jealousy as also involving grief and self-criticism, we should perhaps view jealousy as a very complex emotion with multiple action tendencies, depending on which cognitive-motivational-relational feature is momentarily in focus. I think it is fruitful to separate the components for analysis as distinct emotional states, any one of which might be dominant at any given moment.

Other terms

I am not sure how to account for the relative absence of synonyms for *envy* and *jealousy*. Storm and Storm, and Shaver et al., list *envy* and *jealousy* together and offer no other terms. For *envy* I could only think of *covet* as a synonym; for *jealousy,* the "green-eyed monster," which expresses jealousy's venality, unpleasantness, and danger.

Dynamics

We may resent it when others have more than we, especially when the negative comparison in *envy* is seen as unfair. Alternatively, when we are threatened with serious illness such as cancer, we can obtain some modest psychological relief by noting that others are worse off than we are (cf. Taylor, Lichtman, & Wood, 1984). And when we blame victims, we are often expiating guilt over the good fortune of having been spared the same fate (Lazarus, 1985; see also Lerner, 1980).

These cognitive and social processes have been studied by social psychologists within the rubrics of social comparison and equity theories, and the historically earlier theme of relative deprivation. In these rubrics, the processes of downward or upward comparison of oneself to others are addressed. They have much to do with the cognitive underpinnings of envy and jealousy, though their emotional aspects tend not to be explicitly addressed in social psychological research and theory.

Although envy can have positive consequences, as when we seek another's admiration by emulation, or when we increase our own effort to accomplish, *jealousy* is almost always poisonous in human relations, something it shares with some forms of anger. More often than not, the anger, and the striving to gain back from the rival what was lost or never possessed, appears ultimately, though not always, to lead to a vicious cycle of expressed resentment, further withdrawal by the love object, more resentment, and ultimately rejection. Though it has certain intrapsychic and spiritual advantages over jealousy, an equally poisonous alternative is to cultivate the role of a martyr, which is an interesting psychic counter to envy and jealousy.

Pathology

Characterological *envy* is a very poisonous state of mind. Those who believe, and are distressed by the belief, that they have less than others—for example, less money, talent, health, happiness, a poorer job, a less desirable spouse, and so on— are apt to be generally miserable and unhappy. First and foremost, what makes this outlook pathological, or pathogenic, is that it is dysfunctional and a source of misery; second, although the outlook may not be valid in a normative sense, accurate reality testing is no advantage if one's condition is always viewed with envy. Third, not only do these dysphoric feelings produce misanthropic misery for the person experiencing them, they are apt to poison relationships with all those with whom the feelings are socially or emotionally connected.

Although *jealousy* can often be justified in reality, as when a beloved spouse is unfaithful, it is most clearly pathological, as is any appraisal, when it is characterological (i.e., a trait) and when it deviates from reality and is, therefore, unjustified. Then everything that happens, including the coping process, is inappropriate. The person who is jealous, especially one who is recurrently so, is typically insatiable in insisting on fidelity, domination, succor, and victory over all rivals. This is symbolized by Shakespeare's Othello who, at the venomous prodding of Iago, fails to grasp the truth of his relationship with his beloved Desdemona, accuses her of infidelity — a foolishness so blatantly delusional, incidentally, that audiences often have trouble accepting it — and ultimately slays her and then himself. Though Shakespeare does not provide explicit clues, one motive that can be readily inferred to explain the foolishness of this otherwise heroic figure is the paranoia of a minority person in a foreign culture — Othello is black, an African Moor, in a society of Iberian whites. Another explanation depends on Othello's character as a soldier and executioner; he is no Hamlet — he acts rather than ruminates.

Although jealousy is normatively common, it is said to stem from neurotic, narcissistic needs that can never be satisfied (cf. Ping-Nie Pao, 1969). Melanie Klein (1957) portrays jealousy as stemming from greed stimulated by fear, which signifies that someone else (e.g., another sibling) has taken over or has been given the "good breast," which by right is felt to belong to the one who is jealous. The jealous person is, in consequence, insatiable and forever resentful at the imagined or actual deprivation. Envy, jealousy, a sense of deprivation, and greed are, therefore, closely connected cognitive-motivational-relational states.

Disgust

Distaste involves the strong, innate impulse to avoid or get rid of something offensive. Typical eliciting substances are "waste products of the human and animal body," to quote Rozin and Fallon (1987, p. 23), who refer to others such as Angyal (1941) and Plutchik (1980) as having adopted a similar outlook. Distaste, then, appears to be a fairly rigid reaction pattern, akin to a sensorimotor reflex. The biological utility of distaste as a reflex, from which disgust is said to have arisen, is that it probably protected mammals from ingesting poisonous substances. Rozin and Fallon's (1987) use of the term *distaste* to apply to the reflex, and *disgust* to refer to the emotion, which depends on learned, ideological or metaphorical causative factors, helps to emphasize the distinction between emotions and sensorimotor reflexes, which I have already examined in Chapters 2 and 5 (see also Smith & Lazarus, 1990).

Disgust is an emotion that, from an evolutionary perspective, could be said to be based on *distaste*, a term having reference to the sensorimotor functions of smelling and tasting. Phylogeneticists have treated it as a basic emotion, with its own special expressive features and elicitors, ever since Darwin's (1872/1965) book on emotion.

Rozin and Fallon (1987) consider disgust an innate food-related emotion that has a characteristic facial expression, an appropriate action tendency (distancing oneself from or expelling the offending object), a distinctive physiological response (nausea), and a characteristic feeling state (revulsion). As they point out, psychologists have mostly ignored disgust, perhaps because it is relatively primitive and seems to have fewer psychological and social implications than do other emotions.

The emotion of disgust seems more restricted in content and more rigid in elicitation, considering the limited range of provoking stimuli, than the garden variety, goal incongruent emotional states such as anger, anxiety, guilt, sadness, envy, and jealousy, in which diverse personal meanings play a central role. If we speculate about the innate status of disgust as an emotion, and suggest it is closer than other emotions to a reflex, one trouble with this position is that research suggests that it is not present at birth — Rozin and Fallon note that it takes up to seven or eight years to fully develop in the growing child. Very young children seem not to be repelled, for example, by feces, as parents who have discovered their child finger-painting with his own excrement on the bedroom wall can attest. However, some degree of repulsion does appear to be a universal in adult humans in response to certain substances when smelled or ingested.

Rozin and Fallon cite three possible motives for rejection of a substance in the process of generating the emotion of disgust: (1) the belief that the object has negative sensory properties, (2) anticipation of harm from its ingestion, and (3) the origin or nature of the food — for example, the prospect of eating a grasshopper or ant is offensive in some cultures just because it is a grasshopper or an ant. Notice that these motives suggest that ideational factors, or cognitive appraisals, play an important role in disgust. We can learn to accept substances that others find offensive, or learn to reject substances that others find acceptable and even attractive. These cognitive appraisals, in my view, make it reasonable to treat disgust as an emotion rather than truly a sensorimotor reflex such as pleasure, pain, and startle.

Core Relational Theme

The core relational theme in disgust, even when narrowly defined, is that *of taking in or being too close to an indigestible object or idea (metaphorically speaking).*

Appraisal Pattern

The motives cited by Rozin and Fallon provide the bases for the primary appraisal pattern in disgust — a strong desire to keep the substance away to preserve one's bodily integrity. The appraisal components of disgust are presented in Table 6.9

I am not confident about whether ego-involvement is necessary or substantial in disgust, though I think a case could be made for this. If the *type of ego-involvement* (3) is at risk of being contaminated by an indigestible or "poisonous idea," there is a substantial potential for disgust, and no other emotion. Like sadness, what is indi-

TABLE 6.9. Appraisals for Disgust[a]

Primary Appraisal Components

1. If there is goal relevance, then any emotion is possible, including disgust.

2. If there is goal incongruence, then only negative emotions are possible, including disgust.

3. If any of the six types of ego-involvement is at risk of being contaminated by a "poisonous idea," then disgust will occur.

No secondary appraisal components are essential.

---

[a]Appraisal components sufficient and necessary for disgust are 1 through 3.

gestible or poisonous in disgust could be linked to any type of ego-involvement and value or its goal relatedness. Disgust (like envy) is basically a very simple emotion in appraisal terms, and no other appraisal components are needed to distinguish it from all other emotions.

Secondary appraisal components do not significantly add to the analysis of disgust. However, to the extent that we are capable of cognitive coping to eliminate the objects' offensiveness, we are able to resist the emotion of disgust and eat objects that other cultures value but we find offensive, such as grasshoppers, fish eyes, ants, and grubs, and we can even learn to enjoy them. I remember vividly an experience in Japan when a live fish, just previously cut up for sashimi and which I had been eating with enjoyment, suddenly and unexpectedly began reflex movements, to which I immediately reacted with nausea and the inability to continue eating. Its motion made it seem, I suppose, that the fish was still alive, and I could not again eat until the fish had once again become inert and I had recognized what had happened to provoke my distress. During the episode, my Japanese companions were quite amused, because they knew of the cultural difference in food tastes between Westerners and Japanese.

Disgust arises when we have been confronted by what reviles us but which cannot be avoided as a result of anticipatory coping. For example, we don't take a job as a paramedic or surgeon if we are bothered by the sight of blood. Those concerned with emotions like disgust have not fully addressed the very important problem of how people learn to be disgusted, or, just as important, how they overcome their revulsions, a process that probably involves distancing from sights and smells that would ordinarily produce distress.

Medical students and nurses, for example, must either learn to do this or are not bothered by it in the first place. Training procedures for medical autopsies, for example, involve institutional cognizance of the problem by adopting routine procedures for distancing. For example, the dead body is covered except for the portion to be dissected; gallows humor is usually absent — the procedure is serious and professional — and the personal identity of the dead person is avoided if possible. In the television show, "Quincy," which is about a medical examiner, the opening scene provides a mild trace of ironic humor when almost all of a group of male interns watching an autopsy faint as Quincy uncovers the dead body. I am told that medical students who show this reaction are apt to be counseled out of medicine.

Action Tendency

Mimicking the involuntary distaste reflex, the action tendency in disgust is nausea and the very strong impulse to eject the offensive substance or idea by *vomiting*. A strong impulse to *avoid contact* with the offensive substance, often coupled with nausea, is a parallel reaction that stops just short of vomiting.

Other Terms

Related words for the emotion family of disgust include *revulsion, loathesomeness, distaste, squeamish, repulsion, sickening, ill,* and in Storm and Storm's list, *yuck* or *yucky,* which was one of my children's favorite words for an unpleasant object or social situation when they were young.

Because Rozin and Fallon hew so closely to biological patterns, which depend on universal or near-universal sources of disgust, we have difficulty understanding how certain sights, ideas, and events — that is, meanings in contrast with concrete substances — come to produce disgust. As I said, most emotions are brought about by highly diverse, culturally based but often idiosyncratic thoughts and objects that have taken on the personal meanings that generate anger, anxiety, shame, and so on. We need a fuller understanding of the metaphorical terms and symbols resulting in disgust, and of the sources of individual differences in how they come to produce that emotion and are managed psychologically.

Dynamics

Distaste is obviously protective in a biological sense. As an emotional response to social contexts, however, disgust can result in the inability to enjoy or appreciate what others, either individually or normatively in other cultures or subcultures, find enjoyable. Disgust, therefore, can serve as a barrier to social relationships, to sexual arousal and enjoyment, and can force avoidance of a host of situations and experiences that do not have to be inherently offensive.

Pathology

In contrast with the treatment by Rozin and Fallon, psychoanalysts have paid considerable attention to conflicts over erotic and hostile impulses that become laden with feelings of disgust, or serve as defenses against these impulses. Sometimes ordinarily disgusting body substances are ignored or even gain erotic value — as in oral or anal sex, the latter being an important feature of homoerotic activity, which is difficult for many people to understand because of the standard negative attitude toward feces.

The emotional reaction of horror seems to have some relationship to disgust. What is horrifying seems to be often subjective and individual, though horror movies generate ambivalent avoidance and approach tendencies in large numbers of people. Psychoanalysts generally regard horror, and to some extent disgust, as closely connected to the sources of anxiety in sexuality, aggression, and death. These sources connote the bad, harmful, dirty parts of ourselves, literally and metaphorically, and the terror of helplessness, castration, death, and decay.

Summary

In this chapter I have applied the general cognitive-motivational-relational theory to each of the main goal-incongruent or negative emotions — namely, anger, fright-anxiety, sadness, guilt-shame, envy-jealousy, and disgust-distaste. Although fright and anxiety are closely related, each was treated as a separate emotion, and the same is true for the other hyphenated emotions.

For each emotion, the same outline was followed, proceeding first with an overview of the emotion, then the core relational theme, appraisal pattern, action tendency, other terms, dynamics, and pathology. The appraisal patterns were presented as a decision tree and following the reasoning of an "if-then" analysis, beginning with the most general decision of whether or not there will be an emotion, whether the emotion will be positive or negative, then progressively narrowing down until the necessary and sufficient appraisal components distinguishing that emotion from all others were reached. Tables summarizing these appraisal patterns were also provided for each emotion.

The same set of applications of the general theory are presented with respect to goal-congruent or positive emotions in Chapter 7.

Notes

1. I credit Professor Perez for this formulation, as noted in a footnote in Chapter 4.

2. The difference in the causal processes underlying guilt and shame to which I have alluded has been given cultural significance by some writers. For example, Ausubel (1955) suggested that Japan is primarily a shame culture whereas Western countries are guilt cultures. This suggestion, however, could be based on a superficial reading of cultural similarities and differences, and the distinction is made more difficult by uncertainties about meanings of emotion concepts and language across cultures. To my knowledge, there has not been a thorough exploration of this problem, though Doi (1985) has struggled with some of the issues in his analysis of the concepts of "inner" and "outer" in Japanese and Western cultures.

3. A suggestion made by George DeVos, University of California, Berkeley.

4. The family triangle or Oedipus complex, as we all know, was regarded by Freud as universal and important in the psychosexual development of the child. In the boy, it was said to lead to hostility to the father and anxiety about his possible retaliation (known as castration anxiety), which, in turn, was said to push the boy to identify with the father-aggressor in order to be safe, and to use him as a model for identifcation. In the girl, there was said to be a parallel process involving penis envy and the image of already being castrated (a view that causes understandable resentment in modern women). The whole process may be translated metaphorically (as in neo-Freudian interpretations) into envy of the father's privileged position of power and authority, a social pattern that characterized the late nineteenth century in Europe when Freud lived and obtained his impressions of middle-class family life. Modern changes in male-female role patterns may well have undermined this process of gender identification, assuming its validity for Freud's locale and generation.

◈ 7 ◈

Goal Congruent (Positive) and Problematic Emotions

In this chapter, I deal with (1) emotions that result from goal congruence, in other words, the positive emotions; and (2) problematic emotions — that is, those presenting special uncertainties that make their status as emotions debatable. The positive emotions include happiness/joy, pride, love/affection, and relief. In contrast with the hyphens used in Chapter 6 to indicate different but closely related states, my use of slashes here between happiness and joy, and love and affection, means that I think these terms refer to nearly the same state. The problematic emotions include hope, compassion, and aesthetic emotions. Later, I will examine what makes them problematic, which varies from case to case.

The positive emotions have been singularly ignored or de-emphasized historically, and it is not entirely clear why this should be so. My best guess is that goal incongruent or negative emotions have a much more obvious and powerful impact on adaptation and subjective well-being than do positive ones. The same reasoning also explains the preoccupation with stress in modern social science, physiology, and medicine; stress can be a powerful disrupter and a source of pathology. When we are concerned with why some people make it through life in relative psychological comfort and harmony, whereas others struggle with chronic or recurrent distress and dysfunction, our attention is centered on anger, anxiety, guilt, shame, sadness, envy, jealousy, and disgust rather than on happiness, pride, love, and relief. The positive emotions, love perhaps excepted, are also usually weaker in intensity and impact than are the negative ones, and in keeping with their lower salience, there are fewer and vaguer terms to refer to them.

There is good reason, however, to believe that in the struggle to survive and flourish, positive emotions, too, have important adaptational functions, serving as breathers (a chance to get away from threat), sustainers (facilitators of coping and preservers of morale), and restorers (permitting healing and recovery). They could, therefore, be said to buffer the destructive consequences of negative emotions (Lazarus, Kanner, & Folkman, 1980). I think it is a good guess that positive emotions are important in the total psychological economy of persons, and because they exist as psychological phenomena, we should be as interested in them as their negative counterparts.

In an interesting article, de Rivera, Possell, Verette, and Weiner (1989) elaborate on this point and provide some data in which an attempt is made, with some success, to differentiate between elation and gladness, though the further differentiation of joy from the other two was not particularly robust. They write:

> Although it is possible that there are fewer positive emotion terms than negative ones . . . and fewer types of positive than negative facial expressions, the English language has more than 100 different labels for positive affective states, and it seems unlikely that different words would continue to be used unless important distinctions were being communicated. Because such distinctions have important consequences for personal well-being, social relationships, cognitive processing, and our understanding of emotion, it seems important to attempt to explicate how positive affect may be differentiated.

My list, any list, of positive emotions cannot be final because of the importance of having empirical support for distinctions made among them. Indeed, distinctions such as those made by de Rivera et al. reveal how easy it is to find grounds for subtle and diverse relational meanings, and how many response variables there are to consider. For rational distinctions among emotions to be taken seriously, there must be more than merely a linguistic basis for them. The dilemma is illustrated by my own decisions; although relief may be thought of as one variant of happiness, I treat it here as a separate emotion. And I have ignored gratitude—though with some misgiving, because, in some instances, it may be a strong emotional state.

Happiness/Joy

Happiness and joy, which are almost but not quite the same, are colloquially said to have many diverse causes, as in the many versions of the aphorism, "happiness is . . . a new car; the love of a good woman (man); engaging in productive work; getting what one wants"; and so on. Compared with *happiness,* the word *joy* seems to refer to a more acutely intense reaction to a more specific event, but the two words overlap a great deal. The word *happiness,* which is the one I will henceforth use, is itself ambiguous. If contentment is happiness, it is a mild and unarousing variant, whereas joy, which I suppose extends to ecstasy, is powerful and all consuming.

Historically and philosophically, happiness has posed certain interesting and distinctive theoretical dilemmas. The capacity for happiness seems unequal among people even under similar positive life conditions and might be considered a great gift not bestowed on everyone. Some have viewed it as an elusive goal in the present, accessible only through memory and hope. Others have located happiness nostalgically in childhood or school days, or in freedom from the responsibilities of child-rearing, as in the joke that happiness finally comes when the children have left and the dog has died. Prescriptions for the pursuit of happiness have sometimes been tied to the necessity of being virtuous.

Some, including myself, are convinced that happiness itself cannot be fruitfully sought as a goal but is, instead, a by-product of other goal commitments. A recent anthology examining ideologies and attitudes about happiness (Veenhoven, 1990) illustrates renewed social science interest in the subject. A statement on its advertising brochure, which cites two objections to the ideology that happiness is a desirable goal, is worth quoting.

> Firstly, the value of happiness is questioned: it is argued that suffering is more valuable and that pleasureable life is superficial and meaningless. Secondly it is claimed that happiness is detrimental to other valued things: that it turns people into contented cows and that it undermines social bonds.
>
> The first objection is a matter of appreciation and cannot be judged. The second is at least partly a matter of fact and can, as such, be verified empirically.

We must remember that two kinds of emotion, acute emotions and moods, vie for our attention with respect to happiness. In all of the philosophical variants, happiness seems to be a general life condition, a stable trait rather than an acute emotional state that comes and goes. In the most common examples, the concept of mood (or subjective well-being, which I discuss below) is, perhaps, more appropriate. Although both depend on an appraisal, acute emotion is a response to an adaptational encounter, mood to an existential state or condition of life.

If, however, we view happiness from the standpoint of the specific adaptational encounter that provokes it—that is, as figure against the larger background of the person's life—and if we assume as I did in Chapter 1 that figure and ground are interdependent, then we must recognize that happiness can be muted even when something positive has happened, and that a general tendency to be happy may also moderate the emotional consequences when something bad has happened. In other words, when good things happen to someone whose general mood is dysphoric, they may remain unappreciated; and when bad things happen to someone whose general mood is euphoric, they may fail to produce the expected distress.

The idea of happiness as a background disposition or mood that moderates the impact of daily hassles and uplifts invites us to consider what has been said about a closely related topic—namely, *subjective well-being* (SWB). (See also Strack, Argyle, & Schwarz, 1991, for a variety of approaches to subjective well-being and happiness.) Subjective well-being seems more akin to a sentiment or trait, a subjective calculus of the positive and negative aspects of one's whole life, than to an emotional state. SWB is measured by having a person make an overall assessment of affective ups and downs, smoothed out or averaged over a given period of time, whether a day, a week, a month, a year, or a longer period. Although we can think of emotion (including mood) as also being based on a subjective calculus, it would be careless (see Chapter 2) to call subjective well-being an emotion. To make the comparison, we would need common measures that provide empirical evidence that they are the same or overlap heavily and that they have common or divergent antecedents. This has not been given much systematic attention.

Recent observations suggest that positive well-being has different antecedents and consequences from negative well-being or distress (cf. Diener, 1984). In other words, what makes us feel good is different from, and perhaps independent of, what distresses us. Another peculiar characteristic of subjective well-being is the perplexing finding that people who are objectively well off (in a consensual sense) often make a negative assessment of their well-being, and people whose objective conditions of life are those of hardship and deprivation often make a positive assessment of their well-being. This is why we must constantly and irritatingly preface the term *well-being* with the word *subjective* to announce that the objective and subjective forms are to a considerable extent independent.

The most sensible explanation of this apparent paradox is that people get used to positive or negative circumstances of life and develop favorable or unfavorable *expectations,* which are often confounded in subsequent assessments. The effect of these expectations, or what Helson (1959) generalized in the concept of "adaptation level," is that when something good happens it doesn't necessarily provide an emotional lift, because things have been good all along; one takes positive conditions for granted and expects them to continue. But when positive events happen to those whose circumstances have characteristically been negative, they are often responded to with stronger than expectable positive feelings. And even when a minor source of distress occurs, its contrast with a positive intraindividual norm and the positive expectations this norm creates leads the negative event to be responded to with stronger than expectable distress. This observation provides grounds for the principle that happiness depends on the background psychological status of the person — that is, the overall pattern of expectations and existential mood — and cannot be well predicted without reference to that background.

Core Relational Theme

Although happiness is notorious for arising from diverse causes in different individuals, it has one simple, common core relational theme, which is that we have gained or are gaining what we desire. Put differently, happiness occurs when we think we are making *reasonable progress toward the realization of our goals,* with the qualification that this progress must also occur against a generally benign existential background. In other words, if our life overall seems negative, then a positive event may have little power to please.

Appraisal Pattern

Following the same basic decision-tree format used for the negative emotions in Chapter 6, the appraisal components for happiness/joy are presented in Table 7.1. To reduce repetition, I have not duplicated its details here, though I have elaborated some of the particular components in the text.

In the statement in Table 7.1 about component 2, *goal congruence* (the opposite of incongruence) — that the possible emotions are limited to positive ones, including happiness — a special qualification is in order; when people feel happy as a result of a positive outcome in an encounter, they also sometimes experience guilt or are preoccupied with the danger that the positive condition may come to an end, and so they experience anxiety, too. For example, if we believe that our good fortune is apt to be resented, or that we will be punished for it, the happy state is mixed with anxiety or guilt, and is in some degree muted.

Generally, these mixed or ambivalent states of mind are much influenced by personality traits as well as cultural and religious factors. For example, in religious ceremonies such as marriage and on other happy occasions, Jews are enjoined not to

TABLE 7.1. Appraisal for Happiness/Joy[a]

Primary Appraisal Components

1. If there is goal relevance, then any emotion is possible, including happiness.

2. If there is goal congruence, then only positive emotions are possible, including happiness.

Type of ego-involvement (component 3) is irrelevant.

Secondary Appraisal Components

Blame and coping potential (components 4 and 5) are irrelevant.

6. If future expectations are positive, we expect the good fortune to continue, and if the overall life outlook is favorable in general, the existential background is that which is essential to feel happy. If future expectations (and the existential background) are guarded or unfavorable, then happiness is apt to be muted or undermined.

All other appraisal components, including type of ego-involvement, are not essential.

---

[a]Appraisal components sufficient and necessary for happiness are 1, 2, and 6.

forget their historical suffering as a people, or the suffering of others who have less reason for happiness. Bitter herbs in the otherwise happy Passover service is illustrative, as is breaking the glass in the marriage ceremony, which symbolizes the fragility of human relations and reminds the couple to work toward preserving their union.

Type of ego-involvement (appraisal component 3) is undoubtedly less relevant to happiness than pride, which depends — as will be seen shortly — on the enhancement of ego-identity, and the attributions of accountability and control, which make it possible to take *credit* for something positive. How important taking credit is for happiness is an uncertainty, which I shall comment on again later.

If there is ego-involvement in happiness, it is probably in a background sense of fulfillment, security, and well-being with respect to any or all of the six types of ego-involvement — for example, esteem, moral values, ego-ideals, meanings and ideas, other persons and their well-being, and life goals (all of which I include in the appraisal pattern as "future expectations").

If we adopt the view that ego-involvement is minimal or unimportant in happiness, three primary appraisal components are capable alone of distinguishing happiness from other positive emotions, making it one of the simpler emotions, cognitively speaking. Although neither the *secondary appraisal* component, credit or blame (component 4), nor coping potential (component 5), seems relevant to happiness, future expectations (6) is, as is indicated in the table — which implies that we are truly happy only when we are existentially fulfilled, secure, and sense a basis for future positive well-being.

Action Tendency

The action tendency in happiness is difficult to pin down with confidence. I propose, tentatively, that it consists of behavioral and bodily manifestations of a sense of pleasure and security in the world, which are manifested psychologically and motor-

ically in expansiveness and outgoingness. We usually want to share the positive outcomes and approach others. The exceptions involve anxiety- or guilt-inducing
threats that our good fortune will soon end or that there will be punishment for it,
which I mentioned under "goal congruence."

The postulated similarity between the action tendencies in happiness and pride
could be used to challenge Hume's classic distinction (see the emotion of pride
below), which has to do with enhancement of ego-identity in pride, but to my
knowledge this has not generated any empirical research. The null hypothesis would
be that pride is always or very often involved in happiness, which would account for
the overlap in expressive manifestions. If people are asked to give examples of
happy encounters, they often give examples that entail pride about their role in a
positive outcome (e.g., Hensher, 1990).

Other Terms

Common synonyms for *happiness* are *joy, overjoyed, enjoyed, satisfied, contented,
gratified, pleased, carefree, jubilant, exuberant, exultant, enthusiastic, blissful,
cheerful, playful, amused, glad, gay, gleeful, jolly, jovial, delighted, euphoric,
ecstatic, elated, enraptured,* and *triumphant.* Notice that most of these are moodlike
terms, exemplified especially by *happy, blissful, carefree, cheerful, playful,* and
euphoric. As in the case of sadness, distinguishing happiness as an acute emotion
from happiness as a mood is difficult without an examination of the figure-ground
relationship of episodes and general life conditions, an analysis that I don't believe
has been attempted.

The alternative terms for happiness sometimes suggest differences in intensity
and sometimes convey additional meaning nuances. For example, *blissful* and
ecstatic suggest a much stronger reaction than *amused* and *content;* on the other
hand, *blissful* seems almost ethereal and less excited than *ecstatic,* and *amused*
(unlike *gleeful*) carries the added meaning of a pleasant, slightly detached reaction,
sometimes involving mild criticism or even irony. *Triumph* implies winning over
adversity and might just as well be a condition of pride, which is the way Storm and
Storm (1987) regard it.

Dynamics

In recent years psychologists have become interested in the effects of positive mood
states on skilled performance and on prosocial behavior (see also Chapter 10). This
interest expresses the counterpoint to an earlier concern with the negative effects of
anxiety and other goal incongruent emotions that preoccupied psychologists several
decades ago. Happiness is also a socially attractive emotion. We want to be with
happy people and avoid being with unhappy people, and these states seem to be
somewhat infectious. Goal congruent emotions, such as happiness, or rather their
complex cognitive-motivational-relational configurations as in the appraisal of challenge, appear to result in generosity, eagerness, expansiveness, and free-flowing use of
one's resources. These stand in marked contrast to the constriction and defensiveness
associated with harm-loss and threat and the goal incongruent emotions they foster.

Pathology

Is happiness ever pathological? Psychoanalyst Greenson (1962) suggests so in his discussion of enthusiasm, which is treated as a mood-related trait. Enthusiasm is a passionate, elated outlook, characterized by high spirits, not quiet or passive like bliss, but active and noisy. It is pathological, one might say, when it is all but continuous and above all compulsive—that is, seemingly pushed from within rather than selectively reactive to circumstances. Examples are hypomania and smiling depression.

Greenson regards compulsive enthusiasm as a regression in the service of the ego, a preconscious or unconscious defense mechanism against a cognitive construction that leads to sadness and depression. Its origins are hypothesized to be a history of overgratification in early life, followed by unexpected and severe deprivations later. I am not sanguine about this hypothesis; it seems to me that the defensive use of positive thinking and displays of enthusiasm would be equally justified by negative early life conditions, including rejection, especially in the light of supportive social attitudes toward those who are cheerful and optimistic rather than dour.

One of the seeming paradoxes of some of the current research on depression, to which I referred earlier, is that depressed persons may judge reality as well as if not better than nondepressed persons do, implying that it is better to have positive illusions, as writers and playwrights (e.g., Eugene O'Neill and Henrik Ibsen) have long suggested (see Alloy, Albright, Abramson, and Dykman, 1990; Goleman, 1985; Lazarus, 1983; and Taylor, 1989). Psychologists in the Western, industrial world tend to adopt the somewhat puritanical outlook characteristic of their culture that we must somehow always pay for self-deception, and that it is better to confront painful realities and be unhappy than to deceive oneself about them. Whether and to what extent the tendency of individuals and societies to depend on positive illusions exacts an adaptational price has not been subjected to rigorous empirical testing. As an aside that reveals my politics, the dour message of the Carter presidency (and the candidate, Mondale) was roundly rejected by a public wanting to think positively, and the pleasing—to some—denial of societal realities during the Reagan years seems to have gone a long way toward undermining our economic and social strength and our national humanity.

In any case, the pathology of putting up a cheerful exterior instead of displaying dour attitudes and emotions seems much akin to the distortion of reality that is involved in denial of distress, and in the reaction formation of claiming compulsively to be happy or at peace. It is, presumably, not real happiness, but only looks like it. Whether the real and simulated versions can be readily distinguished and have different adaptational consequences remains to be demonstrated.

I should remind readers of the difficulty of evaluating what is pathological or healthy, which was discussed in Chapter 2 in connection with depression. In the case of happiness, the problem is whether there are solid grounds for saying that a pattern is healthy or sick by virtue of there being an underlying contrary process in a person who is displaying enthusiasm as a coping strategy or making compulsive claims about happiness. One would have to show, I think, that particular dysfunctions arise from this. For example, perhaps overenthusiastic persons slink back into their private worlds when others are not around and feel miserable. Or perhaps, too, the social denial prevents these persons from confronting the underlying depressive process and gaining curative insight about it that might help them work the problem out.

Pride

Shaver et al. (1987) place pride within the emotion family of happiness, which reflects a common juxtaposition of both, as in the statement "He (she) is my pride and joy" (see Figure 2.2). In Storm and Storm's (1987) analysis, too, pride is classified as a positive emotion without "interpersonal reference," a surprising interpretation given the highly social nature of that emotion; on their list *pride* is grouped with *triumphant, victorious, accomplished, special, brave,* and *courageous.*

Historically, as I have said, *pride* has its own special meaning, and it has been traditional among philosophers since Hume (1957) to distinguish *pride* from *happiness.* The crucial difference is that the causal event associated with pride is not only positive, an uplift, it also confirms or enhances personal worth. For other discussions of pride, the reader should consult Isenberg (1980) and Taylor (1980).

Core Relational Theme

The core relational theme for *pride* is *enhancement of one's ego-identity by taking credit for a valued object or achievement, either our own or that of someone or group with whom we identify*—for example, a compatriot, a member of the family, or a social group.

Appraisal Pattern

The appraisal components for *pride* are shown in Table 7.2.

For pride to occur as opposed to happiness and relief, we must receive or *take credit* (component 4) for the positive event and experience ego-enhancement. As I have been saying, this component is crucial to the distinction between pride and happiness. As Taylor (1980, pp. 385–386) put it:

TABLE 7.2. Appraisals for Pride[a]

Primary Appraisal Components

   1. If there is goal relevance, then any emotion is possible, including pride.

   2. If there is goal congruence, then only positive emotions are possible, including pride.

   3. If the type of ego-involvement is enhancement of one's self- and social esteem, then the potential emotions are narrowed to pride, happiness, and relief.

Secondary Appraisal Components

   4. If credit is to oneself, then pride occurs.

   No other secondary appraisal components are relevant.

---

[a]Appraisal components sufficient and necessary for pride are 1, 2, 3, and 4.

I may take pleasure in some beautiful house, say, and not feel proud at all. A further minimum condition to be fulfilled if I am to experience pride is that the beautiful house be in some way mine.

As long as some aspect of one's ego-identity is enhanced by a perceived value, which is what Hume defined as the *cause* of pride, the person will react with pride rather than merely happiness. In Hume's analysis, the beautiful house is the *object* of pride, not its cause. That we take credit for it — it is ours and it expands our identity — is the cause, which is what pride is all about.

Action Tendency

As in the case of happiness, it is difficult to specify with confidence a clear action tendency for pride. It seems reasonable to propose that the expressive impulse in pride involves both expansiveness and the urge to point publicly to its source — for example, by telling people, bragging, showing off. As suggested by Isenberg (1980, p. 356), "Pride is a 'swelling'; the proud man 'swaggers or 'struts'." And one is said to be "bursting with pride," as in the fictional case of the captain in Gilbert and Sullivan's *H.M.S. Pinafore,* who sings that his bosom swells with pride at the thought of his role and his ship, and so do his cousins whom he reckons by the dozens and his aunts. The expansiveness of pride is in striking contrast to the impulse to hide in shame; in feeling proud we have lived up to or even gained as measured against a personal and social standard to which we aspire rather than having failed or disappointed those whose approbation we value.

Sometimes pride is contrasted with the feeling of humility (not, of course, the affectation of being humble as a means of creating an impression). Humility is not equivalent to shame, however, but involves appreciating one's limitations, just as pride involves appreciating one's merits (cf. Isenberg, 1980). Humility is also something that we (and the clergy) may aspire toward, a sort of "higher" emotion or state of mind. With pride we may feel arrogant and act accordingly, but we don't feel arrogant about the things that we feel humble about, except perhaps defensively. Remember that these statements about the sources of pride, humility, and shame are not about the objective truth, but about how it is subjectively evaluated by the person experiencing the emotion.

Other Terms

There seem to be few synonyms for *pride.* Perhaps *triumph* is one, as suggested by Storm and Storm (1987), though it also has additional connotations that change the meaning somewhat. For obscure reasons, the single English word *pride* is made to carry the entire, distinctive burden of meaning for this positive emotional state.

Dynamics

The dynamics of pride overlap those of happiness, but in pride one shows off to others, which is not as important a feature of happiness. However, showing off can become socially awkward; self-aggrandizing may put the other person in a one-down position, which doesn't seem so relevant in the case of happiness, though others are often envious of happiness. Pride is a competitive emotion, because it centers on ego-identity and its enhancement, just as anger involves the protection of this identity. Though pride commonly has positive social connotations, one must tread softly between "overweening" pride, which may be responded to in a hostile way by others, and the failure to acknowledge pride, which may be interpreted as a disingenuous expression of the desire to be superior by understating.

The complexity and richness of social values about pride are nicely illustrated by patriotic tunes and national anthems, which sometimes contain some ambivalence about how far to blow one's own societal horn, so to speak. In the song, "You're a Grand Old Flag," one line says we are "the land of the free and the brave," but a second adds "with never a boast or a brag." Within the same lyric is contained a boast and an admonition not to boast.

Analyses of public reactions to rich and famous celebrities of the entertainment world, and the strategies they use to prevent loss of public favor are interesting practical illustrations of the social dangers of arrogant pride. The public is apt to feel ambivalent about the wealth and fame of celebrities — that is, it is admiring and envious at the same time. People feeling envy may handle it by creating self-serving myths — for example, that celebrities are unhappy and lonely figures who should be pitied rather than envied. In turn, celebrities often present themselves with great displays of modesty, even pointing to and exaggerating their misfortunes and the pathos of having an ailing child, a bad marriage, or having to pay a heavy price for their success. Alcoholism, drug addiction, depression, psychosis, or suicide among celebrities makes very good media copy. And reporters often nourish this public ambivalence in their interviews with celebrities by showing a curious admixture of positive regard and hostile derogation, even thinly veiled contempt, which some celebrities put up with as a useful way of mitigating the problems inherent in ambivalent public reactions.

Our religious culture conveys a negative outlook about pride in the dictum "pride goeth before a fall," which carries both moral overtones and a warning. The implication is that we should not brag at the expense of others; humility, which is a kind of opposite of pride, is a greatly respected value in some cultures. In Japan, for example, if one's child or spouse is complimented, the loved one's virtues are to some extent shrugged off, as if to deny pride by saying, "My wife or child is not so wonderful." In the United States, in contrast, it is appropriate to acknowledge the compliment with pleasure, being proud of the positive virtues of a loved one, but of course, without overdoing it. Thus, "overweening" pride seems to be defined a little differently in different cultures.

Pathology

When it is in defense of a vulnerable ego-identity, pride expresses something very different from the genuine article, which is not humility but an underlying doubt about one's value as a person. If we have little to be proud of, we may identify with a famous group, whether religious, sporting, political, ethnic, or national. The exaggerated need to puff ourselves up through this identification and to exclude or even denigrate outgroups is also referred to as *ethnocentrism,* which is a major factor in prejudice (Allport, 1954).

There is another sense in which pride may have pathological overtones — namely, in what is sometimes referred to as *stubborn pride,* which probably stems from the compulsion to overcome negative feelings about ourselves. After an argument, it is often difficult or impossible for many people to forgive and make up when their pride has been wounded. Even though it is self-defeating to do so, the "proud" person stubbornly persists with anger, or wants the other person to come all the way toward reconciliation rather than meeting halfway. For this type of behavior we often use the ironic expression, "Cutting off one's nose to spite one's face."

Love/Affection

The two words, *love/affection* with a slash between them, mean that I am treating *love* and *affection* as alternative words for more or less the same emotional state. I will hereafter refer only to love. One could easily consider love as a problematic emotion. Although laypeople often consider it *the* prototypical emotion, it consists of not one but a variety of states of which two are especially important — companionate and romantic love. One problem is that romantic love gets tied up with all sorts of cultural values, and the outlook toward it has changed greatly from one era to another. Another problem is that when romantic love involves sex, it draws on a physiological drive that services reproduction as well as the other functions that emotions play. Most emotions are not so clearly dependent on a specific goal or need. In any event, I think love does involve a clear-cut emotional state, though we need to be as clear as possible about what that state is.

Love commonly means a *social relationship* rather than an emotional process or state, a relationship that could involve the emotion of love at some times and not at others, as well as anger, guilt, shame, and jealousy (e.g., Fehr, 1988). There is no better example of an emotion term that in its everyday and professional usage may refer to a trait *or* a state. When we say, for example, that two people are lovers, we are referring to a stable social relationship in which there might be a disposition to feel love under appropriate conditions, a feeling that is not necessarily constant. If we were to ask such people whether they love their paramour, they will, of course, answer "Yes," but they are expressing a sentiment not an emotion; if we ask them whether they feel love at any given moment, they might well say "No." Most social psychological analyses of love and attraction refer to a social relationship, not an emotion.

When love means an emotion, however, it is a process or a *momentary state,* a reaction that comes and goes — though in a love relationship one assumes that feelings of love will recur at least occasionally and perhaps often, depending on the stage of the relationship and its quality. If the relationship is defined by someone else on the assumption that love is involved, this judgment might be in error at any given moment even though it is accurate in the aggregate — that is, as a sentiment; the partner's feelings may include anger and guilt rather than love, especially in a relationship that is in an early stage of breaking up. In a genuine love relationship, some of the time—and in spite of the tendency of poets to idealize it—there will be hope, passion, anger, indifference, boredom, guilt, distress, and even love, depending on moment to moment and day to day patterns of interaction with the partner. A relationship may also change over its course from one of romantic love to one of companionate love, or vice versa.

As implied in the previous sentence, there are different kinds of love, with different emotional overtones. One of these is *liking,* which Sternberg (1987) has described as feeling closeness, bondedness, and warmth toward another person, but without passion or major commitment. Another is *romantic love* in which there is an idealization of the partner and strong sexual attraction, though the latter is not a necessary condition, with perhaps some degree of commitment. *Companionate love* is still another; in Sternberg's analysis, it involves intimacy and commitment but not sexual passion, though a Freudian would say that this kind of love has been "desexualized." It is, perhaps, the kind of love that we feel toward our children, parents, and close friends. Although these kinds of love do not exhaust the possibilities, they are among the most readily and commonly distinguished. Because the psychological conditions involved in each kind are different, an issue could also be raised, as it can be about virtually all emotions, about whether they should be subsumed under the same emotion family or treated separately.

Sternberg (1986, 1987) has provided a review of theories of love and has offered an analysis of his own in which he attempts to bring together the divergent strands and outlooks within a single, integrated system. His "triangular theory" of liking and loving consists of three components—intimacy, passion, and decision-commitment—which he schematizes as the three corners of a triangle whose relative weighting and pattern defines each of eight divergent phenomena of love. However, to my mind his analysis fails to distinguish love as a social relationship from love as an emotion—that is, as a relational theme or meaning that comes and goes, that can be latent at one moment and actively aroused at another (see also Hendrick & Hendrick, 1989, for other criticisms).

The eight types of relationships in Sternberg's system include *nonlove,* which refers to casual interactions among people; *liking,* which arises when intimacy occurs in the absence of the passion and decision-commitment components; *infatuated love,* which is "love at first sight" and involves sexual passion in the absence of intimacy and decision-commitment; *empty love,* which arises from the decision-commitment that one loves another but without intimacy and passion, as in a stagnant relationship that has been going on a long time and in which mutual involvement and attraction have been lost; *romantic love,* which involves a combination of intimacy and passion without commitment; *fatuous love,* which is a combination of passion and decision-commitment without intimacy; and *consummate love,* which adds decision-commitment to passion and intimacy. In consummate love, according to Sternberg, all three angles of the triangle are involved—intimacy, passion, and decision-commitment—though there can be divergence from case to case in the relative emphasis on each component. Sometimes, for example, there is strong decision-commitment and weak passion, or strong passion but weak decision-commitment, and so on.

In treating love as an emotion rather than as a social relationship, we must also be aware that one person in a relationship can experience the emotion in one way, whereas the other person can experience it differently or not at all. To the extent that diverse kinds or patterns of affection constitute distinguishable entities, a cognitive-motivational-relational theory of love as an emotion must specify the core relational themes, appraisal components, and action tendencies in any given individual experiencing it.

Working within Sternberg's typology, but changing it a bit to avoid old meanings and confusions, this may be readily illustrated in the case of the two kinds of loving most commonly distinguished — namely, romantic and companionate love. The reader must bear in mind that although the basic social relationship and overall commitment may be viewed as continual, as between friends, lovers, and parents and children in a stable relationship, in the appraisal analyses that follow I am speaking of love not as a social relationship but as an emotional state that is relational.

Core Relational Themes

The core relational theme for love is *desiring or participating in affection, usually but not necessarily reciprocated.* In *romantic love* this consists of viewing the partner at a given moment in a highly positive way, probably but not necessarily with desire or passion, and the seeking of and yearning for sexual intimacy, which may have already been attained. In connection with the role of sex in romantic love, it would be gratuitous for me to comment on the debate over the distinction between love and sex and whether they can or should be separated.

Notice, however, that erotic feelings may come and go independent of otherwise positive feelings and sentiments. It is also possible to have a romantic involvement that excludes erotic feelings and sexual consummation, as in the asexual romanticism portrayed in English fiction about knights and their maidens, which is not identified by Sternberg. The ideal was debased in the story of Launcelot and Guinevere, King Arthur's queen, which involved an adulterous sexual relationship that helped to break up the fictional Round Table and Arthur's utopian kingdom. All this was celebrated in the popular musical *Camelot.* Another literary example is Don Quixote; the name of Dulcinea, his loved one, is translated as "dream." We all understand, I think, that the idea of a love match in marriage is an invention of the late eighteenth century.

If I may linger a bit longer on this, Kenneth Clark (1970) regards romance as a Romanesque invention. About this he writes amusingly (1970, p. 68):

> But the chivalrous romances of the Gothic time, from Chrétien de Troyes in the thirteenth century to Malory in the fifteenth, with their allegories and personifications, their endless journeys and night-long vigils, their spells and mysteries, all hung on the thread of courtly love, were a specialty of the medieval mind. . . . For two hundred years the *Roman de la Rose* was with Boethius and the Bible the most read book in Europe. I don't know how many people who have read it through today, except in pursuit of a degree. But of course the effect of these romances on nineteenth-century literature was decisive, whether as a quarry or an escape, especially in England: "The Eve of St Agnes," "La Belle Dame sans Merci," *The Idylls of the King,* to say nothing of that crucial masterpiece of the late nineteenth century, Wagner's *Tristan and Isolde.* We may not read the Gothic romances, but they still play a part in our imaginative lives.

If a romantic feeling shifts toward what Sternberg calls "consummate love," the person also makes a commitment to sustain the relationship and to take responsibility for the loved one's well-being. To define it this way, however, is to accept our cultural values, which have varied historically and from society to society in attitudes about romantic commitment. Commitment, however, has little or nothing to do with love as an emotion. Instead, it is a declaration of stable concern, as in the decision to get married and have children, which is also valued as helping to preserve society and facilitate child-rearing. In some societies, the decision to marry is an economic and social one rather than an emotional one. Commitment is, in a sense, an intention to ignore inevitable periods or moments in which the emotion of love is not experienced, and to stick with the relationship regardless of emotional flux, though the commitment may loosen permanently and be dissolved if love seldom or never appears, or if the relationship is otherwise unsatisfying or punishing.

If a person wanting love from another keeps yearning or thinking about the loved one, then this emotional state, usually called "unrequited love," occupies much more psychological time and space than if the emotion arises only in certain settings or in the presence of the other. Many a relational or marital disappointment has developed from unrealistic and romanticized notions about love as a continual state of mind, one in which the partnership never falters from mutual idolatry. Loving, and being loved, can be both painful and ecstatic, and poets have often written about it from both extremes—that is, either idyllically or misanthropically. For some, love is the only human value worth cultivating; for others, it is a case of human folly or a socially acceptable form of psychopathology. In our culture we are seldom neutral about love, because it plays such a central role in our values and mythologies, and in our literature and dramas. Both high and low culture are replete with themes of love and its vicissitudes.

The core relational theme for *companionate love,* too, centers on feelings of intimacy and loving, pleasure in mutual contact, as well as a commitment to the partner's well-being. Compared with romantic love, however, companionate love lacks erotic passion. In parenting, the commitment may be very strong and relatively one-sided; that is, it depends less on reciprocal efforts than is the case in the ordinary companionate relationship. Although incestuous versions are not uncommon, even in parenting, there are social taboos against physical passion in parent-child love relationships, which normally keep the experience companionate, at least on the surface, and not incestuous. Although Freudians view it differently—they regard the absence of erotic desire in companionate love as a result of a defensive process mandated by incest taboos—companionate love eschews the erotic feature so common in romantic love.

Appraisal Patterns

The appraisal components of *love*—both romantic and companionate—are presented in Table 7.3.

I suspect that there is much ego-involvement in love, which consists of wanting affirmation for any or all aspects of one's ego-identity. This could be debated, however, and though the possibility exists for what has sometimes been called "selfless

TABLE 7.3. Appraisals for Love[a.b]

Primary Appraisal Components

1. If there is goal relevance, then any emotion is possible, including love.

2. If there is goal congruence, then only positive emotions are possible, including love.

3. If the type of ego-involvement is desire for mutual appreciation, which is affirming to our ego-identity, then the emotion possibilities narrow to love (or at least liking); if to this is added sexual interest or passion, then love is romantic rather than companionate.

No secondary appraisal components are involved, except perhaps future expectation, which when positive favors love but when negative (that is, the other does not reciprocate) prevents or undermines love.

[a]Appraisal components sufficient and necessary for love are 1, 2, and 3.

[b]Appraisals are the same for companionate and romantic love except for the role of sexual passion, though it can be absent in romantic love, for one reason or another, as discussed in the text.

love," I am somewhat skeptical that it exists without considerable defensiveness. If the *type of ego-involvement* is also desire for mutual regard, which is affirming to our ego-identity, with or without sexual passion, the possible emotions for the whole pattern narrow to love. Romantic love and companionate love are distinguished from each other only by the erotic component.

As indicated in the table, the only *secondary appraisal* component relevant to love is *future expectations,* which when positive favors love, but when this is negative — that is, when a partner does not reciprocate — love dissolves in disappointment and an unstable love relationship. In psychologically healthy persons there is a waning of attachment and a decision to cope with the loss (a kind of grieving) either by trying to reinstate love or by giving it up. No other appraisal component is needed to distinguish love from other positive emotions.

What seems clear is that in *companionate love* what is desired from the loved one, with the exception of physical passion, is psychological intimacy, security, and confidence about mutuality, the same things that are desired in romantic love. Parents, too, desire mutuality, although their commitment to the child may be more resistant to disappointment; if it is lacking, they are unhappy, but they do not necessarily withdraw commitment. A psychologically healthy person restricts love commitments to relationships in which there is evidence of reciprocity on the part of the loved one and on the actualization of that person's own needs in the relationship, though these are often not clear.

Action Tendency

The action tendency in *romantic love* is the urge for both social intimacy and physical affection from the loved one, which, whether homosexual or heterosexual, draws upon characteristic male and female psychosexual characteristics and depends on gestures of warmth, tenderness, interest, and concern for the other. There is a strong impulse to approach, touch, and interact with the other and for mutual sexual gratification. What is attractive in the other is, of course, highly cultural and individual. In *companionate love,* the same applies with respect to social and personal intimacy, but although this kind of love is overtly nonsexual or at least desexualized, it still draws on expressions, sometimes more restrained, of physical and psychological warmth, tenderness, interest, and concern for the other, and there may be suppressed or repressed erotic features.

The desire for intimacy, commitment, and reciprocity appears to be a feature of human biology, reinforced by social experience throughout life, whether or not such tendencies have a sublimated sexual basis as Freud suggested. These manifestations of affection communicate to the loved one that he or she is valued and secure in the relationship. Intimate relationships appear to be important sources of social support for most people, and their absence increases vulnerability to the destructive effects of isolation and loneliness on well-being and health.

Other Terms

There is an extensive vocabulary of love, as might be expected in Western culture. Terms commonly placed within the rubric of love include *adoration, passion* or *hunger, affection, fondness, liking, attraction, caring, tenderness, compassion,* and *sentimentality,* to run down Shaver et al.'s (1987) list and to add a few to it. If we add the terms presented by Storm and Storm (1987), we must also include *lust, desire, horny, passion, sensual, sexy, seductive, attraction, devotion, reverence, comforting, concern,* and *fondness* in the vocabulary of love. Some of these terms fall more within the rubric of liking or companionate love, whereas others fit romantic love better. Still others, such as *devotion* and *reverence,* are also frequently found in religious emotions and have strong cultural overtones as well.

Dynamics

Manifestations of love, whether companionate or romantic, are among the most highly valued of social offerings as well as the most troubling and obnoxious when not wanted. Proffering love may be self-validating and reassuring for the recipient, or it may create a delicate problem of how to respond when the attentions are not desired. For the one who initiates love, the possibility or reality of rejection may be a major source of threat, which could generate either anxiety and anger or the inability to initiate affectionate actions. All of this, of course, is much influenced by the cultural outlook, and what is being described is an understanding largely derived from the American scene (perhaps the European, too), though as Reiss (1990) points out, Americans as a whole have particular hangups about sexuality.

In the beginnings of courtship in both kinds of love, a positive response and a sense of confidence about the possibilities for a genuine and mutual love relationship encourage and strengthen the process of developing psychological intimacy and reinforce emergent feelings of affection; the absence of a positive response is apt to be distressing and discouraging, though there is a mystique about pursuit, more common among men but shared by some women, that for some may sustain efforts to engage the other person in spite of rejection. In healthy affectionate relationships, courtship is normally gradual and dependent on evidence of reciprocity, whereas in troubled versions the person may move too rapidly, or too slowly, toward intimacy and commitment without evidence of mutuality, perhaps entangling that person in a one-sided relationship that is impossible to consummate. Loss of love, especially in a long-term relationship, promotes grief that is akin to grieving at death (see Kemper, 1978, for a detailed psychosocial analysis of the process of establishing and falling out of love).

Pathology

Pathology-centered theories of love emphasize the idea that some powerful and deep need, based on insecurity or personal deficiency, lies at the core of a one-sided attachment that cannot be relinquished. This kind of pathology is celebrated in Somerset Maugham's novel, *Of Human Bondage,* in which an insecure man with a clubfoot becomes an emotional slave of a shallow and thoughtless woman who does not reciprocate his feelings, and whose unattractiveness underscores the bondage.

Freud suggested that love attains its power and intensity from the reawakening and rediscovery of early childhood relationships. Following this line of thought, Bergmann (1971) has treated love as a reinstatement of the symbiotic relationship between child and parent in the fusion of two independent individuals, each with their own selves and self-love. He infers that when the parent-child relationship has been disturbed, the person seems to reinstate a similar pathological relationship with later love partners, tending to seek domination, distance, dependency, or relating with ambivalence. Such persons remain childish in their relationships, may be unable to love, or do not believe that they are lovable. To connect this to a cognitive-motivational-relational theory, what would be concluded from the psychoanalytic position is that interpersonal goals and appraisals relevant to love are influenced, perhaps unconsciously, by early relationships.

Relief

I believe that relief might be considered a bonafide emotion, and a goal congruent or positive emotion at that, but there has been little research on it, and it is little noticed as such. Therefore, I give only minimal attention to it and consider only its core relational theme, appraisal pattern, and action tendency.

Core Relational Theme

As an emotion, relief, uniquely among the emotions, depends on an unfolding event, a change in the person–environment relationship, rather than a single particular relational dilemma. For relief to occur, there must have been first a goal incongruent encounter, which is then *changed* for the better, producing subsidence or elimination of emotional distress. In short, in relief, *a distressing goal incongruent condition has changed for the better or gone away.* Therefore, one could say that relief is a goal congruent or positive emotion, but it always begins with a goal incongruent or negative emotion.

TABLE 7.4. Appraisals for Relief[a]

Primary Appraisal Components

1. If there is goal relevance, then any emotion is possible, including relief.

2. If there is goal incongruence, then the emotion possibilities are limited to only negative emotions; only when incongruence is reduced or changes toward congruence will relief occur.

No other appraisal components are essential, including secondary appraisals.

---

[a]Appraisal components sufficient and necessary for relief are 1 and 2.

Appraisal Pattern

The appraisal components for *relief* are presented in Table 7.4.

What makes relief unique among the emotions is that it occurs only if goal incongruence has been eliminated or relieved so that emotional distress will subside. If there has been relief, then any other negative emotion (whether it is anger, anxiety, guilt, shame, sadness, envy, jealousy, or disgust) associated with the goal incongruence will be eliminated. We experience what is often called "blessed relief" because some terrible harm, loss, or threat has vanished, or something hoped for was realized, a process of going from goal incongruence to congruence.

No other appraisal components are necessary to characterize relief and to distinguish it from other emotions, making relief cognitively the simplest emotion. For example, ego-involvement is irrelevant, as is blame or credit and coping potential; future expectations could be involved in some instances, though they are usually not crucial. For example, it would be difficult to feel much relief if one expects that very shortly the negative relationship will be reinstated.

Action Tendency

One of the problems with the effort to identify an action tendency in relief is that any action is made moot, because the conditions requiring action are no longer relevant. Inasmuch as the reason for preparing for action has vanished, a shift from muscle tension to relaxation is in evidence. This provides a breather from the usual cares. The person slumps down visibly, not with discouragement but with a cessation of vigilance, and one sees a kind of decompression or loss of tension and wariness in the whole body. On the other hand, I think it is appropriate to refer to this as an action tendency, just as lack of action is tantamount to sadness, which has no ameliorative act because such an act is seen by the person as useless, and just as there can be action tendencies even in positive emotions in which there is no goal incongruence.

Is relief an emotion? If we treat relief as an emotion, then, with the possible exception of sadness, it is the one sure case in which, instead of increased arousal, there is just the opposite (cf. Kemper, 1987). There are only two appraisal components for relief—goal relevance and the cessation of goal incongruence—which, whatever its basis, helps make relief different from all other emotions.

Problematic Emotions

Here I refer to three emotion-related concepts that are often treated by others as emotions and that have great importance for our emotional lives — hope, compassion, and aesthetic emotions. Each of these, however, presents special reasons for uncertainty about its status as an emotion, which is why I call them *problematic*. One reason is that hope and compassion seem superficially to be goal congruent or positive emotions, yet on closer inspection they seem to arise from conditions of incongruency; also, aesthetic emotions include both positive and negative variants. I elaborate on the reasons for uncertainty in each case.

I also have considered the possibility that tranquility be viewed as an emotion, somewhat but not exactly akin to relief. It is certainly an important and attractive state of mind. Like relief, it is a kind of demobilization — also a breather — it implies that all is well and there is nothing we need to be doing right now. On this basis, however, one could think of it as an antiemotion, because if we assume that a person is usually in some state of arousal, then tranquility might be an antidote. In any case, although my decision could be questioned, I ultimately decided not to treat tranquility as an emotion.

Hope

Far less has been written about hope, and the yearning that I think is associated with it, than about other emotions. I do not know why this is so, especially because hope is so important in the psychological economy of people as an antidote to despair. For other discussions, the reader should consult Breznitz (1983), Stotland (1969), and most recently, Averill, Catlin, and Kyum (1990). Hope is not routinely treated as an emotion, though I think perhaps it should be.

A test of whether a state should be regarded as an emotion is whether we can construct a core relational theme and an appraisal pattern for it. Another test, one that is more equivocal, is that we can specify an action tendency. A third test is whether or not physiological changes can be identified. In the case of hope, there is no problem with the core relational theme and appraisal pattern, but there is considerable uncertainty about the action tendency and physiological changes apparent with the expression of it, a not unusual state of affairs with some emotions.

Core Relational Theme. I propose that the core relational theme for *hope* is yearning for amelioration of a dreaded outcome. Another way to put it more epigrammatically is *fearing the worst but yearning for better*. In discussions with others, I found that some believed that hope should not be limited to negative or threatening conditions but that it also applies in any *situation* in which something is desired but the prospects are uncertain. Perhaps so, and I have reflected this feature in my discussion of appraisal components. However, in my judgment, hope is not usually a positive state of mind but a wishing or yearning for relief from a negative situation, or for the realization of a positive outcome when the odds do not greatly favor it.

We think of hope as positive for two reasons: First, it is certainly more positive than the lack of hope or despair, with which it is typically contrasted. Second, its social consequences are often positive, as when hope sustains constructive efforts or mitigates emotional distress and dysfunction. Recognizing that hope is not optimism, which contains much more risk, no writer that I know has suggested that hope has negative consequences. Nevertheless, the process leading to hoping may prevent us from letting go of what we wish for and cutting our losses when a commitment has been irrevocably destroyed. The capacity for hope may prevent the person from accepting the way things are and getting on with other commitments, if they remain viable. I shall speak of hope as opposed to despair shortly.

To illustrate concretely the positive-negative confusion, when we have symptoms of illness, we are anxious but hope that we are not seriously ill; when we face an important exam, we are anxious about a negative outcome but hope that we will not fail; when we see that our stamina is failing in an important race, we are also anxious about not making it to the end but hope that we can. We dispell negative emotional tendencies with hope.

Whether we think of hope as positive or negative depends on which side of the issue we attend to. Remember that in Chapter 1, I defined positive and negative *not* on the basis of the feeling tone of the reaction but on whether it is goal congruent or incongruent. Hope usually (Do I dare say always?) arises from a condition of harm or threat. When we are confident that things will work out positively, we feel something akin to *optimism,* not hope. Optimism leaves out the components of yearning and uncertainty that are embodied in hope. The danger in optimism is twofold: First, it primes us for disappointment from the probable reality; second, if expensive decisions are made on an optimistic and, therefore, imprudent assessment, when things go sour the cost can be great.

Averill, Catlin, and Kyum (1990) have presented an historical account of hope in which it is viewed as a negative emotion, as I view it. They characterize Pandora as the Greek mythological equivalent of Eve in Judeo-Christian religious doctrine. In both legends the ills of humankind were unleashed; in the case of Pandora it happened when she opened a forbidden box, and in the case of Eve it happened when she ate the forbidden apple. Averill et al. (1990, p. 3) write:

> When Prometheus stole fire from heaven and gave it to humankind, Zeus ordered that a woman be fashioned who would bring misery to the race of men. She was presented to Epimetheus (the brother of Prometheus) who, ignoring a warning not to accept any gift from the gods, took her as his wife. Pandora brought with her a box containing every human ill. When Epimetheus opened the box, all the ills escaped, save one — hope.
>
> The Tale of Pandora is ambiguous. Was hope another ill like the others that had escaped, or was it a benefactor left behind to aid humankind? The Greeks seemed ambivalent about hope; but in general they viewed it more as a bane rather than a boon.

These authors also point out that Plato spoke of hope as easily led astray, and Euripedes referred to hope as a curse upon humanity. In contrast, the Judeo-Christian outlook treats hope as highly valued, one of the three theological virtues along with faith and charity.

Averill et al. also provide extensive questionnaire data on hope, reporting on findings from four studies in which students were asked to characterize hope, to compare hope with other emotions such as anger and love, to examine metaphors of hope such as those used in folk sayings, maxims, and everyday slang, and finally, to compare Korean and American student perspectives.

They conclude that it is misleading to speak of hopeful feelings as if they formed a single emotional state. One person may be hopeful amid anxiety over the prospects of losing something, whereas another may have the same feeling in the context of new optimism about an improbable occurrence. This leads the authors to adopt the view that hope varies with the conditions that initiate an encounter, and that the experience is as varied as the things for which a person might hope. I would put this differently; hope cannot be distinguished from what is hoped for any more than anger can be divorced from what one is angry about.

Hope, they argue, is also different from optimism, as I have already suggested. Our values are that we should not hope for events that are too unlikely or, conversely, when the likelihood of an event approaches certainty. This suggests a curvilinear relationship between hope and the probability of what is hoped for. Averill et al. write that "folk wisdom contains ample warnings against . . . vain and foolish hopes." On the other hand, optimism increases linearly with the probability of attainment. Hope is also a powerful social tool, they say, "a command to 'keep the faith,' to remain loyal and committed to action, secure in one's moral righteousness, even when rational considerations and empirical evidence might call for skepticism." It motivates and sustains the person in times of difficulty.

Americans, influenced by the Judeo-Christian religious tradition, which is oriented to faith and individual action, view hope as a transitory state, a way of coping, an emotion; whereas Koreans, influenced by Confucianism whose ideal is harmony with oneself, others, and nature, view it as a relatively stable part of personality, a trait closely linked to intellect and will and, therefore, a more voluntary process. Americans mention *faith* and *prayer* as synonyms of *hope,* whereas *moralistic, ideal,* and *ambition* were the Korean synonyms. These findings and speculations, and others not mentioned here, provide an empirical backdrop for my own speculations on the core relational theme and appraisal pattern in hope.

Appraisal Pattern. The appraisal components for *hope* are presented in Table 7.5.

Sometimes we use the expression "I am hopeful" that . . . this or that good thing

TABLE 7.5. Appraisals for Hope[a]

Primary Appraisal Components

    1. If there is goal relevance, then any emotion is possible, including hope.

    2. If there is goal incongruence, then any negative emotion is possible, and hope, too, which I have called problematic; if there is goal congruence, then hope is not necessary.

    Most secondary appraisal components are not involved. However:

    7. Future expectations must be uncertain to sustain hope; put differently, conditions must be unfavorable but not hopeless.

---

[a]Appraisal components sufficient and necessary for hope are 1, 2, and 7.

will somehow happen. A possible exception to the idea of hope as mobilized by goal incongruence is the expression "fond hope," which could convey a positive rather than a negative outlook. Consider also what Averill et al. say about the change in the name, Cape of Storms, on the southern tip of Africa, where so many ships were destroyed and so many sailors lost their lives, to Cape of Good Hope, which is what we know it as today, a euphemism for a place of disaster.

I don't think that *ego-involvement* (3) is relevant to hope, unless it is hope about the preservation or enhancement of one's ego-identity, or some particular aspect of it, in the first place. I suppose we could also say that our ego is involved when we are capable of hope rather than despair under conditions of adversity, and this type of ego-involvement might encourage hope as a coping style.

Action Tendency. One of the reasons for being uncertain about the proper status of hope as an emotion is the difficulty of postulating a unique action tendency. If we ultimately take the position that an action tendency is what makes an emotion embodied, and therefore a true emotion, then we must either identify an action tendency and its physiological correlates or abandon the concept of hope as an emotion. Yearning for a positive outcome, unfortunately, is little more than what we mean by the presence of a transactional motive state, and does not suffice for an action tendency. What is needed is a threatened goal and a yearning that the goal will be attained despite the negative circumstances.

Perhaps approach — moving toward rather than away from an idea or image of a desired outcome — is the best we can do in proposing an action tendency for hope (cf. Arnold, 1960). From the perspective of expressive gestures, we *look up* in hope rather than down as in sadness, which may also share the religious metaphor of God or gods in heaven, which is up in contrast with hell, which is down. Another possibility is that the key to hope is to remain vigilant, mobilized, and committed and not give up on the desired outcome.

Because the outcome toward which we want to move is often both complex and diffuse at the same time — for example, staying alive rather than being dead, staying healthy, being accepted, loved, successful, and so forth — the search for an action tendency seems a bit forced in the case of hope, as it does in anxiety, which is a response to an ambiguous threat; though, like hope, anxiety can be concretized (see Chapter 6). We can and do, of course, fantasize what we hope for, and this could involve action scenarios that flesh hope out concretely. Perhaps we should regard hope as one of those emotions that Ortony et al. (1988) reserve for the absence of a clear action tendency. Nevertheless, I don't want to give up on the action tendency yet, and I am certainly not sanguine about abandoning hope as a bonafide emotion. Like a few other problematic emotional states, hope could also be thought of as a cognitive (emotion-focused) coping process rather than an emotion, but I am not entirely satisfied with this solution, either, for reasons I discussed in Chapters 4 and 6.

Other Terms. I have been unable to think of a synonym for the idea of hope, although Breznitz (1986) and Averill et al. (1990) have reviewed a number of metaphors of hope. For example, Breznitz suggests that hope can refer to a small psychological enclave in which, though everything else seems lost or negative, there still remains something positive; for example, in the late stages of a terminal disease the possibilities for hope narrow from a cure or remission and the resumption of a normal life to having a good, pain-free day or a few hours of surcease. Other metaphors include a bridge to find our way out of danger or despair, an intention to look at the positive features of our life or situation, a performance in which we have the ability to carry out an intention, and an end in itself, which makes us feel better about life.

Averill emphasizes that implicit theories of hope are reflected in maxims, folk sayings, and colloquialisms (see also Lakoff & Kovecses, 1983). To study this empirically, he asked college students to list slang expressions related to hope and then categorized the metaphors. For example, hope as a *vital principle* is illustrated by the familiar expressions "Where there's life there's hope" and "Never say die." Hope as a *source of light and heat* is illustrated by the "light at the end of the tunnel" and "a ray of hope." Hope as being *elevated in space* is illustrated by "having high hopes," "on the wings of hope," and "His hopes were shot down." Hope as a *form of support* is illustrated by "buoyed up by hope" and "grasping at straws." Hope as a *physical object* is illustrated by "hold out hope to" and "abandon all hope." Hope as *deception* is illustrated by "Hope is what dreams are made of" and "Hope can cloud your eyes." Hope as *pressure* is illustrated by "His balloon burst" and "He was crushed." And some miscellaneous examples include "prisoner of hope" and "take heart."

Dynamics. There is little research or theory on which to draw to understand the conditions under which hope occurs. Breznitz (1989; personal communication) has been doing experiments with Israeli soldiers who are required to make debilitatingly long marches. In this research, Breznitz manipulated conditions that encourage hope or despair and studied how far the soldiers would go despite seeming to be near exhaustion. The manipulations involved false information about how far they have marched and still have to go. When the distance yet to go seemed unmanageable, many more quit than when it seemed within reach, despite the fact that the total distance actually marched was the same. Nevertheless, the soldiers did best when given accurate information about their situation; presumably this made it possible to predicate their decision to continue or abandon the march realistically.

Undoubtedly, personality traits such as optimism (cf. Scheier & Carver, 1987) are also relevant to individual differences in patterns of hope, but they have not yet been assessed in experiments under comparable environmental conditions. It is also reasonable to think of hope as being sustained by coping mechanisms that deal with situations that might otherwise be regarded as hopeless, as in the effort of some terminal cancer patients to pay attention to those who seem worse off than they, or what Taylor and Lobel (1989) refer to as downward social comparison. Nor is it clear to what extent or when hope should be considered akin to denial, since sometimes hope is made out of whole cloth, so to speak (Goleman, 1985; Lazarus, 1983; Taylor, 1989). In keeping with this outlook, Snyder, Harris, Anderson, Holleran, Irving, Sigmon, Yoshinobu, Gibb, Langelle, and Harney (1991) have also examined and measured hope in the dispositional or trait sense, defining it as a set of beliefs that one's goals can be met and the ability to plan appropriate steps to achieve these goals.

Pathology. What I have said about hope seems compatible with Erikson's (1963) view of the polarity in old age between integrity and despair and his observation that people may oscillate between one pole and the other in the struggle to deal with the ending of life. The capacity to retain hope in the face of despairing conditions is probably a major coping resource. Put this way, hope would seem to be often, if not always, a self-generated, emotion-focused (cognitive) coping process that is influenced positively or negatively by the environmental conditions being faced, as well as by personality traits. Since the stakes can be high when hoping becomes important, there is the potential for much "heat" in such cognitive coping activity, which makes it unlikely that as a cognitive coping strategy hope is ever cool and detached. This thought should encourage us to treat hope as an emotion as well as a form of coping.

It has also been suggested, as I indicated earlier, that optimism, hope, and positive thinking draw on illusions characteristic of psychologically sound people, whereas pessimism, despair, and depression are apt to comprise the unrelentingly realistic outlook of people experiencing mental anguish (see Alloy, Albright, Abramson, & Dykman, 1990; Taylor & Brown, 1988). From this standpoint, the inability to hope and thus the tendency to give in to despair should be the major pathology of hope. Disillusionment, which Socarides (1977) ironically suggests is the desire to remain disappointed (with the implication of a self-deceptive defense), is also relevant to loss, sadness, depression, and perhaps even bitterness, and seems to have a logical connection with the pathology of hope. If one fears to be catastrophically disappointed by confronting inevitable "feet of clay," self-defensive alternatives are either to cling to illusions, and therefore to preserve hope, or to give in to disillusionment and minimize the potential for disappointment.

Compassion

Although most recent work uses the concept of empathy as an emotion, some writers such as Blum (1980) prefer the term *compassion,* as I do, to the term *empathy.* For Blum, a key to compassion is an altruistic concern for another's suffering and the desire to alleviate it. I begin my discussion, however, with the concept of *empathy,* which is socially and developmentally important, because it has been in vogue in the literature of emotion. As the reader will soon discover, I do not consider empathy an emotion; instead, it should be regarded as an emotional capacity and a process.

Is there a difference between *sympathy, empathy,* and *pity?* Certainly not a clear one. *Sympathy* is often defined as feeling concern about the suffering of someone else, whereas *empathy* is regarded as sharing another's feelings by placing oneself psychologically in that person's circumstance. The former seems, perhaps, more cool or distant than the latter in common usage. The perspective taken in both is always that of the other person rather than the one who is feeling compassion, sympathy, or empathy, as Blum suggests.

The distinction breaks down, however, in dictionary definitions of the three words. For example, *sympathy* is frequently defined as the inclination to think and feel like someone else, sharing the feelings or interests of another, as when we are *in sympathy with* someone or a group, or are sensitive to or affected by another's emotions, especially sorrows. *Empathy* is defined as the imaginative projection of a subjective state to another, or the vicarious experiencing of another's feelings.

Pity is also a synonym of sorts. It can mean sympathetic heartfelt sorrow for one who is suffering as well as compassion. Often, however, it connotes a disdainful or contemptuous feeling in which the other person is regarded as reprehensible, inferior, or responsible for his or her own suffering. Another meaning of pity is to give mercy to one who may or may not be worthy of it. In pity, the person holds himself or herself apart from the afflicted person, and there may be a degree of condescension.

Despite the tradition that has grown up in psychological thought that the words *pity, sympathy,* and *empathy* are different, it is difficult to see a real difference if we take these definitions seriously. The usage of words is often greatly influenced by culture, limited to a particular generation, and sometimes even arbitrary, and I have not seen empirical studies of common usage that might help us sort out the emotional processes involved.

Hoffman (1978, 1982a, 1982b, 1984, 1985) notes that *empathy* has been defined in two ways: first, as the cognitive awareness of another person's internal states, though later he uses the expression "empathic distress" to suggest that this awareness is a hot rather than cold cognition; and second, as a vicarious affective response to another person, which emphasizes putting oneself in the position of another and experiencing that person's emotion. Although the emphasis in analyses of empathy tends to be placed on another's distress or on the tragic, empathy could just as easily involve the sharing of another's positive emotions and the conditions that bring them about.

Hoffman thinks that to the extent one person identifies with the plight of another, there should be something of an emotional match between the person who empathizes and the person with whom there is empathy, which blurs the distinction between self and other. In addition to vicarious experiencing, one can also speak of a pseudovicarious experience in which we react emotionally to another's state because we think we might soon be in a similar position, in which case the focus of attention is really on ourselves rather than the other. This latter kind of experience should not be considered the same as empathy or sympathy.

Core Relational Theme. Specifying the core relational theme for empathy immediately confronts us with a dilemma, which has pushed me to speak of *compassion* rather than empathy. Excluding from consideration the special case of pseudovicarious responding, what is the personal stake in empathy? To the extent that altruism is assumed, no personal stake should be involved. On the other hand, to the extent that we act out the self-concept of a caring person, the stake is to live up to it. If we believe in doing unto others as we would want them to do unto us, then responding helpfully to others in distress increases the likelihood of reciprocal actions when we ourselves are in need, an outlook more akin to a pseudovicarious reaction, and often referred to as "enlightened self-interest."

In any case, and using the point of view I have presented in this book, the core relational theme for empathy (or sympathy) would have to involve a sharing of another person's emotional state, distressed or otherwise. Recently Eisenberg, McCreath, and Ahn (1988) have expressed doubts about the measurement of empathy/sympathy in children because researchers have not adequately distinguished among distressed and anxious reactions, and the dependency on self-report leaves unclear the nature of prosocial actions in contexts where empathy might come into play.

However—and here is the key dificulty—if one shares another's distress, then a paradox arises in that the emotion experienced by another could vary greatly and include sadness or despair, happiness, love, jealousy, envy, guilt, anxiety, anger, hope-yearning, or some mixture of these emotions. Therefore, empathy would not be a particular emotion at all, but a variable emotional reaction the content of which depended on what was experienced by the other person with whom one is empathizing.

From this standpoint, empathy is not an emotion but either an *ability or disposition* to share another's emotions, and a *process* whereby this sharing occurs. It is, of course, a very important, prosocial ability and process, because it expresses the variable capacities of people to put themselves in the position of another's distress. It is also emotional, without being an emotion, strictly speaking. Here the process of shaping the emotional distress is determined by another person whose distress is being observed, not by the one who is empathizing.

The only emotional state with a single core relational theme that would work in this arena of relating and reacting to another's suffering is, I believe, *compassion.* This is not a sharing of another person's emotional state, which will vary depending on what the other person's emotional experience seems to be, but an emotion of its own. This reasoning is why I prefer to speak of compassion rather than of empathy, sympathy, or pity.

In *compassion,* the emotion is felt and shaped in the person feeling it not by whatever the other person is believed to be feeling, but by feeling personal distress at the suffering of another and wanting to ameliorate it. The *core relational theme* for compassion, therefore, is *being moved by another's suffering and wanting to help.*

Appraisal Pattern. The appraisal components for *compassion* are presented in Table 7.6.

I don't think that *ego-involvement* is necessary for compassion, though it might well be present and a factor in it. For example, if we believe that we are better persons for compassion and any efforts we make to help victims, or that it makes us morally superior, then acts of compassion, and perhaps even the emotion of compassion, are enhanced or made more likely.

My stance on the secondary appraisal component of *blame* is that only if we have no reason to blame ourselves or victims for their plight will our emotional experience be clear and unequivocal compassion. To put this differently, when we blame victims to reassure ourselves about a just world, we distance ourselves from them, or dehumanize them, which defeats compassion; even the word *victim* suggests helplessness to prevent the harm.

Finally, although *future expectancy* is not crucial for compassion, the future

TABLE 7.6. Appraisals for Compassion[a]

Primary Appraisal Components

1. If there is goal relevance, either because of the capacity for vicarious experience (see my discussion of aesthetic emotions), enlightened self-interest, altruism, or a moral value that threatens us with guilt, then any emotion is possible, including compassion, which is problematic as a positive state.

2. If there is goal incongruence in regard to another person's plight, then the emotion possibilities are limited to anger, anxiety, guilt, shame, disgust, and compassion.

Secondary Appraisal Components

4. If there is self-directed blame, then the probability of guilt is increased; if blame is directed at the victim, then the probability of anger is increased; if there is no blame, then compassion is likely, depending on the dispositional characteristics of the person.

No other secondary appraisals are essential. If future expectancy is that expressions or actions of compassion will be appreciated, that emotion is favored.

[a]Appraisal components sufficient and necessary for compassion are 1, 2, and 4.

gratitude of the victim could provide some positive reinforcement for expressions or actions of compassion and, for some persons and conditions, might be a primary goal. However, I do not wish to get into the arguments over whether there can be altruism in people, or whether altruism might be an innate though weak human urge.

The motives implied under appraisal components (2) and (3), which refer to goal incongruence and type of ego-involvement, though obscure, also remind us of the phenomenon of "curiousity convergence" (see Fritz & Mathewson, 1957; Janis, 1951). Why do people converge around and inspect the tragedy of a disaster and stare at the people who have suffered it? Commonly they drive around the disaster area, making a nuisance of themselves by getting in the way of rehabilitative efforts. I doubt if compassion is what drives this behavior, though it cannot be ruled out. A more convincing explanation of the behavior, one that was adopted by the writers just cited, is to view it as a form of vigilance, or anticipatory coping, in which we take the opportunity to think of what might happen, and how we should act, if the same disaster happened to us. Many of us who fly often, for example, read in detail about airplane disasters because we recognize our own vulnerability and want to be prepared, to know what it's like and what to do if the same thing happens to us.

Action Tendency. In compassion, the action tendency is the impulse to reach out to mitigate the other's plight, to help the other person, to express sympathy, and yet to maintain sufficient detachment to avoid being overwhelmed with distress ourselves. If we should experience survivor guilt along with compassion, as long as it does not chill the wish to help the victim, it may support compassion, because we wish to pay or atone for our own good fortune at not being a victim.

Other Terms. There are very few synonyms for compassion. Pity is one, though it has other connotations, as I indicated. Other terms include *empathy-sympathy,* and *feeling sorry for,* both of which are found on the list provided by Storm and Storm (1987), though only *pity* is found in the list by Shaver et al. (1987). These terms are acceptable as long as we don't define *empathy* and the others as the sharing of another person's feelings, which removes the reaction from the rubric of a single, predictable emotion.

Dynamics. People who display compassion are, one would think, highly valued by others, especially if these people offer effective support and succor to those who are needy, though these people may also stimulate some guilt or shame, or even annoyance, if they are "too good to be true," or the recipient is demeaned by it. It is also said that altruistic service to others makes the donor feel good. Displays of compassion may also backfire, as when they are performed for effect and are reacted to as not authentic. Even when they are genuine, if performed clumsily they only make the recipient feel worse (see, for example, Silver & Wortman, 1980; Tait & Silver, 1989; and Wortman & Lehman, 1985). This touches on an important clinical issue to be addressed in Chapter 10 having to do with the quality of social support, which is concerned with how to be emotionally supportive without exacerbating distress.

Pathology. Some persons are unable to regulate their compassionate feelings and become overinvolved with another person's suffering, so much so that not only do they experience severe distress themselves, but they may be unable to offer useful help. The point can be well illustrated if we look at how nurses, for example, to do their job must be able to control their own distress in viewing suffering patients and children who are sick or dying. It is generally believed that professional persons can offer better service when they are not overinvolved in their client's suffering; they are thus less likely to suffer burnout if they are capable of achieving some detachment (see Hay & Oken, 1972; Maslach, 1982).

On the other hand, the recipients of professional detachment are apt to feel that their caregivers are too cold. Two of the most important reasons consistently given for burnout are (1) the inability of social service arrangements to ameliorate suffering, because of poor financial support or organization, and (2) the absence of appreciation on the part of recipients and of the society at large for these efforts. From their perspective, social service professionals must constantly operate under unsupportive conditions, and sometimes above and beyond the call of duty, which exacts a high emotional price.

At the other extreme are those who are unable to feel compassion, which is well illustrated by sociopathic personalities who either are born with or acquire an inability to feel compassion for another's suffering. A variant of this defect is the self-protective mechanism of blaming victims and, in so doing, dehumanizing them so that they have no claim on our compassion. It is protective because, as I have already noted, it is commonly felt that we need not feel compassion for those who have brought disaster on themselves. A good example may be the way a large number of people view victims of AIDS. They may think, "Why should I be bothered and have to pay for their disease when it could have been prevented if they had behaved properly in the first place?" Another example is that during the Vietnam War, Western audiences could watch combat deaths on television with little or no emotional response — because, it was argued, they had become habituated to killing. Although distancing and dehumanization protect us from distress, we also pay a societal price in the loss of humanity they entail (see Bernard, Ottenberg, & Redl, 1965).

Aesthetic Emotions

Aesthetic emotions occur when we react emotionally to movies or drama, a painting, sculpture, music, a natural scene, or a religious experience. Although never in the mainstream of psychology, this phenomenon has long engaged the interest of a small number of psychologists and philosophers, who have taken various positions on how it should be understood. The issues are too complex to more than touch on here, but they are important for emotion theory.

One philosophical tradition excludes aesthetic reactions from the rubric of emotion. The notion of disinterestedness, and a later variant, psychic distance, was first introduced by the third Earl of Shaftesbury (1671–1713) and became an important tenet of eighteenth-century British aestheticians (cf. Edmund Burke, 1757). Aesthetic appreciation was considered exclusive of any kind of selfish or personal desire. In other words, from this standpoint aesthetic emotions require detached or uninvolved appreciation in which the viewer has no personal stake.[1] However, if appreciation is uninvolved, it is difficult to view it as an emotional as opposed to an exclusively intellectual, aesthetic process.

Arnheim (1958) has taken the opposite position — that to feel an aesthetic emotion one must be actively engaged in experiencing a painting or piece of music, not merely looking at it in a detached fashion. From this standpoint, aesthetic states are warm, involving, and organismic, which is in tune with the idea that emotions involve personal meaning or stakes and action impulses to make them embodied.

Still another school of thought is to be found in the writings of Clynes (1977), who implies that appreciation of music is innate and has to do mainly with human neurophysiology (something like a sensorimotor reflex). Seashore (1938) provided substantial evidence that musical talent is inherited and developed a test for its assessment (see also Tomita, 1986). Clynes appears to have demonstrated that the emotions generated by music have characteristic and universal expressive motor patterns, with anger having a different pattern than, say, love or fear, which can be studied in much the same way that patterns of facial activity are studied.

Music presents a special problem for aesthetic emotions because one is seldom clear about whether the emotions experienced are generated by the physical sounds and our genetic resonance to them, by what these sounds have become conditioned to, or by the contents of what is experienced, as in opera. Thus, when we are moved by the brief but tremendously emotional aria "Ridi Pagliaccio," often translated as "Laugh Clown Laugh," we are caught up not only by the powerful music and emotional vocal expressions but also our knowledge of the story, which is itself highly emotional. Pagliaccio is acting in a play about a clown whose wife is unfaithful, but he is experiencing the very same situation in his own life with a fellow actor and his own wife. When he sings of his pathos at having to act comically as a clown while his heart is breaking, the audience reacts to the whole scenario, which includes not only the music, gestures, and vocal expression — Caruso's voice broke at a point in the aria, adding to the emotion — but also the contents of the story, which even without the music carries emotional meaning that we could understand even if it were presented only as a drama without music.

Aesthetic emotions have also been regarded as a product of conditioning; having been often connected with negative and positive emotional experiences, certain sights and musical sounds eventually, through conditioning, come to elicit the emotional reactions that have been associated with them. Therefore, when we hear musical selections, for example, which have in the past been associated with conditions of fear, anger, or despair, or with joy, lightheartedness, or contentment, we feel these emotions, and composers draw on these associations to elicit certain emotions in their audiences. These divergent explanations are, of course, not mutually exclusive, and all could play a role in aesthetic emotions.

Some interesting problems arise in connection with the capacity of drama and films to produce strong emotions in their audiences. The most difficult consists of the fact that we react to what is happening to others on the stage or screen with the full knowledge that we are safe from harm at the moment and in a theater or in front of our television screens. How is this possible? Presumably, it is because what we see is believable and tied to our own life experience, and although we may suspend reality somewhat in that what we are seeing is a play, we identify with the experience of the actors because it deals with scenarios that to some extent have applied, do apply, or could be applied to our own lives. What we see is, in effect, a story, but not *just* a story; the story portrays a personal reality about which it may be difficult to remain detached.

In Arthur Miller's *Death of a Salesman,* for example, we could be the tragic, suicidal father — perhaps he is like our own father in important ways — like one of the sons, or like the mother. The playwright creates a complex, believable, and powerful story that many of us experience as happening to ourselves. One assumes that if what happens and the characterizations have little or no personal meaning, we would not experience emotion while watching, and the play would fail if the audience in general was unmoved. What is remarkable is how little interest psychologists have shown in this capacity of humans to experience emotions vicariously through drama and film (see, however, a recent but brief interchange between Walters, 1989, and Frijda, 1989).

Aestheticians may have overstated the point about the suspension of reality in a theater at the expense of the reality of the psychological connection between what is dramatized and the person's own life. On the other hand, it may be that in drama we are able to explore our past, present, or future reactions to complex, harmful, or threatening encounters in a "safe" context in which the dreaded events are happening to others on the stage, though it is also personally meaningful. Therefore, our emotions in the theater may be milder than if the drama is happening now to us. We can also conjure up our own images of these events in preparing for them, or even see live versions of them, as in the phenomenon of curiosity convergence I mentioned earlier. It seems to me that these extremely interesting issues have not been given much attention by scientists, yet they have tremendous theoretical and practical significance for our lives.

From the perspective of a cognitive-motivational-relational theory, the key prob-

lem with the aesthetic and religious emotions is that they constitute not one emotion—such as anger, anxiety, joy, awe, or wonder—but any emotion whose nature
depends on the personal meaning imputed to aesthetic and religious experiences.
This is why I use the plural term, *aesthetic emotions*. It is also the same problem I
pointed to earlier in the case of empathy; no specific emotion is involved, and empathy results in whatever emotion is shared with the other person by the empathizing
observer. No new or special emotion is implied in aesthetic emotions other than traditional ones about whose causation and process of generation we have already
explored. Therefore, there is no standard or normative *core relational theme* for aesthetic emotions, because such a theme would depend on the particular emotion generated. By the same token, there is no common set of *appraisal components* or
action tendencies, because the emotions generated are diverse.

Yet, as in drama, we are moved by the personal meaning conveyed in the sight
or sound of the events portrayed. In representational paintings, for example, the
emotion is probably attributable to universal themes of human tragedy or joy and
religious experience. We are moved by paintings of people being slaughtered in
combat, or experiencing an agony that all can understand and dread, as in the
famous painting by Goya entitled *Third of May* in which the artist portrays an exe-
cution during the Napoleonic wars. Clark (1969, p. 95) writes of it that

> No execution scene has ever revealed this extreme moment with such barefaced hon-
> esty. What is described here is the heroism of the final and hopeless gesture of the
> outstretched arms and staring features of the white-shirted victim as he is mown
> down by a faceless firing-squad. . . . His death is absurd, and he knows it.

If we truly examine the painting with care and involvement, the emotion we
experience could be anxiety, rage, or despair, among others, depending on the personal significance—if any—of what is being viewed. We are made anxious because
of the recognition that we, too, could face violence against our persons; we rage
because of the injustice; we despair because of the reflection of the long human history of senseless barbarism—all three with deep existential significance, which we
somehow sense. We wonder what Goya felt in being motivated to create this painting and suppose that it must have been great anger and perhaps despair. We also
marvel at the artist's power of imagination and craftsmanship. Readers can judge for
themselves in Figure 7.1, which, though a somewhat limited, black-and-white pho-
tographic reproduction, still suggests the graphic emotional impact of the painting.

To ask a rhetorical yet searching question, why should it surprise us that paintings of a ship on a wide sea, a sunset, birds in flight, or the great religious paintings
of the Middle Ages result in emotion? Their artistry conveys a sense of mystery,
loneliness, peacefulness, belonging, or spiritual order to those who look at them.
Religious paintings, or the power of music, reassure some of us about immortality or
the existence of a sustaining God. Why, then, should we be surprised that a scientist
might feel awe, wonderment, or joy from discovering a new principle about the natural order of things? Imagine the human reaction, for example, to the first observation under a microscope of microbes swimming in a spoonful of water, or that of
countless stars that seem to stretch on forever as revealed by the telescope, which
magnified the power of the human eye far beyond anything hitherto seen.

FIGURE 7.1. Francisco Goya's painting, *The Third of May,* illustrates representational art as a provoker of emotions in viewers. (*Source:* Scala/Art Resource, New York. Converted print. Madrid, Prado.)

It is also difficult to know what to say about states like awe, wonder, and faith-trust, because they can be used in more than one sense. Earlier, for example, I listed awe with the emotion family of fear-anxiety, because it often contains these emotional qualities. However, some people find the visual features of the universe or the remarkable functional capacities of living creatures awesome and not fearful. *Wonder* might be a better word for such a state, which seems also to combine easily with faith-trust. One can, of course, experience faith and trust in a love relationship as well as with respect to God, or in the more secular sense of faith, trust, and wonder at a universal order in the physical and biological world.

A second possible mechanism, one that is far more ephemeral, is that archetypal symbols carrying unconscious or barely sensed meanings that all or some people share are created in less concrete, nonrepresentational painting, music, and so forth. The role of symbols, which may have unconscious meanings, also touches on what is poorly understood in the human psyche—namely, primitive and perhaps unconscious symbols and ideas, illustrated in some of the writings of Carl Jung (1960) and by the searchings of mystics. The meanings conveyed by these symbols might be shared or highly individualized. To understand the emotions that flow from them, we would need to know more about the deeper and relatively inaccessible aspects of the human mind.

I must conclude that no special concepts are needed for aesthetic emotions that are not found in cognitive-motivational-relational formulations about emotion in general and about the individual emotions in particular, except those having to do with the principles that allow us to identify vicariously with what is being portrayed. This may be one reason why the aesthetic emotions have remained outside the pale of psychological study and, in a sense, sui generis, in the eyes of those philosophers and psychologists willing to consider them.

The main mystery is to understand how and under what conditions we can be aroused emotionally by paintings, music, drama, literature, religious or spiritual thoughts and experiences. I believe there is no special problem that is not inherent in the emotion process in general, and if we understand this process we will also understand aesthetic emotions. Except perhaps in the case of music, which presumably involves something more in a psychophysiological sense, we are reacting emotionally to the portrayal of the emotional realities of our lives. The more what is portrayed touches that reality, and the more we are involved in or struggling with it in our lives, the more we respond as we would and do in real life.

This is probably why throughout the history of humankind drama, art, and music have played such a consistent and important role. We are not speaking of something strange or esoteric, but of the psychological representation of and involvement in life itself.

Summary

In this chapter I have applied the general cognitive-motivational-relational theory to each of the main goal congruent or positive emotions — namely, happiness/joy, pride, love/affection, relief — and to each of a set of borderline emotions — namely, hope, compassion (as an alternative to empathy), and aesthetic and religious emotions, which I called problematic.

As in Chapter 6, the same outline was followed for each emotion, proceeding first with an overview of the emotion, then the core relational theme, appraisal pattern, action tendency, other terms, dynamics, and pathology. The appraisal patterns were presented as a decision tree, following the reasoning of an "if-then" analysis that begins with the most general decision of whether or not there will be an emotion, whether the emotion will be positive or negative, and then the analysis progressively narrows down until the necessary and sufficient appraisal components distinguishing that emotion from all others are reached. Tables summarizing these appraisal patterns are also provided for each emotion.

Note

1. I credit my awareness of this British outlook to Jaakov Garb, a graduate student at Berkeley, who is interested in the aesthetic emotions experienced by scientists.

PART FOUR

Emotional Development

The topic of emotional development is both phylogenetic and ontogenetic in thrust. Both perspectives are concerned with change in the emotion process over the life-span of individuals, subgroups, or species. In contrast with phylogenesis, which refers to the evolution of the emotion process across species, the ontogenesis of emotion refers to development and change in the emotion process over the life-span of a prototypical individual or subgroup of a species.

The developmental perspective is distinctive in that unlike all other ways of approaching psychological issues it looks at any process of interest, say, intelligence or emotion, on a time line from birth to death. Baltes (1987, p. 611) writes:

> Life-span developmental psychology involves the study of constancy and change in behavior throughout the life course (ontogenesis), from conception to death. The goal is to obtain knowledge about general principles of life-long development, about inter-individual differences and similarities in development, as well as about the degree and conditions of individual plasticity or modifiability of development

Baltes (1987) provides a useful set of theoretical propositions characteristic of life-span developmental psychology, a set that includes both biological and socio-cultural factors. Although Baltes concentrates on intelligence, these propositions are equally relevant to the study of emotion. They are summarized here in Table IV.1.

Interest in the development of emotion has followed the waxing and waning of interest in emotion itself. We saw in Chapter 1 that there have been historical periods in which the status of emotion was in doubt, so the topic was nearly absent from the theoretical and empirical work of social and biological scientists in those periods. The recent reawakened interest in emotion as an important multidisciplinary concept has led, in turn, to a remarkable growth in theory and research on emotional development in infants and young children. In addition, the recent burgeoning of interest in aging, and the realization that people change in complex ways over the entire life course, has also stimulated a modest expansion of work on changes in the emotion process in adulthood and old age. The preponderance of scientific activity on emotional development, however, centers on the period from birth to adulthood.

Table IV.1. Summary of Family of Theoretical Propositions Characteristic of
Life-Span Developmental Psychology

Concepts	Propositions
Life-span development	Ontogenetic development is a life-long process. No age period holds supremacy in regulating the nature of development. During development, and at all stages of the life-span, both continuous (cumulative) and discontinuous (innovative) processes are at work.
Multidirectionality	Considerable diversity or pluralism is found in the directionality of changes that constitute ontogenesis, even within the same domain. The direction of change varies by categories of behavior. In addition, during the same developmental periods, some systems of behavior show increases, whereas others evince decreases in level of functioning.
Development as gain/loss	The process of development is not a simple movement toward higher efficacy, such as incremental growth. Rather, throughout life, development always consists of the joint occurrence of gain (growth) and loss (decline).
Plasticity	Much intraindividual plasticity (within-person modifiability) is found in psychological development. Depending on the life conditions and experiences by a given individual, his or her developmental course can take many forms. The key developmental agenda is the search for the range of plasticity and its constraints.
Historical embeddedness	Ontogenetic development can also vary substantially in accordance with historical-cultural conditions. How ontogenetic (age-related) development proceeds is markedly influenced by the kind of sociocultural conditions existing in a given historical period, and by how these evolve over time.
Contextualism as paradigm	Any particular course of individual development can be understood as the outcome of the interactions (dialectics) among three systems of developmental influences: age-graded, history-graded, and nonnormative. The operation of these systems can be characterized in terms of the metatheoretical principles associated with contextualism.
Field of development as multidisciplinary	Psychological development needs to be seen in the interdisciplinary context provided by other disciplines (e.g., anthropology, biology, sociology) concerned with human development. The openness of the life-span perspective to interdisciplinary posture implies that a "purist" psychological view offers but a partial representation of behavioral development from conception to death.

(*Source:* P. B. Baltes, "Theoretical propositions of life span developmental psychology." *Developmental Psychology, 23.* Washington, DC: American Psychological Association. Copyright © 1987 by the American Psychological Association. Reprinted by permission.)

Chapter 8 is concerned with developmental processes in the individual who is influenced over the life-course by sociocultural factors that are grafted onto and interact with the newborn's physical constitution, and its temperament, to produce a distinctive personality that greatly influences the emotional life. Chapter 9 is concerned with the sociocultural influences that shape the development of the emotion process. These have to do with how living in a society with distinctive cultural and social arrangements affects the emotional life.

❖ 8 ❖

Individual Development

Those who study the relationships among cognition, motivation, and emotion tend to divide into two groups, those devoted to adulthood and those focused on infancy and early childhood. The two groups rarely interact. Yet it is especially important to chart emotional development, and the processes that affect it, because what seems to happen in early childhood is by no means the same as what happens in adulthood. Not to compare these periods of life systematically risks distortion of our understanding of the emotion process in the adult, which draws on both immature and mature cognitive and motivational activity. In effect, adults use processes that are sometimes in the repertory of infants and young children, and sometimes not. Therefore, the study of the emotional life must draw on both periods, and a synthesis of them would increase the accuracy and depth of our understanding.

In this chapter I address the individual course of development of the emotions from infancy onward as it is influenced both by biological factors and by experience with the physical and social environment. This confronts us with prodigious tasks, the most difficult of which is to decide on the variables whose development we should examine.

As Campos, Barrett, Lamb, Goldsmith, and Stenberg (1983)[1] observe, it was once fashionable to study the emergence of emotions in infancy with concepts that had been much influenced by Bridges (1930, 1932). Bridges proposed that newborns show only general excitement, but in the weeks and months that follow, and as a result of maturation, the learning of new motoric abilities, and cognitive development, certain emotions begin to be differentiated. For example, distress is differentiated from excitement at 3 weeks, anger from distress at 4 months, disgust from anger at 5 months, and fear from disgust at 6 or 7 months. Positive emotions follow a parallel developmental sequence in which delight appears at 3 months, then elation followed by affection emerge after about 6 months. The pattern of emotional differentiation Bridges proposed is shown in Figure 8.1.

As Campos et al. point out, more recent observations, especially those based on the newer measures of facial and vocal expression, provide evidence of emotion in the newborn earlier than Bridges suggested. For example, some emotions—such as fear, anger, and joy—show expressive manifestations much earlier, whereas others, such as shame, come later. Unlike fear, shame requires a grasp of the meanings of social signals from others (such as a parent). In effect, for shame to occur, the child must understand criticism in order to grasp the personal significance of blame, as

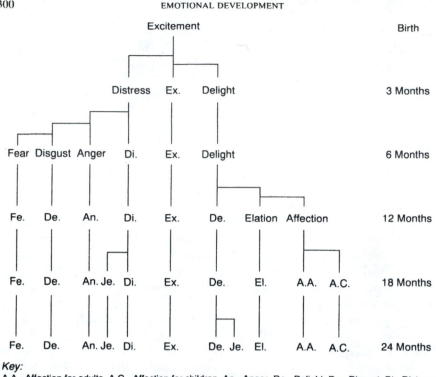

Key:
A.A.=Affection for adults, A.C.=Affection for children, An.=Anger, De.=Delight, Dg.=Disgust, Di.=Distress, El.=Elation, Ex.=Excitement, Fe.=Fear, Je.=Jealousy, Jo.=Joy.

FIGURE 8.1. The Bridges developmental analysis of emotions. (*Source:* K. M. B. Bridges, "Emotional Development in Early Infancy." *Child Development, 3.* Chicago: University of Chicago Press. Copyright © 1932 The Society for Research in Child Development, Inc. Reprinted by permission.)

well as praise to grasp the significance of credit. Contemporary theories of emotional development (for example, Campos et al., 1983; Sroufe, 1979) eschew Bridges' idea that the specific emotions are differentiated out of general excitement and propose instead that the emergence of emotions depends on cognitive development, a position compatible with my own analysis.

One could say, as Campos et al. do, that the systematic study of facial expression gave the study of emotional development in preverbal infants a shot in the arm by providing a set of objective, believable, and nonverbal expressive criteria that to some extent cut across cultural boundaries. The downside of this is that what is charted in this developmental progression is evidence mainly of a single peripheral response, facial expression, which is a component of emotion rather than emotion per se. Unless we assume a one-to-one correspondence between expression and experience, when we see a smile, a distress face, an interest face, an anger face, and the like, we are still left in the position of having to make inferences about what is occurring emotionally.

On the question of what is developing, it would help to recall my discussion of observable and nonobservable variables of emotion at the start of Chapter 2. Please recall that the observables include actions, physiological reactions, subjective reports, and environmental events and contexts; the nonobservables include action tendencies, subjective experience, person–environment relationships, and coping, attributional, and appraisal processes. These constitute what almost everyone today would include in the emotion process. Because the observables serve many masters other than emotion, when we begin to speak about these variables as emotional, we have entered the world of theoretical inference. This means that theories and research on emotional development depend heavily on how the theorist-researcher asks and answers the question about what is emotion and what it is that is observed to be developing; no easy task to trace emotional development, I would think. Many working assumptions need to be made.

I have argued that appraisal and coping draw on goal hierarchies and belief systems, which affect how the individual relates to the world and evaluates as well as manages (copes with) adaptational encounters that have the potential of provoking emotions. My concerns here, therefore, center on the development of these variables and processes, which depend heavily on learning and the epigenetic development of intellectual capacities, as well as on biosocial factors such as temperament. I want also to reflect the approaches of others, even those that differ from mine, in my account of emotional development.

This chapter now turns to the mother-infant relationship, viewed historically, followed by several theories of infant emotional development, and then to questions of biology and temperament. An extended discussion of four mechanisms of learning and their relevance to emotional development follow, after which I consider recent research and thought on cognitive-emotional development beyond the period of infancy. I close with a summary of the developmental course of the emotion process based on what I have said here and in earlier chapters.

Approaches to the Study of Mother-Infant Relationships

There have been several broad ways of thinking about mother-infant relationships that can serve as a recent history for current concerns about emotional development. I deal with them very briefly. In accord with their emphasis on the newborn and early childhood, Campos et al. (1983) review recent shifts in theory and research on the effects of parenting on the child's intellectual and personality development, both of which undoubtedly influence emotional development.

A micro level of analysis is found in the study of mother-infant relationships presented here, focusing as it does on how parental caretakers deal with their individual infants and toddlers. These studies parallel, in a sense, the macro level of analysis employed in the sociological and anthropological study of social influence in Chapter 9, which follows, because the latter focuses on how the larger society and its culture influences behavior and personality and, thereby, the emotional life. Campos et al. discuss four different approaches to the study of mother-infant relationships beginning chronologically in the 1930s.

Psychoanalysis and Social Learning

The first approach combined a *psychoanalytic* (psychosexual) framework and a *social learning* outlook pioneered at Yale (e.g., Whiting & Child, 1953). Research growing out of these overlapping ways of thinking made comparisons of breast and bottle feeding, demand and schedule feeding, gradual and abrupt weaning, and relaxed and severe toilet training. These variables of childrearing reflect the three Freudian stages of psychosexual development, oral, anal, and phallic/genital.

Ethological-Attachment Theory

The second approach is identified with the elaborate theorizing of the late *John Bowlby* (1951, 1969, 1973, 1980) about mother love in infancy as a key factor in mental health and the emergence of a healthy ego. Bowlby's influential work combined a psychoanalytical and a phylogenetic adaptational focus. The affectional bond between infant and adult is said to involve trust, confidence, and security on the part of the infant. The period of infancy is characterized by four key functions: *seeking contact* with the mother for protection and care (coordinated by the attachment system), *avoidance of events* or people that are potentially dangerous (coordinated by the fear/wariness system), *playful social interaction* (managed by the affiliation system), and *exploration* of the nonsocial environment (managed by the exploration system).

The absence or deprivation of mothering was considered by Bowlby to be traumatic to the infant, but later work (e.g., Yarrow, 1961) called some of the psychoanalytic interpretations of the cognitive deficits reported in Spitz's (1946) studies of abandoned infants into question. Bowlby's theorizing also led to the very vigorous research, which continues in the present, on the quality of the mother-child relationship and secure or insecure attachment of the child to the mother. This has been extensively studied in the Ainsworth strange situation (1969; also Ainsworth, Blehar, Waters, & Wall, 1978), an experimental procedure that tests the child's reaction to the mother's return after having left for an interval. Among the most important features of Ainsworth's research that made it unique was a central concern with the consequences of a mother's sensitivity to a baby's signals about its well-being and how available the mother was to the baby.

Theories About the Essence of What a Mother Provides

The third approach grew out of the question of what was important and unimportant in the early mother-child relationship. In contrast with the Freudian psychosexual stages and Bowlby's focus on the quality of the mother-child relationship, infrahuman monkey and rat mothers were evaluated as a *physical source of comfort, security, and stimulation*. This approach was most visibly represented in the work of Harlow (e.g., Harlow & Zimmerman, 1959), who demonstrated that the tactile comfort provided by monkey mothers was more important to the infant than were feeding and oral stimulation from the nipple. In what were in those days considered electrifying studies whose results carried considerable surprises, monkey babies spent most of their time clinging to their mechanical furry but milk-dry mother substitutes, coming to the substitute wire mother with its productive (milk-producing) nipple only occasionally to suck. Later studies by Denenberg (1964) with rats also suggested that handling and stimulation in early infancy were important factors in the rat's later emotionality and adaptational adequacy. The conclusion of this animal research was that the mother is, in effect, mainly a provider of tactile comfort, security, and handling or stimulation to the child.

Theories About Adaptational Fitness

The fourth approach to parenting, especially the mother-child relationship, was largely ethological and guided by the premise that *social activity* facilitates adaptation not by promoting social interaction but by increasing *evolutionary, adaptive fitness.* Ethologists see species-specific behavior as having evolved to serve social communication and regulation; thus, smiling initiates and maintains adaptive social interaction (Brazelton, Tronick, Adamson, Als, & Wise, 1975). One of the problems with this history is that each conceptualization of what was important in the mother-child relationship was offered in an either-or fashion so typical of psychology although it is quite possible that each conveys an important perspective on a complex truth.

Theories of Emotional Development

Four recent analyses of infant emotional development, those of Izard (1978; see also Buechler & Izard, 1983; Izard & Buechler, 1980), Sroufe (1979, 1984), Campos, Barrett, Lamb, Goldsmith, and Stenberg (1983), and Lewis and Michalson (1983), are illustrative of the available ways of thinking.

Izard's Theory

Izard makes three key assumptions: (1) Some discrete emotions, which are present at birth (e.g., startle-interest, disgust, and distress), at least at the motor-expressive level, have the function of signaling the child's urgent needs for a caretaker. These states are evidenced by facial expressions, which Izard sees as linked tightly to emotional experience. (2) Emotions emerge as they become adaptive for the infant, and particularly in infant–caregiver communication. (3) The developmental onset occurs in close connection with changes in motor, perceptual, and cognitive capacities; these capacities make emotions possible but are not causal. Thus, fear develops when infants can locomote (and therefore may need to avoid something), anger when infants can reach out (and therefore strike out).

Concerning point (2), Izard is rare among emotion theorists in his assertion that there is a precise correspondence between emotional expression and emotional experience, with expression being tantamount to experience. In other words, a fear face means that there is a fear experience, an anger face that there is an anger experience, and so on. Little is presently known, however, about the relationship between emotional experience and expression, and about how and when they become connected. Campos, Campos, and Barrett (1989) argue that convergent operations are needed to evaluate any possible isomorphism between expression and experience, or between one response system and another, and I think there is a widespread sense of doubt among researchers and theorists that there is, indeed, such isomorphism. This is what makes it so problematic to assert what children at early stages of life are actually feeling as emotions on the basis of expressive reactions.

Izard also believes that emotion is often more important for perceptual and cognitive development than the other way around; it has long been presumed (e.g., Freud, Piaget) that emotions resulting from adaptational pressures mobilize cognitive development. This idea has a long history and is expressed by many researchers, such as Dunn (1988), who believes that the adaptational pressures of family relationships create the best context for studying the child's understanding of social relationships and the interpersonal rules of emotion.

Anger, surprise, and joy emerge, according to Izard, from birth to 4 months, joy at from 1 to 3 months in conjunction with the ability to discriminate social from nonsocial objects. Anger is possible and useful when the child begins to show new voluntary means-ends activities, which allow it to cope when frustrated. Fear and shyness emerge after 6 months of age — if they occurred earlier, says Izard, they would be disruptive because the younger infant does not have the means to cope with them — and coping plays a role in the infant's reaction to strangers. Coordinated with new motoric skills that emerge then, too, the child can begin to crawl to the mother for safety and away from what threatens it. Shyness and the sense of self begin to emerge together a little later and are functionally related. Izard shares with other modern theorists an emphasis on the functional nature of emotion, which is also a basic premise for this book; emotions are not just epiphenomena but serve important adaptational functions.

Sroufe's Theory

Sroufe (1979) has proposed that the newborn shows at least three emotions at birth, *wariness-fear, rage-anger,* and *pleasure-joy.* More than Bridges and Izard, he emphasizes that what changes in early development are the cognitive capacities of the baby, the ability to express emotion (e.g., laughter), and the ability to cope — for example, by locomotion, which permits the baby to move toward and away from what distresses it. Along with Lewis and Michalson (1983; see also Lewis & Brooks-Gunn, 1978, 1979), and myself, Sroufe believes that an adult form of the emotion process does not become possible until there is an emergent sense of self, which he places at around 9 months, but which I suspect is much earlier and gradual.

According to Sroufe, an infant comes into the world preadapted with certain basic reactions, but its emotional life becomes much more complex through cognitive development, which organizes the emotions on the basis of *distinct meanings* rather than differentiation from generalized excitement, as Bridges had suggested. More specifically, a baby can tell the difference between a strange face and the mother's face at 2 weeks of age. At 4 months, based on the history of interaction with the mother who is now familiar, an unfamiliar person will get a negative reaction (say, wariness). At 7 months the reaction is different; not only is a stranger perceived as discrepant with the past but fear is generated by the specific negative experiences the child has previously had with strangers, making the latter version cognitively more sophisticated. Later on there will be vague apprehension (anxiety) without any specific basis in fact, presumably based on a rudimentary inference about the situation, which is a still more sophisticated process. For Sroufe, anxiety emerges at 12 months, and shame, which he links to fear, at 18 months.

The Theory of Campos, Barrett, and Their Co-Workers

Campos, Barrett, et al. (Campos & Barrett, 1984; Campos et al., 1983; and Campos, Campos, & Barrett, 1989) caution that Sroufe does not tell us precisely how advances in cognitive development are related to emotional development. What they find most lacking in Sroufe's approach, however, is a focus on motivation, particularly the psychological links among goal strivings, thwarting, coping, and emotional states, which I developed in depth in Parts Two and Three of this book in connection with an analysis of the patterns of primary appraisal. Campos et al. (1983, p. 818) state their concern about this omission in what I believe is a powerful analysis, as follows:

> Like Sroufe, we believe that discrete emotion systems may be observable in the neonate. Moreover, we also agree that critical developments in cognitive capacities influence emotions, in that cognition is part (but only part) of what affects the child's appreciation of the significance of an event for his own biologically determined or voluntarily determined objectives. However, we stress that emotional development should not be viewed as a mere exemplar of cognitive development; instead, we feel that just as significant as changes in the development of general cognitive and perceptual capacities are changes in the goals of the organism with development.
>
> Moreover, if, as we believe, the elicitation of an emotion is determined by a particular relationship between a type of goal and a type of appreciation of how events relate to the goal, then it is possible for this relationship to be invariant across development while both goals and cognitions change. For example, anger may be elicited in persons of any age: The neonate may show anger following the appreciation that a preadapted end state is blocked (e.g., impeding the baby's movement when it is exercising reflexive movements — cf. Stenberg, 1982); an 8-month-old may show anger when she anticipates that an event will impede progress toward a visible goal; a 2-year-old may be angered by the content of a verbal remark that may thwart progress toward a symbolic goal, like play; a 10-year-old may be angered by an insult; and so forth. Similar considerations apply to other fundamental emotions.

Campos, Barrett, and their co-workers argue, in effect, that emotions such as anger and fear are tied to specific eliciting conditions, whose effects depend on particular types of experience and cognitive competencies as these emerge. Thus, the infant responds with anger to arm restraint, but other conditions that normatively provoke anger in an adult will not in a baby. Similarly, fear may be elicited by the visual cliff in an infant who has begun to crawl, but this does not generalize to other sources of fear, such as strangers, until certain other cognitive abilities and experiences have been added, which allow the child to distinguish people it doesn't remember from those it does (see also Yonas's, 1981, research on aversive reactions to a looming stimulus by 3-month-old infants). This can be contrasted with the much more complicated and symbolic adult fear—anxiety might be better here—about threat to personal meanings or an impending event that symbolically threatens a central social goal, such as being able to provide for one's family .

With their main concern centered on infant development, Campos, Barrett et al. conclude, as I and many others also do, that there is no universal, external emotion provoker for each emotion. In the adult, it will not be an external stimulus but a relationship between person and environment, which I refer to as a *core relational theme,* that provokes an emotion. This allows me to acknowledge logically that the rules of emotion generation differ across species and across developmental stages because of major differences in the *person* side of the person–environment relationship (e.g., in goals, comprehension, and beliefs). In any event, what emerges in adult emotion can be defined in universal, relational terms, as in the reconciling solution provided in Chapter 5, which considers both universals and sociocultural sources of variation that affect appraisal.

I mention in passing that Campos et al. (1983; also Bertenthal, Campos, & Barrett, 1984), like Izard, view cognitive and motoric development as a determinant as well as a consequence of the onset of emotional reactions. As I indicated in a discussion of their research in Chapter 4, even after an infant is clearly able to perceive depth and, therefore, heights, wariness about height as a danger does not develop until the child has 4 or 6 weeks of locomotor experience (crawling). That this wariness depends not on age but rather on locomotion experiences suggests to me that the child must come to appraise that there is physical danger—all the more so if the infant has fallen or the mother expresses anxiety or alarm about this possibility; crawling provides a perceptual-motor basis for this appraisal. Figure 8.2 (pp.308–309) illustrates some of these observations.

The visual cliff experiment presents an infant with a glass surface on which to crawl or walk; below this there seems to be a substantial drop from a height on one side, but the other side looks shallow. A baby that can perceive depth and has experience crawling senses the danger of falling. In Figure 8.2(a), a nine-month-old baby has been slowly lowered onto the glass plate on top of the deep side, and the camera, shooting up at the baby from below, clearly reveals the baby's fear face.

In Figure 8.2(b), another baby has been placed on the solid side and is encouraged by its mother to come to her across the surface of the steep side, which it does without hesitation. In Figure 8.2(c), placed on the side that looks steep, a baby is wary and fearful. In Figure 8.2(d), a baby copes by walking around the side and holding onto the top of the glass to prevent the possibility of falling. The baby obviously has sufficient cognitive development and experience to cope effectively with the threat of falling and seems to sense that holding onto the glass will keep it safe.

I close the discussion of Campos et al.'s theory with their seven postulates describing the most important features of emotional development. These postulates, listed here, with liberties taken to enrich them and make them more compatible with my own views and my conversations with J. Campos—they are not verbatim quotes—overlap considerably with what I have been saying throughout this book about motivation, coping, and appraisal (1983, p. 818):

1. There is a common set of differentiated emotion states that is a constant potential for emotional experience throughout the life-span of the human species.

2. As cognitive development proceeds and as new goals appear in the life of the child, new emotions emerge on the basis of a richer understanding of the world.

3. The effectiveness of specific eliciting circumstances changes as the organism develops.

4. The relationship between emotional expression and emotional experience becomes more complicated and coordinated as the organism develops.

5. Coping responses change as the organism develops, and with these come emotional changes, too.

6. Emotions become socialized as the organism develops.

7. Receptivity to others' emotional expressions increases as the organism develops.

Lewis and Michalson's Theory of the Development of Self

Shifting now to Lewis and Michalson (1983; also Lewis & Brooks-Gunn, 1978, 1979), their view of emotional development is distinguished by an emphasis on the normative development of the *self* (their preferred term) and an emphasis on developmental patterns that is similar to that of Piaget. The self consists of both subjective or existential properties and objective or categorical properties, such as gender, height, competence, age, and so on. I say *normative* because there is always considerable variation around any norm. The precise age boundaries these authors propose for each period or stage are subject to debate and modification depending on the observations used to identify them. Figure 8.3 presents the stimulus drawings used in this research.

Lewis and Michalson's view identifies five periods or stages, one from about birth to 3 months, a second from about 4 to 8 or 9 months, a third from about 9 to 12 months, a fourth from 12 to 18 months, and the fifth after 18 months of age. In some cases detailed here, at the risk of disturbing the descriptive flow, I make some evaluative comments about a particular period before moving on to the next.

The *first period* occurs between birth and 3 months of age. At this stage the self is relatively undifferentiated from the actions and reactions of others, but such differentiation is beginning, as the connections between the child's actions and the responses of others to it are being perceived and assimilated.

In the *second period,* from roughly 4 to 8 or 9 months, the capacity to differentiate the self from others emerges, and the child is beginning to recognize its own agency and therefore to have intentions. One could say that only when an ego-identity (my term) can be distinguished from other persons and things, even if in a rudimentary sense, can adult forms of emotional experience occur. It takes an elemental sense of one's identity, for example, to appraise even immaturely and vaguely a personal stake in a transaction.

To experience emotions, one also has to have some elementary understanding that what is happening has relevance for one's well-being and, eventually, what the specific relevance is and what might be done about it. The consequences depend on personal vulnerabilities and goals whose vicissitudes are important sources of edu-

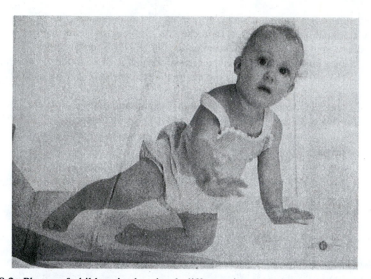

FIGURE 8.2. Photos of children in the visual cliff experiment. Baby reactions to deep (dangerous-appearing) and shallow (safe-appearing) sides. The sides are identical except that one looks shallow and solid while the other looks deep and dangerous. There is a safe-looking ledge between them where the baby is placed before being encouraged by the mother to come to her across one or the other side. (*Source:* Courtesy Joseph J. Campos.)

(a) A 9-month-old baby (above) being lowered to the glass table-top surface on the deep side, showing a fear face. Photo taken from below.

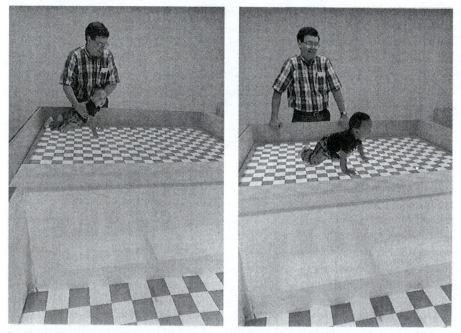

(b) A similar baby dealing with both sides of the visual cliff: When the baby is placed on the shallow side, the baby crosses without fear and with evident enthusiasm.

(c) When the baby (above) is placed on the ledge between the shallow side and deep side, and the mother encourages it to come to her across the deep side, most babies are normally fearful and show avoidance. Notice this baby looking down the deep side with wariness, built on an understanding of the danger.

(d) Some babies show well-developed coping behavior. This one detours carefully along the side of the table to avoid falling, even holding onto the top of the glass surrounding the table top with obvious caution, as it nears the mother.

(a) Birthday party.   (b) Mother with pink hair.

(c) Dog runs away.   (d) Awful-tasting food.

FIGURE 8.3. Stimulus pictures for emotional stories. (*Source:* M. Lewis and C. Saarni, *The Socialization of Emotions.* New York: Plenum Publishing Corp., 1985. Reprinted by permission.)

cation (see also Campos et al.,1983; Campos, Campos, & Barrett, 1989; Lewis, Sullivan, Stanger, & Weiss, 1989, for some empirical research; also some research on children between 6 and 8 months of age by Parrott & Gleitman, 1989, on the cognitive complexities involved in the child's game of peek-a-boo, and Stenberg & Campos, 1990).

(e) Sister knocks over tower of blocks.   (f) Lost in grocery store.

FIGURE 8.3. (Continued)

To linger a bit on this second stage, the emphasis on a personal identity in emotion poses some interesting dilemmas. Should we assume that an infant can only experience an emotion when it recognizes itself as a distinct creature and the possible implications of the social or physical provocation? There is, of course, no way to ask an infant whether or not it is making such a judgment or experiencing an emotion, so the question is extremely difficult to answer without inference and speculation (see also Lyons, 1980).

I think there are several proposals possible about what capacities are present very early on, and these are consistent with the strongest position on the role of appraisal in emotion. One is that certain reflexes (such as pleasure and pain), on which later appraisals are built up through conditioning and the resulting formation of expectations, are available at the outset. The infant learns, among other things, that pleasure or pain is the expectable outcome of this or that physical and social condition, or, as I would say, that the outcome of a relationship with those conditions has a subjectively defined bearing on personal well-being. Also relevant are the capacity to recognize the familiar so that the baby can sense a discrepancy, the ability and experience to grasp the contingencies between antecedent conditions and effects that generate meaning and hence emotion, and a sensitivity to social signals and their meanings (see, for example, Watson, 1985).

Personal meanings arise from all this—that is, from a number of processes—and with the development of abstract intelligence, conditioned expectations become complex, symbolic, existential, and ultimately capable of being verbalized to some extent; they may also remain preconscious or unconscious. We know almost nothing about whether and how what is learned by automatic processing (e.g., by conditioning) becomes conscious. I say more about conditioning shortly.

In any case, the first positive and negative reactions are *not* emotions but concrete reflexes and a vague sense of the familiar and unfamiliar, which is ultimately built into bonafide emotions via primitive, categorical expectations or by evaluations of the conditioned signals that say that this or that harm or benefit is or may be upcoming.

As to ego-identity, when all is said and done, it seems to me essential to postulate some such principle in adulthood to organize hierarchically the multiple goal commitments relevant to the motivational principle. The mind must have some mechanism for choosing which goal to center effort on and which goal to subordinate or suppress in any transaction. When we see an adult who cannot do this, we say he or she is disorganized, immature, childish, mentally ill, or brain damaged.

Whether an infant or a very young child — say, at Lewis and Michalson's stage two or before — has an emergent identity is hard to determine, but that it does is plausible and consistent with observations such as those of Watson (e.g., Bahrick & Watson, 1985; see also Papousek & Papousek, 1974) that at 5 months infants are aware of the contingency between their leg movements and what is shown of this movement on a TV monitor. The experiment compared infants that experienced a perfectly contingent live display of their own movements with those experiencing a noncontingent display of the baby's own movements or those of another baby. The recognition occurred even when the infants' view of their bodies was occluded, so that the findings cannot be interpreted as based on an intramodal visual comparison of two sights, the body and the video display. Is this an ego-identity? Probably not, but it may well signal the rudimentary and inchoate beginnings of one, which is enough for a limited range of emotions.

There is also some recognition by infants that arm restraint, for example, which leads 4-month-old infants to show marked anger (Stenberg & Campos, 1990), is performed by an agency external to themselves (the 4-month-old looks at the experimenter's restraining hand and the 7-month-old looks at the face of the experimenter). There must be some sort of "me," if not I, rather than someone else in this. I suggested in Chapter 3 that differentiation of oneself from others may well be a universal property of all living organisms, including plants. It may take several months for some rudimentary identity to mature, and many years for the kind of complex, differentiated, and comparative identity we think of as characteristic of mature adults, but the process must surely start early.

Therefore, when an infant becomes capable of reacting with anger or fear, there must be some differentiation of its own identity from that of other creatures or objects. Whatever the process is by which an executive agency becomes capable of making appraisals and choosing courses of action, a person ultimately emerges with a distinctive sense of a personal identity, a sense that makes it possible to evaluate and act on the significance of what is happening for personal well-being, whether this is a result of automatic, involuntary appraisals or of deliberate and reflective processes (see Chapter 4).

To return now to Lewis and Michalson, the *third period* is said to involve the emergence of self-permanence, which they propose occurs between about 9 and 12 months of age. Children can now not only differentiate the self from others through the effects of their actions on others, but this distinction is maintained independent of action and context. There is, in effect, an existential self in Lewis and Michalson's terms, which allows for a categorical self as well.

The *fourth period,* from 12 to 18 months, marks continued consolidation and development of the self. From 18 to 22 months, children can recognize themselves in the mirror independent of actions, as well as in still photos and movies.

The observational work of Dunn and her colleagues (Dunn, 1988; Dunn & Munn, 1985), among others, confirms that complex emotions are possible around the fourth period discussed by Lewis and Michalson (1983) because of the child's increasing grasp of social rules and meanings. This doesn't mean, of course, that they could not occur earlier, depending on what form they might take or what is considered simple or complex. Dunn has observed the emotional interchanges among very young children and their mothers, and among siblings, and concludes that an elementary understanding and mastery of the social rules of emotion are already emerging at 18 months. She suggests that compared with cool laboratory contexts in which emotional knowledge has typically been studied, the child's personal interests in family transactions fire acquisition of this understanding for the purpose of having control and influence over relationships with siblings and parents. Family interchanges, she says, are the most emotional of all encounters of living.

Among many other examples, she observes 18-month-old children recognizing the distress of their siblings and attempting to alleviate it by some form of comforting or to exacerbate it when they are resentful rivals. She observes teasing—deliberate attempts to upset or annoy another—as early as 14 to 16 months. This inferential, observational evidence of an understanding of the rules of emotion transcends the inability of the child to verbalize how it works.

Finally, in Lewis and Michalson's *period five,* beginning around 18 months of age, because of advancing symbolic behavior, children are now capable of articulating an elaborate categorical self as distinct from others. This is a time when the child begins to comprehend some of the complex, sometimes subtle, possibilities inherent in social relationships that may be relevant to personal well-being. Children are now or shortly will be capable of more complex emotional experiences such as empathy, guilt, embarrassment, shame, and pride, which depend on being able to recognize, even if only in a rudimentary way, the inter- and intrapersonal significance of what is happening. As I said earlier, the recognition of social signals and their meaning— for example, as criticism or praise—should facilitate the ability to experience guilt and shame. To put this in my theoretical terms, primary and secondary appraisals, including blame and credit, on which the emotional meanings conveyed in social relationships are predicated, surely become more elaborate at this time of life.

Lewis and Michalson's view of self-development presents some problems, however. One of them is its dependence on a strictly Piagetian approach to cognitive development in which formal cognitive capacities such as object permanence are said to create particular emotions in what seems like an all or nothing fashion. This understates the specific contextual considerations that can lead to fear, for example, rather than taking into account functions that develop in tandem that may produce the cognitive achievement of object permanence, or whatever. Thus, a baby views height as dangerous because of specific experiences with locomotion, and other specific experiences of such events as looming and pop-up toys can produce fear for presumably quite different reasons, regardless of the stage of cognitive development. The child's later fears, and its anxieties, come about through a different process, as Sroufe and Campos have suggested. In effect, there can be many kinds of fear rather than a general and uniform fear process, just as there are many kinds of anger, and these can vary in their cognitive and experiential requirements.

A second problem is that self or ego-identity does not occur as a sudden transition but probably develops gradually, so the emotions that depend on it might occur on the basis of a rudimentary version before there is a mature version. Stern (1985) has proposed — and defended the idea with extensive observations of infants — that the beginnings of an emergent self occur as early as the first 8 weeks of life and proceed to more complex and sophisticated versions thereafter. Therefore, although there is utility in the idea that cognitive abilities set the stage for emotional development, similar emotions can be brought about in different ways at earlier stages. Whether or not we should refer to these as the same emotion is an open question, which I discussed in Chapter 2. Lewis and Michalson make the points of change to the self too abrupt to be convincing. A better view might be that there is a glimmer of a self or ego all along, from almost the very start of postnatal life or maybe even before.

To close this discussion of theories of early emotional development, I offer six general *summary statements,* which reflect what might be a modest consensus as well as my own conceptual predilections:

1. The newborn comes into the world with several forms of differentiated emotional expressions rather than mere excitement.

2. These expressions have adaptational significance because they influence the caregiver, as Bowlby, Campos, Izard, and Sroufe all have maintained.

3. Cognitive development dramatically increases the range of environmental events (and person–environment relationships) to which a child will react with an emotion, as well as the ability of the child to cope with the conditions generating an emotion and the emotion itself. Thus, increased orientation to the environment and to oneself as well as motor development and emerging skills allow a child to get away from or approach threatening or benign objects and regions in the environment, increase its range of control, and increase its ability to manipulate encounters and to communicate its needs.

4. Some emotions emerge later than others — for example, shame, guilt, pride, envy, jealousy, and probably anxiety. There seems to be no clear consensus about when early emotions such as fear, anger, and sadness appear, because there has been little systematic effort to look for them or study their appraisals. Nor has there been much programmatic study of the way self or ego develops, and how dependent emotions are on it remains highly controversial. Thus, anger seems to be clearly observable at about 4 months, and might occur earlier, but no one has looked for it systematically, and what research there is depends on facial expression. What was called sadness has been observed in 3-month-olds in association with severe neglect and abuse, but is probably not prevalent until later. Fear has been reported in some 3- to 4-month-olds, but might be different in manner of elicitation and in the underlying appraisals.

What limits consensus, too, is what I have said about the isomorphism between expression and feeling, because a lack of it would make it much more difficult to judge the inner state from outer manifestations. In adults, this isomorphism is defeated to a degree by coping efforts at self-presentation, which allow the person to dissimulate in emotional displays (cf. Ekman, 1977; 1985).

5. To date I am not aware of much research applying the concept of appraisal to the toddler (age 1 to 3 years), though Campos and Stenberg (1981) have. I believe, however, that developmentalists could do more along these lines.

6. Similarly, there has been little research and theorizing about the early development of processes involved in the regulation of emotion as a result of socialization and the maturation of an infant's own motor and cognitive resources. Questions should be asked about when a child begins to use emotions instrumentally to get what it wants, and when it has a range of coping strategies for controlling its social relationships and its emotions. What these strategies are and the conditions influencing their development and selection remain promising arenas for future research.

Temperament as a Biological Factor

Psychologists, even those most concerned with sociocultural influences, have long recognized that social experience is grafted onto a constitutional substrate with some degree of heritability. Interest in temperament, and its connection with emotion, has been growing (see, for example, Kohnstamm, Bates, & Rothbart, 1989). Thayer (1989) regards moods as strongly influenced by energy levels, fatigue, and other bodily states, which he treats under the rubric of temperament, and at times he even seems to equate mood with such states. However, as is traditional in the treatment of moods, he also sees them as providing the predisposition for generalized tension or arousal, which could affect acute emotions. This is a concept of mood that seems quite close to what is often meant by temperament. He writes (1989, p. 118), for example:

> The phenomenon of low energetic arousal producing a disposition for increased tense arousal is well known in everyday life experiences. For example, many parents of small children are aware that these young people are least patient and most irritable when tired. Increased fearfulness, one aspect of tense arousal, is also greatest when children are tired. A good illustration of this occurred once when I took my then five-year-old to Disneyland. Upon arriving in the early afternoon, she chose to go on a very fast ride, and she loved it. She took the ride several more times that day, but the last time in the evening—past her usual bedtime—the ride proved frightening. She refused to take it again until another daytime visit.

In my discussions of the role of cognition in acute emotions and moods in Chapters 4 and 5, I argued that moods cannot be explained without reference to appraisals of the personal significance of one's long-term relationship with the environment. When we feel tired, though our daily round is not over, we are apt to react with anxiety or some other kind of distress, because demands that are normally manageable now seem more whelming if not overwhelming. In other words, my interpretation of Thayer's example quoted here is that, when we are fatigued, demands that might have been challenging and exhilarating are now too much to handle, leading to a sense of threat and anxiety feelings. The role of physical fatigue is to alter for the worse the power balance that is sensed between demands and coping resources; fatigue per se, though influential, is not as I see it the direct cause of the distress; the appraisal of a *weakened capacity to cope* is.

I don't resonate with the extreme biological position that treats temperament as a set of innate traits or genotypes manifesting themselves in patterns of appraisal and coping throughout life (see Goldsmith & Campos, 1986). I prefer the more moderate stance that these tendencies, whether innate, constitutional, or acquired, *interact* with social experience; the ways parents and other environmental forces treat the developing child and respond to its temperament help shape the emotional life. We must examine directly how variables and processes at the biological and social levels interact and play themselves out as the child grows up. This interactive view might better be called *transactional* (see Lazarus & Folkman, 1987). I will discuss it further under the heading of the concept of "goodness of fit."

If we ask, however, how temperament has been defined, we find a great diversity and vagueness. Almost any form of individual difference among infants seems to be a suitable candidate. Often cited is Allport's (1937, p. 54) definition of temperament as:

> The characteristic phenomena of an individual's emotional nature, including his susceptibility to emotional stimulation, his customary strength and speed of response, the quality of his prevailing mood, and all pecularities of fluctuation and intensity of mood.

Campos et al. (1983) comment approvingly that this definition implies several important notions—for example, that temperament, mood, and emotion are closely related; that temperament is stable or traitlike; that it has to do with dispositions affecting behaviors; that it is closely linked to biological factors; and that it concerns parameters of emotional responsiveness such as latency, amplitude, and duration of reactions. However, these authors also complain that the definition does not point us toward the functions that temperament plays in the life of the infant or adult, including the ways in which it influences the reactions of others.

Temperament, they say, refers to stable individual differences in adults as well as infants in specific parameters such as hedonic tone and arousal and with regard to discrete emotions like anger or fear. Their definition is that *temperament refers to individual differences in the intensive and temporal parameters of behavioral expressions of emotionality and arousal, especially as these differences influence the organization of intrapersonal and interpersonal processes.* Whether these individual differences are inherited or acquired needs, of course, to be demonstrated.

In a review of research on genetic factors using pencil and paper measures, Goldsmith (1983) has concluded that there is substantial evidence of a moderate heritability for individual differences of all sorts. More recent evidence supports the original conclusions of Buss and Plomin (1975) that the strongest evidence is found for the broad individual difference dimension of sociability, followed in strength by emotionality and activity. They also consider specific fears, certain components of sensation seeking and physical anxiety, anger, task persistence, and fidgeting as good candidates for further psychobiological research on the heritability of individual differences (see also the research of Plomin & Rowe, 1979).

About temperament as an aspect of emotion, Campos et al. write (p. 830):

> Thus all human beings will manifest fear, joy, anger, interest, increased or diminished activity, and so forth. These are the normative aspects of emotion. However, some show a very low threshold for fearfulness and others a high one. Some will show anger long after the provocation has passed, others will calm quickly. Some will be very active in most situations, whereas others are quiescent.

Buss and Plomin accept Allport's definition of temperament as well, adding five inclusion criteria for valid dimensions of temperament — namely, that it be *heritable, stable, predictive of adult personality, adaptive* in the evolutionary sense, and perhaps *present in other animals.* Consistent with the evidence from their review, the temperamental dimensions they emphasize are emotionality, activity, sociability, and impulsivity.

Mendoza and Mason (1989) write about temperament in a species sense, suggesting that temperamental characteristics vary among species. They cite descriptions by Yerkes and Yerkes (1929) of chimpanzees as active, lively, highly expressive, and impulsive — in contrast with the sluggish and brooding orangutan and the shy, retiring, and discrete gorilla. They also refer to the interplay of species and individual temperamental characteristics with social patterns.

Caspi, Elder, and Bem (1988, 1989) presented longitudinal findings from the archives of the Berkeley Guidance Study (Macfarlane, Allen, & Honzik, 1954) that shyness (moving away from others) and ill-temperedness (moving against the world) persist over the life-course from very early childhood. These authors believe that this consistency arises from the child's tendency, early on, to evoke and maintain reactions from others with whom they interact. In other words, the temperament is important not only with respect to its influence on a person's own behavior, but in its capacity to influence others to respond, which is another variation on the theme of person–environment relationship and fit.

Studies comparing identical twins reared together and apart, such as one by Plomin, Pedersen, McClearn, Nesselroade, and Bergeman (1988; see also Plomin & Rowe, 1979), have also provided evidence for the heritability of temperament and its consistency over the life-course (see also Goldsmith & Campos, 1986). And Campos, Campos, and Barrett (1989) have reviewed and discussed this kind of stability over time in a special issue of *Developmental Psychology* devoted to emotional development and regulation. They point out that the modern view of emotions as processes that establish, maintain, or disrupt the relationship between the organism and the environment on matters of significance has fostered a new interest in emotion regulation, and stable patterns of irritability and inhibition are important from a developmental perspective (see West & Graziano, 1989, in a special issue of the *Journal of Personality*).

Kagan's Research

For many years Kagan (1989) has been a strong advocate of the role of inherited temperament in development, seeming to adopt a biological trait conception of this influence rather than an interactive one (which requires specifying how the infant's environment operates on what is innately given). Though recognizing that coping may override innate temperamental inclinations, Kagan (1989) seems enthralled by the power of innate temperamental characteristics to influence human adaptation.

The temperamental quality of greatest interest to Kagan and his colleagues is what he refers to as "inhibition." He observes that some 20- to 30-month-old children consistently became quiet, vigilant, and restrained—which Kagan interprets as being inhibited, fearful, and shy—in novel situations such as encounters with unfamiliar children and adults, whereas others constantly acted spontaneously and in an outgoing fashion. About 10 to 15 percent fall into one or another of these extremes. He writes (1989, p. 668) that "It is reasonable to suggest that some of the temperamental differences among children are analogous to the biobehavioral differences among closely related strains of dogs, cats, or monkeys." In one study, which adumbrates this theme of biological genotypes, the most extremely inhibited children even showed a higher proportion of blue eyes whereas the extremely uninhibited children had a higher proportion of brown eyes (Rosenberg & Kagan, 1987). Kagan sees this as support for the temperamental typology he has been studying and its inheritance, because the correlated eye color is clearly a function of genetics.

Much of the research Kagan reports contrasts these two extremes of inhibitedness and outgoingness, observed at 21 months and at 7½ years, with later temperamental style predicted from what was observed at infancy. The use of extremes, and the failure to find similar effects for the great majority of cases in the middle, means that the population about which he can generalize is a very restricted one. Kagan found that these two extreme groups retained the same adaptational profiles over an extended time—helping, he thinks, to support his assumption about genetic origins. Early on, in laboratory measurement situations involving play and interaction with unfamiliar adults and children, or in laboratory situations with strange or ominous toys, some children were quiet, shy, and emotionally subdued even in the presence of their mothers. Other children were spontaneous and outgoing. These two extreme groups showed similar patterns five years later. Inhibited and uninhibited children are shown in Figure 8.4.

Moreover, the physiological response patterns of the two groups seemed to implicate brain centers commonly associated with emotion, such as the limbic system and the hypothalamus. For example, inhibited children had more reactive heart rates, greater motor tension, and higher levels of morning cortisol secretion. There were, in effect, signs of strong sympathetic nervous system activation in these encounters with the environment in response to environmental challenge. For additional studies along these lines, see Davidson and Fox (1989; also Fox, 1989; Kagan, Reznick, & Snidman, 1988; Kagan, Reznick, Snidman, Gibbons, & Johnson, 1988).

Although Kagan emphasizes the continuity of temperament over time, he acknowledges that children also cope with these innate patterns in the course of their

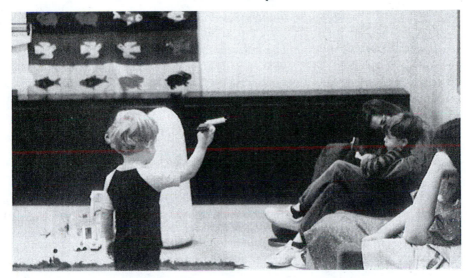

FIGURE 8.4. An inhibited boy and an uninhibited boy. (Courtesy of Professor Jerome Kagan)

development, but he doesn't help us understand how this might work. He writes (Kagan, 1989, pp. 673–674), for example:

> Attributing some of the variation in social behavior to inherited biological processes alters the traditional post-Enlightenment view of our relation to nature. It is difficult to resist the conclusion that temperamentally inhibited five-year-olds are potential victims of circumstances over which they have no control rather than agents who can, at will, alter their behavior toward others. A resolution of this tension is possible if we award to each child's conscious will the power to cope with his or her temperamental bias. I recall an adult subject in the Fels longitudinal study who had been an extremely inhibited boy. He told me that as an adolescent he had been very apprehensive with girls but decided to overcome his fear by inviting the most attractive girl in the class to the senior high school dance. Human behavior is, some of the time, the product of the imposition of deliberative processes on the invisible, uncontrollable forces that both biology and history have created.

It is by no means clear how temperament acts to dispose people to their particular emotional patterns, or what leads them to try to overcome socially undesirable temperamental tendencies. Do inhibited children become fearful or angry adults? Kagan assumes they do, and the research of Caspi et al. (1988, 1989) that I cited earlier suggests he could be right, at least in terms of the probabilities. This is also a position that leads him and his colleagues to dispute the long held view that anxiety in the presence of a stranger, seen typically at around 7 to 10 months of age, is a positive developmental step, an early sign that the infant can distinguish familiar and unfamiliar persons. Kagan assumes that in those children showing such wariness or fear it reflects their inborn temperament more than it does their emotional security as a result of successful or unsuccessful mothering and mother-child bonding.

Rothbart and Derryberry's Research

It might be worthwhile also to cite and illustrate briefly some of the work of Derryberry and Rothbart (e.g., 1984, 1988), which offers considerable contrast with that of Kagan, for example, and those concerned primarily with the genetics of temperament. They have attempted to measure adult individual differences by means of pencil and paper procedures in order to identify the basic factors of temperament by correlational methods. They define temperament (1984, p. 132) as

> Constitutional differences in reactivity and self-regulation, with "constitutional" referring to the relatively enduring biological makeup of the individual, influenced over time by heredity, maturation, and experience. By reactivity we mean the functional state of the somatic, endocrine, autonomic, and central nervous systems as reflected in the response parameters of threshold, latency, intensity, rise time, and recovery time. By self-regulation we mean higher level processes functioning to modulate (enhance or inhibit) the reactive state of these systems.

To this they add (p. 132):

> Self-regulatory processes are best approached in terms of emotions or affective-motivational processes. Indeed, the construct of temperament has traditionally focused upon individual differences in emotionality. When viewed as regulatory, however, affective-motivational processes can be seen to extend beyond the traditional response-oriented domain of emotion, influencing a variety of perceptual and cognitive processes as well. For example, an emotion such as fear regulates somatic, autonomic, and endocrine response systems, while at the same time modulating sensory channels converging upon these response systems. Thus, the regulatory systems of temperament play a high-level role in coordinating attention and response and influence nearly every aspect of experience and behavior.

Derryberry and Rothbart suggest that, although cognition has been treated as primary in controlling lower level emotional processes, these processes do not function in isolation, but develop within physiological contexts established by ongoing moods and acute emotions. The authors also examine theoretically the role of emotion in guiding attention, and the relationship of such sensory regulation to the hierarchical control of the response.

One of the tasks in the study of temperament is to develop a useful set of temperament constructs for measurement. The key problem in defining and measuring temperament is that what is observed behaviorally and physiologically is rarely, if ever, a pure result of biological inheritance but is much influenced by how the environment acts. Therefore, innate tendencies and environmental influences are always confounded to some unknown degree in the measures themselves. The earlier in life one makes the measurements, the less this confounding. These authors also present a set of scales for measuring temperament. I have reproduced their scale constructs in Table 8.1 (pp.322–323) for the purpose of illustration.

The Concept of Goodness of Fit

One reason we should give attention to temperament is that we know that newborns arrive on the scene with markedly different temperaments with which patterns of mothering or, more correctly, parenting, undoubtedly interact. Campos et al. (1983) cite Thomas and Chess's analysis of how temperament might affect the emotional life, which is based on the *goodness of fit* between the infant's temperament and the caregiver's predilections and patterns (see also Lerner & Lerner, 1983). Murphy and her colleagues (e.g., 1962, 1974; Murphy & Moriarty, 1976) observed that some infants are highly excitable and easily overstimulated, while others are phlegmatic and well insulated from stimulation. It is a truism that the former children will probably benefit from styles of parenting that protect their vulnerability to stimulation, while the latter probably need to be prodded to interact with the environment. Murphy provided some evidence that infants' patterns of coping with stimulation—for example, turning away or approaching—potentiate parallel but more complex cognitive and behavioral modes of coping, such as psychological avoidance and denial or confrontational modes in later years.

Consider, for example, a highly activated and irritable child that is vulnerable to stimulation. If the parent is able to protect that child from overexcitement and threatening experiences, the child's attention and ability to learn and to control itself are not as likely to be impaired as if the parent fails to serve as a buffer or even adds to the overstimulation. This kind of child might perhaps be overemotional; whether this would apply equally to all emotions, positive and negative, is not clear.

If, on the other hand, we begin with a lethargic child and the parent ignores it and leaves it to its own dispositions, we might speculate that it will lack the stimulation and richness of environmental experience needed to make full use of its mental capacities, with a result tantamount to inadequacy. If, instead, the parent stimulates the child, the lethargy is apt to be compensated for and there will be a fuller use of its mental capacities.

The same kind of analysis is possible with other temperamental variables—for example, with the severe inhibition or lack of inhibition studied by Kagan. Here, too, a key consideration should be the fit between the child's temperament and the expectations and child-rearing predilections of the parent or caretaker. The inhibited child, presumably fearful in the presence of the unfamiliar, might well be expected to have a low threshhold for experiencing any and all goal incongruent or negative emotions. It may also be protected by parental efforts, so that the withdrawals from the environment are less frequent, severe, or damaging, allowing more exploration of the environment.

Such a child may also develop counterphobic modes of coping to compensate for its fearful inclinations, and may actually develop even greater coping competence and skills than a child that does not have to struggle against its inner constraints; in fact, one of the doctrines of stress theory is that learning to cope depends on having enough stress, not trauma, at the right times in development. The overreactive child may also have to learn ways of dampening or otherwise regulating the autonomic hyperarousal to which it may be vulnerable. Whether this will have an

TABLE 8.1. Definitions of Temperament Scales and Sample Items

Temperament scales	Definitions	Sample items
External sensitivity	The amount of detection or perceptual aware-ness of slight, low-intensity stimulation arising from the external environment	I often notice small changes in the tempera-ture as I enter a room.
Internal sensitivity	The amount of detection or perceptual aware-ness of slight, low-intensity stimulation arising from within the body	I'm rarely aware of the sensations in my stomach.
Cognitive reactivity	The amount of general cognitive activity in which the person engages, including daydream-ing, problem solving, anticipatory cognition, and the ease with which visual imagery or verbal processes are elicited by stimulation	A continuous flow of thoughts and images runs through my head.
Autonomic reactivity	The amount of cardiovascular, electrodermal, gastrointestinal, and respiratory activity elicited under exciting or arousing conditions	My palms usually sweat during an important event.
Motor tension	The amount of tension experienced in various muscle groups throughout the body	My shoulder muscles are usually loose and relaxed.
Motor activation	The extent to which the motor system becomes activated in the form of stereotypical, non-directed actions	I often tap and drum with my hands or feet while reading, writing, or watching TV.
Rising reactivity	The rate at which general arousal rises from its normal to its peak level of intensity	I often find myself becoming suddenly excit-ed about something.
Falling reactivity	The rate at which general arousal decreases from its peak to its normal levels of intensity	I usually fall asleep at night within ten minutes.
Discomfort	The amount of unpleasant affect resulting from the sensory qualities of stimulation, including irritation, pain, and discomfort resulting from the intensity, rate, or complexity of light, movement, sound, and texture	The feeling of rough clothing against my bare skin rarely bothers me.
Fear	The amount of unpleasant affect related to the anticipation of pain or distress, including uneasi-ness, worry, and nervousness related to poten-tially threatening situations	I feel very uncomfortable about having to speak in public.
Frustration	The amount of unpleasant affect related to the interruption of ongoing tasks and behavior or to the blocking of a desired goal	I rarely become annoyed when I have to wait in a slow-moving line.
Sadness	The amount of unpleasant affect and lowered mood related to the exposure to suffering, dis-appointment, and object loss	I seldom become sad when I watch a sad movie.
Low pleasures	The amount of pleasure or enjoyment related to stimuli, activities, or situations involving low stimulus intensity, rate, complexity, nov-elty, and incongruity	Walking barefoot through cool grass gives me great pleasure.
High pleasures	The amount of pleasure or enjoyment related to stimuli, activities, or situations involving high stimulus intensity, rate, complexity, novelty, and incongruity	I would enjoy parachut-ing from an airplane.

TABLE 8.1. (Continued)

Temperament scales	Definitions	Sample items
Relief	The amount of pleasure or enjoyment derived from stimuli or situations involving the attenuation or termination of highly arousing stimulation	I greatly enjoy the relaxed feeling that comes when I no longer have to worry about something.
Attentional focusing	The capacity to intentionally hold the attentional focus on desired channels and thereby resist unintentional shifting to irrelevant or distracting channels	My concentration is easily disrupted if there are people talking in the room around me.
Attentional shifting	The capacity to intentionally shift the attentional focus to desired channels, thereby avoiding unintentional focusing on particular channels	It is usually easy for me to alternate between two different tasks.
Behavioral inhibition	The capacity to suppress positively toned impulses and thereby resist the execution of inappropriate approach tendencies	I can easily resist talking out of turn, even when I'm excited and want to express an idea.
Behavioral activation	The capacity to suppress negatively toned impulses and thereby resist the execution of inappropriate avoidance tendencies	Even when I'm very tired, it is easy for me to get myself out of bed in the morning.

(*Source:* D. Derryberry and M. K. Rothbart, "Arousal, affect, and attention as components of temperament." *Journal of Personality and Social Psychology, 55*, 154–155. Washington, DC: American Psychological Association. Copyright © 1988 by the American Psychological Association. Reprinted by permission.)

effect also on the goal congruent or positive emotions is difficult to foresee. Will such a counterphobic person be able to sustain intimate friendships and love in the face of susceptibility to threat from the outside, or will that person be more wary than others? These are questions that need to be asked and answered if we are to use temperament as a factor in emotional development.

And what about the uninhibited child? Is it reasonable to think of this temperament as an asset or as a liability? Kagan (personal communication) seems to believe that uninhibited children are delightful to other children and adults and hold the world in the palms of their hands, as it were, which would imply the likely development of a rich and adaptive pattern of positive and negative emotions in later life. Some child clinicians, however, think that a child that is too open may get itself into trouble more easily than a child that is appropriately wary. Does the parent of the uninhibited child need to increase the child's wariness so that it does not act too quickly in situations that call for caution, because those situations involve physical or social dangers? If the answer is positive, then such a child might end up more traumatized and threatened in the long run than the child that begins warily.

In this chapter, which has a number of other important agendas, there is no great need to extend this discussion of temperament, to review other theories, or to examine the diverse ways in which temperament has been measured. Campos et al. (1983) have already provided extensive, up-to-date detail on this and should be consulted by the interested reader; they examine many issues, such as measurement, biological influences, continuity over time, and effects on cognition and social inter-action.

Finally, as in the case of theories of infant development, it might be useful to summarize what seems to be a broad consensus on a number of issues concerning temperament and emotion:

1. Temperament is a broader topic than the scope of what we have covered here, going beyond its connections with emotions per se and including activity level and tempo, which are not directly emotional. And yet it also includes individual differences in emotionality and fearfulness — for instance, the proneness to react behaviorally with a smile or to become sad.

2. Temperament has strong biological components, but these are not necessarily genetically given — or more correctly, it needs to be demonstrated for each temperamental variable that it is heritable. There are also some real methodological traps in trying to do this. Using concordance data to explain individual differences in numerous personality variables that look relevant to temperament (e.g., introversion-extroversion), heritability is reported to be roughly 25 percent. However, this percentage is based on the use of pencil and paper tests, and so it is not possible to say whether the variables studied are genetically determined or the result of styles of responding to questionnaires. Thus, the issue of the heritability of temperament remains unsettled.

3. Temperament appears to be quite stable over time, though modifiable. However, a child may be located in a social niche that fails to elicit the temperamental trait.

4. Temperament may be modified when a child develops ways of compensating for temperamental traits; moreover, people with whom the child interacts have an influence, too — another instance of the person–environment relationship. As I noted earlier, temperament does not occur in a vacuum, and its importance in emotional development and adaptation is probably partly a function of the reactions it stimulates in others — for example, the caregivers — so that its role is always transactional. *Goodness of fit* implies that some caregiver-child relationships are adaptive for the child, whereas others may be maladaptive.

Learning and Emotional Development

The sociocultural influences I discuss in Chapter 9 depend to a great extent on learning, and as we move from infancy to childhood and adulthood, the primary mechanism of learning shifts from the relatively elemental and concrete (e.g., classical and operant conditioning) to mechanisms that depend more on abstract intelligence and symbolic meanings. Confronted with an adaptational encounter involving social pressures, the significance of what is being communicated socially (knowledge) for personal well-being must be grasped (primary appraisal) as well as the possibilities available for coping (secondary appraisal), which in turn depend on goal hierarchies and belief systems acquired during development. We refer globally to individual differences in what is acquired as personality.

More than any other social science, psychology has had a sustained interest in social learning and personality development. When, for example, a psychotherapist deals with a client with a dysfunctional emotional pattern, the treatment is basically an effort to get that client to unlearn an inadequate pattern of appraisal and coping, and to acquire a new pattern that will be more serviceable. Similarly, education, child-rearing, the prevention of psychopathology, and the promotion of emotional health are also based in large measure on how we understand the learning process.

When all is said and done, learning is crucial to the emotion process. Nevertheless, this is not the place to do more than to touch on the main themes of the psychology of learning as it might apply to the emotion process. My account must be very general because research attention has hitherto not been directed at the mediating processes of appraisal and coping or at the role of motives and beliefs in emotion. To connect learning with emotional development requires large inferential leaps. To make the discussion of learning, which may seem dated and not very compelling now, reasonably current and to connect it with research on emotion, I cite some recent studies that draw on the different mechanisms of learning.

Four main mechanisms of learning have been emphasized in psychology— namely, associative (reinforcement) learning, imitation and identification, role taking, and the search for meaning and ego-identity. All play a role in the emotion process. Because of their specialized education, psychologists are more or less familiar with much I will say here. However, I review these mechanisms briefly for those who are not as familiar with them, and for psychologists who have forgotten.

Associative (Reinforcement) Learning

The oldest tradition in learning theory is based on the principle that an individual's psychological structure, which organizes actions and reactions, is acquired as a result of associations or connections made between stimuli and responses, which are "stamped in" as a result of rewards and punishments. In contrast with the simple association of two ideas—for example, a stimulus and a response—the more cognitive and modern version is that of *learned expectation* in which one idea becomes a signal or sign for another and evokes it.

Expectation, which is dependent on feedback from the environment, makes comprehensible the natural selection of organisms and their adaptational patterns. This feedback teaches us how to survive or flourish and contributes to the establishment of a personality. For example, when a child engages in behavior that is rewarded by the parents, or when an emotion is followed by positive and negative consequences, these behaviors and attitudes are apt to become habitual responses in similar contexts. Reward and punishment connect learning theory to emotional development in part by tying learning to pain and pleasure, and to contingencies in the world with negative and positive consequences, which in turn contribute to the learning of social motives.

At the turn of the century, conditioning and reinforcement became the dominant principles of learning by association. The origin of *classical conditioning* is found in the famous experiments of the Russian physiologist Ivan Pavlov (1849-1936). Pavlov, you will remember, placed dogs in a harness to study the neural reflexes involved in salivation and digestion. He noticed that the flow of saliva was influenced not only by food placed in the dog's mouth but also merely by the sight of food. The dog's salivary response, which is innate, became conditioned, as Pavlov put it, to a tone that had become connected or associated with the food and eating; prior to this learning, the tone would not have resulted in salivation, and only the presence of food would. And so Pavlov, a physiologist, became one of the most influential psychologists in the world because he had inadvertently discovered a psychological principle of great importance.

In classical conditioning, there has to be an unconditioned stimulus (in this case, food) that innately and without learning produces the unconditioned response (in this case, salivation). The conditioned stimulus (e.g., a light, tone, or noise) must be paired on numerous occasions with an unconditioned stimulus and response (food and salivation) in order for the light or tone, say, to become a signal to the animal of the upcoming opportunity to eat. The appearance of the food is said to be the reinforcement for the expectation of food that has been generated by the conditioned stimulus. In the course of experience, additional stimuli, some similar to the original and others that may have been present during the learning process, will also become conditioned to the same response. Conditioning is selective, however, and with experience the animal ultimately comes to discriminate the relevant from the irrelevant.

Many psychologists regard this as a prime mechanism for the acquisition of fear and other emotions, based in part on Watson and Rayner's (1920) account of Little Albert and his conditioned fear of white rabbits and other furry white animals (see also Jones, 1924). Classical conditioning arrangements of the relevant variables have been drawn upon by many behavior therapists — for example, Wolpe (1958) — in the treatment of "conditioned" fears. As will be noted in Chapter 11, diverse strategies have been created to produce *deconditioning,* and theories about how this works have also been promulgated, many of which now emphasize the cognitive processes that presumably take place in the client's mind (see also Garfield & Bergin, 1978; A. Lazarus, 1971; Marks, 1977, 1978; Rachman, 1976, 1978; Rachman & Hodgson,1974, 1980).

There has traditionally been a close liaison between conditioning and animal research, but in the area of emotions — for example, the development of fears (phobias) — animal research on experimental neuroses has not served as a good model, because investigators have not documented similarities in the emotional patterns between animals and people. A recent analytic review by Mineka (1985) attempted to overcome this and to link this research with therapeutic models, thereby also providing a good account of the classical conditioning approach to phobias and other forms of pathology.

A *phobia* is defined by Mineka as a persistent and recognizably irrational fear of an object or situation, along with a compelling desire to avoid that object or situation and the significant distress it produces. Considerable research has been done showing that monkeys learn to fear certain objects through classical conditioning paradigms. When the conditioned stimulus consists of objects such as snakes and spiders in contrast with electric outlets and stoves, the former activating innate fear tendencies, conditioned fears seem to be more easily learned and very hard to extinguish or decondition. Snakes and spiders were probably dangerous and threatening to our evolutionary ancestors and so in evolution have generated an innate disposition toward fear, or what has come to be called "prepared" conditioning. I quote from Mineka's (1985, p. 242) conclusions:

There is a great deal of animal research that has illuminated important features of [anxiety] disorders and had a meaningful impact on theories of their origin and the variables that maintain them. It seems that the major reasons for dissatisfaction with conditioning models in the past have been that they have been too simplistic . . . none of the anxiety disorders can generally be thought to originate from a single or even a few trials of classical fear conditioning or avoidance learning occurring in a vacuum, as has often been proposed in the past. Instead, there appear to be a multitude of experiential variables that can occur prior to, during, or following a conditioning experience, that affect the amount of fear that is experienced, conditioned, and maintained over time. . . . For example, early experience with control and mastery can reduce the level of fear that is experienced in several different fear-provoking situations later in an infant monkey's life . . . the dynamics of fear conditioning are powerfully influenced by the controllability and predictability of the US. . . . Thus, it is only with an acknowledgment of this kind of complexity that conditioning models will continue to prosper and maintain their usefulness in the future.

Be that as it may, the discovery of classical conditioning was a momentous one because it provided a way to study learning in all animals, including humans. For many learning psychologists (cf. Rescorla, 1988), such conditioning is *the* mechanism on which all learning rests, even the most complex forms of learning in higher mammals. It is possible to regard the process of conditioning as the most elementary basis of learning, and to identify it especially with automatic, unconscious, or preconscious appraising (see also Chapter 4). My own predilection is to say that classical conditioning is one of several forms of learning. Basically, conditioning is not so much a theory of learning — the process can be interpreted in many different ways — as it is a systematic arrangement of the basic variables and processes that govern learning.

Another important arrangement of variables resulting in learning was described later by B. F. Skinner (1938, 1971) and referred to as *"operant conditioning"* (often called "instrumental conditioning"). When you teach a dog to obey commands such as "stay" or "come" you are using operant conditioning. Unlike classical conditioning, in which there is a natural, biological basis for the response to the stimulus (food automatically triggers salivation; an emotional experience automatically produces hormone secretions), when a dog is trained to come on command, the animal must have first made the response by disposition or accident before it can be gotten to do it on signal or command, because there is no reliable stimulus to which the response is attached biologically. The operant response is something the animal can do naturally and does often. If you want it to be elicited by your signal, the dog must come for other reasons before it can be taught to do it when you want it to.

When the desired act is made and often rewarded, the dog will learn to repeat it habitually on signal. It is as if the dog has learned the expectation that doing the act leads to reward. From the standpoint of operant conditioning, we react with fear or anger because we have learned in some specific context that certain rewarding or punishing consequences follow from what we have done. If you want to get rid of an unwanted emotional response to certain eliciting conditions, which came about through conditioning, you must unlearn the expectation that leads to the emotion by the reverse of conditioning, in effect, discovering that the punishing consequence

does not follow your actions or reactions, and perhaps, too, that a rewarding consequence may occur instead.

Operant conditioning has been used as a method of revealing something about
the conditions of emotional development. For example, a fascinating brief research
report in *Science* by DeCasper and Fifer (1980) used it to study the early bonding of
mother and infant. The newborn was allowed to suck on a nonnutritive nipple; the
baby could produce either the mother's voice or an unrelated woman's voice by
varying its rate of sucking. As early as 3 days of age, the neonate was found to have
a preference for the maternal voice, because it quickly began to adjust its rate of
sucking, which increased the time the mother's voice was heard. The mother's voice
was a powerful reinforcer, showing that there is bonding of the infant to the mother
in first few days after birth, or perhaps even in the prenatal period.

This kind of experimental observation suggests the importance in emotional
development of what is happening in the earliest developmental periods, a time of
learning that many interested in emotional development who were concerned with
cognitive factors might easily ignore or downplay. It also reinforces the judgment
that, even in the earliest days of life, not only hedonic factors (pleasure) are rein-
forcers but merely the sensing of familiarity; the mother's voice alone has become a
positive feature of the child's life.

Sullivan and Lewis (1989), too, have used instrumental conditioning (they refer
to it as contingency learning) as a method for studying emotional development. In
their procedure, infants use an arm pull to produce a reinforcing slide of an infant's
smiling face which pops up in front of the infant being studied; the slide is accompanied by children's voices singing the television *Sesame Street* theme song. An
experimental group had control over the result, the so-called contingency condition,
and a comparison group experienced no contingency between the arm-pull activity
and the appearance of the slide and singing. The two groups were matched with
respect to the frequency with which they were rewarded, one for its action and the
other not. The measured effect consisted of facial expressions of emotions scored by
Izard's coding procedures.

Their findings confirm the idea that positive emotional expressions—such as
excitement, interest, surprise, and enjoyment—are associated with mastery or control over the environment, because these emotions increased under the contingency
condition when the baby was able to generate the appearance of the slide and the
singing by its own actions. However, negative emotional expressions—such as sadness, anger, fear, and fussing—were not different under the control and contingency
conditions. They occurred during the final minute of the session and might well
have been related to what was happening within these conditions; perhaps, for
example, the sudden onset of the stimuli, which had a prominent auditory component, itself could have produced some negative reactions. I cite this research mainly
to indicate use of an interesting operant conditioning methodology for studying
learning and emotion in preverbal infants.

What happened in psychology with the change to a cognitive emphasis around
the 1970s, which is illustrated in the concept of appraisal, is not that the pairing of
stimulus and response with rewards and punishments in the fashion of classical or
operant conditioning came to be considered an incorrect description of the learning

process, but rather that this pairing was now said to produce an *expectation* of reward or punishment on the part of the person or animal. It is this expectation that is said to make associative learning under reinforcement work. Expectation is a cognitive concept that refers to what is going on in the mind. For the cognitive psychologist, conditioning is best understood in terms of events such as expectation, knowledge, and appraisal in the mind of the individual.

Actually, for Pavlov and most early learning theorists, conditioning had to do with the formation of expectations, but behaviorists later removed the cognitive component from accounts of conditioning — in a sense, Watson and Skinner de-cognized conditioning. So one could say that we have now returned to what was the original view.

Be that as it may, this modern change in what had become the dominant emphasis was heralded, in part, by the work of Edward Tolman (1948), who thought of learning, even in relatively simple animals such as rats, but certainly in humans, as involving a cognitive map or representation of a situation. It was also heralded by the phenomenologists (many of whom I listed in Chapters 1 and 4), who were not particularly interested in learning per se but represented an advance guard for a cognitive-phenomenological and motivational viewpoint in the 1930s.

Cognitivists think that people develop action-consequence contingencies in their minds, whether these are accurate or inaccurate. In a sense, what we learn are *meanings* rather than merely *associations* among events. If we believe fallaciously that some action will lead to reward or punishment, and never catch on to our misapprehension, then we will probably continue to perform that action, and it will not be eliminated. To put it another way, the process of conditioning, and what is going on psychologically during the process, is considerably more complicated than was originally assumed (cf. Rescorla, 1988).

Moreover, with respect to the emotion process, these meanings can be fruitfully characterized by the six appraisal components used earlier to explain and predict the individual emotions. These are, in effect, what is learned that results in the emotions. Thus, via classical and operant conditioning, we can learn to have certain goals and not others, discover the contingent conditions between such goals and harm or loss and benefits, develop concepts of blame and credit, the options for coping, and the conditions on which future expectations of diverse kinds rest.

The incompleteness of models of learning based on simple conditioning has been pointed out in many ways — for example, by the frequent observation that punishment fails to control delinquent behavior in children and adolescents. Very often the parent who severely and consistently punishes the child for aggressive, antisocial acts succeeds only in fixing and even encouraging such acts rather than eliminating them. This must mean that other expectations or meanings, which the psychologist must understand in order to account for the seemingly paradoxical reaction, have been generated.

For example, parents of delinquents and criminals are likely to have been punitive, physically cruel, and rejecting in their treatment of their children (cf. Glueck & Glueck, 1950; McCord & McCord, 1956, 1958). Children then evidently cease to be impressed by punishment, and the motivation to comply with parental pressure is undermined when there is nothing the child can do to please the parent. There are also aberrant developmental phenomena such as masochism, in which sexual arousal depends on, or is at least facilitated by, physical or psychological punishment. The line between pleasure and pain, and hence between reward and punishment, is more difficult to draw than has often been supposed. We are led to search for other principles that can do a more thorough job of helping us understand the mechanisms of acquisition and change in personality over the life-course, that are relevant to emotional development and experiences. Examples of such other principles include the second mechanism of learning, imitation, and identification.

Imitation (Observational Learning) and Identification

Punishment often fails because different, sometimes contradictory processes like imitation and identification may be at work simultaneously. For example, when children observe their parents punishing them for their aggressiveness, or whatever, the parents are also providing a model that the children imitate and identify with. As Brown (1965, pp. 394–395) put it so clearly:

> Parents who beat their children for aggression intend to "stamp out" the aggression. The fact that the treatment does not work as intended suggests that the . . . theory is wrong. A beating may be regarded as an instance of the behavior it is supposed to stamp out. If children are more disposed to learn by imitation or example than by "stamping out" they ought to learn from a beating to beat. This seems to be roughly what happens.

The difference between imitation and identification should be clarified. Actions that are superficially in conformity with the way a model acts, and with social pressures, are closer to what is meant by imitation. We watch someone else and do what we observe them doing. However, ways of thinking, acting, and feeling that begin as imitation may ultimately become an integral part of the child's personality by the process of identification, internalization, or introjection, all these terms being more or less synonyms for a common process. Imitation does not connote the internalization of social patterns, whereas identification does.

On this point, Kelman (1961) has suggested that socialization can involve various degrees of involvement — from mere *imitative compliance,* which is the superficial adoption of an outlook for the purpose of creating an impression (cf., Goffman, 1959, 1971), to full *internalization,* which is a relatively permanent, often unconscious, personality acquisition. In compliance, we do or say what is expected of us only because we think it will impress others and make them respond to us positively. This is often sensed as a dishonest act, yet it is embedded so firmly in the fabric of our social lives that it usually takes place with little or no conflict or distress, and perhaps even without much awareness (see also D'Andrade, 1984, discussed in Chapter 9).

At the other end of the continuum is complete internalization or identification. In this form of socialization, ways of thinking, feeling, and acting are not "skin deep" but have become an integral part of our personal outlook. The most important processes of internalization probably occur quite early in life and are resistant to change even when rejected on the surface. In all likelihood, our emotions are based more on internalized values and beliefs than on superficial compliance, and insight about their source within us is often difficult to achieve, because we cannot always be clear about which set of rules we are obeying.

Because imitation and identification shape our thoughts, feelings, and actions, often without our being aware of it, psychologists and educators have long distinguished between formal and informal education. *Formal education* is illustrated by teaching at school and by what parents tell children about how they *should* think, feel, and act. However, children also learn by *informal* modeling. Internalization more often occurs through these informal learning experiences, and what is internalized can contradict what is learned from formal education, which often produces superficial compliance. Internalizing an injunction appears to be a more complex task than merely complying with one. We engage in much lip service about the injunctions we are formally taught; this is after all what we mean by hypocrisy.

One developmental implication of this is the unresolved question of when a child is capable of acting out of compliance as opposed to internalization in ways that bear on both the provocation of an emotion or its social regulation. Another developmental implication is that it would be valuable to know when a child can differentiate between compliance with pressure to act or react in a particular way and personal conviction, and how this knowledge influences its emotional life.

Psychologists have struggled to discover the principles whereby parents and others become models for children to imitate and identify with. Imitation and identification are not indiscriminate processes; a child does not automatically pick up any parental characteristic by a kind of osmosis. Parents can see that their children have acquired some of their psychological traits but not others; some come from the mother, some from the father, still others from adults within and outside the family who have also served as models, and some seem unique and self-generated. Why has the child picked up some traits — probably including emotional traits — and not others from various persons used as models, and why do some persons serve as models and others not? The question is very important, and the answer is still fragmentary.

One theory, psychoanalytic in origin, points to obvious similarities between the child and the parent. For example, Freud assumed that sexual identification took place because the boy sees himself physically as like his father, and the girl sees herself as like her mother. A second theory, also psychoanalytic, emphasizes the need of the relatively powerless child to neutralize the threat imposed by the powerful parent or parent-substitute by identifying with and imitating the parent, a process Freud called "identification with the aggressor." The young boy comes to identify with the father by attempting to deal with the Oedipus conflict and the castration threat generated by hostile, competitive struggles with the father. Because the father is too powerful to deal with effectively, an adaptive solution is to join forces with him and to neutralize the danger, and in so doing to banish or hold in control the child's wish to have his mother for himself. A third theory, favored by social learning theorists, emphasizes the parent's power to control the good things of life (Bandura, Ross, & Ross, 1963; Bandura & Walters, 1963; see also Bandura, 1977a, 1977b). Other things being equal, the child imitates the parent who is most capable of creating desirable outcomes; it follows that the child will want to be like him or her to achieve this mastery over the environment.

Though classical conditioning was, for a time, the primary model of emotional learning, it has been argued by Bandura (1989) and others that what is sometimes called vicarious classical conditioning or *observational learning* may account for a higher proportion of fears and phobias than classical conditioning. Regrettably, if we exclude the learning of coping, the observational learning of emotional patterns, which overlaps with imitation, has not been much studied in humans as far as I know, partly for methodological reasons and partly because Bandura's work and similar research took place before interest in the emotions had been rekindled.

There is, however, some research with monkeys on this question, which was carried out by Mineka, Davidson, Cook, and Keir (1984). In an observational learning experiment, Mineka et al. produced fear of snakes in monkeys that had not previously displayed it by having them watch other monkeys display such a fear (see also Cook, Mineka, Wolkenstein, & Laitsch, 1985). To test for the fear, the task involved reaching over a box in which there was a live snake, a toy one, or a model of one. Adolescent rhesus monkeys acquired an intense and persistent fear of snakes merely by observing other monkeys behaving fearfully in the presence of the snake. This fear was not specific to one context and showed no evidence of lessening in a three-month follow up.

Now if we combine what Mineka (1985) said about *prepared conditioning*, which I discussed earlier, with this experimental observational learning procedure, we can examine her evidence for the idea that monkeys can learn fear quickly and perhaps permanently to objects where there is a species readiness to react with fear, such as a snake, by observing another monkey displaying fear to these objects; however, they will not learn fear to objects where there is no such readiness or genetic preparedness, such as a flower.

This was shown by the ingenious method of cutting and splicing films of monkeys showing fear so that it appears as though they are reacting with fear when confronting a real or toy snake or a flower. Monkeys raised in the laboratory that had not acquired such fear, as evidenced in the test situation of having to reach across a snake to get food, after watching the film of fearful monkeys in the same situation on 12 occasions, became afraid of the snake, but did not become afraid of the flower even though they had watched a filmed monkey showing fear to the flower. This observationally learned fear of a snake also was difficult to extinguish.

Clearly, modeling, or imitation and identification, is a powerful way to learn fear, and presumably other emotions. In addition, a study by Hornik, Risenhoover, and Gunnar (1987) on observational learning in human infants, though less precise in the experimental controls that could be used, has also demonstrated that 12-month-olds responded to signals of fear and disgust from their mothers displayed in as brief a period as 30 minutes, and that the fear-inducing effects of these social signals were retained beyond the period of the signals. And so we have good reason to believe that what may be observed in monkeys as imitation, often labeled nowadays as observational learning or social referencing, has a strong counterpart in human infants as well.

Thus, it is feasible that through such a learning mechanism we can acquire the bases on which the six appraisal components will operate in any transaction. For example, we can learn which goals we should be committed to by observing other significant persons, how to evaluate frustration or positive experiences relevant to them, how to evaluate blame and credit, coping potential, and future expectations. This brings us to the third learning mechanism, the playing of social roles.

The Playing of Social Roles

Although conventional wisdom suggests that personal outlooks generate or influence actions, there is abundant evidence that the opposite is also true — namely, that behavior to which we have become committed influences outlooks and values. Lieberman (1956) has shown, for example, that the attitudes of factory workers changed sharply when they were either promoted to the role of foreman or elected to the position of union steward. Those who were made union stewards became more prounion, while those who became foremen shifted in favor of management. Later, however, when economic conditions forced some of the foremen to go back to the rank and file, their outlooks reverted. In short, changes in behavior or, more strictly speaking, in the social roles people play, seem to result in changes in outlook. It is difficult to know, however, whether what was displayed by these workers was superficial compliance or internalized value commitments resulting from their changing work roles. The ease with which the changes occurred suggests perhaps the former.

There have been many observations of this kind of process, influenced by the work of Leon Festinger. Typical was a field experiment at Yale University performed by Cohen (see Brehm & Cohen, 1962) following a student riot in the turbulent 1960s in which the New Haven police intervened, leading to accusations of police brutality and highly emotional and bitter feelings on the part of most of the student body. Cohen selected students at random and asked them to write a convincing essay titled "Why the New Haven Police Actions Were Justified," thus forcing them to argue in favor of the police when their own views had been hostile to the police. Some of the students were offered ten dollars to write the essay, some five dollars, others one dollar, and still others fifty cents. Having written the essay, each student was also asked to indicate his actual opinion of the police actions, and the opinion of a comparison group that had not written the essay was also obtained in the same way.

Cohen found that there was no difference in attitude between students who were paid either five or ten dollars for writing the essay; both groups still considered the police actions very unjustified. However, students who had been paid one dollar became significantly more favorable to the police actions following writing their essays, and those paid only fifty cents were even more so. In short, the less they were paid, the more they changed in the positive direction.

The usual explanation of this type of finding emphasizes the need to justify writing the favorable essay. Although emotions were not directly studied, the need to justify implies a way of coping with the threat of loss of social and self-esteem and the emotional distress it would cause. If you have been paid handsomely, there is no problem to resolve, because you can easily attribute your stance to the money you

have received rather than to a favorable attitude. It's similar to doing a positive commercial on television for which you have been well paid. If, on the other hand, you
have been paid very little, then to go on record in favor of the police must be justified in some other way, because otherwise it seems to reflect on your actual feelings
in the matter or makes you appear rather foolish. By admitting a moderately favorable attitude, you justify or rationalize your willingness to write favorably. This
explanation, however, is not so much about playing roles as about how to rationalize
one's conduct when it seems to deviate from one's beliefs.

Another possibility, however, one that is more in keeping with role playing is
that when you take the role of an adversary, you marshall arguments in favor of the
other person and come to think about things differently, producing perhaps a real
shift in attitude (see Janis, 1968). In the experiment by Cohen, the students had to
take the role of the police to write a justification, and it might be argued that doing
so helped them see the police side of the controversy. This kind of explanation is
consistent with the therapeutic use of role playing as a way to help a person understand the outlook of another person—for example, a spouse in a divorce action. If
you can really come to see it from the other's standpoint, you are likely to be less
hostile and oppositional, and might even change your position altogether. Role playing is also a useful way of practicing what you want to do expertly—handling
stressful encounters with difficult others or managing distressing emotions, for
instance.

A corollary of this idea has important developmental implications. It is that the
positions we have in society and the roles we play at work and in the family have a
powerful effect on the way we think, feel, and act as we grow up. Harkness and
Super (1985) use the term *developmental niche* to refer to the physical settings in
which a child lives, including daily routines, activities, the company of others, the
culturally regulated conditions of child care and rearing, and the psychology of the
caretakers. For example, mothers react differently to the emotional expressions of
their children, especially negative emotions; some find spontaneity desirable, whereas others favor discipline and self-control (Malatesta & Haviland, 1985). Presumably, these different parental attitudes toward emotional expression shape children's
social handling of emotional reactions, and perhaps even their emotional experiences.

A problem with this analysis is that Harkness and Super have offered a purely
environmental approach to the developmental niche in which the child grows up. A
more transactional version of this idea is that young children who grow up in families with older siblings must actively establish niches for themselves in the family—
for example, as the bright and promising child, the obedient or disobedient child,
father's or mother's little helper, the surrogate father or mother, or the helpless
child. In the course of doing so, they leave less room for later children to occupy this
niche, and those who follow must develop other social patterns. The niche they
establish, with its social roles, has important consequences for the development of
lifelong emotional patterns. This transactional version of the developmental niche is
analogous to the ecological niche that diverse animal species establish in making a
livelihood for themselves in the world.

And as with the other mechanisms of learning, playing social roles contributes to the six appraisal components of the theory, both those concerned with goals and those related to frustration, blame and credit, coping potential, and future expectations. For example, the experience of being blamed provides object lessons when it happens again or when we want to blame another, and similarly for the appraisal of credit for a positive accomplishment. Thus, when we have been attacked for taking credit by someone who is offended by it, or when we have done the same to another, there is an opportunity via role playing and empathy to acquire sensitivity to others and ourselves, which might alter the way we react emotionally in similar future situations.

The Search for Meaning and an Ego-Identity

The chief limitation of the three mechanisms of learning described so far is that, with the possible exception of some versions of imitation and identification, they imply a passive person, shaped by external rewards and punishments, imitating or identifying with what is seen in parents and other models, and engaging in actions influenced largely by the social roles he or she is given or permitted. An alternative, or perhaps supplemental, view is that very early in life a child begins to develop a sense of individual identity, actively searching for meaning (cf. Frankl, 1959), struggling to create workable and consistent schemata with which to understand who and what one is in the world. I have already considered theories of emotional development that draw on this idea. This is the last and most complicated mechanism of learning, which I have called the search for meaning and an ego-identity (see also the motivational principle in Chapter 3).

The essential theme here is that, as individuals struggle to fashion their views of themselves and the world in which they live, they evolve a self-consistent, integrated system of motives, beliefs, and scripts or story lines, which are serviceable in directing their lives and dealing with the conditions of life that are encountered. When people fail in this developmental task, they experience confusion, tension, and distress akin to that of Biff in Arthur Miller's play *Death of a Salesman*. Biff, the favorite son, is unable to evolve a workable idea of who he is in the context of the external world to a large extent because his father has created an unrealistic and heroic mythology about him. The source of his emotional distress is a conflict between the expectations of others, in Biff's case those of his father (and of himself as well), and the reality of his actual social identity. As will be seen in Chapter 11, this is a potent kind of existential malaise for which people seek professional help.

Meaning and identity, once found (or rather, created or adopted), can also be lost, or threatened with loss, which could have profound emotional significance. Remember, for example, my treatment of anxiety as the threat of such loss in Chapter 6, and the potential for despair when the threat has been realized. It would not be fruitful here for me to examine closely the overlaps and possible distinctions among three concepts that tend to used interchangeably—the self, ego, and identity (see, for example, Lapsley & Power, 1988; and a review of this book by Klein, 1990).

Loevinger (1976) has long been one of the most influential theorists on ego development. Though her work does not center on the role of the ego in emotion, she has provided an analysis of her own and a scholarly review of other such theories, including Erikson's, whose name is almost synonymous with the concept of ego-identity. My discussion of the search for meaning and ego-identity would not be complete without presenting a table from Loevinger (1976, pp. 77, 92), which portrays ego stages and types proposed by a number of writers alongside the ego levels of her own system. Table 8.2 does this for writers such as Ferenczi (1913), Erikson (1950), Ausubel (1955), Fromm (1941), Riesman (1950), and Graves (1966).

Early on, psychological development involves gaining gradual freedom from concrete environmental stimuli and from the tyranny of drives or impulses. As chil-

TABLE 8.2a. Ego Stages of Ferenczi, Erikson, and Ausubel

Approximate Ego Level	Author		
	Ferenczi (1913)	Erickson (1950)	Ausubel (1952)
Autistic	Magical-hallucinatory omnipotence	Trust	
Symbiotic	Omnipotence by magic gestures Animism	vs. mistrust	Ego omnipotence
Impulsive	Magic words and thoughts		Crisis of ego devaluation
Self-Protective		Autonomy vs. shame and doubt	Beginning of satellization
Conformist		Initiative vs. guilt Industry vs. inferiority	Satellization
Conscientious-Conformist			Crisis of desatellization
Conscientious		Identity vs. role diffusion	Desatellization
Individualistic		Intimacy vs. isolation	
Autonomous		Generativity vs. stagnation Ego integrity vs. despair	

(*Source:* J. Loevinger, *Ego Development.* San Francisco: Jossey-Bass, 1976. Reprinted by permission.)

TABLE 8.2b. Ego Types of Fromm, Riesman, and Graves

Approximate Ego Level	Author		
	Fromm (1941)	Riesman (1950)	Graves (1966)
Autistic			Autistic behavior
Symbiotic	Symbiosis		
Impulsive		Anomy	Animistic existence
Self-Protective		Tradition-directed conformity	Awakening and fright Aggression and power
Conformist	Conformity	Other-directed conformity	Sociocentric attitudes
Conscientious		Inner-directed conformity	Aggressive individualism
Individualistic	Autonomy		Pacific individualism
Autonomous		Autonomy	

(*Source:* J. Loevinger, *Ego Development.* San Francisco: Jossey-Bass, 1976. Reprinted by permission.)

dren mature, they become increasingly capable of manipulating objects and events symbolically, becoming free of concrete dependency on them. Piaget (1952) spoke of the development of intelligence as always moving toward increased spatial and temporal distance between the person and the environment. And although young children cannot inhibit impulse expression very well, in the course of development they increasingly become capable of interposing thought between impulse and action, which allows them to delay action and attune it to the requirements of the situation (cf. Werner, 1948). This permits them to have more control over their choices and the direction of their lives, and to coordinate their internal psychological makeup with their external environment (see also Chapter 4 for an alternative life-course view).

Later development brings with it increasing integration of the constructs of the mind. Cognition, emotion, and motivation become welded into a system that, though often under tension, remains in touch with the environment and in control of actions. The connections among action and the demands, constraints, and resources of the environment, as well as among cognition, emotion, and motivation, are forged and changed dialectically by continuous adaptational transactions with the environment. Block (1982) has pointed out that this movement toward integration is not smooth but involves periodic crises and transitions in which the established psychological structure, when no longer viable, requires reorganization to work better or at all. Fischer and Pipp (1984, p. 89), too, have emphasized the need, as well as the difficulty, of maintaining integrity:

> With development, the capacity for integrating components of thought and behavior grows, and at the same time the capacity for active fractionation increases (e.g., dissociation and repression). The mind is therefore both fractionated and integrated; there is neither a unitary conscious system nor a unitary unconscious one, but there are conscious and unconscious components that can be coordinated or kept separate.

People may seek disconnection when threatened, as in their use of denial and of distancing from sources of their emotional distress. However, when disconnection occurs among the components of mind and between the mind and the environment, there are contradictory thoughts, feelings, and actions, and action is inconsistent and disorganized. What a person thinks may be out of touch with the emotions that are experienced or the motives that shape action. This must mean that this person is being governed by one set of thoughts that are unconscious, but there is a conscious set of thoughts, which are different. The person does not feel like doing what intellectually he or she thinks should be done; or the person says, "I made myself do it." As Epstein (1984; 1990) suggests, an overall self attempts to integrate various subidentities, but when there is complete insulation among the subsystems, there is psychopathology. Schwartz (1979) seems to mean something similar by his use of the term *disregulation* to refer to the loss of communication among the parts of the brain, which allows the normally integrated system of feedback loops to go out of control.

For optimal functioning and mental health there must be integration and harmony among the components of the mind (Lazarus, 1989c) — namely, motivation, thought, and emotion — and between the mind and the environment, and the mind and action. Disconnection among them puts the person at risk for psychopathology, which involves, among other things, recurrent or chronic emotional distress and dysfunction.

What I have said earlier about integration and disconnection has a close parallel with the organization of an ego-identity, the term I prefer, which is of the utmost importance in emotional experience. The reader might also want to see Higgins (1987) on self-discrepancy theory, which is a broad — I believe too broad — system for relating different types of negative psychological situations (because they are self-discrepant) to different kinds of emotional discomfort (such as sadness and fear). In some ways, this line of thought has some superficial parallels with cognitive-motivational-relational theories such as mine. Andrews (1989b) has also presented what he calls a self-confirmation model for depression and its treatment, which is clearly relevant to cognitive-motivational-relational theories of emotion.

Finally, I noted in Chapter 3 that motivation and cognition in emotion overlap with the concept of self or ego-identity, and relate to emotion because it is what happens to one's commitments that affects emotion. Therefore, development of an ego-identity and its role in emotion are important issues for emotional development. Another way of thinking of identity in the emotion process is to evaluate for any individual the values and commitments that are central and those that are peripheral, because it is the central ones that will lie at the heart of the strongest and most pervasive emotions (cf. Gruen, Folkman, & Lazarus, 1989).

Alongside a concern about the development of ego-identity, and its role in the appraisals connected with the emotions, should be a parallel concern for the coping process, including the defense mechanisms, which should also be relevant to emotional development. The developmental aspects of coping and defense have not generated much interest. I think the main reason is that psychologists have not seen that the coping process, which came into being as an important idea in the context of psychological stress, also applies to the emotions. As I noted in Chapter 3, coping is not only a response to emotion and a means of regulating it, it also changes the subsequent emotional state by changing either the actual person–environment relationship or how that relationship is attended to and interpreted (see Folkman & Lazarus, 1988). In other words, coping is truly central to the emotion process, and to understand this process requires that we study it along with appraisal and explore its development.

The initial theory of defense goes back to Freudian thought (cf. Cramer, 1987; Lazarus, 1983; Sjöbäck, 1973), but empirical study of the development of defenses is rare and can be illustrated by a few early studies reported by Miller and Swanson (1960), and a later major longtitudinal study by Vaillant (1977). Swanson (1988) has recently focused on the family and social structure in the development of defense, but it is too early to know whether this will prompt additional investigation.

The lessons here for the six appraisal components should also be clear. A vulnerable ego-identity will influence our reactions to frustration, as I indicated in Chapter 6, so that, for example, we may be more prone to take offense and hence react with anger than someone who has a firmer identity, to defensively project the blame that should be laid on our doorstep, to anticipate the failure to bring effective coping resources to encounters that are very demanding, and hence to be more pessimistic about the outcome. From the theoretical perspective adopted in this book, all mechanisms of learning have their consequences for the emotions as states and traits by virtue of how they influence these appraisal components.

Multiple Mechanisms of Learning and Social Influence

The four mechanisms examined thus far have been ordered from potentially the simplest to the most complex. Simpler animals cannot search for meaning and identity, but they can learn via classical and operant conditioning. And when conditioning occurs in intact human adults, it often depends on elaborate cognitive processes as well as the simplest ones.

Therefore, we should recognize that in psychological development the processes of learning, and the sociocultural influences on emotion, probably depend on many different mechanisms operating at the same time at different levels of complexity, from the simplest and most concrete to the most complex and abstract. The cognitive processes involved in the search for meaning are clearly complex, abstract, and symbolic; however, when modeling or classical conditioning are in focus, the cognitive processes are apt to be simpler and more concrete, corresponding to what I have referred to in Chapter 4 as automatic processing.

One of the problems in thinking about personality and emotional development has been the tendency to use the simplest level of explanation to account for the most complex and abstract levels of functioning, as when conditioning becomes the explanation for all learning. In the very young child, who has little or no self-awareness and limited cognitive resources, the learning process is apt to be relatively simple and automatic, whereas in a more mature child or adult, more advanced kinds of learning are apt to be involved.

The problem takes the reverse form when the focus is on adults instead of young children. We tend, erroneously I think, to assume that adults will use only the most complex and advanced forms of thought rather than childish ones. However, as was suggested in Chapter 4 and in the discussion of the work of Labouvie-Vief et al. (1989) and others about the possibilities of parallel rather than hierarchical organization of developmental levels of functioning, adults in particular circumstances may utilize the simplest forms of learning and thinking, though capable of far more complex ones; it is probably inaccurate always to call this regression, though it can sometimes be that.

This multilevel perspective is used in theories of emotion that take into account more than one level of information processing such as Leventhal's (1980, 1984). It is also found in Hoffman's (1984) discussion of the development of empathy. Hoffman refers to six different modes of empathy, ranging from the simplest process of involuntary conditioning and mimicry to far more complex and cognitively demanding ones such as imagining oneself in another's place (a process that would seem to require some awareness of the implications of what is happening experientially to someone else). Psychologists are becoming less preoccupied with identifying a single, true mechanism of learning and social influence and more attuned to multiple mechanisms, depending on the stage of cognitive development and on the person's condition at the moment. Whatever the mechanisms involved, however, the study of emotional development is about how we come to grasp the personal significance of social events in our lives, and how this understanding generates a specific emotion.

What has been said in this chapter assumes that the psychological structure that develops through childhood and into adulthood is relatively stable and predictable from one time of life to another. This has been much debated, and before leaving the topic of learning and emotional development, I should comment briefly about it. One view is that once established, adult personality is rather stable and not easily changed without great personal struggle. Another view is that we have been much too sanguine about stability, and further, that whatever is stable is less influential in shaping behavior and emotion than is the social context.

Such bald statements do not help us much, because change does occur and psychotherapy is devoted to producing change. We need to know what changes and what remains stable, and the conditions under which change may occur. The emotion theory I have been presenting does not hinge on the resolution of this question, however (see also West & Graziano, 1989).

Research and Thought on Cognitive-Emotional Development

As psychologists have come to recognize the important role that cognition plays in the emotion process, they have also become increasingly interested in what children of different ages know about the rules of emotion, and in the personal significance of social relationships on which the emotions depend. Although there is beginning to be much research and thought about this, our knowledge is very fragmented. Typical questions raised in such work are indicated by two recent chapter titles: "What do children know about emotions and when do they know it?" (Michalson & Lewis, 1985); and "What do children know about the situations that provoke emotion?" (Harris, 1985). I would like to begin this section by first addressing what a person needs to know about emotions in general, and his or her own emotion process in particular, in order to function well in encounters that are emotional or potentially emotional.

The theoretical position on emotion I have presented centers on meaning. It states that the emotion process depends on an appraisal of the significance of what is happening in the environment for the person's well-being. The fundamental consequence of this position is that the person must ask and answer—though not necessarily consciously—a number of personal questions about what is happening, foremost among which are the following: "Is my well-being compromised or in danger?" Or, "Is this a situation of benefit?";"How important to me is what is happening?"; "In what ways, if any, is my well-being engaged, harmed, threatened, or benefited?" A second set of questions, closely intertwined with the first, is "What can be done about this situation, and what are the consequences of any actions I might take?"; "Can I change the provoking negative condition or sustain the positive one?"; "How?"; "If not, can I tolerate or even benefit from it, and how?"; "What are the future consequences, and how might these be resolved or ameliorated?" All these questions (and others, too) are not necessarily asked at once or in sequence, but depending on how matters progress, they are relevant to the appraisal process in any adaptational encounter—actual, potential, or imagined.

Scherer (1984a, 1984b) has formulated an overlapping set of questions, which he refers to as *stimulus evaluation checks*. Certain problems are inherent in his formulations. For example, Scherer views these questions as following a fixed sequence, and some of what he lists as evaluation checks are not in my view necessary to an emotional reaction, but are part of the reaction itself. Nevertheless, they are propositions about the knowledge or belief base that a child or adult acquires through experience and that is necessary for a fully established, adult emotional process.

Three classes of knowledge seem essential for a mature emotion process:

1. The *social signals* about what is happening and their emotional significance for oneself and the other person must be recognized and interpreted. It is important, for example, to know what generates positive and negative emotions in the other person, and the significance of what that person is expressing in the transaction. If, for example, the pursuit of our agendas requires assent, approval, and support from another person, then we must know what to say or do to facilitate a favorable relationship and to avoid resistance. And when the other person responds, what is being communicated needs to be interpreted accurately; for example, we need to decide whether positive statements are consistent with or contrary to other forms of evidence. We must be responsive, for example, to expressive evidence of negativism, veiled annoyance, guilt, or uneasiness, and try to understand it. And we must act appropriately in response to this knowledge.

The socialization of emotion, starting in infancy but becoming much more complex with the acquisition of language and abstract understanding, involves the labeling of emotions, the fit between emotions and social roles, social referencing (in which a child comes to understand facial expressions of the mother and others), and awareness of the experience of emotion in others, which could be considered a form of empathy.

2. A person also needs to know the rules of emotional expression and action, or what are often called *display rules* and *feeling rules*. What can or cannot be expressed and done in any given situation? To any given individual? What are the social constraints on such expression? What sanctions are apt to be invoked by that individual, or by society?

3. Finally, we need to know *how emotions can be handled,* in ourselves and in the other persons who are party to the transaction. What can be done with our anxiety, anger, or guilt, say, when it is counterproductive? What are the situations in which we are vulnerable to dysfunctional emotions? And in regard to the other person, with whom we are dealing? There has been a growing attention to how children cope (see, for example, Compas, 1987), but this research has focused on stress rather than on the emotion process, which has impeded the integration of the theoretical and research literatures on stress and emotion.

Though condensed into three classes of knowledge, these three points present an enormous amount to assimilate about the emotion process, and this assimilation is achieved only gradually over development, if at all. Over and above personal agendas and their sociocultural environments, children and adults differ greatly in their knowledge and beliefs about the emotion process, how accurately they understand it, and how effectively they can use it. We tend to assume, probably correctly, that social competence depends in large measure on the quality and serviceability of this knowledge, and the ability to act on it. Although the details of this, especially in the first few months and years of life, still elude us and constitute a potentially rich agenda for developmental research (cf. Tronick, 1989), recent research has begun to suggest that children learn about the emotion process, even their understanding of metaphor and irony (Winner, 1988), at an earlier age than was originally assumed.

Against this set of concepts about what a person needs to know to function emotionally, psychologists have been learning much about the child's grasp at different ages. This research has been summarized by Michalson and Lewis (1985), Harris (1985), and Lewis and Saarni (1985), among others, and because of the intensity of interest, any review is apt to be dated rapidly. Let us look at some of the highlights.

One broad and important generalization is that social and psychological understandings, which underlie knowledge and appraisal and lead to positive and negative emotions, seem to be acquired quite early, and are much richer than what children can express verbally when asked. What has been learned in this research fits very well the cognitive-motivational-relational analysis of the emotion process I have been offering.

Three-year-old children appear to understand who the appropriate people are to deal with for different purposes—for example, to play with, to get help when hurt, to get information. Very young children also display empathic awareness about the emotions of others; for example, 2-year-olds comfort, hold, and pat a father who is sad, though it is not clear whether they understand the father's emotions or are merely responding superficially, perhaps imitatively, to the expression of sadness. Young children also appear to have considerable knowledge of emotional situations, which is often studied by telling them a story with an accompanying picture—about a birthday party, say, or a broken toy.

If they are asked, for example, how the child in the story feels, or how they would feel, by age 4, sometimes even by 3, they seem to understand what adults would consider an appropriate emotional response—such as fear, sadness, or anger. They even understand that more than one emotional response may be elicited by the situation. By 4, children can correctly use a limited number of emotion terms such as *happy, sad, mad, angry,* and *scared.* There is evidence that children can discriminate emotions even before they can label (and maybe understand) them, differentiating facial expressions as early as 8 months of age. Both differentiating and labeling emotions, especially labeling, improve with age. As early as 2 years of age, children are beginning to understand the emotions involved in crying and laughing. Michalson and Lewis's (1985, p. 127) summary of this research gives some of the flavor of what is known:

> When one looks at the emotion lexicon of children from 2 to 5 years old, one is rather impressed with what children know about the representation of facial expressions and the vocabulary that corresponds to them. With the exception of fear and disgust, 40% or more of the children comprehended emotion labels, specifically, "happiness," "surprise," "anger," and "sadness." That children as young as 2 years old matched the labels with the faces suggests that one does not need to use emotion terms themselves and instead can rely on pictorial representations of the terms to examine children's knowledge of emotional expressions and their contexts.

The vigor of this research movement to study what children understand about emotions is also nicely illustrated by programmatic research at the University of Chicago (e.g., Stein & Levine, 1987, 1989, 1990; Stein & Trabasso, 1990; and Trabasso, Stein, & Johnson, 1981). A premise of this research is Piaget's proposition that children's values and goals, and their understanding of what happens in social encounters, begin to develop early, perhaps in the first months and years of life. Stable cognitive structures begin to emerge, according to these researchers' estimate, from roughly 2½ months to 7 or 8 months of age. These permit the child to anticipate future events. Stein and Levine (1987, p. 172) write, for example, that "Emotions such as anger, sadness, fear, and happiness are more likely to result from evaluation processes focused on assessing the relationship between the precipitating event and the attainment of desired end states."

In their research with children from age 3 to 10, children are asked to remember and interpret stories that involve emotional situations. One of the primary conclusions from this work, which involves careful questioning of the child in a Piagetian style about its understanding of the stories, is that children as young as 3 to 5 years of age understand much more about causal relationships between events than they are usually given credit for. As they mature, they understand well by 5 or 6, for example, that the primary antecedent causes for events are states, goals, and actions, goals being the most frequent. And the consequences are actions and changes in states. Even though the youngest of these children do not well understand internal states, and refer to external events as causes of emotional reactions, it is "goals that drive the desire to maintain a particular state and the outcome that reflects the current status of goal attainment or failure" (Stein & Trabasso, 1990). They conclude from their research about the child's understanding of the bases of emotions as follows:

> Children's sensitivity to goals was also evident in their wishes and plans. First and foremost, children's wishes contained information that focused on the desire to reinstate failed goals or on the desire to maintain achieved goals. Three year olds . . . also generate wishes and plans with these dimensions included. . . . Wishes and plans in response to a new success incorporated the desire to maintain the new goal as well as the old one. Wishes and plans in response to augmented failure incorporated the desire to reinstate both the augmented goal and the original goal.

I have already alluded earlier to ongoing research by Dunn (1988) with children less than 2 years of age, which has also added to this growing body of knowledge about children's understanding of the personal and social rules of emotion. Although verbal expression is limited in these very young children, Dunn suggests that these children must have a great deal of knowledge about the ways emotion is generated, because they are capable of making jokes about what is going on, teasing another child, getting a parent's goat, and so on in their ordinary play. To tease, for example, is to understand another child's psychological vulnerability, and to intentionally annoy parents repeatedly requires an understanding of what the parents want and how to frustrate them. What, for example, do you say about a precocious child of 2 I observed, who when scolded said, "Don't talk to me that way, Mommy;

I don't talk to you that way." Surely, despite the tender years, this child's understanding of social relationships and their emotional implications has great depth.

A second major generalization, consistent with the first, is that ways of conceiving of oneself, the world, the adaptational tasks of life, and the emotions change as the mind grows and changes (see, for example, Labouvie-Vief, DeVoe, & Bulka, 1989). According to some observations, young children appear first to adopt a "situation-response" theory, in which they link the emotion to the eliciting situation. However, as they grow older, they begin to think of emotions also in terms of what is going on in the mind (e.g., Harris, 1985; see also Harris, Olthof, & Meerum-Terwogt, 1981; and Harris & Olthof, 1982).

Six-year-olds know, for example, that a quarrel provokes anger, and positive experiences make one happy. At 11 and 15 years of age, they continue to acknowledge this linkage, but are more likely than 6-year-olds to refer in their explanations to the mental processes that mediate the reaction. It is not clear whether the change is the result of adult "theories of the mind" or their own grasp of the social rules; perhaps it is both. They say, "I'm happy when I feel good inside; I'm sad when I think about bad things" (Harris, 1985, p. 163). The children studied by Harris also know quite clearly that one can pretend to be happy or afraid, but the older children had a more complex understanding about how pretense could be managed and the conditions under which this might occur (p. 165):

> For the younger children, pretense consisted simply of acting in a way that was not appropriate to the situation: laughing after a quarrel or smiling when you were on your way to the dentist. The other children, in contrast, were much more likely to mention the mismatch that would result from such pretense, the mismatch, that is, between what one should actually feel inside and what one would display outside. They talked of trying to hide their feelings or admitted that their feelings would still show through anyway. . . . These complicated relationships should be easier for older children to conceptualize because they make a threefold distinction between situation, inner mental feelings, and overt reaction.

It is difficult to resist the sardonic comment that even children have a more sophisticated grasp of the way the mind works than does the doctrinaire behaviorist who eschews reference to psychological processes that intervene between the situation and the response. Again and again research suggests far more sophistication than used to be assumed about very young children, in fact from a year or two onward, about the emotion process. As children grow older, they also are increasingly capable of recognizing that more than one emotion can occur in any situation, sometimes seemingly conflicting emotions (see also Berndt & Perry, 1986; Boggiano, Main, & Katz, 1988; Donaldson & Westerman, 1986; Strayer, 1985).

On this latter point Harris (1983) tells us that a young child may recognize that there can be more than one component to an emotional situation, each of which give rise to a different and potentially conflicting emotion. Such a recognition makes them more willing to admit to the possibility of ambivalence. He also notes that there is no established explanation of this increasing willingness with age to admit to the existence of mixed emotions. One possibility is an appreciation in such a child of the role of cognitive processes in emotion.

The explanation I offered in Chapter 1 for multiple emotions in any encounter was based on the inevitable complexity of most adaptational encounters. An encounter contains many pieces of business, making it possible to feel good about some and bad about others. As children develop more commitments, and more complex beliefs about themselves and the world, they are also more capable of distinguishing among the multiple facets of their emotional transactions. Few experiences in life communicate with only single, uncomplicated issues relevant to well-being, and even well-being itself has multiple and sometimes conflicting aspects, as in the diverse adaptational outcomes of social functioning, morale, and somatic health.

In my opinion, the details of when particular emotions first appear, and which ones, pale against the realization that a grasp of the social meanings underlying emotions begins very early and precedes mastery of language. It remains difficult to distinguish between emotional expression and emotional experience. The chapter and verse of the unfolding of emotion developmentally will be immeasurably advanced when we begin to have data on what it is that has to be known by the child to experience fear, anxiety, anger, guilt, shame, pride, and so on — that is, the contents of knowledge and appraisal that underlie each emotion, and what it is that a child of this or that age knows.

For this reason, I believe that theory-driven research is advantageous and would profit from drawing on the propositions in Chapters 6 and 7 about the appraisal patterns and the knowledge on which they depend for each emotion or, for that matter, for someone else's propositions. The theoretical premise would be that if a child cannot make certain appraisals, because it lacks either the knowledge or the ability to evaluate the personal relevance of that knowledge, the emotions dependent on those appraisals will not appear in that child's repertoire until each of the appraisals necessary and sufficient for that emotion is within the child's understanding.

Overview of the Development of the Emotion Process

I am now prepared to pull together in the form of a summary that is somewhat schematic and brief the major factors involved in emotional development that have been discussed in this chapter.

I begin with the constitutional status of the infant when he or she comes on the scene, characterized in perhaps a somewhat oversimple way as *temperament.* On the bedrock of temperament is grafted the pattern of child rearing provided by parents and other caretakers, who try to impose on the child their agendas as parents, and who, in turn, are influenced and even controlled by the child in a bidirectional fashion. Most of those who argue that temperament is innate and important fail to provide us with clear theoretical directives about how it might produce diverse types of emotion and degrees of emotionality, or even with bare outlines of the developmental role of temperament, assuming there is one, in interaction with diverse patterns of parenting. Earlier in the chapter I offered some speculations about how temperament might affect the emotion process.

What happens to the child in this transactional process of mutual influence depends in some degree on the formal *stage of cognitive development* at which any environmental input takes place. In the earliest process of emotion in young children, inner and outer are undifferentiated, but very soon the children come to interpret what is happening and regulate their expressions of emotion in accordance with contingencies and social signals, and ultimately in accordance with social situations. Young children then define emotions by the conditions that elicit them but gradually recognize the inner agency of mind. In adolescence, they become more reflective and recognize clearly an inner and outer life, and the rules that apply to them.

These developmental changes in cognitive activity are important in respect to the way meaning, on which emotions depend, is generated, as well as in the social regulation of emotions. The child experiences anxiety when it senses that its modest constructions of meaning are in danger; anger when it understands that an external agent has offended its goal requirements, and eventually when it has a rudimentary self, that this self has been demeaned; shame when there is evidence of disapproval and disappointment by parental figures and ultimately the internalization of this disapproval; and so on.

As the child moves toward adulthood, the complexity of meanings and the emotions they can generate makes childhood emotions look more and more like adult emotions. The outlook and agendas of the parents in these transactions play a role as features of the environment. While simple, automatic types of learning are never outmoded, the complex, abstract, and deliberate processes become important later in development. Language, although not critical for meaning, greatly assists in memory and in the abstractions helping to articulate and sharpen the essential meanings.

As the child begins to grow up, *lifelong personal agendas and styles* of relating to the world are acquired as characteristics of personality, including *goal hierarchies* and *systems of belief and commitment about one's ego-identity.* The process of developing an ego-identity is gradual so that it may be emergent and elemental almost from the beginning before it is fully elaborated, though capable of change perhaps in early adulthood. I think the term here should be *ego-identity* rather than *self,* because these personality characteristics are not merely self-concepts but concepts about self in the world, including roles, commitments, relationships, and a set of niches or places in that world in which to function. They arise from the biological and social universals in being human, the normative meanings found in the person's culture, the social rules of conduct of the society into which the child is born, and the individual life history.

Although the acquisition process continues throughout life, as a rule we assume that the most important and stable goal hierarchies and beliefs are established during the formative years before adulthood. Particularly important in adaptation are the emotional *transitions* forced by living and aging; sound adaptation may require reorganizations of goal commitments, ways of thinking, and coping over the life course because of a changing world and our changing functional abilities.

To me personally, as I age, it is instructive to see a growing interest in how people cope with their losses of function in old age. Baltes's (1987) observations about the strategies whereby older persons compensate functionally for memory problems and physical losses in strength and quickness open up a wide field for the study of emotion and adaptation later in life. Most encouraging is the suggestion that often such persons continue to be effective and productive as a result of these compensatory strategies.

At any point in development the personality is recognizable through, and portrayed in, countless adaptational *encounters with the environment,* which provoke acute emotions and contribute to longer lasting moods. It is in these encounters that all manner of social demands, constraints, and resources are manifested and in which immediate social influences on thoughts, feelings, and actions are operative.

The processes of *appraisal* and *coping,* which mediate between the person and the environment, take place in these encounters and shape the emotional response. I have argued in Chapter 4 and here that these mediating processes begin very early. The norm for any sentient creature is to be constantly appraising the significance of what is happening for well-being, whether automatically or deliberately, though the scope of this significance and its abstractness is apt to be limited in simpler mammals and in the early months of infancy and childhood.

In primary appraisal, the person's stakes in the transaction, which are based on the interplay of motives and beliefs on the one hand, and environmental forces on the other, are the central concerns. In secondary appraisal, the options for coping and future prospects are the central concerns. When faced with a transaction of relevance, particularly one that is appraised as harmful or beneficial, the coping process alters the person–environment relationship, both in actuality and in the way it is apprehended by the person. These processes of appraisal and coping make every transaction a constantly changing one, though recurrent patterns distinguish one person from another in content and style, and younger persons from older ones.

We are now ready to proceed to an examination of the social influences on the emotion process, which is the subject matter of Chapter 9.

Summary

A key theme opening this chapter was that to study emotional development one must decide on the relevant variables and processes, not an easy task and one that is apt to be geared to theory. Much modern research on this has depended mainly on one response indicator, which, though it offers considerable advantages, must still be regarded as a single peripheral response in a sea of variables and processes that comprise the cognitive-motivational-relational configuration of emotion.

Four historical approaches to the role of the mother-child relationship in emotional development were reviewed, including those of Whiting and Child, Bowlby, Harlow and Dennenberg, and a more recent ethological approach. These approaches at the individual parent-child level are analogous to the more macro, sociocultural analyses of Chapter 9, yet to come.

Four recent theories of emotional development were summarized, including those of Izard, Sroufe, Campos et al., and Lewis and Michalson. Some of these theories are of interest especially because of a recognition of the role of an emerging self in emotion.

There followed a discussion of biological factors—particularly temperament, which is beginning to carry the main weight of constitutional givens in emotion. Discussion included Allport's definition of temperament, some research on its heritability, and the way temperament might interact with parenting and coping to influence emotions over the life-course. Kagan's research and that of Rothbart and Derryberry were briefly considered.

Emotional development, from the standpoint of my cognitive-motivational-relational theory, is mainly about the individual's acquisition of personality characteristics that influence appraisal and coping. These factors can be viewed primarily from the biological standpoint of innate tendencies or from the social standpoint of variable experience. Both are obviously involved in emotional development.

If we are to understand emotional development, we must also understand the learning process as it relates to appraisal, coping, and emotion. Four main mechanisms of learning were reviewed: associative (reinforcement) learning, including classical and instrumental conditioning, imitation (observational learning) and identification, the playing of social roles, and the search for meaning and ego-identity. Some examples of current interest in and research on emotion from these learning standpoints were also included when possible, including Loevinger's work on ego-development. The point was made that many different mechanisms of learning could be operating at the same time in adulthood, a position that is compatible with what was said in Chapter 4 about automatic and deliberate cognitive processing.

Research and thought on cognitive-emotional development were examined by considering first what a child must know about an emotion and the social transactions relevant to the emotion process to experience it. The current interest in what children understand about emotional situations was examined and some general findings emphasized.

Finally, the chapter provided an overview of the development of the emotion process which summarizes the main variables, both in the personality and in the environmental context, which I think shape appraisal and coping and, therefore, the emotional reaction.

Note

1. Since it is among the most recent analytic reviews, covers tremendous ground, and displays impressive scholarship, I have drawn on this work heavily in this discussion and adapted it to my own special concerns.

❖ 9 ❖

Social Influence

Two positions can be taken with regard to emotional development, reflecting the field's preoccupations with biological influences on the one hand and social influences on the other. One position views development as an unfolding of individual genetic potentials, which follow inherited or preprogrammed patterns. The other position sees emotional development as learning from experience, which partakes of societally defined rules of behavior and culturally defined meanings. Both positions are, of course, equally applicable and, as I suggested in Chapter 5, a sound theory of emotion looks to the interplay of both. The reader should read this chapter in the context of what I said about the interface between the biological and sociocultural aspects of emotion.

The purpose of this chapter is to speak of emotional development from a sociocultural point of view.¹ This calls for an exploration of social and cultural influences and how these affect emotion. To play a role in the emotion process, society and culture must influence the variables and processes of appraisal and coping, and those that shape them, both at various points of development and as contemporaneous forces that operate in adaptational encounters. We have as yet comparatively little direct knowledge about this influence on theory-specific mediating variables and processes, but there are abundant clues and observations from sociology, anthropology, and psychology on which we can rely to speculate and generate hypotheses.

As to the structure of the chapter, after discussing the sociocultural outlook and how it affects the individual, and making distinctions between culture and social structure, the body of the chapter consists of two main sections: The first discusses how culture influences the emotions of individuals; the second how social structure influences them. I end each section with a brief examination of the six appraisal components, which are the heart of my theory. The social structure section ends with a brief discussion of how emotions are educated.

The Sociocultural Outlook

We live in the midst of a complex web of human relationships, all of which have the potential for generating emotions. These range from intimate familial ties to more distant social relationships involving religious and ethnic groups, local communities, and nations. Most of us are barely conscious of how elaborate the rules governing our social behavior are (Goffman, 1959, 1971). We obey formal and informal rules of pedestrian and vehicular traffic; follow accepted ways of behaving on crowded streets, in elevators, on subways or buses; learn the proper behavior for organized social activities—such as weddings, funerals, and college classrooms—and with members of the same or opposite sex. These rules comprise the relatively stable social realities that existed before each of us arrived on the scene and that will still exist, though perhaps in changed and changing ways, after we are gone. Similarly important as part of our immediate world are the relatively stable, hence predictable, conditions of the physical environment such as the streets and highways, buildings, geography, transportation systems, and climate.

Society and its culture are constantly evolving human products, growing out of older, traditional ways of thinking, feeling, and doing. As Berger and Luckman (1966) have theorized, sociocultural arrangements came into being long ago as matters of convenience or necessity, but once established tend to persist and to be handed down from one generation to the next as habitual patterns and social institutions with more or less stable rules of conduct. They are the social world into which children are born and comprise the social conventions that must be obeyed but over which people living in these societies have only limited control. From birth on, contemporary children, like subsequent generations, must learn about this social order, just as they must learn about the physical environment. We are all products of this social and physical environment, and throughout our lives our modes of thought, our emotions, and our behavior are shaped by it—in the formative years as well as over the whole of life.

Nevertheless, just as their perceptions of physical reality may differ, people living within the same social setting do not always perceive social reality in the same way. To some extent, each individual's social reality is a unique and private subjective world that is never completely shared by others. We have our own projects, meanings, thoughts, feelings, wishes, and acts. What each of us knows is not exactly like what anyone else knows; therefore, the way social reality is constructed in our minds differs from person to person and from subgroup to subgroup. The sociologist, anthropologist, and psychologist must take this into account in their efforts to understand social influences on emotion.

Thus, although there is considerable overlap among the ways different groups and individuals conceive the world, social reality is not exactly the same for members of different nationalities and subgroups living within the same society. As we have increasingly come to realize, an American black living in an urban ghetto has a different conception of the social environment of his country than does an affluent white American living in a small, all-white suburban township. Even the same religion is experienced differently by sharecroppers, factory workers, merchants, millionaires, and intellectuals. And in addition to these variations based on social groupings, individuals also differ greatly on the basis of their unique life experiences.

In this connection, Smith (1981) suggests that there has been a revival of an ethnic sense of identity over the last two centuries, which has profound consequences for the social bases of emotion, for generational conflict, and for the nation-states of the future. There are monoethnic* nations, such as Japan, and multiethnic nations, such as our own. With the rise of ethnic identity, in Eastern Europe and the United States, for example, there is increasing concern about the ability of multiethnic nations to govern themselves, with each group vying against the others and displaying national aspirations of its own.

There is also the problem of the dissolution of cultures and political arrangements over time. As I was growing up there was much academic interest in the fall of the ancient civilizations of Greece and Rome. The classic film *The Seventh Seal* by Ingmar Bergman depicts the breakdown of the existing social order in Europe of the Middle Ages, which was coincident with the "black death" (bubonic plague), both of which must have wreaked havoc on the emotional lives of people living in those times. Barbara Tuchman's writings (e.g., *A Distant Mirror* and *The March of Folly*) about the cultural dissolution of the fourteenth century and its foolish and tragic parallels in the twentieth century also suggest the importance of a distinction between stable and unstable social systems in considering society's impact on the emotional lives of people.

Recently I had an experience that highlights some of the variables and issues of social control. My wife and I and another couple drove to the opera in San Francisco from our homes in the East Bay for a Sunday matinee. Because of the damage done in a recent earthquake that had closed some routes, we allowed two hours to reach the opera house for a trip that would normally be about 40 minutes. Unexpected construction on the bridge—the California Department of Transportation had closed one lane of the Bay Bridge, which led to an enormous traffic jam—resulted in our arriving at the opera house a few moments after the curtain had gone up. The usual tradition in such a case is not to seat the late arriver, and we were barred from entering by a small and uncertain-looking usher with no supervisor within earshot. She had already taken one of many vacant seats—unheard of at a Sunday matinee and indicative of the postearthquake transportation mess—to enjoy the opera.

Considering the circumstances, the outrageous price of our tickets, and the fact that we would miss one third of the opera if we were not seated—one of our party also could not stand on her feet long because of a medical problem—we all decided to protest the usual rule. We forced our way in and took our seats to the noisy protestations of the usher (who would have been wiser not to have fussed, because she created more disturbance than our movements would have made without her). Do I need to add in a book on emotion that the incident provoked strong emotions in most participants, including ourselves—a mixture of anger, anxiety, guilt, and shame, depending on which of the dramatis personae is the focus of our attention.

I note that rules like this are attempts to create the conditions of gracious living and are reasonable when it is possible to control one's arrival time and behavior. Such rules force people who are chronically inconsiderate of others to be more plan-

---

*I am aware that this word is a neologism. However, in contrast with multiethnic, which is in the dictionary, its meaning should be clear, and I could not think of a better word to convey the intended meaning.

ful. I, too, am usually annoyed by late arrivals after a play has started. Such rules are also vestiges of a class-oriented society that limits certain activities to those who can afford the conditions permitting gracious living. In our central cities, these conditions have mostly disappeared. Anyway, as the reader might guess, we were given highly disapproving glances and comments from some of the audience, and we returned their nasty glances and offered a few choice comments of our own.

What is interesting about this somewhat shabby experience is the decline of the force of social rules when they no longer are appropriate to the circumstance, and especially when these rules are no longer accepted by a sizable population. In California, for example, almost everyone drives at speeds of 65 miles or more per hour despite the posted 55-mile-per-hour limit, except of course when a patrol car is visible, and if you drive at 55 you are apt to be pushed from behind to speed up. Social scientists know that these practices erode the citizen's respect for law and create a kind of lottery for who will get caught and fined, with somewhat low odds, especially if one is vigilant. There is even an ego trip about being successful at speeding without being caught.

Rules that are regularly and widely violated are, in effect, a formula for, if not a manifestation of, social change. The increased anonymity of social contacts in our type of society increases the problem. No longer are signals of disapproval much of a personal threat when, after an opera performance, everyone scatters and returns to their anonymous lives at home. When those to whom disapproval is directed are not responsive, we are well on our way to social change. Also interesting are the individual differences in willingness to abide by the traditional rules. Some readers will be horrified at our reaction and behavior at the opera; others will be empathetic and share our disapproval of the rigidity with which the rules were carried out under the circumstances.

Be that as it may, the social scientist's task of describing social reality objectively is difficult — and, indeed, there are many truths, not one. Though there may be much overlap between the realities different individuals respond to as defined by consensus, the reader already understands that I regard the important reality for a person experiencing an emotion to be the private one resulting from individual perception, knowledge, and appraisal. To the extent that meanings differ from individual to individual and group to group, the emotional development and behavior of individuals are apt to vary. There is an intellectual tension between an emphasis on sociocultural norms and individuality. Nevertheless, theory and research on emotion in the social sciences must look to the task of identifying the precise ways in which the social environment shapes an individual's or group's thoughts, emotions, and actions in different contexts over the life-course.

Society, Culture, and the Individual

When we try to connect a social system to a psychological one, such as the emotion process in individual persons, we have the problem of translating a macro level analysis (that is, the social system) to a micro level (the mind of the individual person). At the social level we must distinguish among the components of the social system that are relevant to the emotions. At the psychological level we must consider the components of the individual mind that are relevant to the emotions (see, for example, House, 1981; and Jessor, 1981).

The inevitable gap between social system variables and their psychological effects occurs for two reasons. First, social stratification provides some groups and individuals with adaptational advantages over others. Second, in addition to great genetic-constitutional diversity in the natural world, and despite its presence within the same society or collectivity, individuals and groups have divergent physical life histories, which produce phenotypical variation in our bodies. The variability is so great that, though our bodies operate in comparable ways, there are large individual differences in our sizes and shapes, and the ways our organs do their jobs, but these are considered to fall within normal limits, making it difficult at times even to tell whether deviations from the norm mean that there is something wrong medically.

The same sort of variability also applies to our minds and their developmental histories. For example, our experiences with influential people such as our parents (both as a couple and as individuals) are quite diverse. Any psychological theory of emotion must therefore go beyond an examination of the social system in which people live and explore the individual variables that influence appraisal and coping, and thus the emotions. And if we combine individual biological inheritance with individual sociocultural experience while we are growing up and adapting, it is a challenge to come up with common rules about the development of our distinctive personalities. In short, though common explanatory rules are what we must seek in science, we must also respect the tremendous diversity that is a fact of our biological, social, and psychological lives and find ways of drawing on it when we try to explain and predict an individual's emotions.

A number of interacting sets of variables are relevant to personality development, and how they operate must be clearly thought through. I have found Labouvie's (1982) analysis of four ways of organizing these variables over time and situations quite useful, and Caspi (1987) has drawn on it to provide a thoughtful guide for sorting out personality and social influences on emotion and adaptation over the life-course. Caspi identified them as developmental time-free and developmental time-specific sets of variables on the one hand, and situation-free and situation-specific sets of variables on the other.

Time-free and *situation-free* variables refer to normative patterns that are stable in persons over a relatively long time frame or across situational contexts; they are not linked importantly to particular times or situations and, as such, are of particular interest to personologists. *Time-specific* and *situation-specific* variables refer to the linkage of variables to particular times and situations. For example, when we are considering sociocultural influences on emotional development and change, the focus is on time-specific and situation-specific variables; when we are considering stable personality variables such as emotion traits, the focus is on time-free and situation-free variables. Each perspective deals with only part of the story of human development. To decide what is stable or changeable is, of course, very difficult (see Chapter 3, and a recent special issue of the *Journal of Personality* edited by West &

Graziano, 1989, which is devoted to arguments and evidence about long-term stability and change in personality).

Time-specific variables are a major concern of developmental psychology because they are unstable and change over the life-course (e.g., Cantor, Norem, Brower, Niedenthal, & Langston, 1987; Caspi, 1987; Labouvie-Vief, Hakim-Larson, & Hobart, 1987; and Whitbourne, 1985). *Situation-specific* variables refer to the variable social arrangements to which people are exposed and responsive, the influence of which is a major concern of social psychology.

As people grow up and age, not only do the developmental tasks they face change, the social (and to some extent the physical) environments under which they live change, too. These tasks are, in effect, time and situation specific. Aldwin and Stokols (1988) point out that it is difficult to separate physical and social changes. For example, natural physical disasters affect the social environment, and changes in the social environment have implications for the physical environment, as when divorce, widowhood, or industrial unemployment forces a change in a person's address. Therefore, neither the social environment, the physical environment, the person, nor the functional person–environment relationship is fixed over the life of the person. Change, with its profound implications for emotion and adaptation, is an inevitable feature of living.

Environmental change may, of course, be monumental in scope, and thus a source of great psychological stress and distress among adults who have been uprooted and transplanted from one culture to another. The culture shock created by having to live in a different society from the one in which we have grown up can be a major challenge to sound mental health and is apt to remain so for a long time, if not for the whole of the lives of those affected (though this seems to be less of a problem when the transition is made in early childhood).

I remember, for example, the times my wife and I have spent abroad in a society different from ours, not as tourists but as visitors, when we had a minimal grasp of the language. The hourly and daily adaptational tasks were enervating, especially in the first month or so. It was a continuing challenge merely to know how to get around, to shop, to bank, to use strange household devices, and to relate to other people. We also had the benefit of hosts concerned with our well-being who contributed immensely to our ability to function. Given our experience, intelligence, resources, and supportive hosts, if this process of adapting was for us an exhausting daily process, imagine what it must be for those arriving from another culture, strangers, poor, many without education and without the benefit of knowing the language. Consider, too, the many waves of immigrants to our own shores, including current migrations, not to speak of those who came as indentured servants or slaves.

A large number of variables have to do with the emotion process, and society and its culture have much influence on them. I consider the most important to be the mediating process variables — that is, appraisals of the personal significance of relationships with others, both intimate and distant, the coping processes that affect them, and the social response. The reader by now should recognize, and I hope appreciate, my bias toward personal meaning, which informs my treatment of the sociocultural influences on emotion in this chapter.

Forms of Social Influence

Two broad forms of social influence are usually contrasted: the living culture into which a person is born, and the social structure. *Culture* provides a set of internalized meanings that people carry with them into transactions with the social and physical environment. After they have been internalized and have become part of the personality, they become time- and situation-free variables. *Social structure* produces a set of immediate demands, constraints, and resources, often described in terms of the roles and role relationships that operate in adaptive transactions. These are, in effect, time- and situation-specific variables. Both types of influence are important in understanding the emotion process.

Although it is often an oversimplification to dichotomize, culture tends to be emphasized by anthropologists (cf., Shweder & LeVine, 1984) and personality psychologists; social structure tends to be emphasized by sociologists and social psychologists (cf., Gordon, 1981; Kemper, 1978, 1981; Hochschild, 1979). Developmental psychologists draw on both, though perhaps more on the former than on the latter. Nevertheless, the rules of social intercourse also operate in contemporary transactions having an emotional impact. I examine these later in my discussion of social structure and emotion.

Anthropologists have a number of different ways of defining culture. Geertz's (1973, p. 89) influential definition is well suited to an emotion theory like mine, which is based on meaning. He defines culture as "an historically transmitted pattern of meanings embodied in symbols, a system of inherited conceptions expressed in symbolic form by means of which men communicate, perpetuate, and develop their knowledge about and attitudes toward life."

Social structure, on the other hand, refers to detailed patterns of social relationships and transactions among people who occupy different roles and statuses within a social system. Some of the implicit questions in the analysis of social structure might include: What are the obligations and privileges of being a father, mother, child, lover, husband, wife, and so forth? What sorts of behaviors violate these role expectations, and how are the violations dealt with? How and with whom can social exchange be initiated? How does one do so? What do the reactions indicate and portend? For example, if one asks for information, the reply may be polite but the interchange restricted to the most superficial aspects. With what kinds of persons and under what conditions is it possible to become personal? What social topics can be ventured? What are the signs that a social relationship below the surface is possible? How can one protect oneself from hurt and insult? How can we achieve what we want from a social encounter?

The contrast between the cultural and social structural ways of thinking about the social world is beautifully drawn by Schneider (1976, pp. 202–203), who writes:

Culture contrasts with norms in that norms are oriented to patterns *for action*, whereas culture constitutes a body of definitions, premises, statements, postulates, presumptions, propositions, and perceptions about the nature of the universe and man's place in it. Where norms tell the actor how to play the scene, culture tells the actor how the scene is set and what it all means. Where norms tell the actor how to behave in the presence of ghosts, gods, and human beings, culture tells the actor what ghosts, gods, and human beings are and what they are all about.

Culture and Emotion

Here I am going to talk about how culture influences the emotions and provide numerous illustrations, which help give a more concrete understanding of the way cultural variables work. Let us begin with the how.

How Cultural Influence Works

The key to cultural influence lies in shared and divergent meanings acquired over the course of psychological development. Because of these meanings, people arrive on the scene of every encounter with the environment having a readiness to understand what is happening and to respond accordingly, even if they cannot say what is guiding their responses. I touched on some of this in Chapter 5 when I considered the competition between biological and sociocultural factors in the emotion process.

D'Andrade (1984) has offered a searching examination of two contradictory ways of viewing the way culture influences people who are socialized within it. On the one hand, it is asserted that people feel strong pressures to follow cultural dictates. This defines culture in a Skinnerian way as an external set of demands, which as Spiro (1961) has pointed out is an antipersonality (actually he said "antipsychological") position because of the assumption that conformity to cultural norms is solely the result of external social sanctions and not the result of internal motivation to comply. The opposite theory, more psychologically and personality centered, is that the power of external directives over individual persons arises, at least in part, from the desire to conform to what others do and say.

As Alfred Adler (1927) was wont to emphasize in his early writings, one reason we are socially committed is that as infants and young children we are all helpless and need benign and supportive parenting to survive and flourish. In later writings, however, Adler shifted his emphasis to phylogenetic explanations like those of modern sociobiologists, which point to the adaptational value of the innate desire to join with others, because survival is facilitated by the added strength against danger that is provided by a group.

The first theory about sanctions as the main motivator is incomplete, because extrinsic sources of power by themselves rarely operate for long as successful modes of social control, and when they do, these periods are most commonly characterized by widespread social anomie, political corruption, and dysfunction. In our present world climate, as we approach the twenty-first century, there is a remarkable demonstration of the long-term weakness of mere coercive power in the Eastern European bloc where the clamor for freedom, democracy, and economic prosperity has precipated historic turnabouts. Only a century or so earlier, the collapse of the arrogant monarchies of Western Europe exemplified the failure of those governing to manifest sufficient concern for the well-being of their ordinary citizens. For what might be a brief moment in history, or the start of a new world order, we can see clearly the ultimate failure of external power alone as a way to produce an appropriate degree of conformity, though at this writing the refusal of the Chinese government, and a number of others, to relinquish coercion by arms, threats, and secret police remains — temporarily we hope — a counterpoint to this assertion.

The desire to conform to and believe in a cultural outlook, which is a prime source of social and political stability, has at least three motivational bases: direct personal reward, internalization of the set of values maintained in the culture, and the power of the group to punish the individual for transgressions. Sociopaths and criminals are notoriously deviant from the rest of the society because they fail to internalize social values.

Cultural influences on personality development become evident when we compare the way people think, feel, and act in different societies. It is difficult, however, to separate personality and culture; culture can only be known by reference to the patterns of thought, feeling, and action shared by members of a society, which can be said to be a kind of group personality. This involves a degree of circular reasoning, in that we define culture by the shared personality characteristics of its people and personality by reference to internalized cultural values.

To my mind the best resolution of the difficulty lies in giving attention to the temporal process whereby a child, born into a society with a particular culture, acquires and internalizes cultural meanings. If we think of a cultural pattern as existing before current members of the society arrived on the scene, we can understand the typical personality characteristics of people living within it as the product of socialization or acculturation — that is, as the effect of growing up in, and adapting to, that culture. However, without longtitudinal studies, this is a difficult thesis to prove. To examine cultural influences on personality development with the data base we have forces us, unfortunately, to depend only on nonlongitudinal studies of the peoples of different cultures (see, for example, Benedict, 1934, for observations of Indian cultures of the Southwestern United States; and Shweder & LeVine, 1984, for other, more recent observations).

D'Andrade (1984, p. 100) offers the following summary of his analysis of the problem of culture and personality, which well expresses my own outlook:

> The general position presented here is that meanings involve the total human psyche, not just the part of us that knows things. Every aspect of meaning systems requires a great deal of psychological processing and often considerable experiential priming. It takes years of learning for a child to acquire the representational functions of meaning systems. Representation occurs only because symbols activate complex psychological processes. In the same way, it takes years of learning for a child to acquire the constructive, directive, and evocative functions of meaning systems, and these functions, too, require complex psychological processes. The representational, constructive, directive, and evocative functions are each a consequence of the way the human brain is organized, a biological and psychological potentiality that is highly elaborated and stimulated by cultural meaning systems.

How do culturally based meaning systems influence our individual understandings of human relationships? To help answer this, D'Andrade reproduced a simple story from Schank and Abelson (1977). Suppose one reads the following: "Roger went to the restaurant. He ordered *coq au vin*. The waiter was surly and the table was right next to a cash register. Roger left a very small tip" (D'Andrade, 1984, p. 103). Now the reader must answer some questions about the social interchange in the story, such as "What did Roger eat? To whom did Roger give his order? Where did Roger sit? Did Roger like the restaurant? What was the tip for?"

Following Schank and Abelson, D'Andrade points out that none of the answers is explicitly contained in the story. Yet, because we know much about the culture in which these social exchanges occur, the questions are easy to answer. For example, we know that a customer in a restaurant usually sits at a table, gives orders to a waiter, and eats what is ordered, and that satisfaction with service can be indicated by the size of the tip. If the waiter and surroundings are not pleasant, satisfaction is compromised, and tables placed next to a cash register are usually considered unpleasant. Without such culturally based information, much of the story is uninterpretable. On the other hand, the story is quite meaningful without additional information to those of us living in this kind of culture, because the information is already in our heads and we take it for granted.

Many shared cultural messages are operating in the inferences we are able to draw from any social context with which we have transactions. We experience and understand the emotions of ourselves and others in social situations on the same basis. Emotional experience is therefore substantially cultural, and in many respects based on shared public as well as private meanings.

In attempting to define the questions about how culture influences emotion, K. G. Heider (1991) begins his book on emotion in three Indonesian cultures with a series of questions of importance in the study of culture and emotion. He asks about how culture influences emotion and observes that different languages have different words for emotion. This raises the question of how much emotional behavior (and one should add emotional experience) is culturally variable. For example, how much overlap is there when Americans use the term *anger* and Indonesians use their term *Marah* — a question that raises a number of other questions about how people of different cultures talk, think, feel, and show emotion. Does the size of the emotion vocabulary vary from culture to culture? Do emotion words cluster differently among different cultures? Are some emotions emphasized more in one culture than another and other emotions neglected? Are there culturally unique emotions? Do the causes and outcomes of emotion vary from one culture to another? Are different facial expressions used for the same emotions in different cultures, and if so, how do we understand this?

What is the anthropological answer to Heider's question about how the emotion process is influenced by culture? Two main ways have been proposed: (1) A cultural variable influences the emotions that will be experienced by virtue of the *personal meanings and significances for well-being* it offers, which is consistent with my emphasis on appraisals. (2) A cultural variable influences how the emotion, once it is generated, is *regulated and expressed socially*, which is consistent with the concepts of display rules and coping.

Heider writes of the first kind of influence, on the emotion-generating process, as the *cultural definition* of the provoking event, which intervenes between the event and the emotional reaction. The second point of influence, between the inner emotional state and the observable outcome in behavior and expression, implies that a culture has a number of reaction or *display rules* and call for coping processes, which operate between the inner state and the behavior.

Levy (1973) makes the same basic distinction but expresses it as the difference between *constitutive* rules and *regulative rules.* He has studied the emotional patterns of Tahitians, whose displays of anger are apt to be met by gossip, instruction for them, and coolness, because Tahitians are wary of anger. Thus, felt anger may be masked by a smile, or the expression of happiness disguised. These displays illustrate regulative rules, which Levy tends to emphasize. About this he writes (1973, p. 287):

> Doctrines about anger and violence . . . lead to [the following] strategies for coping with anger; try not to get into situations which will make you mad. Don't take things seriously or withdraw if possible. If someone else is mad at you, try not to let it build up. If you do get angry, however, express it by talking out your anger, so that things can be corrected and you will not be holding it in. Express your anger, if possible, by verbal rather than physical means. If you use physical means try to use symbolic actions, not touching the person. If you touch him, be careful not to hurt him.

I prefer the language of constitutive and regulative rules to that used by Heider, and will use it here. Levy (1973, 1978, 1984) seems to believe that inner emotional states are comparatively little influenced by culture — that is, by constitutive rules — because of biological universals. For example, the death of a child is probably defined as sad in most cultures, and sadness is usually expressed with a pan-cultural sad face and weeping. Nevertheless, this reaction may be altered in accordance with culturally specific meanings that operate between the antecedent event and the private emotional experience. This is, in effect, a constitutive influence. If, for example, the death is believed culturally to be the result of witchcraft, the private reaction may be anger rather than sadness; but if the child is considered to be taken directly to heaven, the culturally based meaning may lead to happiness rather than to sadness or anger.

I have already discussed (in Chapter 5) Levy's interesting observations about sadness and guilt as "hypocognized" in Tahitian culture and anger and shame as "hypercognized." He speaks of these as regulative responses of the culture to the social problem posed by human emotions. Emotions are of interest to the cultural anthropologist mainly because they affect behavior, thought, and meaning systems. In other words, for Levy emotions are not so much shaped by culture as themselves influencing how the culture deals with them.

In some ways, Levy's view is similar to what I have said in Chapter 5 about core relational themes shaping the emotional response because they are biological universals. In other words, once we have appraised that we have been exposed to a demeaning offense, we are bound to react with anger, though we also have all sorts of ways of dealing with the anger. And once we have appraised that our ego-identity has been enhanced, we are bound to react with pride, and so on for each core relational theme and its emotion. Nevertheless, I also assume that culture influences the meaning, hence appraisal itself. The biological rules always operate, but the substance of relationships on which the meaning of the encounter (and hence the core relational theme, appraisal, and the emotion itself) depends is often defined culturally.

Anthropological research and thought on emotion have recently been reviewed by Lutz and White (1986). About the ways culture influences emotion, these authors emphasize, as I do, "how people make sense of life's events" rather than more superficial behavioral patterns. In an instructive analysis, they suggest four possible ways in which cultural meanings and social structure play roles in shaping emotion. Some of these center on constitutive rules and others on regulative rules:

1. A culture emphasizes certain general problems of living and de-emphasizes others. These authors point to Japanese sensitivity to the social group as an audience for their mistakes, the Ilongot experience of inadequacy as a challenge to be overcome, and the North American's focus on what an error says about one's character. These examples seem to me to represent a constitutive rule shaping the emotion itself.

2. Cultural interpretations define the exact nature of a problem of living — for example, what is considered dangerous, a thing worth having, or a loss, and whether a threat is controllable. Also a constitutive rule, I think.

3. Cultures deal differently with contingencies between a violation of the social code and what will result, thus defining what is justifiable anger, fear, shame, or admiration. All persons need to learn how others will respond to how we have acted and what we have said or felt. Hochschild (1979) refers to these as "feeling rules." These rules are both constitutive and regulative; they have to do with the social acts that make us angry, shameful, or whatever, as well as expression and suppression. Guttfreund (1990) has also documented that when bilinguals of Spanish origin speak in their original tongue, rather than English, they express more emotion than they do in their adopted tongue, reflecting differences in the regulative rules of each culture.

4. Life's problems are scripted by a culture for the kinds of solutions that are countenanced or condemned. Are we allowed or encouraged to cry at a loss? Can we preserve our integrity against an attack by physical or verbal retaliation? Should we walk away from another's violation as the Utku do (Briggs, 1970) or dramatically call attention to it as the Kaluli do (Schieffelin, 1976)? These cultural rules seem to be regulative rather than constitutive.

In connection with regulative rules about how emotional encounters may be responded to, it is evident from the media attention in the United States to the trial of Bernard Goetz, and the woman who has been called Lady Goetz for carrying a weapon illegally in a shooting that she claims was self-defense, that our own society is in the throes of evaluating what a threatened public should and should not do in the face of the growing danger of being mugged or killed on city streets. New regulative standards of conduct seem to be needed to fill the current vacuum in a world that has changed.

Within a culture, too, children must have means to learn about the meanings and values that are important to its people, whether in a constitutive or a regulative sense. Dorr (1985) has recently examined the role of television in modern societies in teaching children and adults about relationships between particular social situations and the emotions that are experienced and displayed in our society. She makes a number of useful points about this, writing, for example (pp. 73–74), that

Nearly all programming teaches explicitly or implicitly about display rules or about the emotions that are likely in different situations. What is taught depends more often on the viewer's cognition than on what television portrays. If Cagney or Lacey [characters in a popular series about female police officers] is fearless in a situation that would turn most knees to jelly, one may decide that it is a situation in which to hide one's fear or, alternatively, a situation in which some people are unafraid. Of course, one may just dismiss the whole episode as entertainment irrelevant to real life. . . . Research suggests — where any learning at all occurs — an adult would learn more about display rules than about situation-emotion relationships per se, whereas a younger child would learn more about relationships than about display rules. . . . The reason is that, in ascribing emotions to others, young children are more likely to focus on what "emotions" are displayed, whereas adults are more likely to rely on their knowledge of what people "usually" feel in a given situation, regardless of what they display.

The most obvious way in which cultural meanings can influence the experience and expression of emotion is through how a person *perceives, understands,* and *appraises* what is happening socially, which in turn depends on acquired beliefs and goals. For example, there is anecdotal evidence that what appears as innocuous in one culture is fear- or anger-inducing in another, or that foods considered delicacies by one people are repugnant and even disgusting by another (see my discussion of disgust in Chapter 6).

Other Examples of Cultural Influence

There are hard data showing that even one's perceptions are influenced by culture — for example, in a person's susceptibility to optical illusions (e.g., Segall, Campbell, & Herskovitz, 1966). Tursky and Sternbach (1967) have also demonstrated ethnic differences in the psychophysiological response to pain. This is an example of a constitutive rule because a response state is shaped by culture, though ethnic differences also shape regulative rules.

Based on interviews, Zborowsky (1958, 1969) described ethnic differences in the interpretation of, and the emotional and behavioral reactions to, pain and illness symptoms. For example, he found that, compared with "Old Americans" (those whose families had lived in the United States for many generations and were fully assimilated), Jewish and Italian American mothers were both overprotective and overconcerned about the child's health. Jewish and Italian patients responded to pain emotionally and tended to exaggerate it. In contrast, "Old Americans" were more stoical and "objective" in their reaction to pain. Mechanic (1963), too, observed that, regardless of their educational or economic levels, American Jews were more likely than either American Protestants or Catholics to visit a doctor and take medications. This is an example of both constitutive and regulative rules, because the distress of being ill and the social reaction to it seem both to be affected. (see also Zola, 1966).

Remember, too, that an anthropological concern with cultural differences parallels, a psychological concern with individual differences. In the latter vein, Kleinman (1988) has made a clinical analysis of the divergent personal meanings of terminal and disabling illness among individuals. Such clinical analyses move the culturally based analyses of Zborowsky, Mechanic, and Zola from society to the individual sufferer. The complexity of the themes in "illness narratives," as Kleinman calls them, which are embedded in and gain their meanings from the individual's life history, can be illustrated by the following account (1988, p. 32):

> A flareup in the heart disease of an elderly business executive in North American society can become a part of his bereavement for the wife who died six months earlier. This illness incorporates his worsening alcohol abuse and his bitter conflict with his children over control of the family business. It assimilates his fear of dying and guilt over being a lapsed believer, along with his lifelong psychological conflict stemming from fears of passive dependence and of being controlled by others — fears that took origin from a demoralizing relationship with a brutally authoritarian father. Having become an integral element of the illness experience, those fears have recrudesced under the threat of serious incapacity and the undisguised aim of his children to persuade him to enter a nursing home. They are also intensified by his powerful need near the close of life to make sense of key losses by working out the denouement of the narrative of his life's course. The detailed empirical and symbolic particularities of this life trajectory, like those of every other, create a unique texture of meaning — external layers written over internal ones to form a palimpsest — for each person's experience of chronic illness.

I suggested earlier that culture influences emotion by shaping social relationships and systems of judgment on which appraisal is predicated. During World War II, interest in the Japanese by U.S. governmental agencies was strong because of uncertainty about the nature of the people who were at that time our enemy and how to deal with them. Ruth Benedict's fascinating book *The Chrysanthemum and the Sword* (1946) was a remarkable effort to understand Japanese culture entirely by available written documents. The book's title juxtaposes, from the standpoint of the West, two seemingly contradictory sides of the Japanese character, on the one hand a sensitivity to beauty in nature illustrated by a favorite Japanese flower, the chrysanthemum, and in the same people a reverence for a fighting spirit, integrity, and loyalty to one's feudal lord as expressed in the legends of the samurai, the feudal lord's retainers.

This book represented a unique attempt to study Japanese culture and personality for very practical reasons, and the information derived from this research was drawn upon for one of the great problems the United States faced toward the end of the war — namely, whether we could expect the Japanese to surrender and accept a postwar occupation; and if so, how to facilitate this outcome. Clearly the cooperation of Emperor Hirohito was essential and helped make this occupation peaceful and successful.

Like many writers before and after, Benedict was struck by the powerful shame-oriented emphasis in the education of children and the role of the social group and community in the socialization of Japanese. This is illustrated in the following passage (1946, pp. 287–288):

> One striking continuity connects the earlier and later periods of the child's life: the great importance of being accepted by his fellows. This, and not an absolute standard

of virtue, is what is inculcated in him. In early childhood his mother took him into her bed when he was old enough to ask, he counted the candies he and his brother and sister were given as a sign of how he ranked in his mother's affection, he was quick to notice when he was passed over and he asked even his older sister, "Do you love me *best?*" In the later period he is asked to forgo more and more personal satisfactions, but the promised reward is that he will be approved and accepted by "the world." The punishment is that "the world" will laugh at him. This is, of course, a sanction invoked in child training in most cultures, but is exceptionally heavy in Japan.

Benedict's very early work has since been updated by research programs designed to study child-rearing practices in Japan compared with those in the United States. The best source I know is a review and analysis by Miyake, Campos, Kagan, and Bradshaw (1986), which cites the work of Benedict and Doi, among others, as well as Vogel and Vogel (1961), Vogel (1967), Lebra (1976), Caudill (1971), Caudill and Weinstein (1969), and Azuma, Kashiwagi, and Hess (1981).

What Benedict noted is the substance of the Japanese concept of *amae,* which appears to have no equivalent in European language and which was discussed in depth later by Doi (1973), who has more recently analyzed contrasts between Western and Japanese views of relationships between the person as an individual and the external social community, and between what is psychologically inner and outer (Doi, 1985). Doi's analysis emphasized *amae* and the experience of oneness with the mother and the social environment, fostered by willing support and indulgence of the baby and efforts to avoid separation.

Amae is described as the wish or need to be loved and approved, a kind of psychological dependency on others. It is usual for Japanese to give this quality a positive connotation, whereas Americans, who have a high regard for individuality and autonomy, regard it as reprehensible and shameful, especially in men. Thus, when Japanese get overtly angry, they are apt to feel distress about this, whereas manifesting anxiety about how another person regards them is familiar and personally comfortable, depending, of course, on the eliciting conditions. However, when Americans get overtly angry it does not have a particularly negative connotation, whereas the expression of anxiety is to some extent foreign and personally uncomfortable.

The Vogels (1961) reported that Japanese children and their mothers spent very little time separated. Japanese mothers also communicate a fear of the world outside the family, especially toward strangers (probably because they are so concerned with preserving closeness between them and the child). Japanese children are often very shy and inhibited when they enter school. Lebra (1976) emphasized the efforts of the Japanese mother to sensitize her child to avoid feelings of loneliness and cope with these feelings by closeness to and dependence on the mother. In Caudill's (1971; Caudill & Weinstein, 1969) research, the first to make comparisons of the Japanese and American child-rearing patterns, the American mothers emphasized the value of autonomy and independence on the part of the child in contrast to the Japanese concern with closeness and dependency. Americans seem to want a vocal, active baby, and Japanese seem to want a quiet, contented baby.

Looking again to Japan, where there has been a rapid shift in recent years away from distinctively Japanese cultural traditions to a way of life at least superficially more similar to that of the Western world, there were and probably remain strong underlying cultural patterns of thought and action that sharply distinguish Japanese society from the U.S. and European cultures. This is well illustrated in the observations of Caudill (1959) on Japanese and Euro-American attitudes toward alcohol and its use. Although both Japanese (especially men) and Euro-Americans drink a great deal, there seemed to be little alcoholism in Japan in the sense of a debilitating disorder when Caudill did his studies. There are some who believe, however, that the problem of alcoholism even in the past might have been understated.

In any case, a whiskey advertisement in a popular magazine of some years ago points up the Japanese attitude and has always entertained me. It shows a pleasant old gentleman smilingly anticipating the pleasure of drinking the six bottles of whiskey he has been saving up, while his gray-haired wife is kneeling on the floor and counting her money. The advertisement caption says, "To each his own happiness," reflecting a typical family pattern in which the wife manages the money and gives her husband an allowance with which to do his drinking. When he comes home drunk, the wife is likely to greet him, help him off with his shoes and clothing, prepare a snack for him, and assist him to bed without a complaint.

Nor was this drinking pattern traditionally subject to much social criticism, although this seems to be changing in light of the proliferation of drunks in Tokyo subways. It was unusual for a Japanese man to drink during the working day. Instead, he waited for evening, or vacation, or some other suitable occasion, and he did not anticipate rejection or criticism from others because of his drinking. This seems both constitutive and regulative to me, because what is affected is probably both the emotions of people to the drinker and how they are supposed to react to him.

In contrast, there has traditionally been considerable shame and guilt associated with heavy drinking in the United States and Europe; such drinking not infrequently produces a deterioration in the person's work and social relations, and may lead ultimately to the plight of the "skid row" alcoholic. In the United States, there is great concern about widespread drinking and drunk driving among teenagers, and television is full of ominous advertisements about the evils of alcohol and the social decay and harms to health it can produce. Drugs such as heroin and cocaine are even more troubling to our society, a topic about which there has been a sense of crisis, extraordinary hypocrisy, and moralistic posturing, perhaps because of the popular concern about violent crime and its connection to drugs.

An interesting, provocative, and almost forgotten research comparison of emotional differences among people growing up in two different cultures is a study by Singer and Opler (1956) of Irish and Italian Americans. Singer and Opler observed the emotional patterns and psychological symptoms of an equal number of Irish American and Italian American male schizophrenics, all suffering from serious mental disturbances, and linked these to known differences in cultural outlook between two ethnic groups living within the same society and sharing a common religious heritage. The choice of these two ethnic groups was predicated on clearly demarcated cultural differences in family structure and values. The researchers wanted to determine the extent to which these differences, even following emigration from their cultures of origin, would be reflected in observable patterns of disturbed behavior.

At the time of the study, the Irish mother usually played a dominant and controlling role in the family. Furthermore, in the Irish family sexual activity was subordinated to procreation, celibacy was encouraged, courtship lacked intensity and was drawn out, and marriage was typically delayed for a long time (probably originally for economic reasons). Sexual feelings were also regarded as sinful and thus were a source of considerable guilt. In contrast, the Italian pattern involved a dominant father. Sexuality was not only acceptable but was cultivated as a sign of healthy maleness, as any woman who has visited Italy and had her bottom pinched can attest. Thus, the Italian cultural pattern encouraged expressive acting out of feelings and a male-dominated family life, whereas the Irish pattern tended to be one of inhibition, delay of gratification, and maternal domination. It should not be surprising, therefore, to find patients of Irish and Italian descent showing quite different emotional patterns, derived from differences in their cultural outlook.

Sixty male schizophrenic patients in a mental hospital in New York City were carefully studied by means of direct observation, case history data, and personality tests. The patients ranged in age from 18 to 45, were comparable in education and socioeconomic status, had been hospitalized at about the same time, and were all first-, second-, or third-generation Americans. Singer and Opler indeed found that the Irish male patient was far more inhibited than the Italian, was more beset by fear and guilt, and felt considerable hostility to female family members, though largely he inhibited these feelings. He was also frequently alcoholic (19 out of 30 patients), a symptom that was very rare in the Italians (found in only one of the 30 patients), although Italians also drank extensively. The Italian patient, on the other hand, was far more emotionally expressive and overtly hostile, and he did not attack female family figures but he usually aimed his hostility at the male parent. Findings like these highlight that ways of thinking, feeling, and acting, and even mental illness, are linked to the culture or subculture from which people come, probably in both a constitutive and regulative sense.

Another set of examples of cultural variation having implications for emotion is the contrast between the values of individualism and collectivism, outlooks that differ in different cultures and among different individuals within those cultures. This has been studied extensively by Triandis, Bontempo, Villareal, Asai, and Lucca (1988; see also Sampson, 1988, for a politically more judgmental discussion of individualistic versus collectivistic social patterns). Although Triandis et al. recognize the oversimplified nature of their analysis, they point out that in individualistic cultures, *individuals* are said to achieve; in collectivist cultures, *groups* are said to achieve. In individualistic cultures people feel proud of their individual achievements, and competitive success and interdependence are viewed in utilitarian/social exchange terms; in collectivist cultures, people feel proud of their group's achievements, and interdependence is viewed in terms of duty, obligation, and morality. This seems to me to be about constitutive rules. Triandis et al. (1988, p. 335) write as follows about this:

> Several themes, such as self-reliance, achievement, hedonism, competition, and interdependence change their meanings in the context of the two kinds of cultures. Self-reliance for the individualistic cultures implies freedom to do one's own thing and

also competition with others. Self-reliance for the collectivist cultures implies not being a burden on the ingroup, and competition is unrelated to it. Competition in collectivist cultures is among ingroups, not among individuals.

Studying nine cultural groups, Triandis et al. found a number of cross-cultural, psychosocial differences that derive from this theme. For example, family integrity, consisting of good and lasting relationships between parents and children, was comparatively high in collectivist cultures. Interdependence, consisting of helping one's own family when in need, living close to friends, and having frequent contacts, was high in the collectivist cultures, and separation from ingroups was more common in the individualistic cultures. Self-reliance and hedonism, on the other hand, were high in the individualistic cultures. The contrast of values here, made for example between Americans and Japanese, is expressed when Americans say the squeaky wheel gets the grease, but in Japan the saying is that the nail that sticks out gets pounded down.

With respect to individual differences, allocentric individuals received more frequent and better quality social support than did egocentric individuals, who reported being more lonely than the allocentrics. Although these authors did not study emotions directly, it takes very little imagination to form hypotheses about the kinds of social experiences in these cultures that might be harmful, threatening, or beneficial, thus resulting in either negative or positive emotions, and hypotheses about emotion-relevant individual differences in personality as a result of selective internalization.

There has been extensive recent work by cultural and psychologically focused anthropologists comparing the meaning systems of many different cultures. This work cannot be adequately reviewed here, but should be mentioned in a general way. Some notable examples among many others include D'Andrade's (1984) observations about the meanings of success in American culture; Rosaldo's (1980; 1983) and a string of others focused on Asia and the U.S. (e.g., Ausubel, 1955; studies and analyses by Marsella and his colleagues on culture and emotion, selfhood, coping, and other phenomena, including Marsella, DeVos, & Hsu, 1985; Marsella, Kinzie, & Gordon, 1973; Marsella, Murray, & Golden, 1974; Marsella & Scheuer, 1988; Marsella, Tharp, & Ciborowski, 1979); examinations of shame, guilt, anger, and depression among Japanese and Westerners, Caucasian Americans, Chinese Americans, Japanese Americans, and the Ilongots of Java; research by Hamilton, Blumenfeld, Akoh, and Miura (1990) on taking credit and accepting blame among Japanese and American children; Ryff's (1987) review of studies of diverse societies, including Japan, the United States, China, and India; Church's (1987) examination of personality research in the Philippines; Sue and Sue's (1987) study of Asian Americans; and Florian and Snowden's (1989) research on the reasons given for fear of death by Vietnamese Americans compared with other ethnic groups in the Unites States (such as Chinese, Mexicans, blacks, whites, and Jews). They conclude that the Vietnamese have a greater concern than any other group with loss of social identity and the consequences of their death to family and friends, and they relate this difference to a lack of direction and fulfillment in their lives, lacks that result from the conditions of their uprooting during the Vietnam War.

Shweder (1985) has also made a searching examination of patterns of depression cross-culturally, making a case that the emotional functioning of people in different cultures is neither basically the same nor entirely unique. He finds universals and cultural specifics in six aspects of the emotion process: the types of emotions experienced, emotion-laden situations, the personal and social meaning of the emotions that are experienced, how emotions are communicated or expressed, the social rules about emotions and their display, and the management of unexpressed emotions, or what I referred to in Chapter 3 as emotion-focused or cognitive coping.

I think it is clear, in summary, that culture is a powerful influence on emotion. Even efforts of a society to regulate emotions will have an influence, if not on the shaping of the emotion then on its social expression. About this there seems to be not much argument. Where arguments arise they are about what variables in the emotion process culture can influence, in what way, and how much. I offered a set of postulates about this in Chapter 5, which deals with the competition between biological universals and sociocultural sources of variability, and gave some examples in that chapter of different ways in which the cultural influences might work.

Culture and Appraisal

Having discussed and illustrated the way culture influences the emotional life, it is now important to relate, if possible, what has been said to the appraisal process by zeroing in on the appraisal components used in Chapters 6 and 7 for each individual emotion. Culture could have a major influence in both a constitutive and regulative sense on the goals we acquire and consider personally important—and on other appraisal components, too. Although distinguishing what is experienced emotionally from what is merely expressed in any instance is, as the reader will understand, extremely difficult (an issue I discussed in Chapter 2), I make an attempt here to examine briefly how culture might affect the components of appraisal.

Recall that the three *primary appraisal* components are goal relevance, goal congruence or incongruence, and type of ego-involvement. Though individuals will differ among themselves, I think we should say (see Chapter 3) that culture influences the values, goals, and goal hierarchies its members acquire and express, including their ego-identities.

Whether a person appraises that a *goal is relevant* or at stake in an encounter will depend on that person's goal hierarchy and the social context of the encounter. Relevance of an important goal means the potential for strong emotions. Consider, for example, whether or to what extent pain or other medical symptoms imply a health stake for which medical attention might be needed and about which one should be anxious, angry, or depressed. What we know of the seriousness of such symptoms will make a great difference in this.

Nevertheless, we know from the cross-cultural comparisons I discussed earlier that Jewish and Italian Americans regard pain and symptoms somewhat differently than "Old Americans" do. It is not certain whether being ill is more alarming to Jews and Italians than it is to Old Americans in a constitutive sense or whether it is dealt with less stoically in a regulative sense. Both mechanisms could apply as a function of the ethnic outlooks. Even more interesting are the clinical observations of Kleinman (1988), cited earlier, in which the meaning of being ill is best understood in the context of the person's life history and the individualized significance of what is happening for that person's values, beliefs, life goals, and ego-identity.

In addition to affecting goal relevance, cultural differences could also affect *goal incongruence,* inasmuch as the issue for this appraisal component is whether or not an important goal is being harmed or endangered. Consider another example from the cross-cultural studies regarding Japanese and American child-rearing already discussed. We saw that the Japanese child is apt to react with distress to anger expressed by its mother much more readily or strongly than does its American counterpart, for whom maternal disapproval and anger are common. The goal of being at one with the mother, or pleasing her, is much stronger in Japanese babies as a result of the mother's commitment to a symbiotic relationship that is fostered by indulgence and gentle, shaming efforts to get the child to avoid disappointing or displeasing the mother. The cultural contrast is further enhanced by the American mother's strong commitment to encourage autonomy and individuation. Thus, the goals inculcated in Japanese child-rearing differ to some extent from those in the United States; in consequence, there is a high likelihood that certain conditions will be goal incongruent in the United States but not so in Japan and vice versa.

The *type of ego-involvement* in the appraisals of Japanese and American babies and young children is also likely to diverge as a result of the different ego-identity patterns emphasized in the two cultures. Consider, for example, the difference between the two cultures in their commitments to the individual (which is characteristic of the U.S. outlook) versus the community, such as the family or nation (which is characteristic of Japan). A Japanese child must subordinate the personal side of its ego-identity to the group; the American must develop a strongly autonomous and independent identity capable of challenging the group.

In Japanese stories in which there is a conflict between, say, a couple in love and the wishes of their families or the social rules, the outcome is most often the tragedy of giving up love and conforming to the society; the Japanese have a feeling of rightness and may enjoy, probably ambivalently, the triumph of society over the individual. In Euro-American stories of similar conflict, most often the couple resists the family's wishes or social rules, and we have a feeling of its rightness and enjoy the triumph of the individual against the world. For us, too, the conflict might end in tragedy, as in Shakespeare's *Romeo and Juliet* and Leonard Bernstein's *West Side Story.* In both cases, Japanese and American, the lovers are apt to be "star crossed," caught up in tragedy not of their own making, a symbol of the problems of the society; yet even in death, individual values are likely to triumph in American lore and community values in Japan. A consequence of this is that the provoking scenarios of anger or anxiety, as well as the way these emotions are responded to by those who experience and observe them, differ in the two cultures.

Though I am not aware of life-span studies on this, the compliance emphasized in Japanese child-rearing makes the Japanese child and perhaps adult uneasy rather than angry in competitive situations that are individual rather than collective, whereas the American child and adult should react with anger more comfortably. These differences could work through either constitutive or regulative processes, or both. For example, it is possible that both cultural groups would get uneasy and angry, but the Japanese might be made uncomfortable about the anger and suppress it, whereas the American would be uncomfortable about the anxiety and suppress it. We do not know to what extent these outlooks change the emotions actually experienced, or whether they affect only the expression or display.

A similar analysis can be made of the *secondary appraisal* components of blame or credit, coping potential, and future expectations, which are probably also influenced by culture in both constitutive and regulative ways. For example, who should get *blamed* or given *credit?* Although I am not aware of explicit research comparisons, Tahitians (Levy, 1973, 1984), who are wary of anger and whose doctrines emphasize avoiding situations of anger and physical aggression, should be more apt to avoid assessing blame than we are in the United States, where the externalization of blame is common. And the Javanese, who are much more negative about pride than are the Minangkabau (Heider, 1991), ought to be less likely than the latter to accept credit. Similarly, in Japan one avoids appearing too pleased at compliments for one's family, and we might wonder whether it is credit and pride that are being avoided or only their social manifestations. Whether a difference like this might exist at the preconscious level or only on the surface is an interesting question, but one that is difficult to answer.

With respect to *coping potential,* what is culturally permissible or appropriate could affect whether and how we respond emotionally to the way another person acts toward us in a constitutive sense, and how we express the emotion could be affected in a regulative sense. The Tahitian approach to anger again provides a useful example. The cultural proscription is to cope with anger by avoiding anger-inducing situations, by not taking an insult seriously, and by expressing anger, if you must, verbally not physically. This sounds to me very much like our own middle-class values about anger and aggression, illustrated in Chapter 1 with a scenario about how a Western movie hero should act; it should apply less for the working class or for those cultures and subcultures with a strong male macho ideology that suggests that it is important to act in a physically aggressive way to preserve one's ego-identity.

With respect to *future expectations,* we acquire from the culture a set of beliefs about the reigning influences in the world—for example, luck, fate, God, or human wit and skill. These expectations are also influenced by the realities of societal power rules—its threats and sanctions—and how they work. In cultures and subcultures that emphasize fate (the Hindus of India, for instance), we might expect quite different emotional reactions to the outcomes of important goals than we would in a Western industrialized culture with its emphasis on control and acting against negative circumstances. In Asia, too, the ideal of renunciation of material and ego-oriented goals is widely venerated. Even more to the point might be the future expectations of members of a pessimistic culture compared with one having a more optimistic outlook, or the contrast between a view of God as punitive and meanspirited or as beneficent and forgiving.

In sum, although actual research on these appraisal components is lacking, there are plausible grounds for expecting culture to influence all six appraisal components in either a constitutive or regulative manner. To the extent that this is so, the emotional experiences and expressions characteristic of the members of these cultures should also be different. Much more difficult would be the comparison of the emotion process across cultures at a preconscious or unconscious level. Cultural values define powerful goals—both socially and biologically influenced—as unacceptable, thereby generating conflict. Goal incongruence is inevitable in such instances, a point made long ago by Freud about sex and aggression. Few have dared to address this empirically, because with the inevitable interpersonal and language barriers, it is difficult enough to know about what is conscious and reportable across cultures, much less what is happening psychologically below the surface.

Social Structure and Emotion

Those who emphasize the social structure center their attention on functional role relationships taking place in immediate social encounters—for example, in the context of work and family, in which there are all sorts of social pressures, opportunities, and socially derived expectations. Goffman's (1959, 1971) pioneering work on impression management centered on the rules that operate in various types of social interaction. He described in exquisite detail how people manage the outward expression of their emotions and the strategies they use in response to folkways, but gave little attention to emotional experience.

To address the way society influences emotional experience as well as emotional expression, Hochschild (1979) coined the terms "feeling rules" and "emotion work," which is an expansion of the term *display rules* coined by Ekman and Friesen (1969; see also Ekman, 1977). It is an expansion because the term *feeling rules* is designed to emphasize not only that we regulate our external expressions of emotion, as when Japanese try to look cheerful even when saddened by a personal loss, because they want to avoid burdening others with their grief, but also that we try to feel what we are supposed to feel in social situations. According to Hochschild, people "psych themselves up"; "squash down their anger"; "try to feel grateful"; and "let themselves feel sad" in response to feeling rules. This is what it means to speak of *emotion work*. In the language of appraisal, in addition to influencing how people overtly express or inhibit their emotions, feeling rules also regulate the emotional state directly by affecting how people appraise the encounter to begin with.

Feeling and display rules influence our emotions, especially when we should feel sad but instead feel happy, and vice versa, when we should feel worse or better than we actually do, or when we feel something for a shorter or longer time than is appropriate. Even when these rules are implicit rather than explicit, they are part of the social fabric and exercise powerful sanctions on how we define encounters, and therefore on our emotions (feelings in Hochschild's usage) and their social expression.

Not only do we tailor our reactions to fit the social rules, we also internalize these rules and believe something is wrong when we fail to conform to them in our actual emotions. Therefore, feeling rules are not only situational but can become part of personality, operating in the same way culture operates on personality development. There is often conflict between both sets of forces, with resentment experienced by the person because the social pressure is viewed as exploitation, as when airline stewards or stewardesses, or other service personnel, are expected to smile or to act friendly and cheerful even when they feel otherwise.

In emphasizing mainly economic exploitation of service personnel who must act differently from the way they feel — in keeping with Marxian concepts of alienation from work — Hochschild considers only the negative side of social pressure. She overlooks that being obliged to conform to the pressure can actually lead us to feel more engaged and cheerful. Mildly depressed persons, for example, can sometimes benefit emotionally by having to function socially despite a dour mood, and their depression may lift.

On a personal level, I sometimes get up in the morning distressed over something and feeling bad, and I don't want to do anything but indulge my dour feelings. However, I must deal with my upcoming eight o'clock lecture class, think about what I will say, and manage the early morning commute. In class I must be cheerful and enthusiastic when I just don't feel up to it. Because I usually enjoy teaching and am a bit of a "ham," however, I usually rise to the occasion and mobilize when I am before the class, and in so doing I usually begin to feel expansive and even excited. In the process of doing what Hochschild calls psyching myself up, whatever was bothering me is forgotten for the time being, and I actually do enjoy myself. The positive state may linger for much of the day and sometimes permanently terminates the gloom. I didn't feel like teaching the class, but doing so — that is, coping with the demands of my job — has benefited my mood. It is, by the way, an example of how playing a role actively can change one's outlook, at least temporarily (cf. Lazarus & Folkman, 1984, Ch. 11).

In this example, it is important to recognize the process by which my mood was changed. The change did not occur because the problem that started me off in a bad mood was gone; rather, the focus of attention was altered temporarily by the requirement that I teach my class. What changed was not my original problem but the situational context of adaptation, which led to a change in what I was concerned with at that moment; therefore, my mood changed, because I was now dealing with a very different set of relational demands, opportunities, and constraints. We have many agendas in our daily lives, and not all of them are relevant or attended to simultaneously. In psychotherapy for dysfunctional and distressing emotions, however, the task is to get people to change how they are dealing with a chronic or recurrent problem, so that when it arises again, as it must, the troubling emotional pattern will no longer occur.

How Social Structure Works

How does the society, with its feeling rules, influence the emotions? As a result of social psychological research beginning in the 1930s, we know a great deal about social pressure and how it works. Although most of this research did not directly concern itself with emotions, or with appraisal and coping processes per se, it takes only a bit of thought to see its connection with the emotion process. Later I will offer more direct evidence about education of the emotions in our society.

The earliest programmatic work on the way social situations affect how we think, feel, and act was done by Sherif (1935) with his experiments on the autokinetic effect. *Autokineses* means self-regulated movement, the tendency of a stationary light to seem to move when there are no external reference points by which an observer can fix its position. The effect once posed a real problem for bomber pilots flying in formation: At night they often used the lights of the plane ahead to set their course; because the lights seemed to move in an erratic, confusing fashion — the dark sky contains no reference points — pilots sometimes became disoriented and flew off course. The problem was ultimately solved by using lights that blinked on and off.

Because the phenomenon is subjective and ambiguous, it was also an ideal perceptual situation for the study of social influence. Sherif capitalized on it to study the influence of other people on the way we see things. Subjects were put in a dark room with a single point of light, and told that the light was moving, and that their task was to estimate how far and in which direction it moved. When working alone, a subject developed his own stable autokinetic movement pattern, and the direction and distance of the movement were measured. When confederates were used, their prearranged reports strongly influenced the subjects' reported movement pattern, establishing a new norm for the subject that persisted even when the subject was again working alone. These experiments provided dramatic early demonstrations of the powerful effect others can have on one's perceptual judgments.

It could be argued that if the judgmental task had been unambiguous, the social pressure would have failed to have any effect. Some years later this possibility was followed up by Asch (1952a, 1952b, 1956) in a series of innovative experiments that had a major impact on subsequent research and theory about social influence. Asch set up a situation in which subjects had to say which of three comparison lines was most similar in length to a standard line. Although the differences could have been made very small and difficult, which would have increased the ambiguity of the task, Asch chose instead to make the task easy and unequivocal; thus, when the task was performed alone, subjects made virtually no errors. This created an even more powerful demonstration of the effects of social pressure.

In a typical experiment, there was a single subject, and from three to eight confederates were employed; these announced, one by one, judgments that were erroneous. Imagine yourself in a room with seven other "peers"; as you await your turn to report what you saw, you hear the others one by one all giving the same judgment which obviously differs from what seems correct. Under these circumstances, the typical subject made errors in the direction of the group judgment more than a third of the time; some yielded or conformed on every trial, others never conformed, and still others did so from time to time. Figure 9.1 shows a typical stimulus in Asch's research and illustrates how easy the task was to say which comparison line most nearly matched line X in length. Table 9.1 presents a distribution of error frequencies made by subjects exposed to social pressure and those who were not. Asch's figure and table were famous for many years, and some version could be found in almost all introductory psychology textbooks of the time.

One must be careful here not to equate Sherif's autokinetic effect with Asch's social conformity effects. In the Sherif research, there is every reason to believe that the subjects' actual perceptions were affected by the social environment — they saw the lights moving and reported this. In the Asch research, although subjects frequently went along with the group judgment, there is little evidence that they actually came to misperceive the stimuli; instead they felt conflicted about what they should report.

FIGURE 9.1. A typical stimulus in the Asch study. Subjects were shown all four lines simultaneously and asked which one of the comparison lines, A, B, or C, was most similar in length to line X. When confederates unanimously reported the incorrect answer (say, C), subjects conformed by giving the same wrong answer about 35 percent of the time. (*Source:* S. E. Asch, *Social Psychology.* Englewood Cliffs, NJ: Prentice Hall, 1952. Reprinted by permission.)

Over subsequent years, a tremendous amount of research was done to expand this pioneering exploration of social influence and to pin down the conditions affecting the incidence of conformity. The following is a summary of the findings of this research over many years: Yielding to group pressure occurs regardless of whether or not the judgmental task is ambiguous, as in statements of opinion, or unambiguous, as in statements of fact. It occurs even when the answers given by the group are clearly ridiculous — for example, that men are 8 to 9 inches taller than women or that male babies have a life expectancy of 25 years. It also occurs even when the subject cannot see the others in the group, as long as it is believed that they are present. As

TABLE 9.1. Distribution of Errors When Subjects Performed Asch's Task Alone and Under Group Pressure

Number of Errors	Frequency of Errors When Subject Was Exposed to Group Pressure	Frequency of Errors When Each Subject Worked Alone
0	13	35
1	4	1
2	5	1
3	6	—
4	3	—
5	4	—
6	1	—
7	2	—
8	5	—
9	3	—
10	3	—
11	1	—
12	0	—

(*Source:* S. E. Asch, *Social Psychology.* Englewood Cliffs, NJ: Prentice Hall, 1952. Reprinted by permission.)

might be expected, degree of conformity is reduced, though by no means eliminated, if the voting situation is made anonymous and the subject thinks he is overhearing the other judgments through an error by the experimenter.

To digress a bit, there is the well-known research by Milgram (1965), which he viewed as an analogue to authoritarian regimes such as Nazi Germany. In this research, subjects obeyed the experimenter's instructions to administer painful electric shocks to others even when these victims cried out in severe pain and begged the subject to stop. This suggested that ordinary social pressure can lead people to accept a manifest evil, as we all know to our everlasting sadness (see also Miller, 1986, on Milgram's work). In recent years other interpretations of this pattern have been offered—implying, for example, that subjects actually interpreted what was happening more benignly on the basis of their subjective judgment that the faculty member doing the study was a responsible person who would not harm anyone. This reinterpretation, however, only reminds us that most evil in the world is supported by ordinary people who go along with what is happening by finding benign ways of interpreting it. In any case, Figure 9.2, which shows the percentage of subjects who continued to administer shocks at different levels of shock intensity and evidence of the subjects' distress, is a graphic representation of early findings of this research.

In summarizing variables of social influence, the size of a majority is important up to a point; yielding is not as great, though it is still substantial, when the majority consists of only two others; increasing the majority beyond two results in a large jump in yielding, but increasing the majority above three or four only adds a slight increment. The more confidence a subject has in the group (e.g., if it is believed to

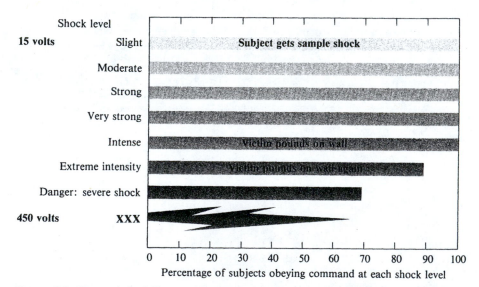

FIGURE 9.2. In a study by Milgram, 65 percent of the subjects were willing to use the highest levels of shock intensity. Virtually all subjects were willing to provide shocks of moderate or strong intensity. (*Source:* S. Milgram, "Behavioral Study of Obedience." *Journal of Abnormal and Social Psychology, 67.* Washington, DC: American Psychological Association. Copyright © 1963 by the American Psychological Association. Reprinted by permission.)

be highly expert or composed of high-status persons) the greater the pressure to conform. However, if there has been a history of disagreement among the confederates of the experimenter, the pressure to conform is less, probably because such a history erodes confidence in the group. And if the subject finds himself with an ally later on who starts to give the same answer that a nonconforming subject would have given, yielding is sharply reduced. Cohesive groups — those with a strong esprit de corps or with which the subject feels closely identified — produce more conformity than do groups without such cohesiveness. Providing a developmental focus, conformity is greater in early adolescence (at ages 13 to 14) than later on (from 18 to 20). Certain personality variables, which have to do with self-esteem, self-confidence, and intelligence, have also been found to dispose the person to remain independent from social pressure (see Maslach, Stapp, & Santee, 1985; and Maslach, Santee, & Wade, 1987).

During the same period, Newcomb (1943; Newcomb et al., 1967) also made extensive field observations of changes in political attitudes on the part of students at Bennington College during their four years of education. Others made similar observations of socially induced developmental changes in outlook. Taking a somewhat different tack by examining governmental records of group decision processes, Janis (1972) was able to show powerful and damaging conformity pressures on presidential advisors responsible for governmental policy blunders such as the Bay of Pigs invasion of Cuba and the Indochina (e.g., Vietnam) wars. Janis called the process whereby the group inhibited dissent to agree on questionable policies *groupthink*. I might also mention as a natural example of the power of the social group to influence the individual the mass suicide and murder of the followers of Jim Jones in Jonestown in 1978 in which 900 people were victimized and died.

As a final example, a classic and complex study by Schachter (1951) during this same period demonstrated how the group punishes deviant individuals, thereby demonstrating a motivational basis of conformity in us all. Schachter created a number of "natural" groups by advertising for college students who wanted to engage in discussions of current social issues. When each group first met, they were asked by the organizer to discuss and make recommendations about a juvenile case that was currently pending in court. A delinquent was to be sentenced for a crime, and the group was asked to determine whether it would recommend clemency or strong discipline to the presiding judge. The case was actually presented in a such a way as to favor clemency.

Following the experimental tradition of Sherif and Asch, Schachter employed accomplices to create pressures to conformity and deviancy. Three accomplices were assigned to each group; these played three prearranged social roles: a *conformer,* who always adopted at the outset the dominant position taken by the group; a *deviate,* who invariably took a position opposite from that of the group; and a *recanter,* who began with a deviant position but later revoked it — seemingly because he was won over to the dominant viewpoint.

Schachter found that the three types of accomplices were treated quite differently. In general, groups punished the deviate for his heresy. At the beginning of the discussions, for example, the group directed intensive conversation toward the deviate and the recanter, presumably in an effort to convert them. However, as time passed without their being able to change the deviate's position, members of the group stopped talking to him. The recanter was ultimately accepted and treated no differently than anyone else.

As part of the same experiment, each group was later told there were too many members for effective future discussions, and each member was asked to evaluate every other member to determine democratically who might be eliminated for membership. The groups usually tended to rate deviates as less acceptable than the other two confederates, thus making their expulsion from the group likely. And when committees were organized to carry out the administrative business of the group, such as determining the topic for discussion, announcing meeting times and places, and the like, deviates were seldom elected to important committees where power might reside, though they were frequently selected for unimportant (powerless) committees where only labor was required. Studies such as this directly point up how social groups use their power to enforce their collective prejudices by punishing the person who does not conform, provide insights into what motivates people to conform, and indirectly suggest the emotional difficulties in resisting the pressure to conform.

Nevertheless, the role of emotion and coping remains mostly implicit rather than explicit in all this research, because the concerns of the researchers center on the external conditions affecting conformity and dissent rather than on the personal struggle of people caught in the social pressure (which must have generated strong emotions). The research on social influence rarely if ever dealt with emotions such as anxiety, shame, guilt, and anger, which are obviously involved in these situations of social influence, or with the coping process that must be a regular feature of them. In all likelihood, one reason for this inattention was the general disinterest of psychology for epistemological reasons, in the emotions, and again we see an example of the fads and fashions of science.

Imagine, for example, what subjects were feeling in Asch's experiments on conformity. Sitting there and seeming to see one answer but also seeing the others one by one give another answer, some probably became merely perplexed: "What is wrong here?" "Have I misunderstood what is going on?" Others are apt to be very anxious and ashamed as the scenario of their deviance unfolds. "I was always a dummy," some say to themselves. "How can I appear to be so foolish? None here will have any respect for me if I stubbornly say what it looks like to me. I will go along with the group to avoid shaming myself, and see if I can figure it out." Still others may get angry: "What right have these people to put me in a situation like this? What's the matter with these other dummies?" And how about the Schachter studies of how the group punishes the deviant? Anxiety, shame, anger, envy, jealousy — all are emotions that could have been generated. Just as obscure in the absence of efforts to measure it are the processes generated to cope with the social and intrapsychic threats and the damage to the subjects' integrity.

Asch's original studies constitute an important, but limited, exception to this lack of concern with the emotions generated in social pressure situations and how people cope with the conflicts and threats these generate. Asch (1952a, 1952b) did careful interviews with his subjects after the experiment, interviews that provided some fertile hypotheses, especially about coping processes. He confronted each subject who yielded to group pressure with his or her performance afterward and asked for an explanation.

Some subjects readily admitted that they believed the other participants had been wrong in their judgments and described great conflict and distress about being deviant. To avoid deviancy, they evidently had consciously chosen to go along with the group. Other subjects also reported experiencing distress but reconciled the difficulty in their minds by assuming that they had somehow misunderstood the task. In effect, they went along with the group, thinking that they themselves had somehow been in error. Finally, a small proportion of subjects expressed surprise and confusion when told of mistakes, reported not remembering experiencing any difficulty during the study, and denied being influenced by the group.

Three distinct processes of coping are suggested by these interview data: (1) Because the group is a powerful agent, capable of disciplining the individual, some subjects felt safer when they avoided exposing themselves as deviant; (2) because people need confirmation from others about their judgments concerning the world, some subjects looked to others in evaluating the adequacy of their own understanding and changed their approach when they seemed to be out of step; (3) because people require approval and acceptance from others, some persons who were deeply threatened when this approval was endangered conformed automatically without seeming even to realize that they were doing so.

The process involved in (3) could be regarded as an example of unconscious conflict and defense. The pattern is like that of the spouse who, when confronted with a demand for divorce, is thoroughly surprised and seems not to have noticed anything wrong in the marriage. An alternative interpretation is that this type of person simply does not pay attention to how another person feels, has the wrong interpretation about what is happening, and is naïve about others. However, if one remembers that the hysteric's defensive style is said to be repression (or denial), which leads to a generalized naïveté based on the narrowing of attention from anything that might be threatening, the two interpretations, naïveté and denial, may not be mutually exclusive. Moreover, what looks like denial may be merely an automatized style of perceiving or relating to the world, generated early in life from not wanting to look at what is threatening, rather than necessarily being an active process of denial or repression (see, for example, the research of Luborsky, Blinder, & Schimek, 1965, on vigilance and avoidance).

Educating the Emotions

To return to the process of emotional socialization, which is a way to describe the central issue at hand, little attention has been given to educational efforts to shape emotions, though this seems to be changing. For example, Pollak and Thoits (1989) have described some of the ways in which staff members of a therapeutic school for disturbed 3- to 5-year-olds communicate what is emotionally appropriate and inappropriate. The authors cite Harris and Olthof's (1982) suggestion that there were three possible ways children come to understand emotions, which they label as *solipsistic, behaviorist,* and *sociocentric. Solipsistic* refers to self-awareness and self-observation. *Behavioristic* refers to learning from other people's emotional reactions. *Sociocentric* refers to formal and informal verbal instruction from the community. Children have to learn the links among specific situational events, expressive gestures, and internal sensations.

Pollak and Thoits's data suggest that the children they studied in this special setting were taught deliberately about emotion by a caretaker's labeling and by making explicit how they should react and why. Elaborate instruction was given by the staff only when a child deviated from emotion norms, expressing inappropriate feelings or feeling displays. The implication is that a similar process occurs in children without emotional disturbances in family life and in school (see also Bloom & Beckwith, 1989, who studied the integration of affective and linguistic expression in early language development).

The problem with the distinction between acquired meanings, or culture, and immediate social pressures on the person in a social encounter is that it is often difficult to tell which is operating and to what extent they reinforce each other or are in conflict. For example, as I said earlier, it is not clear whether we should classify Hochschild's feeling rules as social structural variables or as cultural characteristics that have been internalized and operate in the immediate transaction. They could operate in both ways. The overlapping functions of these influences blur somewhat the distinction between cultural or personality-based feeling rules and those arising situationally out of the social structure.

Consider, too, how public figures must deal with grief or other kinds of distress in their personal lives. When I visited Australia some years ago, I came upon a fascinating political encounter centering on Bob Hawk, who was then a candidate for prime minister for the first time. In a television interview, he had been asked about his daughter-in-law, who was having a struggle with drug addiction at the time, and in the interview Hawk shed some tears. There followed a great amount of public news speculation about whether this show of emotional distress would mar his candidacy. Did it show him as less of a man in a macho society?

It turned out that Hawk was elected several times afterward, suggesting that his overt emotional distress did not harm his political career and might even have helped it. On the other hand, some readers may remember the destruction of Edmund Muskie's presidential aspirations in the U.S. election in which he cried on news film. Both episodes reveal powerful social pressures on public figures, but we would understand the similarities and differences better if the conditions operating in them were also better documented.

Perhaps the emotion work that a public figure must do is especially difficult, given the strong biological pressures that underlie the facial expression of a felt emotion; to turn it off or reverse it may require much effort. It is quite likely that facial expression is much shaped by neurophysiological structures as well as being a learned channel of social communication. Lanzetta (Englis, Vaughn, & Lanzetta, 1982; Lanzetta & Orr, 1980, 1981, 1986; Orr & Lanzetta, 1980, 1984), for example, has shown that it is very difficult to condition a negative response to a happy face and a relaxation response to a fear face. This might also be considered an example of what is today referred to by some as "prepared conditioning," which I discussed briefly in Chapter 8 in connection with the ease with which some fears can be conditioned and their resistence to extinction, presumably as a result of innate, phyloge-netic influences.

From a political standpoint is it seemly to cry and shout, or abandon emotional controls, as some people do at funerals? As a public figure, how should Jackie Kennedy have comported herself at the funeral of her husband, President John Kennedy, after his assassination? How much grief should she have displayed? How much did she actually feel? What is the right amount of distress? There are social class and cultural differences in this that are internalized, as well as situational social demands made by others. What about the stewardess in the airplane who feels dour but is expected to show cheerfulness and warmth? To what extent is the social pressure, backed up perhaps by the threat of economic rewards and punishments, a response to an external social feeling rule or an internalized value about how one should behave?

We must be reminded, too, that we are not passive in assimilating social rules and values and internalizing them as we are growing up. The imagery of osmosis — that is, of a passive recipient partaking of what is presented in the environment — does a disservice to the selectivity with which children model their parents, choosing roles and patterns of behavior on the basis of how serviceable they seem to be to the child (see, for example, Bandura, Ross, & Ross, 1963).

The implication is that we arrive on the scene of social transactions as persons with previously acquired values and meanings, and confront the requirements of social situations that push us one way or another. Sometimes the feeling rules and the internalized cultural values push the person in the same direction and sometimes in opposite directions. The resultant appraisal and coping processes, and the emo-tions they generate, will depend on the interplay of both sets of variables.

A problem with this analysis is the difficulty of making the distinction I made earlier between emotional expression and emotional experience. We can observe the expressions, but it is more difficult to get inside the mind of the person to know the experience. Social influence probably affects both, though we can only know the experience by inference from what is expressed, reported, and observed. One of the most difficult questions for those interested in feeling rules, for example, is to what extent actual feelings, as opposed to emotional displays, can be influenced and changed. Psychotherapists are dedicated to changing dysfunctional and distressing emotions when these are recurrent and frequent. (I shall deal with attempts at inter-vention in Chapter 11.) To manifest a good grasp of the principles involved in the emotion process and its development, emotion theory must to some extent address how malleable emotional expression and experience are.

To understand what is happening to the emotions in immediate social encoun-ters, one must keep in mind that each participant is reacting to cues or signals from the other that give indications about how things are going from the point of view of their individual personal agendas. When there is something at stake in the encounter, appraisals of these cues set in motion a complex chain of cognitive, emo-tional, and coping activities, which are part of the emotion process.

Kemper's (1978) attempt to use variations in two types of social relationships, status and power, as explanations for a number of emotions illustrates how this might work. Although his definitions are somewhat idiosyncratic from the point of view of traditional sociology, he defined *status* as what one gives and receives voluntarily and without pressure from others; when we receive sufficient status we feel happy, content, joyful, glad, esteemed, rewarded, approved, accepted, liked, or loved — each of which is a variant of feeling good. *Power,* in contrast, is the ability to require another to do one's bidding. One can have adequate power and feel safe, secure, and potent; excess power and feel guilty; or insufficient power and feel anxiety or fear. One can also have excess status and feel shame or insufficient status and feel sad, angry, or depressed. Giving less to another than is deserved will result in combined guilt and shame; guilt because one has harmed another and shame because excessive power over the other person negates one's claim to probity, decency, or fairness. For an extensive review and analysis of research and theory on the origins and socialization of guilt, I recommend a very recent chapter by Zahn-Waxler and Kochanska (1990).

Kemper obtains considerable mileage in explaining varied emotions from the analysis of these two social structural factors, power and status. However, to fully understand what happens in an emotional encounter, whether it is temporary or ongoing, requires a more in-depth examination of the relational and cognitive changes to what is happening and the consequent emotional flux. In any social exchange involving emotion, the parties are obtaining information about their relationship and making appraisals of the significance of what is happening for their well-being. Each is responding emotionally to signals given off by the other, both verbal and expressive, and judging whether these have been accurately interpreted. The mutual actions and reactions, and feedback from them, constitute the basis for the appraisals and the emotions they generate.

If we adopt a phylogenetic focus, we see that ethologists, comparative psychologists, and social psychologists have long been well aware of the communicative value of emotional states as revealed in instrumental action and expression (cf. Frick, 1985; Heider, 1958; Marler, 1984). Developmental psychologists have also noted the communication of emotion through a mother's facial expressions and, in turn, communication by the infant or young child to the mother (cf. Campos, Barrett, Lamb, Goldsmith, & Stenberg, 1983; Dunn, 1988; Lewis & Michalson, 1983; Sroufe, Schork, Motti, Lawroski, & LaFreniere, 1984; and Trevarthen, 1984). How emotional signals are appraised depends on the rules for social exchange as well as on the culturally based or inherited, hence universal, meanings of a gesture or other kinds of expression. The role of biological inheritance is clearer and easier to see in simple creatures, and far less applicable to humans.

It is important here, too, not to understate the power of parents to influence their children's understanding of social situations and how they are supposed to act and react emotionally. I implied this kind of emotional communication in Chapter 1 when I spoke of the common tendency of parents to frighten their children by getting visibly distressed about the dangers of carelessly running out into the street where there may be fast-moving cars. These emotional communications are often intended to instill prudence in the child where even one trial learning may be fatal.

However, even without an intent to influence, affective communications by parents or other significant adults are powerful instruments of emotional education, creating social-emotional atmospheres that are quickly and accurately sensed by children. When people come to visit, for example, imagine how the adults react. In one culture or family, the adults get very excited, whether in the positive sense that the visitors are welcome and to be responded to warmly or in the negative sense that visitors are a threat (with some being especially unwelcome) to be avoided or responded to coolly. In the latter case, rather than excitement, suddenly on learning about the visit or finding them at the door unexpectedly, the adults act stiffly, even if politely. The neo-Freudian psychiatrist Harry Stack Sullivan (1953) made much of the transmission of anxiety from mother to child by such inadvertent but powerful communication.

What a child picks up, of course, is often perverse — for example, when a mother who acts as if she feels safe and secure inadvertently communicates to the child that the world is actually dangerous. Or to take another example, when compulsive attention, given by an anxious parent in an effort to provide a safe, well-structured world, is reacted to by the child as oppressive, the parental pattern may then be countered by an opposite one of seeking spontaneity and disorder. Whether they are imitated or resisted, these kinds of emotional communication are likely to play an important role in emotional education. They are learned by children, perhaps internalized, and typically passed on in one form or another to subsequent generations.

Social Structure and Appraisal

As I did previously with culture, I should now sum up the theme of social structure as an influence on the appraisal process, which in my system is the final common path whereby experience in the social world from infancy on shapes the emotion process.

Culture and social structure interact in complex ways, however, operating sometimes in concert, sometimes in conflict. Social structure, like cultural values and meanings, can also be internalized so that it becomes a characteristic of personality. This makes the analysis anything but clean and free of confounding. For example, because adaptational transactions unfold over time, the patterns of social influence on appraisal and the emotions experienced accumulate a brief history of their own during an encounter and across recurring encounters. Therefore, new encounters may recapitulate similar encounters of the past for each person and for each pair of persons. This history itself teaches each person or pair something that could influence subsequent appraisals and coping patterns. Thus, although the mix of variables continually changes, constantly revising the implications for well-being, and therefore changing the emotions experienced and expressed, recurrent encounters with the same persons can create a structure of goals, expectations, and coping strategies, which may take on a stable pattern over time whenever the pair experiences similar encounters.

Therefore, in the background of every transaction, there always exist three sets of forces — namely, (1) cultural meanings that have shaped the motives, beliefs, and understandings a person has of what is happening, (2) immediate social pressures, which are communicated by the behavior of the dramatis personae in the unfolding encounter, and (3) a past history of similar or related encounters that has taught important lessons, which influence the subsequent psycho- and sociodynamics. Still, the chief way in which social structure influences the emotions is in the social roles and statuses of people engaged in contemporaneous transactions in the diverse social encounters of living.

As to how this influences *primary appraisal,* which has to to with *goals* and their fate, it is essential that we read the implications of what is happening in social encounters to appraise whether what is happening is *goal relevant,* whether it is *incongruent or congruent,* and how it bears, if at all, on *type of ego-involvement,* which depends on which of the six forms of ego-identity — namely, esteem, moral values, ego-ideal, meaning and ideas, other persons and their well-being, and life goals — is engaged in the appraisal process.

Consider, for example, the question raised about the feeling rules operating for President Kennedy's wife, Jackie, at her husband's funeral. What goals were operative? To make a proper display? To help the children cope? To cope with the loss herself? To offer warmth and respect to the deceased? To hide resentment toward a man who treated the marriage vows lightly. As I suggested, ethnic and class factors are relevant to these goals, some of which involve our posture in the world. It makes a difference which ones are operating and how we read and respond to the feeling rules and display rules. To satisfy one goal, it may be necessary to thwart another, producing goal incongruence or what is often called conflict. The power of the group, in this case, family and friends as well as a watching world — for we are speaking of a celebrity — to evaluate and criticize and so to shape our behavior under these circumstances is part of the context of this kind of encounter, which affects our overt reactions and perhaps our covert ones, too.

With respect to *secondary appraisal,* assigning *blame or credit* depends not only on one's personality, but also on how another has behaved in a social encounter. A criticism implying blame may be accepted or appreciated as useful when phrased sensitively, but resented if clumsy and assaultive or self-serving. Prideful reactions that seem to be demeaning or unworthy will inhibit the giving of credit to someone who might deserve it. In such instances, how we feel may be at loggerheads with what we are willing to express because of the power that others have over our well-being. The findings of the conformity studies are relevant here, as are those dealing with how the group treats someone who deviates from the group standard. They are contemporaneous influences on these and other appraisal components.

Among the research cited in this chapter the most relevant to *coping potential* is that of Asch on the different ways subjects in the conformity-pressure contexts handled the situation. The correct response was suppressed by many subjects because it deviated from that of the group, sometimes with awareness of the pressure, sometimes being construed as a personal misunderstanding, and sometimes with the conflict denied and unrecognized. We can see that coping potential — that is, what seemed the best way of managing the encounter — was appraised differently by those who displayed each of these three reaction patterns, as is implicit in Asch's interview data.

With respect to *future expectations,* we have reason to assume that those who conformed to the social pressure saw themselves as at risk and that disguising the conflict was a more pleasant or safer alternative than accepting deviancy. There is a widespread preference in our society not to confront another person when there is conflict, which was obviously not in evidence in the minority of research subjects who remained independent of the social pressure.

Summary

This chapter looked at emotional development from a sociocultural point of view. The social rules governing human behavior and the emotional lives of us all are highly complex and operate silently in the main. A major social science problem is to connect the macro level of analysis of the social system with the micro level of the individual person and to say how one influences the other. Society influences emotion by affecting the variables and processes involved in the emotion process, including outputs such as behavior and expression, inputs such as feeling and display rules, stated values, and mediating processes such as appraisal and coping.

There are two broad forms of social influence: the culture in which we live and the social structure. *Culture* provides meanings that are internalized, and *social structure* provides the immediate demands, constraints, and resources that operate in every adaptational transaction. A good part of the discussion centered on ways of thinking about culture and its consequences for emotion as well as examples of this influence. Cultural influences were connected with the six appraisal components, which form the theoretical heart of my analysis.

A great deal of attention was also paid to ideas and research on the way social structure affects emotion, including the classic social psychological research on conformity to social pressure. Here, too, social structure was then connected with the six appraisal components of the theoretical system.

There has been very little research explicitly on the socialization of emotions, and we need to know more about how adults model or teach us what and how to feel, and what and how to express emotions in social intercourse. Examples of how this worked were given, including deliberate and inadvertent emotional communications by parents.

I also pointed out that the distinction between cultural and social structural influence is blurred, because typically they operate in concert in the same social transaction. In any case, in every transaction there are cultural meanings, immediate social pressures, and a past history of similar encounters, all of which must be understood to understand sociocultural influences on the emotion process.

Note

1. In addition to many other sources, which I enumerate in the text, I have also drawn on my book, now out of print, *The Riddle of Man,* published in 1974.

PART FIVE

Practical Applications

The final two chapters of this book deal mainly with practical applications of the thinking presented throughout. Chapter 10 is concerned with the consequences of emotion for health. Till now I have been treating emotion as a dependent variable, a set of reactions that needs to be explained. In Chapter 10 the tables are turned, and emotion is treated as an independent variable — that is, as a causal factor in health outcomes. Chapter 11, which closes the book, deals with the implications of the principles I have presented for several enterprises, including research and the clinical assessment, treatment, and prevention of psychopathology.

❖ 10 ❖

Emotions and Health

In previous chapters I treated emotion mainly as a *dependent variable*, focusing on the conditions that affect the emotion process and how it is generated and unfolds. There is no doubt, for example, that being ill is a powerful negative life condition affecting our emotions. Nevertheless, an overriding reason for our interest is the conviction that, when generated, emotion has profound consequences for health and functioning. When we ask whether and how emotions influence being well or ill, in the short or long term, the order of things is reversed and emotion — that is, the whole cognitive-motivational-relational configuration — becomes an *independent variable.*

I dealt with this a bit in Part Three in my discussions of the dynamics and pathologies of different kinds of emotion, and of the influence of emotion on coping in Chapter 3. However, the focus was always on the short term — that is, on the immediate encounter. When attention is directed at the long term, we deal with somatic health, subjective well-being, and social functioning.

The possibility that the emotion process affects short- and long-term health and well-being has been of major interest to a variety of academic disciplines, including physiology, neurology, biochemistry (especially endocrinology), sociology, anthropology, and psychology, as well as applied subdisciplines, such as medicine, psychiatry, nursing, clinical psychology, social work, and counseling. It is a central theme of psychosomatic medicine, a field that is also referred to as behavioral medicine, medical psychology, or health psychology.

This is not a chapter on health psychology, the issues of which go beyond emotion and include behavioral and life-style sources of illness and how it might be prevented and treated. I do not attempt to review research suggesting, for example, that conditions of life (such as social support) and personality characteristics (such as hardiness) serve as buffers to stressful circumstances of life. Such reviews may be found in several sound textbooks about health psychology (e.g., Feist & Brannon, 1988; Taylor, 1986) and diverse articles on the topic (e.g., Kiecolt-Glaser & Glaser, 1988; Lazarus, 1990a; Lobel & Dunkel-Schetter, 1990; Matarazzo, 1980; Rodin & Salovey, 1989; and Taylor, 1989). My objective is to analyze the role of emotion in adaptational outcomes and to explore issues that arise in research.

I begin with somatic health (or illness) and deal with its assessment, the methodological difficulties in proving a causal role for emotion, and the mechanisms whereby emotion and coping might have an influence. I follow this topic with comparable treatments of the two other adaptational outcomes — namely, subjective well-being and social functioning.

Emotion and Somatic Health

Everyone has some idea of what the terms *health* and *illness* mean, but researchers are not really very clear or precise about these concepts — nor, for that matter, are medical specialists. Two large but overlapping questions dominate debate. The first concerns whether health should be regarded as something more than the mere absence of illness. The second concerns whether it is more useful to separate or combine the three main components of health — the physiological, psychological, and social — which also represent three different levels of scientific analysis.

The position that health is not merely the absence of ailments but consists of an overall condition of well-being has gained widespread support in recent years. The definition adopted by the World Health Organization (WHO) in 1946 illustrates this by treating health as a state of complete physical, mental, and social well-being, thereby explicitly denying that it is just the absence of physical disease or infirmity as well as combining the three components in the definition (see also Seeman, 1989, for a related conception of positive health).

A number of recent writers whose outlook toward health is characterized by the term "holistic medicine" have adopted a parallel position. If, as Feist and Brannon (1988) have pointed out, one takes seriously that the word *health* has its origins in the old High German word *hale* or whole, that in China and ancient Greece health was thought of as being in balance with nature, and that a vital organismic task is to maintain a viable internal equilibrium even when it is disrupted by external demands and pathogens, the term *holistic* makes good sense, implicitly combining physiological, psychological, and social well-being.

Antonovsky (1979, 1987, 1990) has argued forcefully that we must study health instead of disease and has offered what he calls a "salutogenic" model of health instead of a "pathogenic" one. *Salutogenesis,* he writes, is concerned with why people stay healthy, in contrast with *pathogenesis,* which is concerned with why people get sick. He maintains that people stay healthy in large measure because they develop a wholesome — no pun intended — "sense of coherence," which is characterized by a pervasive, enduring feeling of confidence that the world is predictable and that there is a high probability that things will work out as well as can reasonably be expected. Whenever I reread this statement my querulous mind prompts the question, "What are reasonable expectations?"

In light of constant war, murder, treachery, disease, and death, I am concerned that health not be said to depend on self-deception or illusion (Goleman, 1985; Snyder, 1989; Snyder & Higgins, 1988; Snyder, Harris, Anderson et al., 1991; Taylor, 1989), because to have a sense of coherence seems to me to suggest that we should avoid recognizing and thinking about how bad things really are for much of the world (Lazarus, 1983). Many of us are offended by the condition of the world, as I think we should be. Should health be some sort of private ease and smugness, particularly for affluent, educated, and well-functioning people, about their relatively comfortable lives? Certainly this is not what Antonovsky intended.

In any case, this concept, which has parallels in terms like optimism and self-confidence, is the opposite of believing in "Murphy's law," an ironic joke that if something bad can happen it surely will. Sense of coherence suggests a style of thinking somewhat analogous to that in *The Power of Positive Thinking,* Norman Vincent Peale's inspirational book, if we assume that the outlook is unpressured, undefensive, and not merely a social ploy or a form of psychological bootstrapping to overcome distress or despair. All this talk of positive thinking, however, seems a bit diffuse to me and to require a searching analysis of just what positive thinking means, the diverse ways in which it is achieved, and its outcomes under different conditions. Since I am a *pessimist who hopes,* does hoping for the better entitle me to membership in the elite club of those who have a strong sense of coherence? Much more could be said about this, but I remind the reader that I have touched on this theme several times before in this book, especially in Chapters 3 and 4 when I dealt with coping and with appraisal and meaning. I am still not sure what is the best solution to life, or if there is a "the" best solution.

Although Antonovsky's approach is very appealing to me and has great soundness in many respects, it suffers, I believe, from two very serious conceptual and scientific problems: First, by defining health to include physiological, psychological, and social factors, we end up with a more muddled concept than we had before when only physical pathology was emphasized. I say this because the combined concept forces us to beg the question, which is important at this stage of knowledge, of whether and to what extent the three components of health are autonomous or interdependent. It is, for example, important and appropriate to hypothesize that the sense of coherence, which is a psychological variable, helps keep a person physically and socially healthy, and vice versa, and if this is so, to explore how this might work.

Whether there is a relationship is an empirical question. But the holistic definition of health assumes the answer, which is that all three components of health converge in overall health. If we assume the answer, however, we are not in a position then to evaluate empirically whether and how one level of analysis influences the other. Without raising this crucial question, the global proposition remains an article of faith rather than merely a hypothesis. Indeed, however pleasing its theme, holistic medicine has tended to be just that, an article of faith rather than a commitment to discover the truth.

We have, in a sense, come full circle from Chapter 1, in which I expressed dissatisfaction with the definitions of emotion typically offered and argued that attention had to be paid to the process of emotion generation to decide all sorts of difficult issues. I also explained there that, if we included our understanding of the emotion process in our definition, this would beg the questions we needed to ask. The same problem now arises again in bringing together the physiological, psychological, and social aspects of health within the same concept. Rather than blindly accept their interdependence, there is good reason to keep them separate for the purpose of research on their functional interconnections.

Second, the sense of coherence is a global and vague personality trait rather than a detailed and specific set of adaptational processes. Although it is presumed to be causal in health, the sense of coherence is also greatly confounded with the adaptational outcome it is supposed to explain, because health itself, as defined holistically, contains the same states and processes as the sense of coherence. It would be a complete tautology to say that healthy people feel good and have a positive sense of themselves and the world because they have a positive sense of themselves and the world and feel good. The problem is to say what healthy people do that makes them different from those who are ill. How, for example, do they hold onto their sense of coherence in the face of adversity? What are their coping secrets?

I am convinced that in psychology some degree of circularity is inevitable. However, when the overlap between antecedent and consequence is very great, understanding is defeated (cf. Lazarus, 1990b; Lazarus, DeLongis, Folkman, & Gruen, 1985). Nor am I opposed to global or molar concepts, as should have been evident in Chapters 3 to 7 in which I discussed core relational themes. However, without some attempt to unpack them into their molecular components, which in the case of emotion consists of specific appraisal components, coping processes, action tendencies, and physiological reactions, molar concepts alone cannot lead to adequate understanding.

For these reasons, I have opted here to keep the three adaptational outcome variables — somatic health, subjective well-being, and social functioning — separate. This allows me to ask questions about whether and how they are functionally related and about the mechanisms that connect them without assuming the answers. Before examining the role of emotion in somatic health, I consider first problems in the assessment of health and, second, problems of research methodology.

Problems in the Assessment of Health

Two problems stand out with regard to assessing health:

1. Health status is always evaluated on the basis of two sources of information, *laboratory evidence* of pathology, such as high blood pressure, electrocardiograms suggesting cardiovascular dysfunction, indicators of a cancerous growth or lesion based on tissue scanning devices or surgery, and other signs of disease and dysfunction obtained in standard medical examinations and confirmed or disconfirmed by more detailed clinical observation. A second source of information, *patient reports* of symptoms and illness history, is usually necessary to confirm the presence of actual disease. All existing methods of assessing illness draw more or less equally on laboratory tests and on subjective reports, although laboratory evidence of a malignant tumor might be a notable exception to this rule because cancers are often clinically silent for a long time; therefore, when the tumor is revealed and biopsy shows cancer cells, it must be taken seriously as a dangerous disease even if the person fails to note symptoms. Nevertheless, people are not usually sick for a very long time without sensing it, which leads them to complain to a physician.

To the extent that diagnosis of illness depends, in part, on subjective reports, there is, of course, room for *confounding* between the emotion process and health status. For psychological reasons one person may expend more energy than another though they have the same disease, may compensate for the disease with determination and a positive sense of well-being, or may function poorly as a result of ways of coping that are inadequate to the demands of living. Until diagnosis based on laboratory data becomes definitive without recourse to patient reports, this type of confounding remains an important problem for research on the role of emotion in illness.

2. At present, there is neither a guiding theory nor an adequate knowledge base about how to organize the findings of health examinations in order to provide a quantitative estimate of health status. As a result of the lack of a comprehensive theory and adequate knowledge, the boundary between pathology and normal individual variation in physiological structure and function remains ambiguous. People differ tremendously in physiology and in the ways their bodies function without these differences having necessary implications for longevity or functioning. Solid information about the borderline between normality and mortality risk or impairment of functioning is lacking, except in the cases of certain unmistakable diseases. Normal in the statistical sense is, of course, not necessarily the same as health. It is, for instance, normal for people over 65 to suffer from one or more chronic ailments that will not be ameliorated by medical treatment.

Given this ignorance and the absence of an adequate theory of health and illness, certain anomalies are created for measurement and research, the most important of which is inability to accurately evaluate the results of medical examinations. In routine examinations, for example, many persons show a borderline EKG reading for, say, bradycardia. Is a heart rate in the 50s, for example, an indication of some disorder for which an implanted pacemaker might be indicated, or a sign of robust cardiovascular health? And when is a fast rate — say, in the 90s — or a larger than usual heart a sign of imminent cardiac insufficiency? To answer this question, we would need to know under what conditions these findings should be taken as a medical problem. Large numbers of borderline findings are obtained constantly on a variety of ordinary physiological functions, but there is little normative data about the bearing of these functions on longevity and functioning. This forces clinicians to draw heavily on intuition and on the presence or absence of patient complaints in making treatment decisions.

To realize how unsettled our knowledge of illness is, one need only consider the morass into which the whole field of health maintenance and prevention has fallen, as manifested in confusion over how high blood pressure should be to warrant drugs designed to lower it, or what to do about serum cholesterol in the population and in individuals. Medicine has unwittingly been taking the social and psychological risk of frightening the public about many health issues, sometimes on the basis of inadequate knowledge. It would not be surprising if people turned against standard advice just as they have after too many false alarms about hurricanes or other disasters, because these alarms damage the credibility of public health agencies and lead to widespread refusal to take sensible preventive action (Breznitz, 1984).

Another problem resulting from the absence of theory and knowledge is that we cannot say how much a symptom such as mucous colitis should be weighted in a health status evaluation compared with, say, hypertension. When people are compared on health status, a decision must be made about the appropriate negative value to place on signs and symptoms with respect to two relatively independent types of outcome, *mortality risk* and *social functioning.* Mucous colitis appears to have no correlation with life-span, but in severe cases it greatly impairs social functioning. On the other hand, hypertension is a major risk factor in heart attacks and strokes; it can shorten life but has no necessary implication for social functioning, especially when it is not recognized and treated by drugs, which also have disturbing side effects and sometimes are dangerous in themselves. The health status scales with which I am familiar and which are currently in use are silent on this problem.

Problems of Research Methodology

Five methodological problems make it difficult to obtain definitive answers about the emotion–health relationship. These include confounding, subjective versus objective measures, the multivariate causation of health outcomes, and the stability of health status over long periods of time, each of which in turn is now discussed (see also Lazarus, 1990a).

1. Because all measures of somatic health depend on self-reports, the *confounding* inherent in subjective data cannot be completely overcome. The supposed cause, reports of stress or emotional distress, overlaps with the supposed effect, impaired health. That it is necessary to accept some confounding is controversial, as was evident in recent published debates (see Dohrenwend, Dohrenwend, Dodson, & Shrout, 1984; Lazarus et al., 1985). A number of other modern writers have also addressed the issue (for example, Kasl, 1983; Leventhal & Tomarken, 1986; Schroeder & Costa, 1984). Although these writers uniformly inveigh against confounding, none provides a viable solution except to use definitions of emotion (and stress) that depend entirely on objective environmental inputs or stressors.

Despite dominant opinion to the contrary, there is no way to separate the person and environment, as appraised by the person, without destroying what is meant by emotion as conceived in a cognitive-motivational-relational theory. Even if a totally objective input measure of environmental variables were possible, it would still mean the abandonment of a position that defines the sources of emotion as relational, and, therefore, a totally different phenomenon would be studied (see also Lazarus, 1990b).

There is no little hubris in the call for objective measures of the environment (stressors) by critics who themselves do not use them in their own research or who define stress and emotion solely in terms of environmental events. Ironically, there is solid evidence that proximal, subjective appraisals are better predictors of emotional reactions than are distal, objective ones (cf. Repetti, 1987; Solomon, Mikulincer, & Hobfoll, 1987), and evidence of a relationship between emotion and health has also been obtained in studies in which confounding has been made negligible (Rowlison & Felner, 1988). The tendency persistently to ignore this type of evidence suggests that the argument is as much ideological as it is scientific (see, for example, Hobfoll, 1989). I am not sure that a completely adequate resolution of the arguments about this is possible or likely.

2. Analysis of the problem of *subjective versus objective* measures suggests to me that, despite the insistance on the latter, measuring the environment objectively

is a shibboleth. The three main reasons for this assertion are straightforward and not novel:

a. Given the complexity of the environment, especially the social environment, and the fact that a person can only attend to and assimilate modest portions of it, we should not be surprised that its emotion-relevant contents for one individual or collectivity is not the same as for another. Two people walking in the same woods, or listening to the same conversation, do not see or hear exactly the same things, not because one is crazy but because personal agendas shape what is relevant for that person to attend to and how events should be perceived and appraised by that person. Therefore, the events on which emotions are centered are to some extent truly not the same for persons with divergent values, beliefs, and motivational agendas. In other words, differences in how reality is construed do not provide evidence of psychopathology, but may only reflect differences in personal values, commitments, and belief systems.

When researchers have attempted systematic, objective descriptions of the behavioral environments of persons, as have Barker and Wright (1951), they produce unwieldy accounts that bog us down in detail and are difficult to apply in research. We would do better, I think, to describe relevant environments of people through subjective lenses and then attempt to compare them with the consensual judgments of others. If the reader is offended by the claim that describing the objective social environment may be impossible, let me point out that the only means ever used to do so is subjective—namely, a *subjective consensus* of how some given sample of persons views it. The problem gets even more difficult when we are speaking of evaluations of the social environment, which is the basic currency of the emotions.

Although there are uses to which such a consensus can be put, there is a serious problem with using it as a basis of describing the objective environment. Any consensus can be just as "wrong" as descriptions by individuals, because to some extent we all live in accordance with illusions and self-deceptions (cf. Goleman, 1985; Lazarus, 1983; Taylor, 1989). Is there any doubt, for example, that Democrats and Republicans, not to speak of other societal subgroups, view and describe the conditions of their society, and of the world, in very different ways?

What constitutes reality seems like an easy question to answer until we look at it closely and in depth. Nowhere is this more obvious than in the religious mythologies that people live by and become deeply emotional and even violent about. Even though readers know intellectually that religions have diverse catechisms, some will have gotten offended by my use of the term *mythology*. Bible stories are accepted by many as literally true rather than being merely allegories, though it is precisely their allegorical meaning that gives them much of their social and psychological power.

Consider the angry social controversy over the film *The Last Temptation of Christ*, which presents Jesus as having had human erotic fantasies—temptations that he resists. This interpretation is deeply offensive to many religious people yet seems plausible and even appropriately spiritual to others. And right on the heels of this controversy came the publication of *The Satanic Verses*, which was felt by many Moslems to be insulting to their faith, and whose author (Salman Rushdie) was condemned to death by the Iranian Ayatollah Khomeini, an action that, in turn, was condemned by those with a Western concern for freedom of speech. People have always been ready to kill others who challenge their dogmas. Reality, especially in areas that are emotionally charged, is far from a simple matter on which we all agree.

b. A far more important reason for the difficulty in developing objective measures, one hinted at already, is that emotions depend much more on inferential meanings than on actual objects and events. Watzlawick's (1976) analysis of "How real is real?" provides convincing examples: For example, although the physical reality of gold is easily established, its psychological significance depends on cultural symbols and economic arrangements — its value is determined daily and announced in London and elsewhere — forged arbitrarily by social agreement, and this significance varies greatly from time to time and person to person. It is not the physical reality of gold that is significant but its inferential meanings, which lead people to invest in it because it is valued and to make many other interpretations about its significance for their well-being.

c. Another important reason is that because people have individual personal agendas and beliefs, which shape their emotions in any adaptational encounter, the meanings conveyed by the "objective" environment may or may not be relevant for an individual in whose emotions we are interested. Therefore, even if we could measure the objective environment in which an individual functions, it is not necessarily the environment to which that particular individual is responding with an emotion.

Arguments about this have had a long history in the social sciences. Like religious dogma, I am not sure that entrenched positions are subject to change. They will certainly not change or be managed gracefully if the hidden assumptions underlying these positions are not recognized and acknowledged, and if the problems of describing the objective environment are not also thoroughly grasped and acknowledged. In any case, having stated the rationale for a subjective approach to emotion as best I can, let us move on to other methodological problems in the study of emotions and health.

3. Health is a *multivariate* outcome, affected by a large number of powerful factors such as the genes we have inherited over which we have little or no control, accidents of living, environmental toxins, and numerous life-style variables such as smoking, drinking, drug use, diet, and exercise. After the variance in health produced by these variables has been taken into account, what remains as variance subject to the influence of the emotion process is probably modest. Health psychologists have yet to assess convincingly how much health is, indeed, influenced by emotional factors. The null hypothesis must always be taken seriously.

Complicating matters further, the medical profession and the other disciplines influenced by the desire to help control illness and promote health tend to be overly sanguine about the possibilities of affecting health outcomes. For a profession devoted to having a positive effect, it is a threat, indeed a deep offense, to believe that one is more powerless over the dark forces of nature than one would wish, a limitation that applies especially to chronic illness. Though referring to stress rather than emotion, Roskies (1983, p. 371) makes the following deliciously sardonic comment about this bias:

In recent years our traditional understanding of the causes of disease has been transformed by a powerful new concept: stress. . . . Stress has now become a shorthand symbol for explaining much of what ails us in the contemporary world, invoked to explain conditions as diverse as nail biting, smoking, homicide, suicide, cancer, and heart disease. . . . Stress serves the same purpose in modern society as ghosts and evil spirits did in former times, making sense of various misfortunes and illnesses that otherwise might remain simple random games of chance.

It would be un-American to accept a new cause for disease without seeking to cure it or control it. Thus, it is not surprising that the ranks of self-help manuals have recently been joined by books devoted to teaching us how to manage stress. Among the array of do-it-yourself guides to increasing sexual pleasure, building the body beautiful, and unlocking hidden mental and emotional capacities, is a new crop of manuals devoted to taming the killer stress. . . . And although the sales pitch varies from threats of dropping dead to promises of maximum well-being, all are dedicated to the premise that the individual can avert or diminish the potential harm of stress by using new, improved coping strategies.

4. Health status, as it is usually measured, is very *stable* over time, except perhaps for those who are sick and deteriorating as in aging or terminal illness, and for those who are sick and getting well. My own data (Kanner, Coyne, Schaefer, & Lazarus, 1981; DeLongis, Coyne, Dakof, Folkman, & Lazarus, 1982) on middle-aged persons shows the correlation of health status from one time point to another a year later to be roughly +.7, which means that it doesn't change much over quite a long time.

This finding creates a problem because to show the causal effects of emotion on health requires change in the dependent variable, as Kasl (1983) has skillfully argued. One must measure the emotion process prior to such change and demonstrate that the change can be predicted by variables of the emotion process, and that changes in these causal variables from time 1 to time 2 account for the effects. This is a very stringent methodological requirement, and most research on emotion and health has not lived up to it.

5. A corollary of point 4 is that we must have a measure that is *representative* of the emotion process over the period studied — that is, from time 1 at the start of research to time 2 when the effects on health status are measured. If the period is long, say, the five or ten years it might take for a pathogenic life pattern to result in illness, this requirement is difficult to realize. In the absence of a demonstration that it is representative of the person, and that it has changed from the prior period before illness came about, a single instance as a sample of numerous emotional encounters is not sufficient. Therefore, observations must be made again and again during this period to assess what has been taking place over the period in question. This, too, is a very stringent requirement, and the failure to meet it in most research makes it difficult to prove that health or illness is a consequence of the emotion process.

Because of these methodological problems, and the practical difficulties of dealing with them, another research strategy has been gaining favor, which is to study the covariation between stress and minor illness symptoms. Short-term ups and downs of infections and chronic ailments such as headaches, colitis, ulcers, and so forth, can be more easily monitored over a reasonable but modest time interval than major changes in health over many years. The time interval can be made brief enough also to monitor what is happening to mediators of health such as biochemical conditions, the immune process, and the appraisal and coping activities that influence emotional states. Although the health problems being measured in this strategy consist of relatively minor ailments, what makes illnesses come and go is easier to study, and this would probably also be relevant to the major illnesses, which are usually measured in standard health status assessments. A number of recent studies have adopted this strategy with promising results (Caspi, Bolger, & Eckenrode, 1987; DeLongis, Folkman, & Lazarus, 1988; Eckenrode, 1984; Stone & Neale, 1984b).

And because of these problems, the proposition that emotion affects health remains an article of faith rather than a proven principle. Although this is a negative message for those who wish to take the relationship seriously, my purpose in stating it is to point up the reasons for doubt and to encourage better research in the future, not to dampen enthusiasm. My personal conviction is that emotions do affect health, and I would like to be able to point convincingly to solid demonstrations and to the chapter and verse of the causal effects. What exists as evidence now, however, is fragmentary rather than programmatic; it consists of bits and pieces of difficult-to-evaluate evidence that is suggestive rather than definitive.

How the Emotions Might Result in Illness

Before we turn to psychophysiological mechanisms, we should examine a behavioral one, often referred to as *illness behavior*, which can mislead us with respect to the presence of physical illness. Illness behavior refers to how people react to or deal with pain, symptoms, illness or the threat of illness—for example, by the tendency to seek or avoid medical care, to exaggerate or minimize the significance of aches, pains, and symptoms, and to be functionally impaired or distressed. Illness behavior is not illness, though it could be a factor in it; rather, it consists of a variety of attitudes and reactions to symptoms, ailments, and bodily states.

I noted in Chapter 9 that medical sociologists and anthropologists have demonstrated that illness behavior is greatly influenced by cultural factors (e.g., Mechanic, 1962/1978, 1983; Zborowsky, 1969; Zola, 1966; among others). Though interesting in its own right and relevant to the organization and delivery of medical care, illness behavior is also an important impediment to the conduct and evaluation of research on the role of emotions in illness because it can fool us into believing that a healthy person is truly ill, or that a sick person is truly healthy. If people who are not ill seek medical care (a group sometimes referred to as the "worried well"), and we include them in the ill category, we are in danger of overestimating illness rates in a research population; similarly, if people who are ill avoid medical care (a group referred to as the "unworried ill"), and we include them in the well category, we are in danger of underestimating illness rates in a research population. In other words, the researcher must rule out or control illness behavior in obtaining data on the effects of the emotion process on illness.

We are now ready to look at how emotions might result in illness. In the discussions that follow I analyze plausible hypotheses about mechanisms of the emotion-illness relationship.' There are two issues about this that must be examined: The first concerns the competition between the specificity and the general susceptibility models of illness causation. The second concerns direct and indirect pathways whereby psychological and social factors result in illness. I shall discuss these in this order here.

Specificity Versus General Susceptibility. For roughly 75 years or more there has been competition between two theories of causation, the specificity model and the general susceptibility model. The specificity model states that there are specific causes — for example, noxious agents in the environment, sources of vulnerability in the organism, or particular emotions — for each illness. The general susceptibility model states that chronic and severe disturbances of the internal equilibrium, which are the result of stress or emotion, increase the person's general susceptibility to every kind of illness.

The specificity model. The idea that each illness has its own special, emotion-centered causation — that is, the *specificity model* — came into being in the late nineteenth century with the discovery of disease-causing bacteria. Koch, Pasteur, and Lister had demonstrated conclusively that infectious illness was the result of hitherto invisible organisms (microbes) that we now know as bacteria and viruses. Each specific illness, such as childbed fever, smallpox, and tuberculosis, was the result of a particular microbe. In effect, each illness had a specific noxious environmental agent.

However, in the past half-century there has been a growing awareness that illness also depends on lack of effective resistance by the host to noxious environmental agents — for example, infection-producing bacteria and viruses. People do not become ill unless their natural resistance to the microbes is weak or weakened. Although these microorganisms are widely present in the environment, those who are immune to diphtheria, for example, do not become ill and those who are resistant to tuberculosis likewise do not become ill. The idea that illness is the result of invasion by hostile environmental forces is correct but an overstatement, because susceptibility to disease depends on the species and the condition of the individual within that species.

Dubos (1959, pp. 106–107) has made this point effectively and clarified its implications in the following statement:

> Koch and Pasteur wanted to show that microorganisms could cause certain manifestations of disease. Their genius was to devise experimental situations that lent themselves to an unequivocal illustration of their hypothesis — situations in which it was *sufficient* to bring the host and parasite together to reproduce the disease. By trial and error, they selected the species of animal, the dose of infectious agents, and the route of inoculation which permitted the infection to evolve without fail into progressive disease. Guinea pigs always develop tuberculosis if tubercle bacilli are injected into them under the proper conditions; introduction of sufficient rabies virus under the dura of dogs always gives rise to paralytic symptoms. Thus, by the skillful selection of experimental systems, Pasteur, Koch, and their followers succeeded in minimizing in their tests the influence of factors that might have obscured the activity of the infectious agents they wanted to study. This experimental approach has been extreme-

ly effective for the discovery of agents of disease and for the study of some of their
properties. But it has led by necessity to the neglect, and indeed has often delayed the
recognition, of the many other factors that play a part in the causation of disease
under conditions prevailing in the natural world—for example, the physiological status of the infected individual and the impact of the environment in which he lives.

I note parenthetically that this quotation can also be viewed as a powerful statement from biomedicine of what I have said in Chapter 3 about emotions and the person–environment relationship. The *relationship* between the environment and the
person is always crucial, and this principle applies equally to the mind as to the
body. The causes of illness are probably specific as well as multiple, and they also
include the opposing *characteristics of the host,* which make illness always a *transaction* between person and environment, and a process that takes place over time.

In this connection, when researchers have sought to explain different illnesses in
psychosocial terms, they do so by reference to divergent and more or less specific
psychosocial processes, seeming thereby to adopt the premise of the specificity
model. The modern version of it takes into account both the noxious environmental
condition and the personality characteristics that create vulnerability to those noxious conditions.

To take one recent example of explanations of illness based on specificity, the
emotional-physiological processes thought to be involved in heart disease are considered to be different from those connected with cancer or infectious illness. Type
A behavior, or the management of hostility, with its specific biochemical implications, is emphasized in heart disease (cf. Glass, 1977), and its role in other forms of
illness has not been much examined, whereas in cancer many psychosocial explanations center on giving up psychologically (Engel, 1968; Schmale & Iker, 1966), or
suppressing felt emotions, which are said to have negative effects on the immune
process.

When the specificity model is applied to explain how psychosocial factors influence somatic health, each kind of illness is often said to have its origins in specific
emotions, presumably because these have distinctive somatic consequences—
remember that emotions are the result of a particular kind of person–environment
relationship. Depression is assumed to have different biochemical consequences
from phobic or obsessional states, and expressed anger is assumed to have different
biochemical consequences from anger that is denied or inhibited. The valence of
emotion is also believed to be important, as when it is argued that positive emotional
states such as happiness (and laughter) will have therapeutic or prophylactic biochemical consequences in contrast to negative emotional states such as anger and
anxiety (Cousins, 1976; Selye, 1974).

Perhaps the positive emotions work through psychological pathways by generating a greater sense of self-efficacy or self-esteem, thereby undercutting the psychophysiological consequences of anger and anxiety, or other negative emotional
states. Benign or positive emotional states result in different patterns of hormonal
secretions—for example, in peptides that bind with morphinelike receptors in the
brain and lower the destructive metabolic impact of catabolic adrenal cortical hormones. So little research on such promising possibilities has been done that there is

as yet only a very modest basis for evaluating the health-related idea of beneficial versus harmful emotions.

Hypotheses about the direction and control of anger, hinted at earlier as a factor, provide an interesting example. They imply specificity in both the choice of emotion and the pattern of anger control. Contrasts have long been made, for example, between anger directed outwardly and anger directed inwardly or inhibited. As Keinan, Behn-Zur, Zilka, and Carel (unpublished) point out, there is much research on this idea but with inconsistent findings, which these authors try to reconcile theoretically and empirically. They first explore three explanations: one emphasizing variations in the aspects of anger expression that have been studied, a second having to do with the pattern of anger expression, and a third with the match between an individual's anger control style and social pressure.

These authors looked at the intensity and frequency of anger experiences and expression in 134 Israeli men who had a medical examination to evaluate their health. They found that intensity was associated with good health but frequency with poor health; that is, it is not so important for negative health outcomes how intense occasional anger is but how often anger is experienced. I am sure that more will be said about this given the lively interest in the relationship between anger and health.

Although there is precious little systematic evidence that each emotion results in a specific pattern of physiological response, and even less about what these patterns are and how they might produce distinctive health consequences, the basic theme in the specificity hypothesis is quite plausible. It is given substance by the oft-cited autonomic nervous system specificity research of Lacey (1967) and Mason (1975; Mason, Maher, Hartley, Mougey, Perlow, & Jones, 1976), which I referred to in Chapter 2 (see also Levenson, 1988). It is also consistent with the notions developed in Chapter 5 about affect programs in which the appraised adaptational status of any emotional encounter was said to be the primary basis for the specific pattern of physiological mobilization against harms and threats. And it is consistent with the idea that a different action tendency or impulse is an important and integral feature of each emotion, thereby providing a theoretical basis for emotion to be embodied, and for specific response patterns in each individual emotion.

Between 1920 and 1950, the dominant version of specificity was psychoanalytic, illustrated by the influential writings of Franz Alexander (1950; also Alexander, French, & Pollack, 1968) and Dunbar (1948). Each psychosomatic illness was said to be the result of a particular type of intrapsychic struggle, which expressed itself in specific symptom patterns such as ulcers, asthma, migraine, colitis, and other classic psychosomatic disorders.

Alexander's view of psychosomatic disorders was different from the modern version of stress disorders (as in Cannon's and Selye's work) in which conflict or ineffective modes of coping produces tension-induced tissue damage as a kind of wear-and-tear phenomenon. He emphasized that repressed meanings play themselves out through conversion to sensorimotor expressions, which in turn resulted in bodily symptoms expressing the psychodynamics of the struggle.

Alexander's vector theory centered on basic biological processes of intake, retention, and expenditure — that is, the wish to take in, to eliminate, and to retain. All vectors have loving as well as aggressive, hateful connotations, and all organs of the body can be disturbed by the emotions involved in these vectors. The vectors, which come into being in the psychosexual stages of infancy, express themselves symbolically in social attitudes; for example, at the oral stage, in being passively receptive or trying aggressively to incorporate; at the anal stage, in giving or wanting to accomplish something, in seeking to hold onto, to accumulate, or to be stingy.[2] The premise here is that bodily symptoms are symbolic expressions of unresolved conflicts in these arenas of psychosexual development.

Let us look at some examples of how Alexander's analysis might work for the main so-called psychosomatic disorders found in medical practice. For *ulcers*, the hypothesized attitude is "I do not wish to take or to receive because I am active, competent, and efficient, and don't want to be passive or dependent." As in the myth of Tantalus, the ulcer personalities are always hungry to receive but don't allow themselves to accept. This type of person wants to be dependent but fights the impulse. For *ulcerative colitis*, the attitude is "I have the right to demand because I always give. I don't have to feel inferior or guilty for my desires because I have given the best I have for what I take." The prototype for an *asthma* attack is the cry of the newborn for the mother with the first breath drawn. The patient cries out for help from mother, fearing separation from her, but wants also to be competent and aggressive. The asthma conflict from this point of view is "I can't love, because this implies loss of my mother's love."

Graham (1962; see also Graham and Graham, 1961) has reported the most systematic research on the psychoanalytic specificity hypothesis, using a similar premise but modifying the attitudes somewhat from those proposed by Alexander. Graham used judges who selected the "correct" attitude from segments of recorded interview data produced by psychiatrists who did not know the hypotheses involved and tried to predict the patient's disease. Their findings were that the judges were able to do so correctly more often than chance. The attitudes hypothesized to be involved in each of six psychosomatic disorders are presented in Table 10.1.

Summarizing his views of psychosomatic specificity, Graham (1962, p. 237) wrote:

> The work reported appears to be in support of the specificity of attitude hypothesis. This implies that: (a) Each psychosomatic disease is associated with its own, specific attitude. (b) Each attitude has its own specific physiological concomitants.

And further,

> (c) Each psychosomatic disease is part of a specific emotion. (d) Each emotion has its own specific and unique physiological components.

The general susceptibility model. In the 1950s this psychoanalytic version of specificity began to be replaced by the general susceptibility model. One factor in this change was the weakness of the clinical research designed to support the idea of an ulcer, colitis, asthma, migraine, and so on, personality. Much of the findings on the personality characteristics of persons with different psychosomatic disorders was inconsistent.

TABLE 10.1. Graham and Graham's Psychosomatic Attitudes

Ulcerative colitis Felt he was being injured and degraded and wished he could get rid of the responsible agent. (Was being humiliated, screwed; wanted the situation to be finished, over and done with, disposed of.)

Bronchial asthma Felt he was left out in the cold and wanted to shut the person or situation out. (Felt unloved, rejected, disapproved of, shut out, and wished not to deal with the person or situation, wished to blot it out, not have anything to do with it or him.)

Duodenal ulcer Felt he was deprived of what was due him and wanted to get even. (Didn't get what he should, what was owed or promised, and wanted to get back at, get revenge, do to him what he did to me.)

Constipation Felt he was in a situation from which nothing good would come but kept on with it grimly. (Felt things would never get any better but had to stick with it.)

Essential hypertension Felt he was threatened with harm and had to be ready for anything. (Felt in danger, anything could happen at any time from any side; had to be prepared to meet all possible threats, be on guard.)

Migraine Felt something had to be achieved and then relaxed after the effort. (Had to accomplish something, was driving self, striving, had to get things done, a goal had to be reached; then let down, stopped the driving.)

(*Source:* D. T. Graham, Some research on psychophysiologic specificity and its relation to psychosomatic disease. In R. Roessler and N. S. Greenfield (Eds.), *Physiological Correlates of Psychological Disorder.* Madison, WI: The University of Wisconsin Press. Copyright © 1962 by The University of Wisconsin Press. Reprinted by permission.)

A second factor was that a credible account could not be given of how the attitude hypothesized to be a causal factor actually resulted in disturbances to tissue function that would be consistent with the symptoms. There is, for example, nothing more complicated than gastrointestinal function, and disturbances in it are common, yet gastroenterologists seem to have only a modest grasp of how the digestive tract works.

A third factor in the demise of this approach was the loss of favor of psychoanalytic concepts in clinical work and the social sciences. For many social and biological scientists, the psychoanalytic formulations were too esoteric and difficult to support or refute empirically. This negative aura about psychoanalysis still remains, though there is also a widespread impression that in one form or another it expresses something very important about the human psyche.

A fourth factor was the penchant in psychology in the 1950s to think of behavior in terms of drive and activation. The notion of general susceptibility harkens back to a period in psychology I barely touched on in Chapter 2, in which the central concepts of interest were drive and activation. *Activation* was a unidimensional concept implying that alertness, physiological arousal, and action could be said to range from low to high (cf. Lindsley, 1951). Stress or emotion was often defined as a marked increase in activation, and it was assumed that the body did not differentiate among different kinds of emotion; emotion was said to result mainly in increased activation.

There has been a long history of debate and research about activation, or what is sometimes referred to as arousal. The concept of activation or general arousal as an important construct lost favor, probably because researchers lost interest in simple drive concepts and began favoring more cognitively focused concepts such as social motivation and appraisal. Nevertheless, some psychologists remain wedded to an arousal concept, especially in considering such phenomena as motor performance. The continuing argument about the utility of this kind of concept can be observed in two recent articles, one by Neiss (1988), who took a negative position, and one by Anderson (1990), who took a positive position, all of which suggests that one must be wary about speaking of certain positions as passé (see also Amsel, 1990; and Revelle & Loftus, 1990).

A fifth, and perhaps the most important, factor was the tremendous success of Selye's (1956/1976) theory of the General Adaptation Syndrome, which centered on very general, systemic, metabolic effects of adrenal cortical hormones. This theory flowed readily from the earlier homeostatic concepts of Claude Bernard and Walter Cannon, which centered on the autonomic nervous system and the catecholamines of the adrenal medulla (see also Weiss, 1977). It gave an empirically credible account of the way stress might affect the tissues of the body via these hormone secretions and the disruptions of homeostasis they created. I have already discussed Selye's work in Chapter 2, which the interested reader might want to consult again.

Let us explore how the general susceptibility model is supposed to work. Its basis is a simple and uncontested fact that emotions involve major changes in the body's neurochemistry. The next, more difficult, and obscure step is to specify the mechanisms whereby these changes increase the likelihood of illness. The answers must come from epidemiological research and from study of the neurochemistry of emotion (or stress) and its effects on bodily organs. The key ideas are summarized here in a version popularized by Selye.

Selye's (1956/1976) analysis and research into the hormones of the adrenal cortex (the outer rind of the adrenal glands) provided great impetus to the generality position. His *General Adaptation Syndrome* involves three universal stages of reaction: alarm, or warning about a noxious environmental or internal condition; resistance or bodily defense; and exhaustion. Although Selye acknowledged that there were also specific factors in this defense, the specifics seemed less important than the general factor and were downplayed. His emphasis was on a common, orchestrated pattern of somatic changes in the face of environmental load. He spoke of these defensive changes as "stress," and of the environmental load as "stressors."

To make an oversimplified analysis, what happens is essentially this: When the nervous system recognizes a stressor because it disturbs the body's equilibrium, an adrenocorticotropic hormone (ACTH) is secreted by the pituitary gland, which stimulates the adrenal cortex to produce corticosteroids that are circulated throughout the body by the bloodstream. Mineralcorticosteroids promote inflammation to isolate the damaged area of the body, and glucocorticosteroids inhibit or relieve inflammation. These hormones facilitate the mobilization required to cope bodily and in action with the destabilizing demands, but when the biochemical effects of these demands are prolonged and severe, the viability of the organism is endangered. Today we know that in addition to ACTH, peptides, which include morphinelike substances that probably protect against pain and may be important in the immune process, are also secreted by the pituitary.

Remember that this process occurs in response to *any stressor* and that the particular agent of harm is said not to be important in shaping the syndrome. All noxious agents are, in effect, equivalent in producing this stage-centered sequence of reactions. This is why Selye referred to it as the General Adaptation Syndrome. Remember also that this defensive mobilization is said to increase susceptibility to *all illness,* not specific ones, because it has catabolic effects that, when extended over time, may be damaging to the body's integrity.

It is still necessary, however, to explain why people develop different illnesses — in one person heart disease, in another cancer, and in still others dangerous infections. The answer is that as a result of heredity and physiological conditioning, different organ systems are vulnerable in different persons, resulting in diverse patterns of illness and mortality. Since general susceptibility to illness is increased, illness occurs in vulnerable organ systems. This is a simple and powerful idea, which could apply along with specificity.

Recent interest in the immune process suggests an important further mechanism to account for illness — namely, that the bodily disequilibrium resulting from stress weakens the person's immune competency, thereby increasing the likelihood of all-cause illness and mortality. Since the immune process is so important in host resistance to pathogens, it is a reasonable assumption that it is also one of the important mechanisms of emotion-based illness. The data base for these assumptions about immune competency, which is too complex to attempt to review here, is the weak link in our understanding, though there is a growing body of evidence about the role of psychosocial factors in illness, and about the psychophysiological mechanisms involved, especially in infectious disease and the immune process (see, for example, Ader, 1981; Campbell & Cohen, 1985; Cohen & Willliamson, 1991; Jaret, 1986; Jemmott & Locke, 1984; Schleifer, Keller, McKegney, & Stein, 1980; and Tecoma & Huey, 1985). We are still a long way, however, from understanding exactly how all this works, because the immune process involves a great many types of cells and processes and is enormously complex.

One can see from this brief history that there has been an oscillation in which one or the other model — specificity or general susceptibility — has been favored. There is reason to believe that the general susceptibility model and the related concept of diffuse activation (see Chapter 2), which came into being partly as an antidote to psychoanalytic specificity (see Lipowski, 1977, for a more detailed discussion), and which was dominant in psychological thought for several decades, has had its day and — in the expectable pendulum reversal — that we are heading back to newer, and one hopes more adequate, versions of the specificity hypothesis. This statement would be debated by a number of colleagues (e.g., Syme, 1984).

I close the discussion with a diagram that summarizes the two models (Figure 10.1). In one model emotion is said to increase general susceptibility to illness because of the general biochemical disequilibrium it creates; in the other, distinct biochemical patterns are said to exist for each emotion, patterns that lead to particular kinds of bodily effects and illnesses.

Direct Versus Indirect Pathways. To properly examine the way psychological and social factors result in illness requires that we also consider the main pathways by which illness is affected by the adaptational relationship between person and environment and the emotions it causes. There are two types of pathways. In the

THE GENERALITY MODEL OF ILLNESS

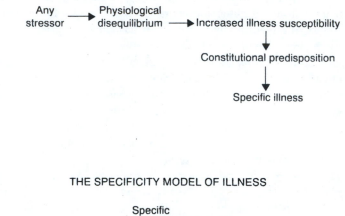

THE SPECIFICITY MODEL OF ILLNESS

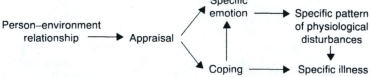

FIGURE 10.1. (*Source:* R. S. Lazarus and S. Folkman, *Stress, Appraisal and Coping.* New York: Springer Publishing Co., Inc., 1984. Reprinted by permission.)

first, certain emotions result *directly* in illness; in the second, illness is produced *indirectly* by faulty processes of appraisal and coping. Both ultimately get to the same place, illness, but by somewhat different routes.

Direct pathways. A direct pathway refers to short- or long-term effects of emotions on the body, which are known from extensive observations of complex and profound neurochemical changes that take place in an individual during an emotional episode. The classic and basic premise is that, *when marked or prolonged,* some of these bodily changes result in illness. I emphasize "when marked and prolonged" because isolated emotional reactions to single encounters (even if very intense) are not likely to have much importance for somatic health or illness. Instead, for emotions to contribute to or result in illness the pathogenic style of responding to life's trials and tribulations, and the troubling emotions it produces, must be chronic or recurrent. Although only a premise, it is the most widely accepted and discussed mechanism in the health sciences.

Depue, Monroe, and Schachman (1979, p. 16) express the premise clearly when they write about appraisal:

> The appraisal process may provide the final common pathway for a host of person and psychosocial variables that modify the impact of the psychosocial environment. In applying this model to the initiation of disease, the factor unifying all of these variables is the appraisal process as it modifies the intensity and duration of the psychological response to a threat in the environment. . . . It initiates what is, for some theorists, the major mediator [between the psychosocial environment and illness]— emotions and their biological concomitants.

Indirect pathways. There are two subtypes, both also involving appraisal and coping: In one, the emotion process contributes to somatic illness indirectly through inappropriate coping, which, I assume, is often based on faulty appraisals.

When chronic or recurrent, *faulty appraisals* should lead to maladaptation. The person is defeated in realizing goals that might otherwise be possible, or is catapulted frequently into adaptational encounters that lead to distress, which would have been unnecessary if there had been sounder appraisals. Notice, however, that this indirect route, which is mediated by appraisal, still brings us back to negative and distressing emotions such as anger, anxiety, guilt, shame, and envy-jealousy, and their physiology. In other words, the ultimate effects on somatic health in this indirect scenario still depend, in part, on the *biochemistry of emotion and its effects on tissues,* which is the same final path postulated for the direct effects discussed earlier.

For example, though it has been challenged repeatedly and now seems less persuasive then it once was (Suls & Sanders, 1988; Offutt & LaCroix, 1988), the presumed connection between Type A and heart disease is believed to depend on biochemical effects on the body. Interpretations of Type A by Glass (1977; Glass, Krakoff, Contrada, Hilton, Kehoe, Manucci, Collins, Snow, & Elting, 1980) are consistent with the assumption that Type A-generated illness arises from biochemical consequences (see also Holroyd & Lazarus, 1982), which, in turn, depend on appraisal and coping styles. Parallel interpretations involving appraisal and coping have been made for hypertension (e.g., Linden & Feurstein, 1981). Whether the route to illness should be based on a general susceptibility or specificity model has not really been addressed in this kind of analysis.

In the second indirect pathway to somatic illness (see Lazarus & Folkman, 1984), *inappropriate coping* is said to increase the probability of mortality and morbidity as a result of risk taking and the damaging use of drugs, alcohol, and tobacco. Here, too, the mechanism takes a detour through coping, which is why it is indirect. In effect, this mechanism depends on potentially pathogenic coping actions, which are often bolstered by self-deceptive ways of thinking that minimize the danger to somatic well-being.

Other kinds of pathogenic coping also belong here, illustrated by dependence on denial, avoidance, and distancing—which, under life-threatening conditions, endanger physical integrity (Lazarus, 1983). Examples would include failing to seek medical attention for a heart attack that is in progress or for a suspicious breast lump that could be cancerous. Cases are not infrequently reported in which, in the middle of a heart attack, men did pushups or ran up several flights of stairs to help convince themselves they were not having a coronary attack. But they were, and luckily were able to report this story after eventually being hospitalized and having survived, though clearly they had added to the danger of sudden cardiac death. These ways of coping increase the odds of more serious or deadly disease since more constructive action could have been taken.

What is distinctive about this indirect pathway is that instead of depending on the biochemical effects of distressing emotions on bodily integrity, which is true of all other hypothesized pathways, the damage to the body is produced by harmful addictive substances and other potentially self-destructive behavior patterns, such as those that could result in spinal cord injury and death or deadly diseases they might have been spared had they acted more prudently and realistically. These actions place people at greater than usual risk of cancer, heart disease, damage to vital organs such as liver and kidneys, and life-threatening or handicapping accidents.

Although the ways are diverse in which appraisal and coping can be maladaptive, and although many cases can be called purely accidental rather than based on risky behavior, maladaptation usually depends on a *mismatch* between appraisal and coping processes and the requirements of the environmental conditions being faced, whether these requirements are acute or chronic. I say more about this in Chapter 11.

Are There Healthy and Unhealthy Emotions?

There is little theory and research about the actual consequences of different patterns of emotion, save what was indicated already in connection with the biochemical (hormonal) consequences of emotions. The proposition offered by Cousins (1976), which has since become emblematic of holistic medicine, is that happy emotional states are capable of preserving somatic health and curing illness, and unhappy or stressful emotional states are destructive or promote illness (see also Selye's distinction between distress and eustress).

Although the Cousins proposition is worthy of being evaluated in programmatic research, it has mainly succeeded in bringing out diverse medical and biological prejudices on either side. Professionals also view what evidence there is quite differently. For example, Pelletier (1977) has written a very readable and optimistic account of the basic premise that the emotional life is important in somatic health. (However, see also Pelletier & Lutz, 1988, which is a somewhat more reserved analysis.)

There is little solid theory about how emotions might actually affect illness by acting on the body's tissues, certainly nothing as noteworthy as Selye's concepts, which are limited mainly to stress. By the same token, very little research has been or is being conducted on the specific biochemical consequences of each emotion, again perhaps for want of good theory and method, or because sufficient interest has not been generated as yet among psychophysiologists. Therefore, I am mainly asserting my own bias when I express the idea that individual emotions should play different roles in somatic health and illness because of their particular somatic effects.

Emotion and Subjective Well-Being (SWB)

Subjective well-being, alternatively referred to as avowed happiness, morale, and life satisfaction, is a traditional and important criterion of the quality of adaptation. Andrews and Withey (1976), Bradburn (1969), Costa and McCrae (1980), Campbell, Converse, and Rodgers (1976), and Diener (1984), among others, have discussed this concept. (The reader might also see a new collection of diverse treatments of happiness and well-being organized by Strack, Argyle, and Schwarz, 1991). Diener's prodigious review and analysis cover roughly the past 20 years of research and thought, and because I only wish to touch on what is relevant about this to the emotion process, the interested reader should consult that review as well as other treatments. (I also mentioned SWB in connection with the emotion of happiness in Chapter 7.)

Theory and Method

Measures of SWB can be thought of as a summing up of recurrent emotional states over the long term — a subjective aggregate of emotional life experiences or, more accurately, of the way a person evaluates the fate of personal life agendas. Whether this is a sound way to view SWB is an unresolved issue. Assuming that it is such a summary, how the task is done by the subject may well depend on the time span under consideration and other factors. If we take appraisal to be the key process in the shaping of emotion in a particular adaptational encounter, it must also be a key to the long-term summary. Moreover, a single encounter cannot tell us dependably about the true aggregate of emotional experiences over time, or how the aggregate is arrived at.

Subjective well-being is not an acute emotion, or a mood, per se, but might be related to them. Whether acute or a mood, emotion is a *state* However, because persons making the judgment are, in a sense, aggregating their emotional lives over a period of time, SWB is always more or less a *trait* rather than a state. The person who rates his or her SWB is not supposed to be influenced by specific emotion states but is expected to take the large view, though it is likely that there will often be such influence (see Schwarz & Clore, 1983).

There has been little interest in making a research comparison between SWB as aggregated by the person who rates it over a week, a month, a year, or longer and a summation of daily emotional experiences. This is the first of several major issues about the nature of subjective well-being that needs to be addressed. One could, for example, examine all the daily emotional encounters that are positive and negative, and evaluate whether the absolute or relative frequency or intensity, or each individual one, is similar to global assessments of SWB. In all likelihood, these two kinds of aggregation will come out differently because they may not be the same thing. Generally, global ratings are skewed toward the positive end of the scale, meaning either that people overlook the negative side of their lives, perhaps wanting to believe that they are generally happy, or wanting others to believe it. I am not sure whether this skewing occurs to the same extent in appraisals of specific emotional encounters, especially those that have happened recently, because it is easier to forget or soften details when one is asked to remember and evaluate events in the distant past.

The closest anyone has gotten to comparing daily evaluations of emotion with summarized global assessments is a study reported by Diener, Sandvik, and Pavot (1989). The authors conceptualized happiness as the relative frequency of positive compared with negative emotions (*affect* is the term they use). Students first rated their positive and negative well-being on three commonly used scales, and then the frequency and intensity of daily positive and negative affect were obtained over a period of six to eight weeks. A substantial correlation was found for frequency and a much smaller correlation for intensity. In other words, if the subjects judged that they had many positive compared with negative experiences, they also gave positive global estimates of their well-being.

These data, however, do not really answer the question about daily emotion and subjective well-being, because both sets of measures, the daily and the aggregated, consist of more or less overlapping summary ratings rather than statements about particular emotional encounters. The correlation could have been the result of a general personality tendency to rate in a given way. The issue dealt with seems to be more a matter of the period being rated than a comparison of individual emotional encounters with SWB. We don't know, for example, what emotions were actually experienced in a given day's ratings of the frequency of positive and negative affect. Frequency as a measure obscures the specifics of experienced emotions in favor of an overall summary of positive and negative, even when it covers a relatively short period such as a single day.

Diener's (1984) review reveals that sociodemographic variables such as gender and income do not play a large role in SWB. By and large, no single set of variables seems to be very powerful in affecting it. This poses a dilemma and presents a second major issue. How do we explain that having a positive or negative sense of personal well-being has little to do with the objective circumstances of our lives? The usual psychological explanation accords with appraisal theory in the proposition that the process is subjective and dependent on what people expect and want rather than on the objective conditions of their lives (see my account of happiness in Chapter 7). A person living with tragedy or deprivation may be frequently or generally happy; conversely, one who seems to live under very favorable circumstances may be frequently or generally unhappy. Helson's (1959) theory of adaptation level, which has to do with what a person is habituated to and accepts as his lot, offers a useful way to think about this dilemma (see also Brickman & Campbell, 1971; Brickman, Coates, & Janoff-Bulman, 1978; and Costa & McCrae, 1980).

A third issue, related to the second, is that well-being and ill-being are often found to be independent. People can rate their SWB as positive and yet rate stress and dissatisfaction in life as high, too. Diener (1984) examines the evidence for independence. His analysis (e.g., Diener, Larsen, Levine, & Emmons, 1985) agrees with mine that evidence of dependence or independence depends on temporal considerations and within-person modes of analysis. Diener et al. write:

> First, positive and negative affect are not independent at particular moments of time. Each type of affect clearly tends to suppress the other. . . . Second, because of the suppressive mechanisms, the two types of affect are not independent in terms of their frequency of occurrence, that is, the more a person feels positive or negative affect, the less that person will feel the other. Finally, when one measures average levels of positive and negative affect over longer time periods, they show a low correlation with each other because mean levels are a result of both frequency and intensity. Thus, their positive relationship in terms of intensity *across persons* cancels their inverse relationship in terms of frequency [italics added].

In effect, the different relationships that are found between positive and negative evaluations of SWB depend, in a large part, on divergent measurement strategies, the most important of which is a frequent failure to examine the ratings intraindividually as well as interindividually and to appreciate that the questions being addressed in these perspectives differ. This is hinted at in Diener et al.'s use of the term "across persons" in the quote. If we compare persons with themselves, for example, we are apt to find that in reporting negative experiences, positive states are suppressed and the relationship between positive and negative well-being is negative. However, if we make the comparison across or between persons, positive and negative well-being are apt to vary independently. I can summarize the generalization emerging here by saying that, although people who often feel bad often feel good, too (interindividual comparison), at the moment they feel bad they are not also likely to be feeling good (intraindividual comparison; see also Chapters 1 and 2 for relevant discussions).

The Causal Connection Between Emotion and Subjective Well-Being

Theoretically speaking, there ought to be a reciprocal causal relationship between emotions and global SWB. This is a variant of the question I asked under somatic health—whether there are healthy and unhealthy emotions. It is also a variant of the figure-ground analysis of happiness in Chapter 7. Diener, Sandvik, and Pavot's (1989) interpretation of one side of this two-way relationship is that positive SWB depends on how often a person experiences positive affective experiences compared with negative affective experiences. This is a bottom-up, response-centered analysis, which is similar to that of Bradburn (1969) and those who postulate that a lack of positive or pleasant events leads to depression (Lewinsohn & Amenson, 1978). Costa and McCrae (1980, p. 699) also imply that summary or trait ratings and repeated individual affect ratings are causally related:

> Few would argue against the position that, for normal people, the major determinants of *momentary* happiness is the special situation in which the individual finds himself. Social slights hurt our feelings, toothaches make us miserable, compliments raise our spirits, eating a good meal leaves us satisfied. The contribution of personality to any one of these feelings is doubtless small. Yet over time, the small but persistent effects of traits emerge as a systematic source of variation in happiness, whereas situational determinants that vary more or less randomly tend to cancel each other out.

This could well be the case. A good logical and empirical case can be made that things work the other way round, with *coping style* tendencies to interpret life positively or negatively determining how one evaluates one's well-being. This is a top-down principle. A person who looks at life dysphorically and pessimistically may well be unable to appreciate or obtain much joy from the good things that happen, or even think of them as good. With a tendency to appraise experiences negatively, we will be unable to appreciate and enjoy positive experiences, which is a dysfunctional clinical syndrome sometimes referred to as *anhedonia*. Perhaps both mechanisms apply.

Furthermore, the person who looks at life positively and optimistically may be easily able to transcend most of the minor harms and threats, and even think of them as good, as in the statement from the Folkman and Lazarus (1988b) Ways of Coping Questionnaire, "I came out of the experience better than when I went in." It is even possible that the trait being measured should not be called SWB at all but rather the tendency to cope by adopting a positive appraisal style. This interpretation that SWB is a consequence of coping is consistent with my view of the emotion process.

One thinks here of misanthropes, pessimists, and generally dysphoric persons. And by parallel reasoning, specific negative experiences might not override a positive general outlook, which makes one think of irredeemable optimists. It is as if the person cannot be dissuaded from a general assessment of well- or ill-being by specific affective experiences. Inspirational books such as Norman Vincent Peale's *The Power of Positive Thinking,* or Horatio Alger's *Success Against Odds,* and the like, encourage people to think positively as an act of will. Nevertheless, some encounters resulting in major life changes or loss have profound significance for overall appraisals and do markedly change overall moods. We need to know what is important and what is unimportant to the individual to make predictions about this, as I suggested in Chapter 3 in discussions of the motivational principle.

This analysis does not address the psychological processes that shape SWB ratings but deals only with peripheral response-response relations. To theorize that one response causes another is acceptable, of course, but is also, in my view, superficial and incomplete. A fuller understanding would come from examining central, meaning-related appraisals and coping processes that influence emotions by altering appraisals via feedback from what happens.

If the issue is redefined in light of cognitive-motivational-relational theory analysis, we then recognize that SWB is a product of appraisal, which both precedes and is an ongoing feature of an SWB. Appraisal of specific adaptational encounters results in particular emotions such as anger, guilt, happiness, and pride, and refers to the way a person evaluates the significance of what is happening for well-being. For appraisals to be aggregated into a global estimate of subjective well-being requires that individual encounters be subordinated to an overall summation of the emotional life over a particular period. Giving a meaningful summary requires a subjective weighting of what is important and unimportant in a person's life, and of the progress being made in actualizing the central agendas of living. Psychologists do not yet understand the basis of this kind of judgment, and the typical aggregated response analysis fails to help us to get to the psychological processes involved.

Fruitful ideas about the meaning of SWB abound, but research has not often been theory driven. Some of the most promising ideas center on patterns of motivation. It has been suggested, for example, that people who take on only long-term projects are apt to have poor morale compared with those whose commitments yield positive feedback in the short term (e.g., Palys & Little, 1983). Others have emphasized just being actively engaged in striving rather than the actual outcomes of an engagement. The notion that positive well-being depends on a sense of progress rather than an outcome is an ancient philosophical theme, expressed by Aristotle and later writers. When people get what they want, satisfaction tends to be short-lived. A relevant aphorism is that satisfaction is always a derivative of other commitments and activity, and cannot be striven for without disappointment. Still others have emphasized the match between what happens and expectations, beliefs, and social comparisons (e.g., Brickman, Coates, & Janoff-Buhlman, 1978; Parducci, 1968). One wonders whether these diverse views truly compete with each other or are in some sense all valid and overlapping so that we need not choose between them.

I conclude that the analysis of subjective well-being is handicapped by the failure to consider the motivational, cognitive, and emotional processes that might contribute to it. As with the emotions, if we remain vague and atheoretical, or focused superficially on the response side, we will fail to understand what subjective well-being is all about, its connections to the emotions, and the role it plays in the total psychological economy.

Coping and Subjective Well-being

In a very decided sense I have been talking about the coping process. But we should not leave the topic of subjective well-being without addressing one variant of this subject — namely, defenses such as repression and denial used in the management of distressing emotional states and the resulting consequences.

The task is made easier by a recent analytic review by Weinberger (1990). Although Weinberger speaks of emotions rather than subjective well-being, it is clear that the study of the so-called repressive coping style is relevant to our present concerns. Clearly, if a person represses anger, anxiety, and other forms of emotional distress — or, rather, the ideation and impulses that generate them — the opportunity is provided for a positive evaluation of subjective well-being at the conscious level even if other appraisals are preconscious or unconscious (see Chapter 4).

Weinberger's analysis is concerned with whether persons assessed as having a repressive coping style actually suffer from negative emotional states which they fail to recognize. In other words, although they appear to have positive well-being and to be clinically sound, they are said to be troubled individuals who claim to themselves and others what is not true. After reviewing a prodigious amount of research, he concludes that at least two kinds of persons report low levels of subjective distress: (1) those who are low in anxiety or are self-assured and also score low on assessment measures of defensiveness; these persons respond well to stress and are aware of distress when it arises, but manage it effectively so what they say is congruent with nonverbal indicators; and (2) those who report little distress but are defensive, as evidenced in many psychophysiological indicators such as voice quality, facial expression, physiological changes, and objective task performance, which are incongruent with their verbal reports and imply that they are at least as anxious as those who report chronic distress.

Weinberger's analysis also seems to suggest the presence of a coping process, which conceals from oneself and the world a negative sense of well-being. The research problem is to distinguish those who are, on the whole, truly comfortable with themselves and their circumstances from those who claim to be but are not. The analysis also points to Freud's concept of the return of the repressed in which it is assumed that repression never puts to rest the internal struggle that generated it; there is always some cost, whether in loss of energy or other symptoms of a failed struggle. (Shedler, Mayman, and Manis, as yet unpublished, have also made an interesting analysis of illusions created by denial and self-deception, which suggests that this way of coping has physiological costs and may be a risk factor for somatic illness.)

There is, however, a theoretical alternative to the Freudian position about the cost of defense, which is that a defense can be successful and well consolidated, especially if it is not challenged by the actual conditions of living, in which case we might never observe any evidence of struggle. Only when there is a failure of defense will there be signs of inconsistency between what a person reports and the observed indicators. Weinberger implicitly adopts the position, widely held in our culture, that one must always pay a price for reality-distorting changes in appraised meaning which result from emotion-focused coping.

In what I have written elsewhere about denial (Lazarus, 1983), I argued that if it can be sustained against all the evidence, self-deception carries no penalty as long as no effective adaptive action is compromised. This, in fact, is the function of illusion. Many illusions are widely shared in our culture and we fight against anyone who attempts to shatter them. It is still an open question whether or not mental health necessarily requires the accurate testing of reality. However, convincing evidence for this alternative would be difficult to generate.

Emotion and Social Functioning

Much of our time and energy is spent adapting behaviorally to the requirements of living, dealing with social and environmental demands, capitalizing on resources and opportunities to further personal or group values and goals, and managing our actions in accord with social constraints, which if violated could lead to harm. To evaluate the effects of the emotion process on adaptation, we must be able to assess how effectively a person functions in the world. I use the general term *social functioning* to include work and problem solving as well as social and family relations.

Assessing social functioning is a difficult task and there are few guidelines. The solution adopted in Lazarus and Folkman (1984) was to focus on coping effectiveness, which was defined as the *fit* or *misfit* between what the person does and the available options. Because the behavior of the environment is a crucial factor, however, a good outcome can result from a coping process that is unsound and a poor outcome from one that is sound. It is therefore important to consider the environmental conditions of social functioning. Some people do well because they experience favorable conditions of life, whereas others do well in spite of hardship; still others do badly because of refractory conditions, or do badly regardless of favorable ones.

Nevertheless, a performance standard of some sort is required, which should vary with the task, the objectives of the person, and the environmental realities. We must also distinguish between the two perspectives I commented on earlier with respect to subjective well-being—namely, that among different individuals and within the same individual. Schönpflug (1983; 1985) would add as a criterion the efficiency with which the person copes, which refers to the costs of a coping strategy in energy expended and damage done by it to other values. As in the case of subjective well-being, we must also distinguish between effectiveness in the short term—that is, in an immediate emotional encounter—and in the long term, in which individual encounters are aggregated and summarized over a given period. Often a coping strategy that has desirable effects in the short term will have undesirable long-term effects.

French, Caplan, and Van Harrison (1982) have emphasized the *fit* or *misfit* between the person and the environment in their analysis of work stress; a good fit leads to good adaptation and a poor fit to poor adaptation. Although the concept is cast in terms of the needs and resources of the person, the fit or misfit also applies to coping and its outcome in social functioning. The analysis of French et al., though impressive and useful, tends to be static in that it emphasizes stable relationships between the person and the environment (especially the workplace) rather than attending to process; stress and emotion change constantly over time under diverse environmental contexts. A stable, favorable fit has to do with adaptation over the long term but doesn't help us understand the dynamics of particular emotional encounters or the emotional ups and downs in them.

In the same vein, it is a half-truth and thereby misleading to carry over from medicine, clinical psychology, and personality psychology an emphasis on personal soundness or dysfunction as a trait. By emphasizing that some people usually or always function well or badly, which is obviously true, we ignore the processes whereby emotional distress arises in specific adaptational encounters (see Lazarus, 1989b). Sound persons perform badly in certain contexts and experience distress from time to time, whereas unsound persons do well and feel good from time to time, depending on what they have to contend with and the resources they can draw upon.

It is also a half-truth, and thereby misleading, to carry over from social psychology and sociology an emphasis on stable and beneficial or destructive work environments as factors in social functioning. If we are to understand how the emotion process affects social functioning, we need to focus on changing as well as stable relationships between any given person and the environments in which that person operates. Moreover, because people strive to fulfill individualized values and goals, their emotions at work depend on which of their goal commitments are harmed, threatened, or benefited in a particular adaptational encounter. Locke and Taylor (1990) identify five such values: material rewards, achievement, a sense of purpose, social relationships, and maintenance or enhancement of self; these authors also note that workers diverge in their individual motivational patterns.

Although much research in the 1950s centered on the impairment of skilled performance as a result of anxiety, there has been a tendency in recent years also to examine the facilitation of performance by positive moods. In both cases, early research and thought have tended to be more or less behavioristic and mechanical, whereas later research has been more cognitively and motivationally oriented. Let us examine the way the emotion process affects social functioning by first looking at impairment produced by negative emotions, and the conditions that generate them, and then looking at facilitation as a result of positive emotional conditions and reactions.

Negative Emotions and the Impairment of Performance

Multiple reviews and analyses, dating back thirty to forty years, by Easterbrook (1959), Holtzman and Bitterman (1956), Horvath (1959), Lazarus (1966), Lazarus, Deese, and Osler (1952), Martin (1961), Sarason (1960), and Winkle and Sarason (1964), attest to great interest in this problem. Janis (1967) also offered an elaborate review and theoretical analysis of his impressive work, and that of others, on the effects of fear arousal on attitude change, emphasizing the role of degree of arousal in generating adaptive and maladaptive patterns of vigilance. There was a concentration of this kind of research in the 1950s and early 1960s, but interest then subsided temporarily, picking up again recently, as is evident in a new journal *Anxiety Research* and books by Krohne and Laux (1982) and Schwarzer (1984), which are concerned with the role of anxiety in performance. A series of books on anxiety, edited by Spielberger beginning in 1966, and then later on stress and anxiety, edited by Spielberger and I. G. Sarason (1975–1986), also illustrates the continuing interest.

One facet of this interest is the concept of *test anxiety* (see also I. G. Sarason, 1972), which has shown continuing vitality probably because being tested in and out of school is so common and assumes so much importance in people's lives. About this Hembre (1988) wrote:

> Last year (1987) the test anxiety construct observed its 35th birthday. Offspring of the omnibus phenomenon *anxiety,* the construct has matured within a huge cocoon of attention, tempting hundreds of researchers to explore its nature, reveal its effects, and develop a treatment. This attention has "intensified" over the years. . . . The construct may seem remarkable less for its age than for its enduring fascination.

An excellent recent review and analysis of the history of thought on the problem by Glanzmann (1985) bring the concern with the effects of anxiety on performance up to date. Although Glanzmann seems to want to preserve what I consider an earlier, outmoded drive theory model, he also appreciates the more recent cognitive approaches and attempts to integrate the two outlooks.

It is important to realize that emotions, even negative ones such as anxiety, do not always impair performance and, in fact, may actually facilitate it, or sometimes fail to change performance, at least on the average (cf. Covington & Omelich, 1987). A good demonstration of this is an old experiment on the effects of failure stress on subsequent intellectual performance (Lazarus & Eriksen, 1952). In addition to other personality measures, two groups of college students were tested on the digit symbol subscale of the Wechsler-Bellevue adult intelligence test. To make the situation stressful, they had been told that their performance would predict their academic prospects and would be placed on their college records. The stressed subjects were told falsely that they had done very poorly and then were retested, presumably to make sure; the control group was told falsely they had done very well and then were also retested, presumably to make sure. At the end of the experiment all subjects were debriefed, that is, told about the experiment, reassured, and allowed to express and discuss their feelings about what had happened.[3]

Comparison of the stressed and nonstressed subjects' performance revealed that there was absolutely no difference in *average performance* following failure or success, but that the *variance* of the two groups on the second testing was markedly greater; that is, some subjects did much better after the failure and others much worse compared with the relatively benign success condition. Findings like this made it abundantly clear that the effects of stressful conditions are not uniform but depend on individual differences in personality—for example, the pattern of motivation and beliefs of those exposed to a stressor—as well as other external conditions that make a difference in the way situations like this are appraised. The main results

TABLE 10.2. Means and Variances of Gross Scores on Test 1 and Test 2

	Experimental		Control	
	Mean	SD	Mean	SD
Test 1	111.4	416.2	113.1	436.8
Test 2	109.4	1096.1	109.4	219.0
t	.70		2.5	
F		2.6		2.0
p	.48	<.01	<.02	<.01

(*Source:* R. S. Lazarus and C. W. Eriksen, "Effects of failure stress upon skilled performance." *Journal of Experimental Psychology, 43*. Washington, DC: American Psychological Association, 1952.)

of this study are presented in Table 10.2, and Figure 10.2 schematizes what it means to speak of an increase of variance without any change in the average.

By the same token, even positive person–environment relationships and emotional reactions do not always improve social functioning and health. Thus, Brown and McGill (unpublished) have obtained evidence that positive life events have negative health correlates for certain kinds of persons in their study, in effect, those with low self-esteem. They speak of this as the "high cost of success." Here, too, we see

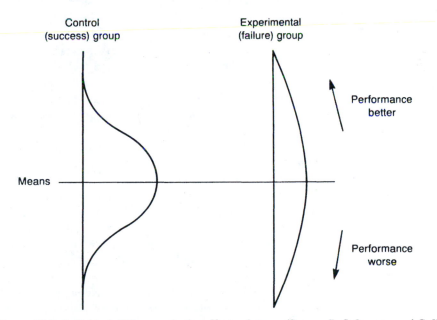

FIGURE 10.2. Individual differences in the effects of stress. (*Source:* R. S. Lazarus and C. W. Eriksen, "Effects of failure stress upon skilled performance." *Journal of Experimental Psychology, 43*. Washington, DC: American Psychological Association, 1952.)

the ubiquitous individual differences, which have inspired the assessment of person-ality variables.

Consider also the informal observation that when we think we are ahead in a high-stakes competition, a highly positive cognitive-emotional state, we may let up a bit and thereby lose. Athletes must learn that being ahead is both a positive and a nega-tive circumstance, and they must guard against its potentially negative consequence. In studying how emotions affect social functioning, we need to know the conditions leading to impairment and those leading to improvement. Consistent with a relational theory, these conditions lie both in the environment and within the person, converging in the person–environment relationship as it is appraised by each person.

It is also important to recognize that an assumption I have been making is that, in the course of evolution, the function of emotions is to promote adaptation not to impair it. The emotion process succeeds, in the main, but sometimes it fails, and when this happens there must be something systematic that helps us explain what has gone wrong. Saying this changes the tenor of what follows from a description of a maladaptive system to an attempt to understand what has gone awry under certain conditions in a system that was designed, albeit imperfectly, to promote adaptation.

A number of mechanisms have been proposed to explain the negative effects on performance of emotions such as anxiety. One of these mechanisms is *interference,* which has been of great interest since the work of Child (1954), Child and Water-house (1952, 1953), and Sarason, Mandler, and Craighill (1952). Mandler and Sara-son (1952) provided an important theoretical statement about interference in drive theory terms. Another drive theory version was offered by Spence and Spence (1966), but it has not been so durable in the face of more cognitive formulations.

The basic notion in Spence and Spence's analysis is simple: Two kinds of drive are relevant to task performance: one task directed, the other aimed at reducing the anxiety and its autonomic arousal. The anxiety is also associated with feelings of inadequacy, helplessness, and concerns about the consequences of negative out-comes. The basic proposition is that as drive—I would say threat—increases, the intensity and number of drive stimuli also rise, eliciting more and more task-irrele-vant responses such as autonomic nervous system arousal and interfering thoughts such as self-deprecations, desire to escape, preoccupation with the consequences of failure, annoyance, and so forth.

State anxiety is usually generated by threatening evaluative conditions, as in a performance test of ability or knowledge. Trait anxiety was measured in early stud-ies by the Taylor (1953) anxiety scale (see also Taylor, 1956), and in more recent studies by the trait-state anxiety scale of Spielberger, Gorsuch, and Lushene (1970). Highly anxious persons, or I would say those reacting to threat with anxiety, have been shown to perform poorly, especially on difficult tasks and when anxiety results in task-irrelevant responses.

A more recent position suggests that there are two separate factors, worry and emotionality, which have become the basis of the *Test Anxiety Questionnaire* of Liebert and Morris (1967). Worry refers to the cognitive expression of concern about one's performance, whereas emotionality has to do with autonomic nervous system reactions or arousal. As I have said elsewhere, it troubles me to see worry separated from the rest of the cognitive-motivational-relational configuration of anxiety, because this turns attention to one part of the whole (however, see Borkovec, 1990, on worry as a way of coping). In any case, it is assumed by some that worry, not arousal, is the source of interference with test performance, and Wine (1971) has proposed an attentional model in which test-anxious persons are said to divide their attention between task-relevant activities and worry, self-criticism, and other concerns, leaving less attentional energy available for the performance itself.

An alternative deficit model (Tobias, 1985) blames poor performance on inadequate study habits or deficient test-taking skills in test-anxious persons. From this standpoint, test anxiety does not impair performance, but the reverse is true — namely, that test anxiety is the result of awareness of one's poor past performances. In other words, many a person who is made anxious by tests has previously done poorly, either normatively or subjectively. Perhaps so. Nevertheless, in my experience, *A* students in college are often exceedingly anxious about their academic performance, suggesting that it is not so much their objective experience but how it is interpreted that makes the difference. In highly competitive academic communities, many *A* students worry that an *A−* or *B+* will lower their grade-point average, thereby endangering their chances for acceptance into graduate school.

Interference interpretations are difficult to disentangle from a different, but related mechanism — namely, *conflict of motives.* The drive interpretations of interference specify two sets of drives that come in conflict, the anxiety drive and the task performance drive. Easterbrook (1959) has argued that anxiety disorganizes the use of stimulus cues called on in learning and performance by narrowing the range of attention from peripheral to central cues in the task. His view of the process, which is readily translated into motivational terms, remains one of the most influential even today.

Although what Easterbrook said sounds superficially like an interference concept, it is also true that when there is threat, hence anxiety, the person must turn attention away from the task at hand and to what must be done to meet the threat. In effect, there is another motivational agenda — namely, to attend to something other than the ongoing task. What is disrupted is therefore not necessarily the performance, strictly speaking, but the motivation or will to attend to it in contrast to the sources of threat. These two interpretations, interference and conflict, are usually conjoined in anxiety situations, and it is difficult to know how important each is in accounting for the impaired performance (cf. Schönpflug, 1983; 1985), or whether they are ever separable.

Glanzmann's analysis, though drive centered, displays an interesting shift toward *cognitive coping processes* as a third possible mechanism for the negative effects of anxiety on performance. Threatening conditions often generate ego-defensive forms of coping, which themselves may result in poor performance as a result of withdrawal of effort. For example, the person may deal with threats to self-esteem in evaluative situations by setting a low level of aspiration, thereby warding off the sense of failure, and minimal effort is then directed to the performance. If the performance is poor, the person can then blame it on lack of effort or maintain that the task was unimportant and not worth the effort. Although anxiety has been the emotion usually studied, other negative emotions such as guilt, shame, and envy-jealousy ought to be just as relevant to performance, because in these states irrelevant thoughts and counterproductive behaviors also occur.

Recent interest in what are called *self-handicapping* strategies, which protect self-esteem, seems to expand research concerns beyond anxiety and interference to include *appraisal and coping*. Although this work is cast quite differently from the older concepts reviewed here and seems quite insular (that is, a precious concern of social psychologists that fails to embed itself broadly within the history of similar ideas long expressed by personality and clinical psychologists), it nevertheless offers a relevant and interesting attempt to explain poor social functioning under conditions of negative emotion.

A recent version of this way of thinking was presented by Baumeister and Scher (1988), who examined what they call *self-defeating* behavior. After a review of relevant social psychological observations, they conclude that there is little evidence that normal persons ever desire harm or failure. On the contrary, self-destructive consequences occur as unforeseen and unintended outcomes of efforts to achieve positive goals, and result from a choice of coping strategies that involve bad trade-offs. They argue, for example, that negative emotions such as anxiety, fear, anger, and embarrassment are the root cause of self-defeating behavior, which is usually intended to produce short-term relief but which ends up producing long-term adaptational harm. Reshaping an old argument, these authors address an important principle of psychopathology — namely, that short-term efforts to preserve a threatened self can lead to harmful long-term outcomes.

The heart of Baumeister and Scher's analysis is a section on what they call *self-handicapping* coping strategies, which can take two forms: (1) creating obstacles to one's own success, which can then be used to externalize the blame for failure; and (2) making excuses, which as Snyder and Higgins (1988) suggest, could sometimes facilitate rather than impair functioning (see also Snyder et al., 1991). Of the two self-handicapping strategies, only creating obstacles seems to result in personal harm. Baumeister and Scher (1988, p. 8) write:

> The self-destructive form of self-handicapping . . . is based on two attributional principles (Kelley, 1971, 1972). These are the discounting principle, whereby failure under extenuating circumstance is not taken as proof of incompetence, and the augmentation principle, whereby success despite obstacles is seen as evidence of especially high ability.
>
> Self-handicapping thus confers attributional benefits on the individual regardless of whether the individual succeeds or fails. The drawback is that self-handicapping objectively increases the probability of failure. After all, impediments do impede performance. Self-handicapping is thus a tradeoff that sacrifices one's chances for success in exchange for attributional benefits (i.e., protection from the implications of failure, and extra credit for success).

An important issue raised by these authors is whether self-handicapping is aimed at protecting a person's *public reputation* or *private self-esteem*. The latter is, of course, what has long been viewed as the basis of ego-defenses, which distort reality in the interests of reducing threats to the self. It is not clear whether the two can be reliably distinguished.

Baumeister and Scher (1988) also analyze a number of counterproductive coping strategies falling within the self-defeating rubric in which a person seeking a positive goal acts in ways that impair the chances of success. These include, among others, perseveration, choking under pressure, and ineffective ingratiation of another person.

In *perseveration*, a person persists at a task or goal long after it would have been better to have quit. People who persist are admired in Western societies, and persistence is widely assumed to increase the chance of success. However, persistance can also be counterproductive, leading Baumeister and Scher to suggest wisely that the real issue is how to decide when persistence will be effective and when it will be useless or even self-defeating—a perception included in the serenity prayer of Alcoholics Anonymous, which calls for wisdom about when to try to change things and when to accept them (see also Janoff-Bulman and Brickman, 1982, who have explored expectation as a central factor in persistence and quitting).[4]

Expectations are also obviously relevant to optimism and pessimism, self-esteem, and efficacy (or the sense of personal control), personality factors that have been proposed to facilitate coping and adaptation and to influence emotion. It is usually argued, for example, that those who lack confidence in themselves are more likely to fail as a result of weak or shaky commitment than are those who have high confidence; Dweck (1975), for example, showed something like this with schoolchildren. However, optimism or confidence, as when we are overconfident, can be self-defeating, too.

Baumeister and Scher's analysis of *choking under pressure* nicely illustrates the change in psychological outlook from mechanical, drive-oriented interpretations of performance deficits to cognitive, attributional ones. The authors suggest that when we choke under pressure, our efforts to succeed lead paradoxically to failure, because optimal performance is prevented by an inward preoccupation. Being too preoccupied with one's own internal state—that is, being too self-conscious—interferes with the performance. The reader will notice that this process, referred to by the authors as a counterproductive coping strategy in the face of threat, also fits historically the earlier analyses of drive-generated, task-irrelevant responses that interfere with performance, as discussed by Glanzmann and others.

Finally, *ingratiation* strategies can also be counterproductive. As the authors point out, most people want to be liked, and they act in ways that are designed to win the approval of others. However, this can produce dislike and rejection rather than approval and liking, particularly when the other person interprets the behavior as what it is, a ploy to win approval or affection. As in the other forms of self-defeating behavior, the success or failure of these strategies depends on a judgment about how the target person will interpret and respond, and often the likelihood of a positive response to ingratiation attempts is overestimated. We might also consider in passing the dilemma of a person with low self-esteem who is excessively in need of approval and therefore characteristically overdoes ingratiation, leading either to no reaction and disappointment or to rejection with its attendant emotional distress.

The reader should not lose sight of the two central themes in modern analyses of negative or threat emotions such as anxiety. First, the patterns described represent efforts at cognitive coping, and these efforts can flow from emotion or precede them. Second, modern research and thought also examine impairment of performance in terms of attributions, appraisals, and coping processes rather than drive and interference. Mathews and MacLeod (1984) illustrate the cognitive theme in their research on how generalized anxiety states lead to the selective processing of information related to schemata of personal danger (see also MacLeod & Mathews, 1988; MacLeod, Mathews, & Tata, 1986; Mathews & MacLeod, 1986; Mathews, Mogg, May, & Eysenck, 1989; and Mathews, May, Mogg, & Eysenck, 1990, for further research on attentional factors in anxiety). More and more the research in this area has come to center on the cognitive processes generated in emotional encounters and how they might operate in the context of performance.

Positive Emotions and the Facilitation of Performance

Positive emotions, and/or the processes generating them, have a favorable effect on performance and social functioning. Variants of this idea have been around for a long time. For example, others as well as I have proposed that, whereas threat constricts functioning in the interests of preserving self-esteem, challenge leads to expansiveness, free-flowing use of intellectual resources, and an eager, joyful state of mind. In the last decade or so, an increasing number of studies have been designed to explore the facilitative role of positive emotional states on social functioning, at least in the short-term adaptational encounters of living.

The basic strategy of this research has been to generate positive moods experimentally, usually by providing small presents, arranging to have subjects find a dime in a public phone, showing happy movies, listening to soothing music, having subjects read positive emotional scenarios, or providing success experiences, which Isen (1970), one of the pioneers in this type of research, has referred to as "the warm glow of success." The consequences of these experimentally produced positive mood states are then examined on a variety of dependent variables, including prosocial behaviors such as being helpful to others (see, for example, Moore, Underwood, & Rosenhan, 1984, also pioneers in this work, and reviews by Carlson, Charlin, & Miller, 1988; Isen, 1984; Forgas & Bower, 1987; and others), cognitive activity including memory and judgment (review by Isen, 1984), and the quality of performance.

Although much of the research on mood and memory has shown that positive moods generate positive memories and negative moods negative memories (see also Chapter 2), recent work of Parrott and Sabini (1990) suggests that this might be the result of the way the studies are conducted, and they offer an empirically based dissent. They propose that, when subjects are unaware that their moods are relevant to the experiment and do not try to induce their moods, they show mood incongruent recall, which they do without awareness of regulating their mood—in other words, without awareness that they have gone from a bad mood to a good one, and vice versa. Though it seems odd that people would want to make themselves feel worse, Parrott and Sabini suggest that the intent is really to achieve a realistic self-concept.

If we leave aside legitimate concerns about what is really being created in the mind in these experiments and take them at face value, and if we keep in mind that these findings are more complicated than any simple generalization can reflect, much of this research can be summarized by saying that positive mood induction results in better problem solving and other kinds of performance, as well as more willingness to be helpful to others, than a variety of comparison conditions. Little attention has been given in this research to the specific quality of the mood that is generated; researchers tend to speak of positive and negative moods, not particular ones. And they do not make a distinction between moods and acute emotions.

An attempt has been made by Carlson et al. (1988) to analyze the diverse theoretical mechanisms that have been proposed for the effect of positive mood on helping behavior and to evaluate them. All seem to depend on the concept of associative *priming* (see Bower, 1981; Clark & Isen, 1982; Forgas, Bower, & Krantz, 1984; and Isen, Shalker, Clark, & Karp, 1978), which illustrates the important role of molecular concepts of cognitive activity in this field. The mood-based generation of positive thoughts is called priming. People are said to store material in memory on the basis of its affective tone. A good mood state is thought to be a cue that increases momentarily the probability that positive thoughts will be generated in any subsequent encounter. When people are in a positive mood, they will evaluate others more favorably through priming and will be more ready to offer assistance.

What I said about what provokes a memory of a past emotion in Chapter 1 is again relevant here. There I said that any component of a cognitive-motivational-relational configuration we call an emotion can call forth such a memory if it is adaptationally relevant in the present context, but the whole configuration is best regarded as an integrated scenario, a meaningful script, and it is best to think of priming and mood effects on memory from a molar, meaning-centered standpoint, not in the molecular fashion that has characterized this kind of research. I don't want to duplicate that discussion here, however.

I find the discussions of the effects of positive mood on social functioning to be too molecular — and unconnected to the molar level — for my taste, and sometimes difficult to follow. It is difficult, for example, to get a feeling for the person's adaptational relationship with the world from the research strategies and writing in this area. And so I offer a simple and molar version of theory that is appraisal- and coping-centered and that derives from what I have said about threat and challenge.

When people are treated warmly or have positive experiences, they are apt also to feel safe, secure, self-confident, and expansive — that is, challenged — rather than threatened or in need of self-protection. Thoughts flow easily (cf. Csikszentmihalyi, 1975). When we walk on a pleasant, safe street our movements are outgoing and free rather than wary, constrained, and inhibited, as we would be if we were threatened or in danger. We are, for the moment, at one with the world and appraise the relationship to the environment as benign or beneficial. This appraisal reduces the need to hold back, at the risk of making a fool of oneself, and minimizes the need to be self-preoccupied, with its common consequence of interference with thinking and acting. In contrast with the impulse to treat others warily when competition is keen, we are inclined to think of others favorably, an outlook so often missing in social transactions in a society with highly competitive, individual rather than community values. Given the appraisals involved in positive mood states, we should not be surprised that performance is better, cognitive activity is much less strained, thoughts and ideas come more easily, and we see others more favorably and open ourselves to them.

It might be useful to look more closely at the emotion (or mood) process rather than merely the mood outcome, which would reveal the discrete types of harms and benefits underlying different moods and which might lead to distinct emotions or moods and action tendencies in the effort to examine how the emotion process influences social functioning. Past research on emotion and social functioning has also centered on single adaptational encounters and has not been explicitly extended to functioning in the long run, which should depend on stable traits and patterns characteristic of an individual or that individual's long-term relationship to the social environment.

The potential promise in the study of the emotions and adaptational outcomes— which include somatic health, subjective well-being, and social functioning—is very great indeed and has contributed to the revival of interest in the emotions. Clinicians have long been convinced that there is a strong causal connection between the emotions and these adaptational outcomes. On the other hand, superficial thinking and careless methodology have tended to trivialize the problem, which is why we are still so far from understanding it fully. I hope that the revival of interdisciplinary interest in the emotions will inspire those who want to study how the emotions affect adaptational outcomes, and that in the next decades we will see far more certain knowledge about how the causal connections work.

Summary

In this chapter I explored emotion as a independent variable that affects three kinds of long-term adaptational outcome: somatic health, subjective well-being, and social functioning.

With respect to emotion and *somatic health,* one first confronts the difficulties of defining health and the absence of solid knowledge about the relationships among the three levels of analysis—the physiological, subjective, and social. Not only must we deal with problems in assessment but also the methodological difficulties of doing sound research on the emotional causes of ill health, including confounding of variables, subjective versus objective measurement, the multivariate nature of health outcomes, the stability of health status over long periods, and the difficulty of finding representative samples of the emotion process during the period that we are evaluating. Generality and specificity theories of these effects were examined, and two different pathways, direct and indirect, were reviewed as mechanisms of effects of emotion on somatic health.

Conceptions of *subjective well-being* were examined and several issues about the nature of SWB discussed, centering especially on the possible connections between emotion, coping, and subjective well-being. Predictably, the outlook I promulgated was that emotions, including acute emotions and moods, as well as subjective well-being, were both products of appraisal. In subjective well-being, however, appraisal is a generalized subjective assessment about one's life overall and so is considerably influenced by issues of self-presentation, general appraisal biases, and coping with the vicissitudes of life.

Issues about emotion and *social functioning* have long been of interest in psychology, especially the study of how negative emotions, especially anxiety and stress, impair performance. Several views of negative emotion and impairment of performance were examined, including more recent approaches centered on coping, especially what are called self-handicapping strategies. A newer concern is the role of positive emotions in facilitating performance and prosocial behavior, and research and thought about this were also examined.

Notes

1. The points made here overlap substantially with a recent treatment of these questions by Lazarus and Folkman (1984), which organizes the arguments somewhat differently.

2. The title of a novel by Philip Roth, *Letting Go,* reflects this kind of view.

3. This kind of research is far less likely to be undertaken or permitted today, at least in the United States, because of greater concern about the sensibilities of human subjects and the use of deception than was the case in 1952 when Eriksen and I did the study.

4. The AA serenity prayer, which seems to have its origins in the Catholic Church of the Middle Ages — though I have heard numerous ideas about its earliest origins — goes something like this: "God grant me the courage to try to change the things I can change, the serenity to accept that which I cannot change, and the wisdom to recognize the difference." This simple epigram contains a great deal of wisdom about coping and adaptation.

❖ 11 ❖

Implications for Research, Assessment, Treatment, and Prevention

In this final chapter it is my intention to spell out the implications of the way I have been thinking about emotions for three practical enterprises: research, assessment, and clinical intervention for the purposes of psychotherapy and prevention. There are a great many themes in the preceding chapters, and some are more significant than others for each of the three enterprises. After a brief reprise of five sweeping and central themes of cognitive-motivational-relational theory that should seem familiar by now, my plan for the chapter is to provide extended discussions of the implications of these themes for research, assessment, and clinical intervention. All five themes combine into a metatheory that has to be understood as a unit to see its implications. This plan is predicated on the assumption that the reader has read what has preceded this last chapter, which is necessary to make this final attempt at integration meaningful and interesting.

Reprise of Main Themes

The five themes I deal with here consist of the system principle,[1] the process-structure principle, the developmental principle, the specificity principle, and the relational meaning principle.

1. The System Principle

In a nutshell, the emotion process involves many variables, which include antecedent and mediating processes as well as responses. The antecedent and mediating process variables are involved in emotion generation; the response variables are the short-term (emotional) outcomes that combine into a cognitive-motivational-relational configuration, which when recurrent or continuous over a long period affect the psychological and behavioral flow, and therefore long-term mental and physical health (see Chapter 10).

424

With respect to emotion generation, no single variable is sufficient to explain the emotional response. It takes a particular confluence of two sets of essential variables — the personality and environmental variables — to set the stage for the personal meaning that is the basis of an emotion. Although it is tempting to center analysis on the more powerful single antecedent variables, such as an environmental demand or a motive trait, the system theory perspective is that a variable's influence on the emotion process is always modified by other variables in the system, especially the mediating process variables of appraisal and coping.

2. The Process-Structure Principle

Emotions follow two interdependent principles: (a) the process principle, which is concerned with flux and change, and (b) the structure principle, which is concerned with stability. I identify these as (a) and (b) to reflect their interdependence. To assess them for research purposes requires that we study emotions in the same persons, intraindividually, over time and across encounters, as well as interindividually.

(a) Process. The hallmark of the process principle is *movement* and *change*. Emotions, especially goal incongruent (negative) ones, are psychological consequences of adaptational struggles (processes), and they demonstrate great variation across time and diverse encounters, because rapid changes in relational meanings are apt to occur at different moments in an encounter and in different encounters, each of which has its own distinctive demands, constraints, and resources (or opportunities).

(b) Structure. Some emotions, and the processes that generate them, are recurrent. Recurrent patterns are explainable in terms of the presence of stable psychological and environmental structures, or more accurately, stable *person–environment relationships*.

3. The Developmental Principle

Some of the biological and social variables that influence the emotions are not fully mature at birth but emerge and change from infancy to young adulthood and perhaps even in old age. The emotion process is not the same, therefore, at different points in the course of development — for example, in a 1-month-old infant, a 4-month-old infant, a 3-year-old child, a 13-year-old child, and a young adult. We are less sure about developmental changes in emotion in later life and old age, though the relational sources of emotion and the coping process ought to change with changes of physiological functioning and social roles if standard analyses of this are sound (e.g., Folkman, Lazarus, Pimley, & Novacek, 1987). In any case, the developmental principle states that the emotions may change in both content and process at different times or stages over the life-course. I examined some of the efforts to plot this change in Chapter 8.

We could also construct a phylogenetic version of this principle, which would state that the emotion process also varies among species. I don't believe we can understand the human emotion process by reducing it to the least common denominator of simpler or very simple species. This kind of reduction would impair our appreciation of the different ways in which all sorts of creatures adapt and react emotionally.

4. The Specificity Principle

Once we have decided that it is useful to distinguish among a number of individual emotions, it becomes necessary to proceed beyond a concept of general arousal to the distinction between positive or negative emotions, and ultimately to identify the distinctive pattern of variables and processes for each individual emotion. The specificity principle was applied in Part Three (Chapters 6 and 7) in the form of a decision tree that proceeds stepwise through a set of appraisals, each of which involves a different relational meaning. Specificity also applies to the organized emotional response configuration, which is distinctive for each individual emotion.

5. The Relational Meaning Principle

Relational meaning is the substantive key to the emotion process. It is expressed by a set of *core relational themes,* which define the interpersonal and intrapersonal harms and benefits inherent in each person–environment relationship. The meaning is fashioned in an *appraisal* process, which is the central construct of a cognitive-motivational-relational theory. *Coping* plays a major role in this meaning, because it influences the deployment of attention and the personal significance for well-being of the person–environment relationship.

Each individual emotion expresses a different relational meaning, which can be further analyzed into a pattern of the six appraisal components: goal relevance, goal congruence or incongruence, type of ego-involvement, harm or credit, coping potential, and future expectations. To understand an emotion requires that we understand the specific relational meaning that has generated it, and how that meaning was fashioned.

Notice that the five principles include four that are very general and abstract and a fifth that defines the essential contents of the theory and has to do with the details of relational meaning, appraisal, and coping. Principles 1 through 4 are essentially metatheoretical. They have to do mainly with premises and perspectives for thinking about emotion and how knowledge about the emotion process is obtained. Principle 5 allows us to talk about practical issues such as research, assessment, and treatment.

Implications for Research

I discuss research implications in two ways—first abstractly, in line with the first four metatheoretical issues, then more concretely, as prescribed by Principle 5. Research problems centered on the effects of emotion on health, functioning, and well-being have already been discussed in Chapter 10. The research possibilities I talk about here are centered mainly on the emotion process itself, not its effects.

Abstract Implications

The implications for research that flow from the first four metatheoretical principles are profound in what they indicate for the treatment of research variables, whether one's research involves laboratory experiments or is field-centered and correlational. In the late 1970s, feeling somewhat constrained about what could be done in the laboratory to generate stress and emotion comparable with the process in normal living, and wary about the so-called controls that were said to be possible in laboratory experiments (see Lazarus & Launier, 1978), I took a rather negative position about experimental methods. I believed then that field studies were more suited to the study of stress and emotion than were laboratory experiments, and still do.

Because it is very difficult to generate emotions reliably in the laboratory, experimental approaches suffer from major constraints, but they also offer the advantages inherent in manipulation and selection of variables under a modest degree of control. The reservation implied in speaking of a "modest degree of control" in socially relevant research is that a laboratory experiment is itself a social event. It involves an experimenter-subject relationship that is not altogether defined by standardized instructions and procedures, and that is apt to be appraised quite differently from individual to individual — because experimenters are not physical objects, and human subjects have their own concerns and beliefs that shape the personal meaning of the experimental situation. We need to be wary, therefore, about our interpretations of the findings of even laboratory experiments.

One of my favorite examples is research concerned with the specificity of hormonal patterns to environmental stressors. Mason and his colleagues (Mason, Maher, Hartley, Mougey, Perlow, & Jones, 1976) wanted to study the effects of fasting, heat, cold, and exercise on a number of neurohumoral systems. However, when the lab temperature was changed rapidly, it was appraised by the animals as threatening; when monkeys were forced to fast, but experimenters brought food to other monkeys, the former got very upset. And when male human subjects exercised on a treadmill, they interpreted what was happening to them — their heavy breathing, fatigue, and poor performance — as threatening. The methodological problem in all this was that psychological threat was confounded with the physical stressors whose hormonal effects the researchers wanted to understand.

Mason et al. decided to try to "clean up the independent variable," in their words, by eliminating this confound, which was the result of appraisals by sentient creatures who constantly evaluate what is happening to them. In the human exercise trials, every effort was made to eliminate the competitive or threatening aspects of the situation. In the fasting trials, the experimental monkeys were given nonnutritive things to eat when the control monkeys were fed. And the temperature changes were accomplished very slowly, so that they would not be obtrusive and threatening.

As a result of this effort, each physical stressor was found to produce a distinctive neurohumoral response pattern. And when the animals (and humans) were threatened psychologically, marked corticosteroid changes occurred, which were not observed in most of the physical stressor conditions. Thus, despite Selye's (1956/1976) emphasis on nonspecific stress hormones, corticosteroids seem to be influenced mainly, though not exclusively, by psychological factors. Only by separating the physical stressors from the psychological ones was it possible to show this.

I am now convinced that, depending on the status of our understanding, certain issues are best tackled by field research and others experimentally (cf. Willems, 1969). Ideally, both approaches should be conjoined in a reasoned, multivariate, multimethod research program. In the main, I favor in-depth measurement rather than psychometric, surveylike approaches. We should make careful naturalistic observations, which would allow us to address the complex meanings of an event for each individual. We should try to get below the surface level wherever possible. And we should arrange our observations longitudinally where possible, to permit the study of process and to increase the grounds for causal analysis (see Lazarus, 1990a, 1990b).

Because many variables of the emotion process are interdependent, and a single one could not possibly be definitive with respect to a complex emotional configuration, the *system principle* implies that ideal research would involve measurement of all or most of the relevant variables and processes. To accomplish this requires that measurements be made of motivations and beliefs, which are the contemporaneous personality antecedents of the emotion process in the Lewinian sense, as well as of the environmental demands, constraints, and resources confronted in the adaptational encounter. These antecedents influence the mediating process variables of the system, appraisal and coping, which in turn shape the emotional response configuration.

A number of historical or background variables might also be considered in system-based research. These might include genetic-constitutional and personal history variables such as child-rearing patterns, early family relationships relevant to ego-identity, experiences relevant to trust or mistrust, authoritarian treatment, rejection, and so on. And as we saw in Chapter 8, the course and stage of psychological development, as well as the species, would also be relevant because the emotion process and contents will vary with it.

I do not mean to suggest that a system theory necessarily requires attention to historical rather than contemporaneous variables. Earlier I alluded to Lewin's (1935) famous contrast between historical and systematic causation. When we look into the historical background of persons for explanations of their actions and reactions, as is done in some forms of psychotherapy, we are using historical causation. Lewin argued that a superior strategy would describe what persons had become at the moment of an encounter to predict their actions and reactions. This is systematic causation, and the system principle is well suited to it.

The ideal of using a system principle analysis in research is, of course, easier to say than do, and it arises from the recognition that interindividual research with a single variable is likely to account for only a very modest proportion of the variance in emotional patterns, though some variables are apt to be stronger predictors than others. Whenever possible, those who adopt a system outlook should use more than one variable in their research and should explore how these variables modify each other in shaping the emotional outcome and its changing characteristics.

A cognitive-motivational-relational theory requires the use of antecedent variables to predict appraisal and coping processes as mediators, as I said in Chapter 5. Otherwise, appraisal theory would be forever mired in post hoc reasoning and never put to a thorough test. This position is certainly antithetical to exclusively contextual approaches, such as "grounded theory" (Glaser & Stauss, 1965, 1968), which abjures general rules and predictions. I am referring to explanatory or interpretive rules, without which there can be no scientific generalizations. I believe the theory of the emotions I have been expounding is potentially explicit enough to reason effectively about appraisals and to make predictions that derive from the confluence of motivational and belief (personality) variables and certain classes of environmental conditions.

Similarly, the theory postulates that certain forms of coping will change appraisals in particular ways, and research could be mounted to evaluate this reasoning, too. Coping and appraisal, especially when emotion-focused or cognitive coping is involved, are so closely related that it is often difficult to separate them; denial or distancing involves reappraisal and changed meaning. This is a methodological problem of considerable importance.

I have consistently avoided falling into the trap of concretely contrasting emotion-focused and problem-focused coping as entities, because they are functions and both can sometimes be expressed by the same thoughts or actions. For example, using a drug to calm us down while we take an exam can serve the function both of reducing distress (emotion-focused coping) and preventing impaired performance (problem-focused coping). Interpreting the coping functions served by thoughts and actions under stress is difficult without more information than the mere endorsement by the subject of the thought or action. The solution requires that the research design draw on the process principle; this depends on an intraindividual observational format over time and across diverse encounters, which could help identify the specific contexts from which to distinguish between the two functions.

System theories greatly enlarge the scope of research from single variables to chains of nested variables, thereby increasing the potential for identifying sources of individual variations, both within and between individuals. As I see it, the theoretician-researcher, especially in the context of discovery in contrast with theory evaluation, must move back and forth fluidly between conceptualization and observation. Science is best regarded as a continuing process of reasoning and observing, observing and reasoning, sequentially or in tandem. The formulas for psychological research that we present to undergraduate and graduate students have little to do with how creative and influential scientists actually ply their trade.

Although all this is difficult to accomplish well, it is by no means impossible if we have the will and creativity. I regret the use of low-cost and superficial measurement in so much psychological research; the pressure to complete a study and publish it will not allow researchers to do justice to theory (see Lazarus, 1990b). It seems that we must constantly lament the tremendous gap between the grand sweep and richness of our theories and what we can usually accomplish in empirical research, especially when measurement is superficial.

The *process-structure principle* mandates that some if not all research be designed intraindividually as well as interindividually, which makes it possible to do two things: First, we can evaluate and distinguish between emotion states and emotion traits, because only by observing emotions in the same persons repeatedly can we evaluate the extent of their stability or flux; second, prospective designs make prediction possible and increase the prospects of making causal inferences. When conducted over extended periods of time, intraindividual research is also developmental, especially if it is centered on periods of a lifetime that involve major developmental changes in the variables and processes being studied.

When, for example, Smith, Novacek, Lazarus, and Pope (unpublished) studied appraisal styles — that is, consistent ways of making appraisals in the same persons across different kinds of emotion-generating encounters — we looked for stability as well as variability in the appraisal process, and tried to predict stability from personality and environmental variables.

And when Novacek and I (1990) studied the goal hierarchies of college students over an academic semester, we sought evidence of motivational stability and variability, finding incidently that health outcomes and subjective well-being were poorer in students who showed motivational instability. We speculated that students who were unstable in goal hierarchy, presumably responding to ongoing academic experiences that provided information about who and what they are in the social world, were also more immature and troubled, because in mature adults a goal hierarchy should ultimately become a stable feature of ego-identity. Only a major crisis would disrupt and change the structure of adult motivation.

And when Folkman, Lazarus, Dunkel-Schetter, DeLongis, and Gruen (1986) and Folkman, Lazarus, Gruen, and DeLongis (1986) studied coping in the same persons over five stressful encounters, each occurring every month, we had an opportunity to evaluate which of eight coping factors were stable (presumably a product of personality traits) and which were unstable (presumably a product of the situational context).

The process-structure principle is especially important when we search for emotion traits — for example, people who are recurrently angry, anxious, guilty, shameful, envious, jealous, prideful, compassionate, hopeful, hopeless, and so on. Such traits, especially when they are dysfunctional, are the center of attention in clinical work. Stability and flux should both be examined to provide a full picture of how emotion works in general and how particular emotions differ among individuals, settings, and periods (see Lazarus, 1989a).

The *developmental principle* offers a distinctive perspective on the emotion process and presents a number of special research implications. Developmentalists are now asking questions about cognitive development in the emotion process, both in content and in formal terms. We need to know more clearly when given emotions emerge. Even more important, we need to know what happens psychologically to create the normative patterns in emotional development as well as individual differences.

The premise under which I have operated is that not only is formal cognitive development relevant, whether considered in Piagetian, Wernerian, Freudian, or other terms, but also that emotions depend on the way children understand human motivation and social transaction. Newborn infants have little capacity to appreciate social rules and culturally influenced meanings, but they eventually grasp, use, and construct these meanings, ultimately creating complex and rich patterns of emotional experience. We need to know much more than we do now about how this works.

The chief research task that emerges from the *specificity principle* is, on the *input* side, to identify the variables that differentiate each emotion, thereby creating a set of subtheories of emotion, as it were. A cognitive-motivational-relational theory provides candidates — hypotheses if you prefer — for the variables and processes that are involved in each. On the *output* side, the specificity principle points us toward patterns of response — that is, action-centered, subjective, and physiological variables, which are distinguishable for each individual emotion (see Chapter 2).

The *relational meaning principle* implicates the contents of *knowledge* and *appraisal,* especially the latter, as the processes that shape the emotion process and the individual emotions. A number of research studies and programs are now emerging to evaluate hypotheses about this. Although there are controversies, reviews of some of this ongoing research (e.g., Smith & Ellsworth, 1985; Lazarus & Smith, 1988; Smith & Lazarus, 1990; Frijda, 1986; Scherer, 1984a, 1984b; Roseman, 1984; Tessor, 1990, and others) suggest surprising agreement about the core relational themes and appraisals underlying the emotions despite their ephemeral nature.

Unfortunately, there has been much less interest in *coping* and emotion. I hope this will change with the growing recognition that relationships with the environment are affected by the coping process, and that coping not only flows from emotion but also precedes it as a causal factor. Remember, however, that appraisal is the key to the emotion process; coping affects emotion through (1) the actual changes it produces in the person–environment relationship, as appraised via feedback; (2) what is attended to; and (3) its effects on the personal meaning of the relationship. The process and contents of coping in each individual emotion are, therefore, among the central research issues of a cognitive-motivational-relational theory.

The relational meaning principle subsumes motivation which, as I said in Chapter 3, defines the business of an adaptational encounter. The significance of what is happening for personal well-being is defined largely in motivational terms — that is, through what a person wishes, needs, and hopes for and against. The three primary appraisal components (see Chapter 4) — goal relevance, goal congruence or incongruence, and type of ego-involvement — are all about motivation. There is no need to treat motivation here as a separate theme, because it is always an intrinsic feature of what I am calling relational meaning, achieved by primary appraisals.

At first blush, there seems nothing terribly radical about the relational meaning principle. People catch on quickly to the idea that the two separate sets of variables — namely, the personality and the environmental variables — are lost in favor of a relational meaning at a new level of abstraction. This new abstraction cannot be defined by either contributing component to the relationship. I said this — I hope not too repetitiously — with considerable care in Chapter 3 and in other places in this book.

Is there a problem in this? Although I have only recently come to speak of core relational themes, I have been lecturing about relational meaning for years, often using the term *transaction,* and I find that it slips from the minds even of listeners who seemed at first to understand and appreciate it. What is difficult to grasp is the difference between *interaction,* which is familiar to everyone, and *transaction,* which cannot be understood merely as the interplay of separate variables. Maybe it was a mistake to have used the term *transaction,* which may not be as clear as relational meaning.

I am often told by psychologists that because other researchers, too, speak of both personality and environmental variables in interaction, they are therefore thinking relationally. This is erroneous, however, because it misses what is meant by relational meaning, which transcends the individual, interacting variables. Our tendency to analyze, to unpack complex ideas and reduce them to elements, may be antithetical to relational meaning. The language of psychology has not been a relational language but one of separate variables, a point I also made in Chapter 1. With their analytic rather than synthetic epistemology, it is difficult for psychologists to come to terms with the idea of relational meaning. It is important to understand that a higher level of abstraction is required for this idea in which individual variables are lost in favor of the new meaning that results from their union. It seems to me that this is, in part, what gestalt meant when it was said that the whole was greater than the sum of its parts, and it is inherent in present-day relational ideas like resonances or affordances (see Chapters 3 and 4).

In connection with the idea that emotion depends on relational meaning, I am tempted to say that an emotional response cannot be defined by a molecular component of an intentional action — as in a facial expression, a muscle movement, or a physiological response element — without reference to the whole, coordinated change. I get the feeling that today emotions are commonly conceived and studied as peripheral events. Instead, emotion draws on what is in the person and in the environment together as a complex relational unit — defined centrally, not peripherally.

Thus, an anger relationship involves the urge to neutralize the agent we blame for our woes by demolishing it, but there is no simple movement whereby the adaptational requirements of an angry relationship can be acted out. Except in blind rage, anger typically involves a shifting relationship between the person experiencing it and another person, and it is, of necessity, dependent on both persons. Anger, as is true for most emotions, is tremendously varied in its adaptational requirements, its manifestations, and the contexts in which it occurs. A complex series of acts is involved that are connected by the intent, the emotion occurring, and informational feedback from its effects. An emotion organizes the response components in myriad ways that depend on what can or must be done in a changing adaptational relationship with the environment.

Therefore, *embodied* cannot mean merely a muscle action potential, the movement of a few muscles of the face, a reaction of the heart muscle, or the electrical conductivity of the skin, though these are all features of embodiment. The data suggest that the Duchenne smile, for example, may be more common in genuine happiness than so-called false smiles; however, this is not happiness, or an absolute criterion of happiness, but only a clue to it. Nor am I suggesting that Ekman, Friesen, and Davidson (1990) are suggesting this, though this sometimes seems to be an implicit message, which should be resisted.

In other words, the central psychological phenomenon of emotion is revealed, in part, by peripheral reactions, but is not totally definable by those reactions. We may, in fact, be misled if we take any peripheral response to be the sine qua non of an emotion. Peripheral measures are needed to study emotion (see Chapter 2); however, they are not relational meanings but only the slaves of it.

If we want to study the action tendencies and physiological response patterns involved in each emotion, those presumably set off by the appraisals and coping patterns involved in the emotion, a molar pattern — a gestalt, as it were — is required, the details of which will vary greatly from one encounter to another. This statement is one of the most profound implications of the idea of relational meaning. If we want to understand the response side of emotion, we must be capable of treating it as a complex amalgam of elements that is molar, intentional, complex, and diverse in detail. Relational meaning incorporates the implications for personal well-being of the relationship between a person and the environment, which draws on goals, beliefs about oneself and the world, the potential for complex coping, and knowledge about the consequences of what we do.

Concrete Implications

Research issues have been addressed in all the chapters of this book, especially in those with a heavy dose of theoretical propositions. It might be useful, nevertheless, to suggest some of the most important research themes that derive from the principles identified — that is, those that go to the heart of the emotion process and the variables of central importance. It would, however, be a futile gesture to try to generate a laundry list of all of the interesting research issues in the field of emotion, or even those on which cognitive-motivational-relational theory has a bearing. I cannot cover everyone's favorite topic, and I hope I will be forgiven for those I have left out. Here I point to four broad research arenas that I consider especially important and promising.

1. In Chapter 3, I spoke of the *motivational principle,* and noted there as well as in this chapter that it is subsumed under the relational meaning principle. You will recall that it states that the things people care about — that is, their goal commitments — define what is harmful and beneficial for them, and therefore what is apt to generate positive and negative emotions in their encounters with the environment. I also identified a person's goal hierarchy, both between and within goals (see Chapter 3), coupled with what a person believes or expects in general and in the specific encounter, as important in the prediction of appraisal patterns and their associated emotions.

Little has been done in recent years to measure goal hierarchies and to use them as variables in the prediction of emotions.[2] One would expect that how people spend their time would be closely related to their goal hierarchies (e.g., Emmons, 1986), though short-term routes to achieve long-term goals can occupy them, too. With his usual clarity, Bruner (1981, pp. 41–42) wrote as follows about the idea of *intention* (see also Heckhausen & Beckman, 1990), which is relevant to our concern here with means-ends relationships:

> What I take for granted . . . is that most of what we speak of in common sense terms as human action is steered by intentions of the following kind and in the following way. An intention is present when an individual operates persistently toward achieving an end state, persists in developing means and corrects the development of means to get closer to the end state, and finally ceases the line of activity when specifiable features of the end state are achieved. The elements of the cycle, then, comprise aim, option of means, persistence and correlation, and a terminal stop order.

When people voluntarily accept environmental demands and constraints, sometimes painful ones, this should be in the service of what is important to them. We might ask, for example, how college students, or any other population, spend their time and how this relates to their motivational patterns, as well as asking what the sources of satisfaction and dissatisfaction in these activities are.

More to the point is the question, implicated in the words *satisfaction* and *dissatisfaction,* of whether and how the emotions experienced by different people in their daily activities reflect their goal hierarchies, as the relational meaning principle suggests. It would be useful to have portraits of the daily emotional lives of people and the contexts in which their emotions are generated. How often do strong emotions arise? Which emotions? How intensely? What are the personality correlates and environmental conditions of these emotional patterns? The closest anyone has come to portraying the emotional life over time are the largely descriptive studies of Wessman and Ricks (1966), which were centered on moods.

In its simplest form, the motivation principle, stated as a hypothesis, predicts that in activites linked to high-priority goals, the emotions experienced should reflect the status of those and other goals in the goal hierarchy, which help define the person–environment relationship: Thus, thwarting in arenas of importance should generate more distress than in unimportant arenas; uncertain threats to important goal attainments should lead to more anxiety than similar threats to relatively unimportant goals; slights to a vulnerable ego-identity should produce anger rather than anxiety; and so on, for each of the positive and negative emotions. Only recently have psychologists regained interest in motivation as a factor in emotion. It was to make research possible on these questions that Novacek and I set out to portray the structure of motivation in college students and to develop a viable measure of goal hierarchies (see Novacek & Lazarus, 1990, for a limited review).

However, to complicate things a bit with the system principle, distress, anxiety, anger, or happiness is also influenced by diverse beliefs and coping strategies, making the emotional outcome difficult to predict without also measuring them. Therefore, even more interesting than the main effects of goal hierarchies on the emotional life of the person in particular settings would be studies of the interplay between these hierarchies and other personality traits such as beliefs about oneself and the world, characteristics of the environment when an emotion occurs, and coping. Complex research designs could be created to test some of the basic propositions of the theory, predicting appraisals and coping as well as the ebb and flow of individual emotions and their patterns over time and in diverse environmental settings, and the interpersonal conditions that account for the flow. It would be all the more impressive if motivational conflicts and unconscious factors, inferred by clinicians who knew the person well, could lead to predictions that were paradoxical with respect to the objective conditions being faced.

This is no game for the faint of heart or for the researcher who wants fast publication. In general, the least interesting hypotheses are those using only one antecedent and one response variable in a single environmental context; the most interesting and fruitful research possibilities, in contrast, would involve studies of the same persons on which there are adequate assessments, compared interindividually on antecedent variables by experimental manipulation or selection, as well as intraindividually, over time, and in demanding environmental contexts — so that both flux and stability could be studied and causal hypotheses tested.

To do otherwise is to relegate psychological research on emotions and adaptation to the testing of banalities or simplistic hypotheses. The current cynicism and malaise about psychological research — there is, for example, doubt that many psychologists even read what is published — cannot be reversed by continuing along lines characteristic of the past, but only by programmatic research based on believable theories about how emotion works. Such theories are, I believe, already derivable from selective use of past findings, what we glean from observation and experience, as well as good sense.

Abortive but promising attempts to do something like what I have just proposed, though less formally than was needed, were initiated in the 1930s by Murray (1938) at Harvard. Attempts were also made at the Institute of Personality Assessment and Research (IPAR) at Berkeley. What, if anything, went wrong with personality assessment in the last several decades? Although there would be argument about this, I believe that those involved in assessment became enamored of a set of psychometric scales that were aimed at measuring traits cheaply and efficiently without reference to functionally equivalent contexts in which they would operate (see Lazarus, 1990b). Traditional personality measurement, based on standard psychometrics, is an outlook that has gone out of date but is still being defended by assessment specialists long after it has ceased to be viable, current enthusiasm about the Big Five[3] notwithstanding. If the reader agrees with me, it would not be amiss to suggest that the field could be considerably revitalized by less emphasis on methodological and psychometric issues and more on in-depth study of theory-driven substantive questions of the sort I have been advocating here.

2. From the standpoint of a cognitive-motivational-relational theory, emotion research must, as increasingly is being done, test the *core relational themes* for each individual emotion, and explore the *appraisal patterns* that are necessary and sufficient for each. The danger is that given the residual behaviorism (I would say scientism, which seems to infect journal editors, the modern bureaucrats of the academy) trying to do this will meet with much resistance.

I have found among journal reviewers and editors a catch-22 mentality likely to defeat the creativity and persistence needed to truly advance our understanding. For example, in a recent interchange on a research report I submitted to a major journal, one reviewer complained that there was nothing new in the research, because the core relational themes and appraisal patterns underlying each emotion were obvious and known to all. Yet another reviewer of the same article complained that the appraisals underlying each emotion could never be proven using self-report data — in effect negating its value not because it was obvious but because the obvious could not be proven.

After over forty years of research experience I doubt that any study can "prove" hypotheses or hunches about appraisal and emotion, whether using self-report measures or any other kind, though studies could offer substantial support for one or another concept. This sounds like Cosmides and Tooby's (1987) sardonic observation, citing popular wisdom, that "arguments against new ideas in science pass through three characteristic stages from it's not true, to well, it may be true, but it's not important, to it's true and it's important, but it's not new — we knew it all along."

3. Research on *action tendencies, physiological response patterns,* and *their relations* in the individual emotions remains, I think, one of the most fruitful arenas for potential research. From the theory standpoint, action tendencies may be a bridge to the embodiment of the emotions. Any programmatic study of them, even if it is accomplished at a micro level, might lead to important extensions of what we know. As I said in Chapter 2 and here, however, I would prefer to look at action tendencies in molar, relational terms, because in emotions the person–environment relationship is crucial — also, so much is going on, and so much of the person is involved.

In this vein, I remember two funny experiences in Japan where my family and I were going to live for a year, which illustrate this point about molar, relational analysis of action tendencies. I arrived in Japan with the expectation that my Japanese host would bow and not shake hands, and as I gathered later, he expected me to shake hands. So when we met I began to bow, he began to shake hands, but in an instant, realizing mutually that the action was inappropriate, I pulled back my bow and he pulled back his handshake, and round and round we went for a few moments of abortive action, a comedy of errors. Had there been a slow-motion film of what was happening, it would have looked like a kind of rhythmic dance. No individual muscle movement, especially in a single individual, would have captured the comical relational aspects of these actions and action withdrawals in response to rapid feedback. We were relating with our whole minds and bodies, dancing to each other's actions and reactions. Thus, the concept of relationship applies to motor as well as psychological processes.

And these reactions were in many respects preconscious and automatic. For example, when I was finally leaving Japan after a year I went to receive a prize for winning a contest on board the cruise ship on which I was returning. I was surprised and amused later to see the photo that the ship's photographer had made of this event; without realizing it, I had made a deep bow as I accepted the prize. Living in Japan, the bow had become an automatic social-relational gesture.

I remember also vividly my impressions of the way Argentine males use their bodies in social contexts, expressing deeply ingrained male-macho attitudes in a fashion I think is almost unique in the world. I don't believe a motor analysis of a single muscle could capture the impression, which is of the whole body in social action, in a relationship with another.

I might add that we need to understand better the bodily perceptions that many people describe as features of their emotions — sinking feelings in the gut, choked throats, waves of hot or cold, invisible tremors, floating or lightness, heaviness, and so on. Minimal research attention has been given to these perceptions and to their connection with the individual emotions. It is possible that a microanalysis of electrical and chemical brain activities, autonomic nervous system responses, or hormonal patterns — which seem to be favored by researchers — will be less revealing than these kinds of unexplained, molar physical experiences would be in distinguishing one emotion from another.

4. Issues that fall within the *developmental* perspective are also among the most promising ones on which to mount research. The evidence suggests that there are

major differences in the way emotions work and as to when they occur at different developmental stages.

The advent of cognitive-motivational-relational theories has changed how developmental questions about emotion are being framed. Whereas before most attention had been centered on the sequence in which emotions emerged — a very difficult thing to study in the uncertainty of finding absolute criteria of emotions in prelinguistic babies and young children — the new tendency is to try to explore what a child can and does understand about getting along in the social world (see Chapter 8). Less attention has been paid to motivational factors than to cognitive ones, which may be unfortunate, though Stein, Levine, and Trabasso's research (see Chapter 8) seems to be an exception.

A cognitive-motivational-relational theory presents a road map of the emotion process in terms of a finite number of person–environment relationships, what people want and think, and how they cope. This greatly enlarges the scope of developmental research, not only in the early years but over the life-course. What has changed are the issues that are being studied, not so much how they are studied. The focus is on the way the variables and processes, which change as development proceeds, contribute to the emotional life.

The core relational themes and appraisal patterns I have presented could generate hypotheses for developmental research on when individual emotions appear, how they work, and what variables influence them. Thus, if we take seriously that shame requires an emergent ego-identity, that positive and negative emotions depend on formative or established goal hierarchies, which seem to develop and change over a long period, or that all emotions depend on what a child — within or across cultures and within or across social structures — understands about the personal implications of social events, these propositions could drive and direct comparative-developmental research.

Implications for Assessment

One of the most difficult issues in research on the emotions is, of course, how to measure the emotions and the other variables of the emotion process (see Chapter 2). When a person reports about an emotion, how do we know it is an emotion or merely cold knowledge about how emotion works, perhaps shared with many others in the culture? Clearly, it would be advantageous to have more than a single response criterion to draw upon in such research. However, other response measures — for example, behavioral and physiological ones — are equally ambiguous with respect to their significance, perhaps even more so than verbal reports, which could be made far more detailed and less subject to ambiguity and distortion than they are in the typical research study. If as much methodological attention were given to subjective verbal reports as is given to facial expression and psychophysiology, the former could be even more useful as sources of knowledge.

Assessment implies a drawing together of multiple measurements into a picture of whole persons relating and adapting to the world in which they live. I have used the term *assessment* rather than *measurement* because I want to convey the idea of a person in the environment rather than a single trait in isolation as the object of study. Most of what is available today are *single-trait measures,* which describe personal characteristics, not persons adapting in the world. This leaves those who would want to study personality and environmental factors in emotion at a great disadvantage in not having suitable measures available for programmatic emotion research and for clinical assessment. It seems to me that emotion researchers who might want to draw on the system principle, whether for clinical assessment or for research, might be wise to start almost from scratch in creating measures of the variables in the system, which could be pulled together systematically in ultimate assessments.

Because emotions, viewed in the broadest sense as complex emotion-generating scenarios rather than merely response states, are so important as organizing principles of human adaptation and maladaptation, and because the topic of emotion has been hitherto at the periphery of theoretical and research interest (see Chapter 1), the reader might indulge me in a fantasy of a sweeping research enterprise or assessment institute, if you will. In such an enterprise, the study of emotions would describe and measure the personality and social factors that could be considered promising candidates for in-depth exploration of the emotion process, and the person–environment relationship characteristic of each emotional state. To make such an enterprise work requires measures of the three kinds of variables: antecedents, mediating processes, and the emotional response outcome. I begin with antecedents existing now.

Antecedent Variable Measures

I spoke of two sets of antecedent *content* variables, the personality and the environmental variables; when conjoined in an adaptational encounter, these are reconciled by the appraisal process, which in turn evaluates the implications for personal well-being of the ongoing and changing person–environment relationship. The two main personality variables have to do with motives and beliefs; the main environmental variables have to do with demands, constraints, and resources (or opportunities).

In addition to content variables, there are also *formal* variables having to do mainly with the timing of encounters, imminence, and ambiguity. These have a bearing on how demands, constraints, and opportunities are experienced, appraised, and coped with, influencing how a person reacts to and handles the adaptational encounter. For example, *imminence* of a harm makes the threat urgent and often changes the coping process from avoidance to vigilance, as when one must obtain an X-ray or CAT scan to check on a cancer recurrence (see Monat, Averill, & Lazarus, 1973). *Ambiguity* increases the likelihood of anxiety. A major stressful event that occurs along with many others in the same period, which has to do with its *timing,* may produce a crisis by pushing a person above a safe level of stress, which of course differs from person to person and within the same person from time to time. Formal variables have not generated much measurement interest.

Motives. To treat motivation as an antecedent requires that goal hierarchies be measured as traits, which become engaged transactionally and can then be referred to as immediate stakes in the adaptational outcome. The approach used by Novacek and me (Novacek & Lazarus, 1990), for example, which is one of several possibilities, looks at goal hierarchies by the standard psychometric procedure of having subjects endorse and rate on importance, expectancy to achieve, effort, and distress each of a large number of statements expressing diverse values and goals, some of them concrete and limited, others sweeping, broad, and abstract. The endorsement ratings were ultimately reduced by factor analysis to six broad goal meanings: power/achievement, affiliation, personal growth, altruism, stress avoidance, and sensation seeking. The results of this analysis provide the basis for a set of scales that can ultimately be used interindividually and intraindividually in research on the role of *explicit motivation* in the emotional life. The six broad goals in the goal hierarchy are illustrated in Table 11.1, along with statements expressing the meaning of each goal.

TABLE 11.1. A Questionnaire Approach to the Measurement of Motivation

---

Self-Report Scale Method Using a Hierarchy of Six Goals

Affiliation
  Wanting to have a close and satisfying relationship with others.
  Needing to feel a sense of belonging.
  Wanting to receive affection and love.
  Wanting to be involved and intimate with others.

Power/achievement
  Wanting to obtain awards and recognition.
  Desiring to be popular and accepted.
  Aspiring to be well-off financially.
  Wanting to compete successfully.

Personal growth
  Wanting to be open-minded.
  Trying to be responsible.
  Aspiring to be a fair and ethical person.
  Wanting to develop a personal philosophy of life.

Altruism
  Wanting to help others in need.
  Needing to be committed to a cause.
  Wanting to make sacrifices for others.
  Wanting to participate in a religious organization.

Stress avoidance
  Desiring an easy life.
  Wanting to avoid blame or criticism.
  Trying to avoid conflict.
  Wanting to avoid stress.

Sensation-seeking
  Wanting to have fun.
  Needing sexual pleasure.
  Wanting an exciting life.
  Trying to have enough free time.

Note: The hierarchy was developed using factor analysis of responses to many items, the clearest of which are sampled here.

(*Source:* J. Novacek and R. S. Lazarus. *Journal of Personality* (1990). Durham, NC: Duke University Press. Copyright © 1991 by Duke University Presss. Reprinted by permission.)

What such measurement assumes theoretically is that strong positive and negative emotions should accompany daily activities that fall within strong goal commitments, and weak emotions should accompany activities that are on the bottom of the goal hierarchy. The emotions should be positive when the person believes reasonable progress is being made toward goal attainment in activities that are relevant to an important goal, and they should be negative when the person believes that goal attainment is being obstructed in these activities.

An achievement-relevant story and the TAT picture to which it was given is presented in Figure 11.1 to illustrate McClelland's approach to the measurement of

---

One of the pictures commonly used on the Thematic Apperception Test to measure achievement motivation is shown here:

Subjects are asked to construct interesting and imaginative stories to such pictures, and given 20 seconds to do so. They are guided through the story plot by four questions: (1) What is happening? Who are the persons? (2) What has led up to this situation; that is, what has happened in the past? (3) What is being thought? What is wanted; by whom? (4) What will happen? What will be done?

Scoring is heavily based on evidence of competition against a standard of excellence, as well as unique accomplishments, long-term attainment of achievement goals, and so forth.

The following story for this picture indicates strong achievement content and is taken from McClelland et al. (1953, p.118):

> Two inventors are working on a new type of machine. They need this machine in order to complete the work on their new invention, the automobile. This takes place some time ago, and the necessary tools are not available. They are thinking that they will succeed. They want to do a good job, and improve transportation. After years of hard work they are successful, and feel elated.

FIGURE 11.1. The TAT Measure of Achievement Motivation. (*Source:* D. C. McClelland, J. W. Atkinson, R. A. Clark, and E. L. Lowell, *The Achievement Motive.* New York: Irvington Publishers, 1953. Reprinted by permission.)

implicit motives and to contrast it with the questionnaire approach. In Chapter 3, I indicated the possibility that the two different cognitive levels implied by these different ways of measuring motivation might lead to contradictory appraisals and emotions within the same person, which is what the psychoanalytic approach also would postulate.

Beliefs. The most difficult problem in measuring this antecedent variable is in choosing which beliefs among many might be most relevant to emotion. Particularly fashionable at present is a class of closely related but not identical concepts that include self-esteem, sense of mastery, self-efficacy, sense of coherence, and optimism. All seem very relevant to the emotion process. For example, in a condition of threat, a sense of mastery or self-efficacy ought to reduce anxiety, and continuing research shaped by Bandura's concept (e.g., Bandura, 1982) has indeed shown this to be the case. Similar arguments could be made for sense of coherence, optimism, and the like.

The mention of self-esteem as a variable leaves me somewhat ambivalent in light of its faddish use in nonacademic circles, and—in my view—the absurd effort to regard it in California politics and education as a basic requirement of successful adaptation. We are treated to superficial sloganeering with respect to the virtues of positive self-regard and how it might be achieved, which undermines the explanatory value and legitimacy of the concept. The worst feature of this is the implication, accepted widely, that if we (i.e., adults, children, minorities, poor people, drug addicts) rehearse positive self-statements we will somehow magically develop self-esteem and succeed at school and in life—shades of Coué many generations ago with his litany of "Every day in every way I am growing better and better."

This implication is a variant of the equally simplistic "Just say no" being advocated as an approach to drugs without regard for the actual circumstances, experiences, and meanings, or lack of meaning, in people's lives. I had thought, naïvely I suppose, that such simplemindedness would have forever disappeared from the modern scene. In school programs dedicated to improving self-esteem there is great reluctance to deal with anything negative (cf. Rohrkemper & Corno, 1988), despite the fact that self-esteem might be usefully defined as "pride in oneself in which one becomes *aware of and accepting of one's imperfections while cherishing one's inherent strengths and positive qualities.*"[4]

An earlier scale of dogmatism (Rokeach, 1960) illustrates a related but different approach; many of its questions point to a conception of oneself as alone, isolated, and helpless in the face of an environment that is hostile and dangerous. Some examples of items from the dogmatism scale are: "Man on his own is a helpless and miserable creature. Fundamentally, the world we live in is a pretty loathsome place. Most people just don't give a 'damn' for others. I am afraid of people who want to find out what I am really like for fear they will be disappointed in me."

With a system of beliefs like this, a person might be expected to view many physical and social situations as threatening that others would not regard as such because they do not share a habitual sense of negativeness and helplessness in coping with a hostile world. Those feeling this way should have a greater tendency to feel vulnerable and defensive than those with a more positive and secure outlook.

Though the environmental situation will play a role, too, the emotions most likely to stem from this kind of belief system would include anxiety and anger.

Thoughout this book I have referred to other antecedent variables that serve as moderators of the person's relationship to the environment by influencing appraisal and coping and, perhaps, mitigating the damaging effects of stress. Many of these constructs can be thought of as beliefs about oneself and world, illustrated by recent constructs, such as hardiness (Kobasa, 1979; see also Orr & Westman, 1990), sense of coherence (Antonovsky, 1990), optimism (Scheier & Carver, 1987), and constructive thinking (Epstein & Meier, 1989). To this list should be added "learned resourcefulness" and a scale of beliefs about self-control (Rosenbaum, 1980, 1990). It would not be fruitful to present these scales here, but mentioning them might be helpful to readers who are particularly interested. There is obviously great interest in this type of personality construct and measure, which can serve as an antecedent variable that probably affects appraisal and coping processes and could influence the emotional outcome of adaptational encounters.

Given my considerable dissatisfaction with single-trait measures, such as these, I am somewhat attracted to the efforts of psychodynamic writers such as Luborsky (1977, 1984) on the core conflictual relationship theme and Horowitz (1988, 1989) on role relationship schemata, which I mentioned in Chapter 3. These concepts refer to molar, organized outlooks — in Horowitz's analysis, a number of such schemata are possible in the same individual — and they are presumed to shape emotional reactions in interpersonal contexts, whether actually, in fantasy, or in expectation. The schemata are identified by in-depth study of individuals (in the case of these authors, the individuals are patients being treated for emotional crises or disorders) rather than by psychometric scales. To illustrate, I reproduce in Figure 11.2 a diagram from Horowitz (1988, p. 53) that shows four patterns related to the theme of procrastination in which a male patient has several different schemata about himself at the same time.

My present bias is that we may ultimately get farther faster in this admittedly costly and clumsy fashion than with traditional psychometrics designed for normative study (see Lazarus, 1990b). In any case, because multiple schemata are present at the same time in a person's mind but are also latent, an interpretive rule is needed to help us say what it is in an adaptational encounter that draws on one or another schema to drive and direct the emotion process.

Because the variables conducive to anger will, to a certain extent, probably differ from those conducive to other emotions such as anxiety, guilt, love, or pride, relational schemata must be chosen for measurement with certain kinds of adaptational encounters and perhaps certain individual emotions in mind. An alternative view, less attractive to me (see Chapters 6 and 7), is that a common set of variables is involved in all negative emotions, and perhaps a different set for positive emotions.

Because of the absence of systematic theory, an especially weak link in the study of antecedent variables is the technology of measuring environmental demands, constraints, and resources. Measurement to date has centered on stressful life events, which provide a modest part of the story, and daily hassles, which provide another (see Lazarus, 1990b; Lazarus & Folkman, 1984). The programmatic

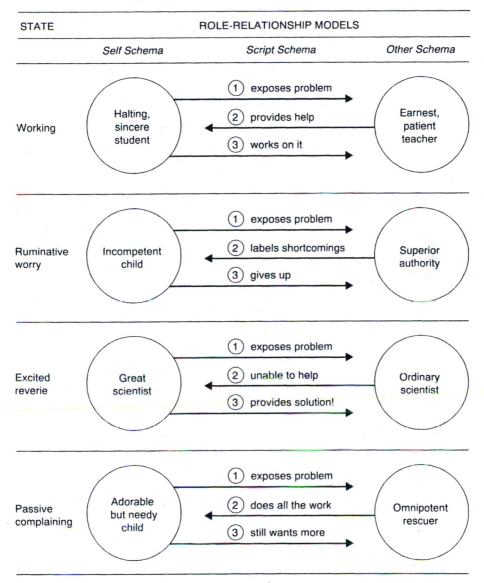

STATE	ROLE-RELATIONSHIP MODELS		
	Self Schema	*Script Schema*	*Other Schema*
Working	Halting, sincere student	① exposes problem ② provides help ③ works on it	Earnest, patient teacher
Ruminative worry	Incompetent child	① exposes problem ② labels shortcomings ③ gives up	Superior authority
Excited reverie	Great scientist	① exposes problem ② unable to help ③ provides solution!	Ordinary scientist
Passive complaining	Adorable but needy child	① exposes problem ② does all the work ③ still wants more	Omnipotent rescuer

FIGURE 11.2. Role-relationship models related to the theme of procrastination. (*Source:* M. J. Horowitz, *Introduction to Psychodynamics.* New York: Basic Books Inc. Copyright © 1988 by Mardi J. Horowitz. Reprinted by permission of the publisher.)

efforts of Moos (1973, 1975; Moos & Billings, 1982) to measure social climates are clearly relevant here.

There has been much debate about whether such measurement should be subjective or objective, and even whether the objective environment is measurable and necessarily relevant to a given individual's person–environment relationships and emotional life. Many psychologists would prefer to measure relationships defined objectively — that is, by an observer rather than by the person being studied. Measurement by the subject makes the criterion of the relational meaning subjective. I am not truly convinced that objective measurement is possible or very fruitful in prediction, and it still must be based on a subjective consensus (Lazarus, 1990b). Although the subjective approach makes the best sense to me when the concern is not strictly normative — for example, when it is directed clinically at individuals — it may be important to keep an open mind about this in other contexts.

Repetti (1987) has developed a scale designed to measure the objective social environment at work by subjective consensus, which I referred to in Chapter 4. Her findings comparing both subjective and objective (consensual) measurement show that the subjective data were more predictive of emotional distress in the context of work. I present her scale in Table 11.2 here.

Because relationally centered measurement is virtually nonexistent in current research, we need to develop measures of person–environment relationships in addition to the separate sets of personality and environmental variables. That is, we need to define and measure the new level of abstraction formed by the conjunction of a person with certain attributes and an environment with certain attributes, and con-

TABLE 11.2. Items Comprising Primary Measures of the Social Environment at Work

---

Global (Factor 1)

1. People go out of their way to help a new employee feel comfortable.[a]
2. Supervisors tend to talk down to employees.[a]
3. There's not much group spirit.[a]
4. The atmosphere is somewhat impersonal.[a]
5. Supervisors usually compliment an employee who does something well.[a]
6. A lot of people seem to be just putting in time.[a]
7. Supervisors tend to discourage criticism from employees.[a]
8. People seem to take pride in the organization.[a]
9. People put quite a lot of effort into what they do.[a]
10. Supervisors often criticize employees over minor things.[a]
11. Few people ever volunteer.[a]
12. It is quite a lively space.[a]
13. Supervisors expect far too much from employees.[a]
14. It's hard to get people to do any extra work.[a]
15. Often people make trouble by talking behind each others' backs.[a]
16. Supervisors really stand up for their people.[a]
17. The social atmosphere in this branch is very friendly.[c]
18. In our branch people show a great deal of respect for one another.[c]
19. There are often conflicts among people who work here.[c]
20. Interactions among fellow employees here are almost always very positive.[c]
21. There is a great deal of tension among people in this branch.[c]
22. People on this job often think of quitting.[d]

Intimacy (Factor 4)

1. People take a personal interest in each other.[a]
2. Employees often talk to each other about personal problems.[a]
3. Employees discuss personal problems with supervisors.[a]
4. Employees at this branch often discuss their personal lives outside of work with each other.[c]

TABLE 11.2. (Continued)

Supervisor Support (Factor 2) and Co-Worker Support (Factor 5)

1. How much (does your immediate supervisor/do other people at work) go out of (his/her/their) way to do things to make your work life easier for you?[b]
2. How easy is it to talk with (your immediate supervisor/other people at work)?[b]
3. How much can (your immediate supervisor/other people at work) be relied on when things get tough at work?[b]
4. How much (is your immediate supervisor/are other people at work) willing to listen to your personal problems?[b]

Job Satisfaction (Factor 3)

1. The work is really challenging.[a]
2. The work is usually very interesting.[a]
3. I frequently think of quitting this job.[d]
4. Generally speaking, I am very satisfied with this job.[d]
5. I am generally satisfied with the kind of work I do in this job.[d]

Note: Each of the items comprising the factor-based measures of the social environment at work and job satisfaction appeared on the Phase 1 Social Environment Survey.

[a]Item is part of the Work Environment Scale by Inset & Moos, 1974, Palo Alto, CA: Consulting Psychologists Press. Copyright 1974 by Consulting Psychologists Press. Reprinted by permission. A 4-point response scale, ranging from *definitely false* (1) to *definitely true* (4), was used to rate each statement describing the social climate.
[b]Item is part of a work social support scale (Caplan, Cobb, French, Harrison, & Pinneau, 1975). A 4-point response scale was used to indicate how well each statement described the respondent's interactions at work: *not at all* (1), *a little* (2), *somewhat* (3), and *very much* (4).
[c]Item was specially written for the study. A 7-point response scale, ranging from *disagree strongly* (1) to *agree strongly* (7), was used.
[d]Item is part of the job-satisfaction scale from the Job Diagnostic Survey by Hackman & Oldham, 1980, Reading, MA: Addison-Wesley. Copyright 1980 by Addison-Wesley. Reprinted by permission. The same 7-point scale was used as in Appendix Note C.

(*Sources:*
(a) Paul M. Insel and Rudolf H. Moos, *Work Environment Scale.* Palo Alto, CA: Consulting Psychologists Press, Inc. Copyright © 1974 by Consulting Psychologists Press. Reproduced by special permission of the publisher. All rights reserved. Further reproduction is prohibited without the publisher's consent.
(b) R. D. Caplan, S. Cobb, J. R. P. French, R. V. Harrison, and S. R. Pinneau, *Job Demands and Worker Health.* Washington, DC: U. S. Government Printing Office, 1975.
(c) R. L. Repetti, "Individual and common components of the social environment at work and psychological well-being." *Journal of Personality and Social Psychology, 52.* Washington, DC: American Psychological Association. Reprinted by permission.
(d) Hackman and Oldham, *Work Redesign.* Reading, MA: Addison-Wesley Publishing Co., 1980. Reprinted by permission.)

---

struct a language to go with this that is relevant to the emotions. This is the purpose of the concept of core relational themes.

To measure relational meanings, researchers must begin almost de novo, because there has been no important tradition of relational analysis and measurement in psychology, though it has been mentioned by mavericks from time to time. An interesting example is some very recent research by de Rivera, Possell, Verette, and Weiner (1989), cited in Chapter 7, which attempts with some success to distinguish among the relational meanings for elation, gladness, and joy on the basis of items that identify situational, bodily, behavioral propensity, and functional variables.

Mediating Process Measures

The central concept of my theoretical analysis of psychological stress is *appraisal*. So in our research, Folkman and I (see Lazarus & Folkman, 1987, for a review) made some limited progress in its measurement, but the procedures we used were much too primitive to survive long in that form. I hope they will stimulate further refinements. A few scattered researchers have taken up the challenge of advancing the measurement of appraisal for use in predictive research (e.g., Hart, 1991; Hart, Comer, & Hittner, 1990; Shalit, 1982; Shalit, Carlstedt, and Shalit, 1986; Larrson, 1987, 1989; Larrson & Starrin, 1984; Larrson, Kempe, & Starrin, 1988).

Our own efforts to measure *primary appraisal* consisted of subjects' reports of personal *stakes* in each stressful encounter (Folkman, Lazarus, Dunkel-Schetter, DeLongis, & Gruen,1986; and Folkman, Lazarus, Gruen, & DeLongis, 1986). A factor analysis produced two main classes of stakes: self-esteem and concerns about the well-being of a loved one. We measured *secondary appraisal* with a number of questions about whether anything could be done to alter the troubled relationship with the environment. However, this research did not deal with individual emotions.

The emotion-centered appraisal theory presented here (see Chapter 4) offers its own opportunities for measurement. The six appraisal components of my analysis require measurement if the theory is to be properly evaluated in research and clinical use. Some efforts to advance the measurement of these appraisal components and to study core relational themes are now under way (e.g., Hensher, 1990; Shopshire & Bonney, 1990), but it is too early to tell how they will work.

In Chapter 4, I also discussed appraisal as a relatively stable cognitive style of a person. I cited the Attributional Style Questionnaire of Peterson, Semmel, von Baeyer, Abramson, Metalsky, and Seligman (1982; see also Seligman, Abramson, Semmel, & von Baeyer, 1979) and Epstein and Meier's (1989) Constructive Thinking Inventory as relevant. Other work on *appraisal styles* includes the sense of coherence of Antonovsky (1987), Kobasa's (1979) on hardiness, and Scheier and Carver's on optimism (1987).

Scales recently developed by my colleagues and me (Smith, Novacek, Lazarus, & Pope, 1990) and research based on them illustrate the measurement of appraisal styles. In a procedure referred to as *responses to situations*, subjects are asked to make evaluative judgments about 12 hypothetical and potentially emotional situations such as: "A close friend beats you out for the opportunity to participate in an activity you had been looking forward to"; "A professor compliments you on a paper you've written"; and "You hear that a friend has been telling people good things about you." Subjects also rate their appraisal thoughts such as: "How important is what is happening in this situation to you?" and "To what extent do you consider yourself responsible for this situation?" These appraisal thoughts cover a range of appraisal components, some of which I discussed in Chapter 4 and used in Chapters 6 and 7.[5] Because the same subjects do this for 12 different hypothetical situations, it is possible to determine to what extent particular patterns of appraisal are consistent for given individuals, thereby measuring what could be called *appraisal style*. The list of situations, appraisal components, and the thoughts that must be rated are presented in Table 11.3.

TABLE 11.3. The Measurement of Appraisal Styles

Situational Appraisal — Components

The following items are used to retrospectively measure the subject's appraisals, in terms of components, within a particular context or event. Each item is rated along an 11-point scale. The actual rating forms used by Smith et al. (1989b) follow the description of all three types of situation-specific measures.

Motivational Relevance

How important was what was happening in this situation to you?

Motivational Congruence

Think about what you *didn't want* in this situation. To what extent were these *undesirable* elements present in the situation?

Think about what you *did want* in this situation. To what extent were these *desirable* elements present in the situation?

Self-Accountability

To what extent did you consider *yourself* responsible for this situation?

Other-Accountability

To what extent did you consider *someone else* responsible for this situation?

Problem-Focused Coping Potential

Think about what you wanted and didn't want in this situation. How certain were you that you would be able to influence things to make (or keep) the situation the way you want it?

Emotion-Focused Coping Potential

How certain were you that you would, or would not, be able to deal emotionally with what was happening in this situation however it turned out?

Future Expectancy

Think about how you wanted this situation to turn out. When you were in this situation, how consistent with these wishes (for any reason) did you expect this situation to become (or stay)?

Situation Appraisal — Themes

The following scales are used to measure the subject's appraisals, in terms of emotion-specific themes, within a particular context or event. Listed below are the items and estimated reliabilities (from Smith et al., 1989b) for the scales used to measure the appraisal themes hypothesized to produce the emotions Smith et al. have studied most intensively to date. The extent to which each item corresponds to the person's thoughts in the situation is rated on a 9-point scale ranging from "not at all" to "extremely."

Other-Blame — Theme for Anger α = .88

I've been cheated or wronged.
Someone else is to blame for the bad situation I'm in.
I've been dealt with shabbily.
Some asshole is interfering with my goals.
Some jerk is trying to take advantage of me.
This bad thing would have been prevented if the other person had been worthy of respect.

Self-Blame — Theme for Guilt α = .87

I have done something bad.
Things are bad because of me.
I am to blame for this bad situation.

Danger/Threat — Theme for Anxiety/Fear α = .71

I feel threatened by an uncertain danger.
I am in danger and might not be able to handle it.
I don't know whether I can handle what is about to happen.

Loss/Harm — Themes for Sadness/Resignation

Loss α = .81

I feel a sense of loss.
Something I cared about is gone.
Something important to me has been destroyed.   (Continued)

TABLE 11.3. (Continued)

Harm α = .92

   I feel helpless.

   I don't see anything I can do to improve this bad situation.

   Just now I seem to be powerless to make things right in this situation.

   Nothing can ever be done to fix this bad situation.

   This situation is hopeless.

   This bad situation is never going to improve.

Optimism — Theme for Hope and Challenge α = .85

   Somehow things might work out in this situation.

   In the end there's a chance that everything will be OK.

   I feel that things are going to get better in this situation.

   If I try hard enough I can get what I want in this situation.

   With some effort I can make things better in this situation.

   I can handle this difficult task.

Relevance — Theme for Interest α = .64

   Something important to me is happening in this situation.

   This situation touches upon my personal concerns.

   There are important things to think about here.

Removal of Threat — Theme for Relief α = .69

   A burden has been lifted from my mind.

   Things have worked out after all.

   A threat or harm has been removed from the situation.

Success — Theme for Happiness α = .95

   Things turned out great.

   I've gotten what I've wanted in this situation.

   Things have gone wonderfully well in this situation.

Concern for Another — Theme for Sympathy α = .91

   I feel sorry for this (other) person.

   It bothers me that this (other) person is in trouble.

   This (other) person needs help.

Irrelevance — Theme for Boredom α = .52

   This situation is totally irrelevant to my concerns.

   I don't care at all about what is happening here.

   What's happening here is a total waste of time.

(Courtesy of C. A. Smith, J. Novacek, R. S. Lazarus, and L. K. Pope.)

The research of the Berkeley Stress and Coping Project from 1977 to 1987 also made a heavy investment in the psychometrics of *coping,* which materialized in the *Ways of Coping Questionnaire* (Folkman & Lazarus, 1988b). Other approaches, some similar to ours (e.g., Moos & Billings, 1982; Billings & Moos, 1981; Stone & Neale, 1984a), others quite different (e.g., Pearlin, Lieberman, Menaghan, & Mullan, 1981; Pearlin & Schooler, 1978), were also emerging during the same period.

Our research subjects filled out a questionnaire or were interviewed about a specific stressful encounter. They were asked to endorse whichever coping thoughts and actions they had used in that encounter and to rate how important each had been. In an earlier version, the emphasis had been on two broad functions of coping — problem-focused coping, in which actions were taken to change the troubled

TABLE 11.4. Sample Items from the Ways of Coping Questionnaire

Factor 1: Confrontive
  Tried to get the person responsible to change his or her mind.
  I expressed anger to the person(s) who caused the problem.

Factor 2: Distancing
  Went on as if nothing had happened.
  Didn't let it get to me; refused to think about it too much.

Factor 3: Self-controlling
  I tried to keep my feelings to myself.
  I tried not to act too hastily or follow my first hunch.

Factor 4: Seeking social support
  Talked to someone to find out more about the situation.
  I asked a relative or friend I respected for advice.

Factor 5: Accepting responsibility
  Criticized or lectured myself.
  I apologized or did something to make up.

Factor 6: Escape-avoidance
  Hoped a miracle would happen.
  Avoided being with people in general.

Factor 7: Planful problem solving
  I made a plan of action and followed it.
  Just concentrated on what I had to do next — the next step.

Factor 8: Positive reappraisal
  Changed or grew as a person in a good way.
  Rediscovered what is important in life.

(*Source:* S. Folkman and R. S. Lazarus, *The Manual for the Ways of Coping Questionnaire (Research Edition).* Palo Alto, CA: Consulting Psychologists Press, Inc., 1988. Reprinted by permission.)

person–environment relationship, and emotion-focused coping, in which cognitive efforts were made to change the meaning of what had happened or to direct attention to one or another aspect. In the latest version, a factor analysis produced eight modes of coping, which have been used as the basis of assessment of the coping process in our and others' research. Sample items for each of the eight scales are presented in Table 11.4.

The coping measured in this procedure is contextual, and to identify stable coping styles requires that coping be observed over time in the same persons (e.g., Folkman & Lazarus, 1985) or across different stressful encounters (Folkman, Lazarus, Dunkel-Schetter, DeLongis, & Gruen, 1986; and Folkman, Lazarus, Gruen, & DeLongis, 1986). There remains considerable interest in identifying coping styles (e.g., Krohne, 1978, 1986, 1989; Krohne & Rogner, 1982). In the past such efforts have not resulted in standardized procedures that have proved useful for clinical work, but perhaps new and more sophisticated relational ones might do better.

The field of coping measurement still remains unsettled, and it is difficult to anticipate where it is likely to go in the future. It has not yet much penetrated the study of the emotions, but I hope it soon will (see Folkman & Lazarus, 1985, for one exception, and Laux & Weber, 1991, for another). Given the theoretical importance of coping in the emotion process, the absence of research on coping in emotion is unfortunate and leaves a large gap in the study of the emotion process.

Response Measures

If we consider only the emotional response without attention to the emotion-generating conditions and processes, we are limited to the measurement of actions and action tendencies, physiological activities, and subjective reports about emotion states. Little needs to be added here to what I said about facial expression, physiological activities, and experienced affect in Chapter 2. There is a thriving enterprise dealing with these response states, much less dealing with other response systems such as voice quality patterns (e.g., Scherer, 1989) and body movements, and very little that looks at the entire emotion response configuration. We are deluged by piecemeal measurements without an effort at synthesis.

Over and above the use of factor analysis to study dimensions, the measurement of *subjective affect* has followed very traditional procedures in which the presence and intensity of emotions are rated using emotion words or scenarios, as in the research by Shaver et al. (1987), which I described in Chapter 2 (see Plutchik & Kellerman, 1989, for reviews and analyses of emotion measurements). Measurement by self-rating scales is more efficient and less expensive than in-depth study, but it is also subject to all the difficulties connected with superficial self-report such as errors of memory, self-deception, presentation of self, individual differences in lexical meanings, and the possible conflicts between surface and depth cognitive processes.

Several researchers have developed rating scales for the measurement of a specific emotion, such as anxiety or anger. One is a set of scales by Endler and Okada (1975; see also Endler, Edwards, Vitelli, and Parker, 1989). Another by Spielberger, Gorsuch, and Lushene (1970) has already been mentioned. It has the special property of having two versions, a state scale that is used for a particular encounter and a trait scale that measures anxiety as a stable property of a person. In Table 11.5, I use the state-trait anger scale of Spielberger, Jacobs, Russell, and Crane (1983; see also Spielberger, Johnson, Russell, Crane, Jacobs, & Worden, 1985) as an illustration, because it is less well known than the anxiety scale and relates to the management of anger and its health-related consequences, which were considered in Chapter 10.

In the preceding discussion of assessment I dealt with measurement of each of a number of individual antecedent, mediating process, and response variables. Because I know of no programmatic efforts to bring them all together as an organized adaptational configuration or system, I close this discussion of assessment by restating the system theory principle: The assessment of the emotion process should ideally make use of all or as many of the types of variables as possible that comprise the total emotion process, all of which combine to provide the personal meanings on which the emotion response configuration depends. Ideally, too, assessments should be made repeatedly over time and across diverse encounters to assess both structure and process, and, when appropriate, to draw on the possibilities of comparative, developmental analysis.

TABLE 11.5.

The State Anger Scale	*The Trait Anger Scale*
1. I am mad.	1. I have a fiery temper.
2. I feel angry.	2. I am quick tempered.
3. I am burned up.	3. I am a hotheaded person.
4. I feel irritated.	4. I get annoyed when I am singled out for correction.
5. I feel frustrated.	5. It makes me furious when I am criticized in front of others.
6. I feel aggravated.	6. I get angry when I'm slowed down by others' mistakes.
7. I feel like I'm about to explode.	7. I feel infuriated when I do a good job and get poor evaluation.
8. I feel like banging on the table.	8. I fly off the handle.
9. I feel like yelling at somebody.	9. I feel annoyed when I am not given recognition for doing good work.
10. I feel like swearing.	10. People who think they are always right irritate me.
11. I am furious.	11. When I get mad, I say nasty things.
12. I feel like hitting someone.	12. I feel irritated.
13. I feel like breaking things.	13. I feel angry.
14. I am annoyed.	14. When I get frustrated, I feel like hitting someone
15. I am resentful.	15. It makes my blood boil when I am pressured.

(*Source:* J. N. Butcher and C. D. Spielberger, *Advances in Personality Assessment, vol. 2.* Hillsdale, NJ: Lawrence Erlbaum Associates, Inc., 1983. Reprinted by permission.)

Implications for Treatment and Prevention

As I said in Chapter 1, a theory is a powerful tool that allows us to reason backward and forward between the propositions about causation and individual emotions as outcomes. The focus may be on emotion generation — that is, from antecedent and mediating variables to emotions as an outcome — but we can also reason backward to make educated guesses from the presence of an emotion to the variables and processes that brought it into being in the first place. This reasoning may also be evaluated empirically like any other. Clinical psychologists and other disciplines concerned with treatment use this kind of backward reasoning because they start with a person who is seeking help for distressing and dysfunctional emotions and then try to understand how things got that way and to produce therapeutic change.

Before we turn to treatment, a few points might first be made about diagnosis for the purpose of treatment. I don't mean diagnosis as labeling but rather the kind that is used clinically to understand what has gone wrong in the person's life and to plan a sensible treatment program. If we think of dysfunction as the result of a failure of appraisal and coping, then examining these failures from a diagnostic standpoint would be appropriate.

Careful attention to diagnosis was once indigenous to clinical practice, but it went out of vogue with a crisis of confidence in diagnostic tests and the movement of clinical psychologists into therapy, where formal diagnosis seemed to be a time-consuming digression. It remains in evidence mostly as ongoing inferences made informally by clinicians, especially during the early stages of treatment as patients present their complaints and reveal the dynamics of their dysfunctions. Typically, patients shop around until they find what seems to them the right match with a particular therapist or therapeutic strategy. More formal attention to diagnosis might increase the possibilities of selecting therapeutic strategies on the basis of the dynamics and patient characteristics rather than, as is often the case, making the assumption that any generalized treatment is equally applicable to every patient.

The therapist might want to know, for example, whether the patient's problems arise from particular kinds of *inappropriate goal commitments and beliefs,* which in turn lead to *appraisals* of threat where it doesn't exist or to benign appraisals where the person should feel threatened. What also is the role of coping in the dysfunction? Is there a recurrent tendency to compound problems by *inept coping?* For example, is coping performed ineffectively or is it inappropriate to the adaptational requirements being faced? Considering what I have said about the shift in psychological thought toward cognitivism, it should come as no surprise that psychotherapists are beginning to think favorably again about some kind of diagnostic assessment as part of treatment.

Of considerable interest today, especially among the cognitive therapists, is assessment of the appraisal and coping thoughts a patient has in connection with personal problems. Kendall and Korgeski (1979; see also Kendall, 1982) point to two important clinical functions of cognitive assessment: first, to investigate the role, say, of irrational beliefs in the development of disorders or in the process of coping; second, to provide confirmation about what is going on in treatment (for example, that the treatment actually has changed the targeted cognitions). These authors provide a brief review of various approaches for sampling what they call "in vivo thoughts," including the use of a portable "beeper," which goes off at varied intervals so that the persons being assessed can record samples of what they are thinking about—their imagery, attributions about events, and self-statements—all of which have been emphasized by Meichenbaum (1975, 1977) and others, whose therapeutic approaches are compatible with a cognitive-motivational-relational approach to the emotion process.

In addition to the beeper technique, which is getting increasingly popular as a research device, an ingenious procedure developed by Perrez and Reicherts (in press) employs a portable computer used by subjects to respond to preprogrammed interview questions about their coping. A major advantage of such a procedure is that the person being assessed can be instructed to do the interview at a moment very close in time to an emotional encounter, thereby minimizing memory problems and retrospective falsification (for another version of this, see also Wheeler & Reis, in press).

Goldfried (1987), too, has shown a sustained interest in advances in cognitive psychology for use in cognitive therapy and has surveyed procedures for making measurements (see also Landau & Goldfried, 1981). I like an analysis he makes based on a quote from Bransford and Johnson (1973) that shows how slight shifts in context create dramatic changes in the personal meaning of an encounter. The passage is as follows (Bransford & Johnson, 1973, p. 415):

The man stood before the mirror and combed his hair. He checked his face carefully for any places he might have missed shaving and then put on the conservative tie he had decided to wear. At breakfast, he studied the newspaper carefully and, over coffee, discussed the possibility of buying a new washing machine with his wife. Then he made several phone calls. As he was leaving the house he thought about the fact that his children would probably want to go to that private camp again this summer. When the car didn't start, he got out, slammed the door and walked down to the bus stop in a very angry mood. Now he would be late.

Goldfried observes that if this passage had begun with the statement that "The unemployed man stood before the mirror . . . " the essential meaning of the statement would be different. And still a different meaning would arise if the passage began, "The stockbroker stood before the mirror." As Goldfried (1987, p. 100) puts it, "If you were to read the passage once again, it would be evident that it takes on a different meaning if the person involved is unemployed or is a stockbroker." We constantly make inferences from what happens about why events occur, and the inferences change automatically with how different details affect the event's meaning. In therapy, clients are helped to change how they view their lives by pointing to facets of their experience that they haven't been attending to, probably because of ego-defensive activity. This process has sometimes been called *reframing* or *restructuring*.

In a very rich analysis, Landau and Goldfried (1981) also suggest that cognitive therapists should look to a body of work associated with the cognitive revolution that provides assessment techniques that could be useful in treatment. They cite a seminal book by Neisser (1967) on cognitive psychology and draw heavily on an important article by Schank and Abelson (1977), both cited in Chapter 4. The latter provides a systematic model of cognitive activities relevant to the emotional life and the way a person deals with adaptational encounters; of particular importance, these authors list illustrative assessment strategies for each type of cognitive activity, which the interested clinical reader may wish to consult.

The heart of Landau and Goldfried's analysis is an overview of two groups of cognitive constructs: (1) motivational influences that include *goals* and *goal themes* and that consist of clusters of related goals; and (2) schemata that include *cognitive maps* (defined as representations of the physical environment), *plans* (defined as general information, including problem-solving strategies, relevant to goal satisfaction), *situational scripts* (defined as representations of the sequence of behaviors to be expected in a particular situation), *instrumental scripts* (defined as fixed sequences of behaviors used to attain specific and frequently encountered goals), *personal scripts* (defined as actions associated with goals that are unilaterally held by one actor — that is, a hidden agenda), and *semantic schemata* (defined as information used to categorize an object or action).

The concept of coping has also found its way into the procedures of cognitive-behavior therapy, stimulated by recent research and theory about the coping process and its measurement. An example is a program of stress management and treatment introduced by D'Zurilla (1986; see also D'Zurilla & Goldfried, 1971; D'Zurilla & Nezu, 1982) and called *problem-solving training*. The heart of this training program is a sequence of staged units as follows: introductory statements of goals and ratio-nale, efforts to increase sensitivity to problems of living and inadequate coping pro-cesses and styles, examination of the role of emotions in problem solving, exploration of particular problems with the aim of reappraising what has been hap-pening and of setting realistic problem-solving goals, generating alternative solu-tions, evaluating the best solution, implementing the solution and verifying its effectiveness, and finally, consolidating the effects of training, facilitating their maintenance, and generalizing what has been learned to other problems.

Whether or not the concepts of appraisal and coping are explicit in treatment programs, in one form or another these concepts are in the minds of all clinicians doing therapy. Casting them in appraisal and coping terms brings the language of a cognitive-motivational-relational theory of emotion into the realm of ordinary clini-cal practice.

The Relevance of the Emotion Process to Psychopathology

As we turn to psychotherapy, the first problem we need to face is that the emotion process is not equally relevant to all forms of psychopathology and, therefore, to all treatment. If, for example, we consult the American Psychiatric Association's revised *Diagnostic and Statistical Manual (DSM III-R, 1987)*, which provides a list-ing of the categories of mental illness referred to in clinical practice, we can see that, although all disorders have emotional implications because of the way they affect patients' lives, by no means all of them involve emotions in a causal role.

The most obvious examples of disorders in which emotions are usually *not* causal are mental retardation, brain damage that is not the result of substance abuse — use of drugs itself as opposed to the consequences of abuse has its own complex causation that probably involves the emotion process — and inherited affec-tive and schizophrenic disorders. It is an open question whether and to what extent personality disorders and some or all schizophrenias have emotional causes. There would be no gain to debate here which disorders do and do not have emotional caus-es. Suffice it to say that in disorders in which the emotion process does *not* play a direct causal role, the study of the emotions is not particularly relevant.

On the other hand, many people arrive in therapy with a diverse set of emotional problems for which they seek help. These include the garden-variety neuroses, eat-ing disorders, problems of substance abuse, anxiety disorders — which include post-traumatic stress disorders — many sexual dysfunctions involving mood disturbances and impaired social functioning, and probably quite a few others about which there might be more argument. Using my own language rather than DSM III-R, I shall here distinguish three different types of patient problems, which probably require somewhat different treatment approaches. Although they overlap substantially, and therefore are not always sharply distinguishable, they are prime examples of adapta-tional problems therapists frequently deal with that could create disturbances in the emotion recurrently experienced or could themselves be influenced by the emotion process.

1. The simplest type of problem is *lack of skill* for handling adaptational demands that have arisen from a recent crisis. For example, a widowed or divorced

woman whose husband, now gone, handled car repairs and bank accounts, and so on, is now faced with a new set of demands—in addition to old demands such as dealing with children and the household—for example, dealing with the husband's now abandoned tasks, her own sexual needs, and loneliness. A comparable set of problems is faced by divorced, separated, or bereaved husbands, people who have been uprooted and displaced, the suddenly unemployed, and the ill or physically handicapped.

Because persons of this sort are apt to be sleepless, depressed, despairing, or anxious, as well as overloaded with demands they have difficulty managing, there are two basic therapeutic tasks, whether these are tackled by means of self-help books (e.g., Yates, 1976) and consultation with friends, or by professional treatment. One is to "psych" themselves up to face the myriad new demands with verve, good spirits, and the conviction that they can master what must be done. Without implying that they do any real good, I note that self-help books always draw heavily on inspirational ideas to help support, encourage, and motivate people to try to change how they deal with things. These books are often titled *You Can Cope,* and the like. The second task is to learn how to do what must be done. Although all sorts of internal obstacles and conflicts may be revealed in the treatment, for this population conflicts are not usually the focus of attention, because the superficial problem is lack of skill and knowledge, which is assumed, sometimes erroneously, to have emerged with the life change rather than because of neurosis.

However, we must not make the mistake of confusing emotional distress in response to personal tragedy with neurosis, that is, intrapsychic struggles about which the person is unaware or only dimly aware that limit coping effectiveness. Lehman, Wortman, and Williams (1987) have observed, for example, that there are long-term effects of life events such as losing a spouse or a child in an auto accident, and many persons subjected to such loss continue to ruminate and experience distress over the entire time they were studied by the investigators, namely, 4 to 7 years; we should probably assume this will continue much longer. The dignity of their distress should not be demeaned by automatically defining these effects as neurotic or as based on personal inadequacies. By the same token, we should not regard lack of distress as evidence of sound coping; Lehman and Taylor (1988) have shown that the threat of an impending California earthquake is commonly dealt with by denial and the failure to take any measures to prepare.

2. When the problems of dealing with life changes that have resulted in crisis are caused or compounded by intrapsychic conflicts or neurosis, the simple information and skill deficits already mentioned overlap with the second type of problem, the *dysfunctional neurosis.* Some proportion of persons with informational and skill deficits are also troubled by neurotic conflicts that involve disturbed emotions resulting from faulty appraisal and coping processes. It is fair to ask why, for example, the knowledge and skill that most well-functioning people have or can attain is lacking or seems so difficult to attain when necessary. This is one of the main reasons why self-help books and well-meaning advice commonly fail to ameliorate personal problems—to some extent the person is defeated by internal struggles that undermine the task of learning and gaining suitable skills.

Dysfunctional neuroses (which I suppose is a redundancy, because neuroses are dysfunctional by definition) are more difficult to treat than the first type of problem, because faulty appraisal and coping patterns, of which the person is apt to be unaware or only dimly aware, must be identified, comprehended, and overcome. This is tantamount to saying that the problems are to some extent created by the patients themselves rather than by the circumstances of their lives. Obsessions and compulsions, anxiety, phobias and panics, and depression are included here. Their difficulties may or may not be accompanied by somatic symptoms such as gastrointestinal disturbances and headaches, which are among the most common psychosomatic ailments impairing the ability to get along in the world.

Usually patients in this category want only to get rid of the symptom that interferes with their peace of mind and functioning, without seeking major adaptational and personality changes. Traditional psychodynamic therapists usually assume that what such patients are troubled about is really symptomatic of hidden, intrapsychic conflicts about which they need to gain insight to revamp the way they live. Not all therapists are sanguine about insight-centered conceptualizations. Later I say more about diverse therapeutic models for tackling these and other problems.

3. A third type of problem, which might be referred to as *existential* for want of a better word, is manifest in persons who arrive at the doorstep of a psychotherapist with vague complaints of unhappiness, disinterest, and general malaise. They do not complain of crisis or dysfunctions but about a lack of meaning and commitment in their lives. The patient asks, "How can I achieve meaning in my life? Tell me how to have something to live for, to commit myself to."

How the Emotion Process Might Be Involved in Psychopathology

We need to be clear about how the emotion process might contribute to adaptational disorders, especially problem types (2) and (3). The most common way of thinking about this is that the emotion process has become distorted early in life by misappraisals resulting from pathogenic ego-defensive efforts to control threat and distress. A long-term pattern of relationships with others has been created, which is fed by other persons (e.g., parents, friends, lovers) and which, by misdirecting the way a person interprets adaptational encounters, obscures the real threats and inadequate coping patterns (cf. Wachtel, 1977) on which the person has become dependent. Since these persons do not on their own confront the real sources of their distress and dysfunction, and therefore do not unlearn the faulty coping patterns and replace them with more effective ones, they need therapeutic help to do so.

From this point of view, it is not so much the emotion, per se, that is the source of trouble, but the process of emotion generation, which implicates inappropriate goal and belief traits — for example, that one must be perfect in all endeavors or is inadequate or unlovable — faulty appraisals of the person–environment relationship, or faulty strategies of coping that leave the person dysfunctional and in distress. For treatment to work, the person must unlearn, as it were, the faulty patterns and acquire new, more functional ones. Whether or not this requires insight on the part of the patient is one of the points of contention between strict behavior therapists and other therapeutic schools of thought, especially the psychoanalytic.

How Emotion Is Viewed by Different Therapeutic Systems

Professionals in clinical practice are among those who have appreciated and contributed to the current explosion of interest in emotion, and a number of recent books dealing with cognition and emotion written by cognitive therapists have appeared. These books are expressly concerned with the role of emotion in psychopathology and psychotherapy — for example, Greenberg and Safran (1987), Guidano and Liotti (1983), Safran and Greenberg (1991). The last-mentioned book will be of particular interest to those who wish to have a firmer theoretical grasp of the role of emotion in therapeutic change, because it consists of a series of chapters, each written from a different therapeutic stance — such as conditioning, cognitive therapy, dynamic therapy, client-centered therapy, and experiential therapy and also commented on by several theorists.

In a useful article on emotion in psychotherapy on which I draw later, Greenberg and Safran (1989) examined the way emotion is viewed by four major therapeutic systems: psychoanalysis, behavior, cognitive, and experiential-humanistic therapies (see also Hollon & Beck, 1979, for another analysis). Summing up the reason for the current concern with emotion, these authors (1989, p. 27) write that "Unless we grapple with the role of emotion in therapy, our understanding of the human change process will remain hollow, missing some of the vital elements of what makes psychotherapy a potentially powerful change process." Drawing on Greenberg and Safran, I explore how emotion is viewed in psychoanalysis, behavior therapy, cognitive therapy, and experiential-humanistic therapy.

From the *psychoanalyst's* perspective, emotion was first conceived of (by Freud) as psychic energy, just as it was conceived of as drive tension in the reinforcement learning theory of Dollard and Miller (1950), which was essentially a translation of Freudian thought into the language and concepts of reinforcement learning.

Freud initially viewed neurotic symptoms as the result of the blockage of innate drives, the therapeutic cure being abreaction, purging, or catharsis. He later de-emphasized catharsis and substituted the idea that in neurosis a threatening drive is repressed and therefore remains undischarged. When the dammed-up drive energy becomes too great to tolerate, it is discharged as emotion. From this standpoint, emotions are expressions of *undischarged innate drives,* which gives them pathogenic and pathological connotations.

In the psychoanalytic model that later emerged, therapy clearly required corrective emotional experiences to expose reality distortions and lead to patient understanding (insight) so that the faulty appraisals and patterns of coping could be abandoned for more functional ones. The painful exploration of the truth was said to be facilitated by the transference relationship with the therapist, which not only helped motivate the patient, who sought the approval of the therapist (as a parent figure), but also provided important information to both patient and therapist about early parent-child relationships.

However, in the 1940s, even insight was viewed as insufficient by itself in the absence of what was then called "working through." This meant that the insight had to be tested, used, and expanded in action-centered emotional confrontations with the patients' sources of threat in the environment and intrapsychically. Without actually living out the distressing experiences that led to dysfunctional ways of coping, the patient might gain intellectual understanding but would not change fundamentally (which means motivationally and emotionally).

Following the epistemology of the less subjective and sparer reinforcement learning theory, rather than focusing on insight about repressed drives, *behavior therapists* try to modify incapacitating emotional reactions such as anxiety through the automatic (cf. Chapter 4) process of deconditioning. The therapy must create a confrontation with the sources of emotional distress, which, because of pathogenic avoidance, had hitherto been distorting the person's adaptation. This is accomplished either by exposure to the sources of anxiety in gradual steps, perhaps in the presence of something reassuring, or by the opposite — that is, the mounting of acute anxiety in the presence of the threat in order to force the patient to discover the truth that the anticipated danger will not materialize. The latter is called *flooding*. These types of deconditioning procedures are particularly appropriate for phobias, panic states, and obsessions. Current exponents of behavior therapy differ in the extent to which they believe innate tendencies versus learning are said to operate in the development of the pathology.

Cognitive therapists usually view emotions, as I do, as the result of the personal meaning of events, the central theme of their therapeutic approach being to change pathogenic ways of thinking about oneself and the world, and thereby to change the troubled emotional pattern. The reasoning is that if cognitions are faulty, then logically they must be changed. But how to do this? A variety of procedures for producing cognitive change are possible, drawing on patterns of action to confront noxious conditions that have resulted in emotional distress, exhortations and disputations with patients about their life assumptions, and insight-producing explorations of distorted meanings that have presumably caused the emotional dysfunction. Relationships between cognition and emotion, and recent controversies about their relationship, have been of particular interest to cognitive therapists because of their emphasis on the thoughts and beliefs underlying the dysfunctional emotional patterns of their patients.

Experiential-humanistic therapists are said by Greenberg and Safran (1989) to regard emotion more positively than do either the cognitive or behavior therapists, viewing it as a vital motivator of adaptation and change. Instead of being regarded as expressions of innate or learned tendencies, emotions are said to provide adaptationally relevant information about self and world. As emphasized in the counterculture of the 1960s, this assumes that we need to get back in touch with our emotions, which have been suppressed by societal rules and internalized patterns of inhibition. Avoidance of painful emotions lies at the core of neurotic problems. The patient must become aware of the meaning of these suppressed emotions and be more responsive to them.

Two versions of this therapeutic approach are cited by Greenberg and Safran: client-centered, or Rogerian, therapy, which emphasizes becoming fully aware of the emotions that were denied and distorted in the past, and gestalt therapy, which emphasizes that the experience and expression of emotion are necessary for change to occur. To these versions of experiential and humanistic approaches, we might add the existential therapies, which in the United States consist of Americanized versions of European existential philosophy.

The Tasks of Treatment

The point made here that patients seeking psychotherapy have different kinds of problems, which require different kinds of treatment, also implies that there are different goals of treatment. Some patients, for example, seem so fragile that therapists use *supportive therapy* to tide them over a crisis or to prevent a worsening of their condition. For these patients the struggle to gain insight or to change their life patterns is viewed by the therapist as dangerous, and is therefore eschewed. Traditional psychoanalysts refuse to accept for psychoanalytic treatment those patients who are deemed to have too vulnerable an ego to undergo insight therapy. Patients who are suffering only from a short-term crisis might also qualify for a more supportive and short-term program with more modest goals rather than seeking an overhaul of their ordinarily functioning personalities. These patients are not necessarily fragile but seem not to need more than temporary professional support.

Many alternative goals are possible for the typical neurotic patient. These include *disappearance* of the damaging symptom, *easing* of emotional distress and dysfunction, acquisition of ambitious *insights,* and *changes* in how the patient copes with chronic or recurrent emotional and interpersonal difficulties. The patient may see the goal in one way and the therapist in another, and part of the therapeutic task at the outset is to find a basis for agreement. One possibility is to have a set of graded goals, which the patient may or may not pursue beyond the most modest ones.

For existentially troubled patients, the problem is not to overcome dysfunctions but to establish *meanings* and *commitments,* a very difficult undertaking. By and large, existential and psychoanalytic therapies both view treatment as a lengthy process of discovering what has gone wrong in the past that has resulted in distress and dysfunction or existential malaise. Anyone who has worked with uncommitted students in academic life knows how difficult it is to overcome this kind of complaint. The student says, "Teach me how to want to do well at something," but the professor usually knows that this cannot come from the outside. But how? What motivation will sustain a search for meaning and an acceptance of commitment? Meaning is something that most of us construct (and commit ourselves to) out of a variety of ideas and influences. Many therapists would say that these patients must discover what turned them off before they can be turned on again in a constructive way. The task of existential treatment is more amorphous than intervention for other kinds of emotional distress.

How Treatment Works

Whereas many therapeutic schools came into being as an attack on earlier schools, as when behaviorists militantly disavowed the psychoanalytic outlook, the present period is singular in that real efforts at rapprochement among diverse therapeutic schools are now being fostered. When we speak of psychotherapy, we are not speaking of a simple process of education or of providing information and skills for those people who are in difficulty because they lack these skills; instead, we are seeking to overcome internal struggles that obscure the truth and obstruct therapeutic change.

Psychodynamic theorists think of this distinction as the difference between surface problems and neurotic symptoms. Although I don't wish to alienate behavioral clinicians, given what I have already said about cognitive mediation and conflict, it should come as no surprise that I believe most psychotherapy deals, in part, with symptoms of inner struggle, which makes the task of change more difficult than it would be in the case of mere education.

Some years ago (Lazarus & Folkman, 1984, Ch. 11) I tried to apply my thinking about stress and emotion to treatment and suggested that several principles that are usually considered antithetical were actually compatible and supplemental ways in which to change the appraisals on which emotions depended. Four principles were examined in my analysis, all of which are in some sense probably true:

1. *Emotions shape thought and action,* which is the familiar concept of emotions as drive. If emotions can influence thought and action, and they can be experienced without defense (cf. Epstein, 1983), the person will think and act more adaptively if they are changed. All sorts of devices may be used to transform emotions, including deconditioning, relaxation, meditation, biofeedback, and the creation of a secure, supportive therapeutic relationship.

2. *Actions shape thought and emotion,* so if we can get patients to behave differently there is a good chance that they will think and feel differently, as when we play a different interpersonal role and then internalize it as our own (see Chapter 8), or discover the bases of another person's perspective, thereby becoming more sympathetic to it.

3. *Thoughts shape emotion and action,* which means that if we change the thoughts, we might also change emotions and actions. This is the central manifesto of the cognitive therapy approach.

4. *The environment shapes thought, emotion, and action,* which, from the perspective of treatment, means that if the environment of a patient can be changed by actions such as job change, divorce, or effective confrontations, the three constructs of mind — cognition, motivation, and emotion — or their relationships with the environment might also change.

Many therapists, including those who identify themselves as cognitive therapists, use combinations of these dicta, as in A. Lazarus's (1981) multimodal therapy, in trying to draw on whatever possibilities for change there might be. These principles, however, do not explain why therapeutic change occurs, but only point to some of the variables involved in such change — namely, cognitions, actions, and emotions. With that in mind (Lazarus, 1989c) I tried to summarize what I believe is the key *principle of therapeutic change.*

Three premises underlie my view of the mechanisms of therapeutic change; they involve the relationships among cognition, motivation, and emotion (see Lazarus, 1989c):

1. Whereas *integration* is tantamount to mental health, disconnection among the constructs of the mind is tantamount to psychopathology, dysfunction, and distress. The three constructs of mind — cognition, motivation, and emotion — should general-

ly be compatible, ideally in harmony; the mind as a system must also be in reasonable touch with environmental conditions; and actions should flow from this harmonious, coordinated system.

2. One of the pathogenic ways in which people manage harms and threats is to seek *disconnection* among these constructs of mind by faulty coping processes, which include what the psychoanalysts have called ego-defense (see Chapter 10). Although denial, for example, is sometimes useful (see Lazarus, 1983), it also creates disconnection. Thus, the essence of psychopathology is *appraisal and coping failure.* That is, we seek disconnection through emotion-focused, sometimes self-deceptive, coping strategies such as avoidance, denial, and distancing, in order to manage the harsh psychological dilemmas of living. Sometimes this is harmless, but at other times it results in dysfunction.

Disconnection is maladaptive when it prevents an essential adaptational action. For example, distancing and denial of threat may result in the failure of a student to prepare for an examination, contributing thereby to performance failure (see Lazarus, 1983; Taylor & Brown, 1988). Such behaviors are especially maladaptive when they become a habitual style of appraising or coping with reality; a single adaptational encounter rarely results in long-term maladaptation, but when the behavior is chronic or recurrent the person is apt to be in trouble. Finally, disconnection is maladaptive when a person is prevented thereby from learning how to cope effectively with important troublesome situations, or from unlearning a pathogenic pattern of coping. Often spoken of in psychotherapy as resistance, it can defeat efforts at therapeutic change.

3. An implication of disconnection and its opposite, harmony, is that not only must those suffering from emotional dysfunction learn to think differently about themselves and their relationship to the world, but this change in thinking must be accompanied by appropriate actions and emotions; it must be an active *emotional insight* (cf. Wachtel, 1977) rather than passive and intellectual, to which I should add that the actions must be directed at efforts to handle matters differently, and presumably better, than before.

In a recent treatment of this (Lazarus, 1989c), I discussed four types of disconnection, all of which involve appraisal and coping. All result in serious mismatches between appraisal or coping and what must be thought and done in the person's special circumstances of living. The forms of disconnection are schematized in Figure 11.3.

One form of disconnection is *within the mind,* what has traditionally been called

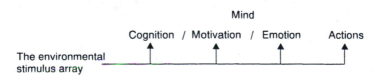

FIGURE 11.3. The four types of disconnection are: (1) within the mind; (2) between mind and environment; (3) between mind and action; (4) between environment and action. (*Source:* R. S. Lazarus, Constructs of the mind in health and psychotherapy. In A. Freeman, K. Simon, L. E. Beutler, and H. Arkowitz (Eds.), *Comprehensive Handbook of Cognitive Therapy.* New York: Plenum Publishing Corp., 1989.)

intrapsychic conflict. In Chapter 4 I gave the example of making one appraisal at a conscious level and another, contrary appraisal, at an unconscious level. In most forms of this kind of disconnection, motives, thoughts, and emotions are out of sync, so to speak.

A second form of disconnection is *between the mind and the environment*. For example, when threat is appraised but is inappropriate, the person needlessly feels anxious, guilty, shamed, and so forth; when threat is not appraised but should be, real threats are overlooked; when the coping process is inappropriate, what is required for an adaptive person–environment relationship is not thought or done.

A third form of disconnection is between *mind and action*. This includes two subvarieties — namely, actions fail to conform to intentions, and intentions are not expressed in action. Observers commonly discuss these by making reference to one or another of the three constructs of the mind. For example, we speak of actions that are inappropriate in the context of *wishes*, actions that are inconsistent with *feelings*, and actions that are inconsistent with the way people *cognize* encounters. These different versions indicate that how disconnection between mind and action is described depends on whether we emphasize motivation, emotion, or cognition, each of which is made to stand for the whole mental process. In a similarly casual fashion, clinicians also refer to disorders of impulse, conflict, or ego-defense as well as lack of skills or knowledge.

A fourth form of disconnection is between the *environment and action*, which harkens back to my earlier discussion of fit or misfit between appraisal or coping and the environment and does not need to be further elaborated.

And so we come down to the essence of the argument, the essential ingredients on which therapeutic change depends. The constructs of the mind must work together and be in appropriate relationship with action and the environment. Therapy cannot depend only on attempts to deal with any single construct — for example, cognition, motivation, emotion, action, or the environmental conditions that are faced by the patient. What is expressed in one must connect functionally with all the rest.

This notion of unity has been expressed by many cognitive therapists in different ways: by Beck (1987), who has emphasized that patients must be helped to *grasp cognitively* what is involved in their *emotional experience;* by Ellis (1984), who has emphasized that *cognition and emotion* are always *unified;* by Meichenbaum and Cameron (1983), who have recognized the futility of trying to change *thoughts without* an *emotional* accompaniment; and even by more behaviorally oriented therapists such as Foa and Kozak (1986), who have emphasized that fearful people must *learn* from the therapeutic confrontation with what they fear that their *fear-inducing expectations are wrong;* they must stop avoiding the sources of fear and, instead, act in ways that make this confrontation possible.

One senses a groundswell of agreement that therapeutic change involves the *interpenetration* of cognitive, motivational (which therapists have not much emphasized), and emotional activities — all focused, I would add, on *actions* that are directed at the *environment* in which the person lives. There are, in effect, five constructs to juggle in treatment: cognition, motivation, and emotion, — which are the main components of mind — as well as actions and an environment.

What I have said here about psychotherapy, though focused on theory, not techniques of intervention, flows from the five principles I have used to summarize the basic themes of my cognitive-motivational-relational theory of emotion. Particularly important is the *relational meaning principle* in which what is significant for persons and their emotions is how things are subjectively thought to be going in their relationships to the environment, especially social relationships, both in particular encounters and existentially. This is what *appraisal* is all about. Though what I have said is also derivable in other ways, the basic theme was not much in evidence before the cognitive revolution in psychology and so owes much to it.

Although there is considerable difference between psychoanalytic thought and the cognitive-motivational-relational analysis I have been presenting, one could also argue that, if we avoid an overly ideological stance, we can see much overlap between what I have been discussing and psychoanalytic thought, which was once the main whipping boy of behavior therapy. The overlap is all the more evident as I have become increasingly concerned with unconscious appraisal (see Chapter 4).

The ideas discussed earlier about how therapy works have actually been around for quite a while in one form or another and are perhaps now beginning to be fully appreciated, because there is less of a spirit of competition between therapeutic systems than there used to be, less of a spirit of "either your theory or mine" among those wanting to advance the treatment of emotional dysfunction. This should be gratifying to those professionals of every stripe who are interested in better understanding and treatment.

Prevention

In interventions that center on prevention rather than treatment, there are, I believe, many more questions than answers, though learning to ask the right questions is the way to begin. The issues in prevention overlap a great deal with those in psychotherapy, especially in secondary rather than primary prevention. Secondary prevention has to do with efforts to keep an already existing dysfunction from getting worse in a crisis.

Primary prevention consists of attempts to minimize vulnerability to dysfunction or prevent its occurrence. When there is still no evidence of dysfunction, prevention seems to differ little from educational efforts to maximize constructive and minimize destructive tendencies. We want to help a child develop into an adult with a substantial supply of coping resources for dealing with inevitable negative life experiences (see Albee & Joffe, 1977; Garmezy, 1981; Garmezy & Rutter, 1983; Rutter, 1979; and Smith, Smoll, & Ptacek, 1990).

One of the major considerations underlying primary prevention has been that children differ greatly in their resources for managing the stresses of living. Some have personality and social advantages that arise from their life circumstances, which help them resist the deleterious consequences of major stress; others have disadvantages and later prove vulnerable. The advantages and disadvantages read like a litany of factors that are difficult or impossible to influence after the fact, such as having loving or hateful parents, being intelligent or unintelligent, or having social skills, money, education, and the like. We are not usually empowered to provide favorable genetics, kind and loving parents, favorable economic conditions, good schools, and the friends that might be good medicine.

The system principle implies that no single variable is a sole primary prevention factor to center on in a child's development. A multiplicity of variables influence the emotional and adaptational outcome — including goal commitments, beliefs, ways of appraising relationships with the environment, coping skills, and ways of getting along in the world that increase the likelihood of a successful long-term relationship with things as they are. The absence of commitments will result in existential malaise; the failure to evolve a normatively sound ego-identity will result in being scattered and undirected; overoptimism or excessive pessimism will undermine appraisal and coping.

Guidelines are still needed to give focus to primary prevention and educational efforts. At numerous points in a growing child's life, what might be called developmental tasks create challenges to children's ability to function, their emotional stability, and their future prospects. Threats are presented by pressures to become more independent, to compete with other children in school and at play, and to deal with injury and illness, loss of a parent as a result of death or divorce, parental rejection, conflict-producing peer pressure, rejection by peers, adult or peer treachery, and so on. Though what children must deal with varies depending on the stage of development, all these and many more demands must be managed in growing up into an adult. At stake are the emerging adult's ego-identity, coping adequacy, reality testing, commitments, and ability to establish intimate relationships, control behavior and feelings, and the attainment of goals. (cf. Erikson, 1963, who has undoubtedly been among the most influential writers to help shape the thinking of those concerned with primary prevention and education).

The principles involved in primary prevention are so general, however, and the number of variables so great, that it is difficult to derive a set of concrete do's and don'ts. As a result, primary prevention has tended to subsist on somewhat pious slogans rather than on a clear program of how children should be raised and educated in our society. For example, we know that stress is inevitable in living. Therefore, although we would not want to generate stress for its own sake, it is crucial that a child learn how to manage it. How much, what kinds of stress, and at what stage of development does stress facilitate or impair a child's coping? Under what conditions does stress become a trauma that impairs later adaptation? These are standard issues of primary prevention, but few concrete guidelines are available in which we might have confidence.

When we observe signs of distress and dysfunction, much of the damage has already been done. The professional task then changes from primary prevention to *secondary prevention,* or treatment in which we must teach vulnerable children and adults therapeutically the coping skills they need to know. Without research comparisons between those who manage well and those who don't, we will not easily discover what it is that successful people do well and unsuccessful people do badly in order to plan what to do to help those who need assistance when they come to our attention.

To make sense of secondary prevention, we need to decide how seriously to regard short-term evidence of dysfunction and distress. Rushing in with treatment may be inappropriate if the distress and dysfunction are temporary and manageable. There are observational grounds for believing, for example, that the great majority of adolescents who show signs of trouble will be free of them in another year or two. Much depends on whether the crisis is the result of a serious loss or a life-threatening illness, and whether it is being responded to appropriately.

We need to know how evidence of dysfunction should be evaluated at different stages of development. What patterns in childhood are pathogenic or merely normal signs of stress in a constructive struggle that will be resolved without help? Is a child who is jealous of a sibling at risk for later psychopathology, or is this merely an expectable and benign pattern called sibling rivalry? Is a child who has recurrent bouts of anger or aggression at risk for later interpersonal difficulty, or can the early pattern of anger be directed constructively? Is a child who responds passively and compliantly rather than aggressively at serious risk, and what should we do about it? Although I don't wish to imply that there is no research on such questions, there are few theoretical and empirical grounds on which to feel confident about answers.

Another set of issues concerning secondary prevention addresses whether the appraisal process can be relearned and a functional balance produced between optimism, pessimism, and reality testing. Are there any rules to tell us how a child should deal, for example, with the loss of a parent, a serious or devastating injury or illness, a sexual assault, or what have you? One answer lies in cultivating and strengthening processes of coping with stress, but we are uncertain about how to do this, and even more uncertain about matching the effort to the child or adult who might have to face a personal disaster in the future. Should the strategy of intervention be to help the person get through the immediate crisis by giving support, or to try to strengthen the person against future life assaults? How might these goals be accomplished?

When a personal disaster does arrive and help is sought, secondary prevention seems much like psychotherapy in that it is centered on providing support and understanding and, where possible, encouraging an exploration of what is at stake and the options available to live through the crisis — what is sometimes referred to as crisis intervention (Caplan, 1961, 1964, 1970, 1974; Horowitz, 1982; Lindsay, 1975; Slaikeu, 1984).

Pennebaker and his colleagues (e.g., Pennebaker, 1989; Pennebaker & Beall, 1986; Pennebaker, Colder, & Sharp, 1990; Pennebaker, Hughes, & O'Heeron, 1987; and Pennebaker, Kiecolt-Glaser, & Glaser, 1988) have been engaged in programmatic research to study the ameliorative effects of writing about or otherwise verbally sharing recent traumatic experiences. Their observations suggest that the coping process can be facilitated and even accelerated by confronting and working through traumas and anticipated traumas. For example, in Pennebaker, Colder, and Sharp (1990), when students wrote about their homesickness and anxieties in coming to college, their visits to physicians for illness in the months after they wrote about these problems were lower than in a control group of students who wrote about superficial topics. This research represents one of the few efforts with ordinary young persons to explore the possibilities that preventive efforts may be able to deal with expectable sources of stress and trauma.

The answer to many of the questions raised here depends on making a distinction between neurosis and a temporary reaction to a severe crisis of living. Early psychiatric wisdom regarded people who were emotionally distressed and dysfunctional as neurotic or suffering from some other psychopathology, and much professional practice still fails to attend to destructive life events or chronic role difficulties as causal factors. Even with severe personal disaster and loss, the standard approach has been to search within the person for an explanation, as if all difficulties and symptoms could be understood from the perspective of personal inadequacy.

More and more, however, clinicians have come to realize that persons who otherwise have been able to manage their lives without severe dysfunction may display symptoms following the death of a loved one, the loss of a job, or social or physical disasters that disrupt their lives and those of their families. Secondary prevention to restrict the damage and get the person back on an even keel is an important clinical service to be performed even with otherwise sound people. In such cases, the older tradition of emphasizing characterological neuroses now seems incomplete and could be thought of as an instance of automatically blaming the victim of destructive life conditions for not functioning well.

Most preventive clinical work today is secondary prevention, directed at those who are generally sound but who have undergone personal crisis or tragedy. The preventive effort is aimed at not allowing this tragedy to take hold of their lives and to result in chronic disability, and to help such persons through the trouble so that they can recommit themselves to productive and satisfying lives. This means accepting the proposition that an important reason for the difficulty lies in the environment, in life events, or pressures of living that are destructive, though these destructive pressures may also be exacerbated by personal defects. Be that as it may, the victim of these environmental pressures or life events may benefit from help to make adaptive decisions that will prevent further psychological disorganization.

Final Thoughts

If there has been a single, central theme in my treatment of the emotions, it is certainly that there is no appropriate sense in which emotion and reason are opposed to each other. Although everyone seems to assume that emotion is irrational, quite the contrary, emotion depends on reason.

However, if we take this position, a philosophical issue arises, namely, whether humans are largely rational or irrational creatures. A prominent stance about this, especially in the twentieth century, is dismissive of the human capacity to reason logically; people are said to think emotionally and therefore illogically, and rationality in human affairs is said to be an illusion.

This way of thinking is characteristic of a number of playwrights whose work collectively became known as the "theater of the absurd," among them Beckett, Duerrenmatt, Genêt, Ionesco, and Pinter. In their plays, life is said to be ridiculous because it is irrational and empty of positive value. We should, of course, keep in mind the penchant of people to be either optimists or pessimists — which means that, for some, absurdity and tragedy dominate; while, for others, idealizing human striving and accomplishment dominates. Those who see people as tragically absurd probably number among the pessimists, which is not to say there is no provocation for such an outlook.

The view that people are illogical thinkers also comes from highly respected research psychologists whose observations suggest that unsound conclusions are common, especially in situations of hope and fear—most notably when the information on which to predicate decisions is ambiguous, as so much of life is apt to be. This further urges us to adopt the negative position on human reasoning. Indeed, it is difficult not to agree that folly and evil abound in human affairs, that pivotal human decisions are commonly faulty, and that in a very real sense humans alone in the animal kingdom get themselves caught in absurd predicaments—perhaps because of their freedom to choose and their emotional propensities—almost as a rule rather than the exception.

Nevertheless, a complication is that it is not always clear what we mean by irrationality. It can refer either to the reasoning process or to the conclusions and outcomes of this reasoning. It is quite possible to have a sound reasoning process but a poor, seemingly irrational, conclusion and outcome, as well as an unsound reasoning process but a good conclusion and outcome. Most often we call the conclusion and outcome irrational when they are self-destructive. Another complication is that conclusions and outcomes are considered irrational by the parties aggrieved by a decision merely because their interests have lost out to those of other social groups. Thus, conclusions and outcomes may be deemed irrational on the basis of whose good they serve, which in a conflict situation is almost bound to be the case.

To those who see people as irrational, I offer the following: We should speak of humans as thinking irrationally only when the reasoning process itself is illogical. It is not necessarily irrational to draw the wrong conclusion. I implied early in this book that much of the time our problems stem not from illogic but from hidden and perhaps faulty premises—that is beliefs, values, and commitments that underlie the erroneous conclusions, which are sometimes hidden from persons holding them or from observers watching them—or from shared illusions that entrap us by encouraging unrealistic judgments about how things are going, even when the reasoning process follows a sound course. In other words, it is not necessarily our logic that fails but the premises on which that logic depends.

If, as I have said, emotions depend on the values, goals, and beliefs to which we are committed and which are important in our lives, these may serve as the faulty premises on which our emotions rest. We make commitments that are bound to produce emotional distress when we fail to attain them or positive emotions when we succeed. Foolish commitments also contribute to meaninglessness, or the "empty self" discussed earlier in this book, which is often pointed to as a cause of the futility and absurdity of life, as in Beckett"s *Waiting for Godot.*

Be that as it may—and I must resist preaching about good or poor values and commitment—the (psycho)logic of our emotions is implacable. We feel bad when commitments—such as they are—fail, but feel good when they succeed, all of this making perfect logical sense. Aside from the wisdom of these commitments, which is another matter, this (psycho)logic is the result of our biological makeup. Indeed, the cause-and-effect logic of the emotions that I have been discussing is what a cognitive-motivational-emotional theory is all about, and the science in this is to describe what is happening and to specify its rules as well as the conditions that affect how the rules operate. The central premise of such a theory is that we react emotionally to how things appear to have turned out in our struggle to attain what we wish.

The values, goals, and beliefs that help generate emotions develop, in part, from the urgings of the society into which we are born. And since similar goals can be found throughout history and across most societies in which people live, there must also be something in human psychology that shapes us in this respect, too. After our basic biological needs are met, we want among other things success, fame (even if only as a celebrity), power, wealth, pleasure, a sense of connectedness to the social system, and warm, nurturant relationships to other people.

To the extent we become heavily invested in an ego-identity, threats to it and its loss in death are dreaded. And to the extent that we dread threats and losses to these commitments, we use the power of our flexible minds to deceive ourselves in the interests of preventing distress, which adds to the sense of irrationality in our species. Perhaps, because of the shortness of our lives, we are too much governed by what is immediate at the expense of the long term. In any case, emotions are the result of commitments, and it is not irrational at all to feel good or bad at the fate of these commitments, but we are irrational only when we cannot appropriately judge that fate.

The only way we can rid ourselves of distressing emotions and attain peace of mind — assuming we might want to — is to renounce or change the very commitments on which they depend, a task that is difficult but facilitated by major losses or a conversion experience, which is a process we don't well understand. The reader knows that such renunciation is the goal of diverse spiritual movements. To desire something and to recognize what must be done to attain it, as well as to recognize when its attainment has succeeded or failed, is to be inevitably emotional. In this way, emotions and reason are inextricably linked in an inescapable logic.

I have come to the close of this long excursion through the difficult terrain of emotion at just the point that, I believe, provides the proper ending, which, if the journey was worthwhile, must also be a beginning. After all, the reason for the trip was to increase our resources so that we can tackle the practical tasks of research on the emotion process and of assessment, treatment, and prevention of dysfunction and excessive emotional distress. Although I am at home with the view that knowledge is its own reward, our central concern must always be knowledge that helps us ultimately to manage our lives more successfully and to ameliorate human suffering and dysfunction. After the journey, it should be easier for the traveler to accept the claim I made at the start, that no issues in social and biological science are more germane to this goal than those that pertain to the emotions.

Summary

In this concluding chapter I tried to summarize my main metatheoretical and substantive theoretical themes and show how they affect three practical enterprises: research, assessment, and clinical interventions for the purposes of treatment and

prevention. I first reviewed briefly the system principle, the process-structure principle, the developmental principle, the specificity principle, and the relational meaning principle. The last of these contains the basic ideas of core relational themes and
appraisal and coping processes.

A number of research issues were reviewed from the vantage point of these principles. Because the first four of the principles are metatheoretical, the discussion of
implications for research began with largely abstract issues, such as the use of many
variables and processes, the problem of stability and flux, the emotion process at
different stages of development, specificity in the process of emotion generation and
in response systems. The relational meaning principle was first discussed in terms of
its implications for molar rather than molecular ways of thinking about affect programs and action tendencies.

At a more concrete level, four arenas of research were discussed: first, the motivational principle, which defines how a person spends time in daily activities and
when an emotion arising from these activities will be positive or negative; second,
research dealing with the role of core relational themes and appraisal patterns in
emotion; third, research on action tendencies, physiological response patterns, and
the relations between them; and fourth, developmental research.

With respect to implications for assessment, antecedent variable measures of
both motives and beliefs were examined, measures of mediating processes such as
appraisal and coping were considered, and finally, some brief thoughts were given
on the measurement of subjective affect.

With respect to treatment and prevention, several major issues were examined —
for example, when the emotion process is relevant or not relevant to psychopathology, how the emotion process might cause psychopathology, and how emotion is
viewed in different therapeutic approaches, including psychoanalysis, behavior therapy, cognitive therapy, and experiential and humanistic therapies. In addition, the
tasks of treatment were reviewed.

Considerable attention was given to how treatment works from the standpoint of
a cognitive-motivational-relational theory of the emotions. The main theme was the
need for integration among the constructs of mind — cognition, motivation, and emotion — and between the mind and action directed toward the environment. The opposite of integration is disconnection, and the reasons for it and the variety of forms of
disconnection were also explored. The chapter ended with a brief examination of
primary and secondary prevention.

Notes

1. Usually one speaks of systems theory; however, our concerns here are with a single
system producing the emotions, so I use instead the singular, *system principle.*

2. The same would also apply to psychological stress, but in accordance with what I said
in Chapter 1 about stress and emotion (see also Lazarus, 1990b), I have chosen to speak here
only about emotion, despite the fact that there is still a thriving research effort on the stress
process.

3. This refers to five trait dimensions that many personality researchers believe cover the
main personality variations needed to describe people and predict their behavior.

4. This useful definition comes from Andrea Parecki, now a graduate student, who is interested in self-esteem programs in the schools.

5. The appraisal components in this research are a bit different from those presented in this book because of changes in my thinking since then.

References

Abelson, R. P. (1963). Computer simulation of "hot cognitions." In S. Tomkins & S. Messick (Eds.), *Computer simulation of personality: Frontier of psychological theory* (pp. 277–298). New York: Wiley.

Abelson, R. P. (1981). Psychological status of the script concept. *American Psychologist, 36,* 715–729.

Abramson, L., Garber, G., & Seligman, M. E. P. (1980). Learned helplessnesss in humans: An attributional analysis. In J. Garber & M. E. P. Seligman (Eds.), *Human helplessness: Theory and applications* (pp. 3–34). New York: Academic Press.

Adatto, C. P. (1957). On pouting. *Journal of the American Psychoanalytic Association, 5,* 245–249. Also in Socarides, 1977.

Ader, R. (1981). (Ed.), *Psychoneuroimmunology.* New York: Academic Press.

Adler, A. (1927). *The practice and theory of individual psychology.* New York: Harcourt.

Ainsworth, M. D. S. (1969). Object relations, dependency and attachment: A theoretical review of the infant–mother relationship. *Child Development, 40,* 969–1025.

Ainsworth, M. D. S., Blehar, M., Waters, E., & Wall, S. (1978). *Patterns of attachment.* Hillsdale, NJ: Erlbaum.

Ajzen, I., & Fishbein, M. (1980). *Understanding attitudes and predicting social behavior.* Englewood Cliffs, NJ: Prentice Hall.

Albee, G. W., & Joffe, J. M. (Eds.). (1977). *Primary prevention of psychopathology. Vol. I: The issues.* Hanover, NH: University Press of New England.

Aldwin, C., & Stokols, D. (1988). The effects of environmental change on individuals and groups: Some neglected issues in stress research. *Journal of Environmental Psychology, 8,* 57–75.

Alexander, C. N., Davies, J. L., Dixon, C. A., Dillbeck, M. C., Druker, S. M., Oetzel, R. M., Muehlman, J. M., & Orme-Johnson, D. W. (1989). Growth of higher stages of consciousness: The Vedic psychology of human development. In C. N. Alexander & E. J. Langer (Eds.), *Higher stages of human development: Perspectives on adult growth.* New York: Oxford University Press.

Alexander, C. N., & Langer, E. J. (Eds.) (1990). *Higher stages of human development: Perspectives on adult growth.* New York: Oxford University Press.

Alexander, F. (1950). *Psychosomatic medicine.* New York: Norton.

Alexander, F., French, T., & Pollack, G. H. (1968). *Psychosomatic medicine.* Chicago: University of Chicago Press.

Alexander, J. (1972). On the affect of horror. *Bulletin of the Philadelphia Association of Psychoanalysis, 23,* 115–128. Also in Socarides, 1977.

Alloy, L. B., Albright, J. S., Abramson, L. Y., & Dykman, B. M. (1990). Depressive realism and nondepressive optimistic illusions: The role of the self. In R. E. Ingram (Ed.), *Contemporary psychological approaches to depression: Theory, research and treatment* (pp. 71–86). New York: Plenum.

Allport, G. W. (1937). *Personality: A psychological interpretation.* New York: Holt, Rinehart and Winston.

Allport, G. W. (1954). *The nature of prejudice.* Reading, MA: Addison-Wesley.

American Psychiatric Association. (1987). *Diagnostic and statistical manual of mental disorders* (DSM III-R). Washington, DC: APA.

Amsel, A. (1990) Arousal, suppression, and persistence: Frustration theory, attention, and its disorders. *Cognition and Emotion, 4,* 239–269.

Anderson, K. J. (1990). Arousal and the inverted-U hypothesis: A critique of Neiss's "reconceptualizing arousal." *Psychological Bulletin, 107,* 96–100.

Andrews, F. M., & Withey, S. B. (1976). *Social indicators of well-being: America's perception of life quality.* New York: Plenum.

Andrews, J. D. W. (1989a). Integrating visions of reality: Interpersonal diagnosis and the existential vision. *American Psychologist, 44,* 803–817.

Andrews, J. D. W. (1989b). Psychotherapy of depression: A self-confirmation model. *Psychological Review, 96,* 576–607.

Angyal, A. (1941). Disgust and related aversions. *Journal of Abnormal and Social Psychology, 36,* 393–412.

Antonovsky, A. (1979). *Health, stress, and coping.* (1979). San Francisco, CA: Jossey-Bass.

Antonovsky, A. (1987). *Unraveling the mystery of health: How people manage stress and stay well.* San Francisco, CA: Jossey-Bass.

Antonovsky, A. (1990). Pathways leading to successful coping and health. In M. Rosenbaum (Ed.), *Learned resourcefulness: On coping skills, self-control, and adaptive behavior* (pp. 31–63). New York: Springer-Verlag.

Arieti, S. (1970). Cognition and feeling. In. M. B. Arnold (Ed.), *Feelings and emotions* (pp. 135–143). New York: Academic Press.

Aristotle. (1881). *Nicomachean ethics* (F. H. Peters, Trans.). London.

Aristotle. (1941). Rhetoric. In R. McKeon (Ed.), *The basic works of Aristotle.* New York: Random House.

Arlow, J. A. (1957). On smugness. *International Journal of Psychoanalysis, 38,* 1–8. Also in Socarides, 1977.

Arnheim, R. (1958). Emotion and feeling in psychology and art. *Confinia Psychiatrica, I,* 69–88.

Arnold, M. B. (1960). *Emotion and personality* (Vols. 1 & 2). New York: Columbia University Press.

Asch, S. E. (1952a). Effects of group pressure upon the modification and distortion of judgments. In G. E. Swanson, T. M. Newcomb, & E. L. Hartley (Eds.), *Readings in social psychology.* Englewood Cliffs, NJ: Prentice Hall.

Asch, S. E. (1952b). *Social psychology.* Englewood Cliffs, NJ: Prentice Hall.

Asch, S. E. (1956). Studies of independence and conformity: A minority of one against a unanimous majority. *Psychological Monographs: General and Applied, 70* (Whole No. 416).

Ausubel, D. P. (1955). Relationships between shame and guilt in the socializing process. *Psychological Review, 62,* 378–390.

Averill, J. R. (1968). Grief: Its nature and significance. *Psychological Bulletin, 70,* 721–748.

Averill, J. R. (1973). Personality control over aversive stimuli and its relationship to stress. *Psychological Bulletin, 80,* 286–303.

Averill, J. R. (1974). An analysis of psychophysiological symbolism and its influence on theories of emotion. *Journal for the Theory of Social Behavior, 4,* 147–190.

Averill, J. R. (1975). A semantic atlas of emotional concepts. JSAS: *Catalogue of Selected Documents in Psychology, 5,* 330. (Ms. No. 421.)

Averill, J. R. (1980), A constructivist view of emotion. In R. Plutchik and H. Kellerman (Eds.), *Emotion: Theory, research, and experience. Vol. 1: Theories of emotion* (pp. 305–339). New York: Academic Press.

Averill, J. R. (1982). *Anger and aggression: An essay on emotion.* New York: Springer-Verlag.

Averill, J. R. (1983). Studies on anger and aggression: Implications for theories of emotion. *American Psychologist, 38,* 1145–1160.

Averill, J. R. (1988). Disorders of emotion. *Journal of Social and Clinical Psychology, 6,* 247–268.

Averill, J. R., Catlin, G., & Kyum, K. C. (1990). *The rules of hope.* New York: Springer-Verlag.

Azuma, H., Kashiwagi, K., & Hess, R. (1981). *The influence of maternal teaching style upon the cognitive development of children.* Tokyo: University of Tokyo Press (In Japanese; cited by Miyake, Campos, Kagan, & Bradshaw, 1986).

Baars, B. J. (1981). Cognition versus inference. *American Psychologist, 36,* 223–224.

Baeyens, F., Eelen, P., & van den Bergh, O. (1990). Contingency awareness in evaluative conditioning: A case for unaware affective-evaluative learning. *Cognition and Emotion, 4,* 3–18.

Bahrick, R. E., & Watson, J. S. (1985). Detection of intermodal proprioceptive-visual contingency as a potential basis of self-perception in infancy. *Developmental Psychology, 21,* 963–973.

Baltes, P. B. (1987). Theoretical propositions of life-span developmental psychology: On the dynamics between growth and decline. *Developmental Psychology, 23,* 611–626.

Bandura, A. (1977a). Self-efficacy: Toward a unifying theory of behavioral change. *Psychological Review, 84,* 191–215.

Bandura, A. (1977b). *Social learning theory.* Englewood Cliffs, NJ: Prentice Hall.

Bandura, A. (1978). The self-system in reciprocal determinism. *American Psychologist, 33,* 344–358.

Bandura, A. (1982). Self-efficacy mechanism in human agency. *American Psychologist, 37,* 122–147.

Bandura, A. (1989). Human agency in social cognitive theory. *American Psychologist, 44,* 1175–1184.

Bandura, A., Ross, D., & Ross, S. A. (1963). A comparative test of the status envy, social power, and the secondary reinforcement theories of identification learning. *Journal of Abnormal and Social Psychology, 67,* 527–534.

Bandura, A., & Walters, R. (1963). *Social learning and personality development.* New York: Holt, Rinehart and Winston.

Bar-Hillel, Y. (1955). An examination of information theory. *Philosophical Science, 22,* 86–105.

Bargh, J. A. (1982). Attention and automaticity in the processing of self-relevant information. *Journal of Personality and Social Psychology, 43,* 425–436.

Bargh, J. A. (1990). Auto-motives: Preconscious determinants of social interaction. In E. T. Higgins & R. M. Sorrentino (Eds.), *Handbook of motivation and cognition* (Vol. 2, pp. 93–130). New York: Guilford.

Barker, R. G., & Wright, H. F. (1951). *One boy's day: A specimen record of behavior.* New York: Harper.

Baron, R. M. (1988). An ecological framework for establishing a dual-mode theory of social knowing. In D. Bar-Tal & A. W. Kruglanski (Eds), *The social psychology of knowing* (pp. 48–82). New York: Cambridge University Press.

Baron, R. M., & Boudreau, L. A. (1987). An ecological perspective on integrating personality and social psychology, *Journal of Personality and Social Psychology, 53,* 1222–1228.

Baumeister, R. F., & Scher, S. J. (1988). Self-defeating behavior patterns among normal individuals: Review and analysis of common self-destructive tendencies. *Psychological Bulletin, 104,* 3–22.

Baumgardner, A. H., & Levy, P. E. (1988). Role of self-esteem in perceptions of ability and effort: Illogic or insight? *Personality and Social Psychology Bulletin, 14,* 429–438.

Beach, F. A. (1955). The descent of instinct. *Psychological Review, 62,* 401–410.

Bearison, D. J., & Zimiles, H. (1986). *Thought and emotion: Developmental perspectives.* Hillsdale, NJ: Erlbaum.

Beck, A. T. (1971). Cognition, affect, and psychopathology. *Archives of General Psychiatry, 24,* 495–500.

Beck, A. T. (1976). *Cognitive therapy and the emotional disorders.* New York: International Universities Press.

Beck, A. T. (1987). Cognitive therapy. In J. Zeig (Ed.), *Evolution of psychotherapy.* New York: Brunner/Mazel.

Beck, A. T. (in press). Cognitive approaches to stress. In C. Lehrer & R. L. Woolfolk (Eds.), *Clinical guide to stress management* (pp. 255–305). New York: Guilford.

Beck, A. T., & Weishaar, M. (1989). Cognitive therapy. In A. Freeman, K. M. Simon, L. E. Beutler, & H. Arkowitz (Eds.), *Comprehensive handbook of cognitive therapy* (pp. 21–36). New York: Plenum.

Becker, E. (1973). *The denial of death.* New York: Free Press.

Bedford, E. (1956–1957). Emotions. *Proceedings of the Aristotelian Society, 57,* 303–304.

Benedict, R. (1934). *Patterns of culture.* Boston: Houghton Mifflin.

Benedict, R. (1946). *The chrysanthemum and the sword.* Boston: Houghton Mifflin.

Benesh, M., & Weiner, B. (1982). On emotion and motivation: From the notebooks of Fritz Heider. *American Psychologist, 37,* 887–895.

Benner, P. & Wrubel, J. (1989). *The primacy of caring: Stress and coping in health and illness.* Menlo Park, CA: Addison-Wesley.

Bennett, D. H., & Holmes, D. S. (1975). Influence of denial (situational redefinition) and projection on anxiety associated with threat to self-esteem. *Journal of Personality and Social Psychology, 32,* 915–921.

Berger, P. L., & Luckmann, T. (1966). *The social construction of reality.* New York: Doubleday.

Bergman, L. R., & Magnusson, D. (1979). Overachievement and catecholamine excretion in an achievement-demanding situation. *Psychosomatic Medicine, 41,* 181–188.

Bergmann, M. S. (1971). Psychoanalytic observations on the capacity to love. In J. B. McDevitt & C. F. Settlage (Eds.), *Separation-individuation: Essays in honor of Margaret S. Mahler* (pp. 15–40). New York: International Universities Press. Also in Socarides, 1977.

Berkowitz, L. (1989). Frustration-aggression hypothesis: Examination and reformulation. *Psychological Bulletin, 106,* 59–73.

Berlyne, D. E. (1960). *Conflict, arousal and curiosity.* New York: McGraw-Hill.

Bernard, M. E., & DiGiuseppe, R. (1989). (Eds.), *Inside rational-emotive therapy* (p. 47–68). San Diego, CA: Academic Press.

Bernard, V. W., Ottenberg, P., & Redl, F. (1965). Dehumanization: A composite psychological defense in relation to modern war. In M. Schwebel (Ed.), *Behavioral science and human survival* (pp. 64–82). Palo Alto, CA: Science and Behavior Books.

Berndt, T. J., & Perry, T. B. (1986). Children's perceptions of friendships as supportive relationships. *Developmental Psychology, 22,* 640–648.

Berne, E. (1964). *Games people play.* New York: Grove Press.

Berscheid, E. (1983). Emotion. In H. H. Kelly et al. (Eds.), *Close relationships* (pp. 110–168). New York: Freeman.

von Bertalanffy, L. (1968). *General systems theory.* New York: Braziller.

Bertenthal, B. I., Campos, J. J., & Barrett, K. C. (1984). Self-produced locomotion: An organizer of emotional, cognitive, and social development in infancy. In R. N. Emde & R. J. Harmon (Eds.), *Continuities and discontinuities in development.* New York: Plenum.

Biernat, M. (1989). Motives and values to achieve: Different constructs with different effects. *Journal of Personality, 57,* 69–95.

Billings, A. G., & Moos, R. H. (1981). The role of coping responses and social resources in attenuating the impact of stressful life events. *Journal of Behavioral Medicine, 4,* 139–157.

Block, J. (1982). Assimilation, accommodation, and the dynamics of personality development. *Child Development, 53,* 281–295.

Bloom, A. (1987). *The closing of the American mind.* New York: Simon & Schuster.

Bloom, L., & Beckwith, R. (1989). Talking with feeling: Integrating affective and linguistic expression in early language development. *Cognition and Emotion, 3,* 313–342.

Bloom, L. J., Houston, B.K., Holmes, D. S., & Burish, T. G. (1977). The effectiveness of attentional diversion and situational redefinition for reducing stress due to a nonambiguous threat. *Journal of Research in Personality, 11,* 83–94.

Blum, L. (1980). Compassion. In A. O. Rorty (Ed.), *Explaining emotions* (pp. 507–517). Berkeley: University of California Press.

Boggiano, A. K., Main, D. S., & Katz, P. A. (1988). *Journal of Personality and Social Psychology, 54,* 134–141.

Bolger, N. (1990). Coping as a personality process: A prospective study. *Journal of Personality and Social Psychology, 59,* 525–537.

Bolles, R. C. (1974). Cognition and motivation: Some historical trends. In B. Weiner (Ed.), *Cognitive views of human motivation.* New York: Academic Press.

Bolles, R. C. (1990). Where did everybody go? *Psychological Science, 1,* 107–113.

Borkovec, T. D. (1990). Worry and emotional processing of phobic imagery. Paper presented at the 24th annual convention of the Association for the Advancement of Behavior Therapy, November 2.

Bower, G. H. (1981). Mood and memory. *American Psychologist, 36,* 129–148.

Bowers, K. S. (1987). Revisioning the unconscious. *Canadian Psychology/Psychologie Canadienne, 28,* 93–132.

Bowers, K. S., & Meichenbaum, D. (Eds.). (1984). *The unconscious reconsidered.* New York: Wiley.

Bowlby, J. (1951). *Maternal care and mental health.* Geneva: World Health Organization.

Bowlby, J. (1969). *Attachment and loss: Attachment* (Vol. 1). New York: Basic Books.

Bowlby, J. (1973). *Attachment and loss: Separation* (Vol. 2). New York: Basic Books.

Bowlby, J. (1980). *Attachment and loss: Loss* (Vol. 3). New York: Basic Books.

Bradburn, N. M. (1969). *The structure of psychological well-being.* Chicago: Aldine.

Bransford, J. D., & Johnson, M. K. (1973). Consideration of some problems of comprehension. In W. G. Chase (Ed.), *Visual information processing.* New York: Academic Press. (Quoted by Goldfried, 1987.)

Brazelton, T. B., Tronick, E., Adamson, L., Als, H., & Wise, S. (1975). Early mother-infant reciprocity. In M. Hofer (Ed.), *Parent-infant interaction.* Amsterdam: Excerpta Medica.

Breger, L., Hunter, I., & Lane, R. W. (1971). *The effect of stress on dreams.* New York: International Universities Press.

Brehm, J. W., & Cohen, A. R. (1962). *Explorations in cognitive dissonance.* New York: Wiley.

Breuer, J., and Freud, S. (1985). *Studies on hysteria.* (J. Strachey, Trans.) New York: Basic Books. (Originally published in 1895.)

Brewin, C. R. (1989). Cognitive change processes in psychotherapy. *Psychological Review, 96,* 379–394.

Breznitz, S. (Ed.) (1983). *The denial of stress.* New York: International Universities Press.

Breznitz, S. (1984). *Cry wolf: The psychology of false alarms.* Hillsdale, NJ: Erlbaum.

Breznitz, S. (1986). The effect of hope on coping with stress. In M. Appley & R. Trumbull (Eds.), *Dynamics of stress* (pp. 295–306). New York: Plenum.

Breznitz, S. (1989). Information-induced stress in humans. In S. Breznitz & O. Zinder (Eds.), *Molecular biology of stress* (pp. 253–264). New York: Alan R. Liss.

Bricker, P. D., & Chapanis, A. Do incorrectly perceived tachistoscopically presented stimuli convey some information? *Psychological Review, 60,* 181–188.

Brickman, P., & Campbell, D. T. (1971). Hedonic relativism and planning the good society. In M. H. Appley (Ed.), *Adaptation level theory: A symposium.* New York: Academic Press.

Brickman, P., Coates, D., & Janoff-Bulman, R. (1978). Lottery winners and accident victims: Is happiness relative? *Journal of Personality and Social Psychology, 36,* 917–927.

Brickman, P., Rabinowitz, V. C., Karuza, J., Jr., Coates, D., Cohen, E., & Kidder, L. (1982). Models of helping and coping. *American Psychologist, 37,* 368–384.

Brickman, P., Wortman, C. B., & Sorrentino, R.(Eds.) (1987). *Commitment, conflict, and caring.* Englewood Cliffs, NJ: Prentice Hall.

Bridges, K. M. B. (1930). A genetic theory of the emotions. *Journal of Genetic Psychology, 37,* 514–527.

Bridges, K. M. B. (1932). Emotional development in early infancy. *Child Development, 1932, 3,* 325–341.

Briggs, J. L. (1970). *Never in anger: Portrait of an Eskimo family.* Cambridge, MA: Harvard University Press.

Briggs, J. L. (1978). The origins of non-violence: Inuit management of aggression. In A. Montagu (Ed.), *Learning non-aggression* (pp. 54–93). Oxford, England: Oxford University Press.

Broadbent, D. E., Fitzgerald, P., & Broadbent, M. H. P. (1986). Implicit and explicit knowledge in the control of complex systems. *British Journal of Psychology, 77,* 33–50.

Brody, N. (Ed.). (1987). The unconscious. *Personality and Social Psychology Bulletin,* Special Issue, 13.

Broverman, D. M. (1962). Normative and ipsative measurement in psychology. *Psychological Review, 4,* 295–305.

Brown, J., & Farber, I. E. (1951). Emotions conceptualized as intervening variables – with suggestions toward a theory of frustration. *Psychological Bulletin, 48,* 465–495.

Brown, J. D., & McGill, K. L. (unpublished). *The high cost of success: When positive life events produce negative health consequences.*

Brown, R. (1965). *Social psychology.* New York: Free Press.

Bruner, J. (1981). Intention in the structure of action and interaction. In L. P. Lipsitt (Ed.), *Advances in infancy research* (Vol. 1, pp. 41–56). Norwood, NJ: Ablex.

Bryant, F. B. (1989). A four-factor model of perceived control: Avoiding, coping, obtaining, and savoring. *Journal of Personality, 57,* 773–797.

Buck, R. (1985). Prime theory: An integrated view of motivation and emotion. *Psychological Review, 92,* 389–413.

Buechler, S., & Izard, C. E. (1983). On the emergence, functions, and regulation of some emotion expressions in infancy. In R. Plutchik & H. Kellerman (Eds.), *The emotions: Emotions in early development* (Vol. 2, pp. 293–313). New York: Academic Press.

Bulman, R. J., & Wortman, C. B. (1977). Attributions of blame and coping in the "real world": Severe accident victims react to their lot. *Journal of Personality and Social Psychology, 35,* 351–363.

Burke, E. (1757). *A philosophical enquiry into the origin of our ideas of the sublime and the beautiful.* London: Dodsley.

Buss, A. H., & Plomin, R. (1975). *A temperament theory of personality development.* New York: Wiley.

Calhoun, C., & Solomon, R. C. (1984). *What is an emotion? Classic readings in philosophical psychology.* New York: Oxford University Press.

Campbell, A., Converse, P. E., & Rodgers, W. L. (1976). *The quality of American life.* New York: Russell Sage Foundation.

Campbell, P. A., & Cohen, J. J. (1985). Effects of stress on the immune response. In T. M.

Field, P. M. McCabe, & N. Schneiderman (Eds.), *Stress and coping* (pp. 135–145). Hillsdale, NJ: Erlbaum.

Campos, J. J. (1988–1989). Crawling onset organizes affective development in infancy. Annual Report, No. 12, Research and Clinical Center for Child Development, Faculty of Education, Hokkaido University, Sapporo, Japan.

Campos, J. J., & Barrett, K. C. (1984). Toward a new understanding of emotions and their development. In C. E. Izard, J. Kagan, & R. B. Zajonc (Eds.), *Emotions, cognition, and Behavior.* New York: Cambridge University Press.

Campos, J. J., Barrett, K. C., Lamb, M. E., Goldsmith, H. H., & Stenberg, C. (1983). Socioemotional development. In M. Haith & J. J. Campos (Eds.), *Handbook of child psychology,* Vol. 2: *Infancy and developmental psychobiology.* New York: Wiley.

Campos, J. J., Campos, R. G., & Barrett, K. C. (1989). Emergent themes in the study of emotional development and emotion regulation. *Developmental Psychology, 25,* 394–402.

Campos, J. J., & Stenberg, C. (1981). Perception, appraisal, and emotion: The onset of social referencing. In M. E. Lamb & L. R. Sherrod (Eds.), *Infant social cognition: Empirical and theoretical considerations.* Hillsdale, NJ: Erlbaum.

Cannon, W. B. (1939). *The wisdom of the body* (2nd ed.). New York: W. W. Simon. (First edition, 1932.)

Cantor, N., Norem, J. K., Brower, A. M., Niedenthal, P. M., & Langston, C. A. (1987). Life tasks, self-concept ideals, and cognitive strategies in a life transition. *Journal of Personality and Social Psychology, 53,* 1178–1191.

Caplan, G. (1961). *An approach to community mental health.* London: Tavistock.

Caplan, G. (1964). *Principles of preventive psychiatry.* London: Tavistock.

Caplan, G. (1970). *The theory and practice of mental health consultation.* London: Tavistock.

Caplan, G. (1974). *Support systems and community mental health.* New York: Behavioral Publications.

Carlson, M., Charlin, V., & Miller, N. (1988). Positive mood and helping behavior: A test of six hypotheses. *Journal of Personality and Social Psychology, 55,* 211–229.

Carlson, M., Marcus-Newhall, A., and Miller, N. (1989). Evidence for a general construct of aggression. *Personality and Social Psychology Bulletin, 15,* 377–389.

Carlson, M., Marcus-Newhall, A., & Miller, N. (1990). Effects of situational aggression cues: A quantitative review. *Journal of Personality and Social Psychology, 58,* 622–633.

Carlson, M., & Miller, N. (1988). Bad experiences and aggression. *Sociology and Social Research, 72,* 155–157.

Caspi, A. (1987). Personality in the life course. *Journal of Personality and Social Psychology, 53,* 1203–1213.

Caspi, A., Bolger, N., & Eckenrode, J. (1987). Linking person and context in the daily stress process. *Journal of Personality and Social Psychology, 52,* 184–195.

Caspi, A., Elder, G. H., & Bem, D. J. (1988). Moving away from the world: Life course patterns of shy children. *Developmental Psychology, 24,* 824–831.

Caspi, A., Elder, G. H., & Bem, D. J. (1989). Continuities and consequences of interactional styles across the life course. *Journal of Personality, 57,* 375–406.

Caudill, W. (1959). Observations on the cultural context of Japanese psychiatry. In M. K. Opler (Ed.), *Culture and mental health* (pp. 213–242). New York: Macmillan.

Caudill, W. (1971). Tiny dramas: Vocal communication between mother and infant in Japanese and American families. In W. Lebra (Ed.), *Mental health research in Asia and the Pacific* (Vol. II). Honolulu: East-West Center Press.

Caudill, W., & Weinstein, H. (1969). Maternal care and infant behavior in Japan and America. *Psychiatry, 32,* 12–43.

Child, I. L. (1954). Personality. *Annual Reviews of Psychology, 5,* 149–170.

Child, I. L., & Waterhouse, I. K. (1952). Frustration and the quality of performance: I. A critique of the Barker, Dembo, and Lewin experiment. *Psychological Review, 59,* 351–362.

Child, I. L., & Waterhouse, I. K. (1953). Frustration and the quality of performance: II. A theoretical statement. *Psychological Review, 60,* 127–139.

Chun, K., & Sarbin, T. R. (1968). Methodological artifacts in subjection research and the tendency to reify: A rejoinder. *The Psychological Record, 18,* 441–447.

Church, A. T. (1987). Personality research in a non-western culture: The Philippines. *Psychological Bulletin, 102,* 272–292.

Clanton, G., & Smith, L. G. (1977). (Eds.), *Jealousy.* Englewood Cliffs, NJ: Prentice Hall.

Clark, D. A., Beck, A. T., & Brown, G. (1989). Cognitive mediation in general psychiatric outpatients: A test of the content-specificity hypothesis. *Journal of Personality and Social Psychology, 56,* 958–964.

Clark, D. A., Beck, A. T., & Stewart, B. (1990). Cognitive specificity and positive-negative affectivity: Complementary or contradictory views on anxiety and depression? *Journal of Abnormal Psychology, 99,* 148–155.

Clark, K. (1970). *Civilisation.* New York: Harper & Row.

Clark, M. S., & Isen, A. M. (1982). Toward understanding the relationship between feeling states and social behavior. In A. Hastorf & A. M. Isen (Eds.), *Cognitive social psychology.* New York: Elsevier.

Clore, G. L., Ortony, A., & Foss, M. A. (1987). The psychological foundations of the affective lexicon. *Journal of Personality and Social Psychology, 53,* 751–766.

Clynes, M. (1977). *Sentics: The touch of emotions.* Garden City, NY: Anchor/Doubleday.

Cofer, C. N., & Appley, M. H. (1964). *Motivation: Theory and research.* New York: Wiley.

Cohen, F., Horwitz, M. J., Lazarus, R. S., Moos, R. H., Robins, L. N., Rose, R. M., & Rutter, M. (1982). Panel report on psychosocial assets and modifiers of stress. In G. R. Elliott & C. Eisdorfer (Eds.), *Stress and human health: Analysis and implications of research* (pp. 147–188). New York: Springer-Verlag.

Cohen, S., & Williamson, G. M. (1991). Stress and infectious disease in humans. *Psychological Bulletin, 109,* 5–24.

Compas, B. E. (1987). Coping with stress during childhood and adolescence. *Psychological Bulletin, 101,* 393–403.

Conway, M. A., & Bekerian, D. A. (1987). Situational knowledge and emotions. *Cognition and Emotion, 1,* 145–188.

Cook, E. W., III, Hawk, L. W., Davis, T. L., & Stevenson, V. E. (1991). Affective individual differences and startle reflex modulation. *Journal of Abnormal Psychology, 100,* 5–13.

Cook, M., Mineka, S, Wolkenstein, B., & Laitsch, K. (1985). Observational conditioning of snake fear in unrelated rhesus monkeys. *Journal of Abnormal Psychology, 94,* 591–610.

Cosmides, L., & Tooby, J. (1987). The latest on the best: Essays on evolution and optimality. In J. Dupre (Ed.), *From evolution to behavior: Evolutionary psychology as the missing link* (pp. 277–306). Cambridge, MA: Bradford/MIT.

Costa, P. T., & McCrae, R. R. (1980). Influence of extraversion and neuroticism on subjective well-being: Happy and unhappy people. *Journal of Personality and Social Psychology, 38,* 668–678.

Cousins, N. (1976). Anatomy of an illness (as perceived by the patient). *New England Journal of Medicine, 295,* 1458–1463.

Covington, M. V., & Omelich, C. L. (1987). "I knew it cold before the exam": A test of the anxiety-blockage hypothesis. *Journal of Educational Psychology, 79,* 393–400.

Cramer, P. (1987). The development of defense mechanisms. *Journal of Personality, 55,* 597–614.

Cronbach, L. J. (1957). The two disciplines of scientific psychology. *American Psychologist, 12,* 671–684.

Croyle, R. T., & Ditto, P. H. (1990). Illness cognition and behavior: An experimental approach. *Journal of Behavioral Medicine, 13,* 31–52.

Csikszentmihalyi, M. (1975). *Beyond boredom and anxiety: The experience of play in work and games.* San Francisco, CA: Jossey-Bass.

Cushman, P. (1984). The politics of vulnerability: Youth in religious cults. *Psychohistory Review, 12,* 5–17.

Cushman, P. (1986). The self besieged: Recruitment-indoctrination processes in restrictive groups. *Journal for the Theory of Social Behavior, 16,* 1–32.

Cushman, P. (1990). Why the self is empty: Toward a historically situated psychology. *American Psychologist, 45,* 599–611.

Dalkvist, J., & Rollenhagen, C. (1989a). On the cognitive aspect of emotions: A review and a model. *Reports from the Department of Psychology, University of Stockholm,* No. 703, September.

Dalkvist, J., & Rollenhagen, C. (1989b). The structure of feelings: A semantic differential study. *Reports from the Department of Psychology, University of Stockholm,* No. 708, October.

Daly, E. M., Polivy, J., & Lancee, W. J. (1983). A conical model for the taxonomy of emotional experience. *Journal of Personality and Social Psychology, 45,* 443–457.

D'Andrade, R. G. (1984). Cultural meaning systems. In R. A. Shweder & R. A. LeVine (Eds.), *Culture theory: Essays on mind, self, and emotion* (pp. 88–119). Cambridge, England: Cambridge University Press.

Darwin, C. (1859). The origin of species. London: J. Murray.

Darwin, C. (1872/1965). *The expression of the emotions in man and animals.* New York: Appleton. (1965, Chicago: University of Chicago Press.)

Davidson, R. J., Ekman, P., Saron, C. D., Senulis, J. A., & Friesen, W. V. (1990). Approach-withdrawal and cerebral asymmetry: Emotional expression and brain physiology I. *Journal of Personality and Social Psychology, 58,* 330–341.

Davidson, R. J., & Fox, N. A. (1989). Frontal brain asymmetry predicts infants' response to maternal separation. *Journal of Abnormal Psychology, 98,* 127–131.

Davitz, J. R. (1969). *The language of emotion.* New York: Academic Press.

DeCasper, A. J., & Fifer, W. Of human bonding: Newborns prefer their mothers' voices. *Science, 208,* 1174–1176.

Deese, J. (1985). *American freedom and the social sciences.* New York: Columbia University Press.

de Klerk, D. (1953). Magnetic properties below one degree K. *Physics Today, 6,* 4.

DeLongis, A., Coyne, J. C., Dakof, G., Folkman, S., & Lazarus, R. S. (1982). Relationship of daily hassles, uplifts, and major life events to health status. *Health Psychology, 1,* 119–136.

DeLongis, A., Folkman, S., and Lazarus, R. S. (1988). Hassles, health, and mood: Psychological and social resources as mediators. *Journal of Personality and Social Psychology, 54,* 486–495.

Dennenberg, V. H. (1964). Critical periods, stimulus input, and emotional reactivity: A theory of infantile stimulation. *Psychological Review, 71,* 335–351.

Depue, R. A., Monroe, S. M., & Schachman, S. L. (1979). The psychobiology of human disease: Implications for conceptualizing the depressive disorders. In R. A. Depue (Ed.), *The psychobiology of the depressive disorders: Implications for the effects of stress* (pp. 3–20). New York: Academic Press.

de Rivera, J. (1977). A structural theory of the emotions. *Psychological Issues* (Vol. 10, No. 4, Monograph 40, pp. 9–169). New York: International Universities Press.

de Rivera, J. (1981). The structure of anger. In J. de Rivera (Ed.), *Conceptual encounter: A method for the exploration of human experience.* Washington, DC: University Press of America.

de Rivera, J., & Grinkis, C. (1986). Emotions as social relationships. *Motivation and Emotion, 10,* 351–369.

de Rivera, J., Possell, L., Verette, J. A., & Weiner, B. (1989). Distinguishing elation, gladness, and joy. *Journal of Personality and Social Psychology, 57,* 1015–1023.

Derry, F. A., & Kuiper, N. A. (1981). Schematic processing and self-reference in clinical depression. *Journal of Abnormal Psychology, 97,* 29–34.

Derryberry, D., & Rothbart, M. K. (1984). Emotion, attention, and temperament. In C. E. Izard, J. Kagan, & R. B. Zajonc (Eds.), *Emotions, cognition, and behavior* (pp. 132–166). Cambridge, England: Cambridge University Press.

Derryberry, D., & Rothbart, M. K. (1988). Arousal, affect, and attention as components of temperament. *Journal of Personality and Social Psychology, 55,* 958–966.

De Sousa, R. (1980). The rationality of emotions. In A. O. Rorty (Ed.), *Explaining emotions* (pp. 127–151). Berkeley: University of California Press.

De Sousa, R. (1987). *The rationality of emotion.* Cambridge, MA: MIT Press.

Dewey, J. (1971). The theory of emotion. In *John Dewey: The early works, 1882–1898* (Vol. 4: 1893–1894). Carbondale: University Press.

Diener, E. (1984). Subjective well-being. *Psychological Bulletin, 95,* 542–575.

Diener, E., Larson, R. J., Levine, S., & Emmons, R. A. (1985). Frequency and intensity: The underlying dimensions of positive and negative affect. *Journal of Personality and Social Psychology, 48,* 1253–1265.

Diener, E., Sandvik, E., & Pavot, W. (1989). Happiness is the frequency, not intensity, of positive versus negative affect. In F. Strack, M. Argyle, & N. Schwarz (Eds.), *The social psychology of subjective well being* (pp. 119–139). Oxford, England: Pergamon Press.

Dobson, K. S., & Neufeld, R. W. J. (1979). Stress-related appraisals: A regression analysis. *Canadian Journal of Behavioral Science, 11,* 274–285.

Dohrenwend, B. S., Dohrenwend, B. P., Dodson, M., & Shrout, P. E. (1984). Symptoms, hassles, social supports and life events: The problem of confounded measures. *Journal of Abnormal Psychology, 93,* 222–230.

Doi, L. T. (1973). *The anatomy of dependence.* Tokyo: Kodansha International.

Doi, L. T. (1985). *The anatomy of self: The individual versus society.* Tokyo: Kodansha International.

Dollard, J., & Miller, N. E. (1950). *Personality and psychotherapy.* New York: McGraw-Hill.

Domjan, M. (1987). Animal learning comes of age. *American Psychologist, 42,* 556–564.

Donaldson, S. K., & Westerman, M. A. (1986). Development of children's understanding of ambivalence and causal theories of emotion. *Developmental Psychology, 22,* 655–662.

Dorr, A. (1985). Contexts for experience with emotion, with special attention to television. In M. Lewis & C. Saarni (Eds.), *The socialization of emotions* (pp. 55–85). New York: Plenum.

Drever, J. (1952). *A dictionary of psychology.* London: Penguin.

Dreyfus, H. L. (1982). (Ed.). *Huserl, intentionality and cognitive science.* Cambridge, MA: MIT Press.

Dreyfus, H. L. (1991). *Being-in-the-world: A commentary on Heidegger's "Being and time, Division 1."* Cambridge, MA: MIT Press.

Dubos, R. (1959). *Mirage of health: Utopias, progress, and biological change.* New York: Harper & Row.

Duchenne, B. (1862). *Mechanisme de la physiognomie humaine on analyse electrophysiologique de l'expression des passions.* Paris: Bailliere. (Not seen.)

Duffy, E. (1941a). An explanation of "emotional" phenomena without the use of the concept "emotion." *Journal of General Psychology, 25,* 283–293.

Duffy, E. (1941b). The conceptual categories of psychology: A suggestion for revision. *Psychological Review, 48,* 177–203.

Duffy, E. (1962). *Activation and behavior.* New York: Wiley.

Dunbar, H. F. (1948). *Synopsis of psychosomatic diagnosis and treatment.* St. Louis, MO: Mosby.

Dunn, J. (1988). *The beginnings of social understanding.* Cambridge, MA: Harvard University Press.

Dunn, J., & Munn, P. (1985). Becoming a family member: Family conflict and the development of social understanding in the second year. *Child Development, 56,* 480–492.

Dweck, C. S. (1975). The role of expectations and attributions in the alleviation of learned helplessness. *Journal of Personality and Social Psychology, 31,* 674–685.

D'Zurilla, T. J. (1986). *Problem-solving therapy: A social competence approach to clinical intervention.* New York: Springer.

D'Zurilla, T. J., & Goldfried, M. (1971). Problem solving and behavior modification. *Journal of Abnormal Psychology, 78,* 107–126.

D'Zurilla, T. J., & Nezu, A. (1982). Social problem solving in adults. In P. C. Kendall (Ed.), *Advances in cognitive-behavioral research and therapy* (Vol. 1). New York: Academic Press.

Easterbrook, J. A. (1959). The effect of emotion on cue utilization and the organization of behavior. *Psychological Review, 66,* 183–201.

Eckenrode, J. (1984). Impact of chronic and acute stressors on daily reports of mood. *Journal of Personality and Social Psychology, 46,* 907–918.

Eibel-Eibesfeldt, I. (1970). *Ethology: The biology of behavior* (E. Klinghammer, Trans.). New York: Holt, Rinehart and Winston.

Eisenberg, N., McCreath, H., & Ahn, R. (1988). Vicarious emotional responsiveness and prosocial behavior: Their interrelations in young children. *Personality and Social Psychology Bulletin, 14,* 298–311.

Ekman, P. (1971). Universals and cultural differences in facial expressions of emotion. In J. K. Cole (Ed.) (1972), *Nebraska Symposium on motivation, 1971* (pp. 207–283). Lincoln: University of Nebraska Press.

Ekman, P. (1977). Biological and cultural contributions to body and facial movement. In J. Blacking (Ed.), *A.S.A. Monograph 15, the anthropology of the body* (pp. 39–84). London: Academic Press. Reprinted in A. O. Rorty (Ed.), *Explaining emotions* (pp. 73–101). Berkeley: University of California Press.

Ekman, P. (1984). Expression and the nature of emotion. In K. R. Scherer & P. Ekman (Eds.), *Approaches to emotion* (pp. 319–343). Hillsdale, NJ: Erlbaum.

Ekman, P. (1985). *Telling lies: Clues to deceit in the marketplace, politics, and marriage.* New York: Norton.

Ekman, P. (1989). The argument and evidence about universals in facial expressions of emotion. In H. Wagner & A. Manstead (Eds.), *Handbook of social psychophysiology* (pp. 143–163). New York: Wiley.

Ekman, P., & Friesen, W. V. (1969). The repertoire of nonverbal behavior: Categories, origins, usage, and coding. *Semiotica, 1,* 49–98.

Ekman, P., & Friesen, W. V. (1986). A new pan-cultural facial expression of emotion. *Motivation and Emotion, 10,* 159–168.

Ekman, P., & Friesen, W. V. (1988). Who knows what about contempt: A reply to Izard and Haynes. *Motivation and Emotion, 12,* 17–22.

Ekman, P., Friesen, W. V, & Davidson, R. J. (1990). The Duchenne's smile: Emotion expression and brain physiology 2. *Journal of Personality and Social Psychology, 58,* 342–353.

Ekman, P., Friesen, W. V., & O'Sullivan, M. (1988). Smiles when lying. *Journal of Personality and Social Psychology, 54,* 414–420.

Ekman, P., Friesen, W. V., & Simons, R. C. (1985). Is the startle reaction an emotion? *Journal of Personality and Social Psychology, 49,* 1416–1426.

Ekman, P., & Heider, K. G. (1988). The universality of a contempt expression: A replication. *Motivation and Emotion, 12*, 303–308.

Ekman, P., Levenson, R. W., & Friesen, W. V. (1983). Autonomic nervous system activity distinguishes among emotions. *Science, 221*, 1208–1210.

Ekman, P., & Oster, H. (1979). Facial expressions of emotion. *Annual Review of Psychology, 30*, 527–554.

Ellis, A. (1962). *Reason and emotion in psychotherapy.* New York: Lyle Stuart.

Ellis, A. (1984). Is the unified-interaction approach to cognitive-behavior modification a reinvention of the wheel? *Clinical Psychology Review, 4*, 215–218.

Ellis, A. (1985). Cognition and affect in emotional disturbance. *American Psychologist, 40*, 471–472.

Ellis, A., & Bernard, M. E. (1985). What is rational emotive therapy (RET)? In A. Ellis & M. E. Bernard (Eds.), *Clinical applications of rational-emotive therapy* (pp. 1–30). Monterey, CA: Brooks/Cole.

Ellsworth, P. C., & Smith, C. A. (1988a). From appraisal to emotion: Differences among unpleasant feelings. *Motivation and Emotion, 12*, 271–302.

Ellsworth, P. C., & Smith, C. A. (1988b). Shades of joy: Patterns of appraisal differentiating pleasant emotions. *Cognition and Emotion, 2*, 301–331.

Emde, R. N. (1984a). Levels of meaning for infant emotions: A biosocial view. In K. R. Scherer & P. Ekman (Eds.), *Approaches to emotion* (pp. 77–107). Hillsdale, NJ: Erlbaum.

Emde, R. N. (1984b). Cognition and affect in emotional disturbance. *American Psychologist, 40*, 471–472.

Emmons, R. A., & Diener, E. (1986). A goal-affect analysis of everyday situational choices. *Journal of Research in Personality, 20*, 309–326.

Emmons, R. S. (1986). Personal strivings: An approach to personality and subjective well-being. *Journal of Personality and Social Psychology, 51*, 1058–1068.

Endler, N. S., Edwards, J. M., Vitelli, R., & Parker, J. D. A. (1989). Assessment of state and trait anxiety: Endler Multidimensional Anxiety Scales. *Anxiety Research, 2*, 1–14.

Endler, N. S., & Okada, M. (1975). A multidimensional measure of trait anxiety: The S-R Inventory of General Trait Anxiousness. *Journal of Consulting and Clinical Psychology, 43*, 319–329.

Engel, G. L. (1968). A life setting conducive to illness: The giving up-given up complex. *Bulletin of the Menninger Clinic, 32*, 355–365.

Englis, B. G., Vaughn, K. B., & Lanzetta, J. T. (1982). Conditioning of counter-empathetic emotional responses. *Journal of Experimental Social Psychology, 18*, 375–391.

Epictetus (1956). *Enchiridion* (G. Long, Trans.). South Bend, IN: Regenery-Gateway. (Original work undated.)

Epstein, S. (1980). The self-concept: A review and the proposal of an integrated theory of personality. In E. Staub (Ed.), *Personality: Basic issues and current research* (pp. 82–132). Englewood Cliffs, NJ: Prentice Hall.

Epstein, S. (1983). A research paradigm for the study of personality and emotions. In M. M. Page (Ed.), *Personality: Current theory and research. Nebraska Symposium on Motivation, 1982* (pp. 92–154). Lincoln: University of Nebraska Press.

Epstein, S. (1984). Controversial issues in emotion theory. In P. Shaver (Ed.), *Review of personality and social psychology: Emotions, relationships, and health* (pp. 64–88). Beverly Hills, CA: Sage.

Epstein, S. (1990). Cognitive experiential self-theory. In L. Pervin (Ed.), *Handbook of personality theory and research.* (pp. 165–192). New York: Guilford.

Epstein, S., & Meier, P. (1989). Constructive thinking: a broad coping variable with specific components. *Journal of Personality and Social Psychology, 57*, 332–350.

Erdelyi, M. H. (1974). A new look at the new look: Perceptual defence and vigilance. *Psychological Review, 81*, 1–25.

Erdelyi, M. H. (1985). *Psychoanalysis: Freud's cognitive psychology.* New York: Freeman.

Eriksen, C. W. (1956). Subception: Fact or artifact? *Psychological Review, 63*, 74–80.

Eriksen, C. W. (1960). Discrimination and learning without awareness: A methodological survey and evaluation. *Psychological Review, 67*, 379–400.

Eriksen, C. W. (1962). (Ed.). *Behavior and awareness — a symposium of research and interpretation* (pp. 3–26). Durham, NC: Duke University Press.

Erikson, E. H. (1950). *Childhood and Society.* New York: Norton.

Erikson, E. H. (1963). *Childhood and society* (2nd ed.). New York: Norton.

Evered, R. (1980). Consequences of and prospects for systems thinking in organizational change. In T. G. Cummings (Ed.), *Systems theory for organizational development* (pp. 5–13). New York: Wiley.

Faris, R. E. L., & Dunham, H. (1939). *Mental disorders in urban areas.* Chicago: University of Chicago Press.

Fazio, R. H., Sanbormatsu, D. M., Powell, M. C., & Kardes, F. R. (1986). On the automatic activation of attitudes. *Journal of Personality and Social Psychology, 50*, 229–238.

Fehr, B. (1988). Prototype analysis of the concepts of love and commitment. *Journal of Personality and Social Psychology, 55*, 557–579.

Fehr, B., & Russell, J. A. (1984). Concept of emotion viewed from a prototype perspective. *Journal of Experimental Psychology: General, 113*, 464–486.

Feist, J., & Brannon, L. (1988). *Health psychology: An introduction to behavior and health.* Belmont, CA: Wadsworth.

Feldman, S. S. (1956). Crying at the happy ending. *Journal of the American Psychoanalytic Association, 4*, 477–485. Also in Socarides, 1977.

Felner, R. D., Farber, S. S., & Primavera, J. (1983). Transitions and stressful life events: A model for primary prevention. In R. D. Felner, L. A. Jason, J. N. Moritsugu, & S. S. Farber (Eds.), *Preventive psychology: Theory, research, and practice.* New York: Pergamon.

Ferenczi, S. (1916). Stages in the development of the sense of reality. In *Sex in Psychoanalysis.* Boston: Gorham Press. (Originally published in 1913.)

Festinger, L. (1957). A theory of social comparison processes. *Human Relations, 7*, 117–140.

Fischer, K. W., & Pipp, S. L. (1984). Development of the structures of unconscious thought. In K. Bowers & D. Meichenbaum (Eds.), *The unconscious reconsidered.* New York: Wiley.

Fishbein, M., & Ajzen, A. (1975). *Belief, attitudes, intention and behavior.* Reading, MA: Addison-Wesley.

Fiske, D. W., & Shweder, R. A. (1986). *Metatheory in social science: Pluralisms and subjectivities.* Chicago: University of Chicago Press.

Fiske, S. T. (1982). Schema-triggered affect: Applications to social perception. In M. S. Clark & S. T. Fiske (Eds.), *Affect and cognition: The 17th annual Carnegie symposium* (pp. 55–78). Hillsdale, NJ: Erlbaum.

Florian, V., & Snowden, L. R. (1989). Fear of personal death and positive life regard: A study of different ethnic and religious-affiliated American college students. *Journal of Cross-cultural Psychology, 20*, 64–79.

Foa, E., & Kozak, J. J. (1986). Emotional processing of fear: Exposure to corrective information. *Psychological Bulletin, 99*, 20–35.

Folkins, C. H. (1970). Temporal factors and the cognitive mediators of stress reaction. *Journal of Personality and Social Psychology, 14*, 173–184.

Folkman, S. (1984). Personal control and stress and coping processes: A theoretical analysis. *Journal of Personality and Social Psychology, 46*, 839–852.

Folkman, S., & Lazarus, R. S. (1980). An analysis of coping in a middle-aged community sample. *Journal of Health and Social Behavior, 21,* 219–239.

Folkman, S., & Lazarus, R. S. (1985). If it changes it must be a process: Study of emotion and coping during three stages of a college examination. *Journal of Personality and Social Psychology, 48,* 150–170.

Folkman, S., & Lazarus, R. S. (1988a). Coping as a mediator of emotion. *Journal of Personality and Social Psychology, 54,* 466–475.

Folkman, S., & Lazarus, R. S. (1988b). *Manual for the Ways of Coping Questionnaire.* Palo Alto, CA: Consulting Psychologists Press.

Folkman, S., & Lazarus, R. S. (1988c). The relationship between coping and emotion. Reprinted from Stein, Leventhal, & Trabasso, in L. J. Menges (Special Ed.), *Social Science in Medicine, 26,* 309–317.

Folkman, S., & Lazarus, R. S. (1990). Coping and emotion. In N. Stein, B. Leventhal, & T. Trabasso (Eds.), *Psychological and biological approaches to emotion* (pp. 313–332). Hillsdale, NJ: Erlbaum.

Folkman, S., Lazarus, R. S., Dunkel-Schetter, C., DeLongis, A., & Gruen, R. (1986). The dynamics of a stressful encounter: Cognitive appraisal, coping, and encounter outcomes. *Journal of Personality and Social Psychology, 50,* 992–1003.

Folkman, S., Lazarus, R. S., Gruen, R., & DeLongis, A. (1986). Appraisal, coping, health status, and psychological symptoms. *Journal of Personality and Social Psychology, 50,* 572–579.

Folkman, S., Lazarus, R. S., Pimley, S., & Novacek, J. (1987). Age differences in stress and coping processes. *Psychology and Aging, 2,* 171–184.

Folkman, S., Schaefer, C., & Lazarus, R. S. (1979). Cognitive processes as mediators of stress and coping. In V. Hamilton & D. M. Warburton (Eds.), *Human stress and cognition: An information-processing approach* (pp. 265–298). London: Wiley.

Fordyce, W. E. (1988). Pain and suffering: A reappraisal. *American Psychologist, 43,* 276–283.

Forgas, J. P. (1982). Episode cognition: Internal representations of interaction routines. In L. Berkowitz (Ed.), *Advances in experimental social psychology.* New York: Academic Press.

Forgas, J. P., & Bower, G. H. (1987). Mood effects on person perception judgments. *Journal of Personality and Social Psychology, 53,* 53–60.

Forgas, J. P., & Bower, G. H. (1988). Affect in social and personal judgments. In K. Fiedler & J. P. Forgas (Eds.), *Affect, cognition and social behavior* (pp. 184–208). Toronto: Hogrefe.

Forgas, J. P., Bower, G. H., & Krantz, S. E. (1984). The influence of mood on perceptions of social interactions. *Journal of Experimental Social Psychology, 20,* 497–513.

Forgas, J. P., & Moylan, S. (1987). After the movies: Transient mood and social judgments. *Personality and Social Psychology Bulletin, 13,* 467–477.

Foulkes, D. (1978). *A grammar of dreams.* New York: Basic Books.

Fox, N. A. (1989). Psychophysiological correlates of emotional reactivity during the first year of life. *Developmental Psychology, 25,* 364–372.

Fox, N. A., & Davidson, R. J. (1984). EEG asymmetry and the development of affect. In N. A. Fox & R. J. Davidson (Eds.), *The psychology of affective development.* Hillsdale, NJ: Erlbaum.

Fox, N. A., & Davidson, R. J. (1989). Frontal brain asymmetry predicts infant's response to maternal separation. *Journal of Abnormal Psychology, 98,* 127–131.

Frankenhaeuser, M. (1976). The role of peripheral catecholamines in adaptation to understimulation. In G. Serban (Ed.), *Psychopathology of human adaptation* (pp. 173–191). New York: Plenum.

Frankl, V. (1959). *Man's search for meaning.* Boston: Beacon.

French, J. R. P., Jr., Caplan, R. D., & Van Harrison, R. (1982). *The mechanisms of job stress and strain.* Chichester, England: Wiley.

Frese, M., & Sabini, J. (Eds.). (1985). *Goal directed behavior: The concept of action in psychology.* Hillsdale, NJ: Erlbaum.

Freud, S. (1922). Some neurotic mechanisms in jealousy, paranoia and homosexuality. *Standard Edition,* XVIII. London: Hogarth.

Freud, S. (1933). New introductory lectures on psychoanalysis. In *The standard edition of the complete psychological works of Sigmund Freud* (Vol. 20). (J. Strachey, Ed./Trans.). London: Hogarth, 1964.

Freud, S. (1936). *Inhibitions, symptoms and anxiety.* London: Hogarth. (First German edition, 1926.)

Freud, S. (1957a). Mourning and melancholia. In J. Strachey (Ed.), *The complete psychological works of Sigmund Freud* (Vol. 14, pp. 243–258). London: Hogarth (Originally published in 1917.)

Freud, S. (1957b). The ego and the id. In J. Rickman (Ed.), *A general selection from the works of Sigmund Freud* (pp. 210–235). Garden City, NY: Doubleday.

Frick, R. W. (1985). Communicating emotion: The role of prosodic features. *Psychological Bulletin, 97,* 412–429.

Fridlund, A. J. (in press). Evolution and facial action in reflex, social motive, and paralanguage. In P. K. Ackles, J. R. Jennings, & M. G. H. Coles (Eds.), *Advances in psychophysiology* (Vol. 4). Greenwich, CT: JAI Press.

Fridlund, A. J., Ekman, P., & Oster, H. (1986). Facial expressions of emotion: Review of literature, 1970–1983. In A. Siegman & S. Feldstein (Eds.), *Nonverbal behavior and communication* (pp. 143–223). Hillsdale, NJ: Erlbaum.

Frijda, N. H. (1986). *The emotions.* Cambridge, England: Cambridge University Press.

Frijda, N. H. (1987). Emotion, cognitive structure, and action tendency. *Cognition and Emotion, 1,* 115–143.

Frijda, N. H. (1989). Aesthetic emotions and reality. *American Psychologist, 44,* 1546–1547.

Frijda, N. H., Kuipers, P., & ter Schure, E. (1989). Relations among emotion, appraisal, and emotional action readiness. *Journal of Personality and Social Psychology, 57,* 212–228.

Frijda, N. H., & Philipszoon, E. (1963). Dimensions of recognition expression. *Journal of Abnormal and Social Psychology, 66,* 45–51.

Fritz, C. E., & Mathewson, J. H. (1957). *Convergence behavior in disasters: A problem in social control.* Washington, DC: National Academy of Sciences, National Research Council, Disaster Study No. 9.

Fromm, E. (1941). *Escape from freedom.* New York: Farrar, Straus & Giroux.

Gal, R., & Lazarus, R. S. (1975). The role of activity in anticipating and confronting stressful situations. *Journal of Human Stress, 1,* 4–20.

Galbrecht, C. R., Dykman, R. A., Reese, W. G., & Suzuki, T. (1965). Intra-session adaptation and intersession extinction of the components of the orienting response. *Journal of Experimental Psychology, 70,* 585–597.

Gardner, H. M., Metcalf, R. C., & Beebe-Center, J. G. (1937/1970). *Feeling and emotion.* Westport, CT: Greenwood Press.

Garfield, S. L., & Bergin, A. E. (1978). *Handbook of psychotherapy and behavior change.* New York: Wiley.

Garmezy, N. (1981). Children under stress: Perspectives on antecedents and correlates of vulnerability and resistance to psychopathology. In A. I. Rabin, J. Aronoff, A. M. Barclay, & R. S. Zucker (Eds.), *Further explorations in personality* (pp. 196–269). New York: Wiley.

Garmezy, N., & Rutter, M. (Eds.). (1983). *Stress, coping and development in children.* New York: McGraw-Hill.

Gassner, S., Sampson, H., Brumer, S., & Weiss, J. (1986). The emergence of warded-off contents. In J. Weiss, H. Sampson, & the Mount Zion Psychotherapy Research Group (Eds.), *The psychoanalytic process: Theory, clinical observation, and empirical research* (pp. 171–186). New York: Guilford.

Geen, R. G., Stonner, D., & Kelley, D. R. (1974). Aggression anxiety and cognitive appraisal of aggression-threat stimuli. *Journal of Personality and Social Psychology, 29,* 196–200.

Geertz, C. (1973). *Interpretation of cultures.* New York: Basic Books.

Gergen, K. J. (1985). The social constructionist movement in modern psychology. *American Psychologist, 40,* 266–275.

Gibson, J. J. (1966). *The senses considered as perceptual systems.* Boston: Houghton Mifflin.

Gibson, J. J. (1979). *The ecological approach to visual perception.* Boston: Houghton Mifflin.

Gilbert, D. T. (1991). How mental systems believe. *American Psychologist, 46,* 107–119.

Gillett, E. (1987a). Defence mechanisms versus defence contents. *International Journal of Psycho-analysis, 68,* 261–269.

Gillett, E. (1987b). The relationship of repression to the unconscious. *International Journal of Psycho-analysis, 68,* 535–546.

Gillett, E. (1990). The problem of unconscious affect: Signal anxiety versus the double-prediction theory. *Psychoanalysis and Contemporary Thought, 13,* 551–601.

Glanzmann, P. (1985). Anxiety, stress and performance. In B. D. Kirkcaldy (Ed.), *Individual differences in movement.* Lancaster, England: MTP Press.

Glaser, B. G., & Strauss, A. L. (1965). *Awareness of dying.* Chicago: Aldine.

Glaser, B. G., & Strauss, A. L. (1968). *Time for dying.* Chicago: Aldine.

Glass, D. C. (1977). *Behavior patterns, stress and coronary disease.* Hillsdale, NJ: Erlbaum.

Glass, D. C., Krakoff, R., Contrada, R., Hilton, W. F., Kehoe, K., Manucci, E. G., Collings, C., Snow, G., & Elting, E. (1980). Effect of harassment and competition upon cardiovascular and plasma catecholamine responses in Type A and Type B individuals. *Psychophysiology, 17,* 453–463.

Glueck, S., & Glueck, E. (1950). *Unraveling juvenile delinquency.* New York: Commonwealth Fund.

Goffman, E. (1959). *The presentation of self in everyday life.* Garden City, NY: Doubleday.

Goffman, E. (1971). *Relations in public.* New York: Basic Books.

Goldfried, M. (1987). Assessment of cognitive activities. In J. P. Dauwalder, M. Perrez, & V. Hobi (Eds.), *Controversial issues in behavior modification* (pp. 97–106). Amsterdam: Swets & Zeitlinger.

Goldsmith, H. H. (1983). Genetic influences on personality from infancy to adulthood. *Child Development, 54,* 331–335.

Goldsmith, H. H., & Campos, J. J. (1986). Fundamental issues in the study of early temperament: The Denver twin temperament study. In M. Lamb, A. Brown, & B. Rogoff (1986). (Eds.), *Advances in infant behavior and development.* Hillsdale, NJ: Erlbaum.

Goldstein, K. (1939). *The organism.* New York: American Book.

Goleman, D. (1985). *Vital lies, simple truths: The psychology of self-deception.* New York; Simon & Schuster.

Gordon, R. M. (1987). *The structure of emotions.* Cambridge, England: Cambridge University Press.

Gordon, S. L. (1981). The sociology of sentiments and emotion. In M. Rosenberg & R. H. Turner (Eds.), *Social psychology: Sociological perspectives* (pp. 562–592). New York: Basic Books.

Graham, D. T. (1962). Some research on psychophysiologic specificity and its relation to psychosomatic disease. In R. Roessler & N. S. Greenfield (Eds.), *Physiological correlates of psychological disorder* (pp. 221–238). Madison: University of Wisconsin Press.

Graham, D. T., & Graham, F. K. (1961). *Specific relations of attitude to physiological change.* Progress report, July 1.

Graves, C. W. (1966). Deterioration of work standards. *Harvard Business Review, 44,* 117–128.

Gray, J. A. (1971). *The psychology of fear and stress.* London: Weidenfeld & Nicholson.

Gray, S. J., Ramsey, C. S., Villarreal, R., & Krakaner, L. J. (1955–1956). Adrenal influences upon the stomach and the gastric response to stress. In H. Selye & G. Hensen (Eds.), *Fifth Annual Report on Stress* (p. 138). New York: MD Publications.

Greenberg, L. S., & Safran, J. D. (1987). *Emotion in psychotherapy.* New York: Guilford.

Greenberg, L. S., & Safran, J. D. (1989). Emotion in psychotherapy. *American Psychologist, 44,* 19–29.

Greenberg, M. S., & Beck, A. T. (1989). Depression versus anxiety: A test of the content-specificity hypothesis. *Journal of Abnormal Psychology, 98,* 9–13.

Greenson, R. S. (1962). On enthusiasm. *Journal of the American Psychoanalytic Association, 10,* 3–21. Also in Socarides, 1977.

Griffin, D. R. (1984). *Animal thinking.* Cambridge, MA: Harvard University Press.

Grinker, R. R., & Spiegel, J. P. (1945). *Men under stress.* New York: McGraw-Hill.

Gruen, R. J., Folkman, S., & Lazarus, R. S. (1989). Centrality and individual differences in the meaning of daily hassles. *Journal of Personality, 56,* 743–762.

Guidano, V. F., & Liotti, G. (1983). *Cognitive processes and emotional disorders.* New York: Guilford.

Guignon, C. (1984). Moods in Heidegger's being and time. In C. Calhoun & R. C. Solomon (Eds.), *What is an emotion? Classical readings in philosophical psychology* (pp. 230–243). New York: Oxford University Press.

Guttfreund, D. G. (1990). Effects of language usage on the emotional experience of Spanish-English and English-Spanish bilinguals. *Journal of Consulting and Clinical Psychology, 58,* 604–607.

Hackett, T. P., & Weisman, A. D. (1964). Reactions to the imminence of death. In G. H. Grosser, H. Wechsler, & M. Greenblatt (Eds.), *The threat of impending disaster* (pp. 300–311). Cambridge, MA: MIT Press.

Hamilton, V. L., Blumenfeld, P. C., Akoh, H., & Miura, K. (1990). Credit and blame among American and Japanese children: Normative, cultural, and individual differences. *Journal of Personality and Social Psychology, 59,* 442–451.

Hammen, C., Marks, T., deMayo, R., & Mayol, A. (1985b). Self-schemas and risk for depression: A prospective study. *Journal of Personality and Social Psychology, 49,* 1147–1159.

Hammen, C., Marks, T., Mayol, A., & deMayo, R. (1985a). Depressive self-schemas, life stress, and vulnerability to depression. *Journal of Abnormal Psychology, 94,* 308–319.

Harder, D. W., & Lewis, S. J. (1986). The assessment of shame and guilt. In J. N. Butcher & C. D. Spielberger (Eds.), *Advances in personality assessment* (Vol. 6, pp. 89–114). Hillsdale, NJ: Erlbaum.

Harkness, S., & Super, C. M. (1985). Child-environment interactions in the socialization of affect. In M. Lewis & C. Saarni (Eds.), *The socialization of emotions* (pp. 21–36). New York: Plenum.

Harlow, H. F. (1953). Mice, monkeys, men and motives. *Psychological Review, 60,* 23–32.

Harlow, H. F., & Zimmerman, R. (1959). Affectional responses in the infant monkey. *Science, 130,* 421–432.

Harre, R. (1986). (Ed.). *The social construction of emotions.* Oxford, England: Basil Blackwell.

Harris, J. D. (1943). Habituatory response decrement in the intact organism. *Psychological Bulletin, 40,* 385–422.

Harris, P. L. (1983). Children's understanding of the link between situation and emotion. *Journal of Experimental Child Psychology, 36,* 490–509.

Harris, P. L. (1985). What children know about situations that provoke emotion. In M. Lewis & C. Saarni (Eds.), *The socialization of emotions* (pp. 161–185). New York: Plenum.

Harris, P. L. (1989). *Children and emotion: The development of psychological understanding.* Oxford, England: Basil Blackwell.

Harris, P. L., & Olthof, T. (1982). The child's concept of emotion. In G. Butterworth & P. Light (Eds.), *The individual and the social in cognitive development.* Sussex, England: Harvester.

Harris, P. L., Olthof, T., & Meerum-Terwogt, M. (1981). Children's knowledge of emotion. *Journal of Child Psychology and Psychiatry, 22,* 247–261.

Hart, K. E. (1991). Coping with anger-provoking situations: Adolescent coping in relation to anger-reactivity. *Journal of Adolescent Research, 6.*

Hart, K. E., Comer, D., & Hittner, J. B. (1990). Threat appraisals and coping with anger-provoking situations. Paper presented at the Western Psychological Association, Los Angeles, CA, April.

Hay, D., & Oken, D. (1972). The psychological stresses of intensive care nursing. *Psychosomatic Medicine, 34,* 109–118.

Hebb, D. O. (1946). On the nature of fear. *Psychological Review, 53,* 259–276.

Hebb, D. O. (1949). *The organization of behavior.* New York: Wiley.

Hebb, D. O. (1954). The problem of consciousness and introspection. In J. F. Delafresnaye (Ed.), *Brain mechanisms and consciousness.* Oxford, England: Oxford University Press.

Hebb, D. O., & Thompson, W. R. (1954). The social significance of animal studies. In G. Lindzey (Ed.), *Handbook of social psychology* (pp. 532–561). Cambridge, MA: Addison-Wesley.

Heckhausen, H., & Beckmann, J. (1990). Intentional action and action slips. *Psychological Review, 97,* 36–48.

Heider, F. (1958). *The psychology of interpersonal relations.* New York: Wiley.

Heider, K. G. (1991). *Landscapes of emotion: Mapping three cultures of emotion in Indonesia.* New York: Cambridge University Press.

Helson, H. (1959). Adaptation level theory. In S. Koch (Ed.), *Psychology: A study of a science* (Vol. 1). New York: McGraw-Hill.

Hembre, R. (1988). Correlates, causes, effects, and treatment of test anxiety. *Review of Educational Research, 58,* 47–77.

Hendrick, C., & Hendrick, S. S. (1989). Research on love: Does it measure up? *Journal of Personality and Social Psychology, 56,* 784–794.

Henle, M. (1962). On the relation between logic and thinking. *Psychological Review, 69,* 366–378.

Henle, M. (1971). On the Scholler of nature. *Social Research, 38,* 93–107.

Henry, J. P. (1986). Neuroendrocrine patterns of emotional response. In R. Plutchik & H. Kellerman (Eds.), *Emotion: Theory, research, and experience* (Vol. 3, pp. 37–60). New York: Academic Press.

Hensher, D. (1990). An appraisal approach to positive and negative emotions. Paper given at the Western Psychological Association annual meeting, April 26.

Hibbert, G. A. (1984). Ideational components of anxiety: Their origin and content. *British Journal of Psychiatry, 144,* 618–624.

Higgins, E. T. (1987). Self-discrepancy: A theory relating self and affect. *Psychological Review, 94,* 319–340.

Hilgard, E. R. (1949). Human motives and the concept of the self. *American Psychologist, 4,* 374–382.

Hilgard, E. R. (1980). The trilogy of mind: Cognition, affection, and conation. *Journal of the History of the Behavioral Sciences, 16,* 107–117.

Hillman, J. (1960). *Emotion: A comprehensive phenomenology of theories and their meanings for therapy.* London: Routledge & Kegan Paul.

Hinde, R. A., & Stevenson-Hinde, J. (Eds.). (1988). *Relationships within families: Mutual influences.* New York: Oxford University Press.

Hobfoll, S. E. (1989). Conservation of resources: A new attempt at conceptualizing stress. *American Psychologist, 44,* 513–524.

Hochschild, A. R. (1979). Emotion work, feeling rules, and social structure. *American Journal of Sociology, 85,* 551–575.

Hoffman, M. L. (1978). Empathy, its development and prosocial implications. In C. B. Keasey (Ed.), *Nebraska symposium on motivation* (Vol. 25). Lincoln: University of Nebraska Press.

Hoffman, M. L. (1982a) Development of prosocial motivation: Empathy and guilt. In N. Eisenberg (Ed.), *The development of prosocial behavior.* New York: Academic Press.

Hoffman, M. L. (1982b). Measurement of empathy. In C. Izard (Ed.), *Measurement of emotions in infants and children.* Cambridge, England: Cambridge University Press.

Hoffman, M. L. (1984). Interaction of affect and cognition in empathy. In C. E. Izard, J. Kagan, & R. B. Zajonc (Eds.), *Emotions, cognition, and behavior* (pp. 103–131). Cambridge, England: Cambridge University Press.

Hoffman, M. L. (1985). Affect, cognition, and motivation. In E. T. Higgins & R. M. Sorrentino (Eds.), *Handbook of motivation and cognition: Foundations of social behavior.* New York: Guilford.

von Hofsten, C. (1985). Perception and action. In M. Frese & J. Sabini (Eds.), *Goal directed behavior: The concept of action in psychology* (pp. 80–96). Hillsdale, NJ: Erlbaum.

Hollingshead, A. B., & Redlich, F. C. (1958). *Social class and mental illness.* New York: Harper.

Hollon, S. D., & Beck, A. T. (1979). Cognitive therapy of depression. In P. C. Kendall & S. D. Hollon (Eds.), *Cognitive behavioral interventions: Theory, research and procedures* (pp. 153–203). New York: Academic Press.

Holmes, T. H., & Houston, B. K. (1974). Effectiveness of situational redefinition and affective isolation in coping with stress. *Journal of Personality and Social Psychology, 29,* 212–218.

Holmes, T. H., & Rahe, R. H. (1967). The social readjustment rating scale. *Journal of Psychosomatic Research, 11,* 213–218.

Holroyd, K. A., & Lazarus, R. S. (1982). Stress, coping, and somatic adaptation. In L. Goldberger & S. Breznitz (Eds.), *Handbook of stress: Theoretical and clinical aspects* (pp. 21–35). New York: Free Press.

Holzman, P. S., & Gardner, R. W. (1959). Leveling and repression. *Journal of Abnormal and Social Psychology, 59,* 151–155.

Holtzman, W. H., & Bitterman, M. E. (1956). A factorial study of adjustment to stress. *Journal of Abnormal and Social Psychology, 52,* 179–185.

Hornik, R., Risenhoover, N., & Gunnar, M. (1987). The effects of material positive, neutral, and negative affective communications on infant responses to new toys. *Child Development, 58,* 937–944.

Horowitz, M. J. (1976). *Stress response syndromes.* New York: Jason Aronson.

Horowitz, M. J. (1982). Stress response syndromes and their treatment. In L. Goldberger & S. Breznitz (Eds.), *Handbook of stress: Theoretical and clinical aspects* (pp. 711–732). New York: Free Press.

Horowitz, M. J. (1988). *Introduction to psychodynamics.* New York: Basic Books.

Horowitz, M. J. (1989). Relationship schema formulation: Role relationship models and intrapsychic conflict. *Psychiatry, 52,* 260–274.

Horvath, F. E. (1959). Psychological stress: A review of definitions and experimental research. In L. von Bertalanffy & A. Rapaport (Eds.), *General systems* (Vol. IV). Ann Arbor, MI: Society for General Systems Research.

House, J. S. (1981). Social structure and personality. In M. Rosenberg & R. H. Turner (Eds.), *Social psychology: Sociological perspectives* (pp. 525–561). New York: Basic Books.

Howes, D. (1954). A statistical theory of subception. *Psychological Review, 61,* 98–110.

Hull, C. L. (1943). *Principles of behavior.* New York: Appleton-Century-Crofts.

Hume, D. (1957). *An inquiry concerning the principles of morals.* New York: Library of Liberal Arts.

Hupka, R. B. (1981). Cultural determinants of jealousy. *Alternative Lifestyles, 4,* 310–356.

Isen, A. M. (1970). Success, failure, attention and reaction to others: The warm glow of success. *Journal of Personality and Social Psychology, 15,* 294–301.

Isen, A. M. (1984). Toward understanding the role of affection cognition. In R. S. Wyer, Jr., & T. K. Srull (Eds.), *Handbook of social cognition* (Vol. 3). Hillsdale, NJ: Erlbaum.

Isen, A. M., Shalker, T. E., Clark, M., & Karp, L. (1978). Affect, accessibility of material in memory, and behavior: A cognitive loop? *Journal of Personality and Social Psychology, 36,* 1–12.

Isenberg, A. (1980). Natural pride and natural shame. In A. O. Rorty (Ed.), *Explaining emotions* (pp. 355–383). Berkeley: University of California Press.

Izard, C. E. (1971). *The face of emotion.* New York: Appleton-Century-Crofts.

Izard, C. E. (1977). *Human emotions.* New York: Plenum.

Izard, C. E. (1978). On the ontogenesis of emotions and emotion-cognition relationships in infancy. In M. Lewis & L. Rosenblum (Eds.), *The development of affect* (pp. 389–413). New York: Plenum.

Izard, C. E. (1984). *Emotion-cognition relationships and human development.* In C. E. Izard, J. Kagan, & R. B. Zajonc (Eds.), *Emotions, cognition, and behavior* (pp. 17–37). New York: Cambridge University Press.

Izard, C. E. (1990). Facial expressions and the regulation of emotions. *Journal of Personality and Social Psychology, 58,* 487–498.

Izard, C. E., & Buechler, S. (1980). Aspects of consciousness and personality in terms of differential emotions theory. In R. Plutchik & H. Kellerman (Eds.), *Emotion: Theory, research, and experience* (Vol. 1, pp. 165–187). New York: Academic Press.

Izard, C. E., & Dougherty, L. M. (1982). Two complementary systems for measuring facial expressions in infants and children. In C. E. Izard (Ed.), *Measuring emotions in infants and children.* New York: Cambridge University Press.

Izard, C. E., & Haynes, O. M. (1988). On the form and universality of the contempt expression: A challenge to Ekman and Friesen's claim of discovery. *Motivation and Emotion, 12,* 1–16.

Izard, C. E., Kagan, J., & Zajonc, R. B. (1984). (Eds.), *Emotions, cognition, and behavior.* New York: Cambridge University Press.

James, W. (1890). *Principles of psychology.* New York: Holt.

Janis, I. L. (1951). *Air war and emotional stress.* New York: McGraw-Hill.

Janis, I. L. (1958). *Psychological stress: Psychoanalytic and behavioral studies of surgical patients.* New York: Wiley.

Janis, I. L. (1962). Psychological effects of warnings. In G. W. Baker & D. W. Chapman (Eds.), *Man and society in disaster* (pp. 55–92). New York: Basic Books.

Janis, I. L. (1967). Effects of fear arousal on attitude change: Recent developments in theory and experimental research. *Advances in Experimental Social Psychology, 3,* 166–224.

Janis, I. L. (1968). Attitude change via role playing. In R. Abelson, E. Aronson, W. J. McGuire, et al. (Eds.), *Theories of cognitive consistency: A sourcebook.* Chicago: Rand McNally.

Janis, I. L. (1972). *Victims of groupthink.* Boston: Houghton Mifflin.

Janis, I. L., & Mann, L. (1977). *Decision making.* New York: Free Press.

Janoff-Bulman, R. (1979). Characterological versus behavioral self-blame: Inquiries into depression and rape. *Journal of Personality and Social Psychology, 37,* 1798–1809.

Janoff-Bulman, R., & Brickman, P. (1982). Expectations and what people learn from failure. In N. T. Feather (Ed.), *Expectancy, incentive and action.* Hillsdale, NJ: Erlbaum.

Janoff-Bulman, R., & Timko, C. (1987). Coping with traumatic life events: The role of denial in light of people's assumptive worlds. In C. R. Snyder & C. E. Ford (Eds.), *Coping with negative life events* (pp. 135–159). New York: Plenum.

Jaret, P. (June 1986). The wars within. *National Geographic,* 702–734.

Jemmott, J. B., III, & Locke, S. E. (1984). Psychosocial factors, immunologic mediation, and human susceptibility to infectious diseases: How much do we know? *Psychological Bulletin, 95,* 78–108.

Jennings, J. L. (1986). Husserl revisited: The forgotten distinction between psychology and phenomenology. *American Psychologist, 41,* 12, 1231–1240.

Jessor, R. (1981). The perceived environment in psychological theory and research. In D. Magnusson (Ed.), *Toward a psychology of situations: An interactional perspective* (pp. 297–317). Hillsdale, NJ: Erlbaum.

Johnson-Laird, P. N., & Oatley, K. The language of emotions: An analysis of a semantic field. *Cognition and Emotion, 3,* 81–123.

Jones, E. E., & Thibaut, J. W. (1958). Interaction goals as bases of inference in interpersonal perception. In R. Taguiri & L. Petrullo (Eds.), *Person perception and interpersonal behavior* (pp. 151–178). Palo Alto, CA: Stanford University Press.

Jones, M. C. (1924). A laboratory study of fear: The case of Peter. *Pediatrics Seminar, 31,* 308–315.

Jung, C. G. (1933). *Modern man in search of a soul.* New York: Harcourt, Brace, & World.

Jung, C. G. (1960). Symbol formation. In H. Read, M. Fordham, & G. Adler (Eds.), *The collected works* (Vol. 8, pp. 45–61). (Trans. from the German by R. F. C. Hull.) New York: Pantheon (copyright held by Bollinger Foundation, Inc.).

Jussim, L. (1991). Social perception and social reality: A reflection-construction model. *Psychological Review, 98,* 54–73.

Kagan, J. (1971). *Change and continuity in the first two years.* New York: Wiley.

Kagan, J. (1984). *The nature of the child.* New York: Basic Books.

Kagan, J. (1989). Temperamental contributions to social behavior. *American Psychologist, 44,* 668–674.

Kagan, J., Kearsley, R. B., & Zelazo, P. R. *Infancy: Its place in human development.* Cambridge, MA: Harvard University Press.

Kagan, J., Reznick, J. S., & Snidman, N. (1988). Biological bases of childhood shyness. *Science, 240,* 167–171.

Kagan, J., Reznick, J. S., Snidman, N., Gibbons, J., & Johnson, M. O. (1988). Childhood derivatives of inhibition and lack of inhibition to the unfamiliar. *Child Development, 59,* 1580–1589.

Kahneman, D., Slovic, P., & Tversky, A. (1982). *Judgment under uncertainty: Heuristics and biases.* Cambridge, England: Cambridge University Press.

Kanner, A., Coyne, J. C., Schaefer, C., & Lazarus, R. S. (1981). Comparison of two modes of stress measurement: Daily hassles and uplifts versus major life events. *Journal of Behavioral Medicine, 4,* 1–39.

Kasl, S. V. (1983). Pursuing the link between stressful life experiences and disease: A time for reappraisal. In C. L. Cooper (Ed.), *Stress research* (pp. 79–102). New York: Wiley.

Kasl, S. V., Evans, A. S., & Niederman, J. C. (1979). Psychosocial risk factors in the development of infectious mononucleosis. *Psychosomatic Medicine, 41,* 445–466.

Kaufman, G. (1989). *The psychology of shame: Theory and treatment of shame-based syndromes.* New York: Springer-Verlag.

Keinan, G., Ben-Zur, H., Zilka, M., & Carel, R. S. (unpublished). Anger in or out, which is healthier?: An attempt to reconcile inconsistent findings.

Kelley, H. H. (1971). Attribution in social interaction. In E. E. Jones, D. E. Kanouse, H. H. Kelley, R. E. Nisbett, S. Vailins, & B. Weiner (Eds.), *Attribution: Perceiving the causes of behavior.* New York: General Learning Press.

Kelley, H. H. (1972). *Causal schemata and the attribution process.* Morristown, NJ: General Learning Press.

Kelly, G. A. (1955). *The psychology of personal constructs.* New York: Norton.

Kelman, H. C. (1961). Processes of opinion change. *Public Opinion Quarterly, 25,* 57–58.

Kemper, T. D. (1978). *A social interaction theory of emotions.* New York: Wiley.

Kemper, T. D. (1981). Social constructionist and positivistic approaches to the sociology of emotions. *American Journal of Sociology, 87,* 337–362.

Kemper, T. D. (1987). How many emotions are there? Wedding the social and the autonomic components. *American Journal of Sociology, 93,* 263–289.

Kendall, P. C. (1982). Methodology and cognitive-behavioral assessment. Paper presented to the British Association of Behavioral Psychotherapists, Symposium on Cognition and Behavioral Analysis, University of Sussex, England, July 1982.

Kendall, P. C., & Korgeski, G. P. (1979). Assessment and cognitive-behavioral interventions. *Cognitive Therapy and Research, 3,* 1–21.

Kendler, H. H. (1990). Looking backward to see ahead. *Psychological Science, 1,* 107–112.

Kiecolt-Glaser, J. K., Garner, W., Speicher, C., Penn, G. M., Holliday, J., & Glaser, R. (1984). Psychosocial modifiers of immunocompetence in medical students. *Psychosomatic Medicine, 46,* 15–22.

Kiecolt-Glaser, J. K., & Glaser, R. (1988). Behavioral influences on immune function: Evidence for the interplay between stress and health. In T. Field, P. McCabe, & N. Schneiderman (Eds.), *Stress and coping* (Vol. 2, pp. 189–205). Hillsdale, N. J: Erlbaum.

Kihlstrom, J. F. (1987). The cognitive unconscious. *Science, 237,* 1445–1452.

Klass, E. T. (1981). A cognitive analysis of guilt over assertion. *Cognitive Therapy and Research, 5,* 283–297.

Klein, G. S. (1958). Cognitive control and motivation. In G. Lindzey (Ed.), *Assessment of motives.* New York: Holt, Rinehart and Winston.

Klein, G. S. (1964). Need and regulation. In M. R. Jones (Ed.), *Nebraska Symposium on Motivation.* Lincoln: University of Nebraska Press.

Klein, M. (1957). *Envy and gratitude: A study of unconscious sources.* New York: Basic Books.

Klein, S. B. (1990). In search of the self, review of D. K. Lapsley & E. C. Power (Eds.), (1988), *Self, ego, and identity: Integrative approaches.* New York: Springer-Verlag, *Contemporary Psychology, 35,* 330–331.

Kleiner, J. (1970). On nostalgia. *Bulletin of the Philadelphia Association of Psychoanalysis, 20,* 11–30. Also in Socarides, 1977.

Kleinginna, P. R., Jr., & Kleinginna, A. M. (1985). Cognition and affect: A reply to Lazarus & Zajonc. *American Psychologist, 40,* 470–471.

Kleinman, A. (1988). *The illness narrative: Suffering, healing and the human condition.* New York: Basic Books.

Klinger, E. (1975). Consequences of commitment to and disengagement from incentives. *Psychological Review, 82,* 1–25.

Klos, D. S., & Singer, J. L. (1981). Determinants of the adolescent's ongoing thought following simulated parental confrontations. *Journal of Personality and Social Psychology, 41,* 975–987.

Kobasa, S. C. (1979). Stressful life events, personality, and health: An inquiry into hardiness. *Journal of Personality and Social Psychology, 37,* 1–11.

Koffka, K. (1935). *Principles of gestalt psychology.* New York: Harcourt, Brace.

Kohnstamm, G., Bates, J., & Rothbart, M. (1989). (Eds.), *Temperament in childhood.* New York: Wiley.

Kohut, H. (1971). *The analysis of the self.* New York: International Universities Press.

Kohut, H. (1976). Creativity, charisma, group psychology: Reflections on the self-analysis of Freud. In J. Sedo & G. Pollock (Eds.), *Freud: The fusion of science and humanism. Psychological Issues* (Monograph 34/35). New York: International Universities Press.

Kohut, H. (1977). *The restoration of the self.* New York: International Universities Press.

Kohut, H. (1984). *How does analysis cure?* Chicago: University of Chicago Press.

Koriat, A., Melkman, R., Averill, J. R., & Lazarus, R. S. (1972). The self-control of emotional reactions to a stressful film. *Journal of Personality, 40,* 601–619.

Krantz, S. E. (1983). Cognitive appraisals and problem-directed coping: A prospective study of stress. *Journal of Personality and Social Psychology, 44,* 638–643.

Kreitler, H., & Kreitler, S. (1976). *Cognitive orientation and behavior.* New York: Springer-Verlag.

Kris, E. (1952). *Psychoanalytic explorations in art.* New York: International Universities Press.

Krohne, H. W. (1978). Individual differences in coping with stress and anxiety. In C. D. Spielberger & I. G. Sarason (Eds.), *Stress and anxiety* (Vol. 5, pp. 233–260). Washington, DC: Hemisphere.

Krohne, H. W. (1986). Coping with stress: Dispositions, strategies, and the problem of measurement. In M. H. Appley & R. Trumbull (Eds.), *Dynamics of stress* (pp. 209–234). New York: Plenum.

Krohne, H. W. (1989). The concept of coping modes: Relating cognitive person variables to actual coping behavior. In *Advances in behavioral research and therapy* (Vol. II, pp. 235–248). London: Pergamon.

Krohne, H. W., & Laux, L. (1982). (Eds.). *Achievement, stress, and anxiety.* Washington, DC: Hemisphere.

Krohne, H. W., & Rogner, J. (1982). Repression-sensitization as a central construct in coping research. In H. W. Krohne & L. Laux (Eds.), *Achievement, stress, and anxiety* (pp. 167–194). Washington, DC: Hemisphere.

Kuiper, N. A., & Derry, P. A. (1982). Depressed and nondepressed content self-reference in mild depressives: *Journal of Personality, 50,* 67–79.

Kukla, A. (1989). Nonempirical issues in psychology. *American Psychologist, 44,* 785–794.

Labouvie, E. (1982). Issues in life-span development. In B. Wolman (Ed.), *Handbook of developmental psychology* (pp. 54–62). New York: Academic Press.

Labouvie-Vief, G., DeVoe, M., & Bulka, D. (1989). Speaking about feelings: Conceptions of emotion across the life span. *Psychology and Aging, 4,* 425–437.

Labouvie-Vief, G., Hakim-Larson, J., DeVoe, M., & Schoeberlein, S. (1989). Emotions and self-regulation: A life-span view. *Human Development, 32,* 279–299.

Labouvie-Vief, G., Hakim-Larson, J., & Hobart, C. J. (1987). Age, ego level, and the life-span development of coping and defense processes. *Psychology and Aging, 2,* 286–293.

Lacey, J. I. (1959). Psychophysiological approaches to the evaluation of psychotherapeutic process and outcome. In E. A. Rubenstein & M. B. Parloff (Eds.), *Research in psychotherapy.* Washington, DC: American Psychological Association.

Lacey, J. I. (1967). Somatic response patterning and stress: Some revisions of activation theory in psychological stress. In M. H. Appley & R. Trumbull (Eds.), *Psychological stress* (pp. 14–42). New York: Appleton-Century-Crofts.

Laird, J. D. (1989). Mood affects memory because feelings are cognitions. *Journal of Social Behavior and Personality, 4*, 33–38.

Lakoff, G., & Kovecses, Z. (1983). *The cognitive model of anger inherent in American English.* Unpublished manuscript, Cognitive Science Program, Institute of Human Learning, University of Caliifornia, Berkeley.

Landau, R. J., & Goldfried, M. R. (1981). The assessment of schemata: A unifying framework for cognitive, behavioral, and traditional assessment. In P. C. Kendall & S. D. Hollon (Eds), *Assessment strategies for cognitive-behavioral interventions* (pp. 363–399). New York: Academic Press.

Lang, P. J., Bradley, M. M., & Cuthbert, B. N. (1990). Emotion, attention, and the startle reflex. *Psychological Review, 97*, 377–395.

Langer, S. (1942). *Philosophy in a new key: A study in the symbolism of reason, rite, and art.* Cambridge, MA: Harvard University Press.

Lanzetta, J. T., & Orr, S. P. (1980). Influence of facial expressions on the classical conditioning of fear. *Journal of Personality and Social Psychology, 39*, 1081–1087.

Lanzetta, J. T., & Orr, S. P. (1981). Stimulus properties of facial expressions and their influence on the classical conditioning of fear. *Motivation and Emotion, 5*, 225–234.

Lanzetta, J. T., & Orr, S. P. (1986). Excitatory strength of expressive faces: Effects of happy and fear expressions and context on the extinction of a conditioned fear response. *Journal of Personality and Social Psychology, 50*, 190–194.

Lapsley, D. K., & Power, F. C. (1988). *Self, ego, and identity: Integrative approaches.* New York: Springer-Verlag.

Larrson, G. (1987). Routinization of mental training in organizations: Some effects on performance and well-being. *Journal of Applied Psychology, 72*, 88–96.

Larrson, G. (1989). Personality, appraisal and cognitive coping processes, and performance during various conditions of stress. *Military Psychology, 1*, 167–182.

Larrson, G., Kempe, C., & Starrin, B. (1988). Appraisal and coping processes in acute time-limited stressful situations: A study of police officers. *European Journal of Personality, 2*, 259–276.

Larrson, G., & Starrin, B. (1984). *Decision making in stressful conditions: A model based on the coping paradigm* (Report C 55064–H3). Swedish National Defence Research Institute, Division of the Behavioral Sciences, Stockholm.

Laux, L., & Weber, H. (1991). Presentation of self in coping with anger and anxiety: An intentional approach. *Anxiety Research 3*, 233–255.

Lazarus, A. A. (1971). *Behavior therapy and beyond.* New York: McGraw-Hill.

Lazarus, A. A. (1981). *The practice of multimodal therapy.* New York: McGraw-Hill.

Lazarus, R. S. (1956). Subception: Fact or artifact? A reply to Eriksen. *Psychological Review, 63*, 343–347.

Lazarus, R. S. (1966). *Psychological stress and the coping process.* New York: McGraw-Hill.

Lazarus, R. S. (1968a). Emotions and adaptation: Conceptual and empirical relations. In W. J. Arnold (Ed.), *Nebraska Symposium on Motivation* (pp. 175–266). Lincoln: University of Nebraska Press.

Lazarus, R. S. (1968b). Methodological artifacts in subception research: A reply to Chun and Sarbin. *The Psychological Record, 18*, 435–440.

Lazarus, R. S. (1974). *The riddle of man.* Englewood Cliffs, NJ: Prentice Hall.

Lazarus, R. S. (1981a). The stress and coping paradigm. In C. Eisdorfer, D. Cohen, A. Kleinman, & P. Maxim (Eds.), *Models for clinical psychopathology* (pp. 177–214). New York: Spectrum.

Lazarus, R. S. (1981b). A cognitivist's reply to Zajonc on emotion and cognition. *American Psychologist, 36*, 222–223.

Lazarus, R. S. (1982). Thoughts on the relations between emotion and cognition. *American Psychologist, 37,* 1019–1024.

Lazarus, R. S. (1983). The costs and benefits of denial. In S. Breznitz (Ed.), *The denial of stress* (pp. 1–30). New York: International Universities Press.

Lazarus, R. S. (1984a). On the primacy of cognition. *American Psychologist, 39,* 124–129.

Lazarus, R. S. (1984b). Puzzles in the study of daily hassles. *Journal of Behavioral Medicine, 7,* 375–389.

Lazarus, R. S. (1985). The trivialization of distress. In J. C. Rosen & L. J. Solomon (Eds.), *Preventing health risk behaviors and promoting coping with illness* (Vol. 8, Vermont Conference on the Primary Prevention of Psychopathology, pp. 279–298). Hanover, NH: University Press of New England. Reprinted in B. L. Hammonds & C. J. Scheier (Eds.), *Psychology and health: The Master Lecture Series* (Vol. 3, pp.121–144). Washington, DC: American Psychological Association.

Lazarus, R. S. (1986). Commentary on LeDoux. *Integrative Psychiatry, 4,* 245–247.

Lazarus, R. S. (1989a). Cognition and emotion from the RET viewpoint. In M. E. Bernard & R. DiGiuseppe (Eds.), *Inside rational-emotive therapy* (pp. 47–68). San Diego, CA: Academic Press.

Lazarus, R. S. (1989b). Psychological stress in the workplace. In S. Matsuoka et al. (Eds.), Proceedings of International Conference on Industrial Health, *Journal of UOEH, 11,* 528–540.

Lazarus, R. S. (1989c). Constructs of the mind in health and psychotherapy. In A. Freeman, K. Simon, L. E. Beutler, & H. Arkowitz (Eds.), *Comprehensive handbook of cognitive therapy* (pp. 99–121). New York: Plenum.

Lazarus, R. S. (1990a). Stress, coping and illness. In H. S. Friedman (Ed.), *Personality and disease* (pp. 97–120). New York: Wiley.

Lazarus, R. S. (1990b). Theory-based stress measurement and commentaries. In L. Pervin (Ed.), *Psychological Inquiry, 1,* 3–51.

Lazarus, R. S. (1991a). Cognition and motivation in emotion. *American Psychologist.*

Lazarus, R. S. (1991b). Progress on a cognitive-motivational-relational theory of emotion. *American Psychologist.*

Lazarus, R. S. (1991c). Emotion theory and psychotherapy. In J. D. Safran & L. S. Greenberg (Eds.), *Emotion, psychotherapy, and change.* New York: Guilford.

Lazarus, R. S., & Alfert, E. (1964). The short-circuiting of threat. *Journal of Abnormal and Social Psychology, 69,* 195–205.

Lazarus, R. S., & Averill, J. R. (1972). Emotion and cognition: With special reference to anxiety. In C. D. Spielberger (Ed.), *Anxiety: Current trends in theory and research* (Vol. 2, pp. 242–282). New York: Academic Press.

Lazarus, R. S., Averill, J. R., & Opton, E. M., Jr. (1970). Toward a cognitive theory of emotions. In M. Arnold (Ed.), *Feelings and emotions* (pp. 207–232). New York: Academic Press.

Lazarus, R. S., Coyne, J. C., & Folkman, S. (1982). Cognition, emotion and motivation: The doctoring of Humpty-Dumpty. In R. W. J. Neufeld (Ed.), *Psychological stress and psychopathology* (pp. 218–239). New York: McGraw-Hill.

Lazarus, R. S., Deese, J., & Osler, S. F. (1952). The effects of psychological stress upon performance. *Psychological Bulletin, 49,* 293–317.

Lazarus, R. S., DeLongis, A., Folkman, S., & Gruen, R. (1985). Stress and adaptational outcomes: The problem of confounded measures. *American Psychologist, 40,* 770–779.

Lazarus, R. S., & Eriksen, C. W. (1952). Effects of failure stress upon skilled performance. *Journal of Experimental Psychology, 43,* 100–105.

Lazarus, R. S., & Folkman, S. (1984). *Stress, appraisal and coping.* New York: Springer.

Lazarus, R. S., & Folkman, S. (1986). Cognitive theories and the issue of circularity. In M. H. Appley & R. Trumbull (Eds.), *Dynamics of stress* (pp. 63–80). New York: Plenum.

Lazarus, R. S., & Folkman, S. (1987). Transactional theory and research on emotions and coping. In L. Laux & G. Vossel (Special Eds.), Personality in biographical stress and coping research. *European Journal of Personality, 1,* 141–169.

Lazarus, R. S., Kanner, A. D., & Folkman, S. (1980). Emotions: A cognitive-phenomenological analysis. In R. Plutchik & H. Kellerman (Eds.), *Theories of emotion,* Vol. 1: *Emotion: Theory, research, and experience* (pp. 189–217). New York: Academic Press.

Lazarus, R. S., & Launier, R. (1978). Stress-related transactions between person and environment. In L. A. Pervin & M. Lewis (Eds.), *Perspectives in interactional psychology* (pp. 287–327). New York: Plenum.

Lazarus, R. S., & McCleary, R. A. (1951). Autonomic discrimination without awareness: A study of subception. *Psychological Review, 58,* 113–122.

Lazarus, R. S., & Monat, A. (1979). *Personality* (3rd ed.). Englewood Cliffs, NJ: Prentice Hall.

Lazarus, R. S., & Smith, C. A. (1988). Knowledge and appraisal in the cognition-emotion relationship. *Cognition and Emotion, 2,* 281–300..

Lazarus, R. S., Speisman, J. C., & Mordkoff, A. M. (1963). The relationships between autonomic indicators of psychological stress: Heart rate and skin conductance. *Psychosomatic Medicine, 25,* 19–21.

Lebra, T. S. (1976). *Japanese patterns of behavior.* Honolulu: University Press of Hawaii.

LeDoux, J. E. (1986a). Sensory systems and emotion: A model of affective processing. *Integrative Psychiatry, 4,* 237–248.

LeDoux, J. E. (1986b). Neurobiology of emotion. In J. E. LeDoux & W. Hirst (Eds.), *Mind and brain* (pp. 301–354). New York: Cambridge University Press.

LeDoux, J. E. (1989). Cognitive-emotional interactions in the brain. *Cognition and Emotion, 3,* 267–289.

Leeper, R. W. (1948). A motivational theory of emotion to replace "emotion as a disorganized response." *Psychological Review, 55,* 5–21.

Leeper, R. W. (1965). Some needed developments in the motivational theory of emotions. In D. Levine (Ed.), *Nebraska Symposium on Motivation,* 1965 (pp. 25–122). Lincoln: University of Nebraska Press.

Leeper, R. W. (1970). The motivational and perceptual properties of emotions as indicating their fundamental character and role. In M. B. Arnold (Ed.), *Feelings and emotions: The Loyola Symposium.* New York: Academic Press.

Lehman, D. R., & Taylor, S. E. (1988). Date with an earthquake: Coping with a probable, unpredictable disaster. *Personality and Social Psychology Bulletin, 13,* 546–555.

Lehman, D. R., Wortman, C. B., & Williams, A. F. (1987). Long-term effects of losing a spouse or child in a motor vehicle crash. *Journal of Personality and Social Psychology, 52,* 218–231.

Lehrman, D. S. (1964). The reproductive behavior of ring doves. *Scientific American, 211,* 48–54.

Lerner, J. V., and Lerner, R. M. (1983). Temperament and adaptation across life: Theoretical and empirical issues. In P. B. Baltes & O. Brim (Eds.), *Life-span development and behavior* (Vol. 5, pp.197–231). New York: Academic Press.

Lerner, M. J. (1970). The desire for justice and reactions to victims. In J. McCauley & L. Berkowitz (Eds.), *Altruism and helping behavior.* New York: Academic Press.

Lerner, M. J. (1980). *The belief in a just world: A fundamental delusion.* New York: Plenum.

Lerner, M. J., & Gignac, M. A. M. (in press). Is it coping or is it growth?: A cognitive-affective model of contentment in the elderly. In L. Montada, S.-H. Filipp, & M. J. Lerner (Eds.), *Life crises and experiences of loss in adulthood.* Hillsdale, NJ: Erlbaum.

Leschak, P. M. (1989). Summer storms: Wind, thunder, rain: enlightenment. *Harpers Magazine,* September, pp. 74–76.

Levenson, R. W. (1988). Emotion and the autonomic nervous system: A prospectus for research on autonomic specificity. In H. Wagner (Ed.), *Social psychophysiology and emotion: Theory and clinical applications* (pp.17–42). London: Wiley.

Leventhal, H. (1980). Toward a comprehensive theory of emotion. In L. Berkowitz (Ed.), *Advances in experimental social psychology.* New York: Academic Press.

Leventhal, H. (1984). A perceptual motor theory of emotion. In K. R. Scherer & P. Ekman (Eds.), *Approaches to emotion* (pp. 271–291). Hillsdale, NJ: Erlbaum.

Leventhal, H., & Scherer, K. (1987). The relationship of emotion to cognition: A functional approach to a semantic controversy. *Cognition and Emotion, 1,* 3–28.

Leventhal, H., & Tomarkin, A. J. (1986). Emotion: Today's problems. In M. R. Rosenzweig & L. W. Porter (Eds.), *Annual review of psychology* (pp. 565–610). Palo Alto, CA: Annual Reviews.

Levey, A. B., & Martin, I. (1990). Evaluative conditioning: Overview and further options. *Cognition and Emotion, 4,* 31–37.

Levin, S. (1971). The psychoanalysis of shame. *International Journal of Psycho-analysis, 52,* 355–362. Also in Socarides, 1977.

Levy, R. I. (1973). *Tahitians: Mind and experience in the Society Islands.* Chicago: University of Chicago Press.

Levy, R. I. (1978). Tahitian gentleness and redundant controls. In A. Montague (Ed.), *Learning non-aggression.* New York: Oxford University Press.

Levy, R. I. (1984). Emotion, knowing, and culture. In R. A. Shweder & R. A. LeVine (Eds.), *Culture theory: Essays on mind, self, and emotion.* Cambridge, England: Cambridge University Press.

Lewin, K. A. (1935). *A dynamic theory of personality* (Trans., K. E. Zener & D. K. Adams). New York: McGraw-Hill.

Lewin, K. A. (1951). *Field theory in social science: Selected theoretical papers.* New York: Harper, 1951.

Lewin, K. A., Dembo, T., Festinger, L., & Sears, P. S. (1944). Level of aspiration. In J. McV. Hunt (Ed.), *Personality and the behavior disorders* (Vol. 1, pp. 333–378). New York: Ronald Press.

Lewin, R. (1984). Why is development so illogical? *Science, 224,* 1327–1329.

Lewinsohn, P. M., & Amenson, C. S. (1978). Some relations between pleasant and unpleasant events and depression. *Journal of Abnormal Psychology, 87,* 644–654.

Lewinsohn, P., Mischel, W., Chaplin, W., & Barton, R. (1980). Social competence and depression: The role of illusory self-perceptions. *Journal of Abnormal Psychology, 89,* 203–212.

Lewis, H. B. (1971). *Shame and guilt in neurosis.* New York: International Universities Press.

Lewis, M., Alessandri, S. M., & Sullivan, M. W. (1990). Violation of expectancy, loss of control, and anger expressions in young infants. *Developmental Psychology, 26,* 745–751.

Lewis, M., & Brooks-Gunn, J. (1978). Self-knowledge and emotional development. In M. Lewis & L. Rosenblum (Eds.), *The development of affect.* New York: Plenum.

Lewis, M., & Brooks-Gunn, J. (1979). *Social cognition and the acquisition of self.* New York: Plenum.

Lewis, M., & Michalson, L. (1983). *Children's emotions and moods.* New York: Plenum.

Lewis, M., & Saarni, C. (1985). *The socialization of emotions.* New York: Plenum.

Lewis, M., Sullivan, M. W., Stanger, C., & Weiss, M. (1989). Self-development and self-conscious emotions. *Child Development, 60,* 146–156.

Lewis, V. L., & Williams, R. N. (1989). Mood-congruent vs. mood-state-dependent learning:

Implications for a view of emotion. *Journal of Social Behavior and Personality, 4,* 157–171.

Lieberman, S. (1956). The effects of changes in roles on the attitudes of room occupants. *Human Relations, 9,* 385–402.

Liebert, R. M., & Morris, L. W. (1967). Cognitive and emotional components of test anxiety: A distinction and some initial data. *Psychological Reports, 20,* 975–978.

Linden, W., & Feurstein, M. (1981). Essential hypertension and social coping behavior. *Journal of Human Stress, 7,* 28–34.

Lindsay, R. S. (1975). *Crisis theory: A critical overview.* Nedlands, Australia: University of Western Australia Press.

Lindsay-Hartz, J. (1984). Contrasting experiences of shame and guilt. *American Behavioral Scientist, 27,* 689–704.

Lindsley, D. B. (1951). Emotion. In S. S. Stevens (Ed.), *Handbook of experimental psychology.* New York: Wiley.

Lipowski, Z. J. (1977). Psychosomatic medicine in the seventies: An overview. *American Journal of Psychiatry, 134,* 233–244.

Lobel, M., & Dunkel-Schetter, C. (1990). Conceptualizing stress to study effects on health: Environmental, perceptual, and emotional components. *Anxiety Research, 3,* 213–230.

Locke, E. A., & Taylor, M. S. (1990). Stress, coping, and the meaning of work. In W. Nord & A. Brief (Eds.), *The meaning of work* (pp. 135–170). New York: Heath.

Loevinger, J. (1976). *Ego development: Conceptions and theories.* San Francisco, CA: Jossey-Bass.

Lorenz, K. (1963). *On aggression.* Wien: Dr. G. Borotha-Schoerler Verlag. English translation by K. Lorenz. New York: Harcourt, Brace & World, 1966.

Luborsky, L. (1977). Measuring pervasive psychic structure in psychotherapy: The core conflictual relationship. In N. Freedman & S. Grand (Eds.), *Communicative structures and psychic structures.* New York: Plenum.

Luborsky, L. (1984). *Principles of psychoanalytic psychotherapy.* New York: Basic Books.

Luborsky, L., Blinder, B., & Schimek, J. (1965). Looking, recalling, and the G.S.R. as a function of defense. *Journal of Abnormal Psychology, 70,* 270–280.

Lutz, C., & White, G. M. (1986). The anthropology of emotions. *Annual Review of Anthropology, 15,* 405–436.

Lynch, J. J. (1976). *The broken heart: The medical consequences of loneliness.* New York: Basic Books.

Lynch, P., Bakal, D. A., Whitelaw, W., & Fung, T. (1991). Chest muscle activity and panic anxiety: A preliminary investigation. *Psychosomatic Medicine, 53,* 80–89.

Lynd, H. (1958). *Shame and the search for identity.* New York: Harcourt, Brace.

Lyons, W. (1980). *Emotion.* Cambridge, England: Cambridge University Press.

Macfarlane, J. W., Allen, L., & Honzik, M. P. (1954). *A developmental study of the behavioral problems of children between twenty-one months and fourteen years.* Berkeley: University of California Press.

MacLean, P. D. (1949). Psychosomatic disease and the "visceral brain": Recent developments bearing on Papez's theory of emotion. *Psychosomatic Medicine, 11,* 338–353.

MacLean, P. D. (1975). Sensory and perceptive factors in emotional functions of the triune brain. In L. Levi (Ed.), *Emotions: Their parameters and measurement* (pp. 71–92). New York: Raven.

MacLeod, C., & Mathews, A. (1988). Anxiety and the allocation of attention to threat. *Quarterly Journal of Experimental Psychology, 40A,* 653–670.

MacLeod, C., Mathews, A., & Tata, P. (1986). Attentional bias in emotional disorders. *Journal of Abnormal Psychology, 95,* 15–20.

Mahoney, M. J. (1989). Scientific psychology and radical behaviorism: Important distinctions based on scientism and objectivism. *American Psychologist, 44,* 1372–1377.

Malatesta, C. Z., & Haviland, J. M. (1985). Signals, symbols, and socialization: The modification of emotional expression in human development. In M. Lewis & C. Saarni (Eds.), *The socialization of emotions* (pp. 89–116). New York: Plenum.

Malmo, R. B. (1959). Activation: A neuropsychological dimension. *Psychological Review, 66,* 367–386.

Mandler, G. (1984). *Mind and body: Psychology of emotion and stress.* New York: Norton.

Mandler, G., & Sarason, S. B. (1952). A study of anxiety and learning. *Journal of Abnormal and Social Psychology, 47,* 166–173.

Manstead, A. S. R., & Tetlock, P. E. (1989). Cognitive appraisals and emotional experience: Further evidence. *Cognition and Emotion, 3,* 225–240.

Marceil, J. C. (1977). Implicit dimensions of ideography and nomothesis: A reformulation. *American Psychologist, 32,* 1046–1055.

Marks, I. M. (1969). *Fears and phobias.* London: Heinemann.

Marks, I. M. (1977). Phobias and obsessions: Clinical phenomena in search of a laboratory model. In J. Maser & M. Seligman (Eds.), *Psychopathology: Experimental models* (pp. 174–213). San Francisco, CA: Freeman.

Marks, I. M. (1978). Behavioral psychotherapy of adult neurosis. In S. L. Garfield & A. E. Bergin (Eds.), *Handbook of psychotherapy and behavior change* (2nd ed., pp. 493–547). New York: Wiley.

Markus, H. (1990). On splitting the universe. *Psychological Science, 1,* 181–185.

Marler, P. (1984). Animal communication: Affect or cognition. In K. R. Scherer & P. Ekman (Eds.), *Approaches to emotion* (pp. 345–365). Hillsdale, NJ: Erlbaum.

Marris, P. (1975). *Loss and change.* Garden City, NY: Anchor Books.

Marsella, A. J., DeVos, G., & Hsu, F. (Eds.). (1985). *Culture and self: Asian and Western perspectives.* New York/London: Tavistock Press.

Marsella, A. J., Kinzie, D., & Gordon, P. (1973). Ethnocultural variations in the expression of depression. *Journal of Cross-cultural Psychology, 4,* 435–458.

Marsella, A. J., Murray, M. D., & Golden, C. (1974). Ethnocultural variations in the phenomenology of emotion: I. Shame. *Journal of Cross-cultural Psychology, 5,* 312–328.

Marsella, A. J., & Scheuer, A. (1988). Coping across cultures. In P. Dasen, J. Berry, & N. Sartorius (Eds.), *Health and cross-cultural psychology.* Beverly Hills, CA: Sage.

Marsella, A. J., Tharp, R., & Ciborowski, T. (Eds.). (1979). *Perspectives on cross-cultural psychology.* New York: Academic Press.

Marshall, G., & Zimbardo, P. S. (1979). Affective consequences of inadequately explained physiological arousal. *Journal of Personality and Social Psychology, 37,* 970–988.

Martin, B. (1961). The assessment of anxiety by physiological behavioral measures. *Psychological Bulletin, 58,* 234–255.

Maslach, C. (1979). Negative emotional biasing of unexplained arousal. *Journal of Personality and Social Psychology, 37,* 953–969.

Maslach, C. (1982). *Burnout: The cost of caring.* Englewood Cliffs, NJ: Prentice Hall.

Maslach, C., Santee, R. T., & Wade, C. (1987). Individuation, gender role, and dissent: Personality mediators of situational forces. *Journal of Personality and Social Psychology, 53,* 1088–1093.

Maslach, C., Stapp, J., & Santee, R. T. (1985). Individuation: Conceptual analysis and assessment. *Journal of Personality and Social Psychology, 49,* 729–738.

Maslow, A. H. (1971). *The farther reaches of human nature.* New York: Viking.

Mason, J. W. (1971). A re-evaluation of the concept of "non-specificity" in stress theory. *Journal of Psychiatric Research, 8,* 323–333.

Mason, J. W. (1975). Emotion as reflected in patterns of endocrine integration. In L. Levi (Ed.), *Emotions: Their parameters and measurement* (pp. 143–181). New York: Raven.

Mason, J. W., Maher, J. T., Hartley, L. H., Mougey, E., Perlow, M. J., & Jones, L. G. (1976). Selectivity of corticosteroid and catecholamine response to various natural stimuli. In G. Serban (Ed.), *Psychopathology of human adaptation* (pp. 147–171). New York: Plenum.

Masserman, J. H. (1946). *Principles of dynamic psychiatry, including an integrative approach to abnormal and clinical psychology.* Philadelphia: Saunders.

Matarazzo, J. D. (1980). Behavioral health and behavioral medicine: Frontiers for a new health psychology. *American Psychologist, 35,* 807–817.

Mathes, E. W., Adams, H. E., & Davies, R. M. (1985). Jealousy: Loss of relationship rewards, loss of self-esteem, depression, anxiety, and anger. *Journal of Personality and Social Psychology, 48,* 1552–1561.

Mathews, A., & MacLeod, C. (1985). Selective processing of threat cues in anxiety states. *Behavior Research and Therapy, 23,* 563–569.

Mathews, A., & MacLeod, C. (1986). Discrimination of threat cues without awareness in anxiety states. *Journal of Abnormal Psychology, 95,* 131–138.

Mathews, A., May, J., Mogg, K., & Eysenck, M. (1990). Attentional bias in anxiety: Selective search or defective filtering? *Journal of Abnormal Psychology, 99,* 166–173.

Mathews, A., Mogg, K., May, J., & Eysenck, M. (1989). Implicit and explicit memory in anxiety. *Journal of Abnormal Psychology, 98,* 236–240.

Matsumoto, D. (1987). The role of facial response in the experience of emotion: More methodological problems and a meta-analysis. *Journal of Personality and Social Psychology, 52,* 769–774.

May, R. (1950). *The meaning of anxiety.* New York: Ronald.

May, R., Angel, E., & Ellenberger, H. F. (1958). (Eds.), *Existence: A new dimension in psychiatry and psychology.* New York: Basic Books.

Mayer, J. D., Saloney, P., Gomberg-Kaufman, S., & Blainey, K. (1991). *Journal of Personality and Social Psychology, 60,* 100–111.

McClelland, D. C. (1951). *Personality.* New York: Sloane.

McClelland, D. C. (1985a). How motives, skills, and values determine what people do. *American Psychologist, 40,* 812–823.

McClelland, D. C. (1985b). *Human motivation.* Glenview, IL: Scott, Foresman.

McClelland, D. C., Atkinson, J. W., Clark, R. A., & Lowell, E. L. (1953). *The achievement motive.* New York: Appleton-Century-Crofts.

McClelland, D. C., Koestner, R., & Weinberger, J. (1989). How do self-attributed and implicit motives differ? *Psychological Review, 96,* 690–702.

McCord, W., & McCord, J. (1956). *Psychopathy and delinquency.* New York: Grune & Stratton.

McCord, W., & McCord, J. (1958). The effects of parental role model on criminality. *Journal of Social Issues, 14,* 66–75.

McGinnies, E. (1949). Emotionality and perceptual defense. *Psychological Review, 56,* 244–251.

McGraw, K. M. (1987). Guilt following transgression: An attribution of responsibility approach. *Journal of Personality and Social Psychology, 53,* 247–256.

McGuire, W. J. (1983). A contextualist theory of knowledge: Its implications for innovation and reform in psychological research. In L. Berkowitz (Ed.), *Advances in experimental social psychology* (Vol. 16, pp. 1–47). New York: Academic Press.

McNally, R. J. (1990). Psychological approaches to panic disorder: A review. *Psychological Bulletin, 108,* 403–419

Mechanic, D. (1963). Religion, religiosity, and illness behavior: The special case of the Jews. *Human Organization, 22,* 202–208.

Mechanic, D. (1962/1978). *Medical sociology* (2nd ed.). New York: Free Press.

Mechanic, D. (1983). *Handbook of health, health care, and the health professions.* New York: Free Press.

Meichenbaum, D. (1975). Self-instructional methods. In F. Kanfer & A. Goldstein (Eds.), *Helping people change.* New York: Pergamon.

Meichenbaum, D. (1977). *Cognitive-behavior modification: An integrative approach.* New York: Plenum.

Meichenbaum, D., & Cameron, R. (1983). Stress inoculation training: Toward a general paradigm for training coping skills. In D. Meichenbaum & M. E. Jaremko (Eds.), *Stress reduction and prevention* (pp. 115–154). New York: Plenum.

Melzack, R. (1961). The perception of pain. *Scientific American, 204,* 41–49.

Mendoza, S. P., & Mason, W. A. (1989). Primate relationships: Social dispositions and physiological responses. In P. K. Seth & S. Seth (Eds.), *Perspectives in primate biology* (Vol. 2, pp. 129–143). New Delhi: Today & Tomorrow's Printers and Publishers.

Merleau-Ponty, M. (1962). *Phenomenology of perception* (C. Smith, Trans.). London: Routledge & Kegan Paul.

Merleau-Ponty, M. (1968). *The visible and the invisible* (A. Lingis, Trans.). Evanston, IL: Northwestern University Press.

Messer, S., & Winokur, M. (1980). Some limits to the integration of psychoanalytic and behavior therapy. *American Psychologist, 35,* 818–827.

Messer, S., & Winokur, M. (1984). Ways of knowing and visions of reality in psychoanalytic therapy and behavior therapy. In H. Arkowitz & S. Messer (Eds.), *Psychoanalytic therapy and behavior therapy: Is integration possible?* (pp. 63–100). New York: Plenum.

Meyer, M. F. (1933). That whale among the fishes — the theory of emotions. *Psychological Review, 40,* 292–300.

Meyer, W-U. (1988). Die Rolle von Überraschung im Attributionsprozess. [The role of surprise in the process of causal attribution]. *Psychologische Redschau, 39,* 136–147.

Meyer, W-U. (in press). Paradoxical effects of praise and blame on perceived ability and affect. In W. Stoege & M. Hewstone (Eds.), *European Review of Social Psychology, 3.* Chichester: Wiley.

Meyer, W.-U, Niepel, M., Rudolph, U., & Schützwohl, A. (in press). An experimental analysis of surprise. *Cognition and Emotion.*

Michalson, L., & Lewis, M. (1985). What do children know about emotions and when do they know it? In M. Lewis & C. Saarni (Eds.), *The socialization of emotions* (pp. 117–139). New York: Plenum.

Middleton, D. R. (1989). Emotional style: The cultural ordering of emotions. *Ethos, 17,* 187–201.

Milgram, S. (1963). Behavioral study of obedience. *Journal of Abnormal and Social Psychology, 67,* 371–378.

Milgram, S. (1965). Some conditions of obedience and disobedience to authority. *Human Relations, 18,* 57–75.

Miller, A. G. (1986). *The obedience experiments: A case study of controversy in social science.* New York: Praeger.

Miller, D. R., & Swanson, G. E. (1960). *Inner conflict and defense.* New York: Holt, Rinehart and Winston.

Miller, G. A. (1953). What is information measurement? *American Psychologist, 8,* 3–11.

Miller, G. A., Galanter, E., & Pribram, K. (1960). *Plans and the structure of behavior.* New York: Holt.

Miller, N. E. (1944). Experimental studies of conflict. In J. McV. Hunt (Ed.), *Personality and the behavior disorders* (Vol. 1, pp. 431–465). New York: Ronald.

Miller, S. M. (1980). When is a little information a dangerous thing? Coping with stressful events by monitoring vs. blunting. In S. Levine & H. Ursin (Eds.), *Coping and health* (pp. 145–169). New York: Plenum.

Mineka, S. (1985). Animal models of anxiety-based disorders: Their usefulness and limitations. In A. Tuma & J. Maser (Eds.), *Anxiety and the anxiety disorders* (pp. 199–244). Hillsdale, NJ: Erlbaum.

Mineka, S. (1987). A primate model of phobic fears. In H. Eysenck & I. Martin (Eds.), *Theoretical foundations of behavior therapy* (pp. 81–111). New York: Plenum.

Mineka, S., Davidson, M., Cook, M., & Keir, R. (1984). Observational conditioning of snake fear in rhesus monkeys. *Journal of Abnormal Psychology, 93,* 355–372.

Mirowsky, J., & Ross, C. E. (1990). Control or defense? Depression and the sense of control over good and bad outcomes. *Journal of Health and Social Behavior, 31,* 71–86.

Miyake, K., Campos, J. J., Kagan, J., & Bradshaw, D. L. (1986). Issues in socioemotional development. In H. Stevenson, H. Azuma, & K. Hakuta (Eds.), *Child development and education in Japan.* New York: H. Freeman.

Monat, A., Averill, J. R., & Lazarus, R. S. (1973). Anticipatory stress and coping under various conditions of uncertainty. *Journal of Personality and Social Psychology, 24,* 237–253.

Moore, B., Underwood, B., & Rosenhan, D. L. (1984). Emotion, self, and others. In C. Izard, J. Kagan, & R. Zajonc (Eds.), *Emotions, cognition and behavior* (pp. 464–483). Cambridge, England: Cambridge University Press.

Moos, R. H. (1973). Conceptualizations of human environments. *American Psychologist, 28,* 652–665.

Moos, R. H. (1975). Assessment and impact of social climate. In P. McReynolds (Ed.), *Advances in psychological assessment* (Vol. 3). San Francisco, CA: Jossey-Bass.

Moos, R. H., & Billings, A. (1982). Conceptualizing and measuring coping resources and processes. In J. Goldberger & S. Breznitz (Eds.), *Handbook of stress: Theoretical and clinical aspects* (pp. 212–230). New York: Macmillan.

Mowrer, O. H. (1976). From the dynamics of conscience to contract psychology: Clinical theory and practice in transition. In G. Serban (Ed.), *Psychopathology of human adaptation* (pp. 211–230). New York: Plenum.

Moyer, K. E. (1968). Kinds of aggression and their physiological basis. *Communications in Behavioral Biology, 2,* 64–87.

Moyer, K. E. (1976). *The psychobiology of aggression.* New York: Harper.

Moyer, K. E. (1986). Biological bases of aggressive behavior. In R. Plutchik & H. Kellerman (Eds.), *Emotion: Theory, research, and experience* (Vol. 3, pp. 219–236). New York: Academic Press.

Murphy, G. (1947/1966). *Personality: A biosocial approach to origins and structure.* New York: Basic Books.

Murphy, L. B. (1974). Coping, vulnerability, and resilience in childhood. In G. V. Coelho, D. A. Hamburg, & J. E. Adams (Eds.), *Coping and adaptation* (pp. 69–100). New York: Basic Books.

Murphy, L. B., & Associates. (1962). *The widening world of childhood: Paths toward mastery.* New York: Basic Books.

Murphy, L. B., & Moriarty, A. E. (1976). *Vulnerability, coping and growth: From infancy to adolescence.* New Haven, CT: Yale University Press.

Murray, H. A. (1938). *Explorations in personality.* New York: Oxford University Press.

Neiss, R. (1988). Reconceptualizing arousal: Psychobiological states in motor performance. *Psychological Bulletin, 103,* 345–366.

Neisser, U. (1967). *Cognitive psychology.* New York: Appleton-Century-Crofts.

Neisser, U. (1985). The role of invariant structures in the control of movement. In M. Frese & J. Sabini (Eds.), *Goal directed behavior: The concept of action in psychology* (pp. 97–108). Hillsdale, NJ: Erlbaum.

Neisser, U. (1990). Gibson's revolution. *Contemporary Psychology, 35,* 749–750.

Neu, J. (1980). Jealous thoughts. In A. O. Rorty (Ed.), *Explaining emotions* (pp. 425–463). Berkeley: University of California Press.

Neufeld, R.W. J. (1975). Effect of cognitive appraisal on d' and response bias to experimental stress. *Journal of Personality and Social Psychology, 31,* 735–743.

Neufeld, R. W. J. (1976). Evidence of stress as a function of experimentally altered appraisal of stimulus aversiveness and coping adequacy. *Journal of Personality and Social Psychology, 33,* 632–646.

Newcomb, T. R. (1943). *Personality and social change.* New York: Dryden.

Newcomb, T. R., Koenig, K. E., Flacks, R., & Warwick, D. P. (1967). *Persistence and change: Bennington College and its students after twenty-five years.* New York: Wiley.

Niepel, M., Rudolph, U., Schütwohl, A., & Meyer, W.-U. (in press). Two characteristics of surprise: Action delay and involuntary attentional focus. In H. Keller & K. Schneider (Eds.), *Curiosity and exploration: Theoretical perspectives, research fields, and applications.* New York: Springer.

Nisbett, R., & Ross, L. (1980). *Human inference: Strategies and shortcomings of social judgment.* Englewood Cliffs, NJ: Prentice Hall.

Nisbett, R. E., & Valins, S. (1972). Perceiving the causes of one's own behavior. In E. E. Jones, D. E. Kanouse, H. H. Kelley, R. E. Nisbett, S. Valins, & B. Weiner (Eds.), *Attribution: Perceiving the causes of behavior* (pp.63–78). Morristown, NJ: General Learning Press.

Nomikos, M. S., Opton, E. M., Jr., Averill, J. R., & Lazarus, R. S. (1968). Surprise versus suspense in the production of stress reaction. *Journal of Personality and Social Psychology, 8,* 204–208.

Norman, D. A. (1980). Twelve issues for cognitive science. In D. A. Norman (Ed.), *Perspectives on cognitive science: Talks from the La Jolla Conference.* Hillsdale, NJ: Erlbaum.

Novacek, J., & Lazarus, R. S. (1990). The structure of personal commitments. *Journal of Personality, 58,* 693–715.

Novaco, R. W. (1979). The cognitive regulation of anger and stress. In P. C. Kendall & S. D. Hollon (Eds.), *Cognitive-behavioral interventions: Theory, research, and procedures* (pp. 241–285). New York: Academic Press.

Oatley, K. (1988). Gaps in consciousness: Emotions and memory in psychoanalysis. *Cognition and Emotion, 2,* 3–18.

Offutt, C., & Lacroix, J. M. (1988). Type A behavior pattern and symptom reports: A prospective investigation. *Journal of Behavioral Medicine, 11,* 227–237.

Ohbuchi, K., & Kambara, T. (1985). Attacker's intent and awareness of outcome, impression management, and retaliation. *Journal of Experimental Social Psychology, 21,* 321–330.

Ohbuchi, K., Kameda, M., & Agarie, N. (1989). Apology as aggression control: Its role in mediating appraisal of and response to harm. *Journal of Personality and Social Psychology, 56,* 219–227.

Opton, E. M., Jr., & Lazarus, R. S. (1967). Personality determinants of psychophysiological response to stress: A theoretical analysis of an experiment. *Journal of Personality and Social Psychology, 6,* 291–303.

Opton, E. M., Jr., Rankin, N., Nomikos, M., & Lazarus, R. S. (1965). The principle of short-circuiting of threat: Further evidence. *Journal of Personality, 33,* 622–635.

Orr, S. P., & Lanzetta, J. T. (1980). Facial expressions of emotion as conditioned stimuli for human autonomic responses. *Journal of Personality and Social Psychology, 38,* 278–282.

Orr, S. P., & Lanzetta, J. T. (1984). Extinction of an emotional response in the presence of facial expressions of emotion. *Motivation and Emotion, 8,* 55–66.

Orr, E., & Westman, M. (1990). Does hardiness moderate stress, and how?: A review. In M. Rosenbaum (Ed.), *Learned resourcefulness: On coping skills, self-control, and adaptive behavior* (pp. 64–94). New York: Springer.

Ortony, A., & Clore, G. L. (1981). Disentangling the affective lexicon. In *Proceedings of the Third Annual Conference of the Cognitive Science Society,* Berkeley, CA.

Ortony, A., & Clore, G. L. (1989). Emotions, moods, and conscious awareness: Comment on Johnson-Laird and Oatley's "The language of emotions: An analysis of a semantic field." *Cognition and Emotion, 3,* 125–137.

Ortony, A., Clore, G. L., & Collins, A. (1988). *The cognitive structure of emotions.* Cambridge, England: Cambridge University Press.

Ortony, A., Clore, G. L., & Foss, M. A. (1987). The referential structure of the affective lexicon. *Cognitive Science, 11,* 341–364.

Ortony, A., & Turner, T. J. (1990). What's basic about basic emotions? *Psychological Review, 97,* 315–331.

Osgood, C. E. (1966). Dimensionality of the semantic space for communication via facial expressions. *Scandinavian Journal of Psychology, 7,* 1–30.

Osgood, C. E., Suci, G. J., & Tannenbaum, P. H. (1957). *The measurement of meaning.* Urbana: University of Illinois Press.

Overmeier, J. B., & Seligman, M. E. P. (1967). Effects of inescapable shock upon subsequent escape and avoidance responding. *Journal of Comparative and Physiological Psychology, 63,* 28.

Owens, J., Bower, G. H., & Black, J. B. (1979). The soap opera effect in story recall. *Memory and Cognition, 7,* 185–191.

Palys, T.S., & Little, B. R. (1983). Perceived life satisfaction and the organization of personal project systems. *Journal of Personality and Social Psychology, 44,* 1221–1230.

Panksepp, J. (1982). Toward a general psychobiological theory of emotions. With commentaries. *The Behavioral and Brain Sciences, 5,* 407–467.

Panksepp, J. (1986). The anatomy of emotions. In R. Plutchik & H. Kellerman (Eds.), *Emotion: Theory, research, and experience* (Vol. 3, pp. 91–124). New York: Academic Press.

Panksepp, J. (1990). Psychology's search for identity: Can "mind" and behavior be understood without understanding the brain?: A response to Bunge. *New Ideas in Psychology, 8,* 139–149.

Pao, P.-N. (1969). Pathological jealousy. *Psychoanalytic Quarterly, 38,* 616–638. Also in Socarides, 1977.

Papanicolaou, A. C. (1989). *Emotion: A reconsideration of somatic theory.* New York: Gordon & Breach.

Papousek, H., & Papousek, M. (1974). Mirror-image and self-recognition in young human infants: A new method of experimental analysis. *Developmental Psychobiology, 7,* 149–157.

Parducci, A. (1968). The relativism of absolute judgements. *Scientific American, 219,* 84–90.

Parisi, T. (1987). Why Freud failed: Some implications for neurophysiology and sociobiology. *American Psychologist, 42,* 235–245.

Parkes, C. M. (1973). Separation anxiety: An aspect of the search for a lost object. In R. S. Weiss (Ed.), *Loneliness: The experience of emotional and social isolation* (pp. 53–67). Cambridge, MA: MIT Press.

Parkes, K. R. (1989). Personal control in an occupational context. In A. Steptoe & A. Appels (Eds.), *Stress, personal control and health.* London: Wiley.

Parrott, W. G., & Gleitman, H. (1989). Infants' expectations in play: The joy of peek-a-boo. *Cognition and Emotion, 3,* 291–311.

Parrott, W. G., & Sabini, J. (1990). Mood and memory under natural conditions: Evidence for mood incongruent recall. *Journal of Personality and Social Psychology, 59,* 321–336.

Pastore, N. (1952). The role of arbitrariness in the frustration-aggression hypothesis. *Journal of Abnormal and Social Psychology, 47,* 728–731.

Patterson, R. J., & Neufeld, W. J. (1987). Clear danger: Situational determinants of the appraisal of threat. *Psychological Bulletin, 101,* 404–416.

Payls, T. S., & Little, B. R. (1983). Perceived life satisfaction and the organization of personal projects systems. *Journal of Personality and Social Psychology, 44,* 1221–1230.

Pearlin, L. I., Lieberman, M. A., Menaghan, E. G., & Mullan, J. T. (1981). The stress process. *Journal of Health and Social Behavior, 22,* 337–356.

Pearlin, L. I., & Schooler, C. (1978). The structure of coping. *Journal of Health and Social Behavior, 19,* 2–21.

Pelletier, K. R. (1977). *Mind as healer, mind as slayer.* New York: Dell.

Pelletier, K. R., & Lutz, R. (1988). Healthy people — healthy business: A critical review of stress management programs in the workplace. *American Journal of Health Promotion, 2,* 5–19.

Pennebaker, J. W. (1989). Confession, inhibition, and disease. In L. Berkowitz (Ed.), *Advances in experimental social psychology* (Vol. 22, pp. 211–244). Orlando, FL: Academic Press.

Pennebaker, J. W., & Beall, S. K. (1986). Confronting a traumatic event: Toward an understanding of inhibition and disease. *Journal of Abnormal Psychology, 95,* 274–281.

Pennebaker, J. W., Colder, M., & Sharp, L. K. (1990). Accelerating the coping process. *Journal of Personality and Social Psychology, 58,* 528–537.

Pennebaker, J. W., Hughes, C., & O'Heeron, R. C. (1987). The psychophysiology of confession: Linking inhibitory and psychosomatic processes. *Journal of Personality and Social Psychology, 52,* 781–793.

Pennebaker, J. W., Kiecolt-Glaser, J. K., & Glaser, R. (1988). Disclosure of traumas and immune function: Health implications for psychotherapy. *Journal of Consulting and Clinical Psychology, 56,* 239–245.

Pennebaker, J. W., & Susman, J. R. (1988). Disclosure of traumas and psychosomatic processes. *Social Science and Medicine, 26,* 327–332.

Pepper, S. C. (1942). *World hypotheses.* Berkeley: University of California Press.

Perrez, M., & Reicherts, M. (in preparation). *Stress, appraisal, and coping: A situation-behavior approach — Theory, methods, results.*

Pervin, L. A. (1983). The stasis and flow of behavior: Toward a theory of goals. *Nebraska Symposium on Motivation, 1982.* Lincoln: University of Nebraska Press.

Pervin, L. A. (1986). Ideographic and nomothetic aspects of affect. In L. Van Langenhove, J. M. De Waele, & R. Harre (Eds.), *Individual persons and their actions: Essays in honor of J. P. De Waele.* Brussels, Belgium: Free University of Brussels.

Peterson, C., Seligman, M. E. P., & Vaillant, G. E. (1988). Pessimistic explanatory style is a risk factor for physical illness: A thirty-five-year longitudinal study. *Journal of Personality and Social Psychology, 55,* 23–27.

Peterson, C., Semmel, A., von Baeyer, C., Abramson, L. Y., Metalsky, G. I., & Seligman, M. E. P. (1982). The Attributional Style Questionnaire. *Cognitive Therapy & Research, 6,* 287–299.

Phillips, D. C., & Orton, R. (1983). The new causal principle of cognitive learning theory: Perspectives on Bandura's "reciprocal determinism." *Psychological Review, 90,* 158–165.

Piaget, J. (1952). *The origins of intelligence in children.* New York: International Universities Press.

Piaget, J. (1976). *The grasp of consciousness: Action and concept in the young child.* Cambridge, MA: Harvard University Press.

Piaget, J. (1980). *Experiments in contradiction.* Chicago: University of Chicago Press.

Plomin, R., Pedersen, N. L., McClearn, G. E., Nesselroade, J. R., & Bergeman, C. S. (1988). EAS temperaments during the last half of the life span: Twins reared apart and twins reared together. *Psychology and Aging, 3,* 43–50.

Plomin, R., & Rowe, D. C. (1979). Genetic and environmental etiology of social behavior in infancy. *Developmental Psychology, 15,* 62–72.

Plutchik, R. (1962). *The emotions: Facts, theories, and a new model.* New York: Random House.

Plutchik, R. (1980). *Emotion: A psychoevolutionary synthesis.* New York: Harper & Row.

Plutchik, R., & Kellerman, H. (1980, 1983, 1986, 1989). (Eds.), *Emotion: Theory, research, and experience* (Vols. 1–4). New York: Academic Press.

Polanyi, M. (1966). *The tacit dimension.* Garden City, NY: Doubleday.

Polivy, J. (1981). On the induction of emotion in the laboratory: Discrete moods or multiple affect states. *Journal of Personality and Social Psychology, 41,* 803–817.

Pollak, L. H., & Thoits, P. A. (1989). Processes in emotional socialization. *Social Psychology Quarterly, 52,* 22–34.

Rachman, S. J. (1976). The passing of the two-stage theory of fear and avoidance: Fresh possibilities. *Behavior Research and Therapy, 14,* 126–131.

Rachman, S. J. (1978). *Fear and courage.* San Francisco, CA: Freeman, 1978.

Rachman, S. J., & Hodgson, R. J. (1974). Synchrony and desynchrony in fear and avoidance. *Behavior Research and Therapy, 12,* 311–318.

Rachman, S. J., & Hodgson, R. J. (1980). *Obsessions and compulsions.* Englewood Cliffs, NJ: Prentice Hall.

Raskin, V. (1985). Jokes: A linguist explains his new semantic theory of humor. *Psychology Today,* October, pp. 34–39.

Reisenzein, R. (1983). The Schachter theory of emotion: Two decades later. *Psychological Bulletin, 94,* 239–264.

Reiss, I. L. (1990). *An end to shame: Shaping our next sexual revolution.* Buffalo, NY: Prometheus.

Repetti, R. L. (1987). Individual and common components of the social environment at work and psychological well-being. *Journal of Personality and Social Psychology, 52,* 710–720.

Rescorla, R. A. (1988). Pavlovian conditioning: It's not what you think it is. *American Psychologist, 43,* 151–160.

Revelle, W., & Loftus, D. A. (1990). Individual differences and arousal: Implications for the study of mood and memory. *Cognition and Emotion, 4,* 209–237.

Rholes, W. S., Riskind, J. H., & Lane, J. W. (1987). Emotional states and memory biases: Effects of cognitive priming and mood. *Journal of Personality and Social Psychology, 52,* 91–99.

Riegel, K. F. (1975). Adult life crises: Toward a dialectic theory of development. In N. Datan & L. H. Ginsberg (Eds.), *Life-span developmental psychology: Normal life crises* (pp. 97–124). New York: Academic Press.

Riesman, D. (1950). *The lonely crowd.* New York: Doubleday.

Robertson, G. C. (1877). Notes. *Mind: A Quarterly Review, 2,* 413–415.

Rodin, J. (1980). Managing the stress of aging: The role of control and coping. In S. Levine & and H. Ursin (Eds.), *Coping and health* (pp. 171–202). New York: Plenum.

Rodin, J., & Salovey, P. (1989). Health psychology. *Annual Review of Psychology, 40,* 533–579.

Rohrkemper, M., & Corno, I. (1988). Success and failure on classroom tasks: Adaptive learning and classroom teaching. *The Elementary School Journal, 88,* 297–312.

Rokeach, M. (Ed.). (1960). *The open and the closed mind.* New York: Basic Books.

Rorty, A. O. (1980a). (Ed.), *Explaining emotions.* Berkeley: University of California Press.

Rorty, A. O. (1980b). Agent regret. In A. O. Rorty (Ed.), *Explaining emotions* (pp. 489–506). Berkeley: University of California Press.

Rosaldo, M. Z. (1980). *Knowledge and passion: Ilongot notions of self and social life.* Cambridge, England: Cambridge University Press.

Rosaldo, M. Z. (1983). The shame of headhunters and the autonomy of the self. *Ethos, 11,* 135–151.

Rosch, E. (1978). Principles of categorization. In E. Rosch & B. B. Lloyd (Eds.), *Cognition and categorization* (pp. 27–71). Hillsdale, NJ: Erlbaum.

Roseman, I. (1984). Cognitive determinants of emotion: A structural theory. In P. Shaver (Ed.), *Review of personality and social psychology: Vol. 5. Emotions, relationships, and health* (pp. 11–36). Beverly Hills, CA: Sage.

Rosenbaum, M. (1980). A schedule for assessing self-control behaviors: Preliminary findings. *Behavior Therapy, 11,* 109–121.

Rosenbaum, M. (1990). *Learned resourcefulness: On coping skills, self-control, and adaptive behavior.* New York: Springer.

Rosenberg, A., & Kagan, J. (1987). Iris pigmentation and behavioral inhibition. *Developmental Psychobiology, 20,* 377–392.

Rosenberg, M. (1965). *Society and the adolescent self-image.* Princeton, NJ: Princeton University Press.

Roskies, E. (1983). Stress management: Averting the evil eye. *Contemporary Psychology, 28,* 542–544.

Ross, L. (1977). The intuitive psychologist and his shortcomings: Distortions in the attribution process. In L. Berkowitz (Ed.), *Advances in experimental social psychology* (Vol. 10, pp. 173–220). New York: Academic Press.

Rotter, J. B. (1954). *Social learning and clinical psychology.* Englewood Cliffs, NJ: Prentice Hall.

Rotter, J. B. (1966). Generalized expectancies for internal versus external control of reinforcement. *Psychological Monographs: General and Applied, 80* (Whole No. 609).

Rotter, J. B. (1975). Some problems and misconceptions related to the construct of internal versus external control of reinforcement. *Journal of Consulting and Clinical Psychology, 43,* 56–67.

Rowlison, R. T., & Felner, R. D. (1988). Major life events, hassles, and adaptation in adolescence: Confounding in the conceptualization and measurement of life stress and adjustment revisited. *Journal of Personality and Social Psychology, 55,* 432–444.

Rozin, P., & Fallon, A. E. (1987). A perspective on disgust. *Psychological Review, 94,* 23–41.

Russell, J. A. (1980). A circumplex model of affect. *Journal of Personality and Social Psychology, 39,* 1161–1178.

Russell, J. A. (1987). Comments on articles by Frijda and by Conway & Bekerian. *Cognition and Emotion, 1,* 193–197.

Russell, J. A., Lewicka, M., & Niit, T. (1989). A cross-cultural study of a circumplex model of affect. *Journal of Personality and Social Psychology, 57,* 848–856.

Russell, J. A. & Mehrabian, A. (1977). Evidence for a three-factor theory of emotions. *Journal of Research in Personality, 11,* 273–294.

Rutter, M. (1979). Protective factors in children's responses to stress and disadvantage. In M. W. Kent & J. E. Rolf (Eds.), *Social competence in children* (pp. 49–74). Hanover, NH: University Press of New England.

Rychlak, J. E. (1981a). Freud's confrontation with the telic mind. *Journal of the History of the Behavioral Sciences, 17,* 176–183.

Rychlak, J. E. (1981b). *Introduction to personality and psychotherapy.* Boston: Houghton Mifflin.

Ryff, C. D. (1987). The place of personality and social structure research in social psychology. *Journal of Personality and Social Psychology, 53,* 1192–1202.

Ryle, G. (1949). *The concept of mind.* New York: Barnes & Noble.

Sachs, O. (1987). *The man who mistook his wife for a hat.* New York: Harper & Row.

Safran, J. D., & Greenberg, L. S. (1991). *Emotion, psychotherapy, and change.* New York: Guilford.

Salovey, P. (Ed.). (1990). *The psychology of jealousy and envy*. New York: Guilford.

Salovey, P., & Rodin, J. (1986). The differentiation of social-comparison jealousy and romantic jealousy. *Journal of Personality and Social Psychology, 50,* 1100–1112.

Sampson, E. E. (1983). *Justice and the critique of pure psychology*. New York: Plenum.

Sampson, E. E. (1985). The decentralization of identity: Towards a revised concept of personal and social order. *American Psychologist, 40,* 1203–1211.

Sampson, E. E. (1988). The debate on individualism: Indigenous psychologies of the individual and their role in personal and societal functioning. *American Psychologist, 43,* 15–22.

Sampson, H., Weiss, J., Mlodnosky, L., & Hause, E. (1972). Defense analysis and the emergence of warded-off mental contents. *Archives of General Psychiatry, 26,* 524–531.

Sandler, J., & Joffe, W. G. (1969). Towards a basic psychoanalytic model. *International Journal of Psychoanalysis, 50,* 79–90.

Sappington, A. A. (1990). Recent psychological approaches to the free will versus determinism issue. *Psychological Bulletin, 108,* 19–29.

Sarason, I. G. (1960). Empirical findings and theoretical problems in the use of anxiety scales. *Psychological Bulletin, 57,* 403–415.

Sarason, I. G. (1972). Experimental approaches to test anxiety: Attention and the uses of information. In C. D. Spielberger (Ed.), *Anxiety: Current trends in theory and research* (Vol. 2, pp. 383–408). New York: Academic Press.

Sarason, S. B., Mandler, G., & Craighill, P. C. (1952). The effect of differential instructions on anxiety and learning. *Journal of Abnormal and Social Psychology, 47,* 561–565.

Sarbin, T. R. (1982). Contextualism: A world view for modern psychology. By V. L. Allen & K. E. Scheibe (Eds.), *The social context of conduct: Psychological writings of Theodore Sarbin*. New York: Praeger.

Sarnoff, I., & Zimbardo, P. (1961). Anxiety, fear, and social affiliation. *Journal of Abnormal and Social Psychology, 62,* 356–363.

Sartre, J.-P. (1948). A sketch of phenomenological theory. *The emotions: Outline of a theory.* New York: Philosophical Library.

Schachter, S. (1951). Deviation, rejection, and communication. *Journal of Abnormal Psychology, 46,* 190–207.

Schachter, S. (1959). *The psychology of affiliation*. Stanford: Stanford University Press.

Schachter, S. (1966). The interaction of cognitive and physiological determinants of emotional state. In C. D. Spielberger (Ed.), *Anxiety and behavior* (pp. 193–224). New York: Academic Press.

Schachter, S., & Singer, J. E. (1962). Cognitive, social and physiological determinants of emotional state. *Psychological Review, 69,* 379–399.

Schafer, R. (1954). *Psychoanalytic interpretation in Rorschach testing*. New York: Grune & Stratton.

Schafer, R. (1976). *A new language for psychoanalysis*. New Haven, CT: Yale University Press.

Schank, R. C., & Abelson, R. B. (1977). *Scripts, plans, goals and understanding*. Hillsdale, NJ: Erlbaum.

Scheele, B., & Groeben, N. (1986). Methodological aspects of illustrating the cognitive-reflective function of aesthetic communication. *Poetics, 15,* 527–554.

Scheff, T. J. (1985). The primacy of affect. *American Psychologist, 40,* 849–850.

Scheff, T. J. (1990a). Socialization of emotions: Pride and shame as causal agents. In T. D. Kemper (Ed.), *Research agendas in the sociology of emotions* (pp. 281–304). Albany, NY: State University of New York Press.

Scheff, T. J. (1990b). *Microsociology*. Chicago: University of Chicago Press.

Scheier, M. F., & Carver, C. S. (1987). Dispositional optimism and physical well-being: The influence of generalized outcome expectancies on health. *Journal of Personality, 55,* 169–210.

Scheier, M. F., Matthews, K. A., Owens, J. F., Magovern, G. J., Sr., Lefebvre, R. C., Abbott, R. A., & Carber, C. S. (1989). Dispositional optimism and recovery from coronary artery bypass surgery: The beneficial effects on physical and psychological well-being. *Journal of Personality and Social Psychology, 57,* 1024–1040.

Scheier, M. F., Weintraub, J. K., & Carver, C. S. (1986). Coping with stress: Divergent strategies of optimists and pessimists. *Journal of Personality and Social Psychology, 51,* 1257–1264.

Scherer, K. R. (1984a). On the nature and function of emotion: A component process approach. In K. R. Scherer & P. Ekman (Eds.), *Approaches to emotion* (pp. 293–317). Hillsdale, NJ: Erlbaum.

Scherer, K. R. (1984b). Emotion as a multicomponent process: A model with some cross-cultural data. In P. Shaver (Ed.), *Review of personality and social psychology: Vol. 5. Emotions, relationships, and health* (pp. 37–63). Beverly Hills, CA: Sage.

Scherer, K. R. (1989). Vocal correlates of emotional arousal and affective disturbance. In H. Wagner & A. Manstead (Eds.), *Handbook of social psychophysiology* (pp. 165–197). New York: Wiley.

Scherer, K. R., & Ekman, P. (1984). (Eds.), *Approaches to emotion.* Hillsdale, NJ: Erlbaum.

Schieffelin, E. L. (1976). *The sorrow of the lonely and the burning of the dancers.* New York: St. Martin's Press.

Schleifer, S. J., Keller, S. E., McKegney, F. P., & Stein, M. (May 1980). *Bereavement and lymphocyte function.* Paper presented to the American Psychiatric Association Meeting.

Schlosberg, H. S. (1941). A scale for the judgement of facial expressions. *Journal of Experimental Psychology, 29,* 497–510.

Schlosberg, H. S. (1952). The description of facial expressions in terms of two dimensions. *Journal of Experimental Psychology, 44,* 229–337.

Schlosberg, H. S. (1954). Three dimensions of emotion. *Psychological Review, 1954, 61,* 81–88.

Schmale, A. H., Jr. (1972). Giving up as a final common pathway to changes in health. *Advances in Psychosomatic Medicine, 8,* 20–40.

Schmale, A. H., Jr., & Iker, H. P. (1966). The affect of hopelessness and the development of cancer. *Psychosomatic Medicine, 28,* 714–721.

Schneider, D. (1976). Notes toward a theory of culture. In K. Basso & H. Selby (Eds.), *Meaning in anthropology.* Albuquerque: University of New Mexico Press.

Schneirla, T. C. (1959). An evolutionary and developmental theory of biphasic processes underlying approach and withdrawal. In M. R. Jones (Ed.), *Nebraska Symposium on Motivation* (Vol. 7, pp. 1–42). Lincoln: University of Nebraska Press.

Schoeck, M. (1966). *Envy.* New York: Harcourt, Brace & World.

Schönpflug, W. (1983). Coping efficiency and situational demands. In G. R. J. Hockey (Ed.), *Stress and fatigue in human performance.* New York: Wiley.

Schönpflug, W. (1985). Goal directed behavior as a source of stress: Psychological origins and consequences of inefficiency. In M. Frese & J. Sabini (Eds.), *Goal directed behavior: The concept of action in psychology* (pp. 172–188). Hillsdale, NJ: Erlbaum.

Schönpflug, W., & Battmann, W. (1988). The costs and benefits of coping. In S. Fisher & J. Reason (Eds.), *Handbook of life stress, cognition, and health* (pp. 699–713). New York: Wiley.

Schroeder, D. H., & Costa, P. T. (1984). Influence of life events on physical illness: Substantive effects or methodological flaws? *Journal of Personality and Social Psychology, 46,* 853–863.

Schwartz, G. (1979). The brain as a health care system. In G. C. Stone, F. Cohen, & N. Adler (Eds.), *Health psychology* (pp. 549–571). San Francisco, CA: Jossey-Bass.

Schwartz, G. E., & Weinberger, D. A. (1980). Patterns of emotional responses to affective situations: Relations among happiness, sadness, anger, fear, depression, and anxiety. *Motivation and Emotion, 4,* 175–191.

Schwartz, G. E., Weinberger, D. A., & Singer, J. A. (1981). Cardiovascular differentiation of happiness, sadness, anger, and fear following imagery and exercise. *Psychosomatic Medicine, 43,* 343–364.

Schwarz, N., & Clore, G. L. (1983). Mood, misattribution, and judgments of well-being: Information and directive functions of affective states. *Journal of Personality and Social Psychology, 45,* 513–523.

Schwarzer, R. (1984). (Ed.). *The self in anxiety, stress and depression.* Amsterdam: North-Holland.

Seashore, C. E. (1938). *Psychology of music.* New York: McGraw-Hill.

Seeman, J. (1989). Toward a model of positive health. *American Psychologist, 44,* 1099–1109.

Segall, M. H., Campbell, D. T., & Herskovits, M. J. (1966). *The influence of culture on visual perception.* Indianapolis: Bobbs-Merrill.

Seligman, M. E. P. (1975). *Helplessness: On depression, development and death.* San Francisco, CA: Freeman.

Seligman, M. E. P., Abramson, L. Y., Semmel, A., & von Baeyer, C. (1979). Depressive attributional style. *Journal of Abnormal Psychology, 88,* 242–247.

Seligman, M. E. P., & Maier, S. F. (1967). Failure to escape traumatic shock. *Journal of Experimental Psychology, 74,* 1–9.

Selye, H. (1956/1976). *The stress of life.* New York: McGraw-Hill.

Selye, H. (1974). *Stress without distresss.* Philadelphia: Lippincott.

Shafii, M. (1985). *Freedom from the self: Sufism, meditation and psychotherapy.* New York: Human Sciences Press.

Shalit, B. (1977). Structural ambiguity and limits to coping. *Journal of Human Stress, 3,* 32–45.

Shalit, B. (1981). Perceived perceptual organisation and coping with military demands. In C. D. Spielberger & I. G. Sarason (Eds.), *Stress and anxiety* (Vol. 8, pp. 189–194). New York: Hemisphere.

Shalit, B. (1982). The prediction of military groups' effectiveness by the coherence of their appraisal. *FOA report C 55053–H3,* Försvarets Forskningsanstalt, Huvudavdelning 5, Stockholm, Sweden.

Shalit, B., Carlstedt, L., Carlstedt, B. S., & Shalit, I. T. (1986). Coherence of cognitive appraisal and coping in a stressful military task: Parachute jumping. In N. A. Milgram (Ed.), *Stress and coping in time of war: Generalizations from the Israeli experience* (pp. 230–235). New York: Brunner/Mazel.

Shanks, D. R., & Dickenson, A. (1990). Contingency awareness in valuative conditioning: A comment on Baeyens, Eelen, & van den Bergh. *Cognition and Emotion, 4,* 19–30.

Shapiro, D. (1965). *Neurotic styles.* New York: Basic Books.

Shaver, K. G. (1985). *The attribution of blame: Causality, responsibility, and blameworthiness.* New York: Springer-Verlag.

Shaver, P. (1984). (Ed.), *Review of personality and social psychology: Emotions, relationships, and health.* Beverly Hills, CA: Sage.

Shaver, P., Schwartz, J., Kirson, D., & O'Connor, C. (1987). Emotion knowledge: Further exploration of a prototype approach. *Journal of Personality and Social Psychology, 52,* 1061–1086.

Shedler, J., Mayman, M., & Manis, M. (unpublished). *The illusion of mental health.*

Shepard, R. N. (1984). Ecological constraints on internal representation: Resonant kinematics of perceiving, imagining, thinking, and dreaming. *Psychological Review, 91,* 417–447.

Sherif, M. (1935). A study of some social factors in perception. *Archives of Psychology, 27* (Whole No. 187).

Shneidman, E. (1989). The Indian summer of life: A preliminary study of septuagenarians. *American Psychologist, 44,* 684–694.

Shontz, F. C. (1975). *The psychological aspects of physical illness and disability.* New York: Macmillan.

Shopshire, M., & Bonney, J. J. (1990). The cognitive relational theory of emotion and the Russell circumplex. Paper presented at the Annual Convention of the Western Psychological Association, Los Angeles, CA., April 26, 1990.

Shweder, R. A. (1985). Menstrual pollution, soul loss, and the comparative study of emotions. In A. Kleinman & R. Good (Eds.), *Culture and depression: Studies in the anthropology of cross-cultural psychiatry of affect and disorder* (pp. 182–214). Berkeley: University of California Press.

Shweder, R. A., & LeVine, R. A. (1984). (Eds.), *Culture theory: Essays on mind, self, and emotion.* Cambridge, England: Cambridge University Press.

Silberschatz, G., & Sampson, H. (1991). Affects in psychopathology and psychotherapy. In J. D. Safran & L. S. Greenberg (Eds.), *Emotion, psychotherapy, and change.* New York: Guilford.

Silver, R. L., & Wortman, C. B. (1980). Coping with undesirable life events. In J. Garber & M. E. P. Seligman (Eds.), *Human helplessness* (pp. 279–340). New York: Academic Press.

Singer, J. A. (1990). Affective responses to autobiographical memories and their relationship to long-term goals. *Journal of Personality, 58,* 535–563.

Singer, J. L., & Opler, M. J. (1956). Contrasting patterns of fantasy and motility in Irish and Italian schizophrenics. *Journal of Abnormal and Social Psychology, 53,* 42–47.

Sjöbäck, H. (1973). *The psychoanalytic theory of defensive processes.* New York: Wiley.

Skinner, B. F. (1938). *The behavior of organisms.* New York: Appleton.

Skinner, B. F. (1953). *Science and human behavior.* New York: Appleton.

Skinner, B. F. (1971). *Beyond freedom and dignity.* New York: Knopf.

Slaikeu, K. A. 1984). *Crisis intervention: A handbook for practice and research.* Boston: Allyn and Bacon.

Slife, B. D. (1981). The primacy of affective judgments from a teleological perspective. *American Psychologist, 36,* 221–222.

Smelser, N. J. (1963). *Theory of collective behavior.* New York: Free Press.

Smith, A. D. (1981). *The ethnic revival: In the modern world.* London: Cambridge University Press.

Smith, C. A., & Ellsworth, P. C. (1985). Patterns of cognitive appraisal in emotion. *Journal of Personality and Social Psychology, 48,* 813–838.

Smith, C. A., & Ellsworth, P. C. (1987). Patterns of appraisal and emotion related to taking an exam. *Journal of Personality and Social Psychology, 52,* 475–488.

Smith, C. A., & Lazarus, R. S. (1990). Emotion and adaptation. In L. A. Pervin (Ed.), *Handbook of personality: Theory and research.* New York: Guilford.

Smith, C. A., Novacek, J., Lazarus, R. S., & Pope, L. K. (unpublished). *Antecedents of emotion: Situations, dispositions, and appraisals.*

Smith, R. E., Smoll, F. L., & Ptacek, J. T. (1990). Conjunctive moderator variables in vulnerability and resiliency research: Life stress, social support and coping skills, and adolescent sport injuries. *Journal of Personality and Social Psychology, 58,* 360–370.

Smith, R. H., Kim, S. H., & Parrott, W. G. (1988). Envy and jealousy: Semantic problems and experiential distinctions. *Personality and Social Psychology Bulletin, 14,* 401–409.

Snyder, C. R. (1989). Reality negotiation: From excuses to hope and beyond. *Journal of Social and Clinical Psychology, 8,* 130–157.

Snyder, C. R., Harris, C., Anderson, J. R., Holleran, S. A., Irving, L. M., Sigmon, S. T., Yoshinobu, L., Gibb, J., Langelle, C., & Harney, P. (1991). The will and the ways: Development and validation of an individual difference measure of hope. *Journal of Personality and Social Psychology, 60.* 570–585.

Snyder, C. R., & Higgins, R. L. (1988). Excuses: Their effective role in the negotiation of reality. *Psychological Bulletin, 104,* 23–35.

Socarides, C. W. (1977). *The world of emotions: Clinical studies of affects and their expression.* New York: International Universities Press.

Sokolov, E. N. (1963). *Perception and the conditioned reflex.* Oxford, England: Pergamon.

Solomon, R. C. (1980). Emotions and choice. In A. O. Rorty (Ed.), *Explaining emotions* (pp. 251–281). Berkeley: University of California Press.

Solomon, Z., Mikulincer, M., & Hobfoll, S. E. (1987). Objective versus subjective measurement of stress and social support: Combat-related reactions. *Journal of Consulting and Clinical Psychology, 55,* 577–583.

Spence, J. T., & Spence, K.W. (1966). The motivational components of manifest anxiety: Drive and drive stimuli. In C. D. Spielberger (Ed.), *Anxiety and behavior* (pp. 291–326). New York: Academic Press.

Spencer, H. (1890). *The principles of psychology* (Vol. I). New York: Appleton (First edition, 1855.)

Sperry, R. W. (1988). Psychology's mentalist paradigm and the religion/science tension. *American Psychologist, 43,* 607–613.

Spielberger, C. D. (Ed.). (1966). *Anxiety and behavior.* New York: Academic Press.

Spielberger, C. D. (Ed.). (1972). *Anxiety: Current trends in theory and research* (Vols. I & II). New York: Academic Press.

Spielberger, C. D., Gorsuch, R. L., & Lushene, R. E. (1970). *Manual for the State-Trait Anxiety Inventory.* Palo Alto, CA: Consulting Psychologists Press.

Spielberger, C. D., Jacobs, G., Russell, S., & Crane, R. S. (1983). Assessment of anger: The state-trait anger scale. In J. N. Butcher & C. D. Spielberger (Eds.), *Advances in personality assessment* (Vol. 2). Hillsdale, NJ: Erlbaum.

Spielberger, C. D., Johnson, E. H., Russell, S. F., Crane, R. J., Jacobs, G. A., & Worden, T. J. (1985). The experience and expression of anger: Construction and validation of an anger expression scale. In M. A. Chesney & R. H. Rosenman (Eds.), *Anger and hostility in cardiovascular and behavioral disorders* (pp. 5–30). New York: Hemisphere.

Spielberger, C. D., & Sarason, I. G. (1975–1986). *Stress and anxiety* (Vols. 1–10). New York: (Hemisphere) Wiley.

Spinoza. (1985). Ethics. In Edwin Corley (Ed.), *The collected works of Spinoza.* Princeton, NJ: Princeton University Press.

Spiro, M. E. (1961). Social systems, personality, and functional analysis. In B. Kaplan (Ed.), *Studying personality cross-culturally.* Evanston, IL: Row, Peterson.

Spitz, R. (1946). Anaclitic depression. *Psychoanalytic Study of the Child, 2,* 313–342.

Sroufe, L. A. (1979). Socioemotional development. In J. D. Osofsky (Ed.), *Handbook of infant development* (pp. 462–516). New York: Wiley.

Sroufe, L. A. (1984). The organization of emotional development. In K. R. Scherer & P. Ekman (Eds.), *Approaches to emotion* (pp. 109–128). Hillsdale, NJ: Erlbaum.

Sroufe, L. A., Schork, E., Motti, F., Lawroski, N., & LaFreniere, P. (1984). The role of affect in social competence. In C. E. Izard, J. Kagan, & R. B. Zajonc (Eds.), *Emotions, cognition, and behavior* (pp. 289–319). Cambridge, England: Cambridge University Press.

Stearns, P. N. (1989). *Jealousy: The evolution of an emotion in American history.* New York: New York University Press.

Stein, N. L., & Levine, L. J. (1987). Thinking about feelings: The development and organization of emotional knowledge. In R. E. Snow & M. Farr (Eds.), *Aptitude, learning, and instruction: Vol. 3. Cognition, conation, and affect* (pp. 165–197). Hillsdale, NJ: Erlbaum.

Stein, N. L., & Levine, L. J. (1989). The causal organisation of emotional knowledge: A developmental study. *Cognition and Emotion, 3,* 343–378.

Stein, N. L., & Levine, L. J. (1990). Making sense out of emotion: The representation and use of goal-structured knowledge. In N. L. Stein, B. Leventhal, T. Trabasso (Eds.), *Psychological and biological approaches to emotion* (pp. 45–73). Hillsdale, NJ: Erlbaum.

Stein, N. L., & Trabasso, T. (1990). Children's understanding of changing emotional states. In C. Saarni & P. L. Harris (Eds.), *Children's understanding of emotion* (pp. 50–77). New York: Cambridge University Press.

Stenberg, C. R., & Campos, J. J. (1990). The development of anger expressions in infancy. In N. Stein, B. Leventhal, & T. Trabasso (Eds.), *Psychological and biological approaches to emotion* (pp. 247–282). Hilldsdale, NJ: Erlbaum.

Steptoe, A., & Vogele, C. (1986). Are stress responses influenced by cognitive appraisal? An experimental comparison of coping strategies. *British Journal of Psychology, 77,* 243–255.

Stern, D. N. (1985). *The interpersonal world of the infant: A view from psychoanalysis and developmental psychology.* New York: Basic Books.

Sternberg, R. J. (1986). A triangular theory of love. *Psychological Review, 93,* 119–135.

Sternberg, R. J. (1987). Liking versus loving: A comparative evaluation of theories. *Psychological Bulletin, 102,* 331–345.

Stone, A. A., & Neale, J. M. (1984a). New measure of daily coping: Development and preliminary results. *Journal of Personality and Social Psychology, 46,* 892–906.

Stone, A. A., & Neale, J. M. (1984b). The effects of severe daily events on mood. *Journal of Personality and Social Psychology, 46,* 137–144.

Storm, C., & Storm, T. (1987). A taxonomic study of the vocabulary of emotions. *Journal of Personality and Social Psychology, 53,* 805–816.

Stotland, E. (1969). *The psychology of hope.* San Fransisco, CA: Jossey-Bass.

Strack, F., Argyle, M., and Schwarz, N. (Eds.). (1991). *Subjective well-being.* Oxford, England: Pergamon.

Strauman, T. J., & Higgins, E. T. (1988). Self-discrepancies as predictors of vulnerability to distinct syndromes of chronic emotional distress. *Journal of Personality, 56,* 685–707.

Strayer, J. (1985). Children's attributions regarding the situational determinants of emotion in self and others. Paper given at the Canadian Psychological Association, Halifax, Nova Scotia, June.

Sue, D., & Sue, S. (1987). Cultural factors in the clinical assessment of Asian Americans. *Journal of Consulting and Clinical Psychology, 55,* 479–487.

Sullivan, H. S. (1953). *The interpersonal theory of psychiatry.* New York: Norton.

Sullivan, M. W., & Lewis, M. (1989). Emotion and cognition in infancy: Facial expressions during contingency learning. *International Journal of Behavioral Development, 12,* 221–237.

Suls, J., & Sanders, G. S. (1988). Type A behavior as a general risk factor for physical disorder. *Journal of Behavioral Medicine, 11,* 201–226.

Swanson, G. E. (1988). *Ego defenses and the legitimation of behavior.* Cambridge, England: Cambridge University Press.

Syme, S. L. (1984). Sociocultural factors and disease etiology. In W. D. Gentry (Ed.), *Handbook of behavioral medicine* (pp. 13–37). New York: Guilford.

Symington, T., Currie, A. R., Curran, R. C., & Davidson, J. N. (1955). The reaction of the adrenal cortex in conditions of stress. In Ciba Foundation Colloquia on Endocrinology. *The human adrenal cortex* (Vol. VIII, pp. 70–91). Boston: Little, Brown.

Tageson, C. W. (1982). *Humanistic psychology: A synthesis.* Homewood, IL: Dorsey.

Tait, R., & Silver, R. C. (1989). Coming to terms with major negative life events. In J. S. Uleman & J. A. Bargh (Eds.), *Unintended thought.* New York: Guilford.

Tangney, J. P. (1990). Assessing individual differences in proneness to shame and guilt: Development of the self-conscious affect and attribution inventory. *Journal of Personality and Social Psychology, 59,* 102–111.

Tavris, C. (1984). On the wisdom of counting to ten: Personal and social dangers of anger expression. In P. Shaver (Ed.), *Review of personality and social psychology: Emotions, relationships, and health* (pp. 170–191). Beverly Hills, CA: Sage.

Taylor, C. (1985). *Philosophical papers* (Vols. 1 & 2). London: Cambridge University Press.

Taylor, G. (1980). Pride. In A. O. Rorty (Ed.), *Explaining emotions* (pp. 385–402). Berkeley: University of California Press.

Taylor, J. A. (1953). A personality scale of manifest anxiety. *Journal of Abnormal and Social Psychology, 48,* 285–290.

Taylor, J. A. (1956). Drive theory and manifest anxiety. *Psychological Bulletin, 53,* 303–320.

Taylor, S. E. (1986). *Health psychology.* New York: Random House.

Taylor, S. E. (1989). *Positive illusions: Creative self-deception and the healthy mind.* New York: Basic Books.

Taylor, S. E., & Brown, J. D. (1988). Illusion and well-being: A social psychological perspective on mental health. *Psychological Bulletin, 103,* 193–210.

Taylor, S. E., Lichtman, R. R., & Wood, J. V. (1984). Attributions, beliefs about control, and adjustment to breast cancer. *Journal of Personality and Social Psychology, 46,* 489–502.

Taylor, S. E., & Lobel, M. (1989). Social comparison activity under threat: Downward evaluation and upward contacts. *Psychological Review, 96,* 569–575.

Tecoma, E. S., & Huey, L. Y. (1985). Minireview: Psychic distress and the immune response. *Life Sciences, 36,* 1799–1812.

Tedeschi, J. T. (1983). Social influence theory and aggression. In R. T. Geen & E. I. Donnerstein (Eds.), *Aggression: Theoretical and empirical reviews* (pp. 135–162). Orlando, FL: Academic Press.

Tedeschi, J. T., Smith, R. B., & Brown, R. C. (1974). A reinterpretation of research on aggression. *Psychological Bulletin, 81,* 540–562.

Tellegen, A. (in press). Personality traits: Issues of definition, evidence, and assessment. In D. Cicchetti & W. Grover (Eds.), *Thinking clearly about psychology: Essays in honor of Paul Everett Meehl.* Minneapolis: University of Minnesota Press.

Tennen, H., & Affleck, G. (1990). Blaming others for threatening events. *Psychological Bulletin, 108,* 209–232.

Tessor, A. (1990). Smith and Ellsworth's appraisal model of emotion: A replication, extension, and test. *Personality and Social Psychology Bulletin, 16,* 210–223.

Tetlock, P. E., & Levi, A. (1982). Attribution bias: On the conclusiveness of the cognition-motivation debate. *Journal of Experimental Social Psychology, 18,* 68–88.

Thayer, R. E. (1989). *The biopsychology of mood and arousal.* New York: Oxford University Press.

Thoits, P. (1984). Coping, social support, and psychological outcomes. *Review of Personality and Social Psychology, 5,* 219–238.

Thomas, A., & Chess, S. (1977). *Temperament and development.* New York: Brunner/Mazel.

Thompson, J. G. (1988). *The psychobiology of emotions.* New York: Plenum.

Tillich, P. (1959). The external now. In H. Feifel (Ed.), *The meaning of death* (pp. 30–38). New York: McGraw-Hill.

Tinbergen, N. (1951). *The study of instincts.* London: Oxford University Press.

Tobias, S. (1985). Test anxiety: Interference, defective skills, and cognitive capacity. *Educational Psychologist, 20,* 135–142.

Tolman, E. C. (1948). Cognitive maps in rats and men. *Psychological Review, 55,* 189–208.

Tomita, M. (1986). Assessment of musical aptitudes: Summary of the research on the existing tests of musical abilities. *Bulletin of the Graduate School of Literature, Waseda University,* No. 32.

Tomkins, J. (1989). Fighting words. *Harpers Magazine,* March, pp. 33–35.

Tomkins, S. S. (1962, 1963). *Affect, imagery, consciousness* (Vols. 1 and 2). New York: Springer.

Tomkins, S. S. (1963). Simulation of personality: The interrelationships between affect, memory, thinking, perception and action. In S. S. Tomkins & S. Messick (Eds.), *Computer simulation of personality.* New York: Wiley.

Tomkins, S. S. (1965). Affect and the psychology of knowledge. In S. S. Tomkins & C. E. Izard (Eds.), *Affect, cognition, and personality: Empirical studies* (pp. 72–97). New York: Springer.

Tomkins, S. S. (1979). Script theory: Differential magnification of affects. In H. E. Howe & R. A. Dienstbier (Eds.), *Nebraska Symposium on Motivation, 1978,* 26. Lincoln: University of Nebraska Press.

Tomkins, S. S. (1981). The quest for primary motives: Biography and autobiography of an idea. *Journal of Personality and Social Psychology, 41,* 306–329.

Tompkins, V. H. (1959). Stress in aviation. In J. Hambling (Ed.), *The nature of stress disorder* (pp. 73–80). Springfield, IL: Thomas.

Torestad, B. (1989). *What is anger provoking? 1. A psychophysical study of antecedents of anger.* Reports from the Department of Psychology, University of Stockholm, March, No. 690.

Tov-Ruach, L. (1980). Jealousy, attention, and loss. In A. O. Rorty (Ed.), *Explaining emotions* (pp. 465–488). Berkeley: University of California Press.

Trabasso, T., Stein, N. L., & Johnson, L. R. (1981). Children's knowledge of events: A causal analysis of story structure. In G. Bower (Ed)., *Learning and motivation* (Vol. 15, pp. 237–282). New York: Academic Press.

Trevarthen, C. (1979). Communication and cooperation in early infancy. A description of primary intersubjectivity. In M. Bullowa (Ed.), *Before speech: The beginnings of human communication.* London: Cambridge University Press.

Trevarthen, C. (1984). Emotions in infancy: Regulators of contact and relationships with persons. In K. R. Scherer & P. Ekman (Eds.), *Approaches to emotion* (pp. 129–161). Hillsdale, NJ: Erlbaum.

Trevarthen, C., & Hubley, P. (1978). Secondary intersubjectivity: Confidence, confiding and acts of meaning in the first year. In A. Lock (Ed.), *Action, gesture and symbol: The emergence of language.* London: Academic Press.

Triandis, H. C., Bontempo, R., Villareal, M. J., Asai, M., & Lucca, N. (1988). Individualism and collectivism: Cross-cultural perspectives on self-ingroup relationships. *Journal of Personality and Social Psychology, 54,* 323–338.

Tronick, E. Z. (1989). Emotions and emotional communication in infants. *American Psychologist, 44,* 112–119.

Tucker, D. M., & Willimanson, P. A. (1984). Asymmetric neural control systems in human self-regulation. *Psychological Review, 91,* 185–215.

Turner, T. (1973). Piaget's structuralism. *American Anthropologist, 75,* 351–373.

Tursky, B., & Sternbach, R. A. (1967). Further physiological correlates of ethnic differences in response to shock. *Psychophysiology, 4,* 67–74.

Uleman, J. S., & Bargh, J. A. (Eds.). (1989). *Unintended thought.* New York: Guilford.

Vaillant, G. E. (1977). *Adaptation to life.* Boston: Little, Brown.

Valins, S. (1966). Cognitive effects of false heart rate feedback. *Journal of Personality and Social Psychology. 4,* 400–408.

Veenhoven, R. (1990). (Ed.), *How harmful is happiness?* Rotterdam: Universitaire Pers Rotterdam.

Vitz, P. C. (1990). The use of stories in moral development: New psychological reasons for an old education method. *American Psychologist, 45,* 709–720.

Vogel, E. (1967). *Japan's new middle class: The salaryman and his family in a Tokyo suburb.* Berkeley: University of California Press.

Vogel, E., & Vogel, S. (1961). Family security, personal immaturity, and emotional health in a Japanese sample. *Marriage and Family Living, 23,* 161–166.

Vogel, W., Raymond, S., & Lazarus, R. S. (1959). Intrinsic motivation and psychological stress. *Journal of Abnormal and Social Psychology, 58,* 225–233.

Vrana, S. R., & Lang, P. J. (1990). Fear imagery and the startle-probe reflex. *Journal of Abnormal Psychology, 99,* 189–197.

Vrana, S. R., Spence, E. L., & Lang, P. J. (1988). The startle probe response: A new measure of emotion. *Journal of Abnormal Psychology, 97,* 487–491.

Wachtel, P. L. (1977). *Psychoanalysis and behavior therapy.* New York: Basic Books.

Wallerstein, R. S. (1983). Defences, defense mechanisms, and the structure of the mind. *Journal of the American Psychoanalytic Association, 31,* 201–225.

Walters, K. S. (1989). Aesthetic emotions and reality. *American Psychologist, 44,* 1545–1546.

Washburn, S. S. L., & Hamburg, D. A. (1968). Aggressive behavior in Old World monkeys and apes. In P. C. Jay (Ed.), *Primates: Studies in adaptation and variability.* New York: Holt, Rinehart and Winston.

Watkins, M. (1986). *Invisible guests: The development of imaginal dialogues.* Hillsdale, NJ: Analytic Press.

Watson, D., & Tellegen, A. (1985). Toward a consensual structure of mood. *Psychological Bulletin, 98,* 219–235.

Watson, J., & Rayner, R. (1920). Conditioned emotional reactions. *Journal of Experimental Psychology, 3,* 1–14.

Watson, J. B. (1930). *Behaviorism.* Chicago: University of Chicago Press.

Watson, J. S. (1985). Contingency perception in early social development. In T. M. Field & N. M. Fox (Eds.), *Social perception in infants* (pp. 157–165). Norwood, NJ: Ablex Publishing Corporation.

Watzlawick, P. (1976). *How real is real?* New York: Random House.

Wegman. C. (1985). *Psychoanalysis and cognitive psychology: A formulation of Freud's earliest theory.* San Diego, CA: Academic Press.

Weinberg, J., & Levine, S. (1980). Psychobiology of coping in animals: The effects of predictability. In S. Levine & H. Ursin (Eds.), *Coping and health.* New York: Plenum.

Weinberger, D. A. (1990). The construct validity of the repressive coping style. In J. L. Singer (Ed.), *Repression and dissociation: Implications for personality, psychopathology, and health* (pp. 337–386). Chicago: University of Chicago Press.

Weiner, B. (1985). An attributional theory of achievement motivation and emotion. *Psychological Review, 92,* 548–573.

Weiner, B. (1986). *An attributional theory of motivation and emotion.* New York: Springer-Verlag.

Weiner, B., Amirkhan, J., Folkes, V. S., & Verette, J. A. (1987). An attributional analysis of excuse giving: Studies of a naive theory of emotion. *Journal of Personality and Social Psychology, 52,* 316–324.

Weiner, B., & Graham, S. (1984). An attirubtional approach to emotional development. In C. Izard, J. Kagan, & R. Zajonc (Eds.), *Emotion, cognition and behavior* (pp. 167–191). Cambridge, MA: Harvard University Press.

Weiner, B., & Graham, S. (1989). Understanding the motivational role of affect: Life-span research from an attributional perspective. *Cognition and Emotion, 3,* 401–419.

Weiner, B., Graham, S., & Chandler, C. (1982). Pity, anger, and guilt: An attributional analysis. *Personality and Social Psychology Bulletin, 8,* 226–232.

Weisman, A. D. (1972). *On dying and denying: A psychiatric study of terminality.* New York: Behavioral Publications.

Weiss, J. (1952). Crying at the happy ending. *Psychoanalytic Review, 39,* 338.

Weiss, J. (1971). The emergence of new themes: A contribution to the psychoanalytic theory of therapy. *International Journal of Psychoanalysis, 52,* 459–467.

Weiss, J. (1986). Part I: Theory and clinical observations. In J. Weiss, H. Sampson, & the Mount Zion Psychotherapy Research Group (Eds.), *The psychoanalytic process: Theory, clinical observation, and empirical research.* New York: Guilford.

Weiss, J. (1990). Unconscious mental functioning. *Scientific American, 262,* 103–109.

Weiss, J., Sampson, H., & the Mt. Zion Psychotherapy Research Group. (1986). *The psychoanalytic process: Theory, clinical observation, and empirical research.* New York: Guilford.

Weiss, J. H. (1977). The current state of the concept of a psychosomatic disorder. In Z. J. Lipowski, D. R. Lipsitt, & P. C. Whybrow (Eds.), *Psychosomatic medicine* (pp. 162–171). New York: Oxford University Press.

Werner, H. (1948). *Comparative psychology of mental development* (rev. ed.). Chicago: Follett. (Originally published in 1926.)

Werner, H. (1956). Microgenesis and aphasia. *Journal of Abnormal and Social Psychology, 52,* 347–353.

Werner, H. (1957). The concept of development from a comparative and organismic point of view. In D. Harris (Ed.), *The concept of development* (pp. 125–148). Minneapolis: University of Minnesota Press.

Werner, H., & Kaplan, B. (1963). *Symbol formation.* New York: Wiley.

Wessman, A. E., & Ricks, D. F. (1966). *Mood and personality.* New York: Holt, Rinehart and Winston.

West, S. G., & Graziano, W. G. (1989). (Eds.), Long-term stability and change in personality. Special issue, *Journal of Personality, 57,* No. 2.

Wheeler, L., & Reis, H. T. (in press). Self-recording of everyday life events: Origins, types, and uses. *Journal of Personality* (Special issue on small events edited by H. Tennen, J. Suls, & G. Affleck.)

Whitbourne, S. K. (1985). The psychological construction of the life span. In J. E. Birren & K. W. Schaie (Eds.), *Handbook of the psychology of aging* (2nd ed., pp. 594–618). New York: Van Nostrand.

White, G. L. (1981). A model of romantic jealousy. *Motivation and Emotion, 5,* 295–310.

White, G. L., & Mullen, P. E. (1989). *Jealousy: Theory, research, and clinical strategies.* New York: Guilford, 1989.

White, P. A. (1990). Ideas about causation in philosophy and psychology. *American Psychologist, 108,* 3–18.

White, R. W. (1959). Motivation reconsidered: The concept of competence. *Psychological Review, 66,* 297–333.

White, R. W. (1974). Strategies of adaptation: An attempt at systematic description. In G. V. Coelho, D. A. Hamburg, & J. E. Adams (Eds.), *Coping and adaptation* (pp. 47–68). New York: Basic Books.

Whiting, J., & Child, I. (1953). *Child training and personality: A cross cultural study.* New Haven, CT: Yale University Press.

Whitman, R., & Alexander, J. (1968). On gloating. *International Journal of Psycho-analysis, 49,* 732–738. Also in Socarides, 1977.

Wicker, F. W., Payne, G. C., & Morgan, R. D. (1983). Participant descriptions of guilt and shame. *Motivation and Emotion, 7,* 25–39.

Wicklund, R. A. (1975). Objective self-awareness. In L. Berkowitz (Ed.), *Advances in experimental social psychology* (Vol. 7). New York: Academic Press.

Wild, C. (1965). Creativity and adaptive regression. *Journal of Personality and Social Psychology, 2,* 161–169.

Wilensky, R. (1983). *Plans and understanding: A computational approach to human reasoning.* Reading, MA: Addison-Wesley.

Willems, E. P. (1969). Planning a rationale for naturalistic research. In E. P. Willems & H. L. Raush (Eds.), *Naturalistic viewpoints in psychological research* (pp. 44–71). New York: Holt, Rinehart and Winston.

Williams, J. W., Jr., Haney, T. L., Lee, K. L., Yi-Hong Kong, Y., Blumenthal, J. A., & Whalen, R. E. (1980). Type A behavior, hostility, and coronary atherosclerosis. *Psychosomatic Medicine, 42,* 539–549.

Wine, J. (1971). Test anxiety and direction of attention. *Psychological Bulletin, 76,* 92–104.

Winkle, G. H., & Sarason, I. G. (1964). Subject, experimenter, and situational variables in research on anxiety. *Journal of Abnormal and Social Psychology, 68,* 601–608.

Winner, E. (1988). *The point of words: Children's understanding of metaphor and irony.* Cambridge, MA: Harvard University Press.

Winterstein, A., & Bergler, E. (1935). The psychology of pathos. *International Journal of Psycho-analysis, 16,* 414–424. Also in Socarides, 1977.

Witkin, H. A. (1965). Psychological differentiation and forms of pathology. *Journal of Abnormal Psychology, 70,* 317–336.

Witkin, H. A., Dyk, R. B., Faterson, H. F., Goodenough, D. R., & Karp, S. A. (1962). *Psychological differentiation.* New York: Wiley.

Wollert, R. (1987). A clinicallly grounded evaluation of attributional theories of depression and psychotherapy. *Canadian Psychology/Psychologie Canadienne, 28,* 218–227.

Wolpe, J. (1958). *Psychotherapy by reciprocal inhibition.* Stanford, CA: Stanford University Press.

Woodworth, R. S. (1938). *Experimental psychology.* New York: Holt.

Woodworth, R. S., & Schlosberg, H. S. (1954). *Experimental psychology.* New York: Holt.

Wortman, C. B., & Brehm, J. W. (1975). Responses to uncontrollable outcomes: An integration of reactance theory and the learned helplessness model. In L. Berkowitz (Ed.), *Advances in experimental and social psychology* (Vol. 8). New York: Academic Press.

Wortman, C. B., & Lehman, D. R. (1985). Reactions to victims of life crises: Support attempts that fail. In I. G. Sarason & B. R. Sarason (Eds.), *Social support: Theory, research and applications* (pp. 463–489). Dordrecht, The Netherlands: Martinus Nijhoff.

Wright, J. C., & Mischel, W. (1987). A conditional approach to dispositional constructs: The local predictability of social behavior. *Journal of Personality and Social Psychology, 53,* 1159–1177. (Special Issue.)

Wright, J. C., & Mischel, W. (1988). Conditional hedges and the intuitive psychology of traits. *Journal of Personality and Social Psychology, 55,* 454–469.

Wrubel, J., Benner, P., & Lazarus, R. S. (1981). Social competence from the perspective of stress and coping. In J. Wine & M. Smye (Eds.), *Social competence* (pp. 61–99). New York: Guilford.

Wundt, W. (1905). *Grundriss der Psychologie* (7th rev. ed.). Leipzig: Engelman. (Not seen.)

Yarrow, L. J. (1961). Maternal deprivation: Toward an empirical and conceptual reevaluation. *Psychological Bulletin, 58,* 459–490.

Yates, M. (1976). *Coping: A survival manual for women alone.* Englewood Cliffs, NJ: Prentice Hall.

Yerkes, R. M., & Yerkes, A. W. (1929). *The great apes: A study of anthropoid life.* New Haven, CT: Yale University Press.

Yonas, A. (1981). Infants' responses to optical information for collision. In R. Aslin & L. Petersen (Eds.), *Development of perception: Psychobiological perspectives* (Vol. 2). New York: Academic Press.

Zahn-Waxler, C., & Kochanska, G. (1990). The origins of guilt. In R. A. Thompson (Ed.), *Nebraska Symposium on Motivation, 1988*. Lincoln: University of Nebraska Press.

Zajonc, R. B. (1980). Feeling and thinking: Preferences need no inferences. *American Psychologist, 35*, 151–175.

Zajonc, R. B. (1984). On the primacy of affect. *American Psychologist, 39*, 117–123.

Zajonc, R. S., Murphy, S. T., & Inglehart, M. (1989). Feeling and facial efference: Implications of the vascular theory of emotion. *Psychological Review, 96*, 395–416.

Zborowsky, M. (1958). Cultural components in response to pain. In E. G. Jaco (Ed.), *Patients, physicians, and illness* (pp. 256–268). New York: Free Press.

Zborowsky, M. (1969). *People in pain*. San Francisco, CA: Jossey-Bass.

Zimbardo, P. G., Pilkonis, P., & Norwood, R. (1974). *Shyness*. Glenview, IL: Scott, Foresman.

Zimney, G. H., & Keinstra, R. A. (1967). Orienting and defensive reponses to electric shock. *Psychophysiology, 3*, 351–362.

Zola, I. I. (1966). Culture and symptoms: An analysis of patients' presenting complaints. *American Sociological Review, 3*, 615–630.

Zuckerman, M. (1979). Sensation seeking and risk taking. In C. Izard (Ed.), *Emotions in personality and psychopathology*. New York: Plenum.

Indexes

Author Index

Subject Index